The Regulation of International Trade

The conclusion of the GATT Uruguay Round negotiations, as well as the emergence of regional trading arrangements, has underlined the significance of international trade regulation in global politics and economics. As new trade issues emerge and we look into the future of the world trading system it is important that we understand its basic working.

The Regulation of International Trade introduces the rules and institutions that govern international trade. The authors examine the theory and functioning of international legal regimes, including those of GATT/WTO (World Trade Organization), the NAFTA (North American Free Trade Agreement), as well as some aspects of the European Union. Attention is also given to the rise of protectionism through the use of internal trade remedy laws, including a detailed comparative analysis of the application of trade remedies to dumping and subsidies in Canada, the USA and the European Union.

The book also contains individual chapters on trade in agricultural products, trade and development, and technical standards. In addition, it contains a detailed discussion of 'new era' trade issues, such as trade and investment, intellectual property rights, trade and environment, trade and labour standards, and trade and competition policy.

Throughout insights of classic and contemporary economics and political economy are related to current issues facing the world trading system. As a comprehensive text *The Regulation of International Trade* will be an invaluable guide to students of economics, trade, politics and international relations.

Michael J. Trebilcock is a University Professor and **Robert Howse** an Associate Professor in the Faculty of Law, University of Toronto. They are co-authors, with **Marsha Chandler**, of *Trade and Transitions*, also published by Routledge.

The Regulation of International Trade

Second Edition

Michael J. Trebilcock and Robert Howse

London and New York

First published 1995
Second edition published 1999 by Routledge
11 New Fetter Lane, London EC4P 4EE

Simultaneously published in the USA and Canada
by Routledge
29 West 35th Street, New York, NY 10001

Reprinted 2000, 2001 (twice)

Routledge is an imprint of the Taylor & Francis Group

Typeset in Baskerville by
M Rules, London
Printed and bound in Great Britain by
TJ International Ltd, Padstow, Cornwall

British Library Cataloguing in Publication Data
A catalogue record for this book is available from the British Library

Library of Congress Cataloging in Publication Data
Trebilcock, M.J.
The regulation of international trade/Michael J. Trebilcock and Robert Howse. – 2nd ed.
p. cm.
Includes bibliographical references and index.
1. Foreign trade regulation. I. Howse, Robert, 1958–.
II. Title.
K3943.T72 1998
341.7′.54–dc21 98-37989
CIP

ISBN 0 415 18497 5 (hbk)
ISBN 0 415 18498 3 (pbk)

Contents

Figures and tables

Figures

Tables

Preface and acknowledgements

The first edition of this book went to press between the December 1993 finish to the Uruguay Round negotiations and the Marrakesh Meeting, at which those results were formalized. The second edition has given us an opportunity to refine and deepen our understanding of the WTO Agreements negotiated in the Uruguay Round, as well, of course as to reflect subsequent developments. These developments include the (now stalled) negotiations on a Multilateral Agreement on Investment, the finalization of negotiations on basic telecommunications and financial services under the GATS, and three years of dispute settlement at the WTO, including a number of important rulings by the new Appellate Body. We have also added separate chapters on areas of emerging importance such as trade and labour rights, trade and competition, and health and safety and other technical standards. The dispute settlement policy chapter has been substantially rewritten in light of three years of WTO practice; funding provided by a Canadian Social Science and Humanities Research Council grant to Robert Howse permitted more extensive reflection on the place of dispute settlement and its jurisprudence in the multilateral trading order than would otherwise have been possible, and those familiar with the first edition of the book will notice in this chapter a considerable evolution in our thinking.

We are grateful for the very constructive comments and criticisms of a number of colleagues who have used various parts of the first edition in their work, including in a number of cases classroom teaching. These include: Petros Mavroidis, Henrik Horn, Joseph Weiler, Armand de Mestral, Larry Herman, Benedict Kingsbury, Pierre Sauve, Ernst-Ulrich Petersmann, Kalypso Nikolaides and Dan Trefler. Several of our colleagues at the Faculty of Law have been of great assistance on specific chapters, especially Brian Langille (trade and labour rights), Rosemary Coombe (trade-related intellectual property rights) and Craig Scott (trade and environment, dispute settlement). Superb research assistance and advice was provided by Dan Markel, a JD student at Harvard Law School, and two graduate students at the Faculty of Law University of Toronto, Jason Levine and Julie Soloway. May Seto coordinated the production process for the manuscript with great skill. All errors and shortcoming are our own.

Preface, first edition

This book is intended to introduce serious students of law, economics, politics, and public policy to the institutions and rules that govern trade between sovereign states. Although we are legal academics, we have not written a traditional legal treatise. Instead, we have sought to bring to bear on our analysis of rules and institutions a wide range of disciplinary perspectives. This includes not only perspectives from the various branches of economics (whether trade theory itself or the theory of finance and industrial organization), but also from contemporary political and ethical philosophy and the international relations and political economy literatures.

Although we do discuss extensively the domestic legal regimes of some of the major trading states, most of the law dealt with in this book is international law. There is, of course, an age-old debate as to whether international law is really law in the true sense of the word, as it is not subject to authoritative enforcement by a sovereign. The GATT/WTO, the main legal and institutional framework for multilateral free trade, has frequently been judged against a domestic law benchmark and found wanting. Some theorists of international relations question whether rules and institutions matter at all, except as reflections of much more fundamental power relationships.

Our own perspective is that rules, norms and institutions matter a great deal. We see their function as the provision of a framework or structure that permits long-term mutually beneficial cooperation between states. Hence, we tend to take a neo-liberal or new liberal institutionalist view of international relations. This book is not, however, intended as an application or vindication of this particular theory of international relations, which would require a sustained discussion of the theory of international economic cooperation not well suited to an introductory text. Still, in examining the function and evolution of particular rules and norms, we have not hesitated to take stances based on a neo-liberal view nor to be critical of alternative policy stances premised on power-based realist or positivist views of international economic relations.

In general, we see the evolution and maintenance of an open, liberal trading order as to the mutual benefit of states. This view is not premised upon a naïve or unquestioning adherence to the economic theory of the gains from trade. On the contrary, throughout our analysis we are highly sensitive to the qualifications to and limits on the case for free trade, as well as the complexities involved in determining the domestic interest in these matters – including concerns about unemployment, worker adjustment, the quality of life and values of human rights and environmental protection. We examine, in a wide range of areas, the multiple challenges that increased economic integration and interdependence pose for domestic and international policymaking. While we frequently see the need to evolve new rules and institutions, or to clarify existing rules and strengthen existing institutions, we also conclude that the basic building blocks of the liberal trading order are not fundamentally defective, and that a protectionist retreat from an open system is likely to reduce both domestic and global welfare.

Compared to the immediacy and directness of the concerns that often result in demands for protectionism – whether job loss within a community or outrage at another state's environmental policies – the basic rules and norms of the global trading order that constrain protectionist responses often appear arcane or obscure. This applies as well to the jurisprudence that has evolved, especially in the GATT, to interpret those rules and norms. We believe that this impression is inaccurate and that in fact there is considerable clarity and coherence to the rules, with interpretation and application to diverse and rapidly changing circumstances being no more difficult and no easier than with respect to other areas of law. But this impression has partly been created because of the often unnecessarily inaccessible and complex presentation of the rules and jurisprudence by trade law experts and officials, and their frequent lack of interest in reaching a broader intellectual and policy community. Ernst-Ulrich Petersmann notes comments by non-experts that 'anyone who reads the GATT is likely to have his sanity impaired' and that there are 'only ten people in the world who understand the GATT and they are not telling'.[1] This book is a modest attempt to show that, to the contrary, international trade law is no more impenetrable or obscure than any other sophisticated body of contemporary law, when it is clearly explained in terms of fundamental concepts, principles and rules.

The topics covered and general organization of this book reflect a number of years' experience in co-teaching an introductory course in international trade regulation at the University of Toronto. The course has typically attracted senior undergraduates both in law and in economics, and we have also been fortunate to have the participation of graduate students in both disciplines, many of whom bring perspectives from undergraduate studies and work experience in a wide variety of countries, both developed and developing. Without this sustained and on-going dialogue with a very diverse and demanding group of students, this book would not have been possible.

We wish to acknowledge excellent research assistance from a number of students or former students at the Faculty of Law, University of Toronto, including Evan Atwood, Ari Blicker, Richard Braudo, John Loukidelis, Karen Powys-Lybbe, Presley Warner, Dan Markel, Julie Soloway, and Jason Levine. In addition, on particular chapters, several colleagues and students read earlier drafts or otherwise assisted us with their reflections and advice. In particular, we wish to thank Isis Calder, Kevin Davis, Gary Horlick, Brian Langille, James Odek, Elie Perkins,

Craig Scott and Diane Varleau. In the production of the second edition of this book, we benefited from the superb administrative and secretarial skills of May Seto and Margot Hall.

1 The evolution of international trade theory and policy

AN INTELLECTUAL HISTORY OF INTERNATIONAL TRADE THEORY AND POLICY[1]

The central question that must be confronted at the outset of any study of international trade is: why do we need a theory of international trade at all? Why is the analysis of the economic, political and social implications of exchange between traders in two national markets different from the analysis of the implications of exchange between traders within a single national market?

Early thinking on foreign trade

In a marvellously accessible and illuminating intellectual history of free trade, *Against The Tide*,[2] Douglas Irwin traces views on the virtues and vices of foreign trade back to early Greek and Roman writers. Their views generally reflected a high degree of ambivalence about trading with foreigners, mainly for non-economic reasons. First, merchants or traders of whatever origins were often regarded as of an inferior social class. This general hostility to merchants and commercial activity was accentuated in the case of foreign traders where contact with strangers could disrupt domestic life by exposing citizens to the bad manners and corrupt morals of barbarians. On the other hand, some early writers (such as Plato) acknowledged the gains from specialization or division of labour, although they were reluctant to extend the implications of this acknowledgement explicitly to foreign trade.

Other writers (such as Plutarch) took the view that God created the sea, geographic separation and diversity in endowments in order to promote interactions through trade between the various peoples of the earth. This doctrine of universal economy was developed by philosophers and theologians in the first several centuries AD, although dominant strands in medieval scholastic thought (reflected, for example, in the writings of St Thomas of Aquinas) continued to be suspicious about commercial activity and to worry that contact with foreigners would disrupt civil life. Natural law philosophers of the seventeenth and eighteenth centuries (such as Grotius) sought to resurrect the doctrine of universal economy, justifying a largely unconstrained freedom to trade on the law of nations (jus gentium).[3]

Mercantilism

However, none of these early views on international trade were primarily based on economic arguments, although (as we will see) they have continued to recur in one form or another even in contemporary debates over free trade. In the seventeenth and eighteenth centuries a school of thought often referred to as mercantilism emerged in Britain and the Continent that was explicitly economic in its foundations. While not hostile to commercial activity generally or to international trade in principle, mercantilists argued for close government regulation of international trade for two principal reasons: (1) to maintain a favourable balance of trade, which argued for aggressive export but restrictive import policies (although how foreigners were to pay for imports without the ability to export was never adequately explained); and (2) to promote the manufacturing of raw materials at home, rather than importing manufactured goods, which would displace domestic production and employment; hence arguments for export taxes on exported raw materials and import duties on imported manufactured or luxury goods.

The origins of the economic case for free trade

These two central tenets of mercantilist theories of international trade were fundamentally attacked and undermined, at least as a matter of theory, if not as a matter of policy, in the second half of the eighteenth century. The first argument for restricting foreign trade reflected a concern that international trade may give rise to an inadequate supply of circulating monetary gold as a result of balance of payment deficits. Silver and gold were mainstays of national wealth and essential to vigorous commerce. Hence the appropriate policy goal was perceived to be the maintenance of a continuing surplus in the balance of payments, i.e. sell more to foreigners than one buys from them. Imperial rivalries also led to political concerns about the transfer of *specie* into foreign hands and in part explains colonization efforts in the eighteenth and nineteenth centuries where colonies were seen as a source of raw materials and an outlet for manufactured goods. However, David Hume, in 1752, demonstrated that through the price-specie-flow mechanism, international trade was likely to maintain an equilibrium in the balance of payments. If a country found itself with surplus currency, domestic prices would tend to rise relative to prices of foreign commodities, and money would flow out of the country. If a country found itself with a shortage of currency, domestic prices would become depressed and would attract foreign currency until the shortage had disappeared.[4]

Adam Smith, in the *Wealth of Nations* (1776), mounted a broader assault on mercantilist theories, in particular the commodity composition argument for restricting trade, and argued that the case for gains from specialization in domestic economic activities applied equally to specialization in international trade:

> What is prudence in the conduct of every private family can scarcely be folly in that of a great kingdom. If a foreign country can supply us with a

> commodity cheaper than we can make, better buy it of them with some part of the produce of our own industry.[5]

Thus, to take some simple examples, if countries with tropical climates can produce bananas or pineapples more cheaply than countries with temperate climates, the latter should purchase these products from the former. Conversely, if countries with industrialized economies can produce hydro-electric generators or telephone systems more cheaply and of better quality than those that could be produced by countries that enjoy a cost advantage in producing tropical produce, the latter should buy these products from the former. In domestic economic activities, most of us accept that it makes no sense for an individual to try and produce all his or her own food, clothing, medical services, dental services, home construction services, etc., but rather to specialize in producing some goods or services for others and perhaps for some limited subset of his or her own needs, while purchasing requirements to meet remaining needs from others who specialize in their production. It is equally easy to appreciate the force of this argument for free trade within nation states. For example, in a large federal state like the US, Michigan specializes in producing automobiles (*inter alia*), Florida citrus fruit and tourism, Texas oil and beef, and California wine and high technology products. If each state of the US were to have attempted to become self-sufficient in these and all its own needs, the US would today be immeasurably poorer. It equally follows, on Smith's theory, that similar specialization is likely to generate mutual gains from trade in international exchanges – the division of labour is limited only by the extent of the market. It is important to note that on Smith's theory, *unilateral* trade liberalization would be an advantageous policy for a country to pursue, irrespective of the trade policies pursued by other countries.

The theory of comparative advantage

A central question left open by Smith's Theory of Absolute Advantage (as it came to be called) was: what if a country has no absolute advantage over any of its potential trading partners with respect to any products or services? Is international trade of no relevance or value to it? David Ricardo, in his book *The Principles of Political Economy* published in 1817, answered this question with a shattering insight that continues to form the basis of conventional international trade theory today. His insight has come to be called the Theory of Comparative Advantage. He advanced this theory by means of a simple arithmetic example. In his example, England could produce a given quantity of cloth with the labour of 100 men. It could also produce a given quantity of wine with the labour of 120 men. Portugal, in turn, could produce the same quantity of cloth with the labour of 90 men and the same quantity of wine with the labour of 80 men. Thus, Portugal enjoyed an absolute advantage over England with respect to the production of both cloth and wine, i.e. it could produce a given quantity of cloth or wine with fewer labour inputs than England. However, Ricardo argued that trade was still mutually advantageous, assuming full employment in both countries: when England exported to

Portugal the cloth produced by the labour of 100 men in exchange for wine produced by 80 Portuguese, she imported wine that would have required the labour of 120 Englishmen to produce. As for Portugal, she gained by her 80 men's labour cloth that it would have taken 90 of her labourers to produce. Both countries would be rendered better off through trade.

Another way of understanding the same intuition is to imagine the following simple domestic example.[6] Suppose a lawyer is not only more efficient in the provision of legal services than her secretary, but is also a more efficient secretary. It takes her secretary twice as long to type a document as the lawyer could type it herself. Suppose, more specifically, that it takes the lawyer's secretary two hours to type a document that the lawyer could type in one hour, and that the secretary's hourly wage is $20, and that the lawyer's hourly rate to clients is $200. It will pay the lawyer to hire the secretary and pay her $40 to type the document in two hours while the lawyer is able to sell for $200 the hour of her time that would otherwise have been committed to typing the document. In other words, both the lawyer and the secretary gain from this exchange. These examples, in an international trade context, generalize to the proposition that a country should specialize in producing and exporting goods in which its comparative advantage is greatest, or comparative disadvantage is smallest, and should import goods in which its comparative disadvantage is greatest.

An unfortunate semantic legacy of Ricardo's demonstration of the gains from international trade that has been perpetuated in the terminology of much subsequent trade literature and debate is that in international trade *countries* are trading with each other. This, of course, is rarely the case. As in purely domestic exchanges, *private economic actors* (albeit located in different countries) are trading with each other. In its most rudimentary form, all that international trade theory seeks to demonstrate is that free international trade dramatically broadens the contract opportunity set available to private economic actors and hence the mutual gains realizable from exchange as parties with different endowments of specialized resources or skills are able to reap the gains from their differential advantages and disadvantages through trade.

It may be argued that in international exchanges, in contrast to domestic exchanges, part of the gains from exchange are realized by foreigners, and that a country would be advantaged by capturing all the gains from exchange for itself. However, this raises the question of whether the domestic gains foregone by foreign trade are greater or less than the additional gains from purely domestic exchange. As a matter of simple economic theory, the gains to domestic consumers from foreign trade will almost always be greater than the additional gains to domestic producers from purely domestic trade. This is so because higher domestic than foreign prices will entail a transfer of resources from domestic consumers to domestic producers (arguably creating matching decreases and increases in welfare), but *in addition* some domestic consumers will be priced out of the market by the higher domestic prices and will be forced to allocate their resources to less preferred consumption choices, entailing a dead-weight social loss. An alternative way in which to conceive of the net domestic loss from foregone foreign exchange opportunities is to ask what compensation domestic producers would need to offer domestic consumers to render them indifferent to these forgone opportunities. Presumably only domestic prices that matched foreign producers' prices would achieve this end.

The factor proportions hypothesis

While Ricardo's theory of comparative advantage still constitutes the underpinnings of conventional international trade theory, his theory has been refined in various ways by subsequent analysis. Ricardo's theory, for example, assumed constant costs at all levels of production which led to the conclusion that a country would specialize completely in the goods where its comparative advantage was greatest (wine in the case of Portugal) or its comparative disadvantage smallest (cloth in the case of England), but this hypothesis rarely seemed to fit the facts. For example, Portugal produced both wine and some cloth. Ricardo's theory was thus modified to take account of increasing opportunity costs. For example, by releasing resources from cloth-making it would not necessarily follow that the addition of these labour inputs to wine-making would continue to increase wine production in constant proportions, especially if the factor proportions in the two activities were different e.g. cloth-making is labour intensive while wine-making is land intensive. In other words, once more than one factor of production was taken into account, it became obvious that combining land and labour at ever increasing levels of output would not necessarily entail similar costs, as the land brought into production at higher levels of output may well (and typically would) be less productive and require more intensive use of labour. On the other hand, the opposite phenomenon may sometimes be true, that is that decreasing costs may be associated with increased scale of operations or levels of output, and may lead to complete international specialization.

Recognition of these considerations led to a reformulation of Ricardo's theory of comparative advantage – often referred to as the Factor Proportions Hypothesis (or the Heckscher–Ohlin Theorem, after two Swedish economists who formulated the theorem in the 1920s). According to the Factor Proportions Hypothesis, countries will tend to enjoy comparative advantages in producing goods that use their more abundant factors more intensively, and each country will end up exporting its abundant factor goods in exchange for imported goods that use its scarce factors more intensively.

While the Factor Proportions Hypothesis seems to explain adequately patterns of international specialization in many activities, particularly agriculture and natural resources, it tends to provide a less satisfactory explanation of patterns of specialization in manufacturing activities in modern industrialized economies, where it is common to observe countries specializing in different segments of the same or closely analogous product markets, and simultaneously exporting and importing products in these sectors. Intra-industry trade has accounted for a very high percentage of the total increase in international trade in recent decades.[7] The Factor Proportions Hypothesis assumes that all countries have access to identical technologies of production and that the list of goods which are traded is somehow exogenously given and unaltered by economic activity. However, patterns of specialization and comparative advantage are not exclusively exogenously determined, but are likely to turn in part on a number of endogenous variables, such as savings and capital accumulation rates in different countries; the levels and patterns of investment in specialized human capital, reflecting the country's commitment to investments in education and research and development; and public infrastructure such as transportation and communication systems, which again reflect patterns of collective investments. On this view, comparative advantage is a much more dynamic notion than the static notion implicit in the original formulation of the Factor Proportions Hypothesis, and moreover recognizes the role that governments can play, through a variety of public policies, in shaping comparative advantage over time.

It is also important to note that classical trade theory, as described above, assumed that physical output from production was (subject to transportation costs) mobile across nations but that factors of production, while in most cases mobile within countries, were immobile across nations. While this obviously remains true of land, it has become dramatically less true of financial capital, technology, human capital, and even people, in large part because of advances in communication and transportation technologies. Thus, trade theory has historically focused on *international trade in goods* (a focus reflected in the initial preoccupations of the GATT), and not international mobility of services, capital or people. This focus has been increasingly challenged, as reflected in a rapidly changing trade policy agenda.

The product cycle theory

Largely reflecting the less static, and more dynamic conception of comparative advantage, noted above, in the 1960s Raymond Vernon of the Harvard Business School formulated a Product Cycle Theory of trade in manufactured goods to explain patterns of international specialization in manufacturing.[8] According to Vernon's Product Cycle Theory, the USA and other highly developed and industrialized economies, reflecting their superior access to large amounts of financial capital and highly specialized forms of human capital, would enjoy a comparative advantage in the research and development intensive stage of product innovation. This stage would focus initially on servicing a small, domestic, custom-oriented market. The second stage in the product cycle would see production expanded to cater to a mass domestic market. The third stage would see products exported to other countries and perhaps parent companies setting up subsidiaries in other countries to undertake manufacture there (the phenomenon of the Multinational Enterprise). A further stage in the product cycle would see the production technology becoming highly standardized and adopted by producers in other countries, particularly countries with lower labour costs, and products perhaps then being exported by these countries back to the USA or other countries where the innovations had originated. According to Vernon, quasi-rents could be earned by domestic firms early in the product cycle, but these rents would be dissipated as the product moved to later stages in the cycle, and comparative advantage shifted to other countries.

The Product Cycle Theory of international trade in manufactured goods seems to explain reasonably well patterns of specialization observable in many countries in the 1950s and 1960s. It has become less compelling over the last two decades, as an increasing number of countries, like Japan and other newly industrializing countries (NICs) have acquired many of the same comparative advantages as the older industrialized economies in early stages of the product cycle, through access to large domestic and international sources of capital that have become increasingly mobile, and through investments of their own in the human capital required to achieve a comparative advantage in the early stages of product innovation and manufacture.

The increasing recognition that comparative advantage is not exclusively ordained by nature but is in significant part, at least in manufacturing and services, the product of deliberate government policies, has led to an increased focus in many domestic policy settings on issues of so-called industrial policy, and at an international level, concerns and accusations over whether foreign governments' domestic policies are unfairly shaping or distorting comparative advantage.[9] These are issues that we take up in more detail in various contexts later in this book. However, beyond these issues, several long-standing qualifications to the case for free trade, in both economic and non-economic terms, should be briefly noted at this juncture.

Qualifications to the case for free trade

Reciprocity

While classical trade theory emphasized the advantages of unilateral trade liberalization over the protectionist base case, taking the trade policies of trading partners as a given, it is obviously the case that a country is likely to realize additional economic advantages from trade liberalization if it can persuade its trading partners also to liberalize their trade policies, thus generating benefits on both the import and export sides. This raises complex strategic issues for the first country. The modern trade literature distinguishes two kinds of reciprocity – passive and aggressive reciprocity.[10] Pursuing a strategy of passive reciprocity, a country might simply decline to reduce any of its existing trade restrictions until its trading partners agree to reduce some of their trade restrictions. However, if the trading partners appreciate that it is in the first country's interests to liberalize trade whatever the former do, they may choose to withhold any concessions in the hope of gaining the benefits of the first country's trade liberalization for free. This is a classic Prisoner's Dilemma problem, which may inhibit trade liberalization and lead to an inefficient outcome in which everyone is worse off. On the other hand, the trading partners may realize that it could be difficult from a political standpoint for the first country to liberalize on the import side without being able to enlist the support of its export-oriented producers and moderate the effects of contraction in its import-sensitive industries with growth in its export industries. In this case, a strategy of passive reciprocity may produce a mutual agreement on trade liberalization.

A strategy of aggressive reciprocity might take any of several forms.[11] Where two countries have previously negotiated a reciprocal trade agreement, in the absence of a supranational authority with the ability to enforce the agreement, the threat of retaliation for breach of or defection from the agreement may be the only effective means of ensuring that the agreement is effectively self-enforcing.[12] Retaliation here is likely to entail withdrawal of previous concessions in the hope that this (or the threat thereof) will induce the breaching country to fulfil its prior commitments. Where countries must deal with each other indefinitely, this tit-for-tat strategy may solve repeated Prisoner's Dilemma games by ensuring cooperation rather than defection.[13]

More controversial forms of aggressive reciprocity (unilateralism) entail threats by one country to withdraw previous concessions or impose new trade restrictions if trading partners persist in engaging in policies that are perceived by the first country to impact unfairly on its interests – e.g. subsidies in the case of imports, or distribution tie-ups in the case of exports. Adam Smith himself was prepared to contemplate retaliatory reinstatement of previous trade restrictions where foreign countries were maintaining restrictions on imports, although he was concerned that where there was no certainty that retaliation ('revenge') would induce removal of the restrictions, retaliation would simply impose unnecessary costs on domestic consumers.[14] The most prominent contemporary example of such a strategy is the discretionary retaliation provisions of the so-called 'Super 301' regime adopted by the USA in the Omnibus Trade and Competitiveness Act of 1988 which may be invoked where a foreign country's policies are found by the US Trade Representative to be 'unreasonable or discriminatory' and to burden or restrict United States Commerce.[15] Here the threat of retaliatory trade restrictions is primarily designed to induce foreign countries to modify policies or practices that the US government believes are unfairly impeding US exports into foreign markets (the so-called 'crow-bar' theory of trade policy). A major problem with this form of aggressive reciprocity (unilateralism) is that it often reflects very divergent understandings of existing obligations – on the one hand, that a foreign country is cheating on at least the spirit of previous reciprocal commitments, or on the other hand, that the country threatening retaliation is attempting to coerce new unreciprocated trade or other concessions from foreign countries and is itself cheating on prior commitments by threatening their withdrawal. While in some circumstances the threat of retaliation may involve 'cooperative' solutions to trade disputes, in other cases 'feuds' (counter-retaliation) or 'stalemates' may ensue.[16] Where cooperative solutions do emerge, they are likely to reflect bilateral 'deals' that are antithetical to a non-discriminatory international trading order and may conduce to 'collusive' or managed forms of trade that diverge substantially from the liberal trade ideal. However, some authors argue that once we take into account the transaction costs entailed in monitoring for cheating on, and ensuring compliance with, complex international agreements that lack an effective third-party enforcement mechanism, these arrangements may be the best that can be achieved. While falling short of the (unattainable) first–best liberal trade ideal, they may prevent the world trading system from degenerating into total autarchy or anarchy.[17]

In any event, while reciprocity in any of its various forms played a marginal role in the classical economic theory of trade, it is absolutely crucial to understanding the evolution of the institutional arrangements, both domestic and supranational, that govern international trade, which are reviewed later in this chapter.

The optimal tariff

A second qualification to the case for free trade, recognized at a relatively early stage in the evolution of trade theory, is the concept of the so-called *Optimal Tariff*. On this theory, countries that account for a very high proportion of international demand for a certain good may, through their governments acting as 'cartel' managers for consumers, possess a significant degree of monopsony power, which they can exercise to their advantage by the imposition of a tariff which changes the terms of trade by forcing firms in exporting countries to reduce the price of their products and in effect absorb the tariff. Consumers in the importing countries continue to pay the same price for the goods, but their governments capture additional revenue from foreign exporters through the tariff. While in theory the concept of the optimal tariff may be correct from a national (although not a cosmopolitan or global) perspective, the empirical evidence suggests that there are few cases where importing countries possess the degree of monopsony power in international markets necessary to implement effectively such a policy.

Infant industries

A third and equally long-standing qualification to the conventional case for free trade pertains to the case of *infant industries*.[18] As John Stuart Mill argued,[19] along with other writers like Alexander Hamilton in the USA in the late eighteenth century and Friedrich List in Germany in the late nineteenth century, in the early stages of a country's economic development there may be a case for the imposition of protective tariffs or quotas to allow infant industries, in particular infant manufacturing industries, to develop, by servicing a protected domestic market, to a scale and level of sophistication that will subsequently permit them to compete both with imports and even more desirably to become effective exporters in their own right. This argument has exerted a significant and enduring influence on international trade theory and policy over the past century and a half. It was centrally relied on by the USA and Canada in maintaining a high tariff policy throughout most of the nineteenth century and the first quarter of the twentieth century. It has been relied on by less developed countries (LDCs) in the post-Second World War era to justify 'special and differential status' under the GATT in protecting their domestic markets and promoting import substitution policies. It is also, more controversially, claimed to have been a central strategic element in the rise of Japan as a major industrial power. In part, the infant industry argument rests on the proposition that an advanced, mature economy cannot be predominantly dependent upon agriculture or natural resources for its exports, but requires a substantial manufacturing base, partly in order to diversify its economic activities and employment base and reduce the risks associated with excessive reliance on a narrow base of commodity exports, which may be subject to high price (and income) volatility and deteriorating terms of trade relative to manufactured imports, and partly for non-economic reasons associated with national pride in being on the technological frontier along with other advanced countries and providing a concomitant number and range of challenging employment opportunities to its more highly educated or trained citizenry. However, it bears pointing out that some countries have sustained high standards of living without substantial manufacturing sectors, e.g. New Zealand and Denmark through agriculture, Middle Eastern oil-producing states through natural resources. Moreover, it has proven extraordinary difficult to specify with analytical rigour the key parameters of the infant industries exception – why private capital markets cannot identify long-term opportunities; why governments are better able to do so; whether there are externalities from investments in infant industries that are not captured in private investment calculi; whether governments are likely to be vulnerable to capture by rent-seeking special interests in the initial decision to promote, and subsequent decisions to sustain, an infant industry.[20]

Strategic trade theory

A contemporary variant on the infant industry argument entails an elaboration on, and application to, the international trade context of the concept of imperfect competition initially developed by Edward Chamberlin and Joan Robinson in the 1930s. Here, it is argued that many modern manufacturing industries fall somewhere between the polarities of the neo-classical economic concepts of monopoly and perfect competition, i.e. essentially oligopolistic industries where prices do not necessarily reflect costs and where quasi-rents can be realized by firms (and hence countries) able to acquire strategically dominant positions in industries in which increasing returns to scale imply that there is room for only a handful of firms in the global market. In this respect, it is argued that an important role can be played by domestic governments through research and development subsidies, export subsidies, procurement policies, related industrial policies, and import restrictions designed to allow a firm to realize economies of scale initially in a protected domestic market, in promoting so-called Schumpeterian industries. This has led to the emergence of Strategic Trade Theory,[21] where it is argued that governments can promote their national interests by assisting firms to establish pre-emptive, first-mover, positions in markets, and to realize learning-curve advantages, in part by maintaining entry barriers to potential competitors. Again, this is a highly controversial aspect of modern international trade theory. Subsequent research has revealed that strategic theory is highly sensitive to a number of key variables: the number of firms in the domestic industry, ease of entry, whether firms choose prices rather than quantities in order to maximize profits, whether targeted industries draw upon a common critical factor of production, the extent of foreign ownership in targeted sectors, and the potential reactions of governments of foreign countries and competitors or potential competitors based there.[22] Nevertheless, the dramatic growth of export sectors in many of the so-called Asian 'Tigers' is often attributed to strategic trade policies.

Revenue-raising considerations

Another long-standing qualification to the case for free trade relates to the *revenue-raising* potential of customs duties. In many industrialized countries, it was not until early in this century that income taxes (direct taxes) provided the primary source of government revenues. Until this time, customs duties and to a lesser extent, export taxes were a major source of government revenues. Even today, in developing countries with large informal economies where internal income taxes are difficult or impossible to administer and collect, import and export taxes constitute a major source of government revenue-raising capabilities.

National security considerations

A long-standing non-economic qualification to the case for free trade relates to *national security* considerations. These may arise on both the import and export sides. With respect to imports, it is argued that there may sometimes be a case for restrictions in order to protect domestic industries which, even though not internationally competitive, may be required in the event of war or other international disruption. Thus, industries such as the steel and ship-building industries have often been protected on this basis, although the concept of national security has proven highly elastic, being invoked to justify restrictions on such unlikely imports as clothes pegs from Poland on the grounds that domestic productive capabilities in clothes pegs would be required in the event of hostilities with the (former) Communist Bloc countries. On the export side, national security considerations have sometimes been invoked to restrict exports of strategically sensitive products or military materiel to 'unfriendly' foreign countries.

Objections to free trade

Apart from the foregoing qualifications to the case for free trade, a number of other more general objections are often raised to free trade: (1) job displacement and wage depression; (2) lowest common denominator effects on domestic social policies; (3) cultural homogenization; and (4) loss of domestic political sovereignty. These will each be briefly considered, drawing primarily, by way of example, on the Canadian experience. Between 1947 and 1986, Canada's merchandise imports grew in value by 552% in real terms and merchandise exports by 564% in real terms. For Canada, post-war multilateral trade liberalization under the GATT has to a large extent entailed bilateral trade expansion with the USA. What have been the effects of this increased trade dependency?

Impact on wages and employment

From 1947 to 1986, per capita GDP in Canada rose in real terms from $7,402 to $19,925 (1986 $) (an increase of 169.2%). Total employment grew from 4,821,000 in 1947 to 12,295,000 in April 1988 (an increase of 155.0%), with manufacturing employment rising 88.7% from 1,131,750 to 2,136,000 during this period. At the same time, of course, Canadian consumers (the silent majority in free trade debates) have enjoyed dramatically wider product choices and lower product prices because of imports. While it would be naïve to suggest that these increases in jobs and incomes are wholly or even primarily attributable to trade liberalization and expansion, at least the opposite proposition so often asserted – that continued trade liberalization is likely to reduce real incomes and employment – is revealed as unfounded. While trade liberalization can have negative impacts on jobs and wages in particular domestic sectors which are vulnerable to imports, the net effect on jobs and wages economy-wide has been strongly positive. For workers in sectors adversely impacted by imports, generous and well-conceived domestic adjustment assistance programmes, rather than trade protection, can often deal more cost-effectively with transition costs (as we will argue more fully in a later chapter).[23]

Contemporary expressions of concern over the effects of trade liberalization on jobs and wages in developed economies tend to focus on competition from low-wage developing countries (the so-called 'pauper labour' argument). However, as Hufbauer and Schott point out,[24] between 1975 and 1990, the dollar value of two-way trade between OECD countries and low-income countries tripled from $59 billion to $200 billion. Yet the per capita income gaps between OECD countries and low-income countries actually increased over this period (from 30 times higher to 58 times higher), reflecting the higher productivity of labour in developed economies. While empirical evidence suggests rising income inequalities and higher levels of unemployment amongst unskilled workers in many developed countries, few of these effects seem attributable to increased trade with developing countries (but rather factors such as technological change).[25]

Impact on social policies

Not only has the post-war period of trade liberalization seen these enormous increases in real incomes and employment in Canada, it has also simultaneously witnessed the emergence of the modern welfare state. Public expenditures in Canada on education rose from $147 per capita in 1947 to $1,237 per capita in 1983–4 in real terms (1986 $), or from 1.99% of GDP to 6.79%. Public expenditures on health care rose from $54 per capita in 1947 to $1,202 per capita in 1985 in real terms (1986 $), or from 0.72% of GDP to 6.18%. Direct financial benefits paid to Canadians under various social welfare programmes amounted to $49,136 million in 1985, compared with 1947 expenditures of $3,838 million on all 'public welfare' programmes (including health) (1986 $). Federal transfer payments to the provinces rose from the equivalent of 0.12% of GDP in 1947 to 4.04% in 1986. Public expenditures on cultural activities have risen from negligible amounts in

1947 to 0.74% of GDP in 1984–5. Over the same period, greatly increased regulatory attention has also been paid to occupational health and safety, consumer protection and environmental issues. Trade liberalization and trade expansion have not been inconsistent with these redistributional, social and cultural policies. History again reveals this fear as unfounded. Indeed the simple truism is often overlooked that only relatively prosperous countries can afford generous social policies. Impoverished third world countries do not have such policies, not because they lack commitment to them in principle, but because they do not have the wealth to afford them. Creating wealth is a precondition to redistributing it.

Thus, nothing in the theory or history of trade liberalization and expansion is inconsistent with increasing real incomes and employment or compassionate and civilized social and cultural policies. In fact, there is every reason to believe that only by exploiting our comparative advantage to the fullest can we sustain increasing prosperity and the social policies that prosperity makes possible. Nevertheless, it is important to acknowledge that concerns that international competition will force countries to the lowest common denominator (a 'race to the bottom') in terms of domestic policies pertaining to, for example, workplace safety laws, employment standards, and environmental laws have recently provoked considerable discussion and debate in the European Union and North America. This is again an issue we return to later in this book, in the context of debates over trade and labour standards[26] and trade and the environment.[27]

Impact on cultural diversity

Another perspective, which figured prominently in the Canada–US free trade debates in the late 1980s, emphasizes the dangers to national cultural identity presented by free trade and international mobility of labour and capital. Distinctive ways of life and cultural values are seen as threatened by the homogenizing effects of economic and technological imperialism. This point of view finds expression in the critique by Rousseau and the nineteenth-century political romantic movement of classical political economy, and also in the Jeffersonian alternative to the commercial republic, as well as in the views of some of the Ancients referred to earlier in this chapter. Even authors like Fukuyama,[28] who have recently proclaimed the triumph of economic and political liberalism and 'the end of history', worry about the blandness, homogeneity, and materialism that this may presage.

One cannot help but find somewhat ominous the romanticized 'closed community' conception held by contemporary critics of economic liberalism. Traditional closed societies may have preserved distinctive customs and beliefs against external influences, but only at the cost of racial, religious, and ideological intolerance, and of significant limits on individual self-development. If we were really to avoid the consequences of contemporary cosmopolitanism, trade barriers would hardly be enough – we would need strict censorship, exit visas, limits on ethnic diversity, and other measures aimed at maintaining the 'closedness' of the community.

In any event, during the post-war decades in which Canada has witnessed such enormous increases in international trade, particularly bilateral trade, it has also simultaneously witnessed the flowering of Quebec nationalism and the increasingly confident assertion of a distinctive French-Canadian cultural and linguistic identity. In the post-war period, Canada has also witnessed an enormous influx of immigrants from a great diversity of cultural backgrounds that has immeasurably enriched Canada's multicultural mosaic, rendering Canada one of the most vibrant and tolerant cosmopolitan societies in the world. This is not the traditional Canada that George Grant so nostalgically recalled in *Lament for a Nation*,[29] but nor have Canadians become part of a homogenized, universalistic American culture as he portended. Canada is and will remain a profoundly different society, as a comparison of daily life in Windsor and Detroit or Toronto and Buffalo should convince the doubtful reader. There are surely deeper measures of a society's cultural evolution than how many minutes are occupied by which country's soap operas on local commercial television networks. While liberal trading policies cannot claim direct credit for our increased cultural diversity and distinctiveness, a close intellectual concomitant of liberal trading policies – more liberal immigration policies – clearly can claim substantial credit. It is not philosophically consistent to urge open and liberal immigration policies but to advocate at the same time closed and illiberal trade policies that deprive potential immigrants of economic opportunities in their home countries, thus leaving them with no option but to sever their roots and emigrate.

Nevertheless, more narrowly focused concerns over the impact of trade and investment liberalization on a country's cultural sectors (e.g. film, television, radio, newspapers, magazine and book publishing) continue to exert considerable influence in international economic relations as reflected in general or qualified exceptions (often contentious) for such sectors in domestic and international policy instruments.

Impact on domestic political sovereignty

All international treaties, whether relating to nuclear disarmament, human rights, the environment, the law of the sea, or trade, constrain domestic political sovereignty through the assumption of external obligations. But unless anarchy in international relations is preferred as an alternative, in most cases we accept that the benefits of the reciprocal obligations involved outweigh the costs associated with any loss of political sovereignty. In the trade context, the additional argument is sometimes made that increased economic interdependence constrains political sovereignty in unacceptable ways in that countries – especially smaller countries with major trading relationships with larger countries, such as Canada and the USA – will be concerned that adopting independent foreign policies, for example, may antagonize the larger trading partner and lead to forms of economic 'blackmail' designed to induce policy conformity. This risk cannot be altogether gainsaid. However, trade treaties that structure relations by reference to durable, well-defined substantive norms and objective dispute resolution procedures reduce the risks of larger countries exploiting raw economic power to bully smaller countries, by subjecting power relations to some form of legal ordering. In addition, smaller countries typically stand to gain disproportionately from trade liberalization. This is due to the simple fact that liberalization will provide access to a larger set of potential new trading relationships than in the case of the larger country gaining enhanced access to the smaller country's market. Nevertheless, sweeping claims for international harmonization of many domestic policies in the name of trade or investment liberalization do legitimately engage concerns over excessive constraints on political sovereignty and democratic accountability by privileging competitive markets over competitive politics (an issue we return to in the final chapter).[30]

Public choice theory and the politics of trade liberalization

Over the last three decades or so, economists have developed an increasing interest in the positive analysis of politics. The basic economic model of politics that has been developed – commonly referred to as 'public choice' theory – models the political process as an implicit market with demanders (voters or interest groups) of government policies exchanging political support in terms of votes, information/propaganda, campaign contributions or other material forms of assistance for desired policies. Government (politicians and their agents, bureaucrats and regulators) will supply policies that maximize the governing Party's prospects of re-election (or in the case of opposition Parties, election). This view of the political process contrasts with that conventionally assumed hitherto by economists, which sees governments as attempting to maximize some social welfare function by correcting for various forms of market failure (monopoly, public goods, externalities, etc.). Implicit in the public choice approach is the view that neither the effect nor intent of most government policies is to advance the common good, but rather to construct minimum winning coalitions, often through redistributional policies, even though the impact of such policies will often, perhaps primarily, be to reduce aggregate social welfare.

Applying the public choice model, Downs[31] and subsequently Olson[32] argued that narrow producer interests would tend to dominate thinly-spread consumer interests in the political process. This is largely a function of the differential mobilization and hence lobbying costs faced by producer and consumer interests. The larger the per capita stakes in an issue, the stronger will be the incentives to overcome information and transaction costs in organizing; and the fewer the affected stake-holders the easier it will be to overcome the free-rider problem that afflicts large interest groups whose individual members have small per capita stakes in the relevant issues. This framework would tend to suggest that highly concentrated industries with few firms, perhaps also highly geographically concentrated, and possibly with highly unionized work-forces, are likely to be able to organize most effectively and, therefore, are most likely to secure favourable policies from government, including trade protection.

A major theoretical difficulty with this model is that it appears to imply no equilibrium in the political process, at least in the context in which it purports to apply, short of a corner solution entailing infinite protection for the affected industries (a total ban on imports). This is manifestly not what we typically observe, even in concentrated industries, which is sufficient to raise some prima facie doubts about the subtlety of the model. As Destler and Odell point out,[33] the weakness in the model is its simplistic assumptions that, on the one hand, domestic producers, who are easily mobilized politically, uniformly favour protectionism and that, on the other, the sole or principal cost-bearers are ultimate end-users or lay consumers, who are politically disabled. More specifically, the model first ignores the fact that imports will often be intermediate inputs into another industry, for example, textiles and clothing, steel and automobiles, and that the industry purchasing the inputs will normally find it rational to resist cost-increasing policies. Second, the model ignores the fact that export-oriented industries may have reason to fear retaliation by foreign countries to restrictions on their exports in the form of reciprocal trade restrictions, thus creating an incentive for such industries to resist domestically imposed trade restrictions. Moreover, the potential for growth in export-oriented sectors is likely to moderate the adjustment costs faced by import-impacted sectors, thus reducing the political resistance to trade liberalization. Third, the model overlooks the fact that importers of final goods – distributors and large retail chains that import and sell large quantities of imports – constitute a major producer constituency that will be disadvantaged by trade restrictions. Fourth, while it is true that consumers may face information costs, transaction costs, and strategic impediments to effective group mobilization, as individuals they still possess votes which constitute a resource that firms, whatever their other political resources, by definition do not possess. The determinants of the political rate of exchange between various political currencies, for example, votes and financial resources, are not well addressed in the public choice model of the political process. Finally, the model fails to disaggregate what may be complex competing interests *within* firms. As Milner argues, domestic firms with strong international ties often face difficult choices as to whether to support or oppose protection. Protectionist measures which may benefit the firm in a sector where it produces domestically could lead to retaliation by foreign trading partners that could harm the firm's exporting or foreign investment interests.[34] Milner also points out that large, multinational firms have more ability to pursue their own adjustment policies, by moving assembly or other activities offshore to counter any wage-price advantages maintained by foreign competitors. On the other hand, such firms may demand trade restrictions as a kind of 'stick' with which to threaten foreign trading partners to open up their markets, although the evidence that using trade restrictions in this manner can procure significant market opening is quite ambiguous.[35] In sum, the behaviour of firms will often be motivated by complex interests that do not necessarily point to a pro-protectionist rent-seeking outcome.

Various non-public choice models of the trade policy process identified by Baldwin,[36] in contrast to the behavioural assumption of short-run economic self-interest adopted by the public choice models, admit of diverse factors: long-run pursuit of self-interest by economic agents and political actors, autonomous behaviour by public officials who are not simply intermediaries acting on the wishes of the electorate or some part of it, and altruism on the part of public and private actors concerned about the welfare of individuals who may be affected by import competition. Conversely, these public and private actors may arguably be concerned about the welfare of individuals in foreign countries, especially poorer developing countries, disadvantaged by denial of access to domestic markets for their goods.

The difficulty with these latter models as positive frameworks for predicting trade policy decisions is that their behavioural assumptions are so vague as to be largely untestable, and are likely to provide a positive rationalization for almost any conceivable set of trade policies (and thus predict or explain nothing).

The empirical evidence on most postulated political determinants of trade protection is as ambiguous as the positive theories that underlie the postulates.[37] This ambiguity applies to industry concentration, geographic concentration, industry size (in terms of number of employees), labour intensity, and extent of unionization. Most studies, however, find a positive correlation between protectionism and low-wage, low-skilled industries.

Baldwin concludes that an eclectic approach to understanding this behaviour is the most appropriate one currently. Until the various models are differentiated more sharply analytically and better empirical measures for distinguishing them are obtained, it will be difficult to ascertain the relative importance of different motivations of government officials under various conditions.[38]

An 'eclectic approach' is, of course, no model at all in terms of yielding testable implications or predictions at the level of positive analysis, and in terms of normative implications, provides very little purchase on those features of the policymaking process which, if modified, are likely to yield superior policy outcomes. Perhaps what can be said is that the evidence does not suggest an iron law of politics that inexorably drives governments, in particular sets of circumstances, to the adoption of particular trade restricting policies.

AN INSTITUTIONAL HISTORY OF INTERNATIONAL TRADE POLICY

The advent of free trade

Trading relationships between merchants from different nation-states go back to the dawn of recorded history. Trade was important to many ancient and medieval powers: Athens, Ptolemaic Egypt, the Italian city-states of Venice, Florence, and Genoa, and the German Hanseatic League. Trade regulation through the imposition of tolls (a major source of state revenue) has almost as long a history, as do trade agreements between nation-states – a commercial treaty between the Kings of Egypt and Babylonia existed in 2500 BC.[39]

However, a functional understanding of modern international trade policy on an institutional level necessarily involves some appreciation of the broader forces at work for free trade in the European economies during the late eighteenth and early nineteenth centuries. From this perspective, international trade institutions need to be seen as one aspect of a more general process leading to access to larger, more unified markets, such that by the mid-nineteenth century only national frontiers remained as effective barriers to trade.[40] This process included the repeal of laws banning the export of certain materials previously considered essential to national welfare, the abolition of local regulations regarding manufacturing techniques, the adoption of (national) standards in weights and measures, and the end of restrictions on personal economic freedom (continuing bans against unions being a conspicuous exception to the general trend). Nation-building itself was in part an effort to ensure free trade within domestic borders where such had not existed before: the dismantling of internal tolls and levies was an essential precondition to industrial development in the European economies.[41]

By the mid-nineteenth century, then, most of the advanced European countries had established free trade within their borders. But many nations continued to practice internationally what they had eschewed internally: protection (trade barriers) continued between nations as they vied for wealth and power in international relations. The first major break with these mercantilist-protectionist policies of the past came in Britain with the repeal of the Corn Laws in 1846, spear-headed by Prime Minister Sir Robert Peel, a late convert to the cause of trade liberalization, and Lord Cobden. The repeal of these laws was in part promoted by the increasing intellectual currency of the ideas of Smith and especially Ricardo, and partly by the practical urgency of responding to the desperation of the Irish Famine. Political agitation fed by the wealth and power of commercial and manufacturing interests also played a role, as it would elsewhere in Europe later in the century.[42] The repeal of the Corn Laws was quickly followed by the unilateral removal or reduction of hundreds of tariffs on most imported goods, ushering in, in Britain, a period of resolute commitment to the principle of free trade that extended into the early years of the twentieth century.

While British trade policy reflected the insights of classical trade theory that *unilateral* trade liberalization enhanced national welfare over the protectionist base case, Britain also, over the course of the century, negotiated a number of free trade treaties with other countries, beginning with the Cobden–Chevalier Treaty of 1860 with France.[43] France in turn, in 1862, negotiated a comprehensive trade treaty with the *Zollverein*, the German Customs Union, as well as with a host of other European nations in the following decade.[44] These treaties were notable for their espousal of the Most Favoured Nation (MFN) principle, which later became the cornerstone of the GATT. Under this principle, countries negotiating trade concessions with one another agreed that they would extend to each other any more favourable concessions that each might subsequently negotiate with third countries. The MFN principle encouraged multilateralism while discouraging trade discrimination, and because of its presence in most French treaties, free trade swept Europe during the 1860s.[45]

Treaties were not the only institutional results of trade policy in this period. At the same time that countries were negotiating cuts in tariffs, they signed conventions, mainly in the realm of transportation and communication, which helped to facilitate trade in other ways. For example, in 1868 the Rhine was declared a free way for ships of all nations, thus greatly facilitating the transport of goods throughout central Europe.[46] Trading nations also promoted international commerce by setting up organizations to sell domestic products abroad. Commercial attachés date from this period, as do state-run international chambers of commerce. Exhibitions were arranged to show off national wares, and commercial museums were set up to inform manufacturers of the requirements and tastes of foreign markets.[47]

However, the heyday of free trade was relatively brief and peaked over the period from about 1850 to 1885. In the 1870s Europe suffered a severe and sustained recession, and also found itself facing increasing competition from non-European grain producers. In 1879, Germany retreated from the principle of free trade, when Bismarck raised tariffs substantially on a number of imported items, partly in response to the economic stringencies of the time, and partly in response to the intellectual influence of writers like Friedrich List, who had returned from the United States persuaded of the virtues of a high tariff policy, particularly in manufacturing sectors, in order to promote infant industries. Germany's retreat from free trade was quickly followed by France and a number of European countries, with Britain alone remaining emphatically committed to free trade.[48]

It is perhaps prudent to reflect here on the character of European free trade during the nineteenth century in light of its sudden decline with the advent of hard times. It is important that the history of international trading institutions is not seen as the inevitable result of economic rationality and the triumph of superior economic thought. On the one hand, free trade did not disappear completely after 1879. Germany continued to negotiate trade treaties, although now economic ends tended to be subordinated to those of foreign policy. But perhaps this was no great change of course – free trade was always as much a tool of foreign policy as of economic development. Prussian attempts to establish the *Zollverein* were at least partly motivated by its nation-building aspirations. Similarly, historians have noted that Germany's treaties with France were part of a policy to isolate Austria (Prussia's main competitor for hegemony in the German world), and an attempt to gain French neutrality with respect to Germany's disputes with Denmark.[49] The Cobden–Chevalier treaty may also have been a product of foreign policy desiderata. It was intended, at least in part, to mollify Great Britain over French meddling on the Italian peninsula.[50]

Moreover, if it is a mistake to see treaties as motivated primarily by considerations of economic efficiency, so too would it be wrong to understand the pursuit of markets solely through the instrumentality of trade treaties. Throughout the nineteenth century, the European powers had pursued colonial acquisitions as a means of exploiting the gains from trade.[51] With the onset of depression, and the collapse of the free trade treaties in the late 1870s, this policy was pursued with a vengeance.[52]

The world thus began the present century with the European powers, with the exception of Britain, preferring in large part to reap the gains from trade other than through free trade with other advanced economies. The story had rarely ever been otherwise in the United States. There, with considerable variations over time, a high tariff policy generally prevailed through the nineteenth century, largely promoted by the Republican Party and influenced by the thinking and writings of prominent Americans like Alexander Hamilton, who had vigorously promoted the infant industry rationale for trade protection, in addition to revenue-raising considerations which for much of the nineteenth century were an important function served by tariffs.

The decline of the international trading order

As the world entered the twentieth century, Britain found its economic hegemony rapidly diminishing, and hence its ability to impress the case for free trade on its major trading partners. The advent of the First World War massively disrupted international trading relationships, and the terms of settlement of the war in part contributed to a general outbreak of beggar-thy-neighbour policies in the 1920s, including competitive exchange rate devaluations and trade restrictions.[53] The Most Favoured Nation system of trade treaties fell into disuse, and trading powers dealt with each other bilaterally instead. In the late 1920s, as the Great Depression set in, many domestic economies, and the world economy at large, largely collapsed. The economic privations of the time prompted many countries to adopt extreme forms of trade protectionism in an attempt to preserve domestic production and employment. The most notorious of such attempts was the enactment by the US Congress of the Smoot–Hawley Tariff in 1930, which raised duties on imports to an average of 60%, and quickly provoked similar retaliatory measures by most of the USA's major trading partners. In the view of most economic commentators, this seriously exacerbated the conditions of the Great Depression, as international trade ground to a virtual standstill.[54] However, a major shift in policy was signalled by the US Administration in 1934, when President Roosevelt was successful in persuading Congress to pass the Reciprocal Trade Agreements Act, which authorized the Administration to negotiate trade liberalizing agreements on a bilateral basis with its trading partners. In the ensuing years, 31 such agreements were concluded. However, the outbreak of the Second World War decisively shattered visions of a more cooperative international trading environment.[55]

By 1944, it had become reasonably clear to the Allies that the war would shortly be won, and policy-makers, particularly in Britain and the USA, turned their minds to strategies for reconstructing the world economy after the war. Hence, in 1944, in Bretton Woods, New Hampshire, USA, an agreement bearing that name was concluded between Britain and the USA that was designed to lay the groundwork for a cooperative international economic environment following the war. The Bretton Woods Agreement envisaged the creation of three key new international institutions: The International Monetary Fund (IMF), which would be charged with maintaining exchange rate stability, and assisting countries facing balance of payment crises to deal with those crises through access to special drawing rights to be provided by the IMF, rather than by resorting to trade restrictions; the International Bank for Reconstruction and Development (IBRD), commonly referred to as the World Bank, whose mandate initially was to provide reconstruction capital from countries like the USA whose economies had not been devastated by the war to the shattered economies of Europe and Japan; the success of the Marshall Plan that the USA subsequently adopted in promoting this objective meant that the World Bank was able quickly to redefine its focus as providing development capital to less developed countries; and the International Trade Organization (ITO), whose mandate was to oversee the negotiation and administration of a new multilateral, liberal world trading regime.[56]

The formation and evolution of the GATT[57]

Following the end of the war, the IMF and the World Bank were duly created, but the ITO did not come into existence, largely as a result of opposition in the US Congress, which was concerned that both the Organization and many provisions in the Havana Charter that would have created it would excessively constrain domestic sovereignty.[58] Instead, a provisional agreement, negotiated in 1947 among some 23 major trading countries in the world as a prelude to the ITO and the adoption of the Havana Charter, i.e. the General Agreement on Tariffs and Trade (GATT), in fact became the permanent institutional basis for the multilateral world trading regime that has prevailed to this day.[59] Under the GATT, some eight negotiating rounds have now been successfully concluded, the latest round (the Uruguay Round) involving more than 100 countries, being concluded in December 1993.[60] The first six of these rounds, concluding in 1967 with the Kennedy Round, focused primarily on reciprocal negotiation of tariff concessions. These negotiations were extremely successful and have led to the reduction of average world tariffs on manufactured goods from 40% in 1947 to 5% today. The Tokyo Round that ended in 1979, while also entailing substantial tariff cuts, for the first time directed substantial attention to various non-tariff barriers to trade, such as government procurement policies, subsidy policies, customs valuation policies, and technical standards. In all of these areas, Collateral Codes to the GATT were negotiated on a conditional MFN basis, meaning that only signatories to the Codes were subject to the rights and obligations created by the Codes.[61] The Tokyo Round closed with the world economy and many domestic economies under increasing pressure from a number of sources, including two oil price shocks, a major world recession in the early 1970s and another beginning in the early 1980s, and the rise of Japan, and other newly industrializing countries (NICs), such as Singapore, Hong Kong, Taiwan, South Korea and Brazil, as major competitive threats in manufactured products. These pressures provoked the rise of the so-called 'New Protectionism' beginning in the early 1970s with countries increasingly resorting to non-tariff barriers to trade, such as quotas, voluntary export restraint agreements, orderly marketing agreements, industrial and agricultural subsidies, and more aggressive unilateral invocation of trade remedy laws, particularly antidumping and countervailing duty laws. In addition, the Short Term Agreement on Cotton Textiles that had been initiated by the USA in 1961 had, by 1973, been generalized to the Multi-Fibre Arrangement (MFA), which permitted countries to negotiate bilateral agreements with exporting countries restricting exports of both natural and synthetic textiles and clothing. This arrangement has been particularly burdensome for many NICs and LDCs which had viewed textile and clothing manufacture, drawing on large pools of unskilled labour and relatively standardized technology, as an attractive entry point into the process of industrialization.

Throughout this period, LDCs in general have played a marginal role in GATT negotiations, which many viewed as a rich man's club. In 1964, LDCs formed the United Nations Commission on Trade and Development (UNCTAD), to address what were perceived to be the special and distinctive economic needs of the LDCs. In 1968, in response to UNCTAD recommendations, Part IV was added to the GATT, providing for so-called 'special and differential status' for LDCs and in particular exempting LDCs from any obligation of reciprocity with respect to trade concessions of developed countries while at the same time urging developed countries to provide unilateral trade concessions to LDCs on trade items of export interest to them. This in turn led to the adoption of the Generalized System of Preferences, where developed member countries of the GATT from the early 1970s onwards granted special trade concessions to LDCs, without seeking reciprocal trade concessions. The special and differential status secured by LDCs under the GATT reflected then widely prevalent thinking in many developing countries that import substitution policies (in effect infant industry promotion policies) were essential to the economic development of these countries, in order to diversify their economic base, provide expanding sources of employment, and reduce dependency on often highly volatile international commodity markets for primary products. With respect to the latter, UNCTAD also promoted the adoption of a variety of international commodity agreements in sectors such as coffee, cocoa, rubber, and tin, in an attempt to stabilize commodity prices and mitigate what were perceived to be deteriorating terms of trade with respect to the exchange of LDC commodities for industrialized countries' manufactured goods.[62]

The Uruguay Round of multilateral trade negotiations under the GATT, which lasted from 1986 to 1993, has proved the most difficult, contentious and complex round of negotiations to have taken place under the auspices of the GATT, in part because of the increasing strains on the world trading system noted above and in part because of the breadth of the negotiating agenda. The Uruguay Round, for the first time, attempted seriously to address the issue of liberalizing international trade in agriculture which had hitherto largely escaped GATT discipline. In addition, the Uruguay Round also sought to reverse the pattern of protectionism with respect to textiles and clothing that had evolved under the Multi-Fibre Arrangement. In addition, several new issues that had previously been viewed as falling outside the ambit of the GATT were for the first time addressed, including in particular international trade in services, trade-related intellectual property issues (TRIPs), and trade-related investment issues (TRIMs).[63]

In a recent extensive review[64] of the evolution of patterns of comparative advantage and international trade policy in the post-Second World War period, Ostry points out that the US as the hegemonic economic power following the war was initially prepared to accept asymmetric tariff reductions as part of its contribution to post-war reconstruction. However, with the resurgence of Western Europe and Japan, the US began to insist on more symmetry in tariff concessions (in the Kennedy and Tokyo Rounds). With rapid and continuing rates of technological diffusion, a declining share of world trade, a loss of comparative advantage in some mass production and technology-intensive sectors, and rising trade deficits with Japan and other NICs, the US in recent years has become increasingly concerned about what it perceives as a lack of reciprocity in international trading relations, and hence has evinced a greater willingness to pursue strategies of unilateralism and regionalism in addition to or instead of exclusive commitments to the multilateral system. In particular, 'system frictions', involving different traditions of government intervention in domestic economies and of forms of industrial organization, have increasingly redirected the focus of international trade policy and conflicts beyond or within the borders of nation states and to divergences in domestic policies that arguably create 'unfair' forms of comparative advantage (or 'unlevel playing fields'). With tariffs now in many cases reduced to minimal levels, the new issues addressed in the course of the Uruguay Round likely portend an increasing and broader focus in the future on domestic policy divergences as potential distortions of international trade – a very different agenda from that which initially pre-occupied the founders of the GATT.

The formation of regional trading blocs

Running parallel with the evolution of the multilateral trading system under the GATT in the post-war period has been another institutional development of considerable significance – the rise of regional trading blocs. While a significant number of these arrangements have been created, to date by far the most important has been the European Union. The European Union finds its genesis in the Marshall Plan adopted by the USA for the reconstruction of war-torn Europe, motivated not only by economic objectives but also importantly by political concerns to promote a degree of economic integration that would make the devastating military conflicts of the first half of the twentieth century less likely to recur. Efforts at formal economic integration began with the European Coal and Steel Community, which was formed in 1952 and was charged with promoting the rationalization and integration of the European steel industry. In 1957, the Treaty of Rome, which contemplated a much more ambitious agenda of economic integration, was entered into, initially by six member countries: France, Germany, Italy, The Netherlands, Belgium and Luxembourg; and subsequently by the United Kingdom, Denmark, Greece, Ireland, Portugal and Spain. In the early years, attention was principally focused on the removal of border impediments to trade, especially tariffs and quotas, but over time the European Union has increasingly committed itself to a much more substantial level of economic and political integration, which would provide for the free movement of goods, services, capital, and people within the Community. In 1986, the Community adopted the Single European Act, which set out an ambitious agenda of policy measures with a view to realizing a single European market by 1992.[65] The Maastricht Treaty, ratified in 1993, provides for further forms of economic and political integration. Apart from the European Union, the European Free Trade Association (EFTA) was formed in

1959, with its initial membership comprising Austria, Denmark, Norway, Sweden, Switzerland and the United Kingdom. The UK and Denmark subsequently joined the European Union, recently followed by Austria, Sweden and Finland. The remaining members of EFTA have pursued a policy of mutual and substantial tariff reductions, although EFTA has had much more modest ambitions, in terms of degrees of economic integration, than the European Union. With the recent collapse of the centrally-planned economies in Eastern Europe, a number of these countries now also aspire to eventual membership in the EU.

On the other side of the Atlantic, the conclusion of the Canada–US Free Trade Agreement (FTA) in 1988 marked an important step in the development of an American regional trading bloc. While the FTA is much less integrating than the European Union, it does provide for the removal of all tariffs over a ten year period as well as most other border measures, for largely unrestricted movement of capital and direct investment, and for the liberalization of some trade in services. In 1992, largely building on and superceding the FTA, a North American Free Trade Agreement (NAFTA) was concluded by the USA, Mexico and Canada (subsequently ratified in all three countries and subsequently, in adapted form, adopted by Canada and Chile), and President Bush spoke of his vision of a trading bloc of the Americas stretching from Anchorage to Tierra del Fuego.

Other regional trading blocs have emerged or are beginning to emerge in Latin America (Mercosur), the Caribbean (CARICOM), Asia and the Pacific Rim (APEC), and Eastern and Southern Africa (COMESA).

The rise of regional trading blocs in the post-war period, alongside the evolution of the multilateral system under the GATT, raises major conceptual and policy issues which will be pursued in greater detail later in this book.[66] While some analysts believe that these trading blocs and the multilateral system can be viewed as complementary and mutually reinforcing, other analysts view regional trading blocs as inherently discriminatory and as a major threat to the future stability and integrity of the multilateral system and to the vision of a cooperative and non-discriminatory world economic order that animated the architects of the Bretton Woods Agreement at the end of the Second World War. Tensions between unilateralism, regionalism, and multilateralism recur in various contexts that are addressed throughout this book.

2 The basic elements of the GATT/WTO, the North American Free Trade Agreement, and the European Union

This chapter is intended to provide a brief orientation to, or topography of, the GATT/WTO (the heart of the multilateral world trading regime), and the two major regional trading blocs in the world: the North American Free Trade Agreement (NAFTA) between the USA, Canada and Mexico, and the European Union. The intention of the chapter is merely to highlight the principal elements of these arrangements, and not to explore them in detail. A number of subsequent chapters in this book will pursue a more detailed analysis of many of these elements. However, given the complexity of these arrangements, there is virtue in having a general road map at hand before embarking on detailed analyses of particular principles or provisions.

THE GENERAL AGREEMENT ON TARIFFS AND TRADE (GATT)[1]

The original GATT of 1947 has now become the GATT of 1994 and the WTO Agreement is an umbrella agreement, establishing the WTO structure, including GATT 1997 and many other Agreements to which all Member States (no longer 'Contracting Parties') must, with few exceptions, subscribe.

Tariffs

The preamble to the GATT commits Members to enter into 'reciprocal and mutually advantageous arrangements directed to the substantial reduction of tariffs and other barriers to trade and to the elimination of discriminatory treatment in international commerce'. Article XXVIII *bis* further provides that

> members recognize that customs duties often constitute serious obstacles to trade and that negotiations *on a reciprocal and mutually advantageous basis*, directed to the substantial reduction of the general level of tariffs are of great importance to the expansion of international trade.

Members commit themselves under this article to sponsoring such negotiations from time to time either on a selective product-by-product basis or by the application of such multilateral procedures as may be accepted by the Members.

Once tariff concessions are agreed to in a particular set of negotiations, these become 'tariff bindings' which are set out in particular Members' tariff schedules that constitute an Annex to the GATT. By virtue of Article II of the GATT, all Parties must adhere to these 'tariff bindings' by not imposing customs duties in excess of those set forth in each country's tariff bindings schedule. This is subject to an exception provided for in Article XXVIII, where at scheduled three yearly intervals, any Member that has made previous tariff concessions can reopen these concessions with other Members who have a substantial interest in the concession with a view to modifying or withdrawing the concession, but in that event other concessions must be offered so that a general level of reciprocal and mutually advantageous concessions not less favourable to trade than those existing between the Parties prior to such reopening is maintained.

Obviously, for tariff concessions to be credible, some agreed customs valuation, classification, and administration system is necessary, otherwise a country in agreeing to reduce, for example, a 20% tariff on imports of a particular category to 10%, could negate the concession by arbitrarily revaluing imported goods of this category upwards by 100%, or by reclassifying them into a higher tariff category, or by imposing administrative charges pertaining to the processing of inbound goods that may operate as a *de facto* tariff. Article VII of the GATT requires that the value for customs purposes of imported merchandise should be based on the 'actual value' of the imported merchandise which in turn is defined as the price at which such merchandise is sold or offered for sale in the ordinary course of trade under fully competitive conditions. This definition proved vague and easy to circumvent, and a special Customs Valuation Code was negotiated during the Tokyo Round (and modestly revised during the Uruguay Round) which stipulates that in the ordinary course of events the 'transaction value' as between an exporter and an importer shall be the value for customs purposes, subject to some limited exceptions where the Parties are not dealing with each other at arms length. Similarly, most of the Members have agreed to harmonize their systems of customs classification (the HS), based on the Brussels Nomenclature, which reduces room for ambiguity or debate as to the proper tariff classification of a particular good. Finally, Article VIII of the GATT restricts the imposition of fees or charges relating to the administrative processing of inbound goods to the approximate cost of services rendered, which shall not represent an indirect protection to domestic products or a taxation of imports for fiscal purposes.

The principle of non-discrimination

The principle of non-discrimination – often viewed as the cornerstone of the GATT – is referred to in the preamble to the GATT and is amplified in two key provisions: Article I, adopting the Most Favoured Nation principle; and Article III, adopting the principle of National Treatment.

The Most Favoured Nation (MFN) principle

Under Article I of the GATT, with respect to customs duties or charges of any kind imposed by any country on any other member country, any advantage, favour, privilege, or immunity granted by such country to any product originating in any other country shall be accorded immediately and unconditionally to a like product originating in the territories of all other Members. Thus, notwithstanding that tariff concessions may be principally negotiated between country A and country B, which may be the principal suppliers and purchasers of the products in question respectively, if either country A or country B makes a binding tariff concession to the other, it must extend exactly the same concession to all other member countries of the GATT, without being able to demand *quid pro quos* as a condition for this extension of the concession, at least if these were not part of the initial negotiations. However, the MFN principle is subject to some important exceptions. Article I itself in effect grandfathers preferences that were in force between certain member countries at the time of the inception of the GATT, subject to a rule that freezes the margin of preference, so that it cannot subsequently be increased. This exception has become less important over time as MFN rates have been negotiated down and differences between the preferential rates and the MFN rates progressively reduced.

A second exception is much more important. Article XXIV permits the formation of regional trading blocs, either in the form of custom unions or free trade areas, subject to two basic conditions: namely that the general incidence of duties after the formation of such an arrangement not be higher than the average levels of duties prevailing on the part of member countries to such an arrangement prior to its formation, and that duties and other restrictions on trade must be eliminated with respect to substantially all the trade between the constituent members of the regional trading bloc. It is under this provision that the European Union, the Canada–US Free Trade Agreement, and NAFTA find their legitimacy. By definition, these arrangements would otherwise violate the MFN principle, because they clearly contemplate more favourable duty and related arrangements amongst constituent members than with respect to external trading partners.

Various regional arrangements either in existence or contemplated at the time of the formation of the GATT, including the possible emergence of a European Economic Community, compelled the initial Contracting Parties to recognize this major exception to non-discriminatory multilateralism. As we will see in later chapters, one view of regional trading arrangements is a pragmatic and positive one: that if full multilateral trade liberalization is not immediately possible, partial forms of trade liberalization on a regional basis may be better than nothing, in that they may sustain or nurture over time forward momentum on trade liberalization. This is often referred to as the 'bicycle theory' of trade liberalization. A contrary view argues that partial trade liberalization may be worse than no trade liberalization at all. This view emphasizes a crucial distinction between trade diversion and trade expansion. A simple example will illustrate the distinction. Suppose at one point in time country A maintains a tariff of 20% on textile imports from both countries B and C. Suppose that some of country C's textile producers are 25% more efficient than A's, and that some of country B's textile producers are 15% more efficient than A's. In this scenario C's more efficient textile producers will successfully surmount A's 20% tariff barrier and sell textiles into A's market 5% cheaper than A's producers. B's producers, on the other hand, will find that the 20% tariff more than neutralizes their 15% efficiency advantage over A's producers and renders their product 10% dearer in A's market than textiles produced in C. If countries A and B at a subsequent point in time agree to form a free trade area and to abolish all tariffs between them but to maintain tariffs against external Parties, including the 20% tariff on textiles that A formerly had in place against C, C finds itself in a position where it can still sell textiles 5% more cheaply than A's producers, but they are now 10% dearer than those produced by B. Conversely, B's producers can now sell textiles into A's market 15% cheaper than A's producers, and 10% cheaper than C's (in effect the tariff retained by A against C neutralizes the efficiency advantage that C's producers enjoy over B's of 10% and imposes a further 10% penalty on C relative to B). The result of the formation of a free trade area in this example is that production of textiles will shift from C, the most efficient producer amongst the three countries, to a less efficient producer, B. In other words, trade has been diverted from C to B, despite C's comparative advantage over both B and A. In this example, partial trade liberalization has actually further distorted the efficient allocation of resources.

In considering institutional arrangements to promote regional economic integration, it is useful to think of an integration continuum. First, there are Free Trade Areas (like NAFTA), where two or more countries agree to remove border restrictions on goods amongst themselves but each reserves the right to maintain whatever external trade policy it wishes with respect to non-member countries. A particular problem raised by this kind of arrangement is importation of goods through low tariff member countries and trans-shipment to higher tariff member countries, which can only be resolved with complex rules of origin. Second, there are Customs Unions where in addition to removing border restrictions on trade in goods amongst member countries, member countries also agree to harmonize their external trade policies *vis-à-vis* non-member countries. Third, there are Common Markets or Economic Unions (like the European Union), where in addition to removing border restrictions on trade in goods amongst member countries and harmonizing external trade policy, free trade in or free movement of services, capital, and people, as well as perhaps a common monetary policy, might be contemplated. Fourth, there are Federalist structures, like the USA, Canada, Australia, and Germany, where economic units form a single state, with the central government being vested with the dominant jurisdiction over economic functions, but with some agreed division of economic powers between the central and subnational levels of government, with constitutional or other arrangements designed to guarantee internal free movement of goods, services, capital, and people, and minimization of internal barriers to trade. Finally, there are Unitary States, where over a given geographic region, one government, to all intents and purposes, possesses exclusive jurisdiction over all significant economic functions, so that problems of inter-governmental coordination of economic policies within the geographic area are eliminated.

The National Treatment principle

The MFN principle set out in Article I of the GATT is designed to constrain discrimination by Members amongst different foreign exporters, i.e. playing favourites among foreigners. The principle of National Treatment set out in Article III of the GATT addresses another form of discrimination, namely where a Member adopts internal or domestic policies designed to favour its domestic producers *vis-à-vis* foreign producers of a given product, even though the latter may all be treated in a uniform way. Article III:4 provides that the products of the territory of any Contracting Party imported into the territory of any other Contracting Party shall be accorded treatment no less favourable than that accorded to like products of national origin in respect of all laws, regulations and requirements affecting their internal sale. In effect, what the principle of National Treatment dictates is that once border duties have been paid by foreign exporters, as provided for in a country's tariff schedules, no additional burdens may be imposed through internal sales taxes, differential forms of regulation, etc. on foreign exporters where domestic producers of the same product do not bear the same burden. The particular application of the National Treatment principle to given situations has been the source of a number of important GATT panel decisions, where difficult decisions arise as to whether a domestic law, regulation or administrative policy, which may be neutral on its face, nevertheless has either the intent or effect of imposing differential burdens on foreign exporters. A specific example of this problem has been addressed in the GATT Code on Technical Standards, initially negotiated during the Tokyo Round, and substantially elaborated in separate WTO Agreements on Technical Barriers to Trade and Sanitary and Phytosanitary Measures during the Uruguay Round, which attempt to promote harmonization of domestic product standards that might otherwise discourage international trade.

An explicit exception to the National Treatment principle is contained in Article III:8 of the GATT, which permits government agencies to favour local producers in purchasing goods for governmental purposes and not with a view to commercial resale. However, this provision is now subject to a detailed government procurement code initially negotiated during the Tokyo Round and expanded during the Uruguay Round that require many departments and agencies of government (although in federal systems, not sub-national levels of government) with regard to government procurement contracts over a certain size to respect the National Treatment principle, and avoid preferences in favour of local producers or unreasonable tendering processes that unfairly disadvantage foreign producers from tendering on government contracts.[2]

Quantitative restrictions

The original framers of the GATT contemplated that the GATT would heavily constrain most border restrictions on trade other than tariffs, so that border restrictions would principally take the form of tariffs which could then be negotiated down over time. In particular, Article XI of the GATT prohibits the use of quotas or import or export licences (i.e. quantitative restrictions) on the importation or exportation of goods into or out of any Member state. Quantitative restrictions on imports clearly protect domestic producers. Less obviously, restrictions on exports may provide local producers for the domestic market with privileged access to 'captive' inputs, or protect local processing plants if exportation of raw materials is constrained. The theory behind Article XI was that if quantitative border restrictions could be avoided, the greater transparency and commensurability of tariffs relative to quantitative restrictions would make their reduction through successive rounds of negotiation more tractable. However, Article XI was markedly unsuccessful in this ambition, and increasingly so over time.

Exceptions to Article XI

First of all, Article XI itself, until recently, contained a major exception for quantitative restrictions on agricultural imports where these are maintained in order to protect domestic supply management or agricultural marketing board schemes. Under the WTO Agreement on Agriculture, these restrictions must be converted into tariff equivalents which in turn are subject to minimum required levels of reduction over a six-year period. In addition, Article XII permits the imposition of quantitative restrictions (albeit, by virtue of Article XIII, on a non-discriminatory basis) if a country is facing serious balance of payments problems. Article XVIII of the GATT also permits less developed countries (LDCs) to impose quantitative restrictions either for balance of payments reasons or infant industry reasons against a very relaxed set of criteria. Finally, a major defining characteristic of the rise of the so-called New Protectionism has been the dramatic escalation in the use of quantitative restrictions, typically negotiated on a bilateral basis under threat of unilateral action, and in clear violation of either the letter or spirit of Article XI and Article XIX (relating to safeguard actions, discussed below). These proliferating forms of quantitative restrictions have occurred under the Multi-Fibre Arrangement (the MFA), and on a more *ad hoc* basis through voluntary export restraint agreements (VEAs) or orderly marketing agreements (OMAs) in sectors such as steel and automobiles. Under the WTO Agreement on Textiles and Clothing, special restrictions on textile and clothing imports are subject to reduction over specified time periods.

The safeguard provision

Under Article XIX (often referred to as the safeguards or escape clause), if as a result of unforeseen developments and of the effect of obligations incurred by a Member under the GATT, including tariff concessions, any product is being imported into the territory of that Member in such increased quantities or under such conditions as to cause or threaten serious injury to domestic producers of like products in that territory, the Member is entitled to suspend or modify obligations or concessions on a temporary basis in order to alleviate the injury. However, where safeguard action is taken, either in the form of reinstatement of a tariff or the imposition of quantitative restrictions, it must be taken on a non-discriminatory (i.e. non-selective) basis, and the Party taking such action must offer compensation (in the form of offsetting trade concessions) acceptable to other Parties whose trade is prejudiced by such action, failing which the latter may retaliate by imposing trade restrictions of equivalent value on exports from the country invoking the safeguard clause. Article XIX was initially envisaged as a kind of safety valve permitting Members to buy temporary breathing-space to moderate adjustment costs when confronted with unexpected surges of imports that were causing serious injury to domestic producers. However, the requirements that action be taken on a non-discriminatory basis and be accompanied by compensating concessions has rendered it an unattractive option for Members with import-impacted sectors relative to bilateral arrangements like the MFA, VERs, and OMAs, extracted under threat of unilateral action, principally through the imposition of antidumping or countervailing duties or in the case of the USA unilateral action under section 301 of the Omnibus Trade and Competitiveness Act of 1988. Article XIX has been substantially refined and elaborated in the WTO Agreement on Safeguards.

Trade remedy laws

Article VI of the GATT recognizes the right of Members to take unilateral action under domestic trade laws where domestic industries are being materially injured because of unfair foreign trading practices, specifically either dumping or subsidization.

Dumping occurs in its most typical form where foreign producers are selling goods into another country's market at prices below those which they would normally charge in their home market (perhaps because they have a protected home market). Where this pricing practice is causing material injury to domestic producers of like products, antidumping duties in the amount of the difference between the export market price and the home market price may be imposed on the imported goods. Many Members of the GATT have enacted antidumping laws, and over the late 1970s and 1980s, such laws were invoked with increasing frequency, especially by such countries as the USA, Canada, Australia, and the EC. Article VI has now been amplified by an antidumping code initially negotiated during the Kennedy Round and modestly revised in the course of the Tokyo and Uruguay Rounds.

In the case of countervailing duties, the complaint is not the private pricing practices of foreign producers, but rather that foreign governments are unfairly subsidizing the production of foreign exports, artificially advantaging them in importing countries' markets. Where foreign government subsidization of foreign exports is causing material injury to a domestic industry producing like products, domestic trade laws enacted in many countries permit the unilateral imposition of countervailing duties on the subsidized imports so as to offset or neutralize these foreign subsidies. Again, over the late 1970s and 1980s, as a characteristic of the New Protectionism, countervailing duties, along with antidumping duties, began to be more frequently invoked, although in the case of countervailing duties almost exclusively by the USA. A special code on subsidies was initially negotiated during the Tokyo Round and extensively revised during the Uruguay Round, partly with a view to disciplining the invocation of countervailing duty laws and partly with a view to providing an alternative multilateral dispute resolution track for adjudicating disputes over all forms of subsidies that may have trade effects.

The issue of subsidies is one of the most sensitive and complex subjects in international trade law. At one level, objections to subsidies are obvious, in that a subsidy can be devised to replicate the effects of almost any tariff. For example, if country A agrees to reduce tariffs on country B's widget exports from 20% to 10%, and binds itself to this concession, this concession can effectively be undermined by country A then providing subsidies to its own domestic producers of widgets in the amount of 10% of production costs. Conversely, if country A declines to negotiate a reduction of its 20% tariff on country B's widget exports, but country B seeks to undermine the reciprocal bargaining process contemplated for tariff reductions under Article XVIII *bis* by unilaterally subsidizing its exports of widgets into country A's market in the amount of 10% of production costs, country A's right to elect which tariffs to bind itself to would be undermined. On the other hand, given that almost all significant domestic policies of governments, e.g. investments in physical infrastructure, education, health, research and development, telecommunications, law and order, directly or indirectly affect the pattern of economic activities that evolve in each country, and by extension the pattern of international trade activities to which each country contributes, the charge of unfair subsidization has no natural limits. A burgeoning political discourse has emerged over the last few years surrounding the notion of 'fair' (or 'unfair') trade, or 'level playing fields'. Professor Jagdish Bhagwati has described the rise of fair trade discourse as 'the truly greatest threat since the 1930s' to the world trading system.[3]

Article XVI of the GATT requires a Member that grants or maintains any subsidy which has the effect of increasing exports or reducing imports to notify the Members of the nature and extent of the subsidization and its likely effects on trade, and where serious prejudice is caused or threatened to the interests of any other Member to discuss with that Party the possibility of terminating the subsidization. With respect to export subsidies, Article XVI provides that where export subsidies are granted on a primary product, these should not result in the exporting country gaining 'more than an equitable share of world export trade in that product', relative to pre-existing shares. With respect to export subsidies on non-primary products, a number of signatories agreed to forsake these where such a subsidy would result in export sales at lower prices than domestic sales. The new WTO Subsidies Agreement attempts to provide much more precise definitions of prohibited, actionable, and non-actionable subsidies.

For clarity of understanding, it is helpful to keep in mind a basic taxonomy of subsidy scenarios. The first scenario is one where country A subsidizes its exports into country B's market. This is the scenario which has classically attracted the potential for countervailing duties under Article VI and complementary domestic trade remedy laws. These subsidies could relate exclusively to exports or to all domestic production, wherever consumed. The second scenario is where country A subsidizes its exports into country C's market, and in so doing displaces country B's exports from country C's market. In this scenario, the subsidized goods are not moving from country A to country B and thus cannot be countervailed by country B, so that country B is remitted to a complaint under the WTO Subsidies Agreement for resolution under the multilateral dispute resolution process. The third subsidy scenario is the case where country A is subsidizing its domestic producers to service principally country A's own domestic market, and in so doing displaces country B's exports from country A's market. Again, as in scenario two, the subsidized goods are not moving from country A to country B so as to attract possible countervailing duties in country B, so that country B is again remitted to the multilateral dispute resolution process.

The considerable, and apparently growing, attraction of antidumping and countervailing duties for import-impacted sectors, relative to the safeguard regime contemplated by Article XIX, reflects the fact that selective (i.e. discriminatory) action is permitted, no compensation is required in the form of counterbalancing trade concessions, and the duties are imposed automatically by administrative rather than political decision (unlike safeguard actions which ultimately require executive political action, typically following discussions and negotiations with affected foreign country governments).

State trading enterprises

Under Article XVII of the GATT each Member undertakes that its state trading enterprises shall, with respect to purchases or sales involving either imports or exports, act in a non-discriminatory manner and make such purchases or sales solely in accordance with commercial considerations. This provision does not apply to imports of products for immediate or ultimate consumption in governmental use and not otherwise for resale.

This provision recognizes that state trading enterprises have the potential for distorting international trade through explicit or implicit subsidy policies or artificial pricing strategies. For example, a state enterprise selling into export markets may artificially subsidize its exports. Conversely, a state enterprise in its purchasing policies may explicitly or implicitly favour domestic producers over foreign producers of the same products. Article XVII, in its initial conception, was principally addressed to a significant number of state-owned enterprises or state-sanctioned monopolies that existed in the jurisdictions of Members at the time of the formation of the GATT, even though these countries were largely committed to market economies. Article XVII is not nearly as well equipped to address the systemic problems of countries which are members of the GATT, or aspire to be, that are predominantly centrally-planned or command economies, or which are in the process (as with Eastern European countries and China) of transition from command to some form of market economy. In these countries, because prices, input costs and wages have traditionally been set by command or administrative fiat, determining, as is required by Article XVII, whether a state enterprise is operating according to 'commercial considerations' involves the intractable counterfactual exercise of determining what the country in question would import or export *if* there were fully functioning markets.

In consequence, where in the past command economies have participated in the GATT, they have done so on special terms that have involved either specific commitments to increase imports from non-Communist countries, or have entailed expectations of partial liberalization of the trade and payments system. Special arrangements of this nature have applied in the case of Poland, Hungary and Romania, and to a much more limited extent to the former Yugoslavia.[4] As well, in many instances, Members have not granted full MFN status to these countries despite their membership in the GATT, and the terms of accession in the case of some of these command economies have permitted imposition of discriminatory safeguards or quantitative restrictions, which were frequently invoked by European Community countries in particular.

With the fall of the Communist bloc, the issue of normalizing the GATT/WTO membership of the former command economies has come to the fore. As well, the question of the admission of Russia and other former Soviet republics looms large, as does the application for re-admission of Communist China, which continues to remain in many important respects a command economy.

Less developed countries

'Special and differential status' is accorded to LDCs under the GATT both with respect to actions which they are permitted to take and with respect to actions that developed countries are expected to take towards them. Under Article XVIII, LDCs have been given broad latitude to impose restrictions on imports, typically through quantitative restrictions such as quotas and licences, for balance of payments reasons or in order to foster infant industries. Under Part IV of the GATT, added in 1964, Article XXXVI:8 provides that developed Members do not expect reciprocity for commitments made by them in trade negotiations to reduce or remove tariffs and other barriers to the trade of less developed Contracting Parties. Article XXXVII in turn provides that developed countries commit themselves to according high priority to the reduction and elimination of barriers to products currently or potentially of particular export interest to less developed Members. These latter provisions led to the introduction of the Generalized System of Preferences in the early 1970s and the unilateral adoption of special preferences by industrial countries with respect to some exports of less developed countries. The degree of success of either of these two elements of the special and differential status accorded to LDCs under the GATT will be the subject of a more detailed discussion in a later chapter.[5] For the moment, it is sufficient to note that with respect to the first element in this status i.e. authorization of import substitution – infant industry promotion policies by LDCs – this reflects a debate going back to John Stuart Mill about the case for protectionism in this context (discussed in the previous chapter). The second element in the special and differential status, i.e. non-reciprocal trade concessions by developed countries, raises the strategic question of whether countries will find themselves willing to engage in unilateral trade liberalization, and reflects the long-standing debate about the virtues of unilateral trade liberalization relative to reciprocal trade liberalization.

General exceptions to GATT obligations

Under Article XX of the GATT, a number of dispensations from GATT obligations are provided with respect to the adoption or enforcement by Members of measures, for example, necessary to protect public morals; necessary to protect human or animal health or life; necessary to secure compliance with laws or regulations which are not inconsistent with the GATT; imposed for the protection of national treasures; necessary for the conservation of exhaustible natural resources, provided that none of these measures are an arbitrary or unjustifiable discrimination between countries where the same conditions prevail or a disguised restriction on international trade.[6] Under Article XXI of the GATT, various national security exceptions are provided for that permit a Member to take any action which it considers necessary for the protection of its essential security interests relating to fissionable materials and traffic in arms and munitions or which reflect the exigencies of war or other emergency in international relations.[7] Article XXV(5) provides that in exceptional circumstances not otherwise provided for in the Agreement, the Members may waive an obligation imposed on a Member by the GATT, provided that any such decision is approved by a two-thirds majority of the votes cast and such majority comprises more than half of the Members. This waiver provision has been invoked on a number of important occasions, including the 1955 US agricultural waiver application and the Canada–USA Auto Pact in 1965.

The federal state clause

International trade commitments entered into by federal states, such as the USA, Canada, Australia and Germany, have posed a problem in international trade law to the extent that commitments made by national levels of government do not constitutionally bind sub-national levels of government who, of course, are not direct signatories of the GATT. Unitary states see this problem as resulting in an unfair form of asymmetry in reciprocal commitments. Article XXIV(12) of the GATT provides that 'each Member shall take such reasonable measures as may be available to it to ensure observance of the provisions of this Agreement by the regional and local governments within its territories'. This clause has been strictly interpreted in several GATT panel decisions and provides very limited grounds for excuse for non-compliance by federal states.[8]

The governance of the WTO

With the failure of the initial Members to endorse the creation of the International Trade Organization and the Havana Charter of which it was part, the GATT, at least on its surface, was born with an anaemic institutional structure relative to many other international organizations, such as the International Monetary Fund and the World Bank. These other organizations were seen as largely addressing and coordinating matters of external economic and political relations, while the ITO and Havana Charter were perceived as possessing the potential for constraining many domestic policies and hence trenching, to a greater extent, upon domestic political sovereignty. However, over the course of time, various institutional structures have evolved that appear to have proven reasonably serviceable in the management of the GATT. A committee of ministers of trade from member countries met periodically, although most of the effective collective decision making was channelled through the Council of Representatives, which met on a monthly basis in Geneva, and was drawn from permanent GATT delegations of member countries, with each country entitled to one vote. The Council of Representatives was supplemented by various specialized committees and working parties as well as dispute resolution panels appointed on an *ad hoc*, case-by-case basis. The full-time staff of the GATT/WTO is headed by a Director-General, appointed on a fixed-term basis by consensus of the Contracting Parties. Article XXV(4) of the GATT provides that decisions of the Members shall be taken by a majority of the votes cast, except as otherwise provided for in the Agreement. Article XXXIII provides for the accession of new members, if supported by a vote of a two-thirds majority of all Members. Article XXX provides for amendments to the GATT provisions. Part I of the Agreement containing the Most Favoured Nation principle and the principle of tariff bindings may only be amended by consent of all the Members. Other provisions may be amended by a two-thirds majority of all the Members, but amendments become binding only with respect to those Members which accept the amendment. Under the WTO Agreement establishing the World Trade Organization (WTO), governance of the GATT will henceforth be vested in the WTO. A Ministerial Conference composed of representatives of all Members must meet at least every two years. Otherwise governance issues are vested in the General Council of the WTO (replacing the Council of Representatives), which also functions as the Dispute Settlement Body and the Trade Policy Review Body.

With respect to specific disputes between Members (which it must be emphasized are governments, not private parties), Article XXII imposes an obligation on Members to accord sympathetic consideration to complaints of other Parties and adequate opportunity for consultation with such Parties. If the Members cannot resolve a dispute through mutual discussions, perhaps assisted by mediation of a third Party, including the Director-General of the GATT or his or her staff, the dispute must then be addressed within the framework of Article XXIII, now substantially elaborated in the WTO Understanding on Rules and Procedures Governing the Settlement of Disputes. Under this Article, if a Member considers that any benefit accruing to it directly or indirectly under the GATT is being 'nullified or impaired' by a policy or practice of another Member, the complaining Party can refer its complaint to the Members as a group, previously the Council of Representatives, now the General Council of the WTO acting as the Dispute Settlement Body, which will appoint a panel to investigate the complaint and make recommendations to the Council for resolution of the dispute. Panels typically comprise three individuals, drawn from countries other than the disputing Parties, who meet privately with the disputing Parties to ascertain the facts and the precise nature of the allegations, and if possible to resolve the dispute informally. If this is not possible, the panel will make recommendations to the Council as to the resolution of the matter. The Council makes decisions on panel recommendations on a consensus basis, previously requiring consensus in favour of adoption of a panel's recommendations but now under the Uruguay Round Dispute Settlement Understanding requiring consensus in favour of rejection. Under the Understanding, panel decisions may now be appealed on matters of law to a standing Appellate Body of seven members. If the Council adopts the recommendations of a panel or the Appellate Body then a Member is required to modify or withdraw its policy or practice to bring itself into conformity with the Council's decision. If it fails to do so, the Council will authorize retaliatory action by the aggrieved Party in the form of a suspension of trade concessions or other obligations the level of which is subject to arbitration. Despite a number of seemingly odd features of this dispute resolution process, when compared with domestic adjudication processes, in many respects it has worked reasonably well over the years. Several hundred complaints have been investigated since the inception of the GATT, as we will see in a later chapter. There has been a high compliance rate with panel recommendations and Council decisions, despite the hypothetical ability of losing Parties (until recently) to veto adoption of adverse panel recommendations. Moreover, aggrieved Parties have almost never found it expedient to pursue retaliatory action against Parties adversely affected by panel or Council decisions.

The WTO Agreements

On 19 December 1993, member countries of the GATT reached a wide-ranging and ambitious agreement on many trade and related issues, after seven years of negotiations which were characterized by much higher levels of rancour and controversy than any of the previous MTN rounds. While the Uruguay Round seemed often at the point of collapse, the WTO Agreement eventually reached signifies substantial progress on a number of important issues.

With respect to goods, substantial average cuts in tariffs (of about 38%) were agreed to. In the case of agricultural products – a key area of controversy – the EU agreed to significant cuts over time in export subsidies, and member countries agreed to abandon quantitative restrictions, which are to be replaced by tariffs. In the case of textiles and clothing, the MFA will be dismantled by degrees, with quantitative restrictions again being replaced by tariffs, which are to be reduced over time. The general safeguard regime has been significantly strengthened by adoption of firm time limits for safeguard measures and for limiting their re-adoption; by improving multilateral notification and surveillance; and by requiring existing grey-area measures to be brought into compliance with the new regime or terminated. A modestly revised Antidumping Agreement was also negotiated, as well as a much more fully elaborated Subsidies Agreement. A revised Government Procurement Agreement provides for somewhat greater coverage of government contracting than the Tokyo Round Code. With respect to intellectual property, substantial harmonization of domestic intellectual property regimes around norms prevailing in the USA and a number of other industrialized countries was agreed to.

With respect to international trade in services, a process for liberalization on a sector-by-sector basis, governed by a conditional MFN principle and an effects-based National Treatment principle, has been set in motion. With respect to trade-related investment measures, local sourcing and minimum export requirements as conditions for approval of foreign investments have been prohibited.

With respect to the governance of the GATT, a World Trade Organization (WTO), now with about 130 members, has been created to oversee an integrated dispute settlement regime and to undertake a pro-active trade policy surveillance role. In addition, membership of the WTO now entails commitment to most of the GATT Agreements, which are fully integrated into the GATT/WTO, and no longer operate on a conditional MFN basis as was the case with most of the Tokyo Round Codes where only signatories to each code were subject to its obligations and entitled to its benefits.

We pursue many of these issues in much greater detail later in this book. Recent estimates suggest that by the year 2002, net world welfare may be around $US270 billion higher, in current prices, than it would be if current levels of protection remained unchanged.[9]

THE CANADA–US FREE TRADE AGREEMENT[10] AND THE NORTH AMERICAN FREE TRADE AGREEMENT[11]

History

Canada and the USA have a long and tangled history of bilateral arrangements pertaining to trade. In 1854, both countries agreed to the Reciprocity Treaty which provided for a measure of free trade with respect to Canadian exports of certain agricultural products and natural resources and US access to Canadian inshore fisheries. However, the USA cancelled this treaty in 1865, in part reflecting US unhappiness with what was perceived to be Canadian complicity with Britain in supporting the Confederacy side in the US Civil War, and in part due to opposition by US agricultural interests. In 1879, Prime Minister John A. MacDonald announced the National Policy, which entailed high levels of tariff protection for manufacturers in central Canada, complemented by policies to support western settlement and provide markets for their goods, which would be encouraged through the development of a national transportation system. In 1911, the Liberal government led by Sir Wilfred Laurier negotiated a tentative free trade agreement with the USA, partly in response to dissatisfaction by farmers in western Canada with the high cost of domestically produced farm implements. However, debate in Parliament forced Laurier to call an election, during which the Conservatives strongly opposed a free trade agreement with the USA on the grounds that this would mean increased competition for Canadian farmers because of the earlier US growing season, would jeopardize relations with Britain, and would risk importing US economic difficulties such as unemployment. The Liberals lost the election, and the agreement was never ratified. In 1934, the US Congress, on the initiative of President Roosevelt, enacted the Reciprocal Trade Agreements Act and in 1935 pursuant to this Act a Canada–US bilateral agreement was negotiated which provided for some modest tariff reductions. In 1948, Canadian and American negotiators negotiated a comprehensive bilateral free trade agreement, but Prime Minister William Lyon Mackenzie King refused to present the agreement to Parliament for adoption on the grounds that it would lead ultimately to union with the USA and separation from Britain. In 1965, Canada and the USA negotiated the Auto Pact which provided for conditional duty-free trade between Canada and the USA in original equipment, auto parts, accessories, and most types of motor vehicles. In a 1975 report entitled *Looking Outward*, the Economic Council of Canada proposed that Canada contemplate substantial trade liberalization with the USA. In 1978, the Senate Committee on Foreign Affairs took a similar position. In 1983, the Department of External Affairs issued a Review of Foreign Trade Policy that recommended that the government consider the advisability of sectoral free trade with the USA in urban transport equipment, textiles, agricultural equipment and petro-chemicals. In 1986, the Macdonald Royal Commission on the Economic Union and Development Prospects for Canada, after undertaking an extensive review of all of Canada's trade policy options, strongly recommended that Canada initiate negotiations with the USA to secure a comprehensive bilateral trade agreement. The Mulroney Conservative government, which was elected in 1984, initiated formal negotiations with the USA in 1986. Negotiations culminated in the Canada–US Free Trade Agreement, which was signed by the two countries on 2 January 1988 and subsequently ratified by the legislative bodies in both countries. As of 1988, two-thirds of Canada's imports came from the USA and three-quarters of its exports went to the USA. About one-fifth of US imports came from Canada and one-quarter of US exports went to Canada. The trading relationship between Canada and the USA is the largest bilateral trading relationship in the world. Subsequent to the FTA, the USA, Canada, and Mexico entered into negotiations to secure a North American Free Trade Agreement (NAFTA), in large part by extending the Canada–US FTA to Mexico. An agreement was reached on 12 August, 1992 and subsequently ratified in all three countries. Because the FTA is now largely subsumed in NAFTA, we will confine our overview to the latter.

Trade in goods

Most tariffs between the three countries will be eliminated over a ten-year period, in accordance with stipulated phase-out schedules, with a few products subject to a fifteen-year transition period. Most import and export restrictions, in particular quotas and import licences, will be eliminated (Chapter 3, Article 300) Canada–US bilateral tariffs will continue to be phased out under the ten-year FTA schedule. Only goods originating within the three countries are entitled to the benefit of the reduced tariffs provided for by NAFTA. Goods which are wholly obtained in either or both countries are deemed to originate in the country from which they are exported and are entitled to NAFTA treatment (Article 401). Goods incorporating third-country materials generally qualify for NAFTA treatment provided sufficient processing has occurred to cause them to have a tariff classification different from that of the component materials (Article 402). In other cases, special content rules must be satisfied as well (Article 402). With respect to automobiles, 62.5% of NAFTA content (rather than 50% under the FTA) is required to qualify for preferential treatment (Article 403). Textiles and clothing must be produced from yarn spun in North America or from fabric made from North American fibres to qualify for preferential treatment (Chapter 4). There are some limited exceptions to these latter rules, through a system of Tariff Rate Quotas (TRQs), which allows preferential treatment of exports up to agreed ceilings even though the rules of origin are not met. The textile and clothing provisions of the Agreement also contain a safeguard mechanism that enables a country to impose trade restrictions to provide temporary relief during a transition period. These rules of origin in the auto, textile and clothing sectors have particular potential for creating trade diversion rather than trade expansion and seem principally motivated by concerns that in their absence foreign firms would use Mexico, with its low-cost labour, as a platform to access the North American market.

With respect to agriculture, the USA and Mexico have agreed to eliminate all non-tariff barriers to trade and to convert these to tariffs or TRQs (Chapter 7, Section A). Tariffs will be eliminated over ten years. Extended periods are provided in the case of sensitive products, such as corn and dry bean exports to Mexico, and orange juice and sugar exports to the USA. Canada and Mexico have agreed to remove all tariff and non-tariff barriers to agricultural trade over ten years except with respect to dairy products, poultry, eggs and sugar. The agricultural provisions also contain a special safeguard provision that can be invoked during the first ten years of the Agreement if imports exceed specified trigger levels. The use of export subsidies for agricultural products is generally discouraged and permitted only in response to non-NAFTA country subsidies, but subject even in this event to consultation procedures. The Agreement provides for efforts at harmonization of grade and quality standards with respect to agricultural products.

Sanitary and phytosanitary (SPS) measures maintained or introduced by any NAFTA country are permitted provided they are not a disguised form of trade restriction and are based on scientific principles and a risk assessment (Chapter 7, Section B). Where possible, NAFTA countries commit themselves to using relevant international standards and to working towards equivalent SPS measures without reducing any country's chosen level of protection of human, animal or plant life or health.

NAFTA members can undertake safeguard action during the transition period if NAFTA imports are a substantial cause or threat of serious injury to a domestic industry (Chapter 8, Article 801). Safeguard action can only be taken once and for a maximum period of three years (Article 801(21)). Where a country takes a multilateral (GATT) safeguard action, NAFTA partners must be excluded unless their exports account for a substantial share of total imports (among the top five suppliers) and contribute importantly to the serious injury or threat thereof (Article 802).

With respect to government procurement (Chapter 10), National Treatment obligations are adopted with respect to purchases by government departments or agencies over $US50,000 of goods and services and over $US6.5 million for construction services. With respect to federal government enterprises, these thresholds are raised to $US250,000 and $US8 million respectively. Each country must give sufficient notice of procurement opportunities to ensure equal competitive conditions for foreign and domestic firms and must set up bid-challenge procedures to enable suppliers to challenge awards.

Trade in services

With respect to trade in services (Chapter 12), both the National Treatment and Most Favoured Nation principles are adopted. The Agreement provides that no local presence is required to provide covered services. A number of reservations have been entered with respect to which services are covered and which are not (Article 1206). With respect to licensing and certification of professionals, the Agreement provides that entry requirements should be related solely to competence and endorses a qualified mutual recognition principle (Article 1210). In the case of land transportation services, the Agreement provides for full access to each country's rail services and for cross-border provision of bus and trucking services to be phased in over a transitional period (Annex 1212). Coastal shipping restrictions are exempted from the Agreement.

The Agreement recognizes the right of establishment with respect to banking, insurance, securities, and other financial services, and adopts the National Treatment and Most Favoured Nation principles with respect to financial services generally (Chapter 14). Canada commits itself to extending the FTA exemption from the 25% non-resident ownership restriction rule in the case of the US to Mexico and the exemption from the aggregate asset ceiling on foreign banks operating in Canada. Mexico has reserved the right to impose aggregrate and individual market share limits on foreign firms in the financial services sector during a transitional period expiring in the year 2000.

North American firms will have access to and use of public telecommunications networks and services on a reasonable, non-discriminatory basis including the right to have private lines, attach terminal equipment, interconnect private circuits, perform switching, signalling and processing functions, use operating protocols of the user's choice, and operate private intracorporate communications systems (Chapter 13). Foreign ownership restrictions in voice-mail and other value-added services will be eliminated.

Cross-border trade with Mexico in electricity and natural gas is substantially liberalized under NAFTA although the Mexican state monopoly in the petroleum industry is maintained (although relaxed with respect to some petrochemicals).

Energy trade between Canada and the US continues to be governed by the FTA. Exceptions to free trade in energy relate to conservation, price stabilization and natural security, but permitted restrictions must be applied on a proportional sharing basis between the two countries so as to ensure that the burden of restrictions applies equally to domestic and foreign markets (Chapter 6).

The Agreement also provides for a regime of temporary entry visas for business persons into any NAFTA country (Chapter 16).

Investment

Both the National Treatment and Most Favoured Nation principles are adopted (Chapter 11). Performance requirements of foreign investors are generally prohibited (Article 1106). A NAFTA member may not expropriate investments of a NAFTA investor except for a public purpose and on payment of compensation reflecting fair market value (Article 1110). Canada has reserved the right to continue reviewing foreign investments above a $150 million threshold as provided in the FTA. Mexico is committed to raising its foreign investment review threshold to $150 million within ten years of the implementation of the Agreement. The investment provisions do not apply to Mexico's petroleum, basic telecommunications and rail sectors, US airlines and radio communications, or Canada's cultural industries. The Agreement also provides that no NAFTA country should lower its environmental standards in order to attract investment (Article 1114). NAFTA investors may seek binding arbitral determinations in international fora for violations of these investment obligations and enforce arbitral awards in domestic courts (Chapter 11, Section B).

Competition policy, monopolies, and state enterprises

Each country commits itself to maintaining laws regulating anti-competitive practices (Chapter 15). In the case of state enterprises and domestic monopolies, these enterprises are not to discriminate against other NAFTA firms or citizens in buying or selling goods and services and are to follow normal commercial considerations in their contractual activities (Article 1502). A tri-lateral committee is to be created to review the relationship between competition laws and trade matters, including presumably trade remedy laws (Article 1504). A side-accord initiated by Canada commits the member countries to attempting to negotiate new legal regimes on dumping, subsidies and countervailing duties within two years of the implementation of the Agreement.

Intellectual property

The Agreement has an extensive set of provisions protecting patent, copyright and trademark rights, and providing for their effective enforcement (Chapter 17). These provisions largely parallel the Uruguay Round Agreement on Trade-Related Aspects of Intellectual Property Rights.

Institutional arrangements

The Agreement provides for the creation of a NAFTA Trade Commission, to be supported by a full-time Secretariat, and complemented by various working groups and committees (Chapter 20). Dispute resolution provisions provide that five person binational panels drawn from a roster of nominees from the disputing countries will adjudicate on disputes between two member countries of the NAFTA, with the third member reserving the option of either participating in the proceedings or pursuing its own process of consultation and dispute resolution (Chapter 20, Section B). In an interesting innovation, disputing countries must select panellists from the other disputing country's roster of nominees (Article 2011). Where complaint procedures are open to a NAFTA country either under the GATT or NAFTA, a complainant country is entitled to choose which regime it pursues its complaint under, except where the complaint pertains to health, safety, or environmental standards, where the respondent country can insist on dispute resolution under NAFTA (Article 2005). In this event, the Agreement provides for the creation of scientific boards to provide expert evidence to panels adjudicating on questions pertaining to health, safety and environmental standards.

The NAFTA renders permanent a special and temporary dispute resolution process initially adopted under the FTA for antidumping and countervailing duty determinations. Under this mechanism, if an aggrieved party so demands, binational panels must be struck as an alternative to pursuing domestic judicial review processes. These binational panels, which comprise five experts drawn from permanent lists provided by each Party (two from each Party with agreement normally on a fifth person as chairperson) may only review final antidumping and countervailing duty determinations for consistency with applicable domestic laws using domestic standards of judicial review. The decision of a panel is binding on the Parties, except for a limited right to request a three-person 'Extraordinary Challenge' committee comprising judges or former judges from the countries in dispute to review a panel's decision. Each Party reserves the right to change or modify its antidumping or countervailing laws, provided that any such amendment expressly stipulates that it shall apply to goods from the other Party. Where a Party complains that such an amendment is inconsistent with the other Party's obligations under the GATT or with the object and purpose of the NAFTA, that Party may request that the amendment be referred to a panel for a declaratory opinion. Where the declaratory opinion reports an inconsistency, the Parties must consult and seek a mutually satisfactory solution to the dispute, including remedial legislation with respect to the statute of the amending Party. If remedial legislation is not enacted within nine months from the end of the ninety day consultation period provided for and no other agreement has been reached, the complaining Party may take comparable executive or equivalent legislative action, or terminate the Agreement with regard to the amending Party on sixty days written notice.

Side-Accords on environmental and labour standards

Subsequent to the negotiation of NAFTA, the current US Administration initiated a further set of negotiations on environmental and labour standards that resulted in trilateral side-accords that set up an elaborate institutional machinery to ensure that existing environmental and labour laws in each of the three countries are effectively enforced with the possibility of fines and trade sanctions as penalties for non-compliance. The Accords also provide for consultative mechanisms designed to promote a higher degree of harmonization of standards in these areas in the future.

THE FRAMEWORK OF ECONOMIC INTEGRATION IN THE EUROPEAN UNION[12]

The 'constitution' of the European Union is the Treaty Establishing the European Community, usually known as the Treaty of Rome.[13] It states the basic principles of economic union – the free movement of goods, persons, services and capital – and contains a variety of legal norms aimed at the realization of these freedoms. In addition to provisions that prohibit customs duties on imports from Member States, quantitative restrictions and 'equivalent measures' are prohibited (Article 30), as are certain State aids to industry.

The Treaty imposes constraints on Member States' governments as well as positive obligations. However, even where the Treaty of Rome requires further positive action in the form of cooperation between governments, this is much more than a 'best efforts' exhortation. In fact, it has the status of a juridical norm. To those accustomed to Anglo-American understandings about the rule of law, this may at first appear strange, since court action is not generally available to force governments to bring into being positive policy measures. It is, however, quite consistent with continental notions of constitutional law as embodying the most general legal norms. In turn, these norms are realized by the enactment of secondary or derivative norms by governments.

The Treaty of Rome establishes several institutional mechanisms for the realization of the Treaty norms: the European Court of Justice, the European Commission, The Council of Ministers, and the European Parliament. Some of the most important 'economic union' provisions in the Treaty of Rome are directly enforceable by the European Court. These provisions allow a citizen (or in some instances a corporation) in a Member State to apply to the judiciary for relief against measures of her own or another State that violate provisions of the Treaty. While direct enforceability or application only exists for some aspects of the Treaty, it has been of major importance in making the Union something more than a common market or customs union. In most free-trade agreements, dispute settlement is an intergovernmental process. As a result, dispute settlement has strong political and diplomatic dimensions. By contrast, the Treaty of Rome is in significant respects a *supranational constitution*, conferring enforceable legal rights on Union citizens.[14]

In addition, a number of provisions of the Treaty are explicitly enforceable by the European Commission, but are subject to judicial review. This is, in particular, the case with competition policy and the prohibition of State aids (subsidies) that distort competition within the Union. The Commission is an executive body consisting of representatives appointed from the Member States, but obliged by law to act independently of their governments. Appointments must be acceptable to all Member States.[15] The Commission must always have a Member from each Member State. Decisions of the Commission must be approved by a simple majority of the Members. In practice, where the Commission makes decisions in individual cases with respect to subsidization, it depends to a large degree on the advice of an extensive technical staff of European civil servants. Decisions of the Commission (e.g. with respect to State aids) are directly binding on Member States, and do not require any kind of political approval or agreement by the governments of the Member States of the Union. The Member States may, however, by unanimous vote, override Commission decisions on some matters (a highly unlikely occurrence).

With respect to harmonization of regulatory regimes through European law, the Commission plays a crucial role, as does the Council of Ministers. The Council consists of political representatives from all major States. It makes regulations and directives upon the initiative of the Commission. Regulations are directly binding in the legal systems of the Member States, whereas implementation of directives requires domestic legislation. Directives allow some flexibility as to the manner of implementation by the Member States, although there is some protection against the possibility that Member States will mis-implement or fail to implement them. In those circumstances, the directive may become directly enforceable in court, even by an individual or firm, if it is adequately specific to give rise to a determinate legal meaning.[16] In addition, the Commission or another Member State can take a recalcitrant Member State to the European Court to force it to implement a directive properly. In some instances, the key issue will be whether the domestic implementing legislation adequately achieves the result intended by the directive. The important point is that directives are not just exhortations to national political authorities to make 'best efforts', but are legally binding with respect to *result*. Whether a given domestic statute *achieves* a result is a question of *law* to be determined by independent supranational authorities.

Directives generally no longer require unanimous approval of the Council. Instead, under the Single European Act of 1986 they must be endorsed by a weighted majority of votes. Harmonization through unanimous agreement between Member States proved to be difficult because of hold-out problems.[17]

We now turn to the substantive law and policy of economic integration developed in the European Union.

Non-discrimination norms vs legitimate public purposes

The major legal limits to non-tariff barriers with respect to goods are contained in Articles 30 and 34 of the Treaty of Rome. They prohibit quantitative restrictions and 'all measures having equivalent effect' on imports and exports. Article 36, in turn, provides specific derogations from these strictures, based on public objectives related to health and safety, public security, and morality, and protection of national cultural treasures, among others.[18]

Early in the jurisprudence of the Union, the scope of Articles 30 and 34 was extended beyond measures that discriminated on their face against non-domestic products to those that merely had a disparate impact. Thus, in the *Cassis de Dijon* case,[19] the Court held that a German law that prohibited the sale of the liqueur cassis with less than 25% alcohol content violated Article 30. It prevented the import of French cassis which had an alcohol content below 20%. However, the Court suggested that where measures are not facially discriminatory but have a disparate impact, they may be saved if they are 'necessary in order to satisfy mandatory requirements relating in particular to the effectiveness of fiscal supervision, the protection of public health, the fairness of commercial transactions, and the defence of the consumer'.

The test of necessity involves consideration of whether alternative measures less restrictive of intra-Union trade might adequately satisfy the 'mandatory requirements' at issue.[20] Hence, if the goal was to ensure that consumers were not misled by an assumption about the domestic product into thinking that the foreign product contained an equivalent amount of alcohol, labelling requirements would suffice. Similarly, in the *German Beer Standards*[21] case, the Court impugned a German law which required any product sold with the label 'Beer' in Germany to meet German purity standards. The Court reasoned that consumers could be informed of the difference between beers through the use of appropriate labelling requirements. Where health risks are claimed as a basis for content requirements that affect trade, and where less stringent requirements are in place elsewhere in the Union, the Court places some burden on the defendant Member State to produce empirical evidence of the risks in question.

State aids

State aids (e.g. subsidies) are dealt with under a separate regime from that in Articles 30, 34, and 36 of the Treaty of Rome. The major relevant provision is Article 92(1) which prohibits 'any aid granted by a Member State or through State resources in any form whatsoever which distorts or threatens to distort competition by favouring certain undertakings, in so far as it affects trade between Member States'. Certain derogations are permitted, including aid to underdeveloped areas or 'to remedy a serious disturbance in the economy of a Member State'.[22] Article 93 makes the Commission responsible for monitoring and enforcement of the State aid prohibitions. A process is mandated whereby the Commission must be informed of any new State aid with sufficient advance notice to determine its consistency with the Treaty. Moreover, it can require the subsidizing State to amend an aid programme to make it consistent with the Treaty. Decisions of the Commission are reviewable by the Court.

Placing review of State aid measures in the hands of the Commission reflects the fact that an approach which emphasizes legal rules and orders is unsuited to dealing with the complex subsidy and tax incentive programmes of advanced, mixed economies. Furthermore, the procedure of *ex ante* review takes into account the possible consequences for workers and other relatively vulnerable constituencies if an existing aid programme were suddenly to be declared invalid by the court. Finally, the possibility of adjustment to an aid programme through negotiation between the Commission and the granting State allows for positive-sum solutions. These solutions might involve, for instance, aid earmarked to sustain existing production in a surplus capacity sector being modified in the direction of a managed exit approach.

HARMONIZATION

The 'Europe 1992' initiative, launched by the coming into force of the Single European Act in 1987, reflects the fundamental recognition that negative constraints on government actions that impede economic mobility are far from sufficient to achieve economic union. An essential thrust of the move towards completion of the internal market by 1992 is the harmonization of regulatory regimes with respect to financial services, securities, insurance, company law, and telecommunications, as well as community-wide standards with respect to product safety, technical specifications, etc. The importance of this aspect of 1992 is well-illustrated by Hufbauer:

> Differing national technical and licensing regimes create major obstacles to a unified market. These are by far the most important barriers, for they restrict market entry on a grand scale. The Cecchini Report puts the gains from opening market entry, and the consequent intensification of competition and realization of scale economies, at about $240 billion. Differing product standards and certification procedures hamper the Europe-wide acceptance of numerous items ranging from autos to pharmaceuticals to packaged cereals.[23]

Various initiatives of the harmonization enterprise being undertaken appear to fall short of truly centralized regulation, in that they involve a process of mutual or reciprocal recognition. In this process, if a firm, product or service complies with domestic regulatory requirements in the Member State which is its 'home', it is allowed into the market of other Member States without being subject to further or different regulatory requirements by the other States. While this approach allows regulatory control to be retained at the level of Member States, a *sine qua non* is the setting of minimum, community-wide standards for regulation. Depending on the area, this can entail quite detailed Community-level regulatory requirements. Moreover, as disputes or concerns emerge whereby the receiving State is dissatisfied with the degree of regulatory protection afforded by the 'home country' regime, an on-going institutional mechanism exists to promulgate new or better defined Community-level standards or rules. The endpoint of the process of mutual recognition may indeed be detailed, unified regulation. This is consistent with the fact that mutual recognition was regarded as a means of speeding up harmonization by generating, from the bottom up, the requirements of harmonization rather than engaging in predicting all the requirements of a uniform regulatory regime.

The Maastricht Treaty and the Treaty of Amsterdam

The Treaty on European Union,[24] better known as the Maastricht Treaty, was signed by the heads of government of the European Union in February 1992 and has now been ratified by all Member States. It is intended as a blueprint for a fundamental deepening of European integration. Undoubtedly the most radical and ambitious aspect of Maastricht is the framework for creation of a single European currency by the end of this century, to replace national currencies of the Member States, including the establishment of a European Central Bank (ECB). The plan for European Monetary Union envisages as a prerequisite for a single currency the alignment of macroeconomic policies of Member States, including the achievement of price stability (low inflation) and the elimination of excessive budget deficits (Article 109j).

As well, the Maastricht Treaty calls for the creation of a common European foreign and security policy (Title V). Where the Council takes a common position on foreign policy, individual Member States are to be bound by it in their own conduct (Title V, Article J.2). However, this requirement is of limited significance, since unanimity is required for Council decisions on foreign policy (Article J.8.2).

Another important feature of Maastricht is a strengthening of the social agenda of the Union, with the Council being given the explicit mandate to adopt directives binding on Member States with respect to working conditions, occupational health and safety, and equality in employment. Importantly, qualified majority voting is to apply with respect to adoption of these directives by the Council (Protocol on Social Policy, Article 2.2). However, with respect to social security, protection of workers in the case of termination of employment, and the work conditions of *Gastarbeiter* the unanimity rule will apply (Article 2.3).

As well, the Treaty would establish immigration policy (i.e. with respect to immigration into Community countries from outside the EC) as a matter of common interest, with measures implementing joint action on these matters to be adopted by the Council according to the qualified majority voting rule (Title VI, Articles K.1, K.3).

Finally, the Maastricht Treaty envisages a number of institutional changes that address (albeit in a rather modest way) concerns about the Union's 'democratic deficit'. An Office of Ombudsman is to be established under the aegis of the European Parliament to address citizen complaints about 'maladministration' by non-judicial Union institutions and officials (Article 138(e)). Also, the Parliament is given a specific mandate to be pro-active – it can request the Commission to submit a proposal to it on any matter where Union action is required to implement the Treaty. In addition, the number of matters on which co-decision (i.e. approval by the European Parliament) is required, as opposed to mere consultation between the Commission and the Council, has been somewhat expanded.[25]

A number of obstacles have emerged to implementing the Maastricht Treaty. First of all, Britain only agreed to Maastricht on condition that it was able to opt out of the social policy and monetary union provisions of the Treaty. Particularly on the single currency and monetary union, this opt out represented a calculated wager that a more pro-European stance would emerge in Britain, and the opt out would thus be temporary.

Perhaps more importantly, the virtual collapse of the existing arrangements for coordination of exchange rates within the European Union (the EMS, European Monetary System)[26] in the autumn of 1992 and the summer of 1993, in the presence of over-heated speculative market activity anticipating currency realignments, cast a shadow on the capacity to move forward with much more radical plans for monetary integration. While some supporters of European Monetary Union saw these crises in the EMS as reinforcing the logic of moving to a single currency in order to eliminate exchange rate instability, many observers have viewed the crises as suggesting that the political pressures on individual countries to adopt different monetary policies remained too great to allow the degree of common macroeconomic policy discipline needed to sustain fixed exchange rates, let alone a single currency.[27] In fact, Monetary Union is proceeding, as discussed in the chapters on Trade, Exchange Rates, and The Balance of Payments.

Furthermore, the initial rejection of the Maastricht Treaty in a referendum in Denmark in the Spring of 1992, and its near rejection in a French referendum in September 1992,[28] have slowed the pace of ratification, although the Union authorities seem determined to find a way around these setbacks. For instance, a set of modifications and qualifications with respect to Denmark's obligations under Maastricht eventually succeeded in securing Denmark's ratification of the Treaty. But the populist backlash against deepening of European integration has led to sober second thoughts in European political circles more generally about the appropriate pace of deepening. One range of concerns that deserves noting is that the provisions respecting immigration policy in the Maastricht Treaty have served as a flashpoint for rejection by the right and far-right in a number of European countries, most notably France and Germany, where immigration is already an extremely sensitive political issue. Some commentators worry that the possibility of loss of national control over immigration policies raised by Maastricht might serve to fuel growing anti-immigrant and racist sentiment in some EC Member States.[29]

It should be emphasized that while Maastricht has become the main focus for public anti-Union sentiment, less public attention has been paid to the increasing activism of the European Commission and Council in implementing the Europe 1992 agenda of harmonization of regulations and standards in many important areas of economic activity (e.g. financial services). An increasing number of harmonization measures, in matters such as product standards and environmental control, are being justified as necessary for the completion of the internal market.

The principle of subsidiarity, as explicitly recognized in the Maastricht Treaty, is that the Union should only act where 'the objectives of the proposed action cannot be sufficiently achieved by the member states' (Article 3b). However, this principle is only to apply to matters that do not fall within the 'exclusive competence' of the Union, and therefore does not limit the scope of Union action with respect to completion of the internal market.

The Treaty of Amsterdam (signed in October 1997) provides mechanisms to allow sub-groups of members of the EU to conclude agreements among themselves and also contains some measures to deal with the 'democratic deficit', including an expansion of the co-decision role of the European Parliament. The Treaty also incorporates the Schengen Agreement, whereby all EU members except the UK and Ireland eliminated their border controls within their common area (the UK and Ireland may continue to impose border controls).

3 Dispute settlement

INTRODUCTION

The legacy of the GATT

As explained in Chapter 2, the General Agreement on Tariffs and Trade was originally intended as only one element of what was supposed to be a much more ambitious institutional structure. By 1950 it was clear that the US Congress would not accept the International Trade Organization, with the result that the only international organization left for the regulation of world trade was a provisional agreement never intended as a framework for such an organization.[1]

From the beginning, then, the GATT was characterized by temporary measures and *ad hoc* solutions to emerging problems. Administrative services for the GATT were provided by the Interim Commission of the ITO and responsibility for oversight and direction was taken on by regular meetings of the Contracting Parties, with Geneva as the *de facto* site.[2]

In contradistinction to the ITO draft charter, the 1947 GATT made no provision for formal, juridical dispute settlement, nor was there any explicit provision for recourse to the International Court of Justice in resolving disputes.[3] The emphasis was on diplomatic methods of consultation and consensus. Article XXII provided for consultations where representations were made by one Contracting Party to another 'with respect to any matter affecting the operation of this Agreement'. Article XXIII provided for the possibility of an investigation, recommendations, and rulings by the CONTRACTING PARTIES (in effect, the GATT Council consisting of all Member States) in the case where a Contracting Party considered that a benefit under the GATT was nullified and impaired. This applied not only in the case where the nullification and impairment flowed from a violation of a provision of the GATT, but in other circumstances as well (which gave rise to what are referred to as non-violation nullification and impairment complaints, discussed later in this chapter). Article XXIII also permitted the CONTRACTING PARTIES to authorize a Contracting Party to suspend concessions under the GATT with respect to another Contracting Party, where it considered that 'the circumstances are serious enough to justify such action'. It is on the legal foundation of these provisions that dispute settlement practice in the

GATT was built throughout its history, and they remain in the 1994 GATT as a basis for the WTO Dispute Settlement Understanding (hereinafter, DSU), which, however (along with various Agreement-specific provisions, discussed below), governs dispute settlement practice not only with respect to the 1994 GATT but all the 'covered agreements' under the WTO umbrella.

The first complaints to come before the GATT were referred to the Chairman of the Contracting Parties at the Second Session in 1948 (without any warrant for such a procedure in the GATT itself), who gave a ruling on the legality or otherwise of the measures complained of.[4] At that same session, a 'working party' was set up for the first time to report on a dispute between the USA and Cuba regarding the latter's textile regulations. The working party, which consisted of GATT representatives from Canada, India, The Netherlands, Cuba and the USA, was to investigate the matter 'in the light of the factual evidence' and to recommend a 'practical solution' to the Contracting Parties. Three days of meetings led to a compromise satisfactory to both of the disputing parties.[5] In contrast to the 'rulings' given by the Chairman, the working parties were really a forum for encouraging negotiation. This was not a third-party investigation for the purpose of coming to objective conclusions on the merits: such a function was precluded by the participation of the disputants, and the fact that the other representatives were acting on the instructions of their respective countries.

The Third Session, in 1949, saw the advent of something like third-party panel dispute resolution. Chile complained to the Contracting Parties about the practices of Australia with respect to fertilizer subsidies. A working party was established, and the report drafted by the neutral countries of the working party was accepted by the Contracting Parties notwithstanding the dissent of the Australian representative.[6] But it was not until the Seventh Session, in 1952, that the Contracting Parties resorted to the panel procedures which have now become the standard means of dispute resolution within the GATT.[7] The use of panels marked an important shift for the GATT. They no longer included representatives from the disputing parties; major trading nations like the UK and the USA were not automatically panel members; and the panel and the GATT Secretariat worked together to develop more formal procedures for the functioning of panels.[8] The GATT Secretariat, in a report to the Contracting Parties, identified this move to panel procedures as an attempt to instil greater objectivity in dispute resolution.[9] One GATT insider has called the institution of panels a Secretariat 'conspiracy' to enhance its influence, and lessen that of the larger countries which tended to dominate working parties.[10] Whatever the real reasons for their creation, panels marked a move away from the GATT as an institution for facilitating negotiation towards a greater emphasis on third-party adjudication.

But the move towards third-party adjudication was not written in stone. No sooner had the panel process been instituted than it fell into a degree of disfavour with GATT nations. During the 1960s, very few disputes were brought before panels – there were only six panel complaints in this period – and from 1963 to 1970 no panels were set up at all. Countries resorted to consultation to resolve disputes, and the more contentious issues were dealt with by working groups, which issued reports with recommendations rather than rendered court-like judgments.[11] Several reasons have been suggested for this move away from legalism in procedure.[12]

The 1960s witnessed a growing perception among GATT countries that the rules of the Agreement were becoming outdated. This period also saw the emergence of the EU, Japan, and several less-developed countries as important trading powers within the GATT. No one in this group found legalism particularly salutary to their interests: strict interpretations of the Agreement would have interfered with domestic programmes designed to manage international trade in various key sectors.[13] Seen in this light, the legalism of the 1950s was probably more a result of the GATT's domination by the USA than some deeply-felt commitment on the part of GATT Members in general. Moreover, the 1960s was a period which saw declining compliance with the spirit of GATT through the use of non-tariff barriers (even as tariffs fell dramatically after the Kennedy Round), and sectoral agreements which effectively managed trade.[14] Faced with trade restrictions that challenged the very assumptions of the GATT, its dispute resolution mechanisms appeared increasingly inadequate to the task of ensuring compliance with the Agreement. The 1970s would see a revival of the use of panel procedures, but this was largely the result of a new aggressiveness on the part of the USA.[15] The real challenges facing the GATT implied the need for new rules.

The Tokyo Round was initiated in part to deal with contentious forms of non-tariff barriers. The USA also hoped to use the Round to strengthen the panels by elaborating their procedures and increasing the predictability of their outcomes. The USA did achieve an important codification of existing practice, and a renewed commitment from GATT countries to use the Agreement's dispute resolution mechanisms.[16] As well, some of the subsidiary codes negotiated during the Tokyo Round included their own dispute settlement provisions, which set deadlines for dispute settlement and allowed resort to dispute settlement as of right.[17] But US efforts towards an even greater emphasis on legalism, for example through the imposition of stricter deadlines, were blocked.[18] In the Tokyo Round, an Understanding on Dispute Settlement (DSU) was negotiated, which in many respects codified and clarified GATT practice as it had evolved to that point, with some relatively minor reforms that addressed some of the concerns that had been raised about the effectiveness of the process. These are summarized by Hudec:

> The Understanding on Dispute Settlement rejects the practice of defendants linking the complaint to resolution of other related issues. It also authorizes the Secretariat to maintain a standing roster of potential panel members, exhorts parties to respond to Secretariat nominations of panel members within seven working days, exhorts parties to 'not oppose nominations except for compelling reasons', and sets a 'normal' time period for the establishment of panels of not more than thirty days after authorization by Council decision.[19]

Finally, in the Uruguay Round a comprehensive agreement on dispute settlement procedures was achieved, including an Appellate Body.

Perspectives on dispute settlement

In order to understand the achievements of the DSU agreed to in the Uruguay Round, it is necessary to examine briefly the various achievements and limitations of dispute settlement practices as they evolved in the GATT on the basis of Articles XXII and XXIII. As noted, often the debate over these practices was cast in terms of 'rules' vs. 'diplomacy', with some Contracting Parties, particularly the United States, arguing for greater legalism, and some other countries, as well as important voices in the global trade policy élite, arguing the advantages of diplomatic flexibility. The demand for legalism usually signalled a concern that panel processes be governed by time limits, that adequate reasons be offered for rulings, and that the adoption of a ruling should not depend on a consensus of all the Contracting Parties (including the Parties complained against), as was considered to be the case under Article XXIII. Those who preferred elements of diplomatic flexibility tended to emphasize the inherently political nature of trade arrangements, and the need for safety valves if the commitment to the system by individual Member States was not to be undermined by dispute outcomes they considered (or their domestic constituencies) considered to be illegitimate. Dispute resolution reform was an important item on the agenda during the Uruguay Round and has resulted in a new Understanding on Rules and Procedures Governing the Settlement of Disputes[20] that largely ratifies, on a permanent basis, the Mid-term Review Agreement, adopted on an interim basis in 1988 during the Uruguay Round negotiations.

Our own perspective on dispute settlement, on which we will elaborate throughout our discussion of the DSU, reflects a modification of the neo-liberal view of the multilateral trading order as a regime whose basis is a mutually self-interested bargain among states. Sustaining such a bargain requires institutions that are capable of identifying and sanctioning (or at least authorizing sanctions against) cheating[21] on the cooperative equilibrium which this bargain represents. Diplomatic, power-based solutions to disputes are unlikely to generate the normative benchmarks necessary to distinguish conduct consistent with the bargain from cheating, and are therefore unlikely to sustain a cooperative equilibrium over time. It is impartial, rules-based dispute settlement that can best perform this function. This is what G.R. Shell in a seminal article on dispute resoluton and international relations theory refers to as the 'Regime Management' model of dispute settlement.[22] However, as we note in several of the chapters of this book, there are elements of the multilateral trading system as it is evolving that are superimposing on a domestic and global welfare-maximizing optimal bargain to constrain protectionism – one that is welfare-maximizing *whatever* the policy choices individual states adopt on non-trade matters[23] – a supranational regulatory regime that embodies certain substantive trade-offs between free trade and other values. Here, we have in mind the TRIPs Agreement, which prescribes minimum standards for national intellectual property laws and regulations, as well as elements of the GATS and the Technical Barriers Agreement that go beyond National Treatment to place constraints or conditions on *non-discriminatory national regulatory outcomes.* As well, when dispute panels have had to weigh environmental and related justifications for largely non-discriminatory measures that have been found GATT-illegal (such as the Process and Production Method-based requirements in the *Tuna/Dolphin* dispute), they have ended up making implicit or explicit trade-offs between the trade liberalization values of the GATT regime and the values that underpin other international and national regimes (in the case of *Tuna/Dolphin*, biodiversity values). Increasingly, in these kinds of situations, dispute settlement may entail more than the evolution and application of a set of norms to identify and distinguish 'cheating' from legitimate state behaviour, and may require a direct regulation of national and international public policy outcomes that implicate diverse values and constituencies. In these circumstances, the regime management goal of sustaining a cooperative equilibrium through the sanctioning of cheating becomes intertwined with the need to produce rulings that have legitimacy with a range of stakeholders whose interests are affected by the way that policy trade-offs are made in interpreting the GATT and the other WTO Agreements. This need is reflected in what Shell calls the Trade Stakeholders Model, which 'views trade dispute resolution as part of a wide-ranging deliberative process by which an emerging global social system can set its priorities.'[24] Shell has very broad global democratic aspirations for this model, which he sees as a means of achieving republican democracy on a world scale. Whether one shares his utopianism or not, the basic idea is a logical consequence of a world where the enforcement of trade norms no longer leaves national (and sub-national) polities, as well as supranational non-trade regimes, unconstrained in their policy autonomy, provided they do not engage in trade discrimination. Since dispute rulings directly[25] impinge on the constituencies that affect the legitimacy of states themselves, the commitment to a cooperative equilibrium by those states will depend not only on the appropriate sanctioning of 'cheating', but also on how dispute settlement is perceived by constituencies to affect their own bargain with the state, or the domestic welfare calculus. Thus, we see the Stakeholder Model as a logical implication of the application of the Regime Management Model to the 'beyond the border' trade regime of the present and future. The implication of the Model is that the WTO dispute resolution process should be open 'to all groups with a stake in the outcomes of trade decisions'.[26] This need not mean, and indeed we would not endorse, standing for all affected actors to bring complaints to the WTO. What it does imply is transparency and publicity in the process, the possibility of intervention through written or oral submissions by affected non-governmental and transnational organization actors, and decisions with clear reasons for factual and legal findings, which can then be subject to meaningful debate by experts and affected groups, both national and supranational.

The DSU negotiated in the Uruguay Round reflects a response to many criticisms of the GATT dispute settlement process,[27] some of which have obvious salience from either a Regime Management or Trade Stakeholder perspective, or both. These criticisms included the following:

1 delay and uncertainty in the process, given the absence of a right to a panel (this remaining at the discretion of the CONTRACTING PARTIES) and the

absence of hard time limits on consultations, responses to requests for panels, and panel proceedings and rulings;
2 an absence of legal rigour and clarity in the panels's rulings;
3 the uncertainty of a panel ruling being adopted, given the consensus rule for adoption (which demanded the consent of the losing party);[28]
4 delay in and partial or non-complete compliance with panel rulings.

Interestingly, from a Regime Management perspective, despite these various shortcomings, the GATT dispute settlement process proved relatively successful through most of the GATT's history in actually achieving compliance, and thereby sustaining a cooperative equilibrium through disciplining, or being seen to discipline, cheating.

From 1947–85, it took about two years to resolve a dispute from the time a complaint was lodged to the implementation of remedial measures.[29] Only ten cases have taken longer than two years, and only one was very protracted indeed.[30] More importantly, a recent detailed review of all GATT disputes between 1948 and 1989 by Hudec *et al.*[31] finds a success rate for valid complaints (resulting in full or partial satisfaction of the complaint) of 88%. While the success rate declined somewhat in the 1980s, the compliance record still stood at 81%. Other trends of note that emerge from the Hudec study are: (1) the explosion of complaints in the 1980s – more than half of all GATT complaints were brought in the last of the four decades of GATT history; (2) for the entire 42–year period, 73% of all complaints were filed by the USA, the EU and its present members, Canada, and Australia. The USA, the EU and its members, Canada, and Japan accounted for 83% of all appearances as defendants. Ninety-two per cent of all complaints involved either the USA or the EU (or its members) as a Party; (3) for the entire period, 52% of all complaints related to NTBs, 21% to tariffs, 16% to subsidies, and 10% to antidumping/countervailing duty measures. Over time, NTBs and AD/CVDs have increased as a percentage of complaints while tariffs have sharply declined; (4) in the 1950s only 23% of all complaints involved agriculture while for the period 1960–84, one-half of the complaints involved agricultural trade measures, many relating to the EU's Common Agricultural Policy. However, compliance rates with rulings in agricultural and non-agricultural complaints are roughly the same; (5) according to the authors, the most important finding of their study is the disproportionate level of non-compliant behaviour by the USA, especially in the 1980s.

There is clearly a link between the increasing ineffectiveness of GATT dispute settlement in the 1980s, defined in terms of perceived or actual compliance (which gives Parties to the bargain the confidence needed to sustain their commitment to it), and the rise in the proportion of disputes related to normative baselines for trade-impacting national (e.g. subsidies) policies. Because some complaints stood on the margins of the text of the GATT itself, the inability of the dispute settlement process to resolve them arguably in those cases reflected the need to evolve the terms of the bargain itself in light of changed circumstances that affected, or arguably affected, the original balance of concessions. Of course, the idea of non-violation nullification and impairment contained in Article XXIII provided a means of adjusting this balance through dispute settlement itself, where despite the absence of a clear violation of the text of the GATT, the behaviour of a Contracting Party undermined the original expectation of benefits. But there were obvious limits to dispute panels playing such a role, given that arguments about expectations often related to controversies over what normative baselines for domestic policy Contracting Parties may have assumed in formulating their expectations of benefits.

But the increasing ineffectiveness of the panel process in the 1980s (despite the appearance of increased legalism defined in term of referring to previous panel decisions as precedents and lengthy reasons for rulings) relates also to the practices in dispute settlement that impeded a transition from a conventional Regime Management Model to a Trade Stakeholder model. These included secrecy in panel proceedings and the way in which panel rulings were developed and drafted, as well as long delays in the derestriction of the rulings and related documents.

In general, panellists under the GATT system were not experts in international trade law, or distinguished jurists of any kind, but rather junior to middle-level trade diplomats, or retired trade diplomats, mostly without formal legal training. These individuals were expected to take advice from the GATT legal Secretariat. The Secretariat, in almost all cases, not only provided the panel with a statement of the Parties' pleadings, but analysis of the merits of each Party's case, and also drafted the panel's decision itself.[32] While commentators close to the process, such as Plank,[33] insist that the rulings nevertheless reflected the panels' own analysis of the issues, one can imagine that non-lawyer junior or middle-level diplomats would not often explicitly challenge the 'professional' advice of the Secretariat as to how a matter should be decided. Also, the Secretariat played a crucial role in the selection of names for appointment to panels, another means of influencing outcomes – for junior and middle-level diplomats, and even perhaps for some academics, service on a panel is an honour or perk, and one can easily imagine that some individuals would not wish to jeopardize their chances of serving more than once in this capacity through a run-in with the Secretariat. Thus, while in appearance, a practice of impartial, disinterested juridical decision-making by a panel of experts, the dispute settlement process was, largely, in reality, dominated by a small, closely knit technocratic élite with a professional interest in the maintenance of the GATT as a regime dominated by liberal trade values. As Keohane and other neo-liberal theorists have pointed out, such élites can play an important positive role in regime maintenance, and as long as the task was that of identifying 'cheating' (explicit or hidden protectionism), the Secretariat's domination of the panel process worked reasonably well from a Regime Management perspective. Academics and independent jurists were unwilling to engage in very much open and critical scrutiny of panel rulings, in part because they believed that to do so would undermine the legitimacy of a process that was effective for Regime Management, and give various protectionist interests with a stake in disrupting the cooperative equilibrium an opportunity to do so. As well, and less idealistically, a further means of control over the system by the Secretariat was epistemic. Because panel reports were only derestricted once adopted, and usually not deristricted if not adopted, by the Contracting Parties, and even if derestricted, often only published in the official reporting service (BISD) much later, many academics and other independent jurists were dependent on good relations with members of the Secretariat to obtain documents critical to timely analysis. In the 1980s, and especially after the *Tuna/Dolphin I* panel ruling, a great deal of pressure was placed on the GATT by the United States to remedy the unavailability of documentation. Various groups began publishing bootleg versions of still restricted panel rulings on the Internet – such versions now regularly show up in *Inside U.S. Trade* and have apparently also sometimes been posted on the web site of the United States Trade Representative.

These developments reflect the fact that once the panels were put in the position of not simply sanctioning 'cheating' but explicitly making trade-offs between different values, the Secretariat-dominated panel process experienced a legitimacy crisis. Faced with such a challenge in the *Tuna/Dolphin* case, which concerned trade sanctions to enforce a regime to protect dolphins for biodiversity purposes (and which applied domestically as well), the response of the system was to approach the problem purely from the professional interest in the maintenance of the liberal trade regime, and view the measures as either covert protectionism ('cheating' disguised as action for non-trade purposes), or unwarranted 'noise' or interference in a self-contained, single value-based regime. In ways that are described in detail in Chapter 15 on trade and the environment, the law and jurisprudence of the GATT were manipulated in order to make the value of liberalized trade trump the value of biodiversity. Ironically, the system had thought that what it was doing was protecting the integrity and coherence of the liberal trading regime, while what it actually provoked was a legitimacy crisis in a crucial element of the system from a Regime Management perspective – dispute settlement. This crisis was, however, diffused (at least temporarily) by the ability of the United States to prevent the adoption of the reports of the panels in *Tuna/Dolphin I* and *II*.

THE WTO DISPUTE SETTLEMENT UNDERSTANDING (DSU)

In light of this critical and analytical history of GATT dispute settlement, we now examine the reforms initiated in the Uruguay Round and consider the potential of these reforms to allow the transition from a Regime Management model of dispute settlement to a Trade Stakeholder model, a transition which, as we have suggested, is implied by the very objective of Regime Management, since the multilateral trade regime is increasingly implicated in prescribing and constraining national and international regulatory choices and, consequently, in trade-offs between liberal trade and other policy values. Already numerous panel and Appellate Body (AB) decisions have interpreted provisions of the DSU, and the following commentary incorporates these interpretations.

Scope of the DSU: Relationship to Articles XXII and XXIII of the GATT 1994 and other WTO Agreements (Articles 1 and 3 and Appendix 2)

The 'rules and procedures' of the DSU apply to all the 'covered' Agreements of the WTO (Article 1) that are listed in Appendix 1 to the DSU. This list is reproduced below.

a Agreement establishing the World Trade Organization

b Multilateral Trade Agreements

Annex 1a: Multilateral Agreements on Trade in Goods

Annex 1b: General Agreement on Trade in Services

Annex 1c: Agreement on Trade-related Aspects of Intellectual Property Rights

Annex 2: Understanding on Rules and Procedures Governing the Settlement of Disputes

c Plurilateral Trade Agreements

Annex 4: Agreement on Trade in Civil Aircraft

Agreement on Government Procurement

International Dairy Agreement

International Bovine Meat Agreement

The DSU applies subject to any certain provisions in dispute settlement in particular covered agreements – in the event of a conflict between a provision of the DSU and a dispute settlement provision of a covered agreement the latter is to prevail (Article 1.2). A list of the relevant provisions of the covered agreements is provided in Appendix 2 to the DSU. This list is reproduced below.

Agreement Rules and Procedures

Agreement on the Application of Sanitary and Phytosanitary Measures 11.2

Agreement on Textiles and Clothing 2.14, 2.21, 4.4, 5.2, 5.4, 5.6, 6.9, 6.10, 6.11, 8.1 through 8.12

Agreement on Technical Barriers to Trade 14.2 through 14.4, Annex 2

Agreement on Implementation of Article VI of GATT 1994 17.4 through 17.7

Agreement on Implementation of Article VII of GATT 1994 19.3 through 19.5, Annex II 2(f), 3, 9, 21

Agreement on Subsidies and Countervailing Measures 4.2 through 4.12, 6.6, 7.2 through 7.10, 8.5, footnote 35, 24.4, 27.7, Annex V

General Agreement on Trade in Services XXII:3, XXIII:3

Annex on Financial Services 4

Annex on Air Transport Services 4

Decision on Certain Dispute Settlement

Procedures for the GATS 1 through 5

The list of rules and procedures includes provisions where only a part of the provision may be relevant in this context. There are some agreement-specific provisions not on this list; these do *not* take precedence over the general provisions of the DSU.

In the event that a dispute concerns more than one covered agreement, and the agreement-specific dispute settlement provisions of the various agreements conflict, the Parties must themselves agree on which rules and procedures apply, failing which the Chairman of the Dispute Settlement Body will decide on the applicable rules, following the principle that the rules of the DSU itself should be used in order to obviate conflict.

Dispute Settlement Body (Article 2)

Article 2 of the DSU establishes the Dispute Settlement Body (DSB), which is the collectivity of WTO Members acting in their dispute settlement capacity and has a role parallel to that of the GATT Council in the pre-WTO multilateral dispute settlement arrangements. Thus, the DSB 'shall have the authority to establish panels, adopt panel and Appellate Body reports, maintain surveillance of implementation of rulings and recommendations, and authorize suspension of concessions and other obligations under the covered agreements.' (Article 2.1).

Consultations and Other Alternatives to Panel Dispute Settlement (Articles 4 and 5)

Reflecting criticisms that the GATT practice with respect to consultations often permitted a Party to delay inordinately the commencement of dispute settlement proceedings, Article 4 provides a set of strict time limits for consultations. A Member must reply to a request for consultations within 10 days of receiving it, and enter into 'consultations in good faith' within 30 days thereafter. If a Member of whom consultations have been requested fails to comply with either deadline then the Member so requesting may 'proceed directly to request the establishment of a panel'. If consultations fail to resolve the dispute within 60 days of the receipt of the request for consultations, the complaining Member may request the establishment of a panel. A panel may be requested before this 60-day period has expired where both the complainant and the responding Member consider that consultations have failed to solve the dispute. The role of consultations was noted by the Appellate Body in *Underwear*,[34] where it held that a Member could not backdate the application of Transitional Safeguards under the Agreement on

Textiles and Clothing (ATC) to the date of request of consultations. One reason the AB gave for this finding was the need to protect the effectiveness of consultations as a means of resolving disputes. However, the consultations here were undertaken under specific provisions of the ATC and not Article 4 of the DSU. Para. 4.8 provides for an accelerated timetable for consultations in 'cases of urgency.' In such cases, consultations are to be entered into within 10 days of the receipt of the request, and if these fail a panel may be requested after 20 days of receipt of the request. In one of the first disputes under the WTO, concerning imposition of tariff surcharges on Japanese automobiles by the US, Japan requested that the matter be treated as a case of urgency within the meaning of 4.8. Japan's argument was that the measures would have an almost immediate impact upon Japanese trading interests.[35] Normally, consultations are requested *after* a measure has been implemented and trade effects are *already* being felt – if Members had intended cases of urgency to extend even to instances where measures have not yet been adopted, but are imminent, then they would have been better advised to make the timetable for urgency the normal timetable. Indeed a non-urgent matter, on the basis of Japan's reasoning, would be a case where the imposition of the measures would be in the non-immediate future – where if anything the action might not be ripe. The reference to 'perishable products' in 4.8 suggests that, in fact, cases of urgency are those where irreparable harm would be caused by delay, something akin to the criterion for granting an interlocutory injunction in many domestic legal systems. With respect to ripeness, the DSU does not state what circumstances may give rise to a right to request consultations.

Establishment and Terms of Reference of Panels (Articles 6 and 7)

Article 6 provides that a panel shall be established at the latest at the DSB meeting following the meeting at which the request first appears as an item on the agenda; a Member may request the convocation of a DSB meeting for these purposes, and one shall be held within 15 days of the request for the meeting, subject to a 10-day advance notice requirement. The DSB may only refuse to establish a panel on the basis of unanimity – since this would mean the very Member requesting the panel would have to object to its establishment, the effect is to create a right to a panel, once the applicable time periods for consultations have elapsed. The DSU does not explicitly state on what substantive grounds such a right may be invoked. However, a reading of the general provisions of Article 3, which refer in several places to concepts such as *prima facie* nullification and impairment where a provision of a covered agreement is claimed to have been violated, and various other provisions (including Article 11, which refers to the panel's role in determining conformity of measures with the covered agreements and Article 26, which deals with non-violation nullification and impairment) suggests that the substantive grounds are those provided in Article XXIII of the GATT, as interpreted in GATT practice. With respect to ripeness, it should be noted that Article XXIII suggests that the breach of an obligation and/or nullification and impairment of benefits is a condition precedent for recourse to panel dispute settlement. In the *Bananas* case, the Appelate Body considered a challenge by the EC to the United States participating in the panel as a complaining party, on the grounds that public international law requires that a state have a 'legal interest' in order to have standing before an arbitral tribunal. The EC claimed that in this instance no such legal interest existed, because the United States had never exported a single banana to the EC. The AB found that the various sources of public international law invoked by the EC did not contradict the recourse to a treaty itself to determine the issue of standing to commence an action under the dispute settlement provisions of that treaty.[36] The AB then referred to the 'chapeau' of Article XIII of the GATT, which refers to the right to bring a matter before the CONTRACTING PARTIES when a Member 'considers' that there has been, *inter alia*, a violation and also to Article 3.7 of the DSU, which states that 'Before bringing a case, a Member shall exercise its judgement as to whether action under these procedures would be fruitful.' From this language, the AB drew the inference that 'a Member has broad discretion in deciding to bring a case against another Member under the DSU . . . a Member is expected to be largely self-regulating in deciding whether any such action is "fruitful"' (para. 135). Despite this emphasis on self-regulation, the AB went on to find that the United States was 'justified' in bringing its claims because it was a producer of bananas and thus the US could have a 'potential export interest' (para. 136). It is unclear whether the AB was here merely endorsing, in *obiter dicta*, the manner in which the US was regulating itself pursuant to Article 3.7, or was implying that despite the large element of self-regulation, there is nevertheless a *de minimus* requirement of objective justification. The request for a panel must 'identify the specific measures at issue and provide a brief summary of the legal basis of the complaint sufficient to present the problem clearly' (Article 6.2). In *Bananas*, the AB upheld the panel's view ruling that, to meet the specificity requirement in Article 6.2, it is sufficient

> for the Complaining Parties to list the provisions of the Agreements alleged to have been violated without setting out detailed arguments as to which specific aspects of the measures at issue related to which specific provisions of those agreements. In our view, there is a significant difference between the *claims* identified in the request for establishment of a panel, which establish the panel's terms of reference under Article 7 of the DSU, and the *arguments* supporting those claims, which are set out and progressively clarified in the first written submissions, the rebuttal submissions and the first and second panel meetings with the parties (para. 141).

A complaining Member may either request special terms of reference for the panel, in which case the proposed terms are to be included in its request for a panel, or accept a standard set of terms, which essentially authorize the panel to consider any relevant provisions of covered agreements in relation to the matter referred to in the request for the panel. More typically specific terms of reference are agreed on the basis of consultation between the Parties, as foreseen by Article

7.2. In the *Desiccated Coconut* case, the AB attributed a very important status to the terms of reference of a panel, holding that

> A panel's terms of reference are important for two reasons. First, terms of reference fulfil an important due process objective – they give the parties and third parties sufficient information concerning the claims at issue in the dispute in order to allow them an opportunity to respond to the complainant's case. Second, they establish the jurisdiction of the panel by defining the precise claims at issue in the dispute.[37]

In *Desiccated Coconut*, the AB also held that in order for a claim to come within a panel's terms of reference, it must have been referred to in the request for a panel (p. 22). A logical implication of the view that the terms of reference establish the panel's jurisdiction is that it may not consider claims of violations that are not mentioned in the terms of reference.[38] However, a panel is not required to restrict itself to the *arguments* raised by Parties in the proceedings, and may develop its own legal reasoning.[39] In order for a panel to be capable of adjudicating a claim that a particular provision of a covered agreement has been violated, the specific provision, and not merely the agreement itself or other provisions of that agreement, must be mentioned in the terms of reference (*Indian Patents*, para. 92). Article 7.2 of the DSU states that 'Panels shall address the relevant provisions in any covered agreements or agreements cited by the parties to the dispute.' In *Shirts and Blouses*,[40] the AB held that '[a] panel need only address those claims which must be addressed in order to resolve the matter in issue in the dispute' (p. 19). However, in this case the argument that the panel was required to address a particular claim was made under Article 11 of the DSU, discussed below, and not Article 7.2. The AB reasoned that another provision of the DSB provided Members with an avenue to seek an authoritative interpretation of a provision of a covered agreement, even where a panel had found it unnecessary to interpret the provision in order to settle a particular dispute (Article 3.9). The AB also emphasized that the DSU does not prohibit a panel from interpreting provisions in addition to those strictly necessary to resolve the dispute. Such remarks would, however, be considered as *obiter dicta*, and might not be subject to appellate review – thus in *Shirts and Blouses*, a statement by the panel relating to the powers of the Textile Monitoring Body was regarded by the AB as 'purely a descriptive and gratuitous comment' and not subject to appellate review.

Composition of Panels (Article 8)

Panels are to be composed of three panellists, based on nominations from the Secretariat from its rosters. WTO Members may from time-to-time propose additional names of qualified persons to add to the rosters. However, a Party to a dispute may not challenge the Secretariat's choice of panellists, except for 'compelling reasons' (8.6). Panellists are to be 'well-qualified governmental and/or non governmental individuals'. These may include persons who have served as diplomatic officials at the GATT, in the Secretariat, or as senior trade officials in national governments. The only non-governmental category explicitly mentioned is that of persons who have 'taught or published on international trade law or policy'. Ironically, given that these criteria are heavily weighted to the traditional trade policy élites, the DSU also states that, in addition to independence, panel members should be selected with a view to ensuring 'a sufficiently diverse background and a wide spectrum of experience' (8.2). From the perspective of achieving a transition from a Regime Management to a Trade Stakeholder model of dispute settlement, these provisions are largely disappointing. The Secretariat retains almost complete control over the composition of panels and as already mentioned, despite the language on diversity and wide experience, is given an explicit basis to continue choosing persons who come from the traditional governmental trade policy élites. Activists, business persons, and individuals with expertise in substantive public policy areas that now interface with international trade rules are not even mentioned as possible candidates for the rosters. One qualification is that in some of the covered agreements, expertise in a substantive public policy area may be an additional criterion relevant to the establishment of the rosters – for instance, the *Decision on Certain Dispute Settlement Procedures for the General Agreement on Trade in Services* provides that a special roster of panellists be established for dispute settlement under the GATS, comprising persons who have expertise related to trade in services 'including associated regulatory matters' (Article 3).

Procedures for Multiple Complaints (Article 9)

Article 9 deals with a situation where more than one Member wishes to complain about 'the same matter'. In this situation a single panel may be struck to examine the multiple complaints 'taking into account the rights of all Members concerned'. The proceedings are to be organized so that all Members enjoy the same rights they would have had in the case of separate panels being struck (9.2). A particular difficulty arises where a Member or Members seek to join a complaint as an additional Party or Parties, one the panel as been struck on the basis of an individual complaint. In such a case, as discussed above, the Terms of Reference will have been determined through the original individual complaint. Thus, in order to join a complaint and still enjoy the right to raise claims not initially raised by the original individual complainant, the other Members would appear to have to do so before the panel's Terms of Reference (its 'jurisdiction') have been determined. However, while a panel cannot amend its own Terms of Reference (*Bananas*), the DSB can. Thus, in *Reformulated Gasoline*, when Brazil requested a panel on US measures which were already the subject of a complaint by Venezuela, the DSB established new Terms of Reference for the joint panel. In this case, it was a particularly straightforward matter, since the original panel had standard Terms of Reference, i.e. not limiting the panel's consideration of any provision in a covered agreement relevant to disposing of the complaint.[41] In cases of a joint complaint, the panel may issue multiple reports, each of which addresses the particulars of the complaint of a single Member (as for example occured in *Bananas*) (Article 9.2). It is to be emphasized that there is no requirement that complaints by two or more Members concerning the same or similar measures of another Member be consolidated in the same panel proceeding. It is an interesting question as to whether the DSB can insist on joinder, even if one or more complainants object – arguably, if joinder were only at the consent of all Parties, then there would not have been the need to protect the rights of each Party in the event of joinder, since a Party who thought their rights would be compromised could simply insist on a separate proceeding. In *Hormones*, there were parallel proceedings by Canada and the United States against the EC. In the case of parallel proceedings, the DSU provides that 'If more than one panel is established to examine the complaints related to the same matter, to the greatest extent possible the same persons shall serve as panelists on each of the separate panels and the timetable for the panel process in such disputes shall be harmonized.' In *Hormones*, Canada and the US participated in *each other's* panels as *third Parties* (a status discussed in the next section of this chapter). An interesting issue arose from decisions taken by the members of the panels with a view to rationalizing the parallel proceedings: a joint meeting was held with scientific experts, all the information provided in the Canadian proceeding was provided to the United States, and *vice versa*, and the United States was invited to attend and even speak at the second meeting of the Canadian panel. On appeal, the EC objected to all these decisions, claiming that they exceeded the normal rights of third parties in WTO panel proceedings. The AB treated all but the last of these decisions not in terms of third-party rights, but rather as related to 'economy of effort' in a situation of parallel proceedings concerning the same matter. Referring to the language in 9.3 of the DSU concerning 'harmonization of timetables', the AB noted 'we can see a relation between timetable harmonization . . . and economy of effort' (*Hormones*, para. 153). The AB further observed: 'Having access to a common pool of information enables the panel and the parties to save time by avoiding duplication of the compilation and analysis of information already presented in the other proceeding [footnote omitted]'. Article 3.3 of the DSU recognizes the importance of avoiding unnecessary delays in the dispute settlement process and states that the prompt settlement of a dispute is essential to the effective functioning of the WTO (para. 153) With respect to the granting to the US of a right to be present at the second substantive panel meeting, the AB deferred to the judgment of the panel that the relationship of this meeting to the joint scientific experts' session was such as to provide a due process case for the US presence there; 'this decision falls within the sound discretion and authority of the panel, particularly if the panel considers it necesssary for ensuring to all parties due process of law' (para. 154).

Intervenors (Third Parties) (Article 10)

Article 10 affords intervenor status to any Member 'having a substantial interest in a matter'(102). Such intervenors ('third parties') have the right to make both oral and written submissions to the panel, and to obtain the submissions of the Parties to the dispute to the first meeting of the panel. 'Third party submissions are to be provided to the parties to the dispute and shall be reflected in the final report'(10). From the perspective of the Trade Stakeholder model, these provisions are highly inadequate, as they provide no intervention rights whatever to non-governmental organizations, or indeed to other international organizations (e.g. in the environmental or health and safety areas) to intervene, even through written submissions. However, pursuant to Article 13 of the DSU, to be discussed further in the next section, panels themselves have wide discretion to obtain and consider information and opinions beyond those contained in the submissions of the complainants and third parties. Now, Article 11 requires the panel to make an 'objective assessment of the matter before it'. In our view, Article 11 would be breached if a panel were to be completely arbitrary in the manner in which it decides to consider or reject information or opinions available to it from sources other than the Parties – it is difficult to see how findings based on such arbitrary selectivity could constitute 'an objective assessment of the matter'. Thus, in our view, the decision made by the *Turtles* panel simply not to consider documents provided by non-governmental organizations was not consistent with a panel's responsibilities under Article 11.[42] In this case, the panel made the bizarre assertion that 'Accepting non-requested information from non-governmental sources would be, in our opinion, incompatible with the provisions of the DSU as currently applied' (para. 7.8). It is not surprising that the panel did not here cite any provision of the DSU or any interpretation of the DSU, either in dispute settlement proceedings or any other context, to support the assertion – the finding is simply without any foundation and was rightly rejected by the AB on appeal. While the AB was less clear on whether amieus briefs could be received at the appellate level unless attached to a party's submissions, in fact, the AB did in practice receive and accept one such unattached submission in the *Turtles* case itself. Perhaps the AB quite reasonably considered the ability to accept such material as implicit in the very notion of appellate jurisdiction, which would be consistent with general appellate court practice. Of course, perfectly consistently with its obligation of 'objective assessment' in Article 11, a panel may decide that information is not relevant and therefore not consider it for purposes of making an 'objective assessment'. But the finding of irrelevancy will itself be a finding of law, subject to appellate review (*Hormones*, para. 143). Wanton disregard of such information may be a violation of the duty to make 'an objective assessment'.

The Jurisdiction and Mandate of Panels (Articles 3, 11, 13, and 19)

Article 11, which we have just discussed with respect to intervenors, is a fundamental reference point for the jurisdiction and mandate of the panel. It states in part:

> The function of panels is to assist the DSB in discharging its responsibilities under this Understanding and the covered agreements. Accordingly a panel should make an objective assessment of the matter before it, including an objective assessment of the facts of the case and the applicability of and conformity with the relevant covered agreements, and make such other findings

> as will assist the DSB in making the recommendations or in giving the rulings provided for in the covered agreements.

The broadness of this mandate is of course qualified by the constraints imposed on the panel by its Terms of Reference, as discussed above. Also relevant to the panel's mandate with respect to legal interpretation is Article 3.2 which states in part: 'Recommendations and rulings of the DSB cannot add to or diminish the rights and obligations provided in the covered agreements.' Article 19.2 states in turn that: 'In accordance with paragraph 2 of Article 3, in their findings and recommendations, the panel and the Appellate Body cannot add to or diminish the rights and obligations provided in the covered agreements.' The significance of these provisions for interpretation will be discussed below in the section on principles of interpretation. The reference to 'covered agreements' throughout raises the issue of how the panel may deal with a situation where a party or third party invokes an agreement other than a covered agreement as relevant to the dispute. In the *Bananas* case, for instance, among the issues in dispute was the consistency with the GATT waiver for Lomé preferences of certain measures by the EC. The legal question was whether the measures fell within the waiver because, in the language of the waiver, they were 'required' by the EC's obligations under the Lomé Convention. The EC argued that, the Lomé Convention not being a covered agreement, the panel should have deferred to the views of the signatories of the Lomé Convention as to what it 'required'. The AB upheld the view of the panel that the Lomé waiver, inasmuch as it incorporated a reference to the Lomé Convention itself, required the panel to examine the provisions of the Lomé Convention, to determine whether in fact the EC measures were 'required' by it. (paras 167–8). While the AB was probably correct to reject a stance of total deference towards the interpretation of the Lomé Convention by states parties, it went on to interpret the Convention largely without reference to the practice surrounding this treaty, which suggests a rather narrow view of the interaction of other international legal regimes with the WTO. As Petersmann notes, in the WTO Agreements there are

> numerous references to other international agreements and general international law rules such as the UN Charter, the International Monetary Fund Agreement, international environmental agreements like the International Plant Protection Convention, international 'standards' promulgated by other 'relevant international organizations open for members to all (WTO) Members', international services agreements, e.g., on international air transport and international telecommunication, worldwide agreement on intellectual property rights.[43]

The coherence of the international legal system would be put at risk if WTO panels and the Appellate Body were to apply or interpret provisions of other agreements referenced in WTO agreements in abstraction from the practice surrounding those agreements, including dispute rulings, views of the institutional organs associated with the treaty, and the opinions of jurists. From the perspective of the evolution of WTO dispute settlement towards a Trade Stakeholder model, since the references to other agreements often relate to benchmarks that are relevant where the panels are dealing with trade-offs between values of liberalized trade and other substantive policy values, the way in which the benchmarks in these other regimes have been evolved by and in response to regime-specific constituencies must be taken into account to ensure an outcome that does not unduly privilege liberal trade over other relevant policy values.

1. Burden of Proof and Standard of Review

The issue of burden of proof is not directly addressed in the DSU, except for Article 3.2 which is a statement of prior GATT practice, as developed in numerous panel rulings: 'In cases where there is an infringement of the obligations assumed under a covered agreement, the action is considered to constitute a case of *prima facie* nullification or impairment. This means that there is normally a presumption that a breach of the rules has an adverse effect on other Members parties to that covered agreement, and in such cases, it shall be up to the Member against whom the complaint has been brought to rebut the charge.' The Appellate Body has observed that

> various international tribunals, including the International Court of Justice, have generally and consistently accepted and applied the rule that a party who asserts a fact, whether the claimant or the respondent, is responsible for providing proof thereof [footnote omitted]. Also, it is a generally-accepted canon of evidence in civil law, common law and in fact, most jurisdictions, that the burden of proof rests with the party, whether complaining or defending, who asserts the affirmative of a particular claim or defence. If that party adduces evidence sufficient to raise a presumption that what is claimed is true, the burden then shifts to the other party , who will fail unless it adduces sufficient evidence to rebut the presumption [footnote omitted] (*Shirts and Blouses*, p. 14; applied by the AB in *Hormones* and *Indian Patents*).

There are some provisions of the WTO Agreements which are in the nature of affirmative defences. These provisions are invoked by the Party complained against. The panel will consider such defences once it has determined that there is a violation of some other provision of a covered agreement (*Reformulated Gasoline*, p. 16), the burden of proof for establishing which is on the complaining Party. After the violation of the other provision is thus established, the burden of proof shifts to the Party complained against to prove the affirmative defence. While in *Shirts and Blouses*, the AB gave the obvious example of GATT Article XX as an instance of an affirmative defence, what constitutes an affirmative defence may not always be so obvious. In *Hormones*, the AB noted: 'The general rule in a dispute settlement proceeding requiring a complaining party to establish a *prima facie* case of inconsistency with a provision . . . before the burden of showing consistency with that provision is taken on by the defending party, is *not* avoided by simply describing that same provision as an "exception"' (*Hormones*, para. 104). In *Hormones*, the panel had made an interpretation of the *Sanitary and Phytosanitary (SPS) Agreement* which suggested that the party complained against generally bore the burden of proof that its measures complied with the *Agreement,* unless they were based on international standards. This would have had the result of making the resort to SPS measures as such a *prima facie* violation of WTO law, unless these measures conformed to international standards. The AB rightly found that such a reading was inconsistent with the text and structure of the *SPS Agreement*, which indicate that the *Agreement* establishes alternative sets of disciplines on Members' SPS measures, depending on whether or not they are based on international standards. The AB noted that according to the *SPS Agreement*, Members have an 'autonomous right' to introduce measures that establish a higher level of protection than provided for by international standards, subject to the disciplines contained in the *Agreement*; logically, then, the burden of proof rests on the complainant to establish a violation, by showing that these disciplines have not been complied with. Once a provision has been characterized overall as an affirmative defence, it appears that the burden of proof is shifted to the defending party with respect to *all* the legal and factual tests in that defence (barring explicit textual language to the contrary). Thus, in *Reformulated Gasoline*, the AB found that with respect to Article XX the burden of proof of showing that a measure is not an abuse of an exception falls on the defending Party, even after that Party has established that the measure qualifies under one of the specific heads of Article XX (p. 22). The AB, however, gave no explicit justification for this finding – one could as easily have argued that once a measure is shown to be in an exculpating category, the burden of demonstrating that it is being used abusively shifts back to the complaining Party, based upon the notion that Members of the WTO should not generally be subject to a rebuttable presumption that they are abusing rights acquired under WTO law. The AB may need to revisit this finding in light of its later observation in *Hormones* that the characterization of a provision as an 'exception' does not in itself exhaustively allocate all the burden of proof within that provision to the defending Party. The issue of standard of review arises where a panel is examining the domestic law of a Member as interpreted by domestic authorities and tribunals to determine whether the law, or the actions of those authorities and tribunals (including fact-finding), or both are in compliance with provisions of the covered agreements. Only the Antidumping Agreement addresses explicitly the issue of standard of review. A certain degree of deference to *findings of fact* by domestic authorities in antidumping matters is provided in Article 17.6 of the Agreement, which states in part that 'If the establishment of the facts was proper and the evaluation was unbiased and objective, even though the panel might have reached a different conclusion, the evaluation shall not be overturned.' In *Hormones*, the AB suggested that the appropriate standard of review for a panel lay somewhere between *de novo* review of the facts at issue before the domestic authorities and 'total deference to national authorities', and referred to the Article 11 responsibility of the panel to make an objective assessment of the facts. It is difficult to see how the AB was able to understand Article 11 as illuminating with respect to where on the spectrum between *de novo* review and total deference the appropriate benchmark is to be found. In the *Indian Patents* case, the AB considered an argument by India that domestic law had to be proven as a fact by the complainant in a WTO panel proceeding, and furthermore that India should be given the benefit of the doubt with respect to whether, under its domestic legal system certain administrative instructions would provide the legal security required by the provision of the TRIPs Agreement in issue, and that, at least, India's guidance in interpreting these administrative instructions should have been sought (para. 64). The AB appeared to take the view that when examining a Member's domestic law solely for the purpose of determining whether it complies with a covered agreement, no particular deference to domestic interpretations of that law is warranted (para. 66). This is, however, rather too simplistic, for in this particular case the very determination of whether India was in compliance with the TRIPs Agreement entailed an assessment of whether the administrative instructions would survive a *domestic* legal challenge under the Indian Patent Act. This entails a predictive judgment about how a particular country's domestic tribunals would understand the interaction between particular administrative decrees and a domestic statute, and it is difficult to see how the AB was able to uphold a panel finding on this matter that was not based on evidence by Indian legal experts on Indian administrative and intellectual property law and how it is applied in the Indian courts. Instead, the AB reviewed the panel's finding as if it were reviewing an ordinary panel intepretation of a WTO provision itself.

2. Findings of Fact

The DSU does not explicitly provide for factual discovery between the Parties prior to the commencement of panel proceedings. However, in *Indian Patents*, the AB suggested that consultations concerning the Terms of Reference should be viewed as, in part, fulfilling this function. The AB noted:

> Parties engaged in dispute settlement under the DSU must be fully forthcoming from the beginning both as to the claims involved in a dispute and as to the facts relating to those claims. Claims must be stated clearly. Facts must be disclosed freely. This must be so in consultations as in the more formal setting of panel proceedings. In fact, the demands of due process that are implicit in the DSU make this especially necessary during consultations. For the claims that are made and the facts that are established during consultations do much to shape the substance and the scope of subsequent panel proceedings. If, in the aftermath of consultations, any party believes that all the pertinent facts relating to a claim are, for any reason, not before the panel, then that party should ask the panel in that case to engage in additional fact-finding (para. 94).

Here the AB was responding to a US argument that the panel should be able to adjudicate a claim not contained in the Terms of Reference, since only on the basis of facts disclosed later did it make sense for the United States to advance that claim – the AB held that it could not go beyond its Terms of Reference, even to remedy such a situation. It added: 'It is worth noting that, with respect to fact-finding, the dictates of due process could better be served if panels had standard working procedures that provided for appropriate factual discovery at an early stage in panel proceedings' (para. 95). In addition to the submissions of the Parties and third Parties, a panel may, as already noted, 'seek information and technical advice from any individual or body which it deems appropriate', subject to certain notification and confidentiality conditions (Article 13.1) and also may 'seek information from any source and may consult with experts to obtain their opinion on certain aspects of the matter'. This may entail the establishment of an expert review group (Article 13.4). The procedures governing such groups are contained in Annex 4 of the DSU. The panel's fact finding is to be guided by the requirement in Article 11 to 'make an objective assessment of the matter before it, including an objective assessment of the facts of the case'. Various of these provisions were considered by the AB in *Hormones*. According to the AB,

> The duty to make an objective assessment of the facts is, among other things, an obligation to consider the evidence presented to a panel and to make factual findings on the basis of that evidence. The deliberate disregard of, or failure to consider, the evidence submitted to a panel is incompatible with a panel's duty to make an objective assessment of the facts. 'Disregard' and 'distortion' and 'misrepresentation' of the evidence, in their ordinary signification in judicial and quasi-judicial processes, imply not simply an error of judgment in the appreciation of evidence but rather an egregious error that calls into question the good faith of the panel [footnote omitted] (para. 133).

However, with respect to statements of experts, the panel has 'a substantial margin of discretion as to which statements are useful to refer to explicitly' (para. 138). Moreover, not every inaccuracy in the panel's representation of statements by experts will 'amount to the egregious disregarding or distorting of evidence before the Panel' (para. 144). From the perspective of a Trade Stakeholder model of dispute settlement, Article 11 as interpreted in *Hormones* offers some real protection against manipulation of panel proceedings by the Secretariat. The panel cannot simply read out of the record or misrepresent information from diverse constituencies – environmental, health, or otherwise – once these have been brought before the panel. In the *Thai Cigarette* case, for instance, which is discussed in Chapter 15 on trade and the environment, the panel chose to ignore a report of the World Health Organization, which dealt with the challenges developing countries face in dealing with increased incidence of cigarette smoking in their populaces; inasmuch as what the panel was doing in *Thai Cigarette* was deciding that the report was irrelevant, this would now be viewed as a legal finding subject to appellate review; inasmuch as the panel, was not making such a legal finding but wilfully disregarding relevant evidence, it would have been prohibited from so doing under Article 11. In *Periodicals*, the AB held that a panel's legal conclusions must be based upon adequate factual analysis, based on the evidence on the record before it, and that it must be logically possible to reach the conclusions of law based upon the evidence. Here, the AB did not rely on Art. 11 of the DSU. Rather, it suggested that in cases where the legal test itself is highly contextual, such as the application of the 'like product' concept in Art. III, inadequate factual analysis could mar a panel's legal reasoning. In some jurisdictions domestic administrative law may similarly extend review for errors of law to these situations where there is a 'mixed' question of law and fact. (*Canada – Certain Measures Concerning Periodicals*, Report of the Appellate Body, 30 June 1997, WT/DS31/AB/R, pp. 22–3.)

3. Findings of Law

Sources of Law

It is obviously the role of panels to apply and interpret the legal provisions of the 'covered agreements'. There are, however, many WTO legal instruments that are not 'covered agreements', but which bear on their interpretation, including at least one Understanding (on commitments in financial services) and numerous Ministerial Decisions and Declarations, as well as Waivers, i.e. agreed derogations from the obligations in covered agreements. Decisions on Waivers in force prior to the entry into force of the WTO are, however, deemed to be part of the GATT 1994, which is a 'covered agreement' (GATT 1994, 1(b)(iii)), as are 'other decisions of the CONTRACTING PARTIES to GATT 1947' effective prior to the entry into force of the WTO Agreement. Whether the Ministerial Decisions taken at the end of the Uruguay Round constitute Decisions in this sense is uncertain: they would arguably have had to have entered into force prior to the entry into force of the WTO Agreement, by virtue of the fact that they were viewed as preparatory to the establishment of the WTO. Under the WTO Agreement a Decision of the Ministerial Conference and General Council will only constitute an authoritative interpretation of a covered agreement where such a decision is taken upon recommendation of the Council responsible for overseeing the agreement in question, and is adopted by three-quarters of the Members (WTO Agreement, IX(2)). By virtue of being authoritative, such an interpretation is obviously binding on panels (and the Appellate Body) and is therefore to be regarded as a superior source of law. Another source of law is other international agreements mentioned or referenced in the 'covered agreements' – as noted above, in *Bananas* the Appellate Body seemed to be suggesting that these should be applied by panels in the same manner as if they were covered agreements themselves. Finally, Article 3.2 of the DSU states that the purpose of dispute settlement is to clarify the provisions of the WTO Agreements 'in accordance with customary rules of international law'.

Palmeter and Mavroidis suggest that 3.2, along with Article 7, which refers to relevant provisions of the covered agreements, has the effect of bringing into the WTO the sources of law stated in Article 38(1) of the Statute of the International

Court of Justice.[44] These are: international conventions, where 'expressly recognized by the consenting states'; custom; general principles of law; judicial decisions and teachings of publicists as 'subsidiary means' of interpretation. In *Reformulated Gasoline* and *Alcoholic Beverages*[45] the Appellate Body held that Articles 31 and 32 of the *Vienna Convention on the Interpretation of Treaties*[46] constituted 'customary rules of interpretation of public international law' for purposes of DSU 3.2. Article 31 of the *Vienna Convention*, which *requires* the use of certain interpretative canons and sources, begins with the general prescription that 'A treaty shall be interpreted in good faith in accordance with the ordinary meaning to be given to the terms of the treaty in their context and in the light of its object and purpose' (31.1). 'Context' here includes an agreement concluded between the Parties in connection with the treaty and any instrument 'made by one or more parties in connexion with the conclusion of the treaty and accepted by the other parties as an instrument related to the treaty' (31.2(a) (b)). 'Taken together with the context', the following shall also be taken into account: subsequent agreements 'between the parties' on treaty interpretation or application; subsequent practice in application of the treaty; 'any relevant rules of international law applicable in the relations between the parties' (31.3(a)–(c)). Article 32 of the *Vienna Convention* permits (but does not require) recourse to the preparatory work for a treaty (*travaux preparatoires)*, either to confirm an interpretation based on the sources prescribed in Article 31, or to determine meaning where there is ambiguity or obscurity, or where the meaning derived from interpretation based on Article 31 sources 'leads to a result which is manifestly absurd and unreasonable'. Clearly, many WTO or GATT Decisions, Declarations, and Understandings – if not part of covered agreements – would constitute 'context' for the interpretation of covered agreements within the meaning of 31.2. Other instruments, however, might be viewed as 'subsequent' agreements or 'subsequent practice' within the meaning of 31.3. Thus, depending on the circumstances, one might view a particular WTO legal instrument that is not a covered agreement either as law that panels must apply by virtue of the legal structure of the WTO itself (see above) or as interpretive sources, to be applied by virtue of the *Vienna Convention* rules, applicable to dispute settlement *both* by virtue of Article 3.2 of the DSU *and* independently, simply by virtue of their status as customary international law.[47] The AB has applied elements of Articles 31 and 32 in a number of its decisions. One very important interpretative principle that it has crafted out of Article 31.1 is that 'interpretation must give meaning and effect to all the terms of the treaty. An interpreter is not free to adopt a reading that would result in reducing whole clauses or paragraphs of a treaty to redundancy or inutility' (*Reformulated* Gasoline, p. 22; applied in *Alcoholic Beverages* and *Hormones*). Here the AB has responded to the tendency of panels to overlook exact textual wording in order to give effect to what they see as the 'object and purpose' of the treaty as a whole. Such a tendency could be seen in the past as quite consistent with the Regime Management model of dispute settlement – the text being understood as a means of constraining cheating on a bargain to reciprocally reduce trade barriers, a too literal interpretation might fail to catch forms of cheating that could undermine the bargain (since it is extremely difficult to specify in advance all behaviours that may constitute 'cheating' on a cooperative equilibrium). Loose interpretation by a professional élite sure of its understanding of the overall purpose of the regime, using what one trade economist colleague described as a 'sniff test for protectionism', may well serve Regime Management goals, by closing 'loopholes' or gaps that could undermine confidence in the bargain by a means less cumbersome than amendment or decision-making by the Parties. If, however, the text of an agreement constitutes or reflects a painstakingly negotiated set of trade-offs between liberal trade values and interests and other policy values and interests – hence between diverse, legtimate constituencies or stakeholders – attention to the exact text is essential to preserve the balance of the bargain. Thus, under the Trade Stakeholder model of dispute settlement, the AB's insistence on careful attention to the exact text appears highly desirable. Indeed, the need for such an approach seems reflected in Article 19.2, which states (as already noted) that 'the panel and Appellate Body cannot add to or diminish the rights and obligations provided in the covered agreements'. Nevertheless, having insisted correctly that a purposive interpretation should not lead to neglect of the text, the AB has on occasion perhaps been too inclined to identify textual fidelity with literal or positivistic textual analysis. If a purposive reading does not mean disposing with textualism, textualism should not mean a neglect of inquiry into purpose and object, when *considering the exact words of the text.* In the *Hormones* case, the AB considered the application of rules of international law in the interpretation of a covered agreement (the SPS Agreement). The EU claimed that the panel should have taken into account the precautionary principle in determining whether its measures with respect to hormone-fed meat were based on a scientific risk assessment; this refers to the notion that in cases where uncertainty surrounds the probability or seriousness of a risk, regulators should take precautions in order to avoid possible harm. The AB held that, while the precautionary principle might have crystallized into a rule of international environmental law, there was considerable uncertainty about whether it had yet attained the status of general or customary international law (para. 123). However, having found that the precautionary principle was, at least, part of international environmental law, the AB ought to have considered the relevance of the precautionary principle, pursuant to 31.3(c) of the *Vienna Convention*, which refers not only to customary or general principles but to '*any* relevant rules of international law applicable in the relations between the parties'. From the perspective of a Trade Stakeholder model on dispute settlement, the openness of the panels and Appellate Body to the use of non-trade international law will be of considerable importance, in bringing the relevant diverse values and constituencies into dispute settlement, where the dispute relates to the interface beween the liberal trade regime and other policy regimes, both national and international. From this perspective, we fully endorse the concerns of Palmeter and Mavroidis about the rationale for rejecting as irrelevant international environmental treaties given by the *Tuna/Dolphin II* panel. The panel suggested that these agreements were irrelevant, because they were not concluded among the Contracting Parties to the General Agreement, and that they did not apply to the interpretation of the General Agreement or the application of its provisions,[48] suggesting that the GATT was a self-contained regime, sealed off from the norms and rules of other international regimes and the values and constituencies that these reflect. As Palmeter and Mavroidis note, this reasoning is clearly inconsistent with 31.3(c) of the *Vienna Convention*, which as noted refers to the relevance of 'any' relevant rules applicable between the parties.[49] In *Turtles*, the AB applied International environmental law (including soft law) in order to interpret the scope of the expression 'exhaustible natural resources' in Art. XX(g) of the GATT. The AB rightly adopted a dynamic approach to Treaty interpretation, recognizing that developments in International environmental law were relevant to giving meaning to words drafted more than fifty years ago. This dynamic approach is clearly consistent with the structure of the Vienna Convention – Art. 31, which deals with *obligatory* sources of Treaty interpretation includes law developed subsequent to the drafting of a treaty, while Art. 32 – which deals with *optional* and *secondary* sources of interpretation – refers to evidence of original intent. In *Alcoholic Beverages*, the AB considered the status of adopted panel reports as a source of WTO law. With Article IX of the WTO Agreement in mind, which as noted above gives the Ministerial Conference and General Council the exclusive authority to adopt interpretations of covered agreements, the AB held that adopted panel reports could not have the status of binding precedents with respect to interpretation of the agreements, even if as Decisions they are binding on the Parties to the dispute. Nevertheless, past adopted panels 'create legitimate expectations among WTO Members, and, therefore, should be taken into account where they are relevant to any dispute' (p. 14). The AB endorsed the panels conclusion that unadopted panel reports 'have no legal status in the GATT or WTO system' although on occasion they might provide 'useful guidance' to a panel (p. 15). In *Argentina – Measures Affecting Imports of Footwear, Textiles, Apparel and Other Items*, the AB, however, criticized the panel for relying on unadopted panel rulings as legal authority (Report of the Appellate Body, Adopted 22 April 1998, WT/DS56/AB,R). In a number of contexts, panels may be required to refer to or interpret municipal law, and indeed review the manner in which that law has been interpreted and applied by the internal tribunals and authorities – this is most obviously the case with respect to the TRIPs Agreement and the Subsidies and Antidumping Agreements, which specify certain standards which a Member's domestic law and legal proceedings must meet. The issues surrounding interpretation of domestic law, or its invocation in interpretation of covered agreements, have been canvassed in the section above on standard of review.

Panel Procedures (Articles 12–15, 18, and 20)

There are few rules of evidence or formal due process that govern panel procedures. Article 12.2 of the DSU emphasizes the importance of 'flexibility' to obtain high-quality panel reports. Some detailed Working Procedures are set out in Appendix 3 of the DSU but these are mostly of a logistical nature. There are normally two meetings between the panel and the Parties and at least two opportunities for Parties to make written submissions. Normally, the complaining

Party makes its first submission before that of the responding Party, so that the latter party's submission can contain a response to that of the former. Reversing the panel, the AB held in *Bananas* that 'There is no requirement in the DSU or in GATT practice for arguments on all claims . . . to be set out in a complaining party's written submission to the panel'; omissions can be corrected in subsequent submissions (paras. 145–6). Perhaps most disappointing from the perspective of a Trade Stakeholder model of dispute settlement, is that the DSU continues GATT practice that panel deliberations are confidential (Article 14). The Rules of Conduct[50] with respect to settlement of disputes go beyond even this language, and refer not only to the confidentiality of dispute settlement deliberations, but also of proceedings. Worse still, Article 18.2 provides that 'written submissions to the panel or the Appellate Body shall be treated as confidential'. While Members may disclose publicly their own position and demand of the other Party a summary of its position for public consumption, stakeholders have no direct access whatever to submissions on disputes that affect them. This, of course, falls far short of the transparency and publicity norms of many municipal legal systems. Concern about these shortcomings, particularly on the part of the United States, has produced some modest progress towards greater publicity and transparency, as reflected in the *Decision on Procedures for the Circulation and Derestriction of WTO Documents*.[51] At least, now, panel reports are to be derestricted rapidly; as well, through the WTO web site (www.wto.org), stakeholders have immediate and free access to documents such as requests for consultations and panels, and the Terms of Reference of the panels. This at least allows for publicity concerning what measures are or may be challenged in dispute settlement and the nature of the complaining Party's legal claims (if not the detailed arguments of the Parties). Also, through the web site there is free access to all adopted panel and AB decisions, and many other now derestricted documents related to dispute settlement – in the past, even unrestricted material was often difficult to obtain without contacts in the Secretariat, and was frequently not published in accessible form until long after being in theory publicly available. Rightly, the United States is pressing for further action on this front; thus, on 19 February 1998 it communicated to the General Council of the WTO its desire to put transparency on the Council's current agenda, in order to review progress in implementing the derestriction decision, as well as to raise additional issues with respect to transparency.[52] Normally, panel procedings are not to exceed in duration a period of six months from the date of composition of the panel to issuance of the final report to the Parties (or three months in cases of urgency). An extension of up to three months is possible in non-urgent cases (Article 12.8–9). The practice of circulating an interim report to the Parties for comment, prior to the drafting of a final report, is reflected in Article 15.

Representation of Parties

Traditionally, in GATT practice, only governmental officials represented the Parties before panel proceedings, although some Parties had resort to outside counsel for opinions and advice. This placed developing countries, who were unlikely to have large armies of in-house expert trade counsel, at a considerable disadvantage in pursuing complaints. However, there was no textual basis for this practice. In *Bananas*, the AB held it could find no legal basis, either in WTO treaty law, or in customary international law for interfering with the choice of a Member as to who represents it before the AB (para. 10) Nevertheless, the AB stressed that it was not deciding the issue of representation in panel proceedings, which had not been appealed. It is difficult to believe that the same principles would not, however, apply to panel proceedings and in the *Indonesian Autos* case the panel so found (*Indonesia – Certain Measures Affecting the Automobile Industry*, Report of the Panel, 2 July 1998, WT/DS 54, 55, 59, 64/R). Opening up the process to non-governmental counsel is a positive development from the perspective of the Trade Stakeholder model; it reduces somewhat the control by governmental and diplomatic élites over the process, and also may erode somewhat the logic of confidentiality, since it is not easy to bind private lawyers to confidentiality of a type to which they are not accustomed, unlike diplomats and bureaucrats.

Relief

A panel, when it concludes that a measure violates a covered agreement 'shall recommend that the Member concerned [footnote omitted] bring the measure into conformity with that agreement' (Article 19.1). As well, a panel may suggest ways in which the Member concerned could implement the recommendations. It is an important issue whether a recommendation that a measure be brought into conformity can encompass a recommendation for specific relief, for example the refunding of antidumping or countervailing duties collected in contravention of the provisions of a covered agreement. As Petersmann notes, five GATT panel reports have recommended this kind of relief, which he refers to as 'restitution in kind'.[53] Given that Article 3.4 of the DSU states that 'Recommendations or rulings made by the DSB shall be aimed at achieving a satisfactory settlement of the matter', and that the principles of GATT Article XXIII dispute settlement are affirmed in Article 3.1, it would be surprising if the language in Article 19 had been intended to narrow the scope of alternatives already available to a panel to achieve a 'satisfactory settlement' under pre-existing GATT practice.

Adoption of Panel Reports (Article 16)

Panel reports are to be adopted by the DSB within 60 days of circulation to Members, *unless a consensus exists against adoption.* Since such a consensus would normally include the winning Party, this amounts to adoption as of right. This is a radical reversal of the GATT practice prior to the WTO, which required a consensus *in favour* of adoption of panel reports. Curiously, Article 16 does not specify how soon after circulation to the Parties of a final report it must be circulated to Members. Article 12.7 merely states that the panel shall submit its findings to the DSB 'in the form of a written report' when the parties have failed to develop a mutually satisfactory solution. This however is arguably subject to Article 20, which stipulates, 'Unless otherwise agreed to by the parties to the dispute, the period of the date of establishment of the panel by the DSB until the date at the DSB considers the panel or appellate report for adoption shall as a general rule not exceed nine months where the panel report is not appealed or 12 months where the report is appealed.'

Appellate Review (Article 17)

Article 17 provides for the establishment of a standing Appellate Body, comprised of seven 'persons of recognized authority, with demonstrated expertise in law, international trade, and the covered agreements generally', a major innovation in dispute settlement. These individuals are appointed for a four-year, once renewable term, and hear appeals in panels of three. If notice of appeal is not filed prior to adoption by the DSB, the panel report will become the binding settlement of the dispute – thus, notice must be filed within 60 days following the circulation of the final report to Members. The AB is to complete its review within 60 days from the filing of the notice of appeal, with the possibility of extension to 90 days. Detailed procedures relating to submissions, hearings and such are contained in the AB's Working Procedures for Appeal.[54] This also contains rules of conduct for AB members concerning, *inter alia*, conflict of interest. Proceedings of the Appellate Body are confidential (DSU 17.10). The 'appeal shall be limited to issues of law covered in the panel report and legal interpretations developed by the panel' (17.6). As already discussed, issues of law may include whether the panel conducted its own operations in accordance with the requirements of the DSU and of the relevant WTO law, and not only panel findings related to claims that the responding Party was in violation of provisions of covered agreeements. Thus, in *Hormones*, the AB reviewed the treatment by the panel of the factual record, and certain of its findings of fact, for consistency with the obligation of 'objective assessment of the facts' in Article 11 of the DSU. In *Hormones* as well, the AB determined that a decision to exclude evidence on the basis of non-relevancy is reviewable for error of law (para. 143) A panel's interpretation of a Member's municipal law for purposes of determining whether that law conforms with the provisions of a required agreement is also reviewable (*Indian Patents*, para. 68). The Appellate Body 'may uphold, modify or reverse the legal findings and conclusions of the panel'. As Petersmann notes, this does not include '(explicit) power for remanding the case back to the panel'.[55] Such remands would not normally be consistent with the concern that pervades the DSU for timeliness in the settlement of disputes; however, where the AB has found that the panel's treatment of the factual record did not conform to the requirements of the DSU, a remand might be an appropriate alternative to merely quashing the panel's findings and any resultant recommendations; in recent cases, such as *Periodicals* and *Turtles*, the AB has instead resorted to what it calls 'completing the analysis', applying its own interpretation of the law to the factual record. Appellate Body reports are to be adopted on the basis of the same negative consensus rule applicable to panel reports, within 30 days of circulation to Members. From a Trade Stakeholder perspective, the AB may be the most important innovation in the dispute settlement system. Appeals make panel decisions contestable and they subject those decisions to scrutiny against juridical norms, making the panel process much less susceptible to manipulation by an inside professional élite. In this connection, it is important that the DSU stipulates that AB members may not be affiliated with any government, and that they are appointed directly by the DSB, without nomination by the Secretariat. Further, the AB has its own legal support services, at least formally separate from those in the Secretariat who advise the panels.

Implementation (Article 21)

Within 30 days of the adoption of a panel or AB report, the losing Party must inform the DSB of the steps it intends to take to implement the recommendations and rulings adopted. Where immediate compliance is 'impracticable', a Member may have a 'reasonable period of time' to bring itself into conformity. A reasonable period of time may be determined by the DSB on the basis of proposals from the losing Party, or by agreement between the Parties, or through binding arbitration. Disagreements over whether implementation measures are adequate are to be referred back to the original panel wherever possible, which is to circulate its report within 90 days of the referral. The *Barings* case has raised some difficult interpretive issues related to how this procedure interacts with procedures for suspension of concessions in Article 22.

Compensation and Suspension of Concessions (Article 22)

Compensation and suspension of concessions are available to the complaining Party if the adopted panel or AB report is not implemented within a reasonable period of time. Compensation is a voluntary alternative to implementing a ruling; suspension of concessions requires authorization by the DSB, subject to a number of conditions and criteria listed in 22.3 and related provisions of this Article.

Exclusivity of WTO Procedures (Article 23)

Article 23 requires Members to resort exclusively to WTO dispute settlement procedures to seek 'redress' for a violation of a covered agreement. In some instances, a complaint may be brought under both WTO procedures and the procedures of some other trading regime, such as NAFTA, in respect of the same measures. Since NAFTA incorporates many provisions of the GATT and (prospectively) some in the WTO,[56] an issue arises as to whether a Member is prohibited from raising issues related to these provisions in a complaint under NAFTA dispute settlement procedures. This issue is further complicated by the NAFTA's own choice of forum rules, which will be discussed later in this chapter.

Non-Violation Nullification and Impairment (GATT Articles XXIII(1)(b), DSU Article 26)

Under Article XXIII(1)(b) of the GATT, as interpreted in GATT practice, a Contracting Party could have recourse to dispute settlement even where no violation of a specific provision of the GATT was complained of, if a benefit was considered to be nullified or impaired by the conduct of another Member. This served the Regime Management goal of maintaining a cooperative equilibrium over time, through vindicating the reasonable expectations of Contracting Parties concerning the benefits obtained from reciprocal concessions even where the conduct threatening to undermine them was not specified explicitly and prohibited in the GATT. This logic is articulated in a general statement concerning non-violation nullification and impairment in the *Oilseeds* panel:

> The idea underlying [non-violation nullification and impairment] is that the improved competitive opportunities that can legitimately be expected from a tariff concession can be frustrated not only by measures proscribed by the General Agreement but also by measures consistent with that Agreement. In order to encourage contracting parties to make tariff concessions they must therefore be given a right of redress when a reciprocal concession is impaired by another contracting party as a result of the application of any measure, whether or not it conflicts with the General Agreement.[57]

It follows from this that to invoke non-violation nullification and impairment, the complaining Party must be able to identify a specific tariff concession or concessions and a benefit flowing from these concessions, or reasonably expected to flow, that has been undermined as a *consequence* of the measures complained of. Article 26 of the DSU stipulates that in the case of non-violation nullification and impairment complaints, 'the complaining party shall present a detailed justification in support of any complaint' and that where non-violation nullification and impairment has occurred there is no requirement to withdraw the measure; instead the panel or Appellate Body is to recommend a 'mutually satisfactory adjustment'.

DISPUTE SETTLEMENT IN THE NAFTA

Background: the Canada–US FTA

The Canada–US Free Trade Agreement (FTA or 'the Agreement') provided two main avenues for the resolution of disputes between its signatories. Chapter 18 of the Agreement set up a Commission to resolve disputes; Chapter 19 detailed procedures for resolving problems in antidumping and countervailing duty cases. The Chapter 18 and 19 mechanisms involved the use of consultation, negotiation, and panels – all of which resembled dispute resolution mechanisms in the GATT under Article XXIII(2). The Agreement also appears to have benefited from experience under the GATT, and to have adopted some of the improvements which were introduced into its procedures post-Tokyo Round.[58]

Chapter 18

Article 1801 of the FTA stated that Chapter 18 is for the 'avoidance or settlement of all disputes regarding the interpretation or application of this Agreement' except insofar as any dispute relates to the provisions of Chapter 17 (Financial Services) or Chapter 19 (Antidumping and Countervailing Duty Cases).[59] It established the Canada–US Trade Commission ('the Commission') to supervise the implementation of the Agreement, to resolve disputes under it, 'to oversee its further elaboration, and to consider any other matter that may affect its operation'.[60]

Articles 1803–4 laid down the procedures for notification and consultation regarding actual or proposed measures that might materially affect the operation of the FTA. The FTA required the Parties to notify each other of such measures in advance of implementation or as soon thereafter as possible. It also gave each Party the right to ask the other for information regarding these measures.[61] Article 1804 allowed each Party the right to consultations regarding any measures or any other matter material to the FTA, and it exhorts the Parties to make every effort to reach mutually agreed upon solutions to problems that arise in these consultations.[62] If consultations did not allow the Parties to resolve their differences within 30 days, then Article 1805 permitted either Party to request a meeting of the Commission, which was to convene within 10 days (unless otherwise agreed) to attempt 'to resolve the dispute promptly'.[63]

If a dispute was not resolved within 30 days of being referred to the Commission, that Commission *must* in the case of a dispute over safeguard actions or[64] (in the case of other actions) *may* refer the dispute to binding arbitration,[65] failing which either Party had the right to request the establishment of a panel of experts 'to consider the matter'.[66] The panel was to be drawn 'wherever possible' from nominated lists of unaffiliated individuals who have been chosen by each country on the basis of their expertise, objectivity, reliability, and sound judgment.[67] A panel would have five members, two from each country and a chair chosen by agreement between Parties, failing which the Commission could intervene. If the Commission could not agree, the chair would be chosen by lot from the roster.

A panel would determine its own procedures, subject to the requirement of at least one oral hearing, as well as the right to present written submissions and rebuttal arguments. Proceedings were confidential and the panel was required to base its decision solely on submissions (unless otherwise agreed by the Parties).[68]

Once the Commission received the final report, it was to agree on a resolution of the dispute in question 'normally' in conformity with the recommendations of the panel.[69] 'Whenever possible', this resolution was to be the non-implementation or withdrawal of measures not conforming with or causing nullification or impairment of benefits accruing under the FTA.[70] If the Commission could not reach agreement within 30 days of the receipt of the final report, or if a Party refused to comply with the findings of a panel under the binding arbitration provisions of Article 1806, then the other Party could suspend the application of equivalent benefits to that Party.[71]

During the lifetime of the FTA, only fine disputes were remitted to panels under Chapter 18: one relating to Canadian salmon and herring landing requirements; another relating to the treatment of non-mortgage interest on land or plant and machinery for purposes of rules of origin; another relating to whether exports of durum wheat to the USA by the Canadian Wheat Board were occurring below acquisition cost; another relating to the adoption of regulations in Puerto Rico that precluded continuing sales of ultra-high temperature (UHT) milk by a Quebec producer to Puerto Rican consumers; and another which concerned a US ban on 'undersized' lobsters.

Chapter 20 of NAFTA

Chapter 20 of NAFTA incorporates the essential structure of dispute settlement provided in Chapter 18 of the FTA. Under the FTA, disputes that fell under Article 18 arising under that Agreement and the GATT could be settled in either forum at the discretion of the complaining Party, although once an election had been made, this excluded the alternative dispute settlement process (Article 1801). Under NAFTA, however, where disputes relate to environmental and conservation matters or sanitary and phytosanitary measures the responding Party may insist that a complaint be heard by a NAFTA, rather than GATT panel (Article 2005). In such cases, a disputing Party may request, or a panel on its own initiative may solicit, a written report of a scientific review board on any factual issue concerning such matters (Article 2015). There is an interesting issue of how these rules interact with the provisions of exclusivity of WTO dispute settlement procedures in Article 23 of the DSU, discussed above. Under *Vienna Convention* principles, the DSU might be argued to modify or prevail over the NAFTA provisions, as an agreement later in time. If this is so, then a NAFTA Party would be prohibited from pursuing its WTO claim in the NAFTA process by virtue of the DSU; this would mean that, by virtue of the election rules, it would be deemed to have chosen the WTO forum, and thereby would not be able to pursue its NAFTA claim at all, since the WTO dispute settlement procedures do not provide panels with the jurisdiction to consider violations of NAFTA provisions (however, since many GATT provisions are incorporated into NAFTA, but for the DSU, a Party might have been able to pursue both sets of claims in NAFTA Chapter 20 dispute settlement).

Other changes from the FTA in NAFTA Chapter 20 include: (1) instead of separate national rosters of respective panellists, as provided under Chapter 18 of the FTA, the NAFTA contemplates a consensus roster of up to thirty persons acceptable to all member countries; (2) instead of disputing Parties selecting nominees from the roster who are their own nationals, NAFTA calls for a process of reverse selection, by which Parties must select from the other country's nationals on the roster; (3) unlike the FTA, NAFTA permits third country and non-member country nationals to serve as a chair of a panel; (4) unlike the FTA, disputes regarding financial services are fully subject to dispute settlement, through specialized procedures designed to ensure appropriate panel expertise (Chapter 14); and (5) under the investment provisions of NAFTA (Chapter 11) any NAFTA investor who alleges that a host government has breached an obligation of the investment chapter may invoke an arbitral tribunal to hear the matter. Investment obligations include requirements for National Treatment and Most Favoured Nation treatment, as well as certain disciplines on specified performance requirements, rules against restricting transfers, and against expropriation without compensation. Procedures may be based on ICSID or its Additional Facility, or on the UNCITRAL Rules for such arbitrations. Procedures are provided to enable consolidation of cases, to avoid procedural harassment, and for the intervention of governments responsible for the Agreement both individually before the arbitral tribunal or collectively through the issuance of Commission interpretations of the Agreement on questions that may be before the arbitral tribunal. Awards for monetary damages are directly enforceable in the domestic courts of the NAFTA members as if they were domestic court judgments. Thus, in the investment context, private Parties are given direct access to international dispute resolution mechanisms for the first time in an international trade treaty. So far, Article 20 procedures in NAFTA have only been invoked in one case, the *Agricultural Tariffication* panel, discussed in Chapter 10 on trade in agriculture in this book; a case that was brought under the investment arbitration procedures, the *Ethyl* case, is briefly discussed in Chapter 13 on trade and investment.

Chapter 19 of the FTA and NAFTA

As a middle power whose main trade partner is the United States, Canada long relied on the rules and processes of international trade law – including the process of GATT dispute settlement – to constrain American protectionism. With the rise of administered protection in the 1970s and 1980s – particularly in the form of harassment of Canadian exporters by countervailing duty and antidumping actions – the multilateral legal framework appeared increasingly incapable of maintaining open borders between Canada and the United States, despite conventional tariffs having been reduced to low levels in the GATT negotiations. Curbing these forms of administered protection was stated to be a central concern of Canada's FTA negotiators.[72]

In the event, the United States did not accept any substantive limitation whatever on the application of trade remedy laws within North America. The Americans did agree to a process of review of domestic countervail and anti-dump determinations by *ad hoc* binational panels, which in the context of American trade authorities, would replace appellate review by the US Court of International Trade (CIT). Canadian trade analysts generally viewed the CIT as extremely deferential to the determinations of the US agencies, the International Trade Administration (ITA) of the Department of Commerce and the International Trade Commission (ITC).[73] Binational review would at least subject these agency decisions to scrutiny against basic US administrative law standards of reasonableness and the requirement to base one's decision on substantial evidence from the record. This binational procedure is set out in Chapter 19 of the FTA and NAFTA.

Article 1904 of the FTA provides that binational panels shall replace judicial review of the 'final determinations' of domestic trade authorities of the two countries in countervail and antidumping cases.[74] At the request of either Party, a panel may consider and issue a binding decision as to whether such a final determination is in conformity with the domestic trade remedy law of the importing country. The standard of review is that laid down by the relevant statutes (as amended from time to time) of each Party, and by 'the general legal principles that a court of the importing Party would otherwise apply'. Requests for panels must be made within 30 days of the issuance of a final determination. While only a Party may request a panel, Article 1904:5 allows interests that would normally be entitled to judicial review under domestic law to petition as of right their government to establish a panel. This means that, in practice, the panel process is largely driven not by governments but private litigants, with producer interests in both countries heavily represented by counsel throughout the process.

In the case of US countervail and antidumping decisions the panel's standard of review is largely derived from the general principles of US administrative law. The standards require that agency determinations represent reasonable interpretations of US law (i.e. not necessarily correct but at least defensible as one of several possible reasonable interpretations of the law) and that findings of fact be supported by substantial evidence on the record, i.e. enough evidence that would allow a reasonable person to draw the inference in question.[75]

Where a binational panel deems that a finding is not in accordance with a reasonable interpretation of the law, or is not supported by substantial evidence on the record, its powers are limited to remanding the matter to the domestic agency that made the original determination, to reconsider its findings in light of the panel's recommendations. *Thus, the binational panel itself is powerless to remove duties, it can only order the domestic authorities in question to redetermine the matter.* Where dissatisfied with a redetermination, the only recourse of an exporter is to have its government request yet another panel. In a number of cases two or three panels have been necessary before the domestic agency in question brought its decision in line with the law (or gave up on finding adequate evidence to support it) and removed or reduced duties.

Panel decisions are made by majority vote, and reasons (majority, concurring, dissenting) are provided in writing. Panellists are chosen from rosters of trade experts provided by the two countries, with two of the five members chosen by each country and the fifth by agreement between them, and in the case of an inability to agree, the fifth panellist may be selected by the two others, or if that fails, by lot from the entire roster. (As will be discussed in Part III, the criteria for panellists have changed with NAFTA.)

Article 1904 of the FTA (13) provides for an 'Extraordinary Challenge' mechanism, whereby a panel ruling may be appeared to an Extraordinary Challenge Committee (ECC), composed of three persons, who must be judges or former judges of a US federal court or a court of superior jurisdiction in Canada. The grounds for an extraordinary challenge are: (a) a panel member was guilty of gross misconduct, (b) the panel seriously departed from a fundamental rule of procedure, or (c) the panel manifestly exceeded its powers, authority or jurisdiction as set forth in Chapter 19. Only, however, where the ECC determines that the panel's decision has been materially affected by one or more of these defects and the integrity of the binational review process is threatened will an Extraordinary Challenge succeed. (As will be discussed in Part III, the grounds of an Extraordinary Challenge have been substantially broadened in NAFTA.)

Experience with the binational review process to date

The early prognosis for the capacity of binational panel review to constrain US protectionism was largely positive. Reviewing several years experience with the process, Trebilcock and Boddez found, in 1993, that 'the panels will use the substantial evidence test in such a way as to reduce barriers by placing greater restrictions on the administrative discretion exercised by the ITC and ITA.'[76] Other, earlier studies reached similar conclusions.[77] In a more recent study, up to and including the *Softwood Lumber* case (but published before its final aftermath), John Mercury found that 'Canadian exporters realized substantial reduction in duties following appeal to binational panels while US exporters enjoyed no such success.'[78] According to Mercury, 'the reduction of duties in nine out of fourteen AD/CVD cases is a significant accomplishment for Canadian exporters', and the average reduction from the initial duty imposed was substantial, amounting to 28.20%.[79] However, what portion of this number can be attributed to binational panel review, as well as how the figure was derived, remain unclear. It should also be noted that the 28.20% average assumed that the impact of removal of 100% of duty in *Softwood Lumber* would not be affected through American legislative action as it has been.

While this seems impressive, it may conceal several major limitations in the success of the process. First of all, while the 28.20% figure appears substantial, it should be remembered that even a reduction of this amount will not necessarily substantially increase market access; even when lessened by this much, depending upon the nature of the market, and elasticities of supply and demand, countervail and antidumping duties will provide producers with a substantial price advantage over imports. The best test of the success of the process from the point of view of Canadian exporters is the extent to which their sales in the US market have increased due to the reduction in price advantage to domestic US producers attendant upon reduction in duties. None of the studies, including Mercury's and the earlier work of Trebilcock and Boddez, examines the success of the binational review process against this criterion.

Second, even where victorious, the complainant to a binational panel must pay its own legal costs. Mercury and Trebilcock and Boddez fail to provide data on these costs, or to estimate the extent to which they mitigate the gains from reduction in duties. Michael P. Ryan, an analyst associated with the Brookings Institution, has estimated costs in the typical case as between US$200,000 and

US$300,000 per litigant,[80] although this would presumably be much higher in complicated, multi-stage disputes like *Pork* and *Softwood Lumber*. Senior practitioners have provided estimates of around US$500,000–US$600,000. But this is anecdotal evidence. As Mercury himself notes, in a number of major cases it has taken two or more remands before the US agencies actually removed the duties. Thus, while panel review is touted as a much more timely process than appeal to the US Court of International Trade, in fact in many of the more controversial cases, including the *Carbon Steel* and *Softwood Lumber* cases, the delay has been almost as great as or greater than the CIT historic average of 734 days.[81] Moreover, costs and delays are exacerbated by the requirement that separate panels review determinations of the existence of subsidization or dumping and determinations of injury. Thus, in the *Softwood Lumber* case, where there were three remands on injury and two on the issue of subsidization, five separate proceedings were implicated in a single dispute.

Binational panels have become impatient with the failure of the US agencies to respond adequately in remand determinations to failures in their initial analysis, or alternately, to shift the ground, either legal or evidentiary or both, of their decision to impose duties, so as merely to evade the panels' criticisms. Thus, in several cases, including *Softwood Lumber*, they have essentially said to the agency that the process cannot go on forever, and that, since the agency has repeatedly failed to support its findings on the basis of law and evidence, it must remove duties. This practice was unanimously upheld in Extraordinary Challenges in the *Pork* and *Live Swine* cases. However, this practice has also led to criticism of the process by politicians and producer interests in the United States.

More importantly, whatever the ultimate significance of the early success that Canadian exporters achieved with the binational panel process, this very success has led to considerable criticism of the process in the US. Much of this criticism has centred on the supposedly undeferential treatment of US agency decisions by the panels. It was thought that the trade experts on the panels, insufficiently impressed with the analysis of the ITA and ITC, were taking the opportunity to use their special knowledge to redo or relitigate as it were the original decisions, rather than merely insuring that they were reasonable in legal interpretation and supported by some factual evidence. At least until *Softwood Lumber*, Extraordinary Challenge panels were unanimous in rejecting the view that a panel's interpretation of the standard of review could easily become a basis for finding that it had manifestly exceeded its jurisdiction, although these decisions did leave the door open, in egregious cases, to finding excess of jurisdiction where a panel clearly misstated the administrative law of the country whose ruling is appealed against, or where it failed to 'conscientiously apply' that law. However, a panel's conscientious, good faith interpretation of the law even where contrary interpretations would also be reasonable, was clearly a mere 'legal issue' and not a grounds for finding manifest excess of jurisdiction. Despite these weaknesses, it is certainly true that in the more routine cases, binational panels have disposed of appeals more expeditiously than the CIT, and the quality of legal and economic analysis employed by the panels has been high.

Changes to the binational panel review process in NAFTA

During the NAFTA negotiations and especially in their final phases, a concerted assault was launched on the binational panel process in the US Congress, focusing on the absence of deference to US agencies and the supposed incorrect application of US law by several panels.[82] While much of this criticism clearly represents 'sour grapes' due to the number of cases which US domestic producer interests had lost, several genuine concerns about the legitimacy and coherence of the process were also in play. First of all, it is generally acknowledged by those with a knowledge of both systems, that the Canadian and American administrative law standards for judicial review of agency determinations are different. This asymmetry is built into the panel process itself, of course, such that where US interests are challenging a Canadian agency determination, the panel must apply the Canadian administrative law standard, as embodied in the *Federal Court Act*, which is one of significantly greater deference to agency decision-making than the US standard. While error of law is a basis for overturning a Canadian agency decision, with respect to errors of fact the threshold is very high indeed: the finding must have been made in a perverse or capricious manner without regard to the evidence before the agency or tribunal. This standard has been interpreted in recent Supreme Court decisions as requiring a very high level of deference to agency decisions.[83] By contrast, it will be recalled, American law requires that any finding not based on substantial evidence on the record be overturned. Thus, American interests do not have equal opportunity to have adverse Canadian agency findings reversed by panels as do Canadian interests with respect to US agency findings. A second area of legitimate concern has been that since each panel is an *ad hoc* decision-maker in a particular dispute, approaches of different panels to legal issues need not be consistent. This leads to lack of legal certainty; ironically, arbitrariness in agency legal interpretation may now be replaced by inconsistent panel rulings. The most obvious case of inconsistency has been panel interpretation of the specificity test in US countervailing duty law, and particularly whether all of a number of factors that go to *de facto* specificity must be considered by the Agency: the *Magnesium* panel considered that this was not necessary, while one of the *Softwood Lumber* panels, which was ruling almost at the same time, answered that all factors must be weighed. And the Extraordinary Challenge procedure does not provide a means of clarifying inconsistent panel rulings so as to produce legal coherence for the future.

A third, related concern that has some legitimacy is that even if the panels are applying the US standard of review in an acceptable manner, they are nevertheless evolving the law in a somewhat different fashion than are the US courts with respect to countervail and antidumping actions that apply to all other countries. At one level, this may be the result of a misunderstanding of the process because, at least in theory, any future binational panel would be bound by the rulings of the US courts in cases dealing with NAFTA non-parties as one aspect of the 'law' that it must apply. Nevertheless, in practice, the fact that two very different kinds of institutions are evolving the US law as it applies to different countries, suggests the potential for some lack of legal coherence.

The changes that US negotiators insisted on in NAFTA reflect the weight attached by the US Congress and the Administration to these various concerns. The grounds for Extraordinary Challenge review have now been extended to include failure 'to apply the appropriate standard of review'.[84] This is, in fact, a very broad rubric, going far beyond the notion in the *Swine* and *Pork* that Extraordinary Challenge review may be available where the standard of review has clearly been incorrectly articulated or not applied conscientiously, i.e. not in good faith. 'Appropriate' is a vague legal category, and leaves ample room for voicing objections to just about any panel ruling. In this respect, it is significant that unlike the FTA, the NAFTA provisions on Extraordinary Challenges explicitly invite the Extraordinary Challenge Committee, in effect, to re-open the whole case through 'examination of the legal and factual analysis underlying the findings and conclusions of the panel's decision' (Annex 1904.13(3)). To permit the Extraordinary Challenge Committee the opportunity to re-examine the whole case, the period for Extraordinary Challenge review has been tripled from 30 to 90 days. The Ways and Means Committee of the US House of Representatives all but suggests that these changes will turn the Extraordinary Challenge procedure into another kick at the can:

> By expanding the period of review and requiring ECCs to look at the panel's underlying legal and factual analysis, the changes to Annex 1904 clarify that the ECC's responsibilities do not end with simply ensuring that the panel articulated the correct standard of review. Rather, ECCs are also to examine whether the panel correctly analyzed the substantive law and underlying facts.[85]

Finally, with respect to the primary panels themselves, the roster of panellists is to 'include sitting or retired judges to the fullest extent practicable' (Annex 1901.2(1)). This represents a major change from the FTA, which allowed for rosters to be dominated by experts in international trade law and economics. The full import of this change can only be understood when one recognizes that the kind of errors in US agency determinations identified by binational panels, especially as they relate to the 'substantial evidence' standard of review, involve the examination of complex methodologies, empirical economic studies, including econometric modelling, and sometimes, dozens of specific calculations. Counsel for these cases are usually highly experienced experts from the trade bar, supported by teams of consulting economists and econometricians.[86]

Softwood Lumber: the binational panel review process at the brink

The *Softwood Lumber* case may be considered as a kind of acid test of the binational panel review process. Very significant exports (several $billion per annum) were at stake in an industry of considerable importance to the Canadian economy. The high trade politics of the dispute were precisely of the kind that require diffusing by a rules-based impartial transnational dispute settlement process, as illustrated by the fact that an early initial US agency ruling in Canada's favour was reversed after enormous Congressional pressure (although, of course, it is impossible to *prove* such a causal relationship). Yet instead of demonstrating the value of the binational panel review process where major Canadian export interests are at stake and protectionist pressures below the border are high, the *Softwood Lumber* case illustrates its fragility, and perhaps futility in such 'high stakes' trade disputes. And indeed the result of the Extraordinary Challenge has been to create a legitimacy crisis for the whole process – ironically, and perhaps characteristic of Canadian timidity – this crisis is mainly located in the United States, whereas the fact that years of hard-won Canadian panel victories have been reversed politically should be leading Canadians to question the worth of the whole exercise.

To appreciate the significance of *Softwood Lumber*, a brief overview of the history of the dispute is necessary.

Since the early 1980s, the American softwood lumber industry has claimed that the stumpage fees payable by the Canadian logging companies to the government are set below the resource rents that would be payable in a competitive market, thereby constituting a 'subsidy' that results in lower log costs for lumber producers than would prevail under competitive market conditions.

In 1983, the US industry brought a countervailing duty action against softwood lumber imports from Canada. In this action, the ITA found that there was no countervailable subsidy in Canadian stumpage programmes. This was based largely on the finding that the programmes were not 'specific' within the meaning of US domestic trade law (the 1983 proceeding is known as *Lumber I*). It is a long-standing rule of US domestic trade law that only 'specific' subsidies are countervailable. The distinction, at its most obvious, is between subsidies directly targeted to particular industries and enterprises (for instance the bail-out of a firm) and generally available benefits (such as education or health care).

The industry re-opened the case in 1986, claiming that it had new evidence that, through administrative discretion exercised by provincial authorities, Canadian stumpage programmes were being explicitly targeted to producers of softwood lumber and therefore 'specific'.

In the 1986 proceeding, the Commerce Department did in fact reverse itself and found that the 'subsidy' was specific within the meaning of US law, and therefore countervailable (this proceeding is generally referred to as *Lumber II*). This reversal was based less on any new evidence of targeting than on a different approach to the law than had been adopted in *Lumber I*). Duties, however, were never imposed since the Canadian government came to a negotiated arrangement with the United States whereby an export tax of 15% would be imposed on softwood lumber exports to the US. This arrangement is referred to as the *Memorandum of Understanding* (MOU). A 1987 amendment to the MOU exempted British Columbia, on the basis of BC's decision to increase stumpage fees (the Atlantic provinces were exempted on slightly different grounds).

Under pressure from US domestic industry interests, Congress in 1988 explicitly expanded the definition of 'specificity' to include subsidies that, although not directly or on their face targeted to specific industries or firms, *in fact* benefit only a small number of industries or firms. The Commerce Department's own internal rules for the application of these statutory requirements [hereinafter, the *Proposed Regulations*] contain a four-factor test for specificity, which encompasses an inquiry into both *de jure* specificity (or targeting) as well as *de facto* specificity. This test is as follows:

> In determining whether benefits are specific, . . . [Commerce] will consider, among other things, the following factors:
> (i) The extent to which a government acts to limit the availability of a program;
> (ii) The number of enterprises, industries, or groups thereof that actually use a program;
> (iii) Whether there are dominant users of a program, or whether certain enterprises, industries, or groups thereof receive disproportionately large benefits under a program;
> and
> (iv) The extent to which a government exercises discretion in conferring benefits under a program.

In 1991, Canada unilaterally terminated the MOU, and shortly thereafter the Commerce Department itself initiated a new proceeding against Canadian lumber exporters, which is known as *Lumber III*. The ITA's final positive determination on subsidy [hereinafter, *Final Determination*] was issued on 28 May 1992, following a preliminary positive determination in March. The ITA found that the stumpage programmes in the various provinces conferred an average subsidy of 2.91% (ranging from 1.25% for Alberta to 5.95% for Ontario).

The Canadian provinces and lumber industry requested review of the positive determination by a binational panel, which issued its decision on 6 May 1993. The panel remanded numerous matters for redetermination or clarification by the ITA. On a number of issues, the panel found that the ITA had misapplied US law, and on other issues it found that there was no evidentiary basis for choices the ITA made with respect to economic methodology, or the conclusions it drew from economic evidence. On yet other matters, the panel found that the legal standard the ITA was applying was unclear, ambiguous or unarticulated. On 23 September, the ITA released its *Determination on Remand*, finding, in fact, even higher rates of subsidization than had been found in the initial determination.

Specificity

In its *Final Determination*, the ITA had found that the Canadian stumpage programmes were specific *based solely on the second factor, i.e. small number of users*. The Canadian complainants had argued, on the basis of classifying the range of products manufactured from softwood lumber, that 27 industries and 3,600 firms benefited from the programme. The ITA, however, took the view that only two or three industries or industry groups benefited. Nevertheless, the ITA ruled that, even on the Canadian view that 27 industries benefited, this was still a small enough number to justify a finding of *de facto* specificity.

The panel, in its original Decision, accepted that there could be some extreme cases where the limited number of users would be, in itself, sufficient to find specificity (such as where only one or two companies were users of a programme). Nevertheless, the panel held that 'Clearly, the 3600-odd stumpage users in this case, representing between two and twenty-seven industries (depending on the definition of industry being used), do not fall into the category of extreme cases' (at 38). Thus, the panel made a remand to the ITA requiring it consider and weigh all four factors in the specificity test in determining whether the stumpage programmes were specific. The panel also held that it was appropriate for the ITA to take into account the extent to which the number of users was merely a function of the 'inherent characteristics of the industry'.

In its *Determination on Remand*, the ITA actually attacked the panel's interpretation of the specificity test. The test, according to the ITA, could be applied sequentially, so that once one of the four factors pointed to specificity it was not necessary to consider the others. With reluctance, the ITA did go on to consider the other three factors.

In weighing the four factors, the ITA found that the evidence of statutory limitation of the programmes to the lumber industry and of administrative discretion was not sufficient as to be dispositive on its own of a finding of specificity. By contrast, the number of users and the dominant/disproportionate user factors pointed much more clearly to a finding of specificity. In particular, 'evaluation of the disproportionality factor provides compelling evidence that stumpage is specific to the softwood lumber industry' (at 48).

Market distortion

In its *Final Determination*, the ITA also rejected a Canadian argument that the existence of a market distortion was a legal requirement for a finding of countervailable subsidy. The ITA criticized one of the economic studies that the Canadian complainants relied on arguing that no market distortion existed.

The two studies the Canadians relied on were the Nordhaus Study and the Nordhaus–Litan Study.

The Nordhaus–Litan Study performed a regression analysis to determine the effect on the quantity of trees harvested when, pursuant to the amended Memorandum of Understanding in 1987, British Columbia actually substantially increased its access fees for stumpage. The study found an elasticity close to zero – i.e. increased access fees had not resulted in a statistically significant decrease in the quantity of timber harvested.

In its original Decision, the panel reversed the ITA and found that, on a correct interpretation of US law, the existence of market distortion was a legal precondition for a finding of countervailable subsidy. As well, the panel found that the ITA's rejection of the Nordhaus Study was not supported by 'substantial evidence on the record'. In particular, the specific criticisms of the Nordhaus Study were based upon misunderstandings or misinterpretation of what the Study said and of Dr Nordhaus's testimony. Moreover, the ITA had not produced *any* competing expert testimony or competing empirical studies of significance.

Finally, the panel described the Nordhaus–Litan Study as the only empirical evidence offered by either side on the issue of market distortion. and noted that the ITA had not even mentioned, let alone rebutted this study.

In its *Determination on Remand*, the ITA stated criticisms of the Nordhaus Study similar to those that the panel had already found not to be supported by 'substantial evidence on the record'. It also put forward what it described as an alternative theory of market distortion – marginal cost theory. And finally, it made some criticisms of the Nordhaus–Litan Study and attempted to perfect that Study by altering some of the variables.

Instead of leaving matters there, the ITA chose – apparently randomly – to change or alter some of the variables in Nordhaus's study and rerun the regressions. It appears that the ITA, without explanation, simply decided to add the size of the harvest as a variable, and with this change it was found that as stumpage access fees decrease, output increases. The complete arbitrariness in the choice of variable gives rise to the suspicion that the ITA was simply prepared to select anything that would give it the result it wanted when it reran the regressions.

After the *Determination on Remand*, the panel was once again convened to examine the ITA's findings. On specificity, the panel found that the ITA had failed to articulate any rational, objective benchmark to sustain the conclusion that the subsidy was specific because there were 'too few' users. In effect, the ITA had not gleaned from the case law any set of legal or economic principles that could provide a benchmark for the meaning of 'too few', and its own tests were inconsistent and based on highly debatable classifications of the industries and firms who benefited from the alleged subsidy. With respect to the market distortion argument of the Canadians, the panel found that the ITA continued to reject this argument without there being any meaningful economic evidence in the record to refute it, and furthermore, that the ITA's reworking of the Canadian empirical study so as to yield a result that suggested that price and output might be affected by the subsidy was not based on a rational methodology. A majority of the panel, the three Canadian panellists, remanded with the *instruction* that duties be removed, since the ITA had been already afforded ample opportunity to furnish reasons and evidence for its conclusions and had failed to do so. In vigorous dissenting judgments, the US panellists – one of whom was the distinguished Yale international law professor Michael Reisman – criticized the Canadian majority for misapplying the US administrative law standard of review. Particularly on the specificity issue, the dissent claimed that determining whether the number of users of a subsidy is too many or too few is inherently a judgment call that is based on accumulated agency experience and expertise, and as long as the result reached is not manifestly irrational, it defeats the intention of Congress to demand that such determinations be justified against strict objective standards or benchmarks. The dissent relied heavily on a recently decided US trade case, the *Daewoo* decision, which emphasized that the role of appellate review is not to perfect an agency's economic methodologies. The majority viewed *Daewoo* as simply restating the existing standard of review, and insisted that what was at issue in *Softwood Lumber* was not imperfection in US agency methodologies but manifest gaps in reasoning and evidence, such that the ITA's conclusions could not reasonably follow from the record.

Not surprisingly, *Softwood Lumber III* was the subject of an Extraordinary Challenge by the United States, both on grounds of undisclosed conflicts of interest with respect to two of the Canadian panellists and also on grounds that the standard of review was misunderstood and/or incorrectly applied by the panel majority. Following the approach in the *Pork* and *Swine* Extraordinary Challenges, the two Canadian members of the ECC rejected the argument concerning standard of review, stating that what was at stake were differences of view about the US law, not the failure to apply the correct standard of review conscientiously. In any case, there was no threat to the integrity of the binational panel process. The majority also applied the test of whether an appellate court *could* have reached the same conclusion as the panel, and suggested it could. The ECC also rejected the US claim based on conflict of interest.

The American member of the ECC, Judge Wilkey launched a broadside attack not only on the panel and the ECC Canadian majorities but on the binational panel process itself. He claimed that 'the Binational Panel Majority opinion may violate more principles of appellate review of agency action than any opinion by a reviewing body which I have ever read.'[87] Judge Wilkey went further, suggesting that this was symptomatic of a systematic and apparently incurable failure of Canadian panellists to understand US administrative law. The implication was that a *binational* panel process simply cannot work on the basis that it is established in the FTA and NAFTA which, of course inherently involves Canadian panellists applying US law in any case where US agencies are at stake.

Judge Wilkey's dissent did not fall on deaf ears in Congress, which in effect reversed Canada's victory by changing the law on specificity and market distortion so that it conformed to the US agency interpretation of the pre-existing law.[88] In light of these changes, Canada felt compelled to negotiate anew voluntary restraints on the export of softwood lumber to the United States, which are now once again in place.

After *Softwood Lumber*, the future of the binational panel process appears uncertain. As one of us has recently argued, the better forum for many these disputes at least with respect to countervailing duty matters may be the WTO, especially given that many of the requirements of US law against which agency decisions are reviewed by binational panels now appear as binding WTO law in the WTO subsidies agreement; in this sense, the WTO process is more secure, since a ruling by a panel cannot be 'repealed' by changes to domestic legislation. At the same time, as an excellent recent study by William Davey suggests, the Chapter 19 process has been quite effective and produced outcomes widely viewed as legitimate by both Canadian and American interests in antidumping matters.[89]

CONCLUSION

The WTO dispute settlement system represents an enormous advance towards the rule of law in international trade and indeed perhaps in the evolution of international law more generally. The entitlement of a complainant to dispute settlement, with or without the consent of the other Party, and the effectively automatic adoption of rulings as legally binding between the Parties, represent important gains over the previous practice of the GATT. Perhaps no advance is more significant, however, than the establishment of a standing Appellate Body, which reviews the legal reasoning of dispute panels. Throughout the GATT's history – admittedly more in earlier than later years – panels, under the wing of the Secretariat, treated the law of the GATT rather freely, in order to obtain outcomes that were thought to be diplomatically viable and to be helpful in sustaining the overall trade liberalization bargain. As the GATT increasingly found itself in a position of deciding matters that entailed a balance of competing or diverse policy values, for example in the trade and environment area, such an approach threatened a legitimacy crisis. Disciplining the activity of panels by requiring a rigorous approach to the legal texts themselves, and the appropriate use of interpretive techniques and sources in public international law (which apply across diverse normative fields touched by international law, whether environment, health and safety, or human rights) is part of the answer to this legitimacy challenge. Unfortunately, another part of the answer – non-governmental stakeholder access to the dispute settlement system – has yet to be put in place. However, the AB has now ruled (*Turtles*) that there is nothing in the text of the Dispute Settlement Understanding that excludes the possibility of a panel using its rather broad powers of inquiry and investigation to allow and consider appropriate submissions by non-governmental organizations and other stakeholders, for instance international organizations in other regimes such as international environmental law.

Dispute settlement under the FTA and NAFTA, by contrast, has become increasingly problematic or ineffective. Very few cases have been brought under the general dispute settlement provisions, partly because due to overlap between many FTA/NAFTA and GATT/WTO provisions it made more sense to pursue dispute settlement at the WTO. With respect to binational panel review of domestic agency determinations on countervailing duty and antidumping matters, the *Softwood Lumber* dispute has displayed the fragility of the Chapter 19 review process in cases where genuine normative conflict underlies the dispute and represents a legitimacy crisis for that process of considerable proportions. Particularly since the WTO Subsidies Code incorporates legal disciplines on the imposition of countervailing duties as a matter of international law that are similar to the constraints imposed in domestic law (which must be based on WTO obligations), review of these matters is likely to increasingly occur as well under the WTO dispute settlement procedures. In our view, this is as it should be – it obviates the danger of competing interpretations of similar or overlapping legal rules and norms by different dispute settlement bodies, and would reflect the basic thrust of Article 23 of the WTO Dispute Settlement Understanding, which provides for the exclusivity of WTO procedures, where WTO rules are at issue.

4 Trade, exchange rates, and the balance of payments

INTRODUCTION

The theory of comparative advantage that we outlined in Chapter 1 suggests that it will benefit a country to produce domestically those products in which it has a comparative advantage and import those in which other countries have a comparative advantage. While the theory shows how a country that does not have an absolute advantage in anything will still be able to export and benefit from trade, it by no means demonstrates that the value of a country's exports of products in which it has a comparative advantage will equal the value of imports in which it has a comparative disadvantage.

To return to the Ricardian example of the exchange of wine and cloth between England and Portugal, what if England's wine imports yield Portugal £100 a year, yet the English cloth it requires costs £200? In this example, to maximize the gains from trade, Portugal must draw down its national reserves of wealth (e.g. gold) in order to obtain the additional £100 it needs to purchase English cloth. It thus seems that the mercantilist objection that liberal trade could reduce accumulated national wealth has not really been met by the theory of comparative advantage.

The philosopher David Hume is thought to be the first to have developed a theory of the balance of payments that could meet this objection.[1] In essence, the theory suggests that since the demand for a country's currency depends on demand for its exports, where the latter rises, so will the former. Where a country has a trade surplus, the extra demand for its exports will increase the value of its currency and therefore make its exports more expensive and its imports cheaper. This, in turn, will reduce the surplus, as demand for exports goes down in response to their relatively higher cost, whereas demand for imports goes up due to their relatively lower cost. In theory, an equilibrium will eventually be reached where trade and payments are balanced at a given exchange rate.

This 'market equilibrium'[2] view of exchange rates and the balance of payments is fundamental to understanding the interface between the legal order of international trade and the international monetary system. The post-war Bretton Woods arrangements contemplated a system of fixed exchange rates tied to the gold standard. Under this system, a country would in theory be required to hold sufficient reserves of gold to back the quantity of its currency in circulation. Where a temporary imbalance of payments occurred (i.e. where a country could not meet payments for imports with its receipts of foreign currency from export sales without selling gold for foreign currency), this would be financed by a country borrowing from the International Monetary Fund.[3] In the case of a structural or persistent imbalance, a country would devalue its currency under the supervision of the IMF, which might recommend domestic policy adjustments to ensure that further devaluations were not required in order to maintain the balance of payments.[4] In the case of a country running a persistent trade surplus, foreign demand for its currency, i.e. by purchasers of its exports, would eventually exceed the amount of its currency that could be backed by gold reserves, therefore calling for a revaluation of the exchange rate and/or domestic policy changes to dampen exports and/or boost imports.

Paul Volcker has said of the Bretton Woods system of IMF-managed fixed exchange rates: 'The irony is that no sooner did it become mechanically operative than worries about its sustainability began. Nor was it purely a coincidence that the first sign of stress appeared about the same time the system began to blossom'.[5] When the European currencies became convertible in the 1950s, the United States was running an enormous trade surplus with its trading partners. However, this was balanced by large outflows of dollars in the form of development assistance to Europe and Japan. As the European and Japanese economies began to recover, the US trade surplus started to decline, while outflows of US currency due to foreign aid and investment continued to increase. By 1960, the United States no longer had sufficient gold reserves to cover all of the dollar holdings abroad, and for the first time there was a crisis of confidence in the US dollar. During the 1960s, and particularly in the early 1970s, the Johnson and Nixon administrations, respectively, largely refused – contrary to what was contemplated by the founders of Bretton Woods – either to devalue the dollar or to alter US domestic policies so as to reduce the payments deficit. Devaluation would have increased the costs of foreign borrowing to finance the Vietnam War, and the appropriate domestic policy changes (tighter macroeconomic policies to dampen US consumer demand for imports) were considered politically infeasible. At the same time, Germany and Japan did not wish to revalue *their* currencies, since this would dampen trade expansion by making exports from these countries to the United States more expensive. Finally, in 1971 the United States unilaterally refused to back the dollar with gold any longer, and proposed that a new system of floating exchange rates be negotiated to replace the Bretton Woods system. The dominant position of the United States in the world economy, as well as the extent of foreign dollar holdings, permitted this unilateralism. In effect, if other countries did not agree to the new system, the crisis in confidence in the dollar would be disastrous for them as well as the United States, since their dollar holdings were enormous and their exports to the United States were a very important source of economic growth. Although between 1971 and 1973 an attempt was made to manage floating rates within a fixed margin or band, by the mid-1970s any attempt at multilateral management of exchange rates was abandoned, although since then there have been occasional negotiated realignments of exchange rates through central bank intervention on the currency markets and through some coordinated adjustment of domestic policies among the major monetary powers, the so-called G-7 (e.g. the Plaza Agreement of 1985 and the Louvre Accord of 1987).[6]

What are the implications for the international trading order of the key relationships between trade, exchange rates, and the balance of payments as they have played themselves out in the post-war period under both fixed and floating rate systems?

First of all, while a decline in the exchange rate seems a logical way to correct a trade deficit (i.e. by making imports more costly and exports less costly), this may be not without significant cost to other pressing domestic policy objectives. In many instances, higher costs for imports may have socially unacceptable effects – for instance, in the case of developing countries, a falling exchange rate could make imported medicines, foodstuffs and other essential requirements prohibitively expensive. More generally, as Fisher notes, 'a depreciation directly affects domestic inflation by raising the prices of imports. Further by increasing the profitability of exports and increasing aggregate demand, depreciation affects wage claims and thereby indirectly increases the inflation rate.'[7] On the other hand, in the case of a country that is running a trade surplus, an appreciation in the value of its currency will lead to unemployment at least in the short run, as sales of exports decline and imports increase – a consequence that may be politically unacceptable.

These are just two illustrations of why countries may be unprepared to accept adjustments to exchange rates in order to move towards a balance of payments equilibrium. A further concern, however, is *liquidity*. Even if countries were prepared to accept the domestic consequences of the indicated adjustments, there is, of course, an assumption that until the adjustment takes place the country running the deficit in trade will have sufficient reserves of wealth, such as gold or the currency of its trading partners, to meet demands for currency to purchase imports that exceed its foreign currency receipts from exports.

Where liquidity is thin, an imbalance of payments inevitably leads either to import restrictions or to limits on the convertibility of currency (exchange controls). Both such measures represent a fundamental threat to liberal trade, and yet may be seen as an unavoidable outcome of free trade between countries that lack reserves of foreign currency or gold.

An equally fundamental challenge to liberal trade is the presence of a variety of factors quite apart from the trade balance that affect exchange rates, such as the movement of capital across national boundaries for investment reasons, remittances of expatriate workers, and speculation on the future value of currencies by currency traders. As Kenen notes:

> The rapid growth of international transactions have [*sic*] been reflected in an even faster growth of foreign-exchange trading. In 1980, daily trading in American currency markets averaged less than $18 billion; in 1986, it averaged almost $60 billion; and in 1992 it averaged more than $190 billion.

> Daily trading in London, the world's largest currency market, averaged $300 billion in 1992.[8]

By contrast, the *annual* value of world trade in goods was $US2,035 billion in 1980 and $US3,506 billion in 1991.[9]

Taken together, the implication of these figures is clear; today the bulk of foreign exchange transactions is not accounted for by payment for traded goods. Indeed, it has been suggested that comparative advantage in trade can easily be wiped out, at least in the short run, by changes in exchange rates due to these non-trade factors.[10] There are several dimensions to the problem. The first is that the *volatility* of floating exchange rates threatens to upset the cost and price calculations of exporters and importers, making trade more risky than purely domestic economic activity that does not involve exchange of currencies. The second, mentioned above, is that non-trade domestic macroeconomic objectives, such as the control of inflation, may deter a country from adjusting its currency so as to permit the achievement of an equilibrium in trade. Lack of macroeconomic policy coordination between major currency countries can thus place considerable strain on the commitment to liberal trade (this is often referred to as the problem of misalignment).

Third, the actual experience of the United States in the mid-1980s, when it allowed the dollar to fall in order to redress its trade deficit, puts in question whether Hume's equilibrium theory still applies in contemporary circumstances. Briefly, an apparently substantial decline in the value of the dollar did not result, even after the required time period for adjustment in consumers' expectations, in a significant reduction in the US trade deficit.[11] Among the reasons often given is that upward pressure on the dollar from high US interest rates (a reflection of the financing requirements of the US budget deficit) made it virtually impossible for the dollar to fall to the point where adjustment in the prices of US imports and exports respectively would lead to an elimination, or significant reduction, of the trade deficit.[12]

It is sometimes argued that a return to fixed exchange rates (where governments determine exchange rates in accordance with economic fundamentals) would help to resolve the instability and imbalance in trade attributable to floating rates. However, in the past, fixed exchange rates co-existed with a financial system where private actors did not trade currency except, largely, to pay for imports and exports. A return to fixed or managed rates would probably entail a reimposition of exchange controls, at least on the capital account (thereby entailing a retreat from the globalization of capital markets). As was demonstrated in the crisis in the European Monetary System in 1992–3 (discussed later in this chapter) even an open-ended commitment by governments to intervene in the markets to sustain fixed rates in the presence of market forces that threaten to destabilize them may not be enough under conditions of free capital flows, where speculators are free to make their own assessment of the credibility and sustainability of these interventions.

A final challenge to liberal trade is much more straightforward – the *substitutability* of currency restrictions for protectionism. Imposing a quota or tax on the sale of foreign currency to purchase an import is likely to have a similar protectionist impact as imposing a quota or tariff on the import of the product itself. Effectively maintaining bargains about the elimination or reduction of tariffs and quotas, therefore, also implies some rules to constrain parallel currency measures. A different but related issue is that of *transaction costs* on trade payments that occur due to government policies that are not motivated by protectionism (for instance, requirements that foreign exchange transactions be reported to the authorities).

Having sketched in brief some of the key relationships between trade and money, and the challenges they present to maintenance of liberal trade, we turn to the legal rules that have been devised to deal with these various challenges.

LIQUIDITY, ADJUSTMENT AND SUBSTITUTABILITY

Liquidity was viewed from the outset of the Bretton Woods system as a fundamental challenge. Few countries had the reserves necessary to be able to wait until a devaluation brought imports and exports back into balance. Therefore, the system had to be designed to permit temporary imposition of both trade restrictions and currency controls in order to manage a balance of payments crisis. At the same time, it was important to ensure that these measures were temporary and did not lead to permanent protectionism. This would involve supervision of a process of domestic policy adjustment with a view to balancing of exports and imports, encompassing domestic policy reforms and/or including exchange rate adjustment.

The legal rules of both the GATT and the IMF, and the institutions of the latter, were designed to reflect this approach to liquidity.

The GATT

Articles XII to XIV of the GATT elaborate a complex code designed to govern and discipline the use of trade restrictions for balance of payments purposes. Article XII:1 states the basic right of any Contracting Party to impose quantitative restrictions in derogation from Article XI 'in order to safeguard its external financial position and its balance of payments'. Article XII:2 establishes that such restrictions shall be limited to what is 'necessary: (i) to forestall the imminent threat of, or to stop, a serious decline in monetary reserves, or (ii) in the case of a Contracting Party with very low monetary reserves to achieve a reasonable rate of increase in its reserves'. As well, such restrictions must be progressively relaxed as the balance of payments improves.

Furthermore, Contracting Parties 'undertake, in carrying out their domestic policies, to pay due regard to the need for maintaining or restoring equilibrium in their balance of payments on a sound and lasting basis' (XII:3). At the same time, no Contracting Party is obligated to take domestic balance of payments measures that would threaten the objective of full employment (i.e. contracting the domestic money supply to dampen demand for imports, XII:3(d)). A process of consultations is envisaged with the GATT Council concerning any new restrictions or increase in restrictions, with periodic review of the necessity of the trade measures and their consistency with Articles XII–XIV. In addition, Article XII contains provisions on dispute settlement, including the authorization of retaliation where a Party persists in trade restrictions that have been found by the Contracting Parties to violate the GATT. Articles XIII and XIV contain respectively the requirement that measures taken pursuant to Article XII:1 be implemented on a non-discriminatory basis and certain narrow exceptions to this non-discrimination requirement, e.g. where discriminatory exchange controls have been authorized by the IMF (see the discussion of substitutability below).

In the case of developing countries, there is a much broader exemption for balance of payments-based trade restrictions. Hence, Article XVII:2(b) states the principle that developing countries should have additional flexibility 'to apply quantitative restrictions for balance of payments purposes in a manner which takes full account of the continued high level of demand for imports likely to be generated by their programmes of economic development'. What this suggests is that even though a developing country could address its balance of payments difficulties through exchange rate adjustments or tighter macroeconomic policies, it should not be expected to do so given the harm to development that may come from the resultant decline in needed imports. It is recognized that quantitative restrictions will allow a developing country to conserve its limited foreign currency resources for purchases of imports necessary for development – whereas an exchange rate devaluation would result in *all* imports becoming more expensive. In this connection, it bears emphasis that balance of payments restrictions in general may be discriminatory with respect to products although not with respect to countries. Indeed, it is explicitly stated that 'the contracting party may determine (the) incidence (of restrictions) on imports of different products or classes of products in such a way as to give priority to the importation of those products which are more essential in the light of its policy of economic development' (XVIIIB(10)). Finally, Article XV:2 provides for deference to the IMF in the determination of what constitutes a balance of payments crisis as well as other financial issues involved in the application of Articles XII and XVIII.

There have been few invocations of Article XII by developed countries since the 1960s.[13] One of the most anomalous features of Article XII is its application to quantitative restrictions exclusively, rather than to re-imposition of tariffs (as contemplated by Article XIX Safeguards against import surges, for example). Perhaps this exclusive emphasis on quantitative restrictions may be in part explained by the assumption that re-imposition of tariffs would not operate rapidly enough to stem a drain on foreign exchange reserves. In the event, Contracting Parties turned out to be *more* inclined to use import surcharges (i.e. tariff-like measures) than to invoke Article XII explicitly in response to balance of payments difficulties. In some cases, the surcharges were made consistent with the GATT through an explicit waiver. In others, they were simply tolerated as a kind of *de facto* expansion of Article XII.[14]

Finally, in 1979 the Contracting Parties, without formally amending the General Agreement, made the 'Declaration on Trade Measures taken for Balance-of-Payments Purposes'[15] which expanded the ambit of Articles XII–XIV and XVIII beyond quantitative restrictions to include 'all import measures taken for balance of payments purposes'. The Declaration also imposes an obligation on Contracting Parties taking such measures to 'give preference to the measure least restrictive of trade', which, as Petersmann suggests, would usually involve a preference for tariffs and surcharges over the quantitative restrictions explicitly mentioned in Article XII.[16]

Through much of the history of the GATT, balance of payments-based trade restrictions were not subject to much direct scrutiny. Developing countries, in particular, made liberal use of such restrictions. However the increasing invocation of these restrictions in the wake of the LDC debt crisis, combined with a new emphasis on the importance of trade liberalization to development in more recent thinking on the subject, had led to increasing concern by the mid-1980s, particularly on the part of the United States and some other developed countries.[17] Another, in some sense, almost opposite source of concern was the continued maintenance of restrictions by countries that were growing rapidly, e.g. the Asian NICs. Thus, in a 1989 case, the United States complained that South Korea continued to impose Article XVIIIB restrictions on imports of beef despite improvements in its balance of payments position.[18] The approach of the GATT panel was quite straightforward – it deferred to the conclusion of the GATT Balance of Payments Committee, in its 1987 consultation with Korea, that the country's current and prospective balance of payments was such that continued restrictions could not be justified. The Committee in turn had acted on the advice of the International Monetary Fund, in accordance with Article XV:2.

The Understanding on the Balance of Payments Provisions of the General Agreement on Tariffs and Trade 1994, incorporated in the Uruguay Round Final Act, is aimed at improving GATT/WTO discipline of trade measures taken for balance of payments purposes. Members commit themselves to publish, as soon as possible, time-schedules for the removal of such trade measures. Such schedules may, however, be modified 'to take into account changes in the balance-of-payments situation' (Article 1). Further (and perhaps the most important modification of the existing GATT regime) Members commit themselves to give preference to trade measures of a price-based nature, such as tariff surcharges, and only to resort to new quantitative restrictions where 'because of a critical balance-of-payments situation, price-based measures cannot arrest a sharp deterioration in the external payments position' (Articles 2, 3). The Understanding further sets out an elaborate set of procedures for review by the Committee for Balance-of-Payments Restrictions of both the time-schedules for elimination of existing restrictions and notifications of any new restrictions. The overall intent appears to be that of placing balance-of-payments trade restrictions under on-going scrutiny, with a view to their elimination as soon as possible. This is consistent with the original GATT regime, where such restrictions are envisaged as temporary, and not an appropriate longer-term solution to payments imbalances. It is also, however, something of a retreat from the more permissive approach to such restrictions reflected in the Tokyo Round declaration.

Pursuant to the Understanding, on 31 January 1995, the WTO General Council established the WTO Committee on Balance-of-Payments Restrictions.[19] From its inception through 1997, the Committee has conducted consultations with numerous Members[20] concerning the existence and possible reduction and phase-out of their balance-of-payments restrictions, including Brazil, South Africa, Slovakia, Poland, Sri Lanka, India, Egypt, Turkey, Tunisia, Hungary, Nigeria, Bangladesh and the Philippines, the Czech Republic, and Bulgaria. In most cases, Members made commitments to eliminate or reduce the restrictions in question, which satisfied the Committee. In some instances, with respect for example to India and Tunisia, there was some controversy within the Committee itself as to how rapidly the balance-of-payments situation of the country would reasonably permit the removal of measures. In other instances, such as Bangladesh, the precariousness of the balance-of-payments situation was easily agreed in the Committee. In several cases, including those of Hungary, the Czech Republic, and Brazil, the Committee considered new measures introduced by Members. The Czech measure, a requirement that importers post a deposit that does not bear interest, was regarded by a majority of the Committee as inappropriate, and was eliminated a month after the Committee made this observation. In general, the Committee appears to be an effective vehicle for scrutinizing balance-of-payments restrictions, although equally clearly there are differences of view on how to interpret situations where the Member's economy has been subject to rapid change. In light of this, it seems appropriate that the Committee has relied upon IMF studies in some controversial cases, and has granted observer status to a number of specialized international organizations, including the European Bank for Reconstruction and Development, the OECD, UNCTAD and the World Bank.

While Articles XII–XIV and XVIII of the General Agreement deal with trade restrictions taken to address a balance of payments crisis, Article XV concerns the trade effects of currency and other monetary restrictions. Here a fundamental concern is the substitutability of exchange measures for trade restrictions. Thus, Article XV:4 states that Contracting Parties shall not 'by exchange action frustrate the intent of the provisions of this Agreement, nor, by trade action, the intent of the provisions of the International Monetary Fund'. Contracting Parties are required to obtain membership in the IMF, or alternatively, to negotiate a 'special exchange arrangement' with the GATT. Article XV:4 is subject to the proviso that any exchange measures explicitly authorized by the IMF are to be considered consistent with the General Agreement (XV:9).

The IMF

The provisions of Article XV of the GATT, taken together, suggest considerable reliance on the IMF to ensure an open payments system that sustains liberal trade. At the time the General Agreement was negotiated and came into effect, however, currency controls were pervasive not only in developing but also in most developed countries. As mentioned earlier in this chapter, the Bretton Woods system was designed in such a way as to permit countries eventually to stabilize their balance of payments without resort to such measures, through lending from the IMF's own resources to sustain liquidity, and through Fund-approved adjustments of exchange rates in connection with appropriate domestic policy reforms. However, it was considered that this state of affairs would not occur, for most countries, until after a considerable transition period.

Countries were therefore provided with an option of accepting the full convertibility obligations of Article VIII of the Fund Articles of Agreement, or joining the Fund through the transitional provisions of Article XIV of the Articles of Agreement. Even the convertibility obligations of Article VIII still permitted a member of the Fund to impose exchange controls with Fund approval.

Thus, Article VIII:2(a) prohibits 'restrictions on the making of payments and transfers for current international transactions' without Fund approval. The expression 'current international transactions' certainly encompasses all import or export sales, but does not include, for example, many forms of foreign investment, securities transactions, etc. In this respect, it is important to note that most developed countries maintained, consistent with Article VIII, restrictions and controls on the *capital* account until the 1980s.[21] Article VIII does not provide any explicit criteria for the authorization of current account restrictions by the Fund, nor does any other provision of the IMF Articles.[22] Article XIV allows a member of the Fund to impose exchange restrictions in 'the post-war transitional period' provided the member declares to the Fund its intent to do so. The Fund may decide that any such measure is no longer necessary, i.e. that the transition period has elapsed, but must in the first instance give the member country 'the benefit of the doubt' (Article XIV:5).

Particularly during the LDC debt crisis, the Fund played an important role in sustaining liquidity in LDC debtor countries and preventing the economic collapse of the debtor states. However, the Fund insisted on macroeconomic and trade policy reforms as a condition for liquidity assistance, thereby forcing painful domestic adjustment as the appropriate response to the crisis in the balance of payments. Similarly, today the Fund encourages the Newly Liberalizing Countries (NLCs) of Central and Eastern Europe to move rapidly towards liberalization of trade and payments. Much of Western assistance is premised on the need for liquidity support to underpin these rapid policy shifts. However liquidity is only part of the problem – the domestic adjustment costs are the other part and these can be enormous.

Interaction between the GATT and IMF rules

A number of legal issues have arisen concerning interaction between GATT rules on trade restrictions for balance of payments purposes and IMF rules concerning exchange controls and monetary restrictions. One such issue is the characterization of measures that can be plausibly viewed as one or the other. This issue was raised but not resolved by a GATT panel in a 1952 case that involved a Greek tax on foreign exchange for imports, which varied depending on 'the usefulness and necessity of the products imported'.[23] Eventually, largely through a decision of the IMF Directors, it was clarified that a measure will be considered an exchange restriction if the *technique* used involves restricting access to foreign exchange, even though the principal intent and effect is to restrict *imports*.[24] Under this approach, the Greek tax would have been deemed an exchange restriction and therefore subject to IMF as opposed to GATT discipline, despite the fact that it was quite directly targeted at imports.

There is some evidence that Contracting Parties have sought to minimize IMF scrutiny of *trade* measures, by advocating a narrow interpretation of Article XV:4, which would limit the IMF's role to that of providing statistical findings concerning a balance of payments crisis.[25] However, in the *Korean Beef Import* case discussed above, a GATT panel took a more expansive view of the IMF's role, deferring to a finding based not just on facts provided by the IMF, but also upon the Fund's 'advice'. In addition, as noted above, the IMF itself, as a condition of assistance, may well impose a requirement that trade restrictions, not just exchange restrictions, be lifted. The overall effect of these developments is that today, whether a Contracting Party chooses to enact trade restrictions or currency measures to address a balance of payments crisis, it will find its actions subject to a similar level and kind of scrutiny by the IMF.

The OECD Invisibles Code

The OECD Code on Liberalisation of Current Invisible Transactions is intended to go beyond the obligations of Article VIII of the IMF Articles in seeking to eliminate all restrictions on 'current invisible transactions and transfers' between OECD member countries. Indeed, members are encouraged to extend the benefit of the Code to all IMF members (Article I(d)). Whereas Article VIII of the Fund Articles applies only to restrictions on payments and transfers themselves, such as rationing of access to foreign currency, the Code applies also to taxes and charges, as well as administrative requirements imposed on the actual *transactions* required to make payments and transfers abroad. These measures fall between the cracks of the GATT and IMF rules, in that they apply neither to imports and exports of products nor do they directly restrict payments on the current account. Obligations under the OECD Code on Invisibles are subject to various reservations filed by individual member states. However, in recent years reservations have been reduced and the Code strengthened.[26]

VOLATILITY

As mentioned earlier in this chapter, the original Bretton Woods arrangements were intended to function with fixed exchange rates. A country would be permitted to adjust these fixed rates in order to correct 'a fundamental disequilibrium'.[27]

The intent of these arrangements was that exchange rate changes would occur only occasionally, and would be supervised by the IMF to ensure that they did not cause undue harm to the trading or other economic interests of other countries, i.e. that they reflected changes in the terms of trade rather than constituting an attempt unilaterally to alter those terms in favour of the devaluing country. Thus a country would be permitted to devalue where its exports had been declining relative to imports, but not in order to create a trade surplus where its existing trade was not in disequilibrium (i.e. competitive, beggar-thy-neighbour exchange rate devaluations that characterized the inter-war period).

Under the system of floating rates that emerged in the 1970s after the collapse of the Bretton Woods fixed rate system, what determines exchange rates is supply and demand with respect to the various currencies. Central banks can and do intervene in the market to alter the value of their countries' currency, in accordance with domestic policy objectives. However, because currencies are no longer fixed in value as against a common, objective standard (such as the price of gold), or subject to adjustment only in accordance with internationally agreed criteria ('fundamental equilibrium'), volatility is much greater.

Blame is often placed on the US for undermining the fixed rate system and thereby introducing fundamental volatility into exchange rates.[28] However, greater volatility was arguably inevitable. With the terms of trade changing rapidly, and moreover with globalization of capital markets, enormous and rapid shifts in capital flows would have probably required very frequent adjustments to exchange rates even under a fixed rate system – or, alternately, curbs on globalization itself. As Spero notes, during the 1980s, 'most developed countries . . . abolished or relaxed exchange controls, opened domestic markets to foreign financial institutions, and removed domestic regulatory barriers. A revolution in telecommunications, information processing, and computer technologies made possible a vastly increased volume, speed, and global reach of financial transactions.'[29]

Those who advocate a return to fixed rates with a view to addressing volatility and sustaining the gains from trade thus also tend to argue for deglobalization, and reimposition of controls on the import and export of capital.[30] However, this perspective fails to consider the extent to which liberalized capital flows themselves contribute to the expansion of trade through globalization of production (Foreign Direct Investment), and the exploitation of comparative advantage in the financial services sector.

There is a serious empirical issue as to the extent to which exchange rate volatility has negatively affected trade.[31] Sophisticated actors on world markets can hedge the foreign exchange risk from their trade transactions by buying and selling in a variety of currencies, or by actively trading in currencies themselves. Nevertheless these possibilities are significantly less open to smaller traders, and there are always transaction costs entailed in the hedging of currency risks. In order to reduce volatility, it has been proposed that a tax be placed on foreign exchange transactions. The tax would be set low enough that it would not affect trade in goods and services but would impose a high cost on 'short term in-and-out transactions' of a speculative nature.[32] However, this kind of proposal presumes that speculation is the driving force behind exchange rate volatility – if, however, such volatility is endemic to globalized capital markets, then short-term transactions may be critical to hedging endemic foreign exchange risk, and therefore the tax may be fundamentally self-defeating.[33]

MACROECONOMIC POLICY COORDINATION AND PROPOSALS FOR MANAGED EXCHANGE RATES

Under the system of fixed exchange rates that prevailed until 1971, changes in macroeconomic policies did not automatically result in changes to exchange rates and thereby did not directly affect the trade interests of other countries or the demand for protection in the country making the policy change. Under the system of flexible rates, however, no rules or institutions have been created for the international management and supervision of macroeconomic policies.

These policies continue to put considerable pressure on the liberal trading order. Occasionally the G-7 countries, i.e. those nations with the major international currencies including the United States, Germany and Japan, have agreed on certain targets and goals. But Germany and Japan, for instance, have often been very reluctant to stimulate spending and expand their money supply so as to increase imports from the United States. At the same time they have been disinclined to revalue their currencies, because this would make their exports more expensive and threaten jobs. The United States, by contrast, has refused to act unilaterally to raise taxes to finance its deficit rather than resort to further foreign borrowing. This has meant continued upward pressure on the US dollar, further exacerbated by interest rates that have reflected a tight monetary policy. The consequence is that US exports remain expensive in terms of other currencies and imports into the USA relatively cheap, creating unremitting pressures for selective trade protection. One recent positive sign, however, is the commitment of the Clinton Administration to reduce significantly the US budget deficit.

Some economists – most notably John Williamson[34] – have developed proposals for targeting zones for exchange rates. This does not represent a return to fixed rates and strict domestic controls on the movement of capital. Rates are still set by supply and demand in the currency markets. Should, however, rates move outside the target zone, countries commit themselves,[35] through central bank intervention and/or policy adjustments, to a return within the zone. This kind of solution seems to offer a number of advantages. First of all, unlike a return to fixed rates, it appears to avoid the kind of limits on financial market liberalization that would be entailed by the (re)imposition of controls on capital movements or restrictions on the markets. In theory, at least, governments sustain the target zones not by constraining the markets but by playing them. Second, since the zones are established by some kind of objective standard, such as a current account target, i.e. what a country's account should look like given a number of external (e.g. trade) and internal (e.g. inflation) factors, the indeterminacy that characterizes open-ended discussions on policy coordination would appear to be avoided.

The problem is, as Cooper notes, that 'the setting of current account targets would be an intrinsically arbitrary exercise in a world of high capital mobility and open markets in goods and services'.[36] Given the multiplicity of reasons why money flows in and out of countries – investment, repatriation of earnings, capital markets transactions such as the purchase and sale of bonds and other securities – how does one begin to determine the balance between in-flows and out-flows that a given country should maintain at a given point in time? A further difficulty, in the absence of exchange controls, is that governmental commitments to maintain the zones must be credible to speculators – otherwise governments will find themselves in the almost impossible position of fighting the expectations of the market. When speculators believe that governments' commitments to their domestic interests are sufficiently pressing that they will not be able to sustain in future their internationally-agreed exchange rate targets, the collapse of the targets can easily become a self-fulfilling prophecy. In sum, without either a return to controls or a move forward to macroeconomic policy harmonization and the kind of supranational control of domestic policies envisaged in the Maastricht blueprint for European monetary union, 'coordination' is likely to remain at the level of a very occasional adjustment in rates which reflects a saw-off between conflicting interests of the major financial powers, or perhaps even more likely, the unilateral threat of protection from the USA if exchange rates are not adjusted appropriately.

More generally, despite the fact that economists still speak of over or undervaluation, it may even be difficult for a country to determine its optimal exchange rate from the perspective of *domestic interests*. For example, until recently the Canadian government has maintained a tight monetary policy to fight inflation, and thereby sustained high interest rates and consequently a high Canadian dollar. As a result, freer trade with the United States has yielded relatively fewer gains for Canadian producers and has resulted in considerable unemployment in Canada. Should the Canadian government have let the Canadian dollar fall against the US dollar, at the cost of lower interest rates and some inflation? (It is important to note that popular discontent with high unemployment was directed at free trade much more than at the government of the day's tight monetary policy.)

With respect to developing or transitional economies, the collapse of the Mexican peso in 1994–5 and the concomitant outflow of foreign short-term capital,[37] and the 1997–8 crisis in Asian capital markets, have led some economists to question whether liberalizing capital controls is a sound policy except at a very mature stage of economic development. Jagdish Bhagwati, for example, draws a sharp distinction between the robust case for liberalization of trade and the much more questionable case for free movement of capital.[38] According to Bhagwati,

> economists properly say that there is a correspondence between free trade in goods and services and free capital mobility: interfering with either will produce efficiency losses. But only an untutored economist will argue that, therefore, free trade in widgets and life insurance policies is the same as free capital mobility. Capital flows are characterized, . . . by panics and manias.[39]

While Bhagwati recognizes the importance of foreign capital to economic development, he believes that foreign direct investment (FDI) is the appropriate vehicle for this, and thinks that there is little evidence that FDI depends on liberalizing capital flows. The IMF points to factors such a 'inadequate financial sector supervision, poor assessment and management of financial risk, and the maintenance of relatively fixed exchange rates' as causes of the Asian crisis.[40] The common ground between Bhagwati's diagnosis and the lessons from Asia proposed by those, like the Fund, who have promoted capital mobility for developing and transitional economies may be this: it appears that liberalization of capital flows should be sequenced after various governance-oriented reforms that assure the kind of regulatory protections against financial instability typical of those mature economies that have learned from managing their own crises. An additional lesson may be that crisis behaviour can result where governments attempt to maintain relatively fixed exchange rates while simultaneously liberalizing capital controls. Without capital controls, if investors no longer have confidence in the government's ability to sustain its currency at a given exchange rate or within a given zone, they can take flight within hours. Indeed, as will be discussed in the next section of this chapter, the crisis in the European Monetary System in 1992 can in part be explained in terms of the risks of maintaining managed exchange rates once capital controls have been removed.

An interesting compromise solution to the debate over free movement of capital is advocated by Haas and Litan. They suggest that, instead of either *laissez-faire* or heavy handed re-regulation, a penalty should be imposed on all foreign lenders in an IMF bailout after a financial crisis in developing country markets – these lenders would face some loss of principal when they refuse to roll over or extend their loans. This, Haas and Litan argue, would better internalize the risk of crisis into the price of credit, and provide investors with greater incentives to monitor borrowing countries for soundness of governance practices and adequacy of financial data.[41]

THE EUROPEAN MONETARY SYSTEM (EMS)

The European Monetary System (EMS) provides an interesting case study of the difficulties of maintaining a system of managed or fixed exchange rates under conditions of increased liberalization and globalization of financial markets and in the absence of an agreed common macroeconomic policy approach.[42] Established in 1978, the EMS applied to many but not all of the members of the European Union (for instance, the UK chose to stay out until quite recently). The core of the EMS was an agreement to maintain currencies within a ±2.25% band of a fixed rate against the ecu, the common EU currency. This agreement was made possible, it is generally thought, by the presence of Germany in the system as a hegemonic financial power. If other members of the system engaged in substantially looser monetary and fiscal policies than the traditionally conservative Bundesbank, confidence in their currencies would weaken, with investors switching their holdings into Deutschemarks. Eventually, to sustain the exchange rate within the 2.25% band, these other countries would have to alter their monetary policies so as to conform with those dictated by the Bundesbank.

In fact, however, this happened only to a limited degree. Until the full liberalization of financial markets in the EU in 1992, a number of the countries with weaker currencies continued to maintain exchange controls. Through these controls, the countries concerned (e.g. Italy) were able to maintain looser macroeconomic policies than those of Germany, since they could limit outflow of capital in response to higher interest rates and a stronger currency in Germany. As well, the system had permitted the fluctuation of some currencies outside the ±2.25% band. In addition, some devaluations and revaluations of currencies actually did occur, despite the commitment in principle to fixed rates. These (albeit infrequent) realignments would eventually create further pressure on the system, by inducing in currency traders and speculators the expectation that at a certain point, where particularly currencies in the system were under sustained pressure, the EMS members would act to realign the fixed rates. The expectation of a devaluation would intensify sale of the currencies already under pressure, and therefore increase that pressure enormously (especially after the lifting of capital controls).

The breakdown of the EMS in September 1992 can be attributed to the interaction of the above factors.[43] In the 1990s, Germany's macroeconomic policies could no longer be considered an adequate benchmark for economically sound price stability goals. Instead, they reflected Germany's special needs to finance German reunification. Because of the politically-motivated refusal of the Chancellor to raise taxes to finance unification, the Bundesbank was required to raise German interest rates beyond a level required by macroeconomic fundamentals, in order to finance unification by borrowing. Under these circumstances, with capital controls removed, other EMS members faced extreme pressure on their currencies. They did not want to raise interest rates to match those set by Germany's extraordinary borrowing requirements for reunification, because this would worsen the recession in their countries. At the same time, the French did not want to devalue the Franc, because a strong Franc was viewed as necessary to maintain investor confidence in the French economy.

One logical solution would have been revaluation of the Deutschemark. Revaluation would, of course, have reduced Germany's exports and increased its imports, therefore countering at least to some extent the effects on other currencies of *capital* in-flows to Germany.[44] And, indeed, such a solution was favoured by the Bundesbank – thereby creating speculation on the markets that currency realignments were imminent. However, the German Chancellor rejected revaluation, probably for political reasons (it will be recalled that, in the short term, revaluation costs domestic jobs, as exports decline and imports rise). Finally, one important factor that continued to hold the system together, and dampen somewhat investor speculation that it was under fundamental threat, was the expectation that the Maastricht plan for a single European currency, once it shifted into full gear, would result in greater coordination of macroeconomic policies in the transitional phase of moving to a single currency, thereby restabilizing the system, or perhaps more accurately putting it on a new, surer footing.

In September 1992, with expectations that Maastricht might be rejected in the French referendum running high, with capital controls now completely removed, and with no resolution in sight to the problem of German interest rates, there was a speculative run on a number of the other currencies in the EMS. Perhaps even more ominous than the speculative run itself, was the discovery by governments and central banks that – with the end of exchange controls – the possibilities of restabilizing their currencies through intervention were dramatically reduced. Even overnight increases in interest rates in the hundreds of percentage points did not succeed, and several countries, including Britain, had to withdraw from the Exchange Rate Mechanism (ERM) of the EMS.

The breakdown of the EMS initially created considerable doubt as to whether plans to proceed with a single currency, as envisaged in Maastricht, are at all feasible. As well, numerous proposals exist for putting the EMS back together again, at least in the short run. However, with the French referendum result narrowly supporting the Maastricht Treaty, and Denmark's eventual acceptance of the Treaty, the project for monetary union received renewed momentum. As for the EMS, it was rehabilitated in a much weakened form by an August 1993 decision to allow currencies to float within a 15% band (Germany and The Netherlands nevertheless undertook to keep their currencies within a 2.25% band).[45]

Finally, it is arguable that the crisis of the EMS reinforces rather than undermines the Maastricht approach of monetary *union*, which requires as a prerequisite to the movement to a single European currency a substantial degree of harmonization of macroeconomic policies. For example, in order for a country to enter the monetary union it must, *inter alia*, have a relatively low rate of inflation, it must not be running an 'excessive' budget deficit, and its interest rates must not exceed a norm based upon the interest rate performance of the three EU countries with the lowest inflation rates.[46]

In part due to the possibility that an insufficient number of Member States would satisfy these various criteria on time, in December 1995 the European Council moved back the starting date for the final stage of transition to a single currency from 1997 to 1999. By 1997, it was evident that all the countries intending to join the EMU (the UK, Sweden, and Denmark decided to opt out) had largely met the convergence criteria related to inflation, public finances, interest rates, and exchange rates, with the partial exception of Greece.[47] Thus, on 2 May 1998 the Council made a final decision to proceed with the final phase of transition in 1999, including the creation of a European Central Bank (ECB), to supervise a common monetary policy.[48] However, the project for the EMU remains fraught with tensions – in fact, the 2 May decision was only able to proceed due to a compromise on who would be the first head of the ECB. The Maastricht Treaty stipulates an eight-year term, but France's insistence on its own candidate resulted in a bizarre compromise whereby the choice of other member states, Wim Duisenberg, made a statement that he would voluntarily end his term early (thus paving the way for a French candidate to serve the remainder of the eight years). This permitted a successful outcome to the 2 May discussions.

Europeans continue to debate whether the loss of macroeconomic policy autonomy is a too high price to pay for currency union. Many believe that Member States have been already constrained in their ability to address the social and economic challenges of unemployment and redesign of the welfare state by the need to meet the convergence criteria for inflation and deficits. While the ECB will only control monetary, and not fiscal, policy, at German insistence the Council has pressed ahead with the 'stability and growth pact', which would limit budget deficits to 3% of GDP on pain of fines. As *The Economist* suggests, it is arguable that this 'foolishly constrains fiscal policy at a moment when the loss of an independent monetary policy argues for more, not less fiscal flexibility'; however, violating the pact does not jeopardize membership in the EMU, and the penalty fines if levied might simply not be paid.[49] Further concerns centre on the lack of democratic legitimacy of the ECB, which might further compound the general problem of the EU's 'democratic deficit'. It is sometimes speculated that the so-called 'euro-11', the informal grouping of finance ministers of the 11 Member States participating from the outset in the EMU, may become a kind of political counterbalance to the unelected bureaucrats at the ECB. This, however, has not allayed fears that a democratic nationalist backlash against monetary union could further fuel the rise of anti-European right-wing populist movements.[50]

CONCLUSION

An examination of the rules and institutions that govern the inter-relationship between trade and finance suggests that despite the 'casino' of currency speculators and globalized capital markets, the Bretton Woods rules and institutions did in many respects prove well-adapted, or at least adaptable, to sustaining a relationship between trade and money conducive to liberal trade. The liquidity and balance of payments adjustment problems are increasingly being addressed through IMF assistance, conditioned upon acceptance of an open trade and payments system. While the LDC debt crisis represented a serious setback, its end result is more rather than less liberalization of trade by the LDCs affected. Moreover, the GATT and IMF rules and the institutional arrangements of the IMF have proven effective in addressing the substitutability problem, whereby countries attempt to undercut trade concessions by resorting to currency measures. With respect to volatility under floating rates, and the corresponding increase in the riskiness of trade transactions, the system has proven less effective in explicitly addressing the challenge. However, in the end it may turn out that hedging techniques are a relatively effective means of private actors themselves reducing foreign exchange risk in trade, although smaller and less sophisticated actors have less access to these strategies. Where the system has been least effective is in addressing the trade pressures that result from and/or intensify conflicts over domestic macroeconomic policies. Yet the major powers have nevertheless avoided a spiral of beggar-thy-neighbour devaluations, even if they find it impossible to agree on a positive strategy for targeting exchange rates.

5 Tariffs, the MFN principle, and regional trading blocs

THE ECONOMIC EFFECTS OF A TARIFF

The economic effects of a tariff on both importing and exporting countries are best understood by first examining the case of a prohibitive tariff – that is a tariff that is so high that it prevents all imports. Here we draw on an example provided by Ruffin and Gregory.[1]

With a prohibitive tariff, the prices paid for shirts in each country are determined by the supply and demand curves in each country. To compare prices, we assume that \$US2 = £1. If there were no tariff, prices would be the same in the two countries. The prohibitive tariff in America raises the price in America from \$US6 to \$US9. Consumers lose area A + B, but producers gain area A. The net loss to America is area B. In Europe, prices fall from £3 to £2, and producers lose area C + D, while consumers gain C. The gain to consumers is less than the loss of producers. The net loss to Europe is area D.

One can next consider a non-prohibitive tariff, which does not preclude all imports of the product. Ruffin and Gregory graph this example as in Figure 5.2.

Before the non-prohibitive tariff, the price of the product is P_w. The tariff raises

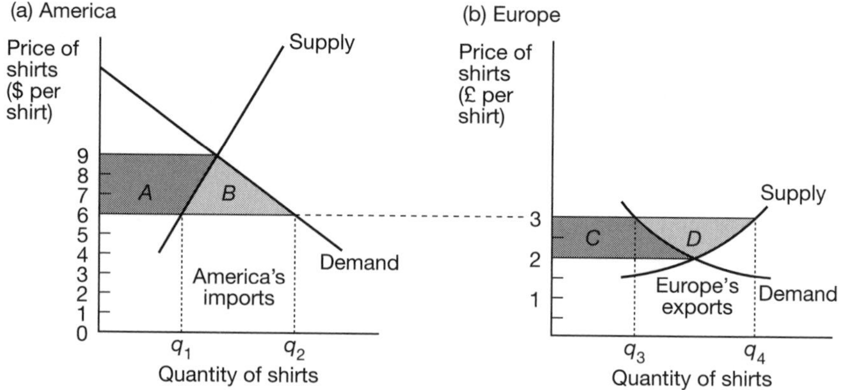

Figure 5.1 The costs of a prohibitive tariff
Source: Ruffin and Gregory, *Principles of Economics*.

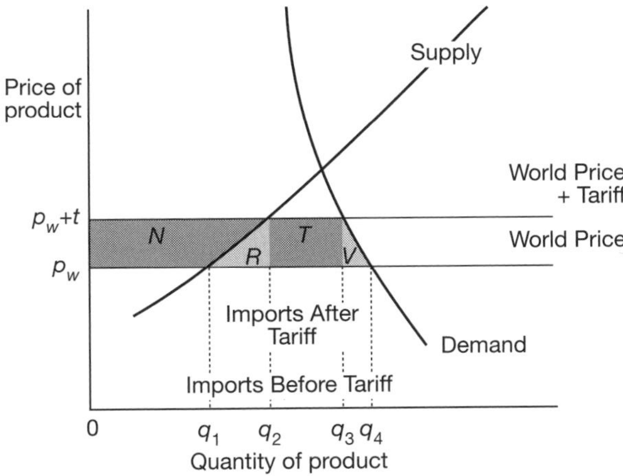

Figure 5.2 The effects of a non-prohibitive tariff
Source: Ruffin and Gregory, *Principles of Economics*.

the price to $P_w + t$; that is, the world price plus the amount of the duty. Consumers lose area N + R + T + V. Producers gain N. The government gains the tariff revenue T, which equals the tariff per unit times the quantity of imports. The net loss is R + V. The tariff lowers imports from $(q_4 - q_1)$ to $(q_3 - q_2)$.

It is also important to note certain economic characteristics of tariffs that contrast with other policy instruments that governments might invoke to protect domestic industries. For example, governments in importing countries may seek to protect domestic industries by quantitative restrictions (or quotas). As protectionist devices, these have the virtues of definitively limiting the volume of imports that will be permitted, and thus provide stronger assurances to domestic producers of protected market shares. On the other hand, they exhibit the corresponding vice, depending on their design, of insulating domestic producers from most forms of foreign competition and thus encouraging inefficiency. In contrast, with a non-prohibitive tariff highly efficient foreign producers may be able to surmount the tariff and still compete effectively with domestic producers, thus creating some incentives for the latter to enhance their productive efficiency. Another difference between tariffs and quotas relates to who collects the scarcity rents that they engender. With tariffs, governments in importing countries collect revenues from non-prohibitive tariffs. With quotas, depending on how they are allocated, domestic holders of import quotas or licences may collect scarcity rents (rather than the government collect tariff revenues). If the quotas are allocated to foreign exporters, these firms will collect scarcity rents by charging more for their goods in the protected market, without being under any obligation to pay customs duties on the imports.

Tariffs should also be distinguished from production subsidies designed to make domestic industries artificially competitive with imports. Such subsidies will distort domestic production decisions by attracting resources into the subsidized activity, but will not necessarily (depending on how they are financed) distort domestic consumption decisions, in that the goods in question will still trade at world prices. Tariffs, in contrast, distort both domestic production and consumption decisions, first by attracting resources into the protected sector and second by raising prices to consumers above world prices, which in general reflect least cost means of production, thus inducing consumers to allocate their resources to less preferred forms of consumption.

As noted in Chapter 2, these characteristics of alternative instruments of protection find rough analogues in the provisions of the GATT. The GATT in Article XI purports to take a strong prohibitory approach towards quantitative restrictions. On subsidies, Article XVI reflects a much more ambivalent position, and while the Tokyo Round Subsidies Code and Uruguay Round Subsidies Agreement (especially the latter) take a somewhat less equivocal stance, only a narrow range of subsidies are subject to outright prohibition. Tariffs are not presumptively good or bad and there is no obligation under the GATT to reduce them, although Article XXVIII *bis* contemplates periodic negotiations on a reciprocal and mutually advantageous basis directed to the substantial reduction over time of the general level of tariffs.

THE MOST FAVOURED NATION PRINCIPLE

The Most Favoured Nation principle, found in Article I of the GATT, has its clearest application to tariff concessions. Under Article I, any concession made by one country to another must be immediately and unconditionally extended to like products originating from other Contracting Parties. While, as indicated in Chapter 1, the Most Favoured Nation principle has a long history, controversy still surrounds the purposes served by the principle.[2]

Schwartz and Sykes[3] argue that in designing an institutional framework in which joint gains may be realized from the exchange of concessions, three considerations need to be taken into account: (1) uncertainty with respect to future changes in trade barriers that may affect the value of current concessions; (2) the free rider problem where participants in multilateral negotiations may refrain from making concessions in the hope that they can take advantage of concessions by others without offering quid pro quos (but at the risk that if every party reasons similarly no concessions will occur); (3) the political weight that attaches to different constituencies and the effects on their interests from trade diversion when nations discriminate in their trade policies. The MFN principle protects expectations of participants in multilateral bargaining by forbidding subsequent more favourable treatment of other participants and avoids the dead-weight loss of trade diversion, but at the cost of preventing nations from discriminating when it might be valuable to benefit certain politically powerful producer interests, and at a cost of substantial incentives for participants in multilateral negotiations to attempt to free ride. Schwartz and Sykes argue that the safeguard regime (Article XIX) may be an appropriate response to the first of these problems and that Article (XXIV) (free trade areas/customs unions) may be an appropriate response to the second problem. Thus, the MFN principle needs to be viewed in a broader institutional context.

The political centrality of the concept of reciprocity in multilateral tariff negotiations is illustrated by the ritual which has followed each previous Round of negotiations, where major participants have announced, principally for domestic political consumption, the balance-sheet on the value of tariff concessions given and received, typically representing that a net gain has been realized. The method commonly employed for calculating the value of concessions has no economic foundation. For example, if country A obtains a 10% tariff cut on widget exports to country B that in previous years have averaged $US10 million, this concession will be valued at $US1 million. But this assumes a demand elasticity in country B of unity, i.e. for every one percentage decline in price, quantity demanded will increase by 1%. This may or may not bear any resemblance to reality. Moreover, to value the concession accurately from country A's perspective requires some knowledge of how other suppliers of widgets are likely to react to these new opportunities. That is to say, without a firm knowledge of these underlying demand and supply elasticities, simply calculating the value of a tariff concession by reference to trade coverage is next to meaningless.

While these political dimensions of the concept of reciprocity are clearly important to the optics of trade policy, we have also acknowledged in Chapter 1 that reciprocity may be an economically rational strategy – while unilateral trade liberalization may be welfare enhancing, reciprocal trade liberalization may generate even greater welfare gains. In any event, for both political and economic reasons, reciprocity has been central to most tariff reductions under the GATT.

A number of important exceptions or qualifications to the MFN principle should be noted at this point.

1 Historical preferences in force at the time of coming into effect of the GATT are grandfathered under Article I of the GATT, although subject to the requirement that the margin of preference cannot subsequently be altered in such a way as to exceed the difference between the MFN rate and preferential rates existing as of 10 April 1947. The provision contemplates that the absolute, not proportional difference between MFN and preferential rates must be maintained when MFN rates are reduced or raised. For example, if the MFN rate is 20% and the preferential rate 10% on imported widgets, and the MFN rate is subsequently reduced to 15% (a 25% reduction), the preferential rate can be reduced to 5% and not merely 7½% (which would be a 25% reduction).
2 The Generalized System of Preferences (GSP) provided for in Part IV of the GATT in favour of developing countries obviously entails preferences that would otherwise violate the MFN principle.
3 Antidumping and countervailing duties imposed by importing countries pursuant to Article VI of the GATT clearly involve duties that are selective and discriminatory.
4 Quantitative restrictions imposed pursuant to Article XII or Article XVIII of the GATT for balance of payment reasons may, by virtue of Article XIV,

temporarily deviate from the principle of non-discrimination in respect of 'a small part of a country's external trade' where the benefits to that country substantially outweigh any injury which may result to the trade of other countries.

5 National security exceptions, recognized in Article XXI of the GATT, may justify the imposition of trade restrictions on a discriminatory basis.
6 Where retaliation is authorized under the nullification and impairment provision of the GATT (Article XXIII) or the safeguard provision (Article XIX), such measures will typically be selective and hence discriminatory.
7 The various non-tariff codes negotiated during the Tokyo Round were typically negotiated on a Conditional MFN basis, meaning that only Contracting Parties who were prepared to become signatories to the codes and thus accept the obligations so entailed were entitled to the correlative benefits. Under the Uruguay Round Agreement, most collateral Codes or Agreements will be fully integrated into the GATT, and membership in the WTO will entail adherence to them.
8 By far the most important exception to the MFN principle is the authorization of customs unions and free trade areas under Article XXIV of the GATT, provided that two basic conditions are met, i.e. trade restrictions are eliminated with respect to 'substantially all the trade' between the constituent territories, and customs duties shall not be higher thereafter than the duties prevailing on average throughout the constituent territories prior to the formation of a customs union or free trade area. Subject to these two conditions, constituent territories are permitted to establish more favourable duty and other arrangements amongst themselves than pertain to trade with non-member countries. This exception is so important that the third part of this chapter is devoted to a discussion of the relationship between regional trading blocs and the multilateral system.

A final comment on the principle of non-discrimination requires a mention of how the National Treatment principle, enshrined in Article III of the GATT, bears on tariff concessions. In the absence of this principle, negotiated tariff concessions could be easily sabotaged. For example, if country A agreed to reduce its tariffs on imported widgets from 20% to 10%, and then imposed differential domestic sales taxes on domestic and imported goods of 5% and 15% respectively, the tariff concession would effectively have been negated. More subtle forms of discriminatory treatment of imports relative to domestically produced goods may equally nullify or impair the benefit of previous tariff concessions to exporting countries and provoke a complaint under Article XXIII.

ALTERNATIVE BARGAINING STRUCTURES

Product-by-product negotiations

In the five negotiating rounds under the GATT prior to the Kennedy Round (1964–7), tariff concessions were negotiated on a product-by-product basis. Under the Principal Supplier rule that was adopted by the participants, countries who were principal suppliers of goods into international markets would prepare 'request' lists of goods where they were seeking tariff concessions from importing countries. Countries preparing request lists would at the same time prepare offer lists indicating products on which they were prepared to make concessions. Because of the MFN principle, requests and offers were typically directed by principal suppliers to principal importers, thus essentially bilateralizing tariff negotiations. A principal supplier would have no interest in directing a request to a minor importer because trade concessions negotiated with such a country, while entailing MFN obligations on the latter's part, would entail no such obligations on the part of major importers. Similarly, the principal supplier of product X would have no interest in making concessions on imports of product Y from a minor exporter, where this concession would have to be generalized to major exporters without being able to extract from these exporters major concessions on products of which the importing country was the principal supplier. According to Finger,[4] product-by-product negotiations achieved very high internalization rates, in the sense that the benefits of trade concessions were confined, to a very large extent, to Parties offering countervailing trade concessions, with very little free-riding (pursuant to the MFN principle) on the part of exporters who offered no reciprocal concessions. To the extent that there were likely to be significant spill-overs benefiting non-reciprocating Parties from tariff concessions, typically product-by-product negotiating rounds concluded with a settling-up session where concessions previously tentatively negotiated were subject to threats of withdrawal or revision unless non-reciprocating countries agreed to offer concessions as well.

While this process may have led to deeper tariff cuts on items that were subject to negotiations, it arguably substantially restricted the range of products with respect to which active negotiations occurred, thus restricting the coverage of the resulting tariff reductions. Product-by-product negotiations had other limitations: first, small exporting and importing countries were largely frozen out of the negotiating process; second, by focusing negotiations on particular products, domestic producer constituencies were encouraged to become active in resisting tariff concessions on products in which they were interested; third, the negotiating process was highly transaction cost intensive because of its focus on line-item negotiations.

Linear-cuts with exceptions

In the Kennedy and Tokyo Rounds, the Contracting Parties chose to substitute for product-by-product negotiations a linear-cutting formula, with a provision for exceptions lists where countries could take products out from the linear-cuts and negotiate, as before, on a product-by-product basis. Obviously, with this approach, the coverage of products embraced by tariff reductions was likely to be much larger, although the degree of internalization of concessions exchanged was likely to have been lower, and according to Finger would have created incentives for shallower cuts. Finger refers to this as the internalization – coverage trade-off. In fact, both the Kennedy and Tokyo Rounds produced average tariff cuts of about 35% –

well in excess of tariff reductions negotiated in the four Rounds that had intervened between the initial GATT negotiations and the Kennedy Round. However, linear-cutting formulae present problems of their own. Now, negotiations must focus on the appropriate formula, and in both Rounds these negotiations proved problematic in various respects. For example, countries that already had low tariffs on average argued that it was unreasonable to expect them to cut these tariffs by the same percentage as high tariff countries, the reasoning being that, for example, a 50% cut of a 60% tariff would still leave a 30% tariff in place, which if one assumes that the initial tariff contained a lot of 'water', might still be largely prohibitive of imports, while a country cutting a 10% tariff to 5% might well find that this would have a significant impact on the volume of imports.

In both Rounds, formulae were finally agreed to which required, in one respect or another, larger cuts of higher tariffs than of lower tariffs. Another problem with the linear-cutting approach was the risk that countries would abuse the right to take items out from the linear-cutting formula and place them on an extravagant exceptions list where they would be subject only to product-by-product negotiations. Indeed, a number of countries with import sensitive sectors like textiles, clothing and footwear adopted this expedient. Also, countries primarily engaged in the exportation of agricultural products or natural resources, where tariffs were in many cases quite low but whose manufacturing sectors were highly protected (like Canada) viewed product-by-product negotiations as more advantageous than linear-cuts and in the Kennedy Round were entirely exempted from the linear-cutting process, but not in the Tokyo Round although subject to extensive exceptions lists. Notwithstanding these problems, as noted above, between linear-cuts and product-by-product negotiated tariff reductions, the average level of tariffs was substantially reduced in the course of both Rounds.

Sector-by-sector negotiations

In both the Kennedy and Tokyo Rounds, efforts were made to negotiate reductions in trade barriers in selected sectors, such as steel, chemicals and forest products. Canada was a prominent proponent of this approach. It was largely a failure. The reasons are not hard to identify. To focus negotiations on a particular sector (e.g. steel), is likely to engage the interest principally of producer interests in this sector and rather than reducing or eliminating trade restrictions instead runs the risk of a managed trade arrangement effectively entailing cartelization of the global industry. Alternatively, because negotiations amongst producer interests in the same sector in different countries tend to have a zero-sum quality to them, no agreement at all will be possible. While a code on trade in civil aircraft and components was successfully negotiated during the Tokyo Round and did reduce some trade barriers, and while the Agreement on Agriculture negotiated during the Uruguay Round will significantly liberalize trade in agriculture, the Multi-Fibre Arrangement that emerged in the 1970s is a stark example of the protectionist scenario. More generally, by attempting to negotiate trade liberalization within sectors, the political room for manoeuvre in cross-product or cross-sectoral exchanges of concessions, as entailed in product-by-product or linear-cutting negotiations, is dramatically reduced.

Non-reciprocal concessions

As recognized in Part IV of the GATT, developing countries are not expected to offer reciprocal commitments in trade negotiations, and developed countries are expected, to the fullest extent possible, to accord high priority to the reduction of barriers to products of particular export interest to developing countries. Pursuant to these provisions, in the early 1970s many industrialized countries adopted the Generalized System of Preferences (GSP), and unilaterally extended preferential tariff rates on certain items of export interest to developing countries. However, these preferential tariffs typically were not bound, usually entail escape clause provisions that permit the termination or reduction of the preferences in the event of import surges, and contain graduation provisions whereby developing countries lose their preferences when in the view of the country extending them they have reached a state of development where they no longer require them. As well, GSP preferences have typically not been extended on items produced by politically sensitive domestic sectors such as textiles, clothing, and footwear, even though these are of major export interest to many developing countries early in the process of industrialization. Moreover, as MFN rates have declined as a result of subsequent multilateral negotiations, the margin of preference between GSP and MFN rates has contracted.[5]

OUTSTANDING TARIFF ISSUES

While the first seven Rounds of tariff negotiations under the GATT since the Second World War dramatically reduced world tariffs on average (from about 40% on manufactured goods in 1947 to about 5%), Laird and Yeats[6] identified a number of tariff issues that remained outstanding at the outset of the Uruguay Round Multilateral negotiations. First, despite low average tariffs, most countries still maintained very substantial tariffs on particular products. Moreover, there was still a good deal of unevenness in tariff levels from one industrialized country to the other with respect to particular items, suggesting that the low tariff–high tariff debate in negotiating modalities for reducing these disparities had not yet been fully resolved (see Table 5.1).

Second, many national tariffs were still not legally bound; this applied particularly to GSP tariffs and also to tariffs in many developing countries. Third, there were different and adverse effects of specific tariffs on developing countries' exports (i.e. a fixed charge per unit), as opposed to *ad valorem* tariffs (a percentage of value). Specific tariffs were still quite common. Fourth, the cost-insurance-freight (CIF) as opposed to free-on-board (FOB) procedures for customs valuation continued to discriminate against geographically disadvantaged developing countries, particularly those that are least developed and land locked. Fifth, a serious problem still existed

Table 5.1 Post-Tokyo, applied and GSP tariffs in selected developed countries

Product group developed	*Australia*	*Austria*	*Canada*	*EU*	*Finland*	*Japan*	*Norway*	*New Zealand*	*Sweden*	*Switzerland*	*USA*	*All*
					Average MFN tariff rates							
All Food Items	4.9	8.0	6.2	3.7	8.9	9.7	2.8	9.7	1.6	10.0	4.1	6.4
Food and live animals	2.8	5.9	6.8	3.2	9.3	10.0	3.0	5.7	1.4	9.0	3.8	6.5
Oilseeds and nuts	4.1	1.9	6.0	10.3	7.9	5.6	4.5	0.9	3.3	7.5	1.4	5.3
Animal and vegetable oils	2.0	0.8	0.0	0.1	0.8	0.3	0.0	0.0	0.0	0.2	0.9	0.1
Agricultural Raw Materials	5.1	2.3	0.0	3.4	1.1	0.7	0.6	1.0	1.7	1.9	0.3	0.8
Ores and Metals	10.2	5.6	2.1	2.8	1.9	2.5	1.5	6.0	2.5	1.4	1.9	2.3
Iron and steel	17.2	8.4	5.4	5.5	3.9	5.0	1.8	8.0	4.8	2.0	4.3	5.1
Nonferrous metals	3.9	6.1	2.2	3.2	1.2	5.5	1.9	4.0	1.0	1.2	0.7	2.3
Fuels	0.0	2.1	1.4	0.1	0.1	1.5	0.0	0.2	0.0	0.0	0.4	1.1
Chemicals	5.4	6.3	6.4	8.4	2.4	5.5	5.9	6.7	5.0	0.9	3.7	5.8
Manufactures excl. chemicals	17.7	14.1	7.0	8.1	8.2	5.7	6.1	22.6	5.4	3.3	5.6	7.0
Leather	17.8	3.3	3.8	10.2	11.8	11.9	4.7	20.9	4.1	1.8	4.2	5.1
Textile yarn and fabrics	15.3	18.2	9.4	17.3	22.7	8.6	12.8	16.2	10.6	6.0	10.6	11.7
Clothing	49.3	30.2	12.6	19.9	32.0	15.0	20.3	93.0	13.6	8.6	20.3	17.5
Footwear	43.9	25.9	11.9	22.5	16.0	14.2	11.2	40.3	14.3	9.6	11.7	13.4
Other Items	0.2	3.3	0.1	4.8	1.3	2.3	2.0	1.2	1.8	0.4	n.a.	n.a.
All Products	n.a.	n.a.	n.a.	n.a.	n.a.	n.a.	n.a.	n.a.	n.a.	n.a.	n.a.	n.a.

Source: Calculations on the basis of the GATT Tariff Study and UNCTAD Series D Trade Tapes.

Table 5.1 continued

Product group developed	*Australia*	*Austria*	*Canada*	*EU*	*Finland*	*Japan*	*Norway*	*New Zealand*	*Sweden*	*Switzerland*	*USA*	*All*
	Average applied tariff rates											
All Food Items	3.1	6.8	3.0	4.4	5.2	9.4	1.4	7.8	0.8	9.1	3.5	5.3
Food and live animals	1.7	4.9	2.9	4.8	5.7	9.7	1.5	3.9	0.8	8.4	3.2	5.3
Oilseeds and nuts	2.0	1.5	4.6	4.9	5.5	4.8	4.3	0.7	2.2	7.4	1.0	4.0
Animal and vegetable oils	2.4	0.8	0.1	0.0	0.8	0.3	0.0	0.0	0.0	0.2	1.0	0.2
Agricultural Raw Materials	0.7	1.6	3.7	0.4	1.0	0.3	0.4	0.7	1.4	0.7	0.3	0.5
Ores and Metals	4.3	0.3	2.7	0.7	0.1	1.8	0.4	4.2	0.2	0.1	2.2	1.5
Iron and steel	7.3	0.5	5.6	2.3	0.1	2.9	0.7	6.4	0.4	0.1	5.0	3.4
Nonferrous metals	2.4	0.2	2.8	0.5	0.0	4.3	0.1	2.1	0.1	0.1	0.7	1.3
Fuels	0.0	1.5	0.2	0.3	0.0	1.2	0.0	0.0	0.0	0.0	0.4	0.6
Chemicals	4.0	0.5	3.0	3.4	0.1	4.8	0.4	4.9	0.4	0.1	3.9	3.1
Manufactures excl. chemicals	11.5	2.0	6.2	4.6	1.3	4.6	1.3	18.3	1.4	0.4	4.9	4.7
Leather	10.9	0.9	11.0	2.1	2.3	10.7	0.8	21.4	0.3	0.1	2.7	3.1
Textile yarn and fabrics	11.3	2.0	18.3	5.3	1.0	7.1	1.6	10.9	1.7	0.6	12.1	7.9
Clothing	35.6	5.1	17.2	7.3	7.7	10.0	3.0	75.6	4.8	1.7	18.1	11.9
Footwear	27.9	1.2	23.4	6.5	3.8	12.5	2.4	28.4	2.8	0.6	9.5	9.0
Other Items	0.1	1.1	4.7	0.1	0.1	0.7	0.4	0.9	0.1	0.2	3.6	3.3
All Products	8.3	2.0	4.4	2.5	1.0	3.1	1.0	11.0	0.8	1.0	3.4	3.0

Source: Calculations on the basis of the GATT Tariff Study and UNCTAD Series D Trade Tapes.

Table 5.1 continued

Product group developed	*Australia*	*Austria*	*Canada*	*EU*	*Finland*	*Japan*	*Norway*	*New Zealand*	*Sweden*	*Switzerland*	*USA*	*All*
	Average tariff for GSP beneficiaries											
All Food Items	1.3	9.0	1.5	5.0	7.0	11.1	0.3	6.2	0.4	6.3	3.6	5.5
Food and live animals	1.0	8.9	1.3	5.1	7.2	11.7	0.3	0.8	0.4	6.5	3.4	5.6
Oilseeds and nuts	0.7	0.1	5.6	6.2	8.8	5.0	3.2	0.0	1.7	9.0	0.3	4.5
Animal and vegetable oils	0.3	0.3	0.0	0.0	10.7	1.2	0.0	0.0	0.0	0.1	0.1	0.4
Agricultural Raw Materials	0.1	1.4	3.1	0.5	5.5	0.5	0.5	0.0	2.1	0.3	0.1	0.5
Ores and Metals	1.6	0.9	0.5	0.5	0.1	1.3	0.3	0.2	0.1	0.4	1.1	0.9
Iron and steel	4.9	2.9	4.0	3.3	0.4	2.0	0.4	2.3	1.0	0.4	3.5	3.0
Nonferrous metals	0.3	1.1	0.9	0.5	0.0	3.1	1.7	0.5	0.1	0.9	0.3	1.1
Fuels	0.0	1.5	0.0	0.2	0.0	1.3	0.0	0.0	0.0	0.0	0.3	0.6
Chemicals	4.2	4.0	6.1	4.1	0.1	5.1	0.2	1.1	0.6	0.4	1.0	3.7
Manufactures excl. chemicals	11.4	18.9	13.8	6.4	9.3	4.2	5.9	14.3	6.9	2.7	6.6	6.7
Leather	9.6	6.6	9.6	2.8	6.1	8.4	5.5	18.0	1.2	1.1	1.4	3.2
Textile yarn and fabrics	6.3	17.5	19.8	7.6	6.0	6.1	11.0	8.5	6.8	2.7	9.0	8.4
Clothing	35.1	27.2	16.2	9.3	23.6	8.6	18.9	82.8	13.2	7.6	17.8	14.6
Footwear	25.6	24.4	23.3	9.1	14.8	7.9	11.6	22.1	13.4	4.4	9.4	10.1
Other Items	0.0	5.2	5.6	0.1	0.1	1.0	0.1	1.7	0.0	0.4	0.4	3.8
All Products	4.3	4.9	4.4	2.1	4.6	2.3	2.8	3.3	2.3	2.3	3.6	2.7

Source: Calculations on the basis of the GATT Tariff Study and UNCTAD Series D Trade Tapes.

as to how to liberalize tariffs for products that are also simultaneously covered by non-tariff barriers (such as quotas). Sixth, developed countries still commonly applied escalating tariffs to imports depending on their stage of processing, in order to protect domestic processing industries, often at the expense of developing countries who would derive substantial advantages from being able to engage in value-added processing of what otherwise are purely commodity or raw materials exports.

The Uruguay Round tariff negotiations

In the Uruguay Round tariff negotiations,[7] Contracting Parties were free to apply any method of reducing tariffs, provided the reduction would be at least equivalent to the over-all reduction achieved in the Tokyo Round (about one-third of prevailing duties). Substantial reductions were in fact achieved. The trade weighted *ad valorem* reductions in tariffs on industrial products were close to 40 percent. In addition, duty-free trade will be assured for 44% of developed economies' exports of industrial products. Significant progress was also made on reducing escalating tariffs on processed goods. After implementation developed countries' tariffs on industrial products will thus fall from 6.3 to 3.8% on average (one-tenth of the average tariff level before the entry into force of the GATT in 1947). Moreover, 99% of developed economies' tariff lines of industrial products will be bound compared with 78% before the Round. Seventy-three per cent of developing countries tariff lines will be bound compared to 21% before the Round. These numbers are, of course, aggregates or averages, and tariffs will continue to be higher in several categories, including textiles and clothing; leather, rubber, footwear and travel goods; fish and fish products; and transport equipment. For example, with respect to textiles and clothing, many tariffs remain in the 15 to 35% range. In the case of agricultural products, as part of the broader Uruguay Round Agreement on Agriculture (discussed in Chapter 10), quantitative restrictions must be converted into tariff equivalents (sometimes running to several hundred percent) and lowered by an equivalent of 36% in six years in the case of developed countries, with a minimum reduction of 15% for each tariff line) (24% overall for developing countries over ten years).

Subsequent to the close of the Uruguay Round, the WTO Ministerial Declaration on Trade in Information Technology Products (ITA) was agreed to at the close of the first WTO Ministerial Conference in December 1996 in Singapore. The ITA provides for participants to eliminate customs duties and other duties and charges on information technology products by the year 2000, on an MFN basis. Six main categories of products are covered: computers, telecommunications equipment, semiconductors, semiconductor manufacturing equipment, software, and scientific instruments. However, implementation was contingent on expanding ITA participation to cover approximately 90% of world trade in IT products by 1 April 1997. On 26 March 1997 participants agreed that this criterion had been met. They also established a Committee as the Expansion of Trade in Information Technology Products, which will monitor the implementation of the ITA.

There are currently 43 parties to the ITA, accounting for 93% of world trade in IT products. The ITA provides for the 'staging' of tariff cuts in four equal rate reductions of 25% each year from 1997 to the year 2000. In addition to regular customs duties, the ITA also provides for the elimination of other duties and charges.

The ITA does not currently cover consumer electronic goods. A further round of negotiations is underway to extend the coverage of the Agreement to computer-based scientific and analytical equipment and other products.

DOMESTIC ADMINISTRATION OF TARIFFS

Each country's customs authorities are responsible for administering the country's customs laws. Primarily their task involves calculating the duties owed by the importer, completing the required paperwork, and collecting the payments. However, calculating import duties involves a number of tasks: valuing the imported goods; locating the goods in the appropriate product classification; and identifying the goods' country of origin. Each stage of the process, from the valuation system to the paperwork and administrative fees, is a potential barrier to trade; domestic administration can increase the level of protection afforded by tariffs or even make the importing process prohibitively complicated. As someone is once reputed to have remarked: 'Let me write the Administrative Act and I care not who writes the rates of duty.'[8] In the areas of customs valuation and classification there has been general acceptance of harmonized rules, but little progress has been made on rules of origin, and administrative fees still remain at each country's discretion. Under Article X of the GATT, every Contracting Party is obligated to publish in accessible form all laws, regulations, rulings, etc., pertaining to classification, valuation, and customs administration and to institute a system of judicial or quasi-judicial review to enable prompt review and correction of administrative actions relating to customs matters. In Canada, tariff schedules are set out in great detail in the *Customs Tariff*, running into several thousand items. Five major tariff rates often exist for a given item: (1) the MFN tariff rate; (2) the FTA or NAFTA rate; (3) the General rate (for non-GATT members); (4) the British Preferential rate (for some Commonwealth countries); and (5) the GSP rate for some developing countries. In turn the Customs Act creates the domestic administrative machinery for the collection of duties through the Department of National Revenue. Internal appeal mechanisms within the Department on classification, valuation and related issues are provided for. Appeals from final Departmental determinations may be made to the Canadian International Trade Tribunal and thence, on matters of law, to the Federal Court of Appeal.

Valuation[9]

Most tariffs today are *ad valorem*, requiring the importer to pay a certain percentage of the good's value in duty.[10] Hence, the value of the imported goods is an important determinant of the ultimate import duty: 'any advance in value is accompanied by a commensurate increase in both duties collected and in the level of protection'.[11] It is in the interest of all countries that valuation techniques be uniform and predictable. A system that is unpredictable or unfair to exporters serves as a non-tariff barrier to trade and undermines the effects of tariff reductions. Further, differences in valuation methods make tariff negotiations more complex.[12] In negotiations, a country must take into account the different effects of tariffs due to the different valuation techniques employed to ensure that it is receiving reciprocal trade concessions.

The current international rules on the valuation of goods for customs purposes are found in the Uruguay Round Agreement on Implementation of Article VII of the GATT.[13] A Customs Valuation Code was initially negotiated during the Tokyo Round in order to 'provide a uniform, neutral valuation system that conforms to commercial realities and prohibits arbitrary values for duty'.[14] A slightly revised Agreement was negotiated during the Uruguay Round.[15] Prior to this, the rules were found in Article VII of the GATT. Article VII was intended to ensure that signatories used fair systems of valuation that conformed with certain principles. It requires that Parties to the Agreement base 'value for customs purposes of imported merchandise . . . on the actual value of the imported merchandise . . . not . . . on the value of merchandise of national origin or on arbitrary or fictitious values'.[16] Actual value is defined as the 'price at which . . . such or like merchandise is sold or offered for sale in the ordinary course of trade under fully competitive conditions'. The article does not specify the valuation method to be used and it gives the importing country discretion over the time and place for determining price.

Prior to the Tokyo Round negotiations over one hundred countries (including Japan and the countries of the EU) had adopted the valuation system called the Brussels Definition of Value (BDV).[17] However, two major GATT trading nations retained separate systems of valuation: Canada and the United States. Because of the Protocol of Provisional Application (the Grandfather Clause),[18] many of the signatories to the GATT were only bound to apply its Articles to 'the fullest extent not inconsistent with existing legislation'. Along with the general nature of Article VII, this provision allowed the perpetuation of very different, sometimes unfair, systems of valuation. For example, the United States used, in part, the American Selling Price (ASP) method of valuation which was viewed as 'a device to keep the American public from seeing in all its nakedness the exorbitant level of duties contemplated by rampant protectionism'.[19] The American system was made up of nine different methods of valuation and was 'stupefying in its complexity'.[20] In addition, Canada's valuation system was long considered to be inconsistent with Article VII of the GATT.[21] Countries which traded with the USA and Canada raised the issue of customs valuation in the Tokyo Round negotiations in an attempt to have them abandon their systems.[22] The original intention of countries using the BDV was that it would become the worldwide system but a compromise was reached with the USA.[23] The Customs Valuation Code that was concluded in 1977 was based in part on the US system and was accepted by the major trading nations.[24] Signatories were obliged to render their legislation consistent with the Code by 1 January 1981 but many countries, including Canada, reserved the right to postpone implementation in order to ensure the maintenance of tariff protection at pre-code levels.[25]

A major objective of the Code was to constrain the exercise of administrative discretion. Both the Tokyo and Uruguay Round Codes establish 'transaction value' as the primary standard of valuation.[26] Transaction value is the price paid or payable for the goods when sold for export to the country of importation, plus certain additions such as the cost of packaging and the value of various items provided to the buyer free of charge in connection with the sale of the goods (assists). There are also some items that can be deducted from the price such as the cost of transportation, handling and insurance from the place of direct shipment. The transaction value can only be used for the purposes of valuation in certain circumstances. It can be used if there are no restrictions on the disposition or use of the goods other than those that are imposed by law or that restrict the resale area or that do not substantially affect the value of the goods.[27] In addition, to use transaction value the price of the goods cannot be subject to any conditions or consideration, such as an undertaking by the buyer to buy more goods at a later date. Sales between related persons (generally officers of each other's companies, partners, direct or indirect controlling interests) are eligible for use of transaction value provided it is demonstrated that the relationship did not affect the price.[28] There are a number of valuation methods outlined in the current Customs Valuation Agreement to be used in the event that the transaction value cannot be used. Authorities must resort to these methods in a particular order; for example, only if the first and second cannot be used can resort be made to the third. In the prescribed order, they are:

- transaction value of identical goods exported to the same country of importation at approximately the same time;
- transaction value of similar goods exported to the same country at approximately the same time;
- deductive value based on resale price in the country of importation; and
- computed value based on the cost of production of the imported goods.[29]

In many cases, the use of one of the alternate methods of valuation will be inappropriate because of information limitations or difficulties in calculation. Generally, resort will be made to the third or fourth methods when the price is affected by the relationship between the Parties to the transaction or when there is no selling price at the time of importation.

Certain methods of valuation are expressly prohibited in the Agreement, such as the use of arbitrary or fictitious values, and the use of the selling price in the country of importation.[30] In the Canadian and American legislation, customs officials are authorized to apply one of the above methods flexibly if goods cannot be valued under any of the above methods; this is the residual or alternative method. Part II of the Agreement also provides for the establishment of a Customs

Valuation Committee comprising representatives of all members that is responsible for furthering the objectives of the Agreement and facilitating consultation and dispute resolution with respect to the valuation system.

Classification

Because there is wide variation in the level of tariffs from product to product, goods must be located in the correct product category to receive proper tariff treatment. As with valuation, the problem with classification for customs purposes is that it can be used as a protectionist device. A country that has agreed to reduce its tariffs in exchange for reciprocal concessions can use the classification system to ensure that the benefit is only received by the reciprocating country. This selectivity can be achieved if the product's classification can be subdivided so that the goods from the reciprocating country are in a distinct category. Then the tariff on the distinct category of goods can be reduced and other countries that would normally receive the benefit of the reduction through Most Favoured Nation treatment receive no benefit.[31] This same technique of product classification is also used to reduce the tariffs on inputs for domestic manufacturers and processors while maintaining the overall level of protection.[32]

The Customs Cooperation Council was established in 1950 and given a mandate to develop and harmonize customs systems of the world. The result of the committee's work is the Harmonized Commodity Description and Coding System. The Harmonized System (HS) was open for signing in 1984 and was implemented in some countries by 1987.[33] The basis of the Harmonized System is that goods should only be classified by their essential or intrinsic nature (i.e. by what they are and not how they are used) and should only fall into one category.[34] In Canada's previous classification system it was not uncommon to find the same good in several different categories carrying different rates of duty.[35] The nomenclature consists of a mandatory six digit classification system that is used by all signatories. Countries who find the classification too imprecise for their needs may use up to four more digits, as Canada has done.[36] Along with the numbers and descriptions, the system includes legal notes that are binding on the signatories. The notes provide definitions of terms and phrases essential to the classifications and set boundaries on the goods to be included in each. In addition, the notes list specific goods to be included or excluded in each category and give directions for locating the appropriate classification for excluded goods. Finally, there are extensive explanatory and interpretive notes.

Rules of origin

The final task in calculating the appropriate duty on imported goods is establishing the country of origin of imports. Tariff treatment is often dependent on the country of origin of the imports. As noted earlier, in Canada there are five major tariff treatments. In order to qualify for a particular tariff treatment an importer must establish the product's origin. Establishing origin is often difficult: goods may be processed, assembled, packaged or finished in a variety of different countries, or shipped to the importing country via another country where they may or may not enter the commerce of that country.

There are presently no comprehensive multilateral rules that govern determinations of rules of origin. Moreover, in many countries, rules of origin are not internally harmonized. That is, there are different rules for establishing origin within the country depending on the context, for example, for tariff purposes or during a dumping investigation. This can pose a difficulty for exporters: a good that originated in country A may pay the tariff rate for country B, where it was processed, but face antidumping duties levied against goods from country A.

The Uruguay Round Agreement on Rules of Origin adopts the following approach with respect to rules of origin. First, the Agreement sets out plans for transition to a harmonized system of origin determination to be developed by a Committee on Rules of Origin and a Technical Committee assisting it within three years of the acceptance of the Agreement. The first step requires all countries to harmonize their own rules of origin.[37] During this period the rules applied by each country must be based on a positive standard (i.e. what confers origin, not what does not confer origin). Once this harmonization is achieved countries will be required to base determinations of origin either on the country where the good was wholly obtained or the country where the good underwent its last substantial transformation. The rule of last substantial transformation is not fully defined in the Agreement[38] but it combines a change in tariff classification with supplementary criteria based on percentage of value added or specific manufacturing or processing operations. The Committee on Rules of Origin has reported substantial progress in its ongoing programme aimed at harmonizing non-preferential rules of origin to be applied by all Member States. The NAFTA also contains a number of new and complex rules of origin designed to clarify and harmonize determinations of content.[39] Goods are deemed to originate in the territory of a NAFTA Party if they are wholly produced or obtained in any of the three NAFTA countries. They may contain offshore materials or components if they are transformed within a NAFTA country so as to be subject to a change in tariff classification. Special regional content rules apply in the case of automobiles, textiles and clothing and some other products.

Customs fees

Aside from the calculation of duties on imported goods, customs authorities are also responsible for processing documentation and collecting duties and administrative fees from importers. Both fees and documents may be barriers to trade. Documentation requirements can make the importation process more costly or prohibitively burdensome. In 1952 a Code of Standard Practices for Documentary Requirements was accepted by the GATT. The Code's main purpose is to restrict the kind and number of documents required. The result of the Code was the abolition in many countries of consular invoices which were previously a heavy burden on international trade.[40]

With respect to fees, there is no international agreement beyond the basic provisions of the GATT. Article VIII provides that:

> All fees and charges of whatever character imposed by contracting parties on or in connection with importation or exportation shall be limited in amount to the approximate cost of services rendered.

The terms of Article VIII are vague and do not significantly constrain domestic practices. For example, importing countries often charge fees equal to a set percentage of the value of imports, leading to total charges far in excess of the cost of services rendered; the protective effect of such fees can be significant.[41] At present, domestic authorities retain a great deal of discretion in this area of customs administration.

MULTILATERALISM VERSUS REGIONALISM

The emergence of regional trading blocs, most prominently the European Union and the Canada–US FTA, and now NAFTA, in the post-war period, collateral to the evolution of the GATT and sanctified by Article XXIV of the GATT, constitutes easily the most important exception to the MFN principle of non-discrimination embodied in the GATT and on that account requires an extended discussion.

While the record of the GATT in reducing tariffs on manufactured products has been impressive, it is also true that it has proven less effective in disciplining tariffs on primary products and non-tariff border measures, especially quantitative restrictions, let alone most other forms of trade-distorting policies of its members. If the reference point against which the GATT is to be judged is the deep integration being realized in the EU, with integration being pursued with respect to not only goods, but also services, capital, and people, coordination of exchange rate and monetary policies, and harmonization of a plethora of domestic fiscal and regulatory policies, it is impossible not to adopt a relatively gloomy prognosis for the future of the GATT.[42] However, it is important to be explicit about the premise on which this prognosis rests. Only with a hegemonic pro free trade presence in the case of the multilateral system, or heavily centralized policy-making institutions in the case of the EU, is it likely that deeper economic integration can be achieved.

Thus, in the case of the GATT/WTO, now with a declining US hegemonic influence and with 130 Members (compared to 23 at the outset) in very different stages of economic development and with widely differing political, economic and cultural orientations – a heterogeneity that is likely to be increased in the future with the admission of countries in transition from command to market economies – it is difficult to imagine the emergence of centralized integrating institutions to whom Member States are prepared to surrender major aspects of their political sovereignty. Thus, if one insists on viewing the GATT, as traditional liberal institutionalists do, as a system of international legal rules designed to constrain domestic self-interest, which system can only be reinvigorated by stressing the importance of a global vision, of farsighted statesmanship that places global welfare and common interest over immediate domestic self-interest and of the importance of the global rule of law,[43] the GATT is now and will always be a disappointment.

However, a somewhat more optimistic (and realistic) view of the GATT is possible. Sometimes referred to as the new liberal institutionalist approach,[44] this view stresses that multilateralism should rather be seen as a decentralized framework for the negotiation and maintenance of mutually advantageous bargains among states. Liberal internationalists seek ways for designing or re-designing processes that, by reducing information, transaction, surveillance and verification costs, will facilitate Pareto-superior deals between or among states that are largely self-enforcing contracts. Performance of these contracts is promoted by reputation effects and tit-for-tat retaliation strategies that tend to solve the Prisoner's Dilemma problem in multi-period games.[45] This is precisely what describes the greatest achievement of the GATT – the dramatic reduction in tariffs, but it bears recalling, over a 40-year period and over eight successive bargaining rounds.

While it has become fashionable to talk of a 'borderless' world economy, the growth of global federalism, the decline in the significance of the nation state, and the rise of consumer sovereignty,[46] it is as plausible to view the rapidly integrating world economy as overlain with 'a splintering world polity'.[47] The rise of regional trading blocs arguably reflects this latter trend. Over 80 regional arrangements have been notified to the GATT under Article XXIV since 1947. Many arose during the 1960s, and a second generation during the 1980s and 1990s.[48] Apart from the EU and NAFTA, other prominent or emerging regional trading blocs include: Mercosur (Argentina, Brazil, Paraguay, and Uruguay) in Latin America; APEC (Asia Pacific Economic Co-operation) in Asia and the Pacific Rim,[49] and CARICOM (the Caribbean Common Market). There is also a commitment in principle to extending NAFTA throughout the Western Hemisphere no later than 2005 (a Free Trade Area of the Americas – FTAA),[50] and preliminary discussion of a Transatlantic Free Trade Area between the US and the EU.[51]

Regional trading blocs have generally enjoyed a bad press from trade economists.[52] The reasons are straightforward enough. At a political or foreign policy level, they necessarily entail playing favourites and risk reducing international relations to mutually destructive factionalism of the kind that was so dramatically evidenced in the 1930s. From an economic perspective, regional trading blocs, whatever their trade expansion properties with respect to intra-regional trade, almost necessarily also entail some measure of trade diversion (in the sense that lower-cost producers outside the regional trading blocs are discriminated against), thus distorting the efficient global allocation of resources and hence reducing global welfare.[53] But this said, the question must be asked, 'compared to what?' Compared to complete, undistorted global free trade, regional trading blocs are clearly second-best. But compared to the world trading system that actually prevails, or is likely to prevail in the foreseeable future, the case against regional trading blocs is not so clear.[54]

In this second-best world, Lawrence and Litan[55] provide a balanced assessment of their strengths and weaknesses. In the end, their assessment is cautiously positive. Central to this assessment is, on the one hand, their view that regional trading blocs may be able to achieve a deeper degree of economic integration than the multilateral system – negotiations typically involve a much smaller number of 'like-minded' nations, and (less explicitly claimed) the necessary centralized or federalizing policy-making and enforcement institutions (as with the EU) are more likely to emerge – and on the other hand, their view that the trade diversion potential of regional trading blocs is often over-stated, given both the size of inherent intra-regional trade flows already involved, at least in the EU and NAFTA,[56] and the empirical evidence on the importance of extra-regional trade to all of the major regions that might conceivably become involved in regional trading blocs. That is, it is reasonable to assume (or hope) that regional trading blocs will remain 'open', rather than become 'closed'.[57]

We are less confident about both sides of this coin. With respect to the trade diversion argument, it is easy to be persuaded of the opposing view. For example, Stoeckel *et al.*[58] point out that the EU has been remarkably unforthcoming about how it plans to standardize external Non-Tariff Barriers (NTBs), especially quantitative restrictions, in 1992 or thereafter. Some member countries have relatively liberal import policies towards, for example, textiles and automobiles; others much more restrictive policies. On the assumption that the EU adopts a compromise between the Union-wide average protection level for each group of manufactures and the 'lowest common denominator' (the most restrictive), Stoeckel *et al.* project that this would lead to a contraction of imports of $US34 billion per year. In addition, because the EU would lose competitiveness due to higher cost imports, exports would fall by $US58 billion per year (9%). Overall, GNP of the EU would fall by over 1% or $US52 billion.[59]

Now, one might argue, as Lawrence and Litan implicitly do, that it would be economically irrational for the EU to constrain extra-regional trade when this has such self-destructive properties. But this can equally be said of most of the plethora of protectionist policies that have ever been adopted by any country anywhere. In the case of the EU, history suggests that economic rationality has not been the only force at play in the evolution of the Common Market. The Common Agricultural Policy (CAP) has transformed the EU at high cost over the post-war period from the world's largest importer of temperate zone agricultural products to the world's second largest exporter, with massive trade diversionary effects.[60] The rise of the New Protectionism (especially quantitative restrictions) in recent years has been particularly pronounced in both the EU and the USA, both of which figure most prominently in discussions of present or prospective regional trading blocs, as the graph from Stoeckel *et al.*,[61] showing the growth in proportion of imports covered by trade restrictions, amply demonstrates (Figure 5.3).

Jagdish Bhagwati, in a recent trenchant critique of regional trading blocs (which he prefers to call Preferential Trade Agreements) entitled 'Fast Track to Nowhere'[62] points to evidence that Mexico's losses from trade diversion due to NAFTA (and its highly restrictive rules or origin) could be as high as US$3 billion a year. The World Bank has estimated that approximately 36% of Caribbean exports to the

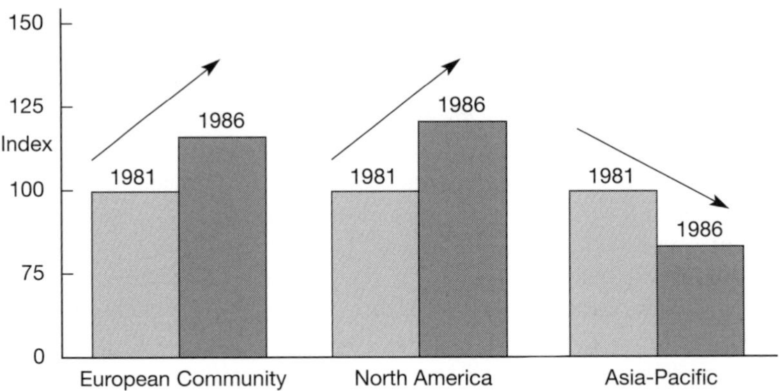

Figure 5.3 Trends in non-tariff barriers in the three regions
Source: Stoeckel *et al., Western Trade Blocks: Game, Set or Match for Asia Pacific and the World Economy?*

US will be subject to potential displacement.[63] Bhagwati argues that as PTA's spread, the world trading system comes to look like a 'spaghetti-bowl' of ever more complicated trade barriers, each depending on the supposed 'nationality' of products (determined by ever more complex and arbitrary rules of origin).

Even if the existence of a hegemonic power is a necessary condition to the maintenance of a liberal trading regime, it clearly is not a sufficient condition – as exemplified by the historical role of the Soviet Union in Eastern Europe and the non-leadership role of the USA in the first third of this century.[64] Similarly, while it may also be the case that the existence of strong centralized institutions in a regional trading bloc is a necessary condition for deep economic integration, it would seem equally hazardous to assume that it is also a sufficient condition.

But this leads us to the first of the two reasons offered by Lawrence and Litan for their relatively positive view of regional trading blocs as conducive to deeper economic integration – negotiations occur among fewer and more like-minded countries than in the multilateral system. Under these circumstances, countries will be more willing to cede the kind of political sovereignty to federalizing central institutions that is required for deeper economic integration. Then presumably once these regional trading blocs have achieved a high degree of economic integration, it is assumed that negotiations between a handful of major trading blocs, all oriented towards progressive trade liberalization, will be conducive to inter-regional economic integration. We are less sanguine than the authors about this scenario.

First, as they would acknowledge, many actual or potential regional trading blocs offer very small prospects for intra-regional trade expansion, even setting aside their effects on external trade. This is true for many actual or potential trading blocs in Africa, Latin America, the South Pacific and the Caribbean, where similarity of natural endowments often sharply limits the potential mutual gains from trade, although the rapid growth in intra-Asian trade suggests more potential for regional trade in manufactured goods.

Second, once one then contemplates more ambitious regional trading blocs, it is difficult to imagine scenarios where a trading bloc is not dominated by one major economic power – either the USA or Japan. It is superficially attractive to characterize the multilateral system as afflicted by the 'convoy problem' in which 'the least willing participant determines the pace of negotiations – the speed of the convoy moving toward free trade is limited by the speed of the slowest ship'.[65] This can be contrasted with the regionalist alternative evoked by Lawrence and Litan through the more appealing metaphor of a geese migration, with the USA (or Japan) as head goose flying in a V-formation with a gaggle of other smaller countries in the same formation eagerly striving to keep up the pace towards at least regional economic integration. But as citizens of one of the smaller countries in such a formation, our judgement, after observing the ferocity of political debates in Canada over adoption of the Canada–US Free Trade Agreement in 1988, is that this entirely ignores political sensitivities to loss of sovereignty. If the virtue of regional trading blocs is their capacity for achieving a deeper degree of economic integration than the multilateral system, this view, as noted earlier, is premised either on a hegemonic theory of trade liberalization or strong federalizing central policy-making and enforcement institutions.

To take the Canada–US or Canada–US–Mexico case, we cannot imagine Canadians (or Mexicans) tolerating an arrangement whereby the USA is free to impose a common set of policies on all three countries across the spectrum of issues being addressed by the EU in its drive to integration (e.g. possibly a common currency, centrally coordinated monetary policy, regulatory and directive powers over many domestic fiscal and regulatory policies). On the other hand, it is equally difficult to imagine the USA accepting a set of federalizing central institutions in which member countries are accorded equal or nearly equal standing (recall the demise of the Havana Charter and the ITO). Thus, we conclude, as the Canada–US FTA and NAFTA largely corroborate, that most regional trading blocs will not be conducive to deep economic integration. We believe the EU is a *sui generis* case. Partly because of the much greater symmetry in size and resources of the participating countries (perhaps about to be tested by the role of a reunified Germany), and partly because of special historical and political considerations largely related to the ravages of recurrent wars, member countries have been prepared to cede significant political sovereignty to federalizing central institutions. Even in the case of the EU, intense internal debates and divisions over the implications for domestic political sovereignty of the Maastricht Treaty suggest growing reservations about this trend.

Third, even if we are wrong, we believe that it is highly speculative to assume that following deep regional integration, regional trading blocs will then readily move to inter-regional economic integration through negotiations with other trading blocs. It is easy to assume that if political forces within each of these blocs have been amenable to regional trade liberalization and perceive the economic gains associated therewith, they would as readily perceive the virtue of just keeping on going, so to speak, and integrating inter-regionally. But the problem here is that regional patterns of integration and specialization that develop may (depending on how much trade diversion is created) significantly exacerbate the adjustment costs of subsequent inter-regional integration, where different patterns of integration and specialization may be entailed.[66] Moreover, regional trading blocs unquestionably place a premium on foreign investment relative to foreign trade (partly because of its domestic employment-enhancement effects), and as foreign firms, principally MNEs, establish substantial presences in each of the major trading blocs, a major political force for broader trade liberalization is attenuated (so-called 'cooperative protectionism').[67]

Fourth, one should not underestimate the sequencing problems in maintaining an 'open' regional trading bloc,[68] in the sense of it remaining open to membership by subsequent Parties. First-movers in such an arrangement face considerable uncertainty in determining the value of the preferences they are receiving in return for putatively deep concessions of their own, when these preferences may be eroded by subsequent admissions to the bloc. This will lead countries to be more reluctant to enter into a bloc in the first place, or to make deep concessions if they do, at least without a right of veto on new memberships (creating hold-out problems). Alternatively, negotiations with all prospective members will need to occur simultaneously, but in this event the large numbers problem said to afflict negotiations in the multilateral system will tend to re-emerge.

Canada had to confront these issues in deciding on its role in the US–Mexico free trade negotiations. The strategy adopted in this case may set the mould for future free trade negotiations between the USA and other Latin American countries. The risk to Canada in staying out of such negotiations was that its preferences in the US market under the FTA would be eroded by similar preferences extended by the USA to Mexico while gaining nothing in return (in contrast to the USA) in terms of enhanced access to Mexico's market for exports and foreign investment. These effects would be exacerbated with each new bilateral agreement that the USA negotiates with another country – in the limiting case, a free trade area from Anchorage to Tierra Del Fuego, in President Bush's words. In turn, there will be strong incentives for export-oriented firms to invest in operations in the USA, relative to other Parties to these bilateral (hub-and-spoke) agreements, because this will assure them of unrestricted access to all affected markets.[69] In recognition of these considerations, Canada joined the negotiations that led to the North American Free Trade Agreement (NAFTA).

The reservations noted above about the economic implications of regional trading blocs constitute strong reasons for being slow to abandon or attenuate the commitment to the non-discriminatory multilateral world trading regime envisaged by the founders of the GATT. Rather, we need a reconceived role (and a more patient set of expectations) for the GATT in promoting Pareto-superior and largely self-enforcing deals between countries on NTB's and other trade distortions in successive bargaining rounds modelled as closely as possible on the tariff-reduction bargaining process that GATT has so successfully facilitated in the past. Reducing most trade distortions to a common metric – a tariff equivalent or effective rate of protection – would be an important first step in pursuing this strategy.

6 Trade policy and domestic health and safety regulation and standards

INTRODUCTION

There has been a dramatic shift in the focus of trade policy concerns from the barriers that lie at the border to the barriers which exist 'within the border'.[1] The GATT/WTO and many other trading arrangements have been largely successful in reducing both the levels of tariffs worldwide and the scale of other border measures such as quotas. This has revealed a new and more subtle category of measures which restrict trade – the numerous commonplace regulations which governments enact to protect the health and safety of their citizens and the environment in which they live. Such regulations vary tremendously across borders: one nation's bunch of grapes is another nation's repository of carcinogenic pesticide residue. This effort to protect citizens from the hazards of everyday life has become a virtual minefield for trade policy-makers, as such differences can often be manipulated or exploited to protect domestic industry from international competition.[2] Even when there is no protectionist intent on the part of lawmakers, through a lack of coordination, mere differences in regulatory or standard-setting regimes can function to impede trade. It has thus become increasingly difficult to delineate the boundaries between a nation's sovereign right to regulate and its obligation to the international trading community not to restrict trade gratuitously. The question of how to address this problem has received increasing attention from trade scholars. As Miles Kahler states, 'the decades-long process of lowering trade barriers resembles the draining of a lake that reveals mountain peaks formerly concealed or (more pessimistically) the peeling of an onion that reveals innumerable layers of barriers.'[3]

There has been a steady growth in the regulations that pertain to health, safety, consumer protection and the environment over the past three decades. In many respects, these regulatory trends can be viewed as part of the elaboration of the modern welfare state in much of the industrialized world, reflecting in part the proposition that greater safety, a cleaner environment, etc. can be thought of as normal economic goods, the demand for which rises as income levels rise, so that greater prosperity (in significant part engendered by trade liberalization) has been accompanied by increased demands for these kinds of domestic policies. As trade liberalization, at least with respect to border measures, has continued to advance, these 'within the border' regulatory measures require new disciplines under international trade rules, particularly in a globalizing economy which, it is argued, has a low tolerance for 'system frictions'.[4]

The allegation that regulations ostensibly designed to protect consumer health and safety are often trade barriers has substantially heightened both domestic and international political conflicts, as trade policy and domestic policy become increasingly linked in domains previously thought to lie outside the arena of trade policy. Regulation in areas which seem purely domestic, such as food inspection, product labelling and environmental policy can all affect how goods cross borders. This has resulted in a polarization of domestic political interests and has drawn new domestic political constituencies into debates over trade policies in the form of consumer and environmental groups or other non-governmental organizations (NGOs) who seek to resist the imposition of constraints on domestic political sovereignty by international trade agreements. As David Vogel notes,

> free trade advocates want to limit the use of regulations as barriers to trade, while environmentalists and consumer advocates want to prevent trade agreements from serving as barriers to regulation. While the trade community worries about an upsurge of 'eco-protectionism' – the justification of trade barriers on environmental grounds – consumer and environmental organizations fear that trade liberalization will weaken both their own country's regulatory standards and those of their nation's trading partners.[5]

This has become a concern in both exporting and importing countries. Domestic producer interests in countries of destination often argue that lax health and safety regulation in countries of origin constitute an implicit and unfair subsidy to foreign producers which should be neutralized, e.g. by countervailing duties or by insistence on foreign countries adopting policies similar to those that obtain in countries of destination.[6] This insistence of across-the-board equivalence raises a number of normative difficulties. How can trade in all goods worldwide really be expected to occur on a level playing field? This proposition seems to be at odds with the theory of comparative advantage which is centrally predicated on nations exploiting their differences (not similarities) in international trade. Few international trade theorists believe any longer that comparative advantage is exclusively exogenously determined, but is significantly shaped by endogenous government polices, including health and safety regulation. Exploiting differences in government policies is no less legitimate than exploiting differences in natural endowments.[7]

A further and at least as potentially a divisive political fault line relating to many of these issues has emerged between developed and developing countries. Many interests in developed countries see the much laxer health and safety standards that often prevail in developing countries as a threat to their more stringent standards by precipitating a race to the bottom. On the other hand, many interests in developing countries see the insistence by interests in developed countries on developing countries adhering to the generally more stringent regulations that prevail in many developed countries (a race to the top) as discriminatory, and an assault on essential features of their international comparative advantage.

This phenomenon has resulted in a number of potential conflicts. For example, the US *Delaney Clause* bars the approval of any food additive found to be carcinogenic. This 'zero-tolerance' approach extends to the pesticide DDT. However, DDT is currently approved for use under the Codex Alimentarius, the international body responsible for establishing standards benchmarks. If Codex levels are exceeded, *prima facie* presumptions that the standard is unduly trade-restricting will arise. The implication is that the US regulation may now be found to be inconsistent with US obligations under the GATT/WTO. This may compel the United States either to allow contaminated food into its market or possibly face retaliatory sanctions.[8] Likewise, labelling has become a sensitive issue, whereby very specific product standards are often required before a specific label can be used, sometimes leading to perverse results. Such was the case when a British sausage maker, wishing to export to Germany, was required to label its product 'pork-filled offal tubes' rather than the more appetizing (and more marketable) title of 'sausages'.[9] Labelling concerns are currently at issue between North America and the EU, particularly in the area of genetically-modified agriculture (biotechnology). Canada and the United States, global leaders in the area, have invested massive resources in the development of this technology which has allowed for large productivity gains. Yet EU markets remain for the most part closed to such products. The EU has further threatened to impose discriminatory labelling schemes, despite the existence of the growing European biotechnology industry.[10]

Within North America, Mexico has recently succeeded in partially overturning an 82-year US ban on Mexican avocados because of the eradication of alleged pests which inhabit the avocado pits. Now imports of Mexican avocados are limited to 19 Midwestern and Northeast states during the winter months only, at the same time that California avocado producers are in low-season. Likewise, Mexican tomatoes have had ongoing difficulties with US market access. Florida's tomato industry has not fared well in the new competitive environment under NAFTA and consequently several actions have been taken to deny Mexican tomatoes access to the US market, including health and safety barriers stemming from concerns relating to irrigation and mulching practices.

From an economic perspective, there is much at stake. The US Department of Commerce recently estimated that in 1993 almost two-thirds of the $465 billion in US merchandise exports worldwide were affected by foreign technical requirements and standards.[11] Market access issues threaten to reduce the gains made in the Uruguay Round in the area of agriculture. The US Department of Agriculture maintains that over 12% of the total $60 billion in US agriculture exports was subject to 'unjustified' trade restrictions involving SPS measures in 1996.[12] Smaller export-driven economies are particularly vulnerable as they lack the resources necessary to comply with multiple regulatory requirements in multiple export markets. The value of a trade agreement and its potential for economic integration is ultimately dependent on the legal and institutional structures that support it. It is now useful to consider how the international legal system has evolved to address these concerns.

This chapter first reviews the legal and jurisprudential foundations to these issues and then explores some of the future policy concerns. Although the focus of this chapter is domestic health and safety standards, environmental issues overlap to some degree with the issues presented. However, this chapter does not deal directly with environmental regulation. For a full discussion of trade and environmental issues, see Chapter 15 of this book.

LEGISLATIVE HISTORY

Successive international trade agreements have attempted to address the issue of standards as non-tariff barriers through increasingly sophisticated legal frameworks. The relevant provisions of three international agreements will be discussed here: GATT/WTO, the NAFTA and the EU. As a starting point, some early work of the OECD is instructive. Although not a trade agreement, the OECD represents the world's major trading economies, and helps to situate the issue in an historical context.

The OECD

The growth in legal instruments addressing the issue of standards in international trade has been relatively recent. Despite this, the Organization for Economic Cooperation and Development (OECD) recognized this as an issue as early as 1972, in the context of environmental regulations in its *Guiding Principles Concerning the International Economic Aspects of Environmental Policies.* These principles have more generally informed trade policy approaches to technical standards. Although these principles do not represent binding legal commitments, they are an early example of attempts to balance the imposition of standards which relate to the valid environmental protection measures of a country on the one hand with the corresponding impacts on trade that measures may have on the other. The principles recognize that valid reasons for divergent standards exist, such as different social objectives or levels of industrialization. The principles also recognize that harmonization, while desirable, would be difficult to achieve in practice. The language in the principles seem to foreshadow the issues that are prominent on the trade agenda today,

> Where valid reasons for differences do not exist, Governments should seek harmonization of environmental policies, for instance with respect to timing and the general scope of regulation for particular industries to avoid the unjustified disruption of international trade patterns and of the international allocation of resources which may arise from the diversity of national environmental standards.
>
> . . .
>
> Measures taken to protect the environment should be framed as far as possible in such a manner to avoid the creation of non-tariff barriers to trade.

Where products are traded internationally and where there could be significant obstacles to trade, governments should seek common standards for polluting products and agree on the timing and the general scope of regulations for particular products.

. . .

It is highly desirable to define in common, as rapidly as possible, procedures for checking conformity to product standards established for the purpose of environmental control. Procedures for checking conformity to standards should be mutually agreed so as to be applied by an exporting country to the satisfaction of the importing country.

(Source: OECD Guiding Principles Concerning the International Economic Aspects of Environmental Policies)

The GATT/WTO

The original GATT as adopted in 1947 does not contain provisions that directly restrict the Contracting Parties' freedom to adopt environmental, health and safety standards.[13] GATT's provisions of general application, however, still apply to such measures. The national treatment provisions found in Article III(4) obligates Parties to treat 'like products' alike within the borders of the importing country. This would thus prevent the discriminatory application of standards between domestic and imported goods, for example, a regulation requiring that milk products be pasteurized regardless of their place of origin would be consistent with the national treatment obligation. But an outright ban on imports of unpasteurized milk products would seemingly conflict with Article XI which prohibits quantitative restrictions against imports. This potential conflict is addressed in the Note to Article III which states that 'any of the measures listed in paragraph 1 which applies to both an imported product and to the like domestic product is to be regarded as an internal measure even if it is collected or enforced in the case of imports at the time or point of importation.'[14] The Note thus resolves this problem by allowing non-discriminatory regulations to apply at the border, essentially making the application of Article III and Article XI mutually exclusive.[15] This implies that an internal regulation which prohibited the sale of unpasteurized milk which had the effect of an absolute ban on imports would be consistent with GATT obligations.

More problematic are the subtle forms of discrimination – those rules which apply equally to foreign and domestic products but discriminate by placing a disparately larger burden on imports. Such *de facto* discrimination is inconsistent with the national treatment obligations under Article III(1), which reads, 'Internal . . . regulations . . . should not be applied to imported or domestic products so as to afford protection to domestic production.' This provision suggests that the complaining Party will bear the onus of proving that a regulation was established to protect domestic industry. This will be a difficult case to make, given the lack of criteria offered to make such a determination. While a violation of Article III(4) is clearly justiciable, it is doubtful whether Article III(1) on its own can be used as a basis for complaint before a GATT panel.[16]

In the event, however, that a regulation is inconsistent with a provision of the GATT, Article XX provides a number of exceptions to such obligations. The portion of Article XX relevant to environmental, health and safety standards reads,

> Article XX
>
> Subject to the requirement that such measures are not applied in a manner which would constitute a means of arbitrary or unjustifiable discrimination between countries where the same conditions prevail, or a disguised restriction on international trade, nothing in this Agreement shall be construed to prevent the adoption or enforcement by any contracting party of measures:
>
> . . .
>
> (b) necessary to protect human, animal or plant life or health; [or]
>
> . . .
>
> (g) relating to the conservation of exhaustible natural resources is such measures are made effective in conjunction with restrictions on domestic production or consumption[.]

GATT case law distinguishes between the *chapeau* language found at the beginning of this text and the areas of substantive exception below it. The purpose of the chapeau language is to prevent Parties from taking undue advantage of the exceptions noted in Article XX, and the burden of proving compliance with the Party relying on such an exception.[17] In general, Article XX has been interpreted narrowly to limit the extent of trade-restrictive environmental, health and safety regulations.[18] In the context of environmental, health and safety regulations, the 'necessary' provision has been interpreted to permit trade-restrictive policies only if no 'less-GATT inconsistent' regulation could be imposed.[19] Esty has commented that this sets a very high hurdle for such policies 'because a policy approach that intrudes less on trade is almost always conceivable and therefore in some sense "available"'. Esty goes so far as to conclude that the strict interpretation of Article XX has effectively eviscerated it as a meaningful exception.[20]

The Tokyo Round

In response to the general perception that the GATT regime was inadequate in dealing with the growing problem of trade distortions arising from disparate national regulations[21], an *Agreement on Technical Barriers to Trade*, or the 'Standards Code' was adopted in 1979 at the Tokyo Round of Multilateral Trade

Negotiations[22] but ratified by only thirty-nine countries.[23] The Standards Code established and elaborated on the principles first introduced in the OECD *Guiding Principles* above. The Standards Code applied to 'all products, including industrial and agricultural products'.[24] It reiterated the national treatment (non-discrimination) obligations of the Contracting Parties in this context and further sought to ensure that technical regulations and standards were not adopted 'with a view to creating obstacles to international trade'.[25] Contracting Parties were urged to work toward the international harmonization of standards[26] and were obligated to adopt such internationally accepted standards, unless inappropriate for reasons which included national security, the protection of human, animal and plant health, technological problems, and climatic and geographical factors.[27] This provision thus shifted the onus of justifying any standard different from the internationally established benchmark to the Contracting Party. Also worthy of note was the obligation to specify standards in terms of their 'performance rather than design or descriptive characteristics'.[28] This provision sought to avoid the potential creation of artificial distinctions based on the intricacies of product design rather than their actual effect.[29] In the event that a Contracting Party did choose to adopt a standard which differed from an international standard or where no such international standard existed, and that standard may have affected trade, notification was required through the GATT Secretariat.[30] With respect to conformity assessment, the Standards Code provided that 'imported products should be accepted for testing under conditions no less favourable than those accorded to like domestic or imported products' and that such procedures should not be more complex or time-consuming than such treatment accorded to like domestic products.[31] The Standards Code also strongly encouraged Parties to adopt a 'mutual recognition' policy, wherever possible, for test results, certificates, and marks of conformity of other Parties.[32]

The Standards Code offered a clear articulation that standards which 'create an unnecessary obstacle to international trade' are not permitted. Such wording implies that there may exist necessary obstacles to trade but no set of criteria was offered in order to determine the dividing line between necessary and unnecessary obstacles to trade. Thus although the Standards Code may be viewed as a helpful first step to reducing the trade-restricting effect of divergent domestic standards, regulations and conformity assessment procedures, its effectiveness was weakened by the fact that it did not address the issue of what exactly constitutes an unacceptable standard. This meant that the complaining Party had the formidable onus of either having to prove 'deliberate protectionist intent, or to demonstrate that the measure went beyond what was "necessary"'.[33] From this legacy came the momentum to make as an objective of the Uruguay Round the development and extension of this legal framework.

The Uruguay Round

The Uruguay Round elaborated the Tokyo Round Standards Code into two new agreements governing standards. *The Agreement on Sanitary and Phytosanitary Measures*[34]

(SPS Agreement) addresses measures designed to protect human, animal and plant life, and health. *The Technical Barriers to Trade Agreement*[35] (TBT Agreement) covers other technical standards and measures not covered by the SPS Agreement. Under the 'umbrella' provisions of the WTO, all Parties to the GATT are obligated to adhere to both of these Agreements.[36] This expanded the number of global imports subject to trade disciplines by approximately $182 billion, according to one estimate.[37]

Agreement on Technical Barriers to Trade

The issues created by technical barriers to trade were recently explored by the US National Research Council. Concerned that standards-related issues were undermining potential gains from trade in the United States, a group of experts were convened to undertake a comprehensive study of the issue. The group, led by prominent trade economist Gary Hufbauer, concluded that 'there is evidence to indicate that significant barriers to global trade are embedded in existing standards and will continue to grow in complexity.'[38] These conclusions were based on the following observations of the group:

> (1) standards that differ from international norms are employed as a means to protect domestic producers; (2) restrictive standards are written to match the design features of domestic products, rather than essential performance criteria; (3) there remain unequal access to testing and certification systems between domestic producers and exporters in most nations; (4) there continues to be a failure to accept test results and certifications performed between domestic producers and exporters in most nations; (4) there continues to be a failure to accept test results and certifications performed by competent foreign organizations in multiple markets; and (5) there is a significant lack of transparency in the systems for developing technical regulations and assessing conformity in most countries.[39]

The TBT Agreement is designed to address such issues. It applies to all products, including industrial and agricultural products, but does not include SPS measures.[40] It covers technical regulations, standards and conformity assessment procedures, as defined in Annex 1 of the Agreement.[41] This could include, for example, regulations governing packaging, recycling or disposal of products, ecolabelling criteria, water or electrical efficiency criteria for household appliances, product noise regulations, and specifications for children's toys. In terms of affirming the right of members to set such standards at the levels they deem appropriate, the preamble to the TBT Agreement contains rather equivocal language.[42] And although there is no positive affirmation of this freedom in the text of the Agreement, members do remain free to choose the level of standards they deem most appropriate, subject to the discipline of the TBT Agreement.

The TBT Agreement is really a more expansive formulation of Article XX, influenced by modern policy concerns and the body of jurisprudence which has interpreted this section. Article 2.1 reiterates a commitment to the cornerstone principles of MFN and national treatment. Article 2.2 of the TBT Agreement states that technical regulations should not be 'prepared, adopted or applied with a view to or with the effect of creating unnecessary obstacles to international trade'. Article 2.2 further states that such regulation should not be 'more trade-restrictive than necessary to fulfill a legitimate objective, taking account of the risks non-fulfilment would create'. This language builds on Article XX by including an open-ended list of permissible legitimate objectives that include *inter alia* the 'protection of human health or safety, animal or plant life or health, or the environment'. To some degree, this amplifies the limited nature of listed exceptions to Article XX. In terms of assessing the risks referred to in the paragraph, Article 2.2 states that 'relevant elements of consideration are, *inter alia*: available scientific and technical information, related processing technology or intended end-uses of products'. This represents a significant departure from the questionable notion in the *Tuna/Dolphin* rulings that National Treatment does not apply to production of these methods (see Trade and Environment chapter), as it may allow differentation based on *how* a product is made, as opposed to the final product itself. Recall that the national treatment and MFN principles apply to 'like' products. Under these rules, therefore, a country could not discriminate based on place of origin between a package of $8\frac{1}{2}\times 11''$ white paper from country A and a package of the same paper from country B. Therefore if an importing country imposed an 'ecotax' on paper manufactured with chlorine bleach, in order to discourage its use and limit the associated harmful environmental effects, it would seemingly be inconsistent with these principles. But Article 2.2 now includes factors for consideration that go beyond the *Tuna/Dolphin* view of determining whether products are 'like' or not, thereby supporting an argument that measures which distinguish between products on the basis of production processes could be now validly justified as national treatment as well.[43]

Members are encouraged to use relevant international standards where they exist, unless such a standard 'would be an ineffective or inappropriate means for the fulfilment of legitimate objectives'.[44] If a Member adopts an international standard, a rebuttable presumption is created that the standard does not create an unnecessary obstacle to trade.[45] Whenever a relevant international standard does not exist or the technical content of a proposed regulation is not in accordance with the relevant international standard and if the technical regulation may have a significant effect on trade of other Members, Members are obligated to publish a notice in a publication at an early stage so as to enable interested parties and other Members to become acquainted with it and to provide opportunities for other Members to make comments in writing on the proposed regulation.[46] Members must also allow a reasonable interval between the publication of technical regulations and their entry into force in order to allow time for producers in exporting countries to adapt their products or methods of production to the requirements of the importing Members.[47]

The TBT Agreement also introduces new obligations in the area of conformity assessment, such as procedures for product testing and inspection and laboratory accreditation.[48] These include the rules that govern who may permissibly certify that a product conforms to certain standards, such as an organization responsible for certifying that a given appliance is deserving of an 'energy efficient' label, or that a given medicine is safe and effective. It is in this area where costs to manufacturers and exporters are most likely to grow in the coming years.[49] There are numerous examples where indefinite delays and/or refusal to certify products, or the lack of recognition of competent laboratory testing in foreign countries has proven to be a significant source of frustration to exporters. This has added needless transaction costs and undermined the goals of economic integration.[50] Many such examples have persisted to serve a protectionist agenda, yet others exist due to a lack of coordination or a lack of effort to address the issue. Articles 5 to 9 set out the basic requirements in this area, and are similar to the obligations described above for technical regulations. Notable is the language encouraging Members to harmonize and/or recognize each others' results of conformity assessment procedures. The effectiveness of such provisions will ultimately depend on their interpretation in the event that a country's conformity assessment procedures are challenged before a panel. One commentator has noted the potential difficulty in interpreting Article 6 which requires 'whenever possible, that the results of conformity assessment procedures in other Members are accepted, even when those procedures differ from their own, provided they are satisfied that those procedures offer an assurance of conformity'.[51]

There are a number of key concerns raised by the TBT Agreement. First, there is a concern among consumer groups that such legislation functions to constrain the ability of Members to set technical regulations and standards at levels they deem appropriate, thereby undermining national political sovereignty and policy autonomy.[52] The TBT Agreement strives to promote international policy convergence, the welfare implications of which are highly ambiguous in many cases.[53] Second, the TBT Agreement does not effectively address the issue of how exactly a panel could go about delineating a validly different standard from a trade-restricting one. While the benchmark of an international standard is clearly given, the subject of risk assessment is not addressed, unlike the comprehensive provisions outlined in the SPS Agreement. This means that if a Member adopts a standard which is more stringent than the international standard it is not required to be justified based on scientific evidence.

It is worth noting, however, that there are benefits of international standardization that go beyond reducing trade frictions. A recent study found that standardization increased technical efficiency, as it made it easier to 'mix and match' among different firms' products.[54] The study also found that allocative efficiency could be increased through standardization, as it reduced information asymmetries between buyers and sellers, and that standardization promotes product compatibility, thereby allowing for increased economies of scale and scope.[55] Moreover, the study found that, based on modern growth theory, standards harmonization 'can offer a competitively neutral form of information exchange capable of promoting cycles of innovation and long-term growth'.[56]

Agreement on Sanitary and Phytosanitary Standards

The WTO Agreement on Agriculture will reduce tariff barriers by an average of 36% over the six years from its inception.[57] This has, and will continue to, increase global trade in agricultural products.[58] As a result, there may be an increase in the number of disputes in the SPS area, because as tariffs continue to fall, there will likely be a corresponding reliance on SPS measures as a source of protection for domestic producers. This underscores the need for a legal framework which can address the fundamental issue of whether a measure validly exists to protect consumers or is merely a sham to protect domestic producers. The SPS Agreement was designed to address this need, and is used primarily as a tool to regulate SPS measures as non-tariff barriers.[59] SPS measures are a highly controversial area of regulation as they concern for the most part the safety of a nation's food supply and consequently have been the focus of intense NGO lobbying efforts. Central SPS issues such as scientific justification and allowable risk are difficult to arbitrate and lie at the heart of a country's sovereignty.

The SPS Agreement adopts the basic structure seen previously in the TBT Agreement and Article XX. It defines an SPS measure to be any number of measures that protect human, animal or plant life or health from pests, contaminants, toxins, disease-carrying organisms, etc.[60] Article 2 sets out the basic rights and obligations of Members. Article 2.1 affirms the right of Members to adopt SPS measures. Members are responsible for ensuring that an SPS measure is applied 'only to the extent necessary' and is based on scientific principles and evidence. Article 5.7 provides a provisional exception to this rule when 'relevant scientific evidence is insufficient', allowing Members to adopt SPS measures 'on the basis of available pertinent information'. Where a Member acts on the basis of Article 5.7, it is required to seek a more objective evaluation based on fuller evidence within a reasonable time. Members are further responsible for ensuring that such measures do not arbitrarily or unjustifiably discriminate against members and that such measures are not applied in a way that would constitute a disguised restriction on trade.

Other provisions amplify the obligations in Article 2.2 and 2.3. Article 3 requires that, to facilitate harmonization, Members base their SPS measures on 'international standards, guidelines or recommendations' wherever possible. Significantly, Article 3.3 makes it clear that a higher level of protection requires scientific justification to be GATT-consistent, whereas any other kind of difference from international standards (i.e. inferior protection) shall be deemed to be GATT-consistent. Measures which conform to international standards will be presumed to be valid. In the absence of harmonization, Article 4 obligates Members to accept the SPS measures of other Members as equivalent, if the exporting Member demonstrates that its measures achieve the same purpose. Article 5 requires that all sanitary and phytosanitary measures be based upon risk assessments that take into account 'risk assessment techniques developed by the relevant international organizations' (Article 5.1).

Many of these concepts pose potential problems in their interpretation and application. First, the requirement that Members may adopt more stringent measures if they are based on 'sound science' seems to imply a 'rigorous cause-and-effect nexus between the empirical evidence and the national regulatory measure chosen'.[61] It is a vague provision which assumes that there exists one objective and correct view of any scientific issue. Science is not a static entity but rather an evolving dialogue within various international communities. As one commentator noted, 'it is by no means obvious . . . that "good science" can be defined with precision in the abstract'.[62] Further, the policy rationale behind many public health measures is precautionary: where there is a small but serious risk, regulators will err on the side of caution.[63] For example, in the United States and Canada, lead was removed from gasoline before the harmful effects were conclusively substantiated with scientific evidence. More recently, there has been strong controversy over BSE disease in cattle and the extent to which measures can be based on tentative scientific evidence. *The Economist* recently noted in reference to this issue that 'responding to a previously unknown disease brings a dilemma. Over-reaction risks diverting scarce resources from real and soluble problems. Under-reaction risks an epidemic.'[64]

The second related area of concern is the distinction between risk assessment and risk management. Measures must take into account international risk assessment methodologies, and be based on scientific research to establish the probability of harm. But the decision on how to manage those risks is more controversial and it is not clear how the SPS Agreement constrains a Member's freedom to make that choice. What constitutes an allowable risk will ultimately reflect the social values of a particular society at a particular stage of development. Is an 'appropriate risk' of a toxic substance one which allows cancer to develop in one out of a thousand, a hundred thousand or one million people? Or should it be zero? Article 5.3 of the SPS Agreement adds a further complication by injecting an economic 'cost-benefit' test into the risk assessment process by taking into account relevant economic factors such as 'the potential damage in terms of loss of production or sales . . . and the relative cost-effectiveness of alternative approaches to limiting risk'.[65] This seems to venture into an uncomfortable area of weighing the value of human health or the environment against more readily measurable economic concerns.[66]

A third concern emanating from environmental and consumer groups relates to the fear that the harmonization process will function to force standards down to the 'lowest common denominator.'[67] Vogel has challenged this proposition, stating that the opposite dynamic can occur, and that trade liberalization has more often functioned to strengthen consumer health and safety standards rather than weaken them.[68] This has been labelled by Vogel as the 'California Effect', referring to the influence that relatively powerful and wealthy green jurisdictions such as California have had in raising health and safety standards through trade. However, the TBT and SPS Agreement strive toward as much harmonization as Members can achieve in an effort to mitigate negative trade effects, which may in fact draw standards downwards. At the very least, high transaction costs are imposed on a country that wishes to pursue a more stringent – or perhaps different – set of regulatory measures that may validly reflect local concerns and tastes. Esty cites the argument that as a matter of political theory, 'decisions should be made at the most decentralized level possible to give maximum scope to local citizens' priorities and preferences . . . those who argue for decentralized decision making believe that access to policymakers and the ability to hold elected officials accountable for their actions is sacrosanct – and lacking in international bodies'.[69] From a welfare perspective, if there are large variances in preferences and the cost of such variance is small (a determination which could be made on a case by case basis), different standards may indeed be welfare-maximizing.[70] Thus the present degree of emphasis on harmonization raises difficult normative issues.

A general characterization of the TBT and SPS Agreements is that they provide a more sophisticated formulation of the principle of non-discrimination contained in Article III of the GATT and a more elaborated set of justifications that must be offered in cases of disparate impact presently dealt with in the exceptions contained in Article XX of the GATT/WTO. While these rules clearly constrain the ability of countries of destination to adopt regulations that have a disparate impact on imports from other countries, they nevertheless leave substantial room for the exercise of national political sovereignty and policy autonomy both in choosing policy objectives (as long as these are not a sham) and policy instruments (as long as these are not disproportionate to the objective, given their effect on trade).[71] In short, if countries generally feel committed to adopting more stringent health, safety, consumer protection, environmental or conservation standards for legitimate (non-trade related) reasons, they remain largely free to do so, subject to demonstrating that there is some rational scientific basis for their actions beyond the impact on international trade, and that such measures do not gratuitously encumber international trade when other less restrictive policy instruments are available to achieve the same objectives.

The NAFTA

The NAFTA provisions with respect to standards are closely similar to the Uruguay Round TBT and SPS Agreements.[72] There are a few important differences, which can be accounted for by the political context in which NAFTA entered into force. The adoption of NAFTA was stalled for two years in an effort to address the concerns of the increasingly powerful NGO community of the United States, particularly consumer, environmental and labour groups.[73] To some extent, the differences that exist between the two agreements reflects the varying degrees of power of the United States in two different trade negotiation contexts. In the trilateral NAFTA negotiations, the United States was by far the dominant economic power, whereas in the case of the multilateral WTO negotiations, its economic power was relatively more balanced. This fact is reflected in the NAFTA as compared to the WTO Agreement, which affords greater latitude to the parties to set health and safety standards at levels they deem appropriate, despite possible trade restricting effects.[74]

TBT Code

NAFTA's TBT Code is found in Chapter 9 and largely reiterates the rights and obligations found in the Uruguay Round TBT Agreement. The right to establish measures 'relating to safety, the protection of human, animal or plant life or health, the environment or consumers' is positively established in Article 904. NAFTA Parties are free to establish the level of protection deemed appropriate and are not obliged to harmonize. This would allow countries to vary in their level of allowable risk.[75] Parties are prevented from establishing standards with a view to, or having the effect of, creating an unnecessary obstacle to trade (Article 904(4)). An unnecessary obstacle to trade will not be deemed to be created where the purpose of the measure is to achieve a legitimate objective, which is defined to include sustainable development as well as the protection of human, animal and plant life, and health. This provides stronger protection for disparate standards than its Uruguay Round counterpart, which states that whenever a technical regulation is created for a legitimate objective and is in accordance with relevant international standards, it 'shall be rebuttably presumed not create an obstacle to trade'.[76] This also represents a departure from the comparable FTA language which used the term 'legitimate domestic objective'. This provision may have been added to permit extraterritorial protection measures, a subject of controversy under the GATT.[77]

The NAFTA TBT Code differs from the Uruguay Round TBT Agreement in that it does not contain an express 'least trade-restrictive' requirement. Both the NAFTA TBT Code and the Uruguay Round TBT Agreement differ from the SPS disciplines in that they permit national regulations to be more stringent than international standards without requiring that those standards be justified by scientific evidence. Article 907 uses permissive language – a Party 'may' take into account available scientific evidence, etc. Again, Article 905 places a premium on the use of international standards by presuming them to be consistent with the obligations under this section.

SPS Code

Trade in agriculture within North America is large and rapidly growing.[78] There is a heavy reliance on the SPS disciplines to facilitate this growth, making the NAFTA model an interesting test case. NAFTA's SPS Code in general contains the same disciplines as outlined above for the SPS Agreement, save for a few exceptions. NAFTA provides a more forceful articulation of the freedom of Parties to adopt such levels of protection as they see fit. Article 712(1) establishes the positive right of a Party to adopt any SPS measure necessary for the protection of human, animal or plant life or health, including measures more stringent than international standards. This is supported by Article 712(2) which states that notwithstanding any other provision, Parties remain free to establish 'appropriate levels of protection'. This has been interpreted as a clear statement that NAFTA countries are not obligated to harmonize their standards.[79] Article 712 contains national treatment language along with the obligation that SPS measures are to be 'applied only to the extent necessary to achieve its appropriate level of protection' and that they may not be applied 'with a view to, or with the effect of, creating a disguised restriction on trade between the Parties'. Article 712(3) requires that SPS measures be based on scientific principles and risk assessment and Article 715 lists the factors that NAFTA countries must take into account when assessing risk and determining appropriate levels of protection. Like the WTO SPS Agreement, Parties are obligated to take international risk assessment methodologies into account along with other scientific considerations. NAFTA also introduces a cost-benefit analysis into the assessment of risk. If a NAFTA Party adopts standards based on international ones, such standards are presumed to be consistent with Article 712 and Parties are obligated to participate in international standardizing organizations. NAFTA 715(3) states that Parties shall 'avoid arbitrary or unjustifiable distinctions' in establishing levels of protection. Article 714 states that the Parties shall, to the greatest extent practicable, pursue equivalence in their SPS measures, as long as levels of protection are not reduced.

NAFTA institutions

NAFTA further established a trilateral intergovernmental institutional structure to support and facilitate the application of the TBT and SPS Codes. A number of committees, subcommittees and working groups meet regularly in order to discuss issues that arise in the context of North American trade.[80] Groups that deal regularly with standards related issues include an SPS Committee and its associated nine technical working groups (including one on pesticides), a Committee on Agricultural Trade and a Committee on Standards-Related Measures with associated subcommittees in the area of land transportation.

The European Union

The Treaty of Rome's central provision with respect to the import restrictions is found in Article 30 which provides that 'quantitative restrictions on imports and all measures having an equivalent effect shall, without prejudice to the following provisions, be prohibited between Member States.' Measures having equivalent effect include trading rules which hinder or have the potential of hindering intra-Community trade.[81] This provision is not absolute – two categories of exceptions exist. First, Article 36 of the Treaty permits exceptions on a number of grounds, including the protection of health and life of humans, animal and plants so long as the measures do not constitute a means of arbitrary discrimination or a disguised restriction on trade. It is possible that this list could be extended to include environmental measures subject to the condition that such measures apply equally to domestic and imported products.[82] Measures which rely on the Article 36 exception must be 'necessary', which has been interpreted in the case law of the European Court of Justice to mean 'that there must be a causal relationship between the measure adopted and the attainment of the objective pursued, and the measure must be the least restrictive method of attaining that purpose'.[83] This requirement thus appears to presage the comparable requirements of the WTO and NAFTA.

The second exception, referred to as the 'rule of reason', is found in the early jurisprudence of the EU.[84] It illustrates how the scope of the Treaty of Rome was extended beyond measures that discriminated on their face against non-domestic products to those that merely had a disparate impact. In its 1979 *Cassis de Dijon* decision,[85] the European Court of Justice held that a German law that prohibited the sale of the liqueur Cassis with less than 25% alcohol content violated Article 30 of the Treaty. It prevented the import of French cassis which had an alcohol content below 20%. However, the Court suggested that where measures are not facially discriminatory but have a disparate impact, they may be saved if they are necessary in order to satisfy mandatory requirements related in particular to the effectiveness of fiscal supervision, the protection of public health, the fairness of commercial transactions, and the defence of the consumer. The test of necessity involves consideration of whether alternative measures less restrictive of intra-Union trade might adequately satisfy the mandatory requirements at issue. Hence, if the goal was to ensure that consumers were not misled by an assumption about the domestic product into thinking that the foreign product contained an equivalent amount of alcohol, labelling requirements would suffice. Similarly, in its 1987 *German Beer Standards* decision,[86] the Court impugned a German law which required that any product sold with the label 'beer' in Germany meet Germany purity standards. The Court reasoned that consumers could be informed of the difference between beers through the use of appropriate labelling requirements. Where health risks are claimed as a basis for content requirements that affect trade, and where less stringent requirements are in place elsewhere in the Union, the Court places some burden on the defendant Member State to produce empirical evidence of the risks in question.

STANDARDS SETTING BODIES

All of the trade agreements listed above rely heavily on the work of international standardizing organizations. As they largely immunize domestic standards from attack, their work is extremely important. The stringency of a country's chosen standard *vis-à-vis* the comparable international standard is key to an initial determination of whether such a measure is or is not consistent with the given trade agreement. This naturally puts such hitherto 'back room' organizations in a new light. How are such institutions governed? To whom are they accountable? To what extent do they permit public participation? How are their standards actually developed?

The international standards system

There are a number of international standardizing bodies mentioned in the text of the trade agreements. In the case of SPS measures, both the NAFTA and WTO refer to the Codex Alimentarius Commission, the International Office of

Epizootics, and the international and regional organizations operating within the framework of the International Plant Protection Convention. In the case of TBT measures, both the NAFTA and WTO refer to the International Organization for Standardization (ISO), the International Electrotechnical Commission (IEC), Codex Alimentarius Commission, the Food and Agricultural Organization (FAO) and the World Health Organization (WHO).

The most important non-governmental international standards development institution is the International Organization for Standardization (ISO), a world-wide federation of national standards bodies from over 100 countries.[87] It was founded in 1946 and has been the most prolific author of international standards to date, generating standards in almost all areas except for electrical standards, which is governed by the International Electrotechnical Commission (IEC).[88] ISO members are comprised of the national bodies 'most representative of standardization in its country'. The technical work of the ISO is highly decentralized and is carried out by over 2,700 technical committees, subcommittees and working groups which are coordinated by a central secretariat located in Geneva.

Within the ISO, each member body has the right to be represented on a committee if it has an interest in a subject. Standards are developed by a consensus process in order to be inclusive of the views of all stakeholders. They represent industry-wide interests, seek to promote global solutions and are voluntary. Standards are developed according to a six-step process. The ISO has developed these rules, on the whole, without controversy. But despite the wide membership, Esty notes that there are only 'limited opportunities for public involvement' and often the only people at the meetings are business representatives from industry. This view is supported by Audley who additionally notes that the fact that only one organization per country can be represented at the meetings compounds NGO efforts 'to overcome technical and financial constraints that already greatly limit their participation in meetings'.[89]

Some difficulties associated with ISO are apparent with the work of ISO 14000, responsible for setting standards for industry environmental management systems. The ISO 14000 certification process requires a combination of adherence to national standards as well as compliance with voluntary standards, as enforced by a third party auditor. Audley notes that the information provided to those auditors 'is not necessarily available to the public, thereby restricting interest groups from access to performance data normally used to watchdog industry performance'.[90]

The lack of public participation has encouraged discussion in other multilateral fora which may shape the work of ISO, thereby improving the process.[91] A recent trilateral meeting of stakeholders in the ISO process outlined the concerns associated with the ISO process, which mainly centred around the ability of developing countries to comply or adapt to standards. International standards are perceived to be largely driven by multinational enterprises, eager to establish global standards and take advantage of decentralized global production processes. Developing countries are particularly concerned that such standardizing processes not be used in a way that excludes them from participation in the global marketplace, noting that 'developed countries are capable of formulating demanding requirements since they have more chances of observing them' and that 'norms in developing countries are a mutilated copy of standards prepared in developed countries; and therefore, they do not project the real possibility for implementing them.'[92] There is further concern that the extra costs of the technology that developing countries require to comply with standards and related certification process may increase the price of their products and undermine comparative advantages.[93] The 'right' of a country to choose its own standards as enunciated in a trade agreement must be evaluated in the context of the economic realities that surround it. As a simple reality of participating in the global marketplace, countries may be forced to standardize to gain market access or because customers and suppliers demand it. Smaller and less economically significant nations will in essence become 'regulation takers', thereby supplanting their own choice of domestic regulation in favour of the dominant market's choice.[94]

The Codex Alimentarius Commission was established in 1962 as a joint undertaking of the UN Food and Agricultural Organization (FAO) and the World Health Organization (WHO). It has over 130 Member States and is responsible for 'protecting the health of the consumers and ensuring fair practices in the food trade' as well as preparing and coordinating all food standards undertaken by international governmental and non-governmental organizations.[95] A recent report by the OECD noted that 'the Codex is believed to become the focal point for regulatory design in the agro-food sector' which has led to an increased interest on the part of firms seeking to promote their own interests.[96] The Codex has been criticized for its closed-door policy and its lack of 'established protocols for ensuring a rational outcome based on scientific evidence'.[97] Codex has evaluated more than 187 pesticides, 523 food additives, and 57 food contaminants. It has also established over 3,019 maximum residue limits for pesticides, many of which are significantly less stringent in the United States, creating a potentially fertile source of trade conflict.[98] In the recent *Beef Hormones* dispute, the Codex standards were key to the ruling against the EU, despite the fact that the Codex standard for hormones 'was adopted by a vote of 33–29 with seven abstentions, [h]ardly a ringing endorsement of the safety of eating hormone-processed meat'.[99]

SELECTED CASE-LAW

Given the increased linkage between trade policy and domestic policy, trade panels are now forced to grapple with issues beyond conventional trade problems in areas such as scientific evidence. Only a fraction of disputes that involve standards-related issues actually reach the panel stage where other avenues have failed such as intergovernmental negotiations or diplomatic intervention, and often involving large industries who are able to devote significant resources to such conflicts.

One particular difficulty is the application of the 'least trade restrictive' test. This question was considered in the GATT panel case of *Thai Cigarettes*, where the Thai government imposed a ban on foreign cigarettes in order to protect the health of its citizens, while allowing the sale of domestic cigarettes through a state-owned industry. In this case, the panel ruled against the Thai government, and found that the same policy goal could be achieved with instruments less restrictive of trade that did not discriminate between domestic and foreign goods.[100] The panel suggested that a ban on advertising or an increase in prices could possibly have been less objectionable policy alternatives to an outright ban. This decision sparked concerns about a GATT panel 'second-guessing' the Thai government's decision about what policy was most appropriate to reduce smoking among its citizens.

The difficulties that can arise in operationalizing a least trade restrictive means or proportionality test are illustrated by the *Danish Bottles* case, where the European Commission challenged a Danish regulation established in 1981 requiring that all beer and soft drinks be sold in returnable containers that could be refilled.[101] These containers had to be pre-approved by the Danish environmental protection agency, in order to ensure that they were suitable for recycling and that a sufficient proportion of the returned containers would actually be reused.

Following complaints by firms in other Member States denied market access for non-compliance with this regulation, the Commission encouraged Denmark to change its laws. In 1984, Denmark permitted non-approved containers on the condition that the total non-complying containers not exceed 3,000 hectolitres annually per firm and that a deposit and return system was established. This legislation also failed to satisfy the Commission, which declared that the deposit and return scheme as well as the agency approval scheme was incompatible with Article 30 of the Treaty of Rome as it 'constituted a measure having an equivalent effect to a quantitative restriction'.[102]

On appeal to the European Court of Justice (ECJ), the Court in September 1988 found Denmark's requirements regarding the mandatory disposal and recycling of empty containers to be legal. The ECJ applied the *Cassis de Dijon* reasoning and ruled the recycling scheme as 'an indispensable element of a system intended to ensure the reuse of containers and therefore . . . necessary to achieve the aims pursued by the contested rules. That being so, the restrictions which it imposes on the free movement of goods cannot be regarded as disproportionate.'[103] Here the ECJ effectively sidestepped the issue of discrimination and a consideration of whether the rule of reason extended to measures that although facially neutral placed a larger burden on foreign firms.[104]

However, the ECJ found the restriction of 3,000 hectolitres per year per firm to be inconsistent with Article 30, stating that although the system for Danish containers offered superior environmental protection, the non-conforming containers were still 'environmentally-friendly' as they were subject to a deposit and return scheme as well. Accordingly, the ECJ applied a 'least trade restrictive' test and found that this restriction failed, as a less trade restrictive alternative existed. One commentator noted that this ruling does not achieve the same high level of environmental protection as the more trade-restrictive alternative. Thus the ECJ seems to have conducted an implicit balancing test between the two objectives of environmental protection and the free movement of goods, resulting in a lower level of protection than originally chosen by the country.[105]

The *Danish Container* case finds close echoes in Canada. Following two GATT panel decisions[106] holding various aspects of Canadian (mostly provincial) regulation of liquor distribution (mostly beer) in violation of Article XI, Article III, and Article II of the GATT and not saved by any of the exceptions in Article XX, the Ontario government in April 1992 announced the imposition of a ten-cent per container tax on non-refillable (albeit recyclable) beer containers, in order ostensibly to promote the use of refillable containers (bottles), which were asserted to be more environmentally congenial. As a background fact, about 90% of Canadian beer is sold in bottles, while about 90% of US beer is sold in containers and in terms of access to the Canadian market, the ability of US breweries to export beer into Canada in cans was crucial to their ability to compete effectively with domestic breweries. The imposition of the can tax provoked a highly acrimonious dispute between the Canadian and US governments, leading the US government to impose retaliatory tariffs on exports of Canadian beer to the US and the Canadian government to counter-retaliate by imposing tariffs on US beer exports into Canada. The dispute was finally resolved through a negotiated agreement, and thus the can tax was never challenged before a GATT panel. Had it been, any such panel would have faced very similar issues to those which arose in *the Danish Container* case, although given the long history of disputes between the EU and the US on the one hand, and Canada on the other, over protectionist policies adopted by Canadian federal and provincial governments towards the brewing industry in Canada, one might have been more readily inclined to conclude that the measure was a 'sham' or 'colourable', in the absence of compelling evidence that recyclable cans (which were already subject, like bottles, to a deposit and return system) were less environmentally friendly than refillable bottles – a proposition that is apparently not scientifically obvious.[107] It further raises questions about the extent to which policy consistency within an administration is an appropriate factor to consider in making this judgment, as a similar requirement was not imposed on pop or juice aluminum cans, whose numbers far outweigh beer cans in Ontario.

The WTO Appellate Body has recently dealt with the question of whether a health regulation was discriminatory as applied to foreign firms in the context of reformulated gasoline. In a recent effort to reduce air pollution, the United States established two gasoline programmes under the auspices of the *Clean Air Act*. The programmes provided that in specific high pollution areas as measured by ozone concentration, only 'clean' reformulated gasoline could be sold, which meant that it had to be blended with ethanol, a cleaner burning octane enhancer produced from corn. This required a significant capital expense on the part of reformulated gasoline producers, so an interim standard was allowed over a five-year phase in period until a fixed standard became effective. This interim standard was calculated using a formula that began with a 1990 baseline and would reduce the amount of olefines (an ozone producing chemical) yearly on a percentage basis.[108] Foreign producers, however, were not permitted to use their 1990 baseline, but a statutory baseline, which often imposed a stricter burden on them. Venezuela and Brazil, the leading exporters of gasoline to the United States, filed a complaint with the GATT/WTO claiming that the regulation violated

Article III as it treated like products differently, based on their country of origin. With respect to the economic and environmental stakes, the Venezuelan company stood to lose $150 million year, after it had undergone significant capital expenses based on previous US regulations in order to be able to export to the United States. As well, the regulation was only moderately effective in achieving the stated standard – clean air.[109] In this way, an 'end-means' test begins to enter into the jurisprudence, which questions the actual efficiency and effectiveness of a regulation in achieving its stated goal.

The WTO panel found that the US regulation violated Article III:4 of the GATT by treating foreign gasoline less favourably than domestic gasoline. Interestingly, the panel declined to rule on whether the US had violated Article III:1, in reply to the argument advanced by Venezuela and Brazil that the measure was 'applied so as to afford protection to domestic production.' This seems to highlight the reluctance of trade panels to impute *male fides* on the part of an offending country. In considering whether the measure was 'saved' by the exceptions of Article XX, the panel first examined Article XX(b) and the question of whether the measure was 'necessary' to protect animal and plant life. The panel regarded its task as asking the question of whether there were less trade-restrictive alternatives available in achieving the policy goal, rather than the necessity of the environmental goal. It found that there were more flexible ways of determining a baseline level for foreign producers than a statutory standard, and hence there were indeed less-trade restrictive alternatives available to the United States in achieving its stated policy goal. In considering Article XX(g), and whether the measure 'related to the conservation of exhaustible natural resources', the panel used the 'primarily aimed at' test as enunciated in the 1987 decision on *Herring and Salmon.* The panel found 'no direct connection between less favourable treatment of imported gasoline that was chemically identical to domestic gasoline and the US objective of improving air quality in the United States' and therefore were 'not primarily aimed at the conservation of natural resources.' The panel found it unnecessary at that point to consider whether the measures were inconsistent with the TBT Agreement.

The Appellate Report largely upheld the panel's findings. It did, however, take issue with its legal reasoning under Article XX(g) stating that 'the phrase "primarily aimed at"' is not itself treaty language and was not designed as a simple litmus test for inclusion or exclusion from Article XX(g), thereby calling into question the precedential value of the *Herring and Salmon* case.

The first decision by a WTO panel on the SPS Agreement entailed the long-standing dispute between the US and the EU in the *Beef Hormones* case.[110] In this case, the United States initially filed a complaint against the EU under the GATT Tokyo Round Standards Code, alleging that a 1988 EU Directive banning the sale of hormone-fed beef in the EU had no basis in scientific evidence of a health danger from human consumption of the hormones. The EU viewed the ban as a legitimate response to public concerns about use of hormones as growth stimulants, while admitting that there was little scientific support for these concerns. The more technical legal disagreement surrounded whether the Code applied to standards which were not product standards in the strict sense but applied to the 'process or production method' (PPM) by which a product was produced (clearly, the ban on hormone-fed beef went to the method of production of the beef). The EU claimed that the Code did not apply to PPMs. The United States, however, invoked a provision of the Code that suggested PPMs would be covered in circumstances where their effect was to circumvent the primary obligations of the Code not to create 'unnecessary obstacles to trade.' A technical panel under the Code was never established to decide the matter, since the EU refused to accept its jurisdiction, arguing that the Code did not apply at all to the kind of measure at issue. The EU was prepared to have a special panel of legal experts address the threshold issue of the Code's jurisdiction over the dispute, but this was unacceptable to the United States.

The US subsequently revived the complaint under the new SPS Agreement. A WTO panel upheld its complaint in an important decision in September 1997.[111] The panel held that for five of the six growth hormones in dispute, international (Codex) standards existed, which the EU ban did not conform to, casting the burden of proof on the EU to demonstrate that its more stringent standards were based on a scientific risk assessment, which it failed to do. In the case of the sixth hormone, for which an international standard did not exist, the panel similarly held that the EU ban was not based on a scientific risk assessment. The panel concluded that the EU measure was unjustified, as it violated three separate provisions of the SPS Agreement: (1) the measure was not based on a risk assessment; (2) the measure was inconsistent in its application as it allowed a chemical with similar effects to be used for swine thereby tolerating a difference in risk levels; and (3) the measure was not based on an international standard.[112]

Charnovitz is critical of this decision, stating that the panel essentially reinforced all the negative stereotypes about the GATT/WTO and the environment, stating that

> [i]nstead of nudging the [EU] Commission, the Hormone Panel bludgeoned it [as it complained about] the EU's legislative process, cast doubt on whether zero risk would ever be permitted under SPS, accused the Commission of disguised protectionism, and contrasted hormone regulation with the regulation of other carcinogens. Such broad criticism increases the number of people who will find fault with the panel's analysis.[113]

The recent Appellate Body decision in this case largely upheld the findings of the panel report and does not change the finding that the ban was inconsistent with the provisions of the SPS Agreement. However, one commentator noted that the areas where the Appellate Body did reject the findings of the original panel 'could make it more difficult for countries to successfully challenge sanitary measures that were stricter than international standards'.[114]

The Appellate Body addressed the issue of burden of proof, a point not clearly resolved in the SPS Agreement, yet 'pivotal to the U.S. government's victory'.[115] The panel essentially regarded the failure to use international standards as a *prima facie* violation of the SPS Agreement, with the burden of proof then shifting to the party taking the measures to justify them pursuant to one of the two routes available. On this point, the Appellate Body found that there was no basis in the SPS Agreement text for giving the various provisions in question this structure. Rather, the Appellate Body noted the language which suggests that harmonization is not a self-standing obligation under the SPS Agreement, but rather it creates a balance between the legitimate rights of states to maintain regulatory diversity or distinctiveness and the need to reduce the trade-distorting impact of regulatory diversity. The Appellate Body suggested that the panel had not properly appreciated this balance – for instance, by holding that measures based on international standards must conform to such standards. The language 'based on' implies, as the Appellate Body correctly suggested, a greater scope for diversity in the detailed measures themselves than the notion of conformity, implying something closer to full-blown harmonization. Finally, the Appellate Body corrected the overly narrow notion of risk assessment adopted by the panel in its interpretation of the SPS Agreement; risk assessment can include real world considerations, such as the degree of risk that may occur due to improper handling or precautions, or ineffective regulatory control of abuses. The Appellate Body stated that,

> [i]It is essential to bear in mind that the risk that is to be evaluated in risk assessment under Article 5.1 is not only risk ascertainable in a science laboratory under strictly controlled conditions, but also risk in human societies as they actually exist, in other words, the actual potential for adverse effects on human health in the real world where people live and work and die.[116]

Ultimately, the Appellate Body found that there must be a reasonable relationship between risk assessment and the measures undertaken, a notion that allows for some deference to complex social trade-offs within the risk regulation process and differences of scientific opinion, while at the same time imposing a requirement that there be some rational relationship between the risks identified, however broadly conceived, and the measures adopted. The Appellate Body concluded, however, that the European Community had in fact not provided a risk assessment related to risks from inadequate control of abuses, and so these considerations could not justify its measures.

In regard to Article 5.5 which speaks to consistency in the application of an SPS measure, the Appellate Body reversed the findings of the panel. The panel had ruled that the EU had violated Article 5.5 in applying the SPS measure inconsistently. In order to establish a violation of Article 5.5, three elements have to be proved. The first is that the Member establishing the measure must have done so in several situations. The second is that 'those levels of protection must exhibit arbitrary or unjustifiable differences in their treatment of different situations' and the third element is that these differences result in a disguised restriction of international trade.[117] These elements were not established by the US.

The *Beef Hormones* decision raises a number of concerns relating to difficulties in the adjudication of scientific issues. Wirth writes,

> Social value choices necessarily intrude into the analysis of physical phenomena by means of risk assessment methodologies through the selection of inferences and assumptions. Consequently, there is unlikely to be a single, unique way to analyze even the purely scientific significance of much empirical data. As a result, in a regulatory context science may be least helpful when there is a genuine scientific dispute.[118]

He further notes that scientific questions do not always lend themselves to a 'yes' or 'no' answer that is demanded by an adversarial adjudication process. At issue is also the fact that technical questions are not necessarily fully understood or appreciated by trade panels, which are often composed of diplomats and lawyers.

Absent full harmonization, the issue of equivalency and mutual recognition becomes especially salient. The problem of mutual recognition of SPS measures was dealt with in the *UHT Milk* case in 1992, where Canada initiated an action against the United States under Chapter 18 of the FTA regarding ultra-high temperature milk.[119] After 14 years of trouble-free exports to Puerto Rico, UHT milk from Quebec was denied entry on the basis that it did not comply with recently adopted Puerto Rican health and safety standards. The Canadian government claimed that these standards, at least as applied to the facts in issue, were a sham, and were more properly characterized as a barrier to trade and an outright violation of the FTA. The US government claimed that it was free to set its own health and safety standards, and that its obligations under the FTA did not diminish that freedom.

In an effort to increase milk sales, Puerto Rico had adopted new regulations requiring that milk originating outside of Puerto Rico must either comply with specific pasteurizing requirements or have been processed under 'substantially similar regulations' and be inspected by a state official certified by the US Food and Drug Administration (FDA). Submissions were made to the FDA demonstrating that the technical standards under which UHT milk from Quebec was produced was at least equivalent to the new Puerto Rican regulations. The FDA denied this request for equivalency and revoked the licence of the Canadian firm which exported the milk on the basis of non-compliance. The FDA was unwilling to conduct an equivalency study and certify Canadian inspectors unless such a study formed part of a broader solution to dairy trade between Canada and the United States. The FDA did not feel that it was able to justify the expense involved to provide relief to only one Canadian firm.[120] Numerous diplomatic and intergovernmental interventions followed. The issue was discussed at the *Technical Working Group on Dairy, Fruit, Vegetable and Egg Inspection* and a 'UHT Subcommittee' was even established under the auspices of this technical working group to consider issues relating to equivalency. These efforts were ultimately unsuccessful.

Canada argued that the regulation violated national treatment, as although the regulations applied equally to domestic and imported milk, the failure to allow a demonstration of equivalency made it impossible for Quebec producers to meet the requirements easily met by US producers.[121] Canada also noted that Puerto Rico failed in its obligation to facilitate trade by establishing equivalency, pursuant to its obligations under the FTA which requires the parties to 'facilitate trade in agricultural products' by working together 'to improve access to each other's markets through the elimination or reduction of import barriers'. Canada further argued that Article 708.1 was breached by the failure to 'make equivalent their respective technical regulatory requirements and inspection procedures' where harmonization was not feasible and by the failure of Puerto Rico to 'establish equivalent accreditation procedures for inspection systems and inspectors' by its insistence that only FDA certified inspectors could be employed to evaluate Quebec UHT milk. Finally, Canada argued that the regulation was a disguised restriction on trade designed to protect domestic UHT production.[122]

The United States argued that it had the right to maintain and upgrade technical regulations for the protection of human, animal and plant life and it is the responsibility of the foreign producer to comply with such legitimate health regulations. The United States further argued that the upgrading of standards does not make them a restriction on trade and the safety and quality of the milk supply is a legitimate policy objective. Alternatively, if the FTA had been breached, then the GATT Article XX(b) exception for health and safety was applicable. The United States further argued that the denial of a licence was fully consistent with national treatment as standards do not vary between imported and domestic product and that equivalency rests with the discretion of the Puerto Rican authorities.[123]

The panel prefaced its remarks by affirming that the setting of standards is a significant prerogative of states and stated that the central issue was one of determining equivalency and the appropriate standard by which equivalency should be judged. The panel ruled that Article III should not be examined on general GATT principles, but rather the case should be decided on the more specific FTA provisions. Consequently, the panel abstained from determining whether national treatment had been violated. The panel rejected Canada's argument that the United States had failed to work together to facilitate access to each other's markets as only a *best efforts* type obligation was imposed on the Parties, the observance of which is fundamentally a matter of acting in good faith, the absence of which was not demonstrated. The panel further noted that as no time limits are specified in the FTA for the resolution of either harmonization or equivalency, the rules are not strictly mandatory. The panel concluded that the Puerto Rican rules did not constitute an arbitrary or unjustified restriction on trade, because in the absence of an equivalency study it was unclear whether any other measure would provide the level of health protection sought by those rules. However, somewhat surprisingly, the panel concluded by finding that there had been 'non-violation nullification and impairment' of Canada's reasonably expected benefits under FTA Article 2011 and recommended that an equivalency study be conducted within a reasonable period (preferably two months), with sharing of costs, and that Quebec UHT milk be readmitted to the Puerto Rican market if Quebec standards were found to have the same effect as the Puerto Rican standards. Interestingly, again, the panel sidestepped the issue of determining whether the measures afforded 'protection to domestic production' or were a 'disguised restriction on trade', perhaps out of concern for embarrassing a party to the dispute.

One commentator has argued that although the question before the panel related to substantive equivalency and comparison of the standards governing the production of milk, this was not the legal issue before the panel.[124] Rather, the panel 'had to consider only the narrower issue of whether an opportunity to prove equivalency had been offered at an appropriate time and in an appropriate manner'.[125] Thus the question before the panel was one of legal process (were the rules followed?) rather than one of substance (are the production methods equivalent?). While it was not for the panel to make technical determinations, the Panel still failed to determine whether the process differences, that is, the failure to grant equivalency in a timely manner, constituted a violation of national treatment obligations. In the case of the obligations imposed on the Parties under Articles 703 and 708 (the provisions which obligate the Parties to work together to achieve market access through harmonization, mutual recognition, etc.), the panel made its decision on the narrowest interpretation possible, supporting the contention that because certain obligations are not 'hard', they are therefore virtually non-existent. The Parties are under a reasonable duty to facilitate trade under these Articles, despite the absence of specific time limitations. This affords wide latitude to Parties in the imposition of health and safety measures which could be barriers to trade. Under such an interpretation, Parties could effectively use stalling tactics, and delay equivalency studies in the name of consumer protection.

FUTURE POLICY DIRECTIONS

Apart from being an issue addressed by the legal texts and jurisprudence of international trade agreements, the interface between trade and domestic regulation has been receiving increasing attention from the international policymaking community. The OECD recently completed a comprehensive two-year project designed to study how countries may address these problems through regulatory reform in a number of areas, including domestic health and safety standards.[126] Such reform is considered to be necessary to enhance competition and reduce regulatory costs, which will in turn 'boost efficiency, bring down prices, stimulate innovation, and help improve the ability of economies to adapt to change and remain competitive'.[127]

The report provides a review of the net negative effects on an economy and on trade that standards and conformity assessment procedures may have. Those issues which call for policy consideration include three categories of the domestic regulation and trade interface: regulations which are excessively trade-restrictive; divergences in regulatory requirements; and regulations biased toward domestic interests. The discussion and analysis of the trade and domestic regulation interface largely build upon and elaborate the principles (i.e., national treatment, least-trade restrictive measures, policy transparency) discussed in this chapter. The report classifies recent approaches to reform into four categories: (1) standards development and conformity assessment procedures; (2) surveillance mechanisms for standards-related measures; (3) development of mutual recognition agreements (MRAs); and (4) increased business concerns and emerging initiatives.[128] From this analysis, a number of policy recommendations were set forth for consideration and subsequent implementation on the part of the OECD ministers.

With respect to the first category, a number of initiatives have emerged in the standards development process in an effort to reduce regulatory inefficiencies, one of which is the proliferation of voluntary standards. The report notes that 'although voluntary standards run a greater risk of being captured by private interests than mandatory standards (which calls for domestic and international surveillance), they are by nature more market driven and more capable of flexibility in the face of technological development'.[129] Consequently, the report recommends that countries periodically review standards development processes according to efficiency criteria.

The report also recommends increased use of harmonization to avoid trade friction, accompanied by an ongoing rigorous review of international standards. The report notes the possible efficiency gains and the increased transparency of a harmonization strategy, which may be appropriate on a case-by-case basis. The report further proposes a rationalization of conformity assessment procedures, urging that countries regulate in proportion 'to the intensity of the social concern or the risk involved' and engage in either pre-market or post-market surveillance according to the relative risk of the product. For example, sensitive medical devices or pharmaceuticals may require approval before entering a market, while lower risk products, such as electrical safety regulations for appliances, may be more appropriately regulated by post-market surveillance mechanisms. The report also recommends increased vigilance regarding anti-competitive actions in the area of conformity assessment procedures. This concerns primarily the accreditation of the laboratories that certify various products, etc. In the past, national accreditation bodies have had a virtual monopoly on the right to test and certify products, to the exclusion of any foreign competition.

With respect to the second category, international oversight of standards-related measures, the report calls for a strengthening of such regimes. International oversight is another term for the TBT and SPS Agreements currently in place under the WTO. It has been referred to by Sykes as 'policed decentralization' which means that 'national authorities are largely free to pursue their own policy objectives but must do so subject to a set of broadly applicable legal constraints'.[130] Increased surveillance could be undertaken by ensuring that such agreements are fully implemented; by extending the scope of measures covered; by clarifying obligations of the parties; and by encouraging the active participation of stakeholders in the process, particularly business stakeholders.[131] The report further encourages increased multi-stakeholder domestic surveillance of the trade impacts of standards and procedures.

The third category, the development of MRAs, is one of the more promising solutions to the tension between trade and domestic regulation. An MRA can apply to standards, conformity assessment or testing data. They have not been widely used to date, and consequently the report recommends the 'expanded recognition of conformity assessment of other jurisdictions through arrangements such as MRAs'.[132] One policy option for MRAs is the adoption of the principle 'once approved, accepted everywhere'. This is a quasi-MFN approach: once a product is deemed to be in compliance with a relevant standard in one country, that product could move freely without further restrictions or requirements.

The report describes the expected benefits of the increased use of MRAs with respect to conformity assessments to include improved trade opportunities and efficiencies as well as the streamlining of domestic regulatory systems. Concerns related to MRAs include the possibility that trade with non-participants will be impeded, and that MRAs will lead to a 'race to the bottom' as countries seek to gain competitive advantages through lax regulatory enforcement.[133] The mutual recognition approach has been a cornerstone principle in the EU's quest for a single market, which has been largely successful, albeit among relatively homogeneous nations. Efforts beyond the EU have been limited as such agreements have been for the most part bilateral and confined to a specific product. The financial implications are significant – the US Department of Commerce forecasts a savings of over $100 million per year if planned MRAs with the EU are implemented.[134] Indeed, comprehensive draft texts of MRAs are already well underway in various fora. The EU, building on its experience within the single market, has either concluded or is in the process of negotiating MRAs with Canada, the United States, Japan, Australia and New Zealand.[135] The draft MRA text between the US and the EU covers in comprehensive detail *inter alia* electrical safety, recreational craft, pharmaceutical good manufacturing processes, and medical devices.[136] Likewise, within the prospective Free Trade Area of the Americas (FTAA), a Working Group has been established to consider the development of future MRAs.[137] Within Asia Pacific Economic Cooperation (APEC), the Osaka 'Action Agenda' included MRAs as one of its non-binding goals, in part to respond to the increasing problem of divergent health and safety standards.[138] This has resulted in the completion of a pilot project which has produced the 'APEC Mutual Recognition Arrangement for Foods and Food Products'. Next on the agenda for APEC MRAs is electronic equipment safety arrangements.[139]

Last, there is potential for reform through emerging initiatives within business sectors. The report notes that 'as product life cycles are shortened by rapid technological development and trade opportunities are expanded by globalization, obstacles arising from product standards and conformity assessment have increased business concerns'.[140] This observation, along with the transparency issues arising from the decentralization of the standards development process and the fact that firms themselves often are the sole owners of specialized technical expertise, have led to the proposition that firms rather than governments may be in a better position to pioneer regulatory reform. Such a dynamic is evidenced by the Trans-Atlantic Business Dialogue (TABD), established in 1995, which has made contributions to the reform process by, for example, developing recommendations toward the 'functional equivalence of regulatory standards'.[141]

CONCLUSIONS

To some extent, the legal texts reviewed in this chapter obscure the difficulties that a panel will be required to make when adjudicating legal questions. Supranational panels will face a number of challenges in ruling on the issues posed in this chapter. Such challenges lie at the heart of trade panels' competence and legitimacy. There are essentially three fundamental 'tests' that a panel may apply when deciding whether a domestic health or safety measure is consistent with a country's international trade obligations.

One central test seen throughout this chapter is the question of whether the measure under consideration is a valid attempt to promote a legitimate policy objective or whether it is really a disguised restriction on trade. This has been more succinctly referred to by Sykes as the 'sham' test. In adjudicating this question, a panel is put in the awkward situation of making a rather brutal characterization – that the country with the offending standard has intended to adopt a policy in bad faith. This raises issues relating to 'diplomatic manners'. As was seen in the *UHT Milk* case, the panel was reluctant to conclude that the US measure was a sham, resulting in a 'non-violation nullification and impairment' ruling in what was arguably a clear case of regulatory protectionism. Panels will further be required to subjectively assess what the 'real intention' of a government was. In many cases, a government's intention will be difficult to discern. Often a unified intent does not exist given the way modern policy is created. This would require evaluating interest group influences, political log-rolling, etc.

A second test is the evaluation of whether a measure is based on a scientific risk assessment. This has the initial appeal of being more objective than the sham test as it relies on hard science rather than softer intuitive judgments regarding intent. But as was seen in this chapter, scientific inquiry is riddled with value judgments. While there has been some success in separating scientific fact from scientific judgment in the trade agreements by distinguishing between risk assessment and risk management, the separation is by no means water-tight. Scientific risk assessments are by nature uncertain and even the choice of methodology necessary to conduct a risk assessment requires to some degree a normative judgment. The result is that trade panels are put in the position of adjudicating conflicting scientific evidence. Needless to say, the lawyers and diplomats that compose these panels do not generally possess the expertise to understand the complex intricacies of such issues, much less rule on them. Thus, what at first seems to be a clear and objective test to guide the panellists seems more likely to strain the limits of adjudicative competence.

A third test is the requirement that panels rule on whether a particular form of domestic intervention is proportionate to the stated regulatory goal, essentially determining whether the 'right fit' exists between the policy instrument chosen and the stated objective (the so-called proportionality test). As the legal test for evaluating whether a measure is 'necessary' is based on whether a least trade-restrictive measure has been employed, a panel will be required to engage in what may be a very complex policy inquiry into the various policy alternatives and their viability in achieving the stated policy goal. In answering these questions, panellists are drawn into an uncomfortable area of second-guessing expert domestic regulators. In the case of, for example, air quality standards, one wonders whether, for example, a diplomat from New Zealand or Sweden is really in the position to second guess the high-level scientific expertise and peer review process of the US Environmental Protection Agency. The attitude of trade panels to these problems so far is not encouraging, a prime example being the *Thai Cigarette* ruling,[142] where the panel relied entirely on its own axiomatic reasoning that alternatives less restrictive than banning imported cigarettes would be available to achieve the health objectives of the Thai government, without considering the various constraints, including institutional and fiscal, on implementation of the less restrictive alternatives, such as regulation of advertising and marketing. The question of proportionality can easily extend into an inquiry about the validity of the stated goal itself, as was seen in the *Danish Bottles* case when in answering this question, the ECJ essentially ratcheted down the level of environmental protection chosen by Denmark through its balancing test.

In designing institutional processes in an international context in which these concepts can be rendered justiciable and operational, more attention needs to be given than hitherto to relative burdens of proof. As a tentative proposition, we would argue that a complainant should bear the burden of proving that a domestic policy measure of another country has a disparate and substantial impact on international trade. If this can be proven, it seems to us that the burden of proof should then shift to the respondent country to demonstrate that notwithstanding this, the policy measure both genuinely engages a legitimate policy objective – the sham principle (and here we would contemplate a much longer list of legitimate policy objectives than is presently embodied in Article XX, reflecting in part, for example, the legitimate policy objectives for domestic subsidies formerly contained in Article 11 of the Tokyo Round Subsidies Code) – and that no less trade restrictive policy instrument is reasonably available for vindicating these policy objectives as effectively – the least trade restrictive means or proportionality principle ('effectively' being understood here to mean both the extent of attainment of the objective in question and the cost to the country in question of achieving it through one instrument rather than another).

As to what constitutes adequate discharge of the burden of proof on these latter issues, there is an important consequential issue of the standard of judicial or panel review to be applied. This has been a bitterly contentious issue in a somewhat analogous context with respect to FTA and NAFTA binational panel reviews of ITA and ITC determinations in the US in antidumping and countervailing duty cases.[143] One view (reflecting a 'correctness' standard) would require that the respondent country bear the burden of adducing substantial evidence on the record that the challenged policy is necessary for the attainment of a legitimate policy objective and that no less trade restrictive means is available to achieve this purpose (arguably a difficult negative to prove). An alternative view (reflecting a 'patently unreasonable' standard) would be substantially more deferential to the country whose domestic policies are under challenge and would simply require that the evidence adduced be sufficient to suggest that the policy choice is not patently unreasonable or a grossly disproportionate adaptation of means to ends, or put otherwise is a plausible means of attempting to achieve the legitimate policy objective in question, even if the reviewing body could itself imagine superior instruments. We favour something close to the latter approach (perhaps a 'clearly unreasonable' standard) because it seems to us more respectful of domestic political sovereignty and policy autonomy than the former view which invites supranational panels to second-guess the domestic policy choices of democratically elected and accountable governments by applying a strict *de novo* cost-benefit analysis of their own. Moreover, by substantially limiting the ability of one country to challenge the domestic policy choices of another in quasi-judicial fora, the 'threat point' of the former in political negotiations over possible policy convergence is sharply reduced, thus also reducing the risk of coerced forms of harmonization reflecting asymmetric bargaining power, or worse, coerced forms of discriminatory managed trade arrangements.

Another way of dealing with the problem of institutional competence in applying proportionality or least trade-restrictive means tests is to rely upon opinions or advice from expert international organizations. Here, also the *Thai Cigarette* case is instructive of the traditional institutional culture of the multilateral trading order – the panel simply refused to consider empirical work by the World Health Organization. Even where, as noted above, WTO legal instruments link the work of specialized international bodies to trade norms, as in the case of ISO, there is very little sustained cooperation and dialogue between the WTO and the institutions in question.[144] In fact, there may be too great a gap between the diplomatic, rules-based trade culture of the WTO and the hands-on, technically-oriented culture of some of the specialized organizations to easily allow for the emergence of deep and effective links. As an organization that has both a rules-based free trade orientation and also a policy cooperation orientation, the OECD may need to reconceive itself as a kind of bridge between these different cultures. But as the current controversy surrounding multilateral investment negotiations at the OECD suggests, a serious problem is posed by the limited membership of the OECD, which excludes most developing countries. This may argue for eventually making the OECD into a truly multilateral body, perhaps beginning with different classes or levels of membership for countries at different levels of economic development. These factors highlight the risk of allowing harmonization efforts to get too far ahead of the institutional structures available to sustain it in a legitimate, as well as an efficient, fashion.

7 Antidumping laws

INTRODUCTION

Among the trilogy of trade remedy regimes – countervailing duty, safeguard and antidumping actions – antidumping actions are by far the remedy of choice. By the end of 1989, twenty-eight countries had adopted antidumping laws.[1] Nearly 1,200 actions were initiated between July 1980 and June 1988.[2] Four countries' actions accounted for 97.5% of all actions brought: 30% were brought by producers in the United States; 27% were brought in Australia; 22% in Canada; and 19% in the European Union. The targets of these actions are more diverse. The EU was the largest single target, defending 27% of the actions, while Canada, the USA and Australia in total were targeted in fewer than 14% of the actions. The second most targeted group of countries were the Newly Industrialized Countries (NICs), representing 18% of the defenders. The actions against the NICs were most often initiated by the USA and Australia, who, along with the EU, also initiated 106 actions against Japan. The EU's main targets were the socialist countries of Eastern Europe, who defended 15% of the world's actions. Overall, western industrialized countries accounted for 58% of the targets and developing countries (other than NICs) only 9%. Finally, of the actions initiated by the major users, the success rate ranged from 44% for Australia to 71% for the EU. More recent GATT data suggest some interesting new trends, with Brazil and Mexico joining the list of major users of antidumping laws.[3]

In antidumping proceedings, the following substantive issues are central (a) whether the foreign exporter is engaged in 'dumping' goods into the importing country's market. Determining whether dumping is occurring and what the margin of dumping is entails comparing a foreign firm's export prices in the importing country's market with either prices charged by the exporter in its home market in the ordinary course of trade, or where insufficient transactions exist in the home country to yield a reliable set of home market prices, with the exporter's average total costs including overheads and a reasonable margin of profit; (b) if dumping is occurring, whether it is causing material injury to domestic producers of like products, which in turn requires interpretations of 'domestic producers', 'like products', 'material injury' and causation.

In this chapter, we review the GATT/WTO provisions on dumping and the domestic dumping regimes in Canada, the USA and the EU. We then develop a fundamental critique of dumping laws and argue for their replacement with harmonized domestic competition laws that focus on cross-border predation.

THE GATT PROVISIONS ON ANTIDUMPING

Article VI of the GATT contains general rules governing the application of antidumping and countervailing duties. The first paragraph of the Article condemns export sales below normal value when they

> cause or threaten material injury to an established industry in the territory of the Contracting Party or materially retard the establishment of a domestic industry.

In addition, the Article describes the basis for determining when sales are below normal value: when the export price is less than 'the comparable price, in the ordinary course of trade, for the product when destined for consumption in the exporting country'.[4] When these criteria are satisfied the importing country is entitled to levy an antidumping duty equal to the difference between the normal value and the export price.

However, the wording of the Article is vague in important respects, leading to inconsistent interpretations and applications of the provision. Moreover, two of the biggest users of antidumping duties – Canada and the USA – did not consider themselves bound by its terms because their domestic antidumping laws pre-dated the GATT and to the extent of any inconsistencies were arguably 'grandfathered' under the Protocol of Provisional Application.[5]

The Kennedy Round Antidumping Code

In the Kennedy Round negotiations, beginning in 1963, many concerns about Article VI were addressed. The result was the 1967 Agreement on the Implementation of Article VI (the Antidumping Code) which laid out detailed criteria and procedures for the invocation of antidumping actions.[6]

Among the procedural rules contained in the Code was the requirement in Article 10(a) that provisional duties only be imposed following a preliminary finding of both dumping and injury. The imposition of retroactive duties was restricted by Article 11 of the Code, and Article 6 established rules of confidentiality and evidence. Finally, a notable feature of the Code is that it stated a preference for the imposition of a duty that is less than the dumping margin when the lesser duty will alleviate the injury.[7]

With respect to substantive issues, the first problem with Article VI is that it does not define the 'industry' whose injury justifies imposing antidumping duties. Article 4(a) of the 1967 Code clarified this issue, defining industry as 'the domestic producers as a whole of the like products or . . . those of them whose collective output of the products constitutes a major proportion of the total of those products'. A like product was defined in Article 2(b) as

> identical, i.e., alike in all respects to the product under consideration, or in the absence of such a product, another product which, although not alike in all respects, has characteristics closely resembling [the dumped product].

These two definitions in combination identify a relatively narrow group of producers which must be injured in order for an action to be successful.

A second ambiguity in Article VI is in the requisite causal link between the dumping and the injury. The 1967 Code specified that the dumping had to be 'demonstrably the principal cause'[8] of the injury.

The Tokyo Round Antidumping Code

Signatories to the Antidumping Code in 1967 committed themselves to ensuring that their domestic trade legislation was rendered consistent with the Code. For the USA this task posed a substantial problem. The Code's test for causality was quite stringent and inconsistent with the US Antidumping Act.[9] The inconsistency between the Code and the Act led to unwillingness on the part of Congress to amend its laws or restrict the discretion of the administering authorities.[10] While the USA claimed that its applications were not inconsistent with the Code, the wording of the domestic law remained unchanged.[11] Having adopted the Code's definitions, the EU sought to ensure compliance by the USA and insisted on reopening the Code during the Tokyo Round.

The main revisions to the 1967 Code related to causality and injury determination. Rather than requiring that the dumping be 'demonstrably the principal cause', the 1979 Code only specified that any 'injuries caused by other factors must not be attributed to the dumped imports',[12] making it more consistent with the US position. The EU also now supported a relaxation of the causation requirements. With respect to injury, the factors to be used in evaluating the impact of the dumping were explicitly laid out, i.e.:

> actual and potential decline in output, sales, market share, profits, productivity, return on investments, or utilization of capacity; . . . effects on cash flow, . . . wages, . . . growth.[13]

Also, the rules on the acceptance and administration of price and quantity undertakings were expanded in the 1979 Code (although their thrust remained the same). Finally, the Code required that except under special circumstances a proceeding should be completed within one year and that the rules permitting retroactive duties be more restricted.

The Uruguay Round Antidumping Agreement[14]

The 1979 Code left unresolved a number of problems and ambiguities.[15] The incompleteness of the Code resulted in inconsistent antidumping practices and procedures throughout the world. The Antidumping Code received further attention in the recent Uruguay Round negotiations. The main changes reflect a growing tension between developed countries, especially the USA and the EU, which bring a substantial percentage of all antidumping actions, and NICs and developing nations who are typically defenders rather than complainants.

Article 2 of the Uruguay Round Antidumping Agreement defines products as being dumped if the export price is less than the comparable price, in the ordinary course of trade, for the like product when destined for consumption in the exporting country. Where there are no sales of the like product in the ordinary course of trade in the domestic market of the exporting country or when because of the particular market situation or the low volume of the sales in the domestic market of the exporting country (a sufficient quantity must normally constitute 5% or more of the sales of the product to the importing country) such sales do not permit a proper comparison, the margin of dumping shall be determined by comparison with a comparable price of the like product when exported to an appropriate third country or with the cost of production in the country of origin plus a reasonable amount for administrative, selling and general costs and for profits. Sales in the domestic market of the exporting country below per unit (fixed and variable) costs of production plus administrative, selling and general costs may be disregarded in determining normal value if made for an extended period of time (normally one year) in substantial quantities (more than 20% of transactions). Thus, all export sales, whether above or below total costs will be averaged to obtain the export price while generally only domestic sales above total costs will be averaged, increasing the likelihood of a finding of dumping.

The existence of margins of dumping shall normally be established on the basis of a comparison of weighted average domestic sale prices and weighted average export market prices or by a comparison of domestic prices and export prices on a transaction-to-transaction basis. This precludes comparing isolated low-priced export transactions with weighted average domestic prices to establish dumping.

Where there are no home market or third country sales on which to base price comparisons, constructed value may be used which includes materials and labour costs and an amount for selling, general and administrative expenses (SG&A) plus profit. These latter costs – SG&A and profit – must now be based on actual data pertaining to production and sales in the ordinary course of business by the exporter. This precludes inclusion of home market sales at a loss in the calculation of the exporter's profits. In the absence of firm-specific data on SG&A and profits, the weighted average of the amounts incurred or realized by other exporters may be used, thus penalizing more efficient foreign producers. Where non-recurring start-up costs are incurred by new facilities, costs should be adjusted to reflect the costs at the end of the start-up period (Article 2.2.1.1).

In determining injury, Article 3.3 permits the investigating authority in the importing country to assess cumulatively the effects of imports from more than one country where they are subject to simultaneous investigation if the level of imports from each country is more than *de minimis* and if it is appropriate to do so. Article 3.5 provides that the demonstration of a causal relationship between the dumped imports and the injury to the domestic industry shall be based on an examination of all relevant evidence, including any known factors, other than the dumped imports, which at the same time are injuring the domestic industry, and the injuries caused by these other factors must not be attributed to the dumped imports. Factors which may be relevant include *inter alia* the volume and prices of imports not sold at dumped prices and the magnitude of the margin of dumping (Article 3.4).

Article 5 expands the procedural rules that govern the initiation and investigation of a dumping action. Article 5.8 requires that an investigation should be terminated when a dumping margin is *de minimis* (less than 2% of the normal value) or when the volume of dumped products is negligible (i.e. if the volume of dumped imports from a particular country accounts for less than 3% of imports of the like product in the importing country unless countries that individually account for less than 3% of imports collectively account for more than 7% of imports). The rules on evidence (Article 6) are also expanded providing for assurances of disclosure and improved opportunities to make a full defence or argument, while still preserving essential confidentiality. Article 6.12 requires that in cases where the product is commonly sold at retail, industrial users and consumer organizations be given an opportunity to provide relevant information regarding dumping, injury and causality. Evidence provided by foreign Parties shall not be disregarded even if it is not clear in all respects (Annex II). Article 11 includes a 'sunset review' clause which limits, subject to review, the duration of duties to five years from their imposition. Article 9.5 requires the individual assessment of exporters who did not export during the period of investigation. This treatment replaces the prior application to uninvestigated exporters of the highest duty levied in a case. Articles 7 and 10 place restrictions on the imposition of provisional and retroactive duties

Under Article 8, proceedings may be suspended or terminated on receipt of a satisfactory voluntary undertaking from any exporter to revise its prices or to cease exports at dumped prices. Price undertakings may not be sought or accepted unless preliminary determinations of dumping and injury have been made and even if then sought and accepted, the exporter may elect to have the investigation completed. In the event of a negative determination, undertakings lapse. Under Article 12, public notification is required of the initiation of an investigation and of any preliminary or final determination along with findings and conclusions reached on all issues of fact and law considered material by the investigating authorities. Article 13 requires countries with antidumping regimes to maintain judicial, arbitral or administrative tribunals for reviewing initial determinations.

Member countries were unable to agree on provisions to prevent circumvention of antidumping duties by exporters subject to duties on given products setting up local assembly plants using imported inputs to make the same products ('screwdriver plants'); this issue has been remitted to the Committee on Antidumping Practices, set up under the Agreement, for resolution.

Complaints over non-compliance with the Agreement may be referred to the integrated Dispute Settlement Body established by the broader Uruguay Round Agreement. Under Article 17.6, dispute resolution panels shall determine whether domestic agencies' establishment of the facts were proper and whether their evaluation was unbiased and objective. However, deferring to US concerns, Article 17.6 then provides that if the establishment of the facts was proper and the evaluation was unbiased and objective, the evaluation shall not be overturned even though the panel might have reached a different conclusion. Also, where a panel finds that a provision of the Agreement admits of more than one permissible interpretation, the panel shall find the agency's determination to be in conformity with the Agreement if it rests upon one of these permissible interpretations.

In 1992, a GATT panel was established to consider the legality of an antidumping duty imposed on imports of fresh and chilled Atlantic salmon from Norway.[16] The panel found inconsistencies with the United States' obligations under the GATT Antidumping Code with respect to the methodology for calculating margins of dumping. However, these inconsistencies did not result in the panel recommending that the duties be repealed, as the panel was not able to conclude that a correct application of the methodology would have resulted in a determination that no dumping had occurred. According to Norway, this represented a departure from previous panel decisions, where, at a minimum, recommendations pertaining to reduced duty margins were made in response to a finding of error in methodologies for calculating duties. Also that year, a panel was established at the request of the United States to consider the imposition of antidumping duties on polyacetal resins from the United States.[17] Here the primary issue was that the Korea Trade Commission had failed to provide adequate evidence in support of its determination of present injury and future threat of injury, according to the GATT Antidumping Code. In this case, the panel recommended that Korea bring the measure under dispute in conformity with its obligations under the Antidumping Code. It is significant that the panel declined to recommend that Korea bring its law into conformance with its obligations under the Code, as the United States had requested. The panel preferred to limit its jurisdiction to the 'law as applied' by Korea, rather than the law itself. In 1995, a panel was convened to consider the legality of EC antidumping duties on cotton yarn from Brazil. Brazil contended that the EC had violated a number of provisions of the Code. In a lengthy and comprehensive decision, the panel dismissed all of Brazil's substantive arguments. In 1997, Mexico requested the establishment of a dispute settlement panel regarding Guatemala's decisions to initiate an investigation into allegations of dumping of portland cement from Mexico. The panel ruled in Mexico's favour, requesting that Guatemala bring its action into conformity with its obligations under Articles 5.3 and 5.5 of the Antidumping Code and revoke its anti-dumping measures on imports of Mexican cement. Guatemala appealed the decision. However, the Appellate Body did not consider any of the substantive issues in the case because it was found that the dispute was not properly before the panel. The measure at issue was not properly identified and thus the panel was not entitled to examine any of Mexico's claims.[18]

ANTIDUMPING LAWS: CANADA, THE UNITED STATES AND THE EU[19]

Canada amended its *Customs Tariff* in 1904 to provide for antidumping duties and in so doing became the first country in the world to establish an antidumping regime.[20] The current legislation is set out in the Special Import Measures Act 1985 (the SIMA).[21] The first specific American antidumping statute, which is still in force, is known as the Antidumping Act of 1916.[22] Because of the onerous predatory intent requirement, there has never been either a successful prosecution or a civil judgment under this Act. This parallels experience under predatory pricing provisions in domestic antitrust laws where convictions or successful civil suits are rare. The US Congress enacted the Antidumping Act of 1921[23] to provide complainants with a greater scope for relief than the 1916 Act. The current American legislation is embodied in Title VII of the Tariff Act of 1930. Institutions of the European Union have had the authority to take action against dumped imports since 1968.[24]

In Canada and the USA, the institutional responsibilities for determining 'dumping' and 'material injury' are separated. 'Dumping' determinations are made by the Deputy Minister of National Revenue (DMNR) in Canada[25] and by the International Trade Administration of the Department of Commerce (DC) in the United States. 'Material injury' determinations are made by the Canadian International Trade Tribunal (CITT) and by the US International Trade Commission (the ITC). The institutional arrangements in the EU are very different from those in the USA and Canada. The principal institution involved in the administration of the EU antidumping system is the Commission, specifically Directorate C in the Directorate-General in Charge of External Relations of the Union, which has the primary responsibility for the enforcement of the antidumping regime. It is responsible for all stages of the investigation, including the decision to initiate a proceeding. Following an investigation, the Commission can impose provisional duties or submit proposals for definitive action to the Council. It also has the authority to accept undertakings by the exporter and terminate the proceeding. Finally, the Commission makes recommendations to the Council with respect to antidumping legislation.

The Council's main role is to approve the provisional determinations of the Commission and to order the collection of the imposed duties. It also has legislative responsibility for the antidumping regulation. The role has usually been a *pro forma* one.

An advisory committee made up of a Commission representative and an official from each member state is consulted by the Commission at various stages in the investigation. The committee's primary involvement is in determining the appropriate relief to be granted for an injury. An undertaking from the exporter cannot be accepted if there is not complete agreement from the Member States. Through their customs authorities, the Member States also help to ensure that duties are collected. Again, in practice the Committee's role is largely *pro forma.*

In certain circumstances the Court of Justice has the authority to review antidumping decisions. It can review the legality of Commission or Council determinations and redress 'manifest errors' in the assessment of facts or violations of procedural rules, although in practice the Court exercises its review function with restraint.

Finally, the European Parliament has an advisory role and issues non-binding opinions on EU legislation. In addition, its Committee on External Economic Relations serves as a forum for discussion of the administration of the antidumping system.

In Canada, once the CITT has determined material injury it may consider the potential effect of antidumping duties on 'the public interest'.[26] If the CITT is of the view that imposing antidumping duties would be contrary to the public interest, it must both publish a report in the *Canada Gazette* and report to the Minister of Finance, who has the discretion to lower or remove the duty.[27] The provision reflects the concern that 'concentration on producer interests alone is too narrow a focus and the consumer interest must be considered'.[28] In practice, however, only three public interest hearings[29] have been convened since the provision was enacted in 1985, and consumer groups did not initiate or participate in any of the hearings. The United States does not have a public interest provision. The EU regulations provide that duties should only be imposed when doing so serves the Union's interest,[30] but the typical reason for invoking the clause is to avoid domestic producers paying more for dumped inputs.[31]

While the CITT's decision is 'final and conclusive',[32] the CITT may review its own findings if it is satisfied that such a review is warranted.[33] There are also appeals to the Federal Court of Appeal[34] and the Supreme Court of Canada, principally on issues of law.[35] In the United States, an appeal lies to the Court of International Trade from both DC and ITC decisions and then to the Court of Appeals for the Federal District.[36] The EU system has a limited right of appeal. As previously noted, the Court of Justice is reluctant to review Commission determinations in this area. The EU antidumping system has been characterized by discretion and secrecy; the reluctance of the Court to review the Commission's determinations increases the appearance (at least) of unfairness in the system's administration.[37] Arguably, the odd bifurcation of institutional functions in Canada and the US serves a similar obfuscatory function.

Under Chapter 19 of the Canada – US Free Trade Agreement and now under Chapter 19 of NAFTA, appeals from final determinations by domestic agencies in antidumping and countervailing duty proceedings may be taken to binational dispute settlement panels. This has proved an important innovation, with implications for the potential scope and role of the dispute resolution processes under the Uruguay Round Antidumping Agreement. It should be noted that Chapter 19 of the FTA was premised on an agreement that the current means of dealing with AD and CVD disputes are unsatisfactory. Article 1906 of the FTA called for an agreement within five years (with the possibility of a two-year extension) on a code between Canada and the USA regarding AD and CVD matters. The Article contemplated the possibility that the Agreement could be terminated (on six months notice by either Party) if no accord was reached on a new regime for resolving disputes in this contentious area.[38] Thus, Chapter 19 was, on its face, a temporary expedient.

It begins with two other important limitations on its power and scope. The following Articles refer to NAFTA, but are largely identical to their predecessor sections in the FTA. Article 1901:1 states that the Article 1904 provisions outlining the procedures for the review of 'final determinations' in AD and CVD cases apply only to goods which the relevant authority in the *importing* Party has determined come from the other Party. Moreover, Article 1902 reserves the power to apply and amend domestic AD and CVD law to each Party respectively.[39] However, Article 1902 imposes limits on the capacity to modify existing AD and CVD law: Parties must notify and consult each other about such changes; for changes to apply to the other Party it must be named; and no change can be inconsistent with relevant GATT provisions or 'the object and purpose of this Agreement and this Chapter'.[40] These restrictions are not as significant as originally anticipated. They had been seen as an attempt to ensure some degree of bilateral accountability in this area. This view is supported by the *Softwood Lumber* case, where the US Congress effectively repealed the decision by legal amendment, in apparent contradiction with the intent of these provisions.

Articles 1903 and 1904 both are designed to allow bilateral review of the amendment and application of AD and CVD law. Article 1903 allows a Party to request that a panel be set up to examine an amendment to determine whether it is consistent with relevant GATT and FTA provisions, or whether, in addition, it 'has the function and effect of overturning a prior decision' made under Article 1904.[41] If the panel decides that an amendment is in fact objectionable, the Parties are then to enter into consultations to remedy the situation within 90 days, and if remedial legislation is not enacted within nine months of the end of this consultation period then the other Party is entitled to take comparable action or terminate the Agreement.[42]

Article 1904 provides a set of procedures allowing binational panels to replace judicial review of the 'final determinations' of administrative agencies in AD and CVD cases.[43] At the request of either Party, a panel can review such determinations and issue a *binding decision* as to whether they conform to the AD and CVD law of the importing country subject to a procedure for an extraordinary challenge of a panel's decision to a binational panel of retired judges on various grounds (such as gross misconduct, bias or conflict of interest).[44] The standard of primary panel review is that laid down by the relevant statutes (as amended from time to time) of each Party, and by 'the general legal principles that a court of the importing Party would otherwise apply'.[45] Requests for panels must be made within 30 days of the publication of a final determination.[46] Only the Parties have the right to request a panel, but Article 1904:5 provides that a Party must ask for a panel when petitioned by a person otherwise entitled by domestic law to redress via judicial review.[47] The administrative agency whose determination is being reviewed has the right to be represented by counsel before the panel, as do all other persons entitled by domestic laws to standing before a court reviewing such determinations.[48] The panel reaches its decision by a majority vote of its members, and it issues its reasons (majority, concurring, and dissenting) in a written report.[49] If a panel finds an error in a final determination it may remand the determination to the relevant domestic administrative agency for 'action not inconsistent with the panel's decision'.[50]

Chapter 19 – its committees and panels – is supported and administered by a Secretariat established under Article 1908. It has three branches, each run by a Secretary, one Canadian (located in Ottawa), one American (located in Washington, DC) and one Mexican (located in Mexico City). The Secretariat operates as a division of the general NAFTA Secretariat, as established by Article 2002 and is responsible for servicing the meetings of panels and committees, and providing general administrative assistance.[51] It is also charged with the task of receiving and filing all official papers connected with the operation of Chapter 19.[52] This institutional feature may enhance the quality and consistency of panel decisions.

The final salient feature of Chapter 19 is its elaborate provisions regarding the composition of panels. Annex 1901.2 sets out the method of choosing these panels, and the pool from which they are to be drawn. A roster is established by consultation between the three Parties of 75 unaffiliated individuals – 25 from each country – who are chosen for their good character, reliability, and objectivity.[53] The roster shall also 'include judges or former judges to the fullest extent practicable'.[54] A panel is composed of five members, a majority of whom must be lawyers. Each Party must choose, in consultation with the other Party, two members; each Party is allowed four peremptory challenges; and if panellists are not chosen within 30 days of the request for a panel, or alternative panellists are not chosen within 45 days then a panellist will be chosen by lot from the Party's candidates on the roster.[55] A fifth member must be chosen within 55 days of the request by the Parties, or, if they cannot agree, within 60 days by the already chosen panellists, or, if they cannot agree, by lot (on the 61st day).[56] The Chair of the panel is picked from among the lawyers by a majority vote of the panellists; if there is no majority vote then the Chair will be chosen by lot.[57]

Early critics of the FTA argued that the provisions did not go far enough to prevent administrative harassment of exporters by domestic competitors. The critics argued that no effective limits had been placed on the discretion of administrative trade agencies, and that panels would be as ready to defer to these agencies in reviewing their determinations as had been the US Court of International Trade and the Canadian Federal Court of Appeal.[58] But the experience with the mechanisms to date suggests that they do represent a significant improvement over what they replaced.

According to a study by Mercury,[59] between 1989 and 1995, when the FTA was largely subsumed into NAFTA, 49 requests for binational panel review were initiated. Panels as of 1995 had rendered decisions in 32 cases (most binational determinations are being appealed to binational panels). About two-thirds of US agency determination that were appealed to binational panels resulted in panel remands to agencies for redeterminations (compared to a remand rate by the Court of International Trade of about one-third). Canadian agency determinations were subject to a markedly lower remand rate, reflecting in part the more deferential standard of judicial review of specialized agency decisions under Canadian domestic law. Panel decisions were mostly unanimous (with a few high profile exceptions where panels divided on national lines) and mostly met the time limits prescribed by Chapter 19. However, delays have occurred as a result of the inability of panels to order relief but only remand matters to domestic agencies for redetermination, sometimes resulting in multiple remands. There have been three Extraordinary Challenges to panel rulings, all initiated by the US, and all unsuccessful. These results have been largely confirmed by Davey, who has found the Chapter 19 process to work on the whole 'reasonably well'.[60]

In the experience under the FTA, the great majority of appeals to binational panels have been of US agency decisions, originally initiated by US Parties. However in 1993, there was a surge in the review of Canadian agency decisions.[61] The Mexicans have been increasingly active, responsible for initiating 12 of the 35 actions under NAFTA to date.

In most respects, the panel procedures under FTA were preserved and made permanent by NAFTA. But two important changes carry the potential to reinstate the more traditional and deferential standard of judicial review that applied prior to the creation of the binational panel review process under the FTA. First is the requirement that the roster include judges, rather than international trade lawyers, economists, or other experts (Annex 1901.2). Second, the Extraordinary Challenge procedure pertaining to panel decisions has been extended to permit a challenge in a case where a panel has failed to apply the appropriate standard of review (Article 1904(13)). Indeed Davey has written in the case of NAFTA panel reviews of US antidumping decisions that, 'while the degree of deference accorded to Commerce seems to have varied somewhat from panel to panel, none of the panels appear to have been overly intrusive in their reviews.'[62] This contrasts with the review of Canadian decisions where 'panel review has probably been somewhat more intrusive than judicial review'.[63]

The second round of bilateral negotiations contemplated by the Canada–US Free Trade Agreement on new rules for antidumping, subsidies, and countervailing duties appeared initially to have been abandoned. In their place, NAFTA provides that the trilateral Free Trade Commission shall establish a Working Group on trade and competition to make recommendations to the Commission within five years of the coming into force of the Agreement 'on relevant issues concerning the relationship between competition laws and policies and trade in the free trade area'.[64] The Parties further agree to consult on '(a) the potential to develop more effective rules and disciplines concerning the use of governmental subsidies; and (b) the potential for reliance on a substitute system of rules for dealing with unfair transborder pricing practices and government subsidization'.[65] A trilateral side-accord of 2 December 1993 committed the three governments to establishing a working group on subsidies and antidumping duties which was to complete its work by 31 December 1995. This working group failed to reach a consensus on a reform agenda.

THEORETICAL RATIONALES FOR ANTIDUMPING LAWS

Economic rationales for antidumping laws

There are three ways in which dumping can be characterized: as international price discrimination, as predatory pricing, or as intermittent dumping. These characterizations, if well-founded, each give rise to possible economic justifications for the existence of antidumping laws.

International price discrimination

Canada was the first country in the world to enact antidumping legislation and there is some evidence that this was prompted by fears of international price discrimination. According to Jacob Viner, Canada's first antidumping legislation was a response to the US Steel Corporation's practice of selling its exports at prices substantially below its domestic prices.[66] US antidumping laws are also often characterized as a means of responding to international price discrimination.[67]

Both Canadian[68] and US[69] antitrust laws prohibit various forms of domestic price discrimination. These laws have intricate and detailed requirements which make the legal definition of price discrimination complex. However, a standard economic definition of price discrimination is as follows:

> It is discriminatory to charge significantly different product prices to two or more customers when there are no significant differences between the costs to the seller of supplying those customers.[70]

A seller thus price discriminates when selling an identical product in different markets for different prices. The seller must have some degree of control over the market price (or 'market power') to be able to price discriminate, and the seller will only have market power under conditions of imperfect competition.[71]

There are essentially two arguments for prohibiting domestic price discrimination.[72] First, a monopolist's[73] total output may decrease when it shifts from a single-price policy to a discriminatory pricing policy. Because a monopolist sells less output than is optimal, a further decrease in its output might exacerbate the scarcity and impose greater welfare losses on society. Once the monopolist price discriminates between the two markets, some existing customers will be forced out of the higher priced market, and new customers will be attracted to the lower priced market. The total output produced and sold will decrease if the higher priced market forces out more customers than the lower priced market attracts.

The second argument against allowing price discrimination reflects two forms of social cost imposed on society. The first costs are those that the monopolist incurs in segregating its markets and computing its customers' elasticities of demand. If price discrimination were prohibited, resources invested in administering the price discrimination scheme could be put to socially beneficial uses such as product innovation, plant expansion or research and development. Second, according to

Posner,[74] the lure of monopoly profits induces competing sellers to seek monopolies. Sellers compete with each other to obtain, for example, licences and protectionist legislation in the hope of achieving a monopoly. In the monopoly contest, sellers may invest resources up to their expected monopoly profits. The monopoly rents gained by the ultimate victor may be wholly offset by the socially wasteful expenditures of the competing sellers. If price discrimination is allowed, expected monopoly profits will be higher, sellers will invest more resources in achieving monopolies, and resulting social costs would be higher than under a nondiscriminatory pricing policy.

These traditional arguments for prohibiting price discrimination are inconclusive. Among antitrust scholars there is no consensus on whether domestic price discrimination should be prohibited.[75] First, whether output will increase or decrease under price discrimination is an empirical question.[76] In a wide range of – perhaps most – circumstances, a monopolist is likely to maximize profits by price discriminating in a way that increases output over that obtaining with a single monopoly price – indeed a perfectly discriminating monopolist will charge each consumer his or her reservation price and produce the competitive output (appropriating all consumer surplus in the process). However, perfect price discrimination is rarely feasible because it entails a monopolist acquiring information on every potential customer's elasticity of demand and preventing arbitrage between low-priced and high-priced consumers. Second, while the costs that the monopolist incurs in acquiring and segregating its market may be wasteful, if the monopolist produces more output under price discrimination those costs may be outweighed by the benefits of the increased output. Third, since some monopolies are efficient, expenditures to secure such monopolies are not wasteful.

Even if one assumes the validity of the arguments for prohibiting domestic price discrimination (although they are often contested), the case for prohibiting dumping is not analogous. Domestic price discriminators and dumpers have different effects on the export country. A seller only 'dumps' if it charges a lower price to its export market customers than it charges to its home market customers.[77] Therefore, while domestic price discriminators create both a higher priced market and a lower priced market within the same country, dumpers create only a lower priced market in the country to which they are exporting.

The importing country benefits from low import prices. The consumers in the importing country enjoy more consumer surplus since they receive more output at a lower price per unit. When the importing country imposes antidumping duties on low-priced imports, its consumers lose these benefits. By increasing the price of dumped goods to the exporter's monopolistic home market price, antidumping duties impose supracompetitive prices on consumers in the export market and force them to settle for an inefficiently low level of output. Those consumers who remain in the market pay higher prices and enjoy less consumer surplus, and some consumers are priced out of the market, generating a dead-weight social cost.

In addition, when dumping occurs, the higher priced market is by definition located in the dumper's home country. The dumper's home country thus bears the dumper's costs of identifying and segregating its markets, and any social costs associated with the dumper's monopoly profits. The efficiency losses associated with domestic price discrimination, which drive the arguments for prohibiting price discrimination, are borne entirely by the dumper's home market. Hence, the arguments for prohibiting domestic price discrimination do not justify a corresponding prohibition against dumping; dumping gives the export country the benefit of the price discriminator's low priced market without the social costs of its high priced market. Even if the importing country were concerned about the dumper's home market abuses through some altruistic motive, forcing domestic consumers to pay the dumper's home market monopoly price seems a wholly ineffective response. On this point, Trebilcock and Quinn note

> Although equality of exploitation has a certain egalitarian ring to it, it seems a little difficult to see any other virtue in replicating other people's miseries, particularly when in so doing we are in no way ameliorating the lot of our fellow sufferers.

Finally, while the potential reduction in output is an argument against price discrimination, and whether total world output will rise or fall under international price discrimination is an empirical question, in the case of dumping prices are by definition lower in the export market, so the output available to the importing country is unambiguously higher with dumping, rendering highly problematic the appropriateness of providing any remedy to producers in the latter country on this account. The losses to consumers will almost always outweigh any gain to producers who are thereby protected. This is borne out by the empirical evidence.[78]

However, recent 'revisionist' literature by WTO officials[79] attempts to provide an economic rationalization for antidumping laws by drawing on the persistent and pervasive influence of concepts of reciprocity in international trade relations. This literature argues that international price discrimination is symptomatic of asymmetric market access and economic distortions in exporters' home markets that antidumping duties should properly seek to redress. An illustrative case is the antidumping complaint brought in Canada by General Motors and Ford against Hyundai for allegedly selling cars in Canada in the mid-1980s at 36% less than it sold them for in South Korea.[80] One might argue that it is unfair for domestic automobile manufacturers to have to face competition in the Canadian market from Korean imports when these manufacturers lacked equivalent access to the Korean market. (The price differential presumably reflected some form of protection of the South Korean market from import competition.) Moreover, to the extent that the imposition of antidumping duties might induce Hyundai to reduce its home market prices, this would remove the economic distortion in the allocation of resources reflected in overproduction for export markets and underproduction for the home market.

There are a number of responses to this line of argument. First, it is far from clear that the imposition of antidumping duties will in fact in many cases remove the distortion in the exporter's home market – the exporter will have to weigh the loss of sales (and profits) in export markets from the imposition of duties against the loss of profits entailed in abandoning supracompetitive pricing in the home market. Second, it is far from clear in most antidumping cases that the gravamen of domestic producers concerns about dumped imports is denial of equivalent access to the exporter's home markets; hence this seems a curiously coincidental or indirect means of addressing market access problems in these markets. Third, to the extent that differences in prices between home and export markets are explained by export subsidies from the home country's government, these are not properly the domain of antidumping laws but countervailing duty laws. Fourth, to the extent that the price differences between the two markets are explained by trade restrictions (e.g. tariffs or quotas) in the home country's market, then their legality should be addressed directly. If the home country has high unbound or bound tariffs, it is entitled to maintain these under the GATT/WTO pending mutual negotiations to reduce them. If it is utilizing quotas, these may be objectionable under Article XI (quantitative restrictions). If it has conferred a state-protected monopoly on the exporter, it is entitled to do so provided that it satisfies the non-discrimination conditions of Article XVII (state trading enterprises). If it is a developing country and is seeking to protect and promote an infant industry, it is entitled to do so provided it meets the conditions of Article XVIII. If the home country's domestic competition laws are being applied to the exporter in a preferential way, then this is likely to be challengeable under the National Treatment principle (Article III). Fifth, operationalizing this focus on market access conditions in exporters' home markets in antidumping proceedings seems intractable. If a precondition to imposing antidumping duties is a judgment by competition authorities in importing countries that conditions in exporting countries' markets would violate importing countries' domestic competition laws, this would seem a clearly unacceptable extraterritorial application of an importing country's domestic laws. If, on the other hand, this judgment is remitted to competition authorities in exporting countries (many of which, however, do not have such authorities) under a theory of positive comity, their judgments will often be viewed as non-credible and self-serving in importing countries.[81]

In short, it is not and never has been a precondition to international trade that the domestic policy environment in exporting and importing countries be in all respects the same – an extreme version of level playing field or reciprocity concepts – subject to the important explicit constraints on discrimination embodied in the above Articles of the GATT.

Predatory pricing

Predatory pricing is the second characterization of dumping that gives rise to an economic rationale for antidumping laws. It consists of 'systematically pricing below cost with a view to intimidating and/or eliminating rivals in an effort to bring about a market price higher than would otherwise prevail'.[82]

US antidumping laws were initially enacted out of a concern for predatory pricing by foreign competitors.[83] Canadian, US and EU antidumping laws penalize predatory pricing in addition to international price discrimination by authorizing the constructed-cost method of calculating the normal value. This penalization of below-cost pricing suggests that predatory pricing may be an additional rationale for current antidumping laws.

Canadian,[84] US,[85] and EU[86] domestic antitrust laws prohibit predatory pricing. A seller who engages in predatory pricing (the predator) ultimately harms competition by driving other sellers from the market and acquiring market power. Once the predator gains market power it restricts its output and captures monopoly profits. Predatory pricing is unlikely to occur frequently.[87] An extensive antitrust literature argues that predatory pricing is not often an effective means of achieving market power,[88] and economic theory suggests that systematic below-cost pricing is infeasible and irrational unless certain structural conditions are present. In order to compensate for the extensive losses suffered while selling at artificially low prices, the predator must achieve a monopoly position by driving its competitors from the market and preventing new competitors from entering. This will be difficult: competitors will only leave the market if there are low barriers to exit, and low exit barriers imply correspondingly low barriers to entry. Thus, even if the predator is successful in driving out its current competitors, it may face competition from a new wave of competitors, thus precluding recoupment of predatory losses incurred. As well, as Hovenkamp[89] and McGee[90] argue, if the initial competitors are driven into bankruptcy, other sellers may acquire their facilities at fire-sale prices and compete with the predator while incurring lower fixed costs. Since it is unclear whether the predator will succeed in creating a monopoly, the potential gains from predatory pricing are uncertain.

Predatory pricing allegations are also difficult to assess. As Areeda and Turner note:

> [U]nhappy rivals may automatically assume predation when a competitor's price is below their costs, disregarding the possibility that the alleged predator's cost is well below theirs and more than covered by his price.[91]

In both Canada and the USA, prices below the seller's marginal cost[92] or average variable cost[93] tend to be presumed predatory, although courts have experienced some difficulty in measuring those costs.[94] Prices above average total cost (including fixed costs) are generally presumed non-predatory. Prices between average variable cost and average total cost may or may not be predatory, depending on the circumstances, such as proof of predatory intent or ability to recoup short-run losses in the long run by raising prices without being under-cut by remaining competitors or new entrants. The rejection of average total cost as an invariable reference point is important because there are many instances in which a seller may be forced to sell below cost. For example, in times of slack or declining demand, the seller may not be able to sell enough output to cover all of its costs. As long as the seller prices its output above its variable costs, the revenue in excess of its variable costs will defray a portion of its fixed costs. Thus, the seller suffers lower losses than it would by halting production (in which case it would suffer losses equal to its full fixed costs).

The gains from predatory pricing are even more uncertain in the international arena. For a predator to achieve a monopoly in its export market it must not only drive out domestic competitors from the export market, but other foreign competitors as well. Foreign producers compete with each other just as vigorously as they compete with domestic competitors in their export markets.[95] Thus, the likelihood of one seller achieving a worldwide monopoly is slim, and vigorous competition among foreign competitors implies a small likelihood, in most markets, of successful oligopoly formation.[96]

Although true international predatory pricing (predatory dumping) may be expected to occur infrequently, where it does occur it harms competition in the export market. Indeed, predatory dumping is more harmful than wholly domestic predatory pricing because resulting monopoly profits are captured by the foreign exporter. On efficiency grounds, antidumping laws are justifiable insofar as they prevent predatory dumping. However, the current antidumping regimes of Canada, the USA and the EU penalize behaviour which may be neither predatory nor prohibited by antitrust legislation. Indeed, Hutton and Trebilcock conclude that of the thirty cases between 1984 and 1989 in which Canada imposed antidumping duties, none could be supported on predatory pricing grounds.[97] A recent unpublished study for the OECD of a much larger sample of cases apparently reaches similar conclusions.[98] Currently, antidumping duties are imposed when 'fully-allocated costs' exceed export market prices. As argued above, below-total-cost pricing need not be predatory. Hence, antidumping laws penalize conduct by foreigners that is not penalized when engaged in by domestic firms.

Moreover, even below-marginal-cost pricing by the exporter need not reflect an underlying predatory intention. When the exporter makes its production decisions, it estimates the price its output will eventually realize in the export market. As long as the estimated export market price exceeds its marginal cost, it will produce output for sale in the export market. If, owing for example to fluctuating exchange rates or changed market conditions, the actual export market price turns out to be lower than estimated the exporter will have no choice but to sell its output at the best available price. This price may be lower than the *ex ante* marginal costs the exporter faced when it made its production decision. However, the exporter will continue to sell in the export market because the output has already been produced and it can recoup a portion of its sunk costs by selling its output.[99] Although the exporter is engaging in below-marginal-cost pricing, there is no predatory intention. The exporter is doing what it can to minimize its losses in the face of its inaccurate *ex ante* estimate of the market price. Hutton and Trebilcock find that frustrated *ex ante* market price estimates accounted for below-marginal-cost pricing in four antidumping actions initiated in Canada against US exporters.[100]

Finally, in some cases below-marginal-cost pricing may actually promote competition. Depending on the product, sellers may engage in below-marginal-cost pricing to compete for market share. Deardorff[101] identifies two product characteristics, 'experience' and 'learning by doing', that make below-marginal-cost pricing likely for some goods. Consumers may pay more for 'experience' goods after their first and subsequent purchases than before their first purchase. This is because the quality of 'experience' goods is only discernible after their first use. To induce consumers to sample their goods for the first time, as a marketing strategy sellers may initially price their goods below their marginal cost. Sellers will recoup their initial losses once consumers pay more for the goods on their subsequent purchases.[102] Sellers produce 'learning by doing' goods when they experiment with new technology or new products. When they first enter the market with new goods, sellers may be inefficient and suffer losses. At this point, marginal costs may exceed the sale price. Sellers gradually reduce their costs as they 'learn' more about efficient production methods. In the meantime, they gain a valuable toehold in the market.[103]

Below-marginal-cost pricing for 'experience' or 'learning by doing' goods is typical for sellers expanding into new markets and cannot be viewed as predatory. In fact, it increases consumer demand, competition, and productive efficiency, and sellers can recoup their costs without acquiring market power. Many sellers, regardless of their degree of market power, may increase their market share by selective below-marginal-cost pricing. These legitimate roles for below-marginal-cost pricing suggest that antidumping laws should not categorically penalize below-marginal cost pricing. Significantly, domestic antitrust laws do not prohibit these kinds of activities in the case of domestic firms.[104]

Again, the recent 'revisionist' literature that seeks to provide an economic rationalization for antidumping laws contests this analysis of the constructed cost aspect of antidumping laws as inconsistent with notions of predation.[105] It is argued that European Commission decisions in domestic predation cases under EU competition laws have rejected pricing above average variable cost as presumptively non-predatory and have in fact adopted an average total cost test, which is close to the constructed cost test employed in antidumping law, and that US courts have adopted divergent cost tests in domestic predation cases under US antitrust law, some of which are consistent with the constructed cost test. It is then argued that pricing below average total cost is irrational unless a firm plans to exit a market or is doing so only on a temporary basis (e.g. because of depressed demand), or is engaged in predatory behaviour towards its rivals.

Several responses are in order. First, while it is true that courts have taken different positions on appropriate cost tests in domestic predation cases, they all nevertheless require proof of some kind that the alleged predator's behaviour is in fact predatory – that it is to say that the intent or effect of its behaviour is likely to entrench or reinforce a dominant market position, permitting it then to behave monopolistically. The constructed cost inquiry in antidumping cases never views as relevant any of the evidence that in a domestic predation case might be viewed as demonstrating predatory (monopolizing) intent or effect. For example, is it seriously arguable that Hyundai was using supracompetitive profits garnered in its protected South Korean market to finance below-cost exports to the North American market with a view to predating (monopolizing) the latter market? Thus, the argument that the constructed cost test is a close surrogate for predation tests in domestic competition or antitrust cases is wholly unpersuasive. It bears repeating that in the OECD and Canadian empirical studies of antidumping cases referred to above, few or no cases were found to satisfy conventional economic conceptions of predation. Second, even acknowledging room for debate about the appropriate tests to be applied under competition or antitrust law in domestic predation cases, surely the National Treatment principle requires that whatever tests are applied to domestic producers should also equally be applied to foreign producers. Manifestly, antidumping laws violate this precept by according domestic producers much greater pricing latitude than that accorded to foreign producers. Domestic firms are rarely found guilty of predation under domestic antitrust or competition law regimes; foreign firms are frequently found guilty of dumping, suggesting the extent of the discrepancy between the two regimes.

More transparently baseless economic rationalizations for antidumping laws are also advanced in this literature.[106] One is that exporters facing recessions in their home markets may export these recessions to export markets by below full-cost pricing and thus antidumping duties are a useful anti-cyclical policy. Given that it is at the same time claimed that antidumping duties often affect only about 1% of imports, (let alone GNP), it is difficult to think of a more futile anti-cyclical policy. It is also argued that where importing countries devalue their currency for balance of payment reasons, this objective may be defeated by exporters into their markets adjusting their export prices downwards (below home market prices) to offset the effect of the devaluation and thus to retain market share. Again, given the very small percentage of imports said to be affected by antidumping duties and the large and complex set of forces that determine exchange rates, it is difficult to believe that such a strategy could have any discernible impact on the balance of payments. Moreover, domestic producers who use imported inputs may be required to adopt the same strategy in order to remain competitive, yet would not be penalized on that account.

Intermittent dumping

The final characterization of dumping that gives rise to an economic rationale for antidumping laws is intermittent dumping. Jacob Viner defined intermittent dumping as systematic dumping which lasts for several months or years at a time.[107] Viner viewed this form of dumping as objectionable because it lasts long enough to injure domestic producers without providing consumers with a constant long-run supply of goods.[108] A situation in which intermittent dumping might occur is in the context of oversupply of perishables. Agricultural producers often make planting decisions long before selling their produce. Because of the cyclical nature of supply in agricultural markets, producers often find they have excess produce and rather than allowing it to rot they sell at low prices. For these agricultural producers, the relevant cost at the time of selling is the cost of packaging and marketing. Hutton and Trebilcock[109] find that the only Canadian antidumping cases that exhibited any indication of intermittent dumping were agricultural cases. They argue that the case of perishables is not a dumping problem and that agricultural price instability should be addressed, if at all, through income stabilization programmes rather than antidumping laws.[110]

Non-predatory intermittent dumping cannot occur unless certain structural conditions are present.[111] First, exporters must be unable to compete with domestic producers under normal market conditions. Otherwise, exporters would provide a permanent source of supply instead of an intermittent one. Second, intermittent dumping must be so extensive that it substantially disrupts domestic production. The losses incurred by selling below-cost products into export markets makes it unlikely that the dumping will last long enough to disrupt domestic production. As well, disruption will only occur if domestic purchasers substitute foreign goods for domestic goods. By substituting foreign goods for domestic goods during the intermittent dumping period, domestic purchasers will disrupt domestic production. As a result, when the intermittent dumping period is over domestic producers will charge higher prices than before to recoup their post-intermittent-dumping readjustment costs. Domestic purchasers can avoid the higher price by not substituting away from domestic goods in the first place, although collective action problems may inhibit this response.

The conditions necessary for non-predatory intermittent dumping to occur are unlikely to arise. Moreover, the effect of non-predatory intermittent dumping on welfare is ambiguous. When foreign exporters dump, domestic producers in the export market must adjust to meet lower import prices. Some domestic producers may be forced out of the market and if the dumping is only temporary domestic producers will then have to readjust to fill the vacuum left by the departing dumper. The adjustment and readjustment costs incurred by domestic producers unquestionably harm *producer* welfare.[112] Corporate resources which would go to skills training, expansion, or research and development are diverted to maintaining the producer's market share in the more competitive market. Losses incurred during the dumping period may force some producers into bankruptcy. Since domestic capital markets may be imperfect, the producers forced into bankruptcy may not be the least efficient.[113]

Adjustment and readjustment costs associated with intermittent dumping may also be passed on to consumers. Intermittent dumping harms consumers if they end up paying a higher long-run average price for goods than they would pay if there were no dumping. If intermittent dumping occurs with sufficient frequency that the domestic producer's cost of capital is higher over the long run (reflecting higher risk) than it would be in the absence of intermittent dumping, this cost will be passed on to consumers. However, the dumping margin may so depress prices during the period of dumping that, notwithstanding the producers' increased cost of capital, the consumer ends up paying lower long-run average prices. The net effect of intermittent dumping on consumer welfare is thus uncertain.

Given both the uncertain effect of intermittent dumping on consumer welfare and the low probability of the structural conditions for intermittent dumping being satisfied, it is questionable whether antidumping laws should seek to prevent intermittent dumping. In any event, the present antidumping laws of Canada and the United States are ill-adapted to addressing problems of intermittent dumping. Antidumping investigations assess dumping margins and material injury without regard to whether the dumping is temporary or permanent. This conclusion is borne out by Hutton and Trebilcock's finding that the possibility of intermittent dumping concerns was present in only four of the thirty Canadian cases they examined in which antidumping duties were imposed.[114]

Non-efficiency rationales for prohibiting dumping

The standard literature on dumping generally considers only economic or efficiency-based rationales for prohibiting dumping.[115] However, efficiency-based rationales may not tell the whole dumping story. Typically, antidumping laws can be justified politically because they address the perceived 'unfairness' of low-priced foreign imports. A US Senate Committee has called dumping 'pernicious',[116] and American courts have characterized dumping as an 'unfair trade practice'.[117] The global increase in antidumping actions may therefore reflect growing domestic political objections to the unfairness of low-priced foreign imports. The previous section showed that the only economic justification for antidumping laws is the prohibition of international predatory pricing, but notions of fairness may offer different justifications.

Fairness is a difficult concept.[118] Bhagwati characterizes the fairness terminology in antidumping laws as 'inherently vague',[119] and remarks that it is 'reflective of the psychological mood of a nation losing hegemony in the world economy'.[120] The perceived unfairness of non-predatory dumping may result from the disruptive impacts of low-priced imports on domestic industry and work-forces. By increasing the net price of imports, antidumping duties make domestic goods relatively more attractive to consumers and allow domestic producers to avoid direct competition with foreign exporters. Direct competition with low-cost suppliers may eventually force domestic producers to leave the market. This exit is likely to result in domestic workers losing jobs and shareholders of affected producers losing capital. Thus, while consumers would benefit from lower prices if antidumping duties were abolished, domestic producers might suffer severe losses from low-priced imports.[121]

Hutton and Trebilcock examine distributive justice and communitarian rationales for antidumping laws.[122] Antidumping laws would be justified on a distributive justice rationale if they were to enhance the welfare of the least-advantaged members of society.[123] The least-advantaged group would include immobile, unskilled, and low-income workers.[124] Antidumping laws would be justified on a communitarian rationale where they minimized the disruptive effect of imports on established communities and their corresponding network of family and social relationships.[125]

However, both theoretically and empirically, antidumping laws cannot be sustained on these non-economic rationales. First, there is no principled reason to distinguish between the harm caused by non-predatory dumping and the harm caused by non-dumped low-priced imports. Undeniably, low-priced imports inflict losses on domestic interests; however, the severity of these losses does not depend on the home-market price of those imports, which is what distinguishes dumped imports from other imports.

Empirically, most Canadian cases in which antidumping duties are imposed do not reflect distributive justice or communitarian rationales. Hutton and Trebilcock show that of the thirty Canadian antidumping cases in which antidumping duties were imposed between 30 October 1984 and 3 February 1989, two cases could be justified by a distributive justice rationale alone, five cases could be justified by a communitarian rationale alone, and four cases could be justified by a combined distributive justice/communitarian rationale. Nineteen of the thirty cases examined could not be justified on any normative rationale, either economic or non-economic.[126] Thus, not only do non-economic rationales fail to justify a prohibition against dumping, but antidumping authorities appear to ignore these rationales when they impose antidumping duties. Indeed, Hutton and Trebilcock find that most Canadian antidumping cases benefit those workers and communities who are already better off than the majority of workers and communities in Canada,[127] suggesting that the current Canadian regime may actually violate distributive justice concerns.

A different line of non-economic rationalization of antidumping laws (and trade remedy laws more generally) has recently been developed by Sykes in a political/Public Choice analysis of these laws.[128] He argues that rather than attempting to ascribe an economic logic to them or to attempt to interpret, apply or refine them in economically rational ways, it is more persuasive to view them as part of a grand and complex political compact amongst major trading nations where in order to facilitate major trade liberalization concessions with respect to border measures such as tariffs and quantitative restrictions, the Contracting Parties by agreement reserved to themselves unilateral opt-out regimes against the contingency that the discrete impacts of import competition in particular sectors would prove politically unsustainable; in the absence of these opt-outs or safety valves, governments would have been more reluctant to assume the political risks of trade liberalization initiatives in the first place.

Sykes' argument is a subtle and disconcerting one, in that it is inherently non-refutable through any decisive a priori analysis. However, several reactions are in order. First, it seems implicitly to rest on a notion that there is a fixed quotient of protectionism in the world (and each of its trading partners) and that if protectionism is suppressed or curtailed in some dimensions it will re-surface in others (like water finding its proper level). This implicit assumption rests on murky theoretical foundations and empirically is sharply at odds with the post-war experience which on any measure has entailed dramatic trade liberalization (not only of border measures, but many other trade restricting measures). Thus, whatever implicit political compact may have motivated the initial founders of the GATT, this compact has surely not remained static and immune from new learning, experience and changing preferences, but has evolved through time and over (many more) countries. Adopting this more dynamic political perspective, there is no reason to believe that trade remedy laws (any more than the host of other protectionist measures that have been eliminated or liberalized) are part of some iron law of politics that is impervious to change. The fact that antidumping laws have not been seriously reformed to date is no more decisive against future prospects of reform than the fact that tariffs were high in 1947 (and had been for many years) was not decisive against their subsequent reduction. This is not to gainsay the continuing political salience of constituencies in importing countries whose interests may be jeopardized by trade liberalization, but it does argue for searching for better ways of accommodating these concerns that do least violence to the net welfare gains from trade. Whether such ways can in fact be found is indeed a major challenge and must await further discussion in later chapters, particularly the discussion of transition costs, safeguard regimes and domestic adjustment policies in Chapter 9.

REFORMING ANTIDUMPING LAWS

Current antidumping regimes might seek to prevent international price discrimination, international predatory pricing and intermittent dumping. However, only predatory pricing gives rise to a legitimate economic rationale for prohibiting dumping: when dumping is merely international price discrimination, the export market benefits. Intermittent dumping can be expected to occur only rarely and its net welfare effects are ambiguous.[129] Yet antidumping laws are ill-designed to identify and penalize true international predatory pricing. Instead, they result in duties being levied upon goods priced at non-predatory levels, thereby imposing costs on consumers in export markets through supracompetitive prices and subjecting foreign firms to burdens that domestic competitors do not bear.

Non-economic rationales for antidumping laws, such as concerns over distributive justice or communitarian impacts of low priced imports, are more appropriately dealt with under safeguard regimes or, better still, under domestic adjustment assistance programmes. This conclusion leads us to propose that antidumping laws should be replaced by either supranational or harmonized domestic antitrust regimes which penalize international predatory pricing without at the same time penalizing non-predatory international price discrimination. Price discrimination laws should play no role in regulating cross-border trade. Amongst Member States of the European Union, this solution has largely been adopted, with the abolition of antidumping duties with respect to inter-member trade and replacement with Union competition laws which bind Member States and their citizens. However, EU competition laws constrain not only predatory pricing but also price discrimination, including cross-border price discrimination.[130] Therefore, the European model is more expansive than our analysis suggests is warranted.

Instead, the more modest goal of harmonizing domestic antitrust laws, ideally under the aegis of the GATT, with respect to international predatory pricing seems a more appropriate goal. In this respect, the 1988 Protocol between Australia and New Zealand, pursuant to the Australian–New Zealand Closer Economic Relations Trade Agreement (ANZCERTA) between the two countries is much more apposite. Both countries agreed that as of July 1990, all antidumping actions between the two countries should cease and that any antidumping duties then in place should be terminated. In their place have been substituted harmonized provisions in both countries' competition law pertaining to abuse of dominant position. These provisions permit a complainant located in one country to complain of abusive behaviour by a firm or firms located in the other country. The courts in the first country are then authorized to hold hearings in the second country and to use the second country's courts to enforce subpoenas and other orders. The provisions on abuse of dominant position clearly focus on cross-border predatory pricing, and not cross-border price discrimination. Canada and Chile have adopted a similar regime under their Free Trade Agreement. Warner has recently proposed a similar harmonized antitrust regime for bilateral Canada–US trade.[131] Here the political trade-offs seem promising. Between 1980 and 1988, US producers brought 22 antidumping actions against Canadian exporters, while Canadian producers brought 50 actions against US exporters. Canada imposed duties in 23 of the 50 actions, while the US imposed duties in 14 of the 22 actions. In principle, such a regime could also be implemented multilaterally, through a GATT cross-border predatory pricing Code, which would require signatories to harmonize their domestic antitrust laws in line with the Code, in very much the same way that at present domestic antidumping laws must conform with the GATT Antidumping Agreement (or domestic intellectual property laws must conform to the WTO TRIPS Agreement). A variant on this approach would be to preserve antidumping regimes at a formal level but seek to agree on harmonization requirements that would incorporate predation concepts explicitly into these regimes (including tests for predation or abuse of dominant position in export markets; definition of relevant (not 'like') product (and geographic) markets; protection of competition, not competitors). The initial US Antidumping Act of 1916 in part exemplifies this approach. This would, in effect, turn antidumping actions into private actions for cross-border predation, with duties rather than damages as the available remedy. In moving in this direction, one of the major forms of the 'New Protectionism' would be radically constrained, while legitimate concerns about domestic impacts of surges in low-priced imports would be dealt with through a well-conceived multilateral safeguards regime[132] and domestic adjustment assistance programmes.[133] In this chapter, we have focused on one area of potential convergence between trade policy and competition policy. Arguments for harmonizing domestic competition policies to facilitate international trade and investment in fact range much more broadly, and we take up these issues in a later chapter.

8 Subsidies, countervailing duties, and government procurement

INTRODUCTION

Under Article VI of the GATT, countervailing duties can be levied by member countries on imports that are causing harm to domestic industries due to subsidization by a foreign government.[1] After antidumping actions, countervailing duty actions are the most frequently initiated trade-remedy actions, accounting for 18% of all import relief measures initiated between 1979 and 1988.[2] However, unlike antidumping actions, one country is the main user: between 1979 and 1988 the United States initiated 371 actions while all other countries initiated only 58.[3] According to Messerlin: 'To the United States, the [GATT Subsidies] Code is an instrument to control subsidies. To the rest of the world, it is an instrument to control US countervailing duties.'[4] The predominance of the USA as a user of countervailing duties illustrates the distinctive view of subsidies held by the USA, and limited international agreement on the status of subsidies as policy instruments. In the USA, subsidies are often viewed as illegitimate distortions of international trade, while in other countries industrial subsidies have often been considered a legitimate instrument of domestic policy. On some measures, rates of industrial subsidization more than doubled in G7 countries between 1952 and 1985: from 1.03% of GDP to 2.13%, while in the US the figure stood at 0.58% in 1985.[5] Levels of subsidization have undoubtedly fallen more recently, as many governments, in the face of recessionary conditions in the late 1980s and early 1990s and rising budget deficits have cut public expenditures and committed themselves to domestic policies of privatization and de-regulation.

Despite US concerns at the use of subsidies by other countries,[6] there is a debate about the incidence of subsidies in the United States itself, particularly at the state level where subsidies (including tax incentives), including locational inducements for new plants, are pervasive. Fry estimates that 'at the end of the 1980s, the total annual tab for targeted assistance at the subnational level was over $20 billion for non-agricultural businesses; expenditures and lost revenues for the states approached $200 billion'.[7] Moreover, many of these state aids are highly visible, rather than being hidden in procurement policies, utility rate rebates, etc.[8]

With respect to subsidies at the federal level, recent empirical work by Bence and Smith, based upon data from the mid-to-late-1980s, concluded that, excluding the defence sector, the average subsidy rate (subsidies as a percentage of the value of industry outputs) was about 0.5% for the United States.[9] However, once defence procurement in the United States is taken into account, the US average rate of subsidies jumps to 2%. Bence and Smith, however, do not explain the methodology used to discern the subsidy component in defence procurement, and hence the 2% estimate should be regarded as speculative. At the same time, it should be noted that neither estimate fully reflects off-budget items such as loan guarantees and tax expenditures.[10]

Parties to the GATT are authorized to levy countervailing duties in response to injury caused or threatened by subsidized imports.[11] However, there are three situations in which subsidies can distort trade, and in only one can countervailing duties be used directly to address any resulting distortions. First, if country A subsidizes its exports to country B, causing domestic producers in country B to be disadvantaged, country B can respond by countervailing those imports. Second, if country A subsidizes its domestic production, disadvantaging the exports of country B to country A, the only actions country B can take are to respond with equivalent subsidies, or complain of nullification or impairment of prior tariff concessions to a GATT dispute resolution panel.[12] Finally, if country A subsidizes exports to C, disadvantaging exports of country B into C's market, again there is little that country B can do unilaterally other than respond with equivalent subsidies.[13] It is necessary to consider both the rules on subsidies and those on countervailing duties in order to address the problems raised in these three scenarios.

GATT PROVISIONS ON SUBSIDIES

Article VI

Article VI of the GATT contains general rules governing the application of antidumping and countervailing duties. In section 3, countervailing duties are defined as 'a special duty levied for the purpose of offsetting any bounty or subsidy bestowed directly or indirectly upon the manufacture, production or export of any merchandise'. The fact that countervailing duties are linked with antidumping duties in this Article suggests that subsidies are actionable for the same reason that dumping is: because they result in below-normal value pricing;[14] however, subsidization is distinguished from dumping on the grounds that the former is a distorting practice of *government* whereas the latter is a pricing policy of a private firm.[15]

Few rules are laid out in this Article. In order for a countervailing duty action to be authorized, the effect of the subsidization must be to cause or threaten material injury to an established domestic industry or to retard materially the establishment of a domestic industry. Section 5 specifies that no product may be subject to both antidumping and countervailing duties and that any countervailing duties should be no more than the estimated bounty or subsidy determined to have been granted. Finally, two specific practices are exempted from countervailing duty actions. First, the exemption of a product from duties or taxes borne by that product (or a product like or competitive with that product) when not destined for export (i.e. when destined for consumption in the country of origin) is not a countervailable subsidy.[16] Second, the maintenance of price stabilization systems for producers of primary commodities is not countervailable if such systems lead to both high and low export prices and are not intended to stimulate exports or cause distortions.[17]

Article XVI

Article XVI of the GATT contains general provisions on subsidies. At the time of the formation of the GATT, Article XVI contained only one provision whose main purpose was to encourage notification and consultation on the use of subsidies. Section A requires Parties to notify the GATT of any subsidies that affect imports or exports, directly or indirectly, and to consult with any Parties whose interests are threatened by or are suffering serious prejudice from such subsidies. This provision of the GATT was: 'something less than an effective brake on the use of subsidies . . . [and] there is no record of any country ever having limited a subsidizing practice as a result of consultations under Article XVI, paragraph 1'.[18]

In 1955, Article XVI was expanded to include a more specific provision on export subsidies.[19] The provision is relatively weak and in any event not all countries accepted it.[20] Under section B, Parties were obliged to seek to avoid the use of subsidies on the export of primary products. Any such subsidy should not be applied in such a way as to result in that Contracting Party having a 'more than equitable' share of world export trade in the subsidized product. With respect to non-primary products, Parties were to seek to avoid the use of subsidies that would result in export sales of a product at prices below the comparable price for the sale of the like good in the domestic market. The different treatment of primary and non-primary products was interpreted by developing countries as discrimination against their trade and they did not endorse this section of the Article.[21] The final amendment to Article XVI was made in 1960 when an illustrative list of export subsidies was developed to aid Parties in interpreting the provisions.[22]

The Tokyo Round Subsidies Code

As was the case with antidumping, the presence of an injury requirement in Article VI of the GATT did not affect the administration of countervailing duty laws in the USA. By virtue of the Protocol of Provisional Acceptance, domestic laws that were in existence at the time of the signing of the GATT took precedence over GATT obligations, leaving the US government 'free to countervail without demonstrable economic justification'.[23] For most nations, subsidies other than export subsidies were considered matters of national or internal policy. Thus, the aim of the Tokyo Round negotiations on subsidies was to secure a binding requirement that countervailing duties only be imposed on subsidized products that were causing material injury to domestic producers. However, the USA, which felt strongly about the unfairness of subsidies, insisted that rules on countervail should only be addressed if an agreement to discipline subsidies more generally was reached.[24] In essence, there was a fundamental difference in approach to the issue of subsidies/countervailing measures.[25] The result of the conflict between the USA and other countries was the two-track approach laid out in the Tokyo Round Code on Subsidies and Countervailing Duties. It should be noted that the Code was a plurilateral, not multilateral, agreement and was in fact adopted mostly by OECD countries and by a small number of the most advanced developing countries, leaving non-signatories uncommitted to the disciplines and disentitled to its benefits.

Track I

Track I of the Tokyo Round Subsidies Code dealt entirely with unilateral responses to subsidies – i.e. the imposition of countervailing duties on subsidized imports causing injury to a domestic industry. Signatories had the authority to impose countervailing duties sufficient to counteract the foreign subsidy, or a lesser duty if this would be sufficient to alleviate the injury.[26] The procedural and substantive provisions are very similar to those on antidumping. Article 2(1) requires that sufficient evidence of subsidization, injury and a causal link between the imports and the injury be furnished before an investigation can be launched. The main weakness in the Code was that there was no clear definition of a countervailable subsidy. Because of the Code's silence on this issue, countries were given a great deal of latitude in defining 'subsidy' for countervailing duty purposes.[27]

Track II

Track II has been the multilateral route for addressing subsidies.[28] It was primarily concerned with obligations undertaken by signatories to reduce the incidence of trade-distorting subsidies and for the most part was an elaboration of Article XVI of the GATT. Countries agreed to notify the Contracting Parties of any subsidies that may impact on exports or imports and undertook to avoid granting export subsidies[29] on other than primary products. Moreover, signatories were expected to avoid export subsidies on certain primary products if they served to increase the signatory's share of world trade beyond what is equitable, account being taking of the share of the signatory in trade during a previous representative period. If an export subsidy was being maintained in a manner inconsistent with the Code, a signatory would request consultation with the offending country under Article 12(1). The matter could be referred to conciliation and panel review under Part VI of the Code if a mutually acceptable solution was not reached in thirty days.

Expanding on Article XVI of the GATT, the Code addressed domestic subsidies in Article 11. Signatories recognized that domestic subsidies were important instruments for the promotion of social and economic policy. The policy objectives recognized in the Code[30] were:

1 the elimination of industrial, economic and social disadvantages of specific regions;
2 to facilitate the restructuring, under socially acceptable conditions, of certain sectors, especially where this has become necessary by reason of changes in trade and economic policies, including international agreements resulting in lower barriers to trade;
3 generally to sustain employment and to encourage re-training and change in employment;
4 to encourage research and development programmes, especially in the field of high-technology industries;
5 the implementation of economic programmes and policies to promote the economic and social development of developing countries;
6 redeployment of industry in order to avoid congestion and environmental problems.

Furthermore, signatories 'do not intend to restrict the right of signatories to use such subsidies to achieve these and other important policy objectives which they consider desirable'.[31] When adopting policies that involve the granting of subsidies, Parties shall 'weigh, as far as is practicable, taking account of the nature of the particular case, possible adverse effects on trade'.[32] While recognized as legitimate, domestic subsidies could be challenged if they caused one of three effects:[33]

- injury to the domestic industry of another signatory;
- nullification or impairment of the benefits accruing to another signatory under the General Agreement;
- serious prejudice to the interests of another signatory.[34]

Unlike the Track I procedure, Track II did not permit the complainant to impose duties unilaterally to counteract an offensive subsidy, but did address all these basic subsidy scenarios identified above. First, the complainant signatory was required to consult with the country providing the subsidy. If no mutually acceptable solution to the matter was reached then a panel would be formed by the Committee on Subsidies and Countervailing Measures.[35] After consideration of the panel's report, the Committee would make recommendations to the Parties to the dispute. If these recommendations were not followed within a reasonable amount of time, the Committee could authorize countermeasures – including the withdrawal of GATT concessions or obligations.

The Code also recognized the role of subsidies in the economic development policies of developing countries and laid out somewhat stricter rules governing actions against them under Track I. There were also restrictions on the rights of other signatories to take action against them under Track II.

The Tokyo Round Subsidies Code proved only modestly effective, and contentious cases involving EC subsidies on the export of wheat flour and pasta and on domestic oilseed production were not satisfactorily resolved, precipitating further negotiations over subsidies disciplines during the Uruguay Round.

There were, however, a number of less contentious cases satisfactorily resolved. In 1991, Brazil challenged a countervailing duty imposed by the United States on non-rubber footwear from Brazil.[36] Brazil argued that the United States had violated its most-favoured nations obligations toward Brazil, by giving it less favourable treatment in the administration of the Subsidies Code than it had accorded to other countries. More specifically, the less favourable treatment was argued to be the failure on the part of the United States automatically to backdate the revocation of countervailing duty orders issued without an injury determination to the date on which the United States was obligated to provide that determination. The panel accepted Brazil's argument and ruled against the United States, ostensibly expanding and refining the definition of most-favoured nation treatment in this context. Another case before a GATT panel in 1991 involved a challenge to countervailing duty determinations on the part of the United States.[37] Here, Norway argued that the United States had violated the Code on a number of counts by imposing duties on Norwegian exports of salmon. The panel found that the United States had acted consistently with its obligations under the Code. An important aspect of this case was the conclusion of the panel that 'the imposition by the United States of countervailing duties in respect of regional development programmes was not inconsistent with [its legal] obligations.'[38] The fact that Norway had been subsidizing its salmon industry as part of a regional development programme was not relevant to the outcome of this case.[39] Another case involving Brazilian duties on milk and milk powder from the EC was also successfully resolved. The EC challenged the duties on a number of procedural and substantive provisions. Here they were bolstered by the third-party support of the United States who sought to ensure that Brazil's procedures were in conformity with the Code. The panel ruled in favour of the EC and recommended that Brazil cease to apply countervailing duties.[40]

The Uruguay Round Subsidies Agreement[41]

The new Uruguay Round Subsidies Agreement, unlike the Toyko Round Code, is an integral part of the GATT/WTO and binds all Member States. Agreement on tighter constraints on subsidies was facilitated by recessionary conditions and rising government deficits during the negotiations. Subsidies are for the first time defined. They will be deemed to exist if there is a financial contribution by government or any public body where the government practice involves a direct transfer of funds (e.g. grants, loans, and equity infusion); potential direct transfers or liabilities (e.g. loan guarantees); government revenue that is otherwise due but is forgone; government provision of goods or services other than general infrastructure; government payments to a funding mechanism or direction to a private body to carry out any of the foregoing functions (Article 1.1). A definition of specificity is also adopted, which closely follows existing US countervailing duty law. This definition includes subsidies that are on their face limited to an enterprise or industry (or group of enterprises or industries), as well as subsidies that are *de facto* specific in terms of how governments exercise their discretion in the administration of a subsidy programme or who actually benefits from it.

Subsidies are classified as actionable, non-actionable, and prohibited. Non-actionable subsidies include general (non-specific) subsidies such as spending on education or infrastructure, as well as some specific subsidies (Article 8). First, specific assistance for research activities conducted by firms or by higher education or research establishments on a contract basis with firms is not actionable if the assistance covers not more than 50% of the costs of basic industrial research or 25% of the costs of applied research.[42] Second, assistance to disadvantaged regions given pursuant to a general framework of regional development, and non-specific within eligible regions, is not actionable subject to certain conditions. Each disadvantaged region must be a clearly designated, continuous geographical area with a definable economic and administrative identity. The region must be considered as disadvantaged based on neutral and objective criteria, indicating that the region's difficulties arise out of more than temporary circumstances. The criteria include some measure of economic development which shall be based on at least one of the following factors (as measured over a three-year period): one of either income per capita or household income per capita, or GDP per capita, which must not be above 85% of the average for the country concerned; the unemployment rate which must be at least 110% of the average for the country concerned. Even these two forms of specific subsidies may be objectionable if a signatory can demonstrate that they have resulted in serious adverse effects to its domestic industry. Third, assistance to promote adaptation of existing facilities to new environmental requirements is non-actionable provided it is a one-off measure, is limited to 20% of the adaptation costs, does not cover the cost of replacing and operating the assisted investment, is directly limited to planned reduction in a firm's pollution and does not cover any manufacturing cost savings, and is available to all firms that can adopt the new equipment or processes. These three kinds of subsidies require notification to the Committee on Subsidies and Countervailing Measures prior to implementation to ensure compliance with the various conditions that attach them.

Two kinds of non-agricultural subsidies are prohibited *per se*: subsidies contingent in law or in fact upon export performance (illustrated in an Annex to the Agreement), and subsidies contingent upon use of domestic rather than imported inputs (Article 3). Subsidies that are neither prohibited nor non-actionable are placed in the actionable category. Actionable subsidies are defined as specific forms of government assistance to firms or industries (Article 5). The list of legitimate grounds for domestic subsidies found in Article 11 of the Tokyo Round Subsidies Code has been dropped. Actionable subsidies may be objectionable if they cause injury to the domestic industry of another country, if they entail nullification or impairment of benefits accruing to another country under the GATT, including the benefits of concessions bound under Article II of the GATT, or if they cause serious prejudice to the interests of another country. Serious prejudice may arise where the effect of the subsidy is to displace or impede the imports of like products into the market of the subsidizing country; where the effect of the subsidy is to displace or impede the export of a like product of another country from or to a third-country market; where the effect of the subsidy is a significant price-undercutting by the subsidized products as compared with the price of a like product of another country in the same market; or where the effect of the subsidy is an increase in the world market share of the subsidizing country in a particular subsidized primary product or commodity as compared to the average share it had during the previous period of three years (Article 6.3). Subsidization in excess of a threshold value of 5% *ad valorem* is deemed to cause serious prejudice unless the subsidizing country can prove otherwise. Prohibited (export) and actionable subsidies are subject to challenge under either the multilateral dispute resolution track or the domestic countervailing duty track. Non-actionable subsidies are immune from challenge under both tracks (Article 10, note 33), although where a non-actionable subsidy is causing serious adverse effects to the domestic industry of a Member State, the Subsidies Committee may recommend a modification to the programme.

Part V of the Agreement sets out detailed rules governing countervailing duty actions. In most respects they follow the Tokyo Round Code. However, countervailing duties may only be imposed in respect of actionable or prohibited subsidies as defined in the Agreement. Article 11.9 also contains a *de minimis* provision which requires an investigation to be terminated if the amount of a subsidy is less than 1% *ad valorem* or where the volume of subsidized imports or the injury is negligible. Under Article 15.5, in determining material injury from subsidized imports, injuries caused by factors unrelated to the subsidized imports cannot be attributed to the imports; a number of these extraneous factors are enumerated in the Article. Under Article 21.3, duties must be terminated within five years of their imposition unless renewed following a review by the relevant domestic agency prior to that date.

With respect to institutional arrangements, the Subsidies Committee constituted under the Agreement shall establish a permanent Group of five Experts to prepare opinions on the existence of prohibited subsidies and to provide advisory opinions to the Committee on the existence and nature of any subsidy. The Group of Experts may be consulted by any signatory and give advisory opinions on the nature of any subsidy proposed to be introduced or currently maintained by that signatory, although such advisory opinions may not be invoked in proceedings before the Committee itself (Article 24). The consolidated dispute resolution mechanisms provided elsewhere in the Uruguay Round Agreement empower the Committee to constitute panels to review subsidy complaints, including, importantly, application by domestic agencies of Member States of domestic countervailing duty laws at variance with the terms of the Agreement (for example, the application of the specificity test).

Under Part VII of the Agreement, substantially enhanced notification and surveillance procedures with respect to subsidies are instituted, requiring signatories to report annually to the Committee the existence of subsidies (as defined by the Agreement), and to provide substantial detail on the nature and effects of the subsidies. The Committee itself is required to engage in regular surveillance of these notifications.

With respect to developing countries, Part VIII provides some partial exemptions from the strictures in the Agreement. The provisions on prohibited subsidies do not apply to least developed countries, and other developing country signatories are provided with an eight-year grace period to bring themselves into compliance with the prohibited subsidy provisions. The presumptive rules, providing when actionable subsidies shall be deemed to result in serious prejudice (Article 6(1)), do not apply to developing countries with respect to whom such prejudice must be demonstrated by positive evidence. With respect to actionable subsidies, the dispute resolution process may not be invoked unless the subsidy entails nullification or impairment of tariff concessions or other obligations under the GATT in such a way as to displace or impede imports of like products into the market of the subsidizing country or unless injury to the domestic industry in the importing market of a signatory occurs as defined in the Agreement. Moreover, countervailing duty actions shall not proceed if a domestic agency determines that the overall level of subsidy granted by a developing country upon the product in question is 2% or less of its value calculated on a per unit basis, and that the volume of the subsidized imports represents less than 4% of the total imports for the like product in the importing signatory. This exemption from countervailing duties only applies where developing countries collectively account for no more than 9% of the total imports for the like product in the importing country. The comparable *de minimis* rule in the case of subsides originating in developed countries is 1% *ad valorem* (Article 11.9). In the case of countries in the process of transformation from a centrally-planned to a market economy, prohibited subsidies must be phased out within a period of seven years from the date of entry into force of the Agreement. Subsidy programmes involving forgiveness of government debt and grants to cover debt repayment are not actionable for the same period under the dispute resolution processes of the Agreement. With respect to other actionable subsidies, the provisions applicable to developing countries, which require nullification or impairment of tariff concessions or other obligations under the GATT, are adopted (Article 29).

Apart from the Uruguay Round Subsidies Agreement, the Tokyo Round Agreement on Trade in Civil Aircraft and a 1992 Agreement between the EU and the US constrain subsidies in the civil aircraft industry. A 1994 Agreement among some OECD members also constrains subsidies in the civil shipbuilding and repair industry.

More recently, the Appellate Body of the WTO has considered issues relating to countervailing duties in a dispute between the Philippines and Brazil over desiccated coconut.[43] Here the dispute was really about when the 1995 WTO Agreement entered into force, an issue central to the outcome of the case. The original panel had ruled that the Article VI of GATT 1994 did not apply in the present case, as the dispute concerned countervailing duties which were imposed before the WTO Agreement came into force. The Philippines appealed this point, arguing that the WTO Agreement was a legal tool available to them as soon as it entered into force. Brazil also appealed the decision of the panel citing a deficiency in the terms of reference. The Appellate Body upheld the decision of the panel on the first issue and therefore found it unnecessary to rule on the second question regarding the terms of reference.[44]

Protectionism in government procurement[45]

Government procurement policies pose a problem closely related to that of potentially trade-distorting subsidies. In most countries, the government is the largest single purchaser in the economy. In common law jurisdictions (like Canada), the government's procurement contracts are usually governed, in principle, by the same contract law that applies to private transactions.[46] The process of government procurement is, however, unlike private contracting in that governments often use their large purchasing power as a tool to promote various domestic political, social, and economic policies. These purposes of government procurement contracting lead to the adoption of a wide range of measures that qualify the objective of obtaining the best product or service for the lowest price.[47] The three most common areas for domestic preference in government procurement are: (1) to protect employment in declining industries; (2) to protect the supply of 'strategic' defence goods; and (3) to support emerging domestic high-tech industries.

Domestic preference in government procurement contracting is usually expressed in the form of either official domestic preference policies (overt discrimination against foreign suppliers) or exclusionary tactics 'hidden' as something else (less visible forms of discrimination).[48] Overtly discriminatory tactics include:

1 Price differentials applied against foreign bids (whereby foreign bids may be accepted only if the lowest domestic bid is more than a certain percentage higher than the foreign one).[49]
2 'Discounts' for the domestic content of the bid.
3 Selective sourcing policies (whereby only domestic firms are invited to bid).[50]
4 Set-asides of certain procurements to specific domestic sectors.
5 Assignments of certain procurements for domestic industries only (for example, defence spending).
6 Requiring foreign contractors to procure from the local market as a condition of the award of the contract.

Less visible forms of discrimination include:

1 Selective tendering procedures, employed to (unofficially) exclude foreign competition.
2 Manipulating the time and method of giving notice of tender solicitations to favour domestic suppliers.
3 Short deadlines for submitting bids, which foreign suppliers are unable to meet.
4 Product or service standards which are only readily met by domestic producers.

The GATT Tokyo Round Code on Government Procurement

The GATT initially refrained almost completely from regulating government procurement policies: paragraph 8(a) of Article III makes government procurement an exception to the National Treatment obligation. However, this issue was re-examined during the Tokyo Round, and it was decided that the eventual elimination of discriminatory procurement practices was desirable.[51] The result of the ensuing negotiations was the Agreement on Government Procurement (the Code), a plurilateral Agreement with about twenty signatories.[52]

The Tokyo Round Code on Government Procurement sought to achieve greater liberalization of government procurement through the establishment of an agreed framework with respect to regulations, procedures and practices regarding government procurement. The Code established the obligation of National Treatment, and also set out detailed rules for transparent procurement procedures that were to be followed in order to ensure that foreign suppliers indeed receive fair treatment.

The Code was, however, quite limited in scope and coverage. It only applied to contracts of a value of SDR 130,000 or more[53] (about US$170,000). Service contracts were not covered at all by the Code,[54] and Article VIII provides for other exceptions, notably in the area of defence spending. As well, the Code only applied to government agencies that 'contributed' to the Code, as listed in Annex I:13; signatories excluded numerous departments from this list. State or municipal governments were also not covered by the Code.

The Code's provisions for National Treatment also raised several difficulties. First, these provisions were only available to suppliers from other signatories to the Agreement, thus requiring rules of origin.[55] Second, these principles did not exempt foreign suppliers from customs duties. Third, Article V:15(b) allowed governments to continue to demand offset industrial benefits (such as local content, licensing of technology, investment requirements, counter-trade or similar requirements) from potential foreign suppliers as a condition for awarding a contract.

The key mechanism of the Code was a set of detailed and transparent tendering procedures. The preferred procedure under the Code was the 'open' tender, in which a notice of each proposed purchase (NPP) is published in the designated publications, containing all of the information necessary for the timely submission of both foreign and domestic bids.[56] 'Selective' tendering procedures were also allowed, either by the use of previously established lists of suppliers, or by a qualification requirement as a precondition for the submission of bids; however, such lists and qualifications were required to be published, and not to be used as a means of excluding foreign suppliers.[57] More problematic is the use of 'single' tendering procedures, where the government only considers tenders from a single source. In order to control the protectionist abuse of single tendering, the Code required a justification to be published in an appropriate publication (as defined by the Code) in the event of a single tendering.[58]

The Code required that a contract shall be awarded to the lowest tender, or to the tender which in terms of the specific evaluation criteria set forth in the NPP is determined to be the most advantageous.[59] The use of technical specifications to refuse the award to a foreign firm, a common device used by governments to exclude foreign suppliers from tender competition, was regulated under Article IV:2(a). Technical specifications prescribed by procurement entities should be in terms of performance rather than design, and should also be based on international standards if possible.

The Code provided for a system of enforcement and dispute resolution. The emphasis has been on the settlement of disputes between the states involved, rather than the granting of a private right of action to an aggrieved supplier: mechanisms for the hearing of private complaints were left to the discretion of the procuring agency.[60] Between governments, Article VII of the Code envisaged a three-stage complaints proceeding: first, bilateral consultations would be held; second, if these produced no result, the Committee on Government Procurement would mediate; and third, if mediation failed, the Committee would constitute an *ad hoc* panel to make recommendations. Panel decisions were non-binding, but the Committee could recommend the authorization of the suspension of the application of the Code *vis-à-vis* the suppliers of the non-complying Party.[61]

Under these provisions in 1991, the United States challenged a procurement on the part of the government of Norway for electronic toll collection for the city of Trondheim.[62] The United States contended that Norway had violated its obligations under the *Agreement on Government Procurement* in choosing a Norwegian supplier of electronic equipment. The dispute primarily centred around the fact that 'the Government of Norway had single tendered the equipment from a Norwegian supplier, excluding viable and eager competition from a capable United States'.[63] Norway justified this classification on the basis that it was a research and development contract and thus excluded from the disciplines of the Agreement. The panel found that a single tendering of this procurement could not be justified in the present case and accepted the argument of the United States.

The Uruguay Round Government Procurement Agreement[64]

The Toyko Round Government Procurement Code was substantially revised during the Uruguay Round negotiations in an attempt to address some of the difficulties in the Code's operation.[65] These revisions have the effect of harmonizing the GATT Code with the NAFTA Agreement on government procurement (see below). There are four key areas of change in the revised GATT Agreement: first, the scope and coverage of the Agreement has been expanded to include service and construction contracts; second, entitites covered have been extended beyond central government entities to subnational government entities and to public enterprises (e.g. public utilities)[66] third, contracting entities are no longer able to demand offsets as a condition for the awarding of contracts;[67] and fourth, the Parties are now required to establish effective bid challenge procedures.[68]

The establishment of mandatory bid challenge procedures, by which aggrieved foreign suppliers may challenge alleged breaches of the Agreement directly, is potentially the most important change in the Uruguay Round Agreement. Under this requirement, each Party to the Agreement will have to establish impartial review bodies to adjudicate procurement disputes in a timely fashion. However, as noted in Article XX:7(c), the compensation provided to the aggrieved supplier may be limited to the costs for tender preparation or protest, a sum which may be insufficient to deter governments from effectively breaching their obligations under the Agreement.

An important new aspect of the Uruguay Round Agreement is the expansion of the scope and coverage of the Agreement to include 'sub-central government' (state, provincial and municipal) entities and public enterprises as well as central government entities. Each Party is responsible for listing in Appendix I all entities within its jurisdiction to be covered by the Agreement, and each Party may withdraw one of the listed entities at will (subject to objections from other Parties, which are to be resolved in accordance with the procedures on consultations and dispute settlement contained in Article XXII). If major changes to the existing structure are requested by one of the Parties, such as transfers of entities between categories within Appendix I, the Committee on Government Procurement (established by Article XXI) will consider the proposed change and determine if compensatory adjustments are necessary.

Unfortunately, the Uruguay Round Government Procurement Agreement (GPA), like its Tokyo Round predecessor, is a plurilateral, not multilateral Agreement (with 23 signatories), and did not undergo the important status change of most of the Tokyo Round Codes, which have now been fully integrated into the GATT/WTO and bind all Member States – presumably a testament to the influence of powerful domestic constituencies who benefit from preferential government procurement. This raises complex questions as to when a procuring government is entitled to discriminate between GPA and non-GPA signatories in awarding contracts, given that the GPA contains no explicit exemption from the general MFN obligation in the GATT. Also, even among GPA Members, numerous derogations and the adoption of a reciprocity rule mean that signatories often deny access to procurements by categories of entities to suppliers from certain GPA signatories or deny access to procurement for certain classes of goods or services where other signatories have not made reciprocal commitments in these same areas. Differential treatment both between signatories and non-signatories and among signatories is likely to raise formidable complexities in identifying the origins of goods or services and also has the potential for creating significant trade diversion.[69] Thus, the Agreement can only be counted as modest progress towards liberalizing government procurement markets around the world.

Government procurement under the Canada–US FTA

As a result of the limited coverage of the Tokyo Round Government Procurement Code, many Canadian and US firms were still subject to the protectionist procurement policies of each other's governments. In the USA, these measures included the Buy American Act, which required that only domestic supplies be purchased for public use, subject to an exception for 'unreasonably' priced domestic alternative products. The American government also protects domestic concerns through various 'set-aside' provisions, notably to benefit businesses owned by 'socially or economically disadvantaged individuals', a category which automatically excludes foreign suppliers.

The Canadian procurement policies are not regulated by statute, but rather by administrative directives. The most important of these is the Canadian Content Premium Policy, under which the Department of Supply and Services will apply a premium of 10% of the difference in foreign content on competing bids in favour of sources with greater Canadian content. As well, when the value of a procurement exceeds $2 million, the 'procurement review mechanism' is triggered, with the purpose of ensuring that the awarding of the contract will achieve the 'maximum benefit to Canada'.[70] These administrative directives are only in effect for government contracts not covered by international agreements, but before the implementation of the FTA they were an important method of ensuring domestic preferment for contracts not covered by the GATT Code.

The FTA represented an attempt to liberalize government procurement that was not covered under the GATT Code from the effects of these domestic preference policies. However, Chapter 13 of the FTA actually changed little from the Code.[71] The most important changes it made were: first, to lower the threshold of eligibility from SDR 130,000 to $US25,000; second, to enable eligible Canadian goods to be treated like US goods (including 'Buy American' differentials);[72] and, third, the establishment of a requirement for domestic procurement review, available to aggrieved suppliers.

In Canada, the Procurement Review Board was established to fulfil this obligation. Governed by both the procedures of the GATT Code and the 'expanded' obligations under Article 1305 of the FTA, the board has the authority to order the government to postpone the awarding of a contract pending the completion of the board's investigation.

Government procurement under NAFTA

NAFTA's Chapter 10 provides for considerably wider coverage than either the Tokyo Round Government Procurement Code or the FTA, both in terms of entities and types of contracts covered. Not only does NAFTA extend the improvements available under the FTA to Mexico, it also extends coverage to many federal government agencies not covered by either the FTA or the Code, although not to subnational levels of government.[73] NAFTA also closed some previously-existing exclusions in the earlier agreements, such as construction and service contracts (which are now covered) and the imposition by procurement entities of offset requirements (which are now prohibited).[74]

Threshold values were, however, raised under NAFTA to $US50,000 (this provision, however, applies only to Mexico: for Canada and the USA, the FTA threshold of $US25,000 still applies). For the newly-covered area of construction services, the threshold has been set at $US6.5 million. For 'government enterprises', as opposed to federal government entities, the thresholds are higher still: $US250,000 for goods and services, and $US8 million for construction services.

One major problem with the NAFTA procurement rules lies in the area of tendering procedures. Article 1009 of NAFTA allows more restrictive 'qualification procedures' than the FTA, which may be used to exclude foreign tenders.

The process of liberalizing North American government procurement markets under NAFTA is still far from complete. Under Article 1024, the Parties have agreed to commence further negotiations no later than 1998, with a view to further liberalization of their respective government procurement markets. Prior to that date, the Parties have agreed to attempt to obtain the voluntary acceptance, by state and provincial government entities, of the principles contained in this chapter. As well, the Parties have also agreed to increase their obligations and coverage under this chapter to a level at least commensurate with the final version of the Uruguay Round Agreement.

Procurement markets in the European Union

The European Union has attempted to regulate the domestic preferment policies of its Member States with regard to government procurement through a series of coordination directives. The legal effect of these directives is that aggrieved suppliers can, at least in principle, invoke the provisions of the procurement directives directly in the national courts of the Member States.

The original directives issued by the commission were the Public Works directive and the Public Supplies directive.[75] These directives were based on three main principles: first, community-wide advertising of contracts, in order to give equal opportunity to firms from all Member States; second, the banning of 'discriminatory' technical specifications; and third, the use of objective and non-discriminatory criteria in tendering and award procedures.

The major problems with these directives were their limited coverage (the so-called 'excluded sectors' included energy, water, transportation and telecommunications), and their high value thresholds (after amendment, ECU 5,000,000 for the Works directive, and ECU 130,000 for the Supplies directive). Another major problem lay in the excessive discretion given to awarding entities to choose their tendering procedures.

Under the coordination directives, three different tendering procedures are allowed: 'open' and 'restrictive' competitive tendering, and non-competitive 'negotiated' tendering. In 'restrictive' tendering, the awarding authority advertises its intention to receive requests to participate in the tender for a specific contract; the authority may then choose the applicants to whom invitations to submit tenders will be sent. This system can obviously be abused, although amendments to the directives now curtail the awarding authorities' discretion somewhat (requiring, for example, justification for the use of 'restrictive' tendering procedures under the supplies directive, and the publication of the reasons for both winning and losing bids under the works directive). An additional opportunity for abuse was created by the fact that non-competitive tendering was originally allowed in exceptional circumstances, although the Member State's use of these exceptions was required to be reported.[76]

Experience with the operation of the coordination directives soon demonstrated that redress for aggrieved suppliers in the offending nation's national courts was uneven. To remedy this situation, the Review directive was implemented.[77] This directive requires members to provide effective domestic review procedures with the power to suspend the awarding of contracts, to set aside awarding entities decisions, and to award damages to aggrieved suppliers.

The Commission also made an attempt to apply the Union procurement rules to the traditionally excluded utilities sectors by implementing the Utilities directive.[78] This directive applies both to public authorities and to private firms operating on the basis of 'special or exclusive rights' granted by a Member State (to avoid the public/private distinction in the legal status of the entities involved). Due to the 'special nature' of the concerned undertakings, awarding entities were allowed considerable discretion in their choice of tendering procedures, and were in addition allowed to use an unspecified 'qualification system' to screen potential tenders.

The Commission, recognizing the special status of the 'excluded sectors', also adopted a Utilities Review directive applicable only to the Utilities directive.[79] Like the regular Review directive, it requires Member States to provide effective review procedures in relation to all decisions taken by their contracting entities. As an alternative to this mandatory remedy, the Utilities Review directive adopted two voluntary procedures: the attestation system, in which the awarding entity submits to systematic review by attestors (independent and objective witnesses to the entity's conformity with the requirements); and the conciliation procedure, in which aggrieved bidders and contracting entities settle their disputes through a non-litigious process of negotiation mediated by a Commission-appointed conciliator. In general, these review procedures allow the Member States wide discretion in determining what procedures they will follow.

DOMESTIC ADMINISTRATION OF COUNTERVAILING DUTY LAWS[80]

Institutional context

Because the USA is almost the exclusive user of countervailing duty laws, it is important to understand the institutions and methodologies it employs to administer those laws. Four institutions are involved in the administration of US countervailing duty laws: the International Trade Administration of the Department of Commerce (DC), the International Trade Commission (ITC), the Court of International Trade (CIT) and the review panels initially established under Chapter 19 of the Canada–USA Free Trade Agreement (FTA) and now NAFTA.

The International Trade Administration is the branch of the DC responsible for the enforcement of antidumping and countervailing duty laws. It is responsible for conducting antidumping and countervailing duty investigations and has the authority to initiate investigations.[81] In countervailing duty cases the DC determines whether the products under investigation are being unlawfully subsidized, and if so, calculates the margin of subsidization and the appropriate duties. Further responsibilities include conducting administrative reviews of outstanding countervailing duty orders and ensuring that these orders are properly administered by customs officials.

The ITC is the body responsible for establishing the existence of actual or threatened material injury due to subsidized imports. The CIT is the American court with competence to review determinations of the DC and ITC (and thereafter the Court of Appeals for the Federal District). Under Chapter 19 of the FTA and NAFTA, binational panels are appointed to hear disputes arising out of countervailing duty determinations between the Parties to the Agreement.

Substantive law

In the USA, laws dealing with unfair foreign subsidization date back to the Tariff Act of 1897. Current US legislation is found in the Trade Agreements Act of 1979 which amended the Tariff Act of 1930. In a countervailing duty action, two central questions must be answered: Is the foreign producer who is selling into the domestic market receiving an actionable subsidy from its home government? Are domestic producers of products like or competitive with those being subsidized suffering or being threatened with material injury as a result of the subsidized imports?

Subsidies

According to the Tariff Act, a countervailing duty will be imposed on imported goods when it is found that the country is directly or indirectly subsidizing the manufacture, production, or exportation of goods imported into the USA.[82] The application of this provision depends on the meaning given to the word ‘subsidy’. Defined broadly, the term could include everything from the provision of basic infrastructure to government-financed education and regional development programmes. Such a definition would effectively undermine liberal trade since virtually every product would benefit from these kinds of government assistance[83] and hence could be subject to a countervailing duty. The US legislation begins its definition in §1677(5) by making clear that the term ‘subsidy’ has the same meaning as the phrase ‘bounty or grant’ and includes but is not limited to export subsidies and domestic subsidies.

Export subsidies

As reflected in Track I of the Tokyo Round Code and the definition of prohibited subsidies in the Uruguay Round Agreement, export subsidies are considered the most objectionable form of government assistance. An export subsidy can be defined as government programmes or practices that increase the profitability of export sales without similarly increasing the profitability of domestic sales.[84] The US legislation has no explicit definition of this concept, and instead refers in §1677(5)(A) to the illustrative list of export subsidies found in the Tokyo Round Subsidies Code (largely reproduced in Annex I to the Uruguay Round Agreement). Some examples of the enumerated practices are:

- the provision by governments of direct subsidies to a firm or an industry contingent upon export performance;
- currency retention schemes or any similar practices that involve a bonus on exports; and
- internal transport and freight charges on export shipments provided or mandated by governments, on terms more favourable than for domestic shipments.

The DC has the authority to find that practices not on the list are export subsidies.[85] Even with the benefit of the list, it is often difficult to identify export subsidies.[86] Because export subsidies will generally result in assessment of larger duties than would be applicable to domestic subsidies, the determination of whether a subsidy is an export or domestic subsidy is important.[87]

Domestic subsidies: the Specificity Test

International rules are more lenient with respect to subsidies not targeted specifically at exports. The hostility to pure export subsidies probably reflects the view that most legitimate domestic policy rationales for subsidies would not differentiate between production intended for domestic consumption and production intended for export. In addition, export subsidies raise concerns over the prospect of mutually destructive international export subsidy wars. However, in the countervailing duty provisions of the Tokyo and Uruguay Subsidies Codes there is no differentiation between domestic or export subsidies. In the USA, practices that cannot be characterized as export subsidies are countervailable if they fall within the definition of domestic subsidies in §1677(5) of the Tariff Act. Countervailable domestic subsidies are defined as subsidies targeted to a *specific* enterprise or industry, or group of enterprises or industries. In addition, the subsidies must provide some opportunity or advantage to the targeted producers that would not otherwise be available to them in the marketplace.[88] The wording of this definition has given rise to the Specificity Test for the assessment of the countervailability of domestic subsidies. This test has developed over time into one that investigates not only *de jure* but also *de facto* specificity. Under this test, where either the purpose or the effect of a government programme is to benefit a specific enterprise or industry, or group of enterprises or industries, the DC will find that a countervailable benefit has been conferred. Included in this definition are forms of assistance such as capital, loans or loan guarantees on terms inconsistent with commercial considerations, goods or services at preferential rates, funds or forgiven debts to cover operating losses, and the assumption of costs or expenses of manufacture, production or distribution.

In the early 1980s, there was a significant degree of controversy in the USA over whether the specificity test should be retained in its current form.[89] The CIT, on review of DC decisions, also created some confusion on this issue. In *Carlisle Tire and Rubber Co.* v. *United States*,[90] the Court upheld the DC's decision in favour of Korean exporters benefiting from a generally available accelerated depreciation programme. The court found that in order for a countervailable domestic subsidy to exist, there must be evidence of a regional or industry preference. However, subsequent cases suggest that this interpretation of the specificity test no longer obtains. For example, in *Cabot Corp.* v. *United States*,[91] the CIT held that the specificity test upheld in *Carlisle* is not the correct legal standard to apply; it would erroneously allow the recipients of subsidies purportedly of general availability to avoid countervailing duties even though the subsidies in fact only benefit specific industries or enterprises.

The *Cabot* decision resulted in a change in DC methodology. It led to the articulation of the DC's current approach: the three-pronged specificity test.[92] The DC now proceeds through a series of steps in its investigation before being satisfied that the subsidy in question is not countervailable. First, a *de jure* limitation on the availability of a subsidy is sufficient to find specificity. Second, if the subsidy is generally available but few enterprises actually use the programme, or if there are disproportionate or dominant users, the DC will find *de facto* specificity. Third, if a foreign government is exercising its discretion in such a manner that a *de jure* generally available programme is *de facto* specifically targeted, the DC will again find *de facto* specificity. This formulation of the specificity test has increased the DC's discretion and thus reduced predictability for exporters in countervailing duty cases. This definition of specificity is largely adopted in the Uruguay Round Agreement definition of actionable subsidies.

There are a number of noteworthy aspects of US countervailing duty laws.[93] First, countervailing duty actions cannot be taken against non-market economies,[94] although given the recent transformation of many of the former command economies, there is considerable room for ambiguity as to which countries presently are non-market economies. Second, subsidies indirectly received by an exporter, such as through a subsidized input source, can be countervailable. However, if it is alleged that an indirect subsidy was received by a company via a subsidy given to another company upstream,[95] the DC will not assume that benefits conferred by the subsidy are passed on to the second company.[96] In cases entailing allegations of these 'upstream subsidies', it must be shown that there is an indirect subsidy before countervailing duties will be assessed. In addition, the upstream subsidy must confer a competitive benefit on the goods under investigation and have a significant effect on their cost of production.[97] It is also not sufficient to show that a subsidy programme exists; the specific product being investigated must have been subsidized.[98] Benefits conferred by private individuals may be countervailable if the evidence indicates that the benefit was conferred at the request of the government.[99] Finally, countervailing duty petitions or orders cannot be suspended or overturned by the executive for political reasons.[100]

Calculation of countervailing duties

According to Article 19.4 of the Uruguay Round Subsidies Agreement: 'No countervailing duty shall be levied on any imported product in excess of the amount of subsidy found to exist, calculated in terms of subsidization per unit of the subsidized product and exported product.' Article 19.4 provides that it is desirable that the duty should be less than the total amount of the subsidy if such lesser duty would be adequate to remove the injury to the domestic industry and that procedures should be established which would allow domestic authorities to take account of representations by domestic interests, including consumers, who may be adversely affected by the imposition of duties.

The task of the DC is to determine the amount of the countervailing duty required to protect US producers from the injury created by the subsidy.[101] In order to achieve this, the value of the subsidy is measured with reference to the benefit conferred upon the targeted industry rather than the cost of the subsidy to the government.[102] However, the DC does not evaluate the effect of the subsidy on the cost of production, quantities produced, or prices charged by the foreign exporting firm. As a result it is not clear that the methodology accurately captures competitively salient benefits to the firm. The subsidy may not result in lower costs or higher production; it may, for example, result in greater inefficiency on the part of the producer. Alternatively, the subsidy may have no effect on the costs of production because of the nature of the subsidy. For example, if the grant is to pay for the decommissioning of an old plant, there would be no effect on the marginal costs of production of the firm.[103]

The net subsidy is found by making certain adjustments to the subsidy amount conferred.[104] The countervailing duty is found by dividing the net subsidy by the total sales of the company receiving the subsidy. If the government practice is found to be an export subsidy then the countervailing duty is calculated by dividing the net subsidy by the total exports of the company receiving the subsidy; since total sales will typically be greater than exports, export subsidies will generally result in higher duties.[105] The DC will not impose duties against subsidies that are *de minimis*, comprising less than 0.5% of the *ad valorem* value of the merchandise (increased to 1% under Article 11.9 of the Uruguay Round Agreement).

Injury[106]

Prior to the Tokyo Round, US law on countervailing (and antidumping) duties did not contain an injury requirement; both forms of duties could be applied without any showing of harm to domestic firms from the foreign action. The purpose of an injury test is to ensure that duties are only imposed in cases in which a causal nexus is found between the unfair foreign practice and harm suffered by the domestic industry. The injury requirement adopted in the Tokyo and Uruguay Round Subsidies Codes is the same as that in the Antidumping Code and antidumping and countervailing duty cases are treated in the same way by the ITC.[107] The subsidized imports must cause material injury or a threat of material injury to a domestic industry, or material retardation to the establishment of a domestic industry. There are three components to the injury test: (1) the definition of domestic industry; (2) evidence of material injury; and (3) a causal nexus between that injury and the subsidized imports.

Domestic industry

The injury proceeding before the ITC requires that the ITC first define the relevant US industry. The Uruguay Round Subsidies Agreement defines 'domestic industry' as 'domestic producers as a whole of the like product or those of them whose collective output of the products constitute a major proportion of the total domestic production of those products'.[108] The US legislation adopts a similar definition.[109] Under the Uruguay Round Subsidies Agreement, no investigation may be initiated if the domestic producers expressly supporting the application account for less than 25% of total production of the product by the domestic industry (Article 11.4). In special circumstances the ITC can divide the industry into separate geographical markets if two conditions are met: (1) the companies in that region must sell all or almost all of their output of the like product in the geographical region; and (2) demand in that region must not be substantially supplied by US producers outside of the region.[110] As is the case with antidumping investigations, a narrow construction of the relevant domestic industry can make a finding of injury more likely.

The 'like product' is defined as 'a product which is like, or in the absence of like, most similar in characteristics and uses with' the product under investigation.[111] In analysing a complaint, the ITC must focus on the narrowest range of products that includes the like product, but in many cases must investigate a broader industry due to the unavailability of data. In addition, there may be more than one like product.[112]

Material injury

There is no precise definition in the Uruguay Round Agreement of 'material injury' but the Agreement directs authorities to examine a number of specific factors such as changes in output, prices, employment or profitability in the domestic industry.[113] In the USA, most cases focus on actual or threatened material injury, which is defined as harm that is not 'inconsequential, immaterial or unimportant'.[114] The injury test requires an analysis of domestic industry conditions. The factors typically considered by the ITC in this determination are the volume of subsidized imports, their effect on domestic prices of like products, and their impact on domestic producers of like products. In its evaluation of the volume of imports, the ITC considers both the absolute level of imports at the time of the proceeding and whether the level is increasing either relatively or absolutely.[115] With respect to the effect on prices, the ITC considers any evidence of undercutting and determines whether there is any indication that the effect of the subsidization has been to depress domestic prices.[116] The presence of certain negative factors such as plant closures or unprofitability will often be sufficient to convince the ITC that the injury test has been satisfied. In other cases the ITC will compare certain economic variables to their levels in previous years, inferring from a decline in such variables the presence of injury.[117] Such variables might include capacity utilization, employment, or return on equity. If these factors do not provide the ITC with evidence of material injury, the investigation will be terminated and no duties will be assessed against the exporters. The ITC's investigations are divided into a preliminary and a final phase. In the preliminary phase the ITC must determine if there is a reasonable indication of injury. Inconclusive or incomplete evidence related to the key elements may support an affirmative preliminary finding of injury but not be adequate to support a final determination of injury. In both cases, the ITC must make its determination on the basis of all the evidence before it.

Causation[118]

There is no precise definition in the Uruguay Round Agreement of 'cause', beyond a list of factors that may be examined,[119] leaving the appropriate standard to the discretion of the investigating authorities. The ITC looks for a causal nexus between the subsidization and the effects on the domestic industry. Factors that are typically considered in this context are the presence of underselling, evidence of lost sales, and import trends in the industry.[120] There are a number of weaknesses with this approach to causation. First, these three factors do not define a test capable of resolution: 'the test mixes analysis of trend information unrelated to dumping or subsidization with analysis of the effects of dumped or subsidized imports'[121] and the US legislation does not 'identify a method of integrating these factors into a cogent analytical structure'.[122] Moreover, the assumption that declining performance alone is evidence of harm caused by imports does not account for other factors that affect performance, or the possibility that the harm is due to import competition and not subsidization. Thus, because the ITC methodology focuses on the imports rather than the subsidization, an affirmative finding might result when the harm is caused by reason of comparative advantages that the imported goods might possess. Finally, the three criteria usually considered – evidence of underselling or lost sales and import trends – do not serve to identify clearly the relationship between the subsidization and the harm. For example, evidence of lost sales suffered by the domestic industry only provides relevant causal information if it can be shown that those sales were gained by the subsidized importers by reason of the subsidization. At present the ITC does not evaluate the kind of evidence or perform the kind of counterfactual that would justify a determination of causation.

Rights of appeal

The Court of International Trade (CIT) is the US Court vested with jurisdiction to review ITC and DC rulings. In practice, the CIT has been highly deferential to these administrative bodies. Underlying this disposition is the view that administrative bodies have extensive expertise and therefore have comparative competence in those matters that fall within their jurisdiction. The CIT typically requires that the agency determination be supported by substantial evidence on the record.[123] The CIT also normally requires that the ITC and DC provide the reasons supporting their determination. However, if those reasons allow the CIT 'reasonably to discern the agency's path,' a decision of 'less than ideal clarity' will be upheld.[124]

Chapter 19 of the FTA and NAFTA provides for the establishment of binational panels to review final agency determinations.[125] Either Party may request review by the binational panel and its determinations are final except in extraordinary circumstances. These panels have authority to determine that there has been either an error of law by the administrative agency or that the evidence on the record was insufficient to support the decision at that level. While a panel cannot overturn the administrative decision, its remanding of the decision to the appropriate agency generally forces compliance due to political repercussions that would result if no action were taken. Evidence to date suggests that the binational panel review process has led to significant improvements in the level of rigour required of the ITA and ITC in countervailing and antidumping duty determinations.[126]

The complexities and opaqueness of US countervailing duty law are well-exemplified in a long-running trade dispute between Canada and the US over Canadian softwood lumber exports to the US.[127]

Three separate countervailing duty investigations have been undertaken by US authorities (in 1982, 1986 and 1991) following allegations by US softwood lumber producers that low stumpage rates (royalties) charged by Canadian federal and provincial governments for harvesting lumber on Crown lands constituted a countervailable subsidy that was injuring US softwood lumber producers. In the first case, the ITA found no countervailable subsidy on the grounds that any subsidy was non-specific. In the two later cases, it reversed itself and found a specific countervailable subsidy and the ITC subsequently found material injury. The material injury determination was the subject of three remands by binational panels under the FTA. The subsidy determination was subject to two remands by binational panels – the second a 3–2 decision on national lines which the US government then challenged before an Extraordinary Challenge Committee of judges under the FTA, which also split 2–1 on national lines. Congress later enacted legislation vindicating the basis of the US agencies' determinations, ending a 15-year saga driven by private parties' ability to invoke (and re-invoke) US countervailing duty laws. Issues that proved contentious in these proceedings included: (a) whether Canadian stumpage rates were 'too low' so as to constitute a subsidy – relative to what? – private stumpage rates in the US, Canadian governments' costs of maintaining Crown lands, costs of reforestation, government stumpage rates in other countries; (b) whether, assuming a subsidy, the subsidy was specific – the US petitioners claimed that it benefited principally two industries, solid wood products, and pulp and paper products, while the Canadian defendants claimed that it benefited 3,600 firms distributed across 27 industries (as defined by output); (c) whether, even assuming a subsidy and that the subsidy was specific, the subsidy was a cause of any injury that US softwood lumber producers could demonstrate was attributable to it; and (d) what standard of review binational panels should apply to domestic agency determinations in terms of degree of deference.

This unbecoming subsidies imbroglio yields several lessons: first, the intractability or indeterminacy of many of the key elements in US countervailing duty law; second, the fact that US new home buyers were the principal beneficiaries of cheaper Canadian lumber imports almost entirely disappeared from view in the process; third, privately-driven trade remedy litigation is open to serious risks of protectionist abuse; and fourth, it may be appropriate to re-evaluate fundamentally the Chapter 19 binational dispute resolution regime (despite its qualified successes) and remit subsidy disputes instead to state-to-state dispute resolution before demonstrably neutral GATT/WTO panels (and the Appellate Body) under the Uruguay Round Subsidies Agreement.[128]

RATIONALES FOR COUNTERVAILING DUTY LAWS

Traditionally, the legitimacy of countervailing duty laws has depended on the characterization of subsidies as harmful in some way and on evidence that offsetting countervailing duties repair that harm. Advocates of countervailing duty laws offer two main characterizations of subsidies that give rise to an argument in favour of countervailing duties. First, subsidies are often characterized as inefficient and as introducing economic distortions into world trade. Second, subsidies are characterized as being unfair and disturbing the 'level playing field' of international trade.

Efficiency rationales

The traditional argument for countervailing duties is that subsidies distort comparative advantage and hence lead to the inefficient allocation of global economic resources. While this may often be true, a plausible characterization of many subsidies is that they correct or compensate for market imperfections or externalities that would otherwise exist, and thus enhance efficient resource allocation.[129] In many cases subsidies serve to produce 'a more efficient resource allocation, that is, resource allocation more consonant with the actual production possibilities and consumer preferences than that yielded by wholly private transactions'.[130] The task of evaluating whether subsidies contribute to or derogate from efficient resource allocation is daunting. According to Schwartz and Harper, the exercise is at best highly indeterminate because of three factors: (a) the pervasiveness of externalities which subsidies may help internalize; (b) what the authors rather opaquely call potential private–public intersectorial economies, which embrace the collective validation of all kinds of preferences that may not be adequately captured in private market transactions (e.g. protection of national security, preserving the family farm and rural lifestyles, promoting regional development, etc.); and (c) the possibility that a positive government benefit to a firm may be designed to offset some other burden that has been imposed by government (e.g. high minimum wage laws, stringent occupational health and safety requirements, plant closing or environmental obligations).

Even if subsidies are truly distortive of international trade, the question that remains is whether countervailing duty laws improve resource allocation. It is clear from the previous section that the methodology currently used by US agencies in the calculation of subsidy margins does not serve to determine accurately the duties needed to offset the effects of trade distortions. Moreover, it has now been convincingly demonstrated[131] that in almost every conceivable set of circumstances, countervailing duties reduce domestic social welfare in the *importing* country, where social welfare is defined as the maximization of producer, consumer and government surplus. Gains to domestic producers from the higher prices induced by the duties are offset by losses to consumers who remain in the market and pay the higher prices, while some consumers who would have purchased the product are priced out of the market and suffer welfare losses. Even accounting for the increase in government surplus in terms of increased revenue from duties, consumer losses outweigh all gains, leaving total welfare lower. Thus, however ambiguous the welfare effects of a subsidy either in the country providing it or globally, there is nothing ambiguous about the welfare effects of the subsidy in the importing country. This analysis suggests that rather than condemning foreign subsidies, importing countries should send expressions of their gratitude to the subsidizing country, noting only their regret that the subsidies are not larger and timeless.

A further efficiency argument that is sometimes directed against subsidies is that government support in the form of export subsidies is intended or at least serves to assist firms in practising predatory pricing. It is argued that subsidies may enable a firm to sell at a lower price in the foreign market in order to eliminate competition and thereafter reap monopoly profits.[132] Predation nationally or internationally is a practice that unambiguously lowers economic welfare. However, in the previous chapter on antidumping laws, we argued that there is little theoretical or empirical basis for allegations of predation in international trade. Moreover, current countervailing duty laws do not consider factors that would support a claim of predation, such as industry concentration and barriers to entry. As in the case of antidumping, concerns over predation (potentially a valid reason for the prevention of some forms of subsidization) do not justify existing countervailing duty laws.

Fairness rationales

The level playing field rationale

Some advocates of countervailing duties argue that subsidies constitute unfair trade and disturb the 'level-playing field' in international trade. Professor Robert Hudec, a distinguished international trade law scholar, provides a useful taxonomy of many of the unfair trade claims that presently enjoy wide currency.[133] He draws a basic distinction between what he calls offensive 'unfairness' and defensive 'unfairness'. With respect to offensive unfairness, the claim is often made that domestic policies adopted by governments in exporters' countries of origin provide them with unfair advantages in competing in importing country markets or in third-country markets. With respect to defensive unfairness, the claim is often made that a country has adopted domestic policies that unfairly favour its own products and unfairly penalize foreign producers who wish to sell into this country's market.

In the case of countervailing duty laws, the complaint of offensive unfairness focuses on the fact that foreign firms are able to out-compete domestic firms in the latter's market as a result of some artificial advantage that the foreign firms enjoy by virtue of government subsidies or other benefits conferred on them in their country of origin. This unfairness claim is difficult both to unravel and to contain.[134] At one level, even in the case of an explicit export subsidy, one can reasonably argue that, as suggested above, consumers in the export market are better off as a result of the foreign subsidy and that it should be viewed as a form of foreign aid that on balance increases the welfare of citizens in the importing country. At another level, the claim of unfairness relating to foreign governments' actions has no natural limits to it. Unless one is prepared to adopt a *laissez-faire* baseline as one's normative reference point, and to view every government deviation from this baseline as a form of unfairness where it has some impact on the pattern of international trade, one is quickly forced to accept that almost everything that modern governments do is likely, either directly or indirectly, to affect the pattern of economic activities within a country and therefore, by extension, the pattern of international trade flows to which that country contributes. For example, such basic activities of governments as investments in physical infrastructure, e.g. roads and communication systems, investments in public education and basic research, investments in law and order, investments in health care systems, etc. all shape in one way or another a country's comparative advantages or disadvantages in international trade.

According to liberal trade theory, only if differing productive conditions exist across countries can gains be derived from international trade; countries will specialize in the production of the goods that they can produce relatively cheaply, and purchase from abroad, at lower cost, goods in which they have a comparative disadvantage. If all countries were to have identical productive conditions, then no country would have a comparative advantage in the production of any good and there would be no gains from trade. Thus, if subsidies disturb the 'level playing field' they serve to increase potential gains from trade.[135] It is at least arguable that differing subsidization policies across countries, like different education levels or different tax structures, are simply one of the factors that contribute to different productive conditions across countries. Moreover, it is to point out the obvious that, given an assumption of scarce resources, a country that chooses to subsidize one set of activities cannot subsidize another set of activities, which some of its trading partners may, as a matter of domestic policy priorities, choose to subsidize instead.

In recent debates where these kinds of claims of offensive unfairness are made, three new areas have emerged.[136] First, it is sometimes argued that the quiescent state of Japanese competition/antitrust law permits Japanese firms, through acquisition of dominant market positions or through collusive arrangements in Japan, to garner supra-normal profits in the Japanese market and to use these to fund subsequent aggressive export initiatives. Second, it is widely claimed that lax environmental laws in many countries constitute a form of implicit subsidy that confer on firms originating in these countries an artificial advantage in export markets. Third, it is often argued that weak labour laws pertaining to such matters as minimum wages, hours of work, child labour, workplace safety conditions, again operate as implicit subsidies to firms located in countries with such policies and confer on them an artificial advantage in export markets. In all three cases, the policy choices for governments in importing countries are either to attempt to persuade or induce the country of origin to harmonize its laws up to the standards prevailing in the importing country; or for the importing country to harmonize its laws down to the level of those prevailing in the exporting country; or to harmonize to some agreed intermediate solution; or to impose unilaterally some border measure, like a countervailing duty, designed to neutralize whatever artificial advantages are claimed to be associated with these domestic policy differences.

As Bhagwati points out,[137] fairness arguments can be pushed to almost any lengths:

> If Bangladesh has a current comparative advantage in textiles, due to lower wages, we no longer need to worry about being scolded as protectionists when we reject imports of Bangladeshi textiles as unfair trade caused by her 'pauper labour'. After all, the low Bangladeshi wages are a result of inadequate population control *policies* and of inefficient economic policies that inhibit investment and growth and hence a rise in real wages. In like manner, if the United States continues to produce textiles, which rely heavily on immigrant labor, often illegal, this is unfair trade, since American immigration *policy* encourages this outcome, and therefore a Structural Impediments Initiative demand for changed immigration policy needs to be made against the United States simply to ensure level playing fields.

This is not to argue that claims of unfairness have no role at all in international trade law. Debates within the European Union over a Social Protocol and the negotiation of side accords to the North American Free Trade Agreement (NAFTA) on labour and environmental standards highlight the importance that these issues have assumed. Issues pertaining to recognition or harmonization of domestic environmental, labour and competition policies are pursued in later chapters. Rather, it must be emphasized that economists, lawyers and other trade policy analysts now face an urgent task in introducing a substantial measure of coherence and discipline into these fairness claims, both at the theoretical and operational level, so that they can be contained within defensible bounds. We return to this question in the concluding chapter of this book.

Unfair impact rationales

Even if there are no efficiency or fair trade rationales that justify countervailing duty laws, there are possible arguments for countervailing duty laws that take account of the disruptive impact of imports on vulnerable members of society. In particular, it may be that distributive justice or communitarian values can be vindicated through the use of this form of protectionism. On distributive justice grounds, countervailing duty laws might be justifiable to the extent that they improve the lot of the least-advantaged members of society.[138] However, countervailing duty laws are not designed to address these concerns. As was suggested in the previous section, the application of countervailing duties focuses on factors ill-suited to uncovering any injury suffered by an industry as a result of foreign subsidies and factors even less well-suited to discovering the impact on the least advantaged stake-holders in these industries. In addition, as noted in the previous chapter on antidumping, it is clear that in practice distributive justice concerns have not been addressed through antidumping cases; it is unlikely that the evidence is any different for countervailing duty cases. Moreover, there is no principled reason to treat some of the least advantaged as more deserving of protection because the threat to their welfare derives from subsidized imports rather than unsubsidized imports, domestic competition, or other internal factors.

Similarly, the vindication of communitarian values would require that policies be adopted that prevent the disruption of long-standing communities. However, countervailing duty laws are also poorly suited to the achievement of this end. Current formulations of the injury test inquire into the adverse impacts on the domestic industry without investigating whether these impacts are being sustained by dependent communities. Finally it must be emphasized that, in general, protectionist trade remedies such as countervailing duties are not the most appropriate policy instruments for vindicating these values. Instead, as we argue in the next chapter, labour adjustment assistance programmes, or short-term safeguard relief where appropriate, more directly and effectively address transition costs suffered by workers. Such an approach would be a non-discriminatory means of dealing with disruptive impacts of competition from any source on the most vulnerable members of our society without excessively burdening consumers with the costs of trade protectionism.

REFORMING SUBSIDY LAWS[139]

There are two basic problems with countervailing duty laws: their unilateral nature serves to increase international trade frictions and perhaps protectionist tendencies; and they fail to distinguish between subsidies that are distortionary and those that are benign. Reform of the laws on subsidies must address both these concerns. There has been some debate in the recent literature about whether reform proposals should focus on the theoretically defensible or the politically feasible;[140] the approaches that follow are grouped into regimes that represent varying degrees of trade liberalization and, correspondingly, varying degrees of political realism.

The US cash-flow approach: the status quo

There are substantial problems with the current administration of countervailing duty laws by the USA. In an exhaustive critique of current and proposed DC practices in the administration of US countervailing duty law, Diamond concludes:

> The rules promulgated and proposed cannot be squared with any known purpose which countervailing duty law may serve. Surrogates are chosen which have no conceivable relationship to the effect which the foreign subsidy has on the ability of the foreign firm to compete. Internal inconsistencies arise when [DC's] intuitive grasp of competitive effects causes it to over-ride the cash-flow principle which it has adopted. Conceptual lacunae arise where [DC] can find no answer to questions regarding implementation and can only declare that the necessary economic and financial principles do not exist.[141]

The thrust of Professor Diamond's critique of current and proposed DC practices is as follows: in determining the existence of a countervailable subsidy, and in determining the appropriate level of the countervailing duty, the cash-flow or benefit-oriented approach adopted by the DC fails to make consistent distinctions between benefits accruing to a foreign firm from a subsidy and *competitive* benefits accruing from a subsidy. Under the cash-flow or benefit-oriented approach, government action confers a countervailable subsidy on a foreign firm whenever such action allows the foreign firm to receive something of value which it would not have received in a free market. The difference which occurs in the firm's cash flow as a result of the subsidy is *prima facie* the benefit which a countervailing duty will be set to neutralize by pro-rating the value gained by the company (and hence the countervailing duty) over the amount of merchandise produced. As Diamond points out, this approach generates all sorts of largely intractable difficulties. It does not distinguish between subsidies that alter a firm's production costs and those that do not – a subsidy to decommission a plant and under-write adjustment costs for displaced workers or to clean up environmental damage is treated in the same way as a wage subsidy or output-related subsidy. In the case of foreign firms with multiple product lines, pro-rating capital subsidies over product lines is arbitrary. Determining the amount of the subsidy in the case of equity infusions or loans is also arbitrary, as is the allocation of the benefit over time (when the subsidy may in fact be received upfront). The issue of causation is also problematic: is it the impact of foreign imports, which happen to be subsidized, on domestic producers that is central, irrespective of the competitive significance of the subsidy, or is it the latter? But if the latter, this requires a prior determination of the competitive significance of the subsidy, which the cash-flow or benefit-oriented approach explicitly eschews. Diamond's description of the contortions of the DC over time in adopting, rejecting, revising, and re-adopting various rules of thumb to address these issues reflects the inherent arbitrariness and, in a conceptual sense, futility of this exercise.

The entitlement approach

As a more coherent alternative to the cash-flow or benefit-oriented approach, Diamond develops an entitlement theory of countervailing duties,[142] building on an approach initially proposed by Goetz, Granet and Schwartz.[143] The entitlement theory is premised on the notion that US producers should be entitled to an outcome which limits the direct impact of the subsidized firm in the US market to what it would have been had the government subsidy not been available. This entails an analysis of the impact of subsidies on foreign exporters' marginal costs of production. If the subsidy reduces marginal costs, leading a firm to equate marginal revenues and marginal costs at higher levels of output to increase its sales in the USA at the expense of US producers, the latters' entitlement to 'fair competition' has been violated and countervailing duties are *prima facie* in order.

This entitlement theory differs from the cash-flow or benefit-oriented approach currently taken by the DC because of its focus not simply on benefits conferred by governments on foreign firms that export into the USA, but on *competitively salient* benefits. Thus, causation and injury requirements would emphasize the extent to which subsidies that reduce the marginal costs of imports cause injury to domestic firms by reducing their market share. The entitlement theory also differs from the economic distortion approach, which would target countervailing duties on foreign subsidies that distort the globally efficient allocation of resources.

Diamond proposes the entitlement theory as some form of potentially coherent and tractable middle ground between the cash-flow or benefit-oriented approach on the one hand, which he views as incoherent, and the economic distortion theory on the other, which he rejects as indeterminate. However, his approach is also problematic at the operational level. The entitlement approach, given the central role it assigns to the impact of a subsidy on foreign firms' marginal costs of production and the causal linkage between this and alleged injury to domestic producers, is highly data intensive, which is likely to exacerbate problems of data manipulation and lack of transparency in decision-making. Measuring marginal costs is a notoriously difficult exercise, exacting in its data demands and inherently error-prone. Firms do not record their costs in this fashion, and so one would likely quickly be driven to the concept of average variable costs as a compromise. Even then, in multi-product firms, problems of joint cost allocation are likely to be pervasive. Moreover, the counterfactual with which the subsidy-impacted marginal cost function of a foreign firm must be compared is likely to be highly speculative. Is it the *status quo ante* of the firm before the conferral of the subsidy, or alternative courses of action that the firm might have taken to reduce its production costs in the absence of a subsidy?

Problems well known in antitrust law and public utility regulation[144] suggest that in the countervailing duty context these difficulties would be even more pronounced. Here one is dealing with *foreign* firms, typically more than one, each with its own cost functions. Nor do the problems stop with estimating marginal cost functions for foreign firms. Even where subsidies are found to reduce the marginal costs of production of foreign firms with respect to exports into the USA, it will still be necessary to address causation and injury issues, and then to determine the correct level of duty. Diamond suggests that injury will largely be a function of the elasticity of domestic demand for the product: the more elastic the demand the less the injury. But again we know from antitrust experience in defining relevant product and geographic markets that these elasticities are often highly speculative. Even in cases where domestic demand is relatively inelastic so that increased sales by subsidized foreign exporters *prima facie* will erode the market shares of domestic producers, it is easy to envisage cases where loss of market share would occur absent the subsidy.[145] Thus, again, a counterfactual which is necessarily highly conjectural is required not only at the foreign firms' end of the process, but also at the domestic end of the process. Moreover, these comparisons presumably cannot be excessively static, but once a duty is imposed would require constant review in the light of changing circumstances over time at either end of the process. Finally, should foreign firms be able to argue that the subsidies they have received are wholly or partially offset by subsidies received by domestic producers, and that only the net subsidy advantage should qualify as a countervailable subsidy? Goetz, Granet and Schwartz are frank enough to acknowledge these complexities:

> Admittedly, the neutralization approach would often be difficult to implement because of the empirical issues that it implicates . . . Experience with this approach might well yield useful generalizations so that 'rules of thumb' could, in some situations, effectively replace detailed case-by-case enquiry. This is not to suggest that coherent implementation of the protectionist rationale will ever be anything but a very costly and error-prone process . . . Facing the implications of mandating this approach may also lead some legislators to become less certain of the desirability of implementing the protectionist [entitlement] rationale. It is no doubt clear by now that this is a result which would not be uncongenial to us.[146]

Taxonomizing subsidies

In the Tokyo Round, no agreement was reached regarding the classification of domestic (non-export) subsidies as acceptable or unacceptable (countervailable). Thus, an approach that has been pursued in the Uruguay Round Subsidies Agreement is to spell out more definitively the different categories of subsidies. Under a first-best regime, our preference would be to abandon this approach. The development of a three-way taxonomy of subsidies as benign ('white'), prohibited ('black'), and ambiguous ('grey') is, in many respects, problematic. First, conventional understanding has it that pure export subsidies are the most objectionable and trade-distorting forms of subsidies and provide the strongest case for both international and domestic countervailing sanctions.[147] This understanding is reflected in the Tokyo and Uruguay Rounds Subsidies Codes. It may be that such subsidies represent a foolish misallocation of resources by the subsidizing state – in effect giving away its goods to foreigners below cost – and may distort the efficient global allocation of resources by squeezing out more efficient third-country producers from the importing country's market, who should perhaps be entitled to make a claim for nullification or impairment under Article XXIII of the GATT. However, in terms of its own economic welfare, the importing country has no grounds for objection. The general economic case for countervailing duties in the case of pure export subsidies is as tenuous as the general economic case against dumping.[148] While we recognize the broader international risk of 'Prisoners' Dilemma' type export subsidy wars, negotiated reductions of, or restrictions on, such subsidies in given contexts, as reflected in the Uruguay Round Agreement on Agriculture, the Tokyo Round Code on Trade in Civil Aircraft, and the OECD Agreement on civil shipbuilding and repair seem an appropriate response to this problem. We also recognize that pure export subsidies will typically be harder to justify in terms of non-trade-related domestic policy objectives, most of which can be better served by subsidies or other policy instruments that are not targeted exclusively on exports, but again it is not clear why this should be of concern to the importing country.

Similarly, generally available subsidies under the Uruguay Round Agreement are not seen as trade distorting with respect to either imports or exports, presumably because they do not disproportionately influence the price of particular categories of goods. However, this view reflects a rather static conception of comparative advantage; most modern international trade theorists believe comparative advantage is a dynamic concept and is not entirely exogenously determined.[149] Clearly, many developed countries owe a significant part of their international comparative advantage to social investments in health, education, law and order, basic research and physical infrastructure. It may be the case that generally available subsidies are more benign than selective subsidies because they are less likely to be the product of rent seeking by special interest groups. It may also be the case that generally available subsidies are reflected more fully in exchange rate adjustments than selective or targeted subsidies. But in an international environment, where exchange rates are determined increasingly by international capital flows rather than goods flows, it is not clear how robust this assumption is, or when one can be confident that generally available subsidies have induced appropriate exchange rate adjustments while more selective subsidies have not.

Finally, in the context of countervailing duty law, there remain selective domestic subsidies with export spillovers. In this case, the economic analysis is the same as that for the case of pure export subsidies: the importing country receives lower priced goods and increases its welfare. To the extent that such subsidies squeeze out a third-country's exports, then the third country should, as in the case of pure export subsidies, have a right to bring a nullification and impairment claim before a GATT dispute resolution panel.

A first-best alternative to countervailing duty law: negotiated reciprocity

The preceding analysis illustrates the normative incoherence as well as the technical difficulties associated with current and proposed countervailing duty laws. Our first-best reform proposal would be to abandon the attempt to develop a taxonomy of subsidies and to admit that 'unfair' subsidies are a largely incoherent idea. The protectionist tendencies that drive countervailing duty actions should be disciplined by being subjected to the strictures of a revamped Article XIX on Safeguards. To advocate the replacement of 'unfair' trade remedy laws with a comprehensive safeguards regime is not to deny that global economic welfare might be enhanced by the reduction of government subsidies to industry. Rather it is the case for countervailing duties that makes no sense, not the case for reducing some subsidies. Although it has been suggested that the appropriate use of countervail may actually lead to a reduction in the use of subsidies, there is little empirical evidence to suggest that the imposition or threat of contingent protection actually alters states' domestic policies.[150]

However, the GATT may have an appropriate role to play in facilitating agreement among states to reduce subsidies. The GATT is more likely to achieve success, not through a ban of some supposedly pernicious subclass of subsidies enforceable through unilateral retaliation, but through facilitating negotiation of mutually advantageous concessions among the Contracting Parties. It is through negotiated reciprocity that the GATT has achieved its greatest success – the dramatic reduction in tariffs which were never classified as prohibited, actionable, or non-actionable. The enhanced notification and surveillance procedures in the Uruguay Round Subsidies Agreement may indeed facilitate such an approach to disciplining subsidies.

When subsidy wars threaten a tragedy of the commons, mutual agreement to halt or constrain subsidization in a particular sector may be possible. In comparison, tariff reductions did not occur because trading states suddenly recognized the cogency of the economic arguments that tariffs distort global allocative efficiency. Similarly, the focus regarding subsidies should be on facilitating, through the GATT, Pareto-superior bargains, where subsidies are reduced reciprocally, or 'traded' against removal of other trade restrictions.

A particularly forceful case for mutual reduction of subsidies exists where several states are sustaining excess capacity in declining industries through constantly increasing subsidization or are competing with each other in granting locational inducements to attract new plants. At some point, the cost of matching the increases of every other state's subsidy becomes a negative sum game, thereby making negotiated restraints attractive. Such restraints might, for example, involve an agreement to focus subsidy policies on orderly reduction of capacity through severance pay settlements to older workers, other public assistance for worker retraining and relocation, or regional subsidies to create jobs in other sectors in the region concerned.

Although there are quite broad prohibitions on subsidies in the Treaty of Rome, from the beginning the European Commission has not viewed the prohibitions on State Aid as reflecting a *laissez-faire* paradigm of non-intervention in markets.[151] Article 92 of the Treaty of Rome prohibits 'any aid granted by a Member State . . . which distorts competition' by favouring certain enterprises, provided that an effect on trade be demonstrated. The Commission only began to intervene actively in the aid policies of Member States during the sectoral crises of the 1970s and early 1980s when Union producers were faced with excess capacity in a variety of sensitive sectors such as steel, autos, and textiles. In this context, subsidization appeared as a beggar-thy-neighbour attempt by each subsidizing country to maximize its share of a declining world market for Community production as a whole. The subsidizing countries then externalized onto other member countries the adjustment costs of sectoral decline. Political norms of interstate cooperation, and the 'race to the bottom' effects of intra-Union subsidies wars, justified intervention. The intervention occurred without the Commission having to decide on an appropriate normative base-line for government intervention in mixed economies, i.e. how much intervention is compatible with free competition, or the *laissez-faire* ideal. Moreover, in many cases, the Commission's response was to accept readjustment of the aid in question with a view to restructuring and reducing capacity. The latter was aimed at alleviating the crisis of surplus capacity within the Union as a whole.[152] Finally, the Commission has taken a positive view of subsidies aimed at development of new environmentally safer production processes, as well as development of disadvantaged regions (as the Uruguay Round Subsidies Agreement now does). Nevertheless, the Commission has insisted on justification of the specific measures in question, and has not sustained measures to prop up failing firms just because they happened to be located in underdeveloped regions. Instead, the Commission has sought evidence that the aid in question will contribute to long-term development of the local economy. Backed by technical expertise and capacity for on-going monitoring and scrutiny of government policies, the Commission has been able to engage in a fruitful (although occasionally tense) dialogue with aid-granting Member States about the relationship between means and ends, in which the broader social goals behind government intervention have been accepted at the outset as legitimate, as well as the principle that one Member State should not impose on another the costs of attaining those goals within its own borders. The Union jurisprudence on subsidies has, therefore, a much less *laissez-faire* tone than that of US domestic trade tribunals applying American countervailing-duty law, which presume the illegitimacy of any foreign subsidy that is not generally available.

Following the EU experience, the GATT/WTO requires better institutional machinery for negotiation and supervision of these kinds of subsidy regimes. However, creating an institutional framework to facilitate such regimes is a more appropriate task for the GATT/WTO than the elusive search for a universal taxonomy of good and bad subsidies. A transparency agency operating under the aegis of the GATT, now to an important extent contemplated in the detailed notification and surveillance mechanisms of the Uruguay Round Subsidies Agreement (Articles 25 and 26), could also play a positive role by monitoring subsidy policies and calculating subsidies in tariff equivalents, or effective rates of protection, thus providing a kind of common bargaining currency. For instance, in the steel sector, the USA might agree to remove some existing voluntary export restraints or contingent protection actions in return for EU commitments to use subsidies to reduce, rather than sustain, excess capacity. Clearly, in order to make such commitments plausible, some kind of independent surveillance mechanism is required to conduct verifications and ensure against flagrant cheating. Current GATT machinery is not designed to handle this verification function but were such machinery developed (perhaps through the new World Trade Organization) we might see more agreements that address domestic subsidies. Thus, the reduction of subsidies should be treated as has tariff-cutting in previous GATT rounds: the aim should be periodic global welfare enhancing bargains based on a broad balance of concessions (negotiated reciprocity).

Second-best reforms

It must be acknowledged that at least in the short run it is unlikely that the first-best solution of removing all *a priori* general constraints on subsidies and leaving their reduction to negotiated reciprocity in particular contexts would be acceptable to the USA. The second-best solution accepts the general taxonomic approach embodied in the Uruguay Round Subsidies Agreement. However, on our preferred approach,[153] the regime would consist primarily of Track II, and unilateral application of countervailing duties (Track I) would be restricted to a narrow class of prohibited pure export subsidies perhaps defined as subsidies where at least 80% of the output of subsidized foreign firms is exported, provided that the subsidies are competitively salient subsidies (as discussed above with respect to the entitlement approach). Track II would be the exclusive avenue of recourse for addressing actionable subsidies; no remedy of any kind would be available in the case of non-actionable subsidies. If a subsidy has some trade effects, but is also serving legitimate non-trade related domestic policy goals, remedial action should only be taken following investigation by a multilateral panel. The panel would determine whether the subsidy is objectionable and the Committee of Signatories to the Subsidies Agreement would mandate appropriate remedial or retaliatory action. In formulating the standards to be applied by subsidies panels, the experience of review panels established under Chapter 18 of the FTA may be helpful.[154] In cases involving disagreements about the legitimacy of government policies that influence trade, the panels have adopted a least restrictive means test. For example, in the case, *In the Matter of Canada's Landing Requirement for Pacific Coast Salmon and Herring* (1989), it was argued that a Canadian requirement that all catches of these fish be landed in Canada before processing was an essential component of resource conservation which was exempted by Article XX(g) from the GATT prohibition on export restrictions under Article IX.[155] However, because the objectives of the policy could have been achieved through sampling and other monitoring requirements less restrictive of trade, the policy was not sustained by the panel.

The paradigmatic formulation of the least restrictive means test is found in the case law under section 1 of the Canadian Charter of Rights and Freedoms.[156] In order for a limit on a Charter right to be sustained, the limit must have a valid objective, and the means chosen to reach that objective must be rationally connected to the objective and must be the least restrictive means, or the means that impairs minimally the right in question. This approach should be adopted to deal with the indeterminate class of reviewable (actionable) subsidies: if a subsidy is causing serious prejudice to other countries (in the sense employed in the Uruguay Round Subsidies Agreement) in any of the three subsidy scenarios outlined at the outset of this chapter (subsidized exports by A to B; subsidized exports by A to C, displacing B's exports to C; subsidized domestic production by A displacing B's imports), but is nevertheless rationally connected to a legitimate non-trade related policy objective (such as those previously set out in Article 11 of the Tokyo Round Subsidies Code), and is the least trade-restrictive policy instrument available to achieve that objective it should be sustained, but not otherwise. This test should encourage governments to seek out domestic policy instruments that will minimize trade distortions.

In summary, we envision that an international subsidies regime could feasibly aspire to define a category of subsidies that are immune from challenge either multilaterally or unilaterally, along the lines of 'non-actionable subsidies' in the Uruguay Round Subsidies Agreement, and another category of subsidies (principally subsidies that are *de jure* or *de facto* pure export subsidies) that are *per se* objectionable both multilaterally and unilaterally. For the wide array of intermediate subsidies that do not fall into either of these two categories, we envisage only a multilateral complaints route, with panels applying a least trade-restrictive means test, and an adverse determination by a Subsidies panel being required before retaliation can be undertaken. Invocation of domestic countervailing duty regimes would not be possible unless and until such a determination had been made.[157] This would largely place all three subsidy scenarios on the same legal footing, subject to the same substantive disciplines and the same multilateral review process. This proposed approach also recognizes the complex welfare judgments entailed in evaluating the economic effects of subsidies and is respectful of the domestic sovereignty of Member States to pursue a wide range of non-trade related domestic policy objectives of their choosing without risking unilateral punitive measures from other countries with divergent perspectives on the wisdom of those policies, while at the same time constraining subsidy policies that are gratuitously or disproportionately trade distorting.

9 Safeguard regimes and domestic adjustment policies

THE GATT SAFEGUARD REGIME

Introduction

Article XIX of the GATT is widely known as the Escape Clause or Safeguard Provision. It allows a GATT signatory in certain circumstances to avoid GATT obligations that cause serious injury to domestic industries of a product like, or competitive with, one whose importation is increasing.[1] When the increase in imports is caused by unforeseen developments and prior GATT obligations, a Contracting Party can modify or withdraw the relevant trade concessions. Measures taken under Article XIX are intended to be temporary, lasting only long enough to prevent or remedy the injury, and applied in a non-discriminatory way to all Parties exporting the product. Finally, they can only be undertaken when Parties with substantial interests have been consulted and agree to the import restraint or receive proper compensation.[2] A new Agreement on Safeguards was negotiated during the Uruguay Round and is discussed throughout this chapter.

As of May 1993, 152 safeguard actions under Article XIX had been notified to the GATT. As with antidumping, over 80% of the actions were taken by four main users: Australia, the USA, Canada, and the EC. Almost a third of the measures have been imposed since the conclusion of the Tokyo Round in 1979. Over this period, the EC has invoked Article XIX 18 times (of which 13 involved processed foodstuffs) and the USA 4 times.[3] Compared with other trade remedies, safeguard actions are infrequently initiated: from 1979 to 1988, 1,833 antidumping actions and 429 countervailing actions were initiated,[4] while in 1988, 261 export restraint arrangements (ERAs) – typically bilaterally negotiated restrictions on exports – were known to be in existence.[5] The predominance of antidumping and countervailing actions may seem surprising since they respond to 'unfair' forms of trade and would seem to carry a heavier burden of proof. Moreover, the number of ERAs is striking and disconcerting; these actions are not legal under the GATT,[6] but have been the preferred form of safeguard action. Because they are often unofficial, secret and discriminatory, ERAs are a serious threat to the integrity of the GATT multilateral trade regime, specifically undermining the integrity of the safeguard regime.

History and background

Article XIX is a direct derivative of the escape clause found in the 1943 Reciprocal Trade Agreement between the USA and Mexico.[7] Prior to 1943, escape clauses to protect against specific risks had been contemplated by trade agreements, but never a general escape clause.[8] Then in 1947, responding to concerns in Congress over impending GATT trade liberalization, a US executive order required that all trade agreements entered into by the USA include a general escape clause similar to the one found in the Reciprocal Trade Agreement.

Among the Contracting Parties, there was general agreement during the initial GATT negotiations that an escape clause was desirable, but there was some controversy about its scope.[9] The rationale for the inclusion of a safeguard provision was twofold:[10] to encourage greater trade liberalization, and to increase the trade regime's flexibility. The goal of the GATT was to remove all trade barriers except customs duties (tariffs), and then to reduce these duties through successive, binding multilateral negotiations. Safeguards were believed to be necessary to protect against unforeseen economic difficulties that might result from liberalization. It was thought that with the existence of a form of relief from obligations in extreme circumstances, countries would be more likely to agree to broad reductions in trade barriers in the first place. Second, it was believed that the flexibility provided by safeguards would increase the long-term stability of the system. If nations were able to protect their import-sensitive industries temporarily within the GATT regime then they would be less likely to abandon the multilateral system in favour of protectionism or some more discriminatory trading system.

Substantive requirements

The escape clause agreed upon in 1947 is 'extraordinarily oblique, even for GATT language',[11] resulting in difficulty in interpretation and uncertainty in application.[12] Very few rules define the required procedure for invocation of the safeguard. The safeguard user must notify the Contracting Parties and afford those with a substantial interest an opportunity for consultation with respect to the proposed action. A striking feature of the regime is that the importing country is responsible for the substantive determinations, and while notification to the GATT is mandatory there is no requirement of surveillance or external confirmation. The lack of international involvement encourages informal, secret negotiation since exporters feel their interests are inadequately protected by the formal mechanism. In addition, actions that are taken under Article XIX must be taken by the executive branch of the government of the Contracting Party and are thus political, not administrative actions like antidumping and countervailing duty actions. The need for executive approval forces an invoking government to justify the action to its constituents and to foreign governments. In addition, it may be difficult if the action is prompted by a genuine emergency to explain why it is necessary to pay compensation in terms of offsetting tariff concessions. By creating greater political costs, the safeguard regime creates incentives to substitute relief through less accountable mechanisms like ERAs.

Increased imports

According to Article XIX, the importing country must show that the imports in question are increasing, either relatively[13] or absolutely, due to unforeseen developments and GATT obligations. While integral to the invocation of the safeguard provision, neither of the two causative factors is defined in the Article. The increased importation of the product must be affected by GATT obligations, but the kind of obligation is uncertain. The Article includes more than simply tariff concessions – a large proportion of the actions involve quantitative restrictions – but there is a debate over whether the Most Favoured Nation (MFN) clause is applicable. Some argue that the MFN requirement of the GATT may be the obligation causing the injury,[14] and so Parties should be able to restrain imports on a selective basis – by suspending MFN treatment. However, others insist that it is unlikely that the MFN obligation is responsible for the increased imports.[15] Leaving aside the MFN issue, this requirement is easily satisfied if all the safeguard user has to show is that *but for* GATT obligations, protective measures would have been taken to prevent the increase in imports; there is little evidence that this clause is more strictly construed.[16]

The second causality requirement is that the increased imports be caused by 'unforeseen developments'. This criterion is the least onerous aspect of the safeguard clause. Indeed, according to some, interpretation has rendered this requirement a virtual nullity.[17] In the *Hatter's Fur Case* in 1951, the USA alleged that imports of Czechoslovakian hatter's fur were causing injury to domestic producers. The change in the preferred style of women's hats was declared sufficiently 'unforeseen' to justify an Article XIX action; this conclusion was supported by a GATT report on the case.[18] Such interpretations suggest that almost anything can be considered an unforeseen development:

> Any increase in imports, even if through normal changes in international competitiveness, could therefore be considered actionable under Article XIX.[19]

Serious injury

The increased imports must cause or threaten serious injury to domestic producers of like or directly competitive products. There are three ambiguities in this requirement: (1) what is needed to establish causation? (2) what constitutes serious injury? and (3) what qualifies as a like or competitive product? First, serious injury is different from material injury (the requirement for antidumping and countervailing actions) but whether it requires proof of more or less harm than material injury has not been established. Second, the range of producers that can be protected by a safeguard action are more diverse than those contemplated by an antidumping action, extending to producers of competitive as well as like products. But what kinds of competitive products are eligible for protection remains unsettled. What has been established, in the *Hatter's Fur Case*, is that the Party invoking safeguard protection is entitled to the benefit of the doubt that serious injury has been sustained or is threatened.

Remedy and compensation

The GATT obligation that is causing or threatening the injury can be suspended or modified 'to the extent and for such a time as may be necessary to prevent or remedy such injury'. Some Contracting Parties, particularly the EU, have argued that GATT obligations can be suspended selectively so that the concession is only withdrawn with respect to the particular trading nations who are causing the injury. This argument is inconsistent with the Article XIX interpretation developed during the Havana Charter negotiations,[20] and with the GATT's apparent historical insistence on nondiscriminatory application of safeguard actions.[21] However, the right to restrain imports selectively has been at the centre of debates over the reform of the safeguard clause and contributes to the greater attractiveness of ERAs and other trade remedies like antidumping and countervailing duties, all of which are selective.

The safeguard remedy seems designed for temporary relief but no precise requirements are specified under Article XIX in this respect. Before taking action the Contracting Party must consult with the Parties substantially affected to try to obtain agreement on the need for such action. Ultimately, the safeguard provision can be invoked without agreement from trading partners but, according to Article XIX(3), if the restrained Parties are dissatisfied with the action they have the right to suspend concessions of substantially equivalent value or other obligations. This aspect of the safeguard regime has been interpreted as establishing a right to compensation. Compensation usually takes the form of other trade concessions by the Party invoking the safeguard relief and requires negotiations between the injured country and all exporting countries. Owing to the generally low level of tariffs, it is becoming increasingly difficult for countries to compensate with equivalent concessions; few tariffs are high enough for meaningful reductions except for products which are already sensitive to imports.[22] Thus, the requirement is often politically difficult to meet and it increases pressure to find alternative escape routes. Sykes argues that the compensation requirement reduces the likelihood that the safeguard provision will be used inappropriately.[23] However, it also reduces the chance that it will be used at all, as countries instead negotiate ERAs or invoke other trade remedies.

Other escape clauses

Article XIX is not the only provision of the GATT that allows signatories to suspend their obligations. Articles XII and XVIII(b) permit the imposition of import controls to relieve temporary balance-of-payments pressures and economic development problems of less-developed countries. In addition, Article XXVIII provides for the renegotiation of concessions during specified renewal periods.

Outside of the GATT there is a further safeguard regime worthy of note: Chapter 8 of NAFTA, which slightly adapts Chapter 11 of the Canada–US Free Trade Agreement (FTA).[24] It differs from the GATT clause in a number of important ways. First, bilateral emergency actions are only permissible within the ten-year transition period.[25] Second, these actions have several features distinguishing them from those allowed under the GATT: they must be limited to three years; there is no right to renew; the increase in imports causing the serious injury has to be absolute, so if the import's share of the market increases due, for example, to a decline in purchases of domestic goods no action can be taken; the increase in imports must constitute a substantial cause of serious injury the only actions permitted under the clause are tariffs, which may be only raised to the lesser of the MFN rate applicable when action is taken or the MFN rate applicable at the time NAFTA came into force.[26] In addition, in order to address the problem of 'side-swiping', the Chapter provides for exemption of member countries from the impact of actions taken by another member country under the GATT multilateral safeguard regime unless their imports account for a substantial share of total imports or are contributing importantly to the serious injury. This shall not normally be considered the case if a Party is not among the top five suppliers of the good in question. As under Article XIX of the GATT, there are notification and consultation requirements and an obligation to provide compensation or risk retaliation.

Theoretical rationales for the safeguard regime

Trade liberalization

In 1970 Kenneth Dam observed that 'the GATT escape clause is a useful safety valve for protectionist pressures'.[27] In his view, the clause, in addition to being a prerequisite for essential US participation, encouraged trade liberalization more generally. According to Dam, the GATT escape clause 'encourages cautious countries to enter into a greater number of tariff bindings than would otherwise be the case'.[28] Sykes develops this observation into the primary rationale for a safeguard regime.[29] His thesis is not unlike the traditional argument for the inclusion in the GATT of a safeguard regime: that broader liberalization will be undertaken when there is an opportunity to suspend those obligations. His approach is novel in its use of public choice theory to explain the role of this trade remedy.

Public choice theory predicts that policy-makers will be more concerned about trade impacts on producers than on consumers because the former are both better organized and more influential than the latter. According to Sykes, the consequence of the self-interested behaviour of policy-makers is that they may not liberalize trade even if the current environment is favourable to such an action. Their reluctance will result from knowledge that unanticipated changes in economic conditions may create circumstances in which political rewards to an increase in protection (or the political costs of an irrevocable commitment to reduce protection) are great.[30]

The safeguard is therefore essential to any liberalizing scheme. This conclusion depends on two important and challengeable assumptions: that adequate substitutes do not exist for the formal safeguard regime, and that signatories feel bound by their obligations and will generally not wish to abrogate them.[31] In Sykes' view, the *ex ante* nature of the safeguard regime implies that it is different from bilateral negotiations over ERAs which occur *ex post*. The increased use of grey-area and other contingent measures to avoid obligations, combined with the infrequent use of Article XIX, challenges both these assumptions. By modelling Article XIX, Sykes shows how the criteria for invoking the safeguard serve to maximize political gains from protection. In addition, he argues that requirements such as compensation reduce illicit use of the escape clause. The optimal safeguard regime would constrain protection to cases in which the gains to the importing country are greater than any losses to other countries (typically where the importing country's domestic industry is declining, entailing job displacement, etc., while foreign suppliers may be expanding industries where restraints will merely curtail future growth).

Economic adjustment

Jackson advances an economic adjustment rationale for safeguards:

> Imports, particularly recently increasing imports, often cause harm to select groups within an importing society, even though they may in the long term and in the broader aggregate increase the welfare of that society. Competing firms will be forced to 'adjust' to the imports . . . a temporary period of time of some relief from imports will allow the domestic competing industry to take the necessary adjustment measures.[32]

This rationale can be reformulated in different terms: the safeguard remedy provides an opportunity for domestic industries to improve their competitiveness with imports. Hufbauer and Rosen have studied the effectiveness of various programmes for facilitating adjustment of US industries being impacted by import competition. Their study focuses on three trade policies: special trade protection, such as exceptional restraints on imports that go well beyond normal border or tariff restrictions; trade-related adjustment assistance to labour in affected industries; and escape clause relief.[33] Hufbauer and Rosen find that among the various policies, the escape clause is the most effective at inducing adjustment. Of the sixteen industries studied ten received tariff increases, two obtained orderly marketing arrangements, and the other four received quota protection. The adjustment of these firms was relatively successful since twelve no longer required protection:[34] one of these adjusted by expanding; the rest contracted either to a competitive core or out of the industry. The relative success of escape clause relief results from three factors: the relief is temporary, which gives firms a strong incentive to adjust quickly; labour adjustment programmes in the USA are inadequate and incapable of effectively inducing or easing adjustment; and the escape clause in the USA is administered by the International Trade Commission and while the President authorizes the granting of relief, the primary mechanism is not political lobbying as it is for special forms of trade protection.

The adjustment rationale does not, standing alone, support a role for safeguards. Its inadequacy stems from the distinction that it draws between competitive impacts from imports and from domestic sources. If there are social gains to be realized from facilitating adjustment to economic changes why should not all firms experiencing competitive pressures from whatever source receive such assistance? The answer is clearly that in competition within domestic industries there are at least two sets of domestic producer interests, differently affected, whereas foreign firms causing harm to domestic industries do not have any political 'allies'. There are few real political losses to be suffered from harming a foreign industry so that there are incentives to provide adjustment assistance to domestic firms suffering from import competition through safeguard relief.

Non-economic rationales

There may be important non-economic rationales for the protection offered by the safeguard regime. Despite the efficiency gains to be achieved through trade liberalization, substantial losses resulting from unconstrained imports may justify protection of domestic interests. Vulnerable domestic interests may include less well-endowed and immobile workers and long-established communities whose viability substantially depends on domestic industries that are facing contraction or collapse due to import competition. Distributive justice and communitarian values would require sensitivity to these vulnerable interests and justify policy initiatives to alleviate adverse impacts.

However, trade protection is a very costly way to vindicate these values. The cost to consumers for each job saved by trade protection typically far outweighs the average compensation per worker in the industry affected.[35] To cite some examples, the cost to US consumers of protection of the specialty steel industry was $1 million per year for each job preserved when the annual compensation was less than $60,000 for those jobs. United States consumers of automobiles paid $160,000 per year for each job saved through protection when annual compensation in this industry was less than one quarter of this figure.[36] In Canada, the statistics are similar: consumers of footwear were 'taxed' through trade protection between $53,668 and $69,460 per job saved, while compensation per year for a worker in the industry was $7,145; consumers of textile and clothing were 'taxed' between $40,600 and $50,982 per year for each job saved when average earnings were $10,000; and consumers of automobiles paid between $179,000 and $226,394 per year for each job saved when average compensation in the industry was between $29,000 and $35,000.[37] Given the substantial cost to domestic consumers of trade restrictions, it is likely that other policy instruments can vindicate distributive justice and communitarian values at lower cost.

Reforming safeguard laws

As noted earlier, the frequency of the use of safeguard protection has been low.[38] To some, this evidence suggests that the safeguard regime is an effective part of a liberal regime: it encourages broad liberalization without leading to substantial avoidance of obligations.[39] On this view, the principal challenge may be to make the regime stricter so that it contributes more positively toward greater trade liberalization. However, this optimistic conclusion requires the drawing of an artificial distinction between Article XIX actions and grey-area measures such as ERAs. The distinction is drawn by Sykes on the grounds that if *ex post* negotiations of import restraints were a perfect substitute for the safeguard regime then there would be no need to have a formal regime at all; the very existence of Article XIX shows that *ex post* negotiation is not a substitute for the safeguard regime. However, his view is inconsistent with the marked tendency of countries to negotiate ERAs in response to injurious import competition rather than resort to Article XIX.[40]

Thus, the challenge for reform of the safeguard regime is a substantial one. On the one hand it is necessary to restore the relevance of the safeguard regime by making it more attractive than alternative escape actions such as ERAs.[41] This can be accomplished by relaxing the criteria for invocation of the safeguard regime and bringing grey-area measures within the ambit of the GATT. On the other hand, if the regime is excessively relaxed then it will no longer serve to lower the overall levels of trade protection. Thus, the challenge is to balance these two objectives: to encourage the use of the safeguard regime rather than illicit substitutes, but to maintain its positive, trade liberalizing influence.

Selectivity

The issue of selectivity in the application of safeguard remedies has been central to ongoing debates over reform of the GATT safeguard regime. In 1947, there seemed to be consensus on the importance of the application of safeguard remedies to all exporters on a non-discriminatory basis. This position seems to have been confirmed in subsequent GATT practice.[42] According to Bronckers,[43] the principle of non-discrimination in the context of Article XIX of the GATT serves two principal purposes. First, it promotes economic efficiency by minimizing the trade distortions associated with safeguard remedies. It achieves this purpose by imposing a common burden on all exporters of the product found to be causing serious injury to domestic producers. By not unduly burdening the most efficient exporter with trade restrictions, distortions in the global allocation of resources are minimized. Moreover, second-order distortionary effects such as trade diversion to unconstrained third countries are avoided. Second, it is argued that the principle of non-discrimination increases the number of adversely affected exporting countries, and their combined pressures against the initial invocation of safeguard relief or for the removal of existing safeguard measures or for the granting of compensation operates as a deterrent against unwarranted or abusive exercise of the safeguard remedy. These pressures coincidentally protect weaker or smaller exporting countries who might otherwise be singled out for trade restrictions, whether their exports were or were not the principal cause of injury to domestic producers in an importing country, and for whom demands for compensation or the threat of retaliation may not be viewed as credible.

Despite these arguments for non-discrimination in the application of Article XIX, there have been recurrent demands, particularly from some developed countries, for selective application of import restraints under the safeguard regime. The case for selectivity was first advanced when Japan acceded to the GATT in 1955. Some Contracting Parties took the view that applying restraints against all exporters when Japanese exports were principally causing the harm in question would lead to a destructive, overall increase in trade protectionism. No change was made in the regime at that time, leaving the issue unresolved. The case for selectivity can be shortly stated.[44] First, if it is appropriate to provide an exceptional form of relief to countries suffering serious injury from imports, obviously the most effective form of relief will target the principal source of the imports, rather than adopting a shotgun approach that restrains imports from all sources, whether or not they are contributing importantly to the injury in question. Second, the increasing invocation of 'unfair' trade remedy regimes, particularly antidumping and countervailing duty regimes, which impose duties selectively on particular sources of imports, and the proliferation of various forms of 'voluntary' export restraints, which also impose restrictions on imports by country of origin, implies a high degree of substitutability amongst these various trade remedies. This suggests the futility of insisting on a principle of non-discrimination under Article XIX.

It was clear prior to the Tokyo Round negotiations that countries were reluctant to use the safeguard regime because it disrupted the trade of nations that was not causing significant harm, and required complex negotiations and compensation schemes. Instead, nations were concluding 'voluntary' ERAs with the main sources of disruptive imports. This practice mainly disadvantages NICs and developing countries who are vulnerable to pressure from the larger economies; they agree to these arrangements in order to avoid more adverse impacts that might result from resort to unilateral formal remedies. There are also benefits to exporters from ERAs, especially the opportunity to reap monopoly rents from the artificial scarcities induced by quotas, although this does not imply that they are necessarily supported by exporting countries. There was a strong desire on the part of developing countries to strengthen the GATT Safeguard regime, making grounds for invocation clearer and stricter. Knowing what alternatives they faced in formal mechanisms, they would then have greater bargaining power in bilateral negotiations. Essential to their view of the regime was the incorporation of safeguards, and alternative escape actions, into a system of nondiscriminatory application. To relax the discipline of Article XIX was thought likely to encourage, rather than constrain the incidence of bilateral, managed trade arrangements, which are antithetical to the founding premises of the multilateral system. An opposing view was taken by the EU which advocated the right to apply Article XIX selectively. Selectivity was believed necessary to enhance stability in international trade. As Winham observes:

> [D]eveloping countries are less well served by stability than by rapid changes in traditional trading patterns . . . the effort to negotiate selective safeguards was motivated by a desire to force developing-country exporters to adjust to a pace of change that would not create dislocation in competing industries in the developed countries.[45]

When safeguard negotiations began in 1978, near the end of the Tokyo Round, selectivity was the focus of discussions but the developing countries and the EU could not reach agreement.[46] Developing countries were prepared to compromise on the issue of selectivity in exchange for multilateral surveillance. This compromise was reflected in the Secretariat Draft of April 1979, which specified that in cases where serious injury would result from unusual (not just unforeseen) circumstances, restraints could be taken selectively, either with the agreement of the exporting country or with the approval of a proposed international safeguard committee. This compromise was acceptable to Canada, the USA, Japan, and developing countries,[47] but the EU was unable to accept such a system of review: the administration of international trade laws in the EU is not very transparent, and because of the competing interests in the Union public scrutiny may have caused political difficulties. The right to make determinations of injury without being monitored by an international agency became an issue of economic sovereignty and put an end to any chances of agreement. Ultimately, the only decision made at the Tokyo Round was that a committee should meet to try to elaborate supplementary rules and procedures to provide 'greater uniformity and certainty'[48] in implementing the Safeguard Clause. Following the negotiations, the committee collected data on safeguard use and met to discuss problems of reform but no further progress was made toward a common approach to the matter.[49]

Developing countries, while committed to the issue of nondiscrimination, were willing to compromise if selectivity was combined with other reforms advantageous to them. The two major adjuncts to selectivity are surveillance and clearer criteria for invocation. One such package that Wolff recommends would entrench very specific criteria for selective restrictions, aimed at ensuring that the exporter being targeted is really the principal cause of the injury and does not suffer excessive prejudice from the selective treatment.[50] In addition to the requirement that the supplying countries involved have increased their market share, the products of these countries must 'differ in terms of quantities, prices, or kind from other imports not being restricted so that these products can reasonably be determined to be the cause of the serious injury or threat thereof'.[51] Further, other countries' imports must not be injurious and if a substantial advantage in terms of acquisition of market share is being conferred on unrestricted suppliers there should be a mechanism for the targeted suppliers to seek redress. Wolff's reforms would also include a provision for multilateral surveillance. This approach to selectivity is consistent with the multilateral emergency provisions in the Canada–US Free Trade Agreement and now NAFTA, in which exports that are 'not contributing importantly to the serious injury' are exempted from restraints.

The Uruguay Round Agreement on Safeguards resolves the issue of selectivity as follows: Under Article 5, safeguard measures shall be applied to a product being imported irrespective of its source. Under Article 9, where a quota is employed, if agreement amongst all affected Parties on the allocation of the shares of the quota is not feasible, shares shall be allocated amongst exporters based on proportions of imports supplied during a previous representative period. This rule may be departed from where: (a) imports from certain Parties have increased disproportionately to the total increase in imports; (b) the reasons for the departure are justified; and (c) the conditions of the departure are equitable to all suppliers. Such a departure may not exceed four years in duration. In the case of developing countries, safeguard measures may not be applied against their exports if in the case of a given country exports do not exceed 3% of all imports of the product in question, provided that developing countries with less than a 3% import share collectively do not account for more than 9% of total imports (Article 19).

Injury

While the ultimate stumbling block to agreement on a new safeguards regime in the Tokyo Round negotiations was the issue of selectivity, the determination of injury was also controversial. The definition of injury in Article XIX is very imprecise and there was disagreement on the appropriate test to adopt. Because of the conflict over selectivity, the issue was not resolved. Approaches to the question vary dramatically. Some advocate a substantial loosening of the criteria for invocation combined with a reduction in the number and scope of measures available.[52] One improvement in this area would be to make safeguard protection on proof of injury available to industries as of right, like protection from dumping, rather than a matter of political discretion. Others advocate a tightening of the requirements.[53] Ways of achieving such a tightening vary. One possible system would have two tiers: governments could negotiate agreements with other states undertaking to satisfy stricter criteria before invoking safeguard relief and in return be relieved of the obligation to pay compensation; those without such agreements would follow the less restrictive criteria and pay normal compensation.[54]

Another proposal contemplates that an industry should only be protected if injury is being suffered by ‘less-endowed and immobile workers or long-established and dependent communities’.[55] This injury test is more attractive than the status quo because the cost of protection borne by consumers would be balanced against the gains by another vulnerable group ‘able to make normatively defensible claims not vulnerable to a utilitarian social welfare calculus’.[56] In addition, the concept of worker and community interests as the only legitimate interests justifying protection suggests a link between revenues from protectionist measures and adjustment programmes which these revenues can help finance. Along with the altered injury requirement could also be a condition that the country invoking safeguard relief show that there are no less drastic (less trade distortive) policy instruments available to vindicate these values.

The injury test adopted in the Uruguay Round Safeguards Agreement is a modest improvement over the ambiguities of Article XIX. Serious injury is defined in Article 6 as 'a significant overall impairment in the position of the domestic industry'. The factors to be considered in this determination are specified: rate and amount of the increase in imports in absolute and relative terms, the share of the domestic market taken by increased imports, changes in the level of sales, production, productivity, capacity utilization, profits and losses, and employment. However, the need for GATT obligations and unforeseen developments to cause the increase in imports appears to have been removed or at least rendered marginal; as long as there is an increase in imports that is causing injury, relief is available.

Surveillance

While the developing countries were prepared to compromise on selectivity, the Tokyo Round negotiations ultimately foundered on the issue of multilateral surveillance. The Uruguay Round Safeguards Agreement now provides for a Safeguards Committee which will monitor the implementation of the Agreement and compliance with its procedural and substantive requirements by Contracting Parties. All decisions to initiate or implement safeguard actions must be notified to the Committee, along with evidence justifying the measures. The Committee will also oversee the phasing out of grey-area measures and report as appropriate to the Contracting Parties through the Council for Trade in Goods on the operation of the Agreements. The general dispute resolution mechanisms of the GATT will apply to the new Agreement (Article 38).

Compensation

One of the problems with the Article XIX regime is the obligation of Parties to pay compensation for invoking safeguard protection. As Tumlir states:

> [I]t is destructive of the spirit of reciprocity for a country in an emergency to be obliged to pay for taking *bona fide* temporary action, to negotiate such a payment and to be threatened with retaliation if it does not offer enough.[57]

In addition to the fact that the compensation requirement forces concessions for *bona fide* emergency actions, the requirement increases the burden of the safeguard regime and the attractiveness of alternative escape routes. Rather than negotiate with a number of exporters over the appropriate compensation for all or face retaliation, a country will find it more attractive to conclude a bilateral arrangement. However, supporters of the compensation requirement, like Sykes, insist that it discourages use of the regime in non-emergencies or in circumstances in which the gains are insufficient to justify the real costs. The Uruguay Round Safeguards Agreement retains the obligation to compensate, but if the escape measure lasts less than three years the right of exporters to suspend concessions of equivalent value is withheld (Article 18), thus reducing their leverage in demanding compensation.

Duration

One of the most significant aspects of the Uruguay Round Safeguards Agreement is the introduction of provisions for limited duration and digressivity of relief. The Agreement specifies that no action shall be maintained for longer than four years (Article 19). It may be extended for up to an additional four years if there is evidence that the industry is adjusting and the protection is shown still to be necessary to remedy serious injury (Articles 11 and 12). Any measure of more than a year in duration must be progressively liberalized so that the amount of protection decreases over the duration of the measure (Article 13). In addition, there are limits on the application of new restrictions to a product that has already been subject to restraint: effectively, no new measure can be introduced for a period of time equal to that during which the previous measure was in effect (Article 14). There is some risk that being aware of the need to progressively remove the restraint, Parties will impose initially tighter restraints than are necessary. The surveillance of the GATT Safeguards Committee is designed to discourage any such overprotection.

Grey-area measures

As noted at the outset of this chapter, the integrity of the safeguard regime has been undermined by measures taken outside the framework of the GATT. The obvious solution would be to bring these other measures into the system and then restrict their use or ban them. Some fear that to legalize other trade measures would be to encourage their use.[58] Some proposals for reform have suggested that the other contingent trade remedies be subject to some of the same criteria for invocation. This harmonization would imply, for example, that the kind of injury required to sustain antidumping measures would be similar, in order to prevent domestic producer interests from attempting to substitute one form of contingent protection for another.[59]

The Uruguay Round Safeguards Agreement makes substantial progress in constraining grey-area measures as follows: Article 22 provides that a Contracting Party shall not seek, take or maintain such arrangements nor encourage or support the adoption or maintenance by public and private enterprises of equivalent non-governmental measures. In addition, those currently in existence shall be brought into conformity with the Safeguards Agreement or be phased out within four years of the coming into force of the Agreement, with an exception permitted for one specific measure per Contracting Party subject to review and acceptance by the Safeguards Committee and subject to termination not later than 31 December 1999.

Conclusion

In many respects, the Uruguay Round Safeguards Agreement is a substantial improvement over Article XIX of the GATT: in bringing existing grey-area measures within its purview and prohibiting further such measures; in establishing firm time limits; in achieving a compromise on the issue of selectivity; and in improving multilateral notification and surveillance. There are a number of other reforms that should be considered in future. First, some relaxation of the principle of non-discrimination seems justified in order to avoid pointless 'side-swiping' of exporters who are not contributing importantly to the serious injury in question. Here, a *de minimis* provision along the lines of that to be found in NAFTA would seem appropriate. Second, a radical reconceptualization of the injury test also seems appropriate, so that while firms or industries may be able to petition for safeguard relief, the success of such petitions should depend on a showing that imports are causing serious injury to less well-endowed and immobile workers or long-established communities, and that alternate remedies less distortive of trade are not available, in the form of various domestic adjustment assistance policies, to redress such injury. Third, the only forms that safeguard relief should be permitted to take should be either tariffs or auctioned quotas, in part because these two forms of relief render the cost to domestic consumers more transparent, and more importantly, because they generate a source of revenue out of which domestic assistance policies can be financed. Fourth, safeguard relief should be available as a matter of administrative rather than political decision (like antidumping and countervailing duties), so that incentives to substitute away from the safeguard regime are reduced.

DOMESTIC ADJUSTMENT ASSISTANCE POLICIES

Each of the major industrialized nations has adopted its own policy approaches to the challenge of economic adjustment, including adjustment to trade liberalization and shifts in comparative advantage. We have reviewed these policies extensively elsewhere.[60] We confine ourselves to some brief comments on one class of such policies – industrial subsidies – and offer a somewhat more extended set of comments on labour market adjustment policies.

Industrial subsidies

In many industrialized countries, beginning in the early 1970s, sectors like shipbuilding, coal, steel, textiles, clothing and footwear, and in some cases, automobiles, experienced substantial competitive pressures from imports. Apart from trade restrictions, countries under import pressure often had resort to various kinds of industrial subsidies. In general, these subsidy policies have not been effective in avoiding the ultimate need for adjustment or moderating its severity. Pure output related subsidies have been the least effective in this respect in that they flatly deny the need for adjustment, and while they maintain output and employment in an industry this typically can only be sustained if the subsidies are endless and often increasing. Other forms of industrial subsidies have been designed to facilitate the modernization of obsolete capital. Here it is argued that state assistance to facilitate capital modernization may be necessary to make a distressed industry internationally competitive again. However, obsolete plants are often the result, and not the cause, of the loss of international competitiveness. Firms which are only able to cover variable costs are constrained to allow their fixed assets to run down and with them their long-term capacity. If an adequate return could be made on new fixed assets, presumably private capital markets would provide the funds required to make the investment. A governmental judgment that such an investment will yield long-run competitiveness and profitability will typically be at variance with these private capital market judgments and should, for this reason, be viewed with extreme scepticism.

Much less frequently, industrial subsidies have been provided to ease exit costs. Japan has most prominently invoked industrial subsidies for this purpose in industries like coal mining and steel. It is argued in this context that if there is some degree of indivisibility in plant or firm size so that efficient industry adjustment to a decline in demand requires that firms exit in some orderly temporal sequence, market forces may not produce this sequence. A case may thus arise, so it is argued, for a governmental role in managing adjustment to the contraction in demand, perhaps through recession cartels, active promotion of mergers, or compensation for scrapping physical capacity. While Japanese policies seem to have registered some successes in this context, there are reasons for caution in assigning a proactive role to government in facilitating firm exit. First, this view assumes that governments can economize on transaction costs in this context in ways not open to private firms, through mergers, specialization agreements, and other means. Also, there are clear dangers of bureaucratic involvement in detailed industrial restructuring in terms of relative institutional competence, and also dangers of fostering anti-competitive forms of collusion in seeking agreement on future industry structure.

More generally, the normative case for subsidies to firms in import-impacted sectors is weak. Firms may be able to diversify away the risk of increased import competition through their investment strategies. More importantly, shareholders in these firms can diversify away this risk through portfolio diversification. This risk is no more serious or unforeseeable than many of the risks which firms and shareholders routinely assume, e.g. technological change, shifts in consumer demand, which they are prepared to bear for an appropriate risk-adjusted return.

Labour market adjustment policies

The case for active labour market adjustment policies is substantially more compelling. Under conditions of close to full employment, there would be little reason to be concerned about the dislocation effects of trade liberalization. The market, in effect, would soon reabsorb the dislocated workers, although even here, from a number of ethical perspectives, it might be appropriate for governments to bear some of the transition costs faced by these workers.

If, more realistically, we assume that re-employment is likely to be far from automatic, then the question arises as to what measures are required to facilitate it. The concept of adjustment is complex. At one level, the adjustment problem may be understood as the time lag between a worker being displaced from one job and finding another that is an adequate replacement. From this perspective, provision of temporary income support and search, counselling, and relocation assistance would seem obvious and appropriate to address the problem.

However, the fact that employment is being created primarily in sectors other than those where jobs are being lost raises serious questions about the adequacy of the unemployment insurance model. It may be necessary to go far beyond this model, and provide training and retraining of workers for new types of employment within the economy. This is well-expressed in the Canadian de Grandpré Report, which contrasts the trampoline approach (which emphasizes training and retraining), with the unemployment insurance model (the 'safety net' approach).[61] The report suggests:

> The 'trampoline' approach seeks to prepare Canadian workers to prosper in a world of increasing technological change and international competition, in which Canada must use its access to the larger North American market to achieve greater economies of scale and higher productivity.[62]

In terms of economic efficiency (i.e. allocative efficiency), it may seem unclear why either income support or a trampoline ought to be provided by the state to trade-dislocated workers. Kaplow, for example, has argued strongly that from an efficiency perspective compensation for regulatory change (of which trade liberalization is one example) makes no sense absent convincing proof that markets are incapable of allocating the risks of such changes.[63]

In fact, however, there are certain inherent limits to the efficient private *ex ante* allocation of the risk of job loss from trade liberalization. It is very difficult to make sound *ex ante* predictions as to the nature and extent of these risks.[64] As a consequence, although worker self-insurance through personal savings undoubtedly exists, such savings are very likely to be too high or too low, given lack of good information about risk. With respect to private insurance, one simply does not observe such markets. Their absence cannot be explained by the presence of basic public unemployment insurance in most industrial democracies, since it is unclear why a market for supplemental benefits would not exist. After all, public insurance benefits cover only a portion of income loss and in some countries only for relatively short periods of time. An additional explanation for the absence of such private insurance would be the arguably quite severe moral hazard problems involved. Full insurance of the risk of dislocation due to trade liberalization would very likely lead some workers and firms to take greater risks, or to underinvest in precautions against the risks in question (e.g. skill diversification). It should be emphasized that these possible market failures do not suggest that government will be any better at *ex ante* allocation of risks of job loss from trade. However, the absence of viable private insurance markets may argue for government intervention based upon the desirability of the existence of insurance that would otherwise not be provided, a desirability to be established on independent normative grounds.

A further possibility would be contractual allocation of risk between employer and employee through bargaining of notice periods in the event of dislocation. While such notice periods are the subject of contractual bargaining in some subset of cases, there is empirical evidence that the existence and nature of such provisions are very poorly correlated to the actual risk of dislocation in the industry and region in question.[65] This suggests that serious information failures may plague *ex ante* allocation of these risks through contractual bargaining between employer and employee.[66] In addition, it is often very difficult for workers to address the risk of dislocation through *ex ante* diversification of their skills. Indeed, powerful incentives exist for workers increasingly to specialize in firm-specific knowledge and skills, as it is these investments that usually have larger pay-offs in promotions and bonuses.

Naturally, firms themselves are likely to invest most heavily in those training programmes that involve highly firm-specific skills. They have little incentive to train workers to be able to move to other sectors or firms, and indeed, arguably, a disincentive since the longer a worker stays with a particular firm, the greater will be that firm's return on the investment in that worker. Of course, if the firm is a conglomerate encompassing a wide range of economic activities (i.e. highly diversified in its operations) it may have an incentive to provide training that is not narrowly job specific, with a view to workers moving between diverse activities within the firm. Yet, even in this case, it is far from clear that in the absence of a long-term employment contract or implicit contract (such as company loyalty in Japan) workers would not take the newly acquired skills and apply them elsewhere.

A somewhat different economic efficiency rationale for adjustment policies stems from the very real danger that, absent appropriate government intervention, trade-induced worker dislocation may result in an erosion of human capital. Workers who lose their jobs due to freer trade, or other structural changes, may out of desperation and in the absence of retraining assistance, seek employment at lower wage levels, and in occupations of lower skill and labour productivity. Empirical evidence suggests that a significant percentage of dislocated workers end up in lower-wage, lower-skill occupations, and, in fact, never regain the earnings levels of their previous employment.[67] Worse still, a protracted period of unemployment – especially when uncushioned by adequate income support – may also entail physical and mental illness, family break-up, alcoholism, and drug use, which in addition to creating added costs for various social safety nets, is almost certain to reduce the productive capacity of workers and reduce the chances that they will return to the workplace, leading instead to dependence on the social welfare system. All of these factors are likely to be aggravated by the problem of 'sour grapes'[68] or adaptive preferences: the longer workers are unemployed or underemployed in an occupation, the less likely they will be to *believe* in their own inherent capabilities, and hence actively to seek better opportunities.[69] In sum, the *human* effects of dislocation on workers and their families may well lead to long-term sub-optimal deployment of workers' capacities, absent positive adjustment measures.

Many of the most important, and most controversial, arguments about the justification for trade-linked adjustment assistance measures centre around the notion that it is desirable to compensate the losers from freer trade. In economic theory, the notion of Kaldor-Hicks efficiency, applied to the analysis of policy change, suggests the desirability of a given policy change where the benefits to the winners from this change outweigh the losses to the losers. However, unless one adopts a very crude or extreme utilitarian position, the complete sacrifice of particular groups in society for the sake of the common good is ethically problematic.

There are important political and social reasons for attempting to spread across society the costs of adopting particular measures to improve the general welfare. The attitudes of particular groups towards the political process, and their sense of citizen solidarity with the community as a whole, may be adversely affected by having to pay the largest part of the price for a given improvement. The common good itself may be lost sight of as acrimonious debates about who wins and loses increasingly dominate the political process. This range of concerns has been evoked by Michelman in his discussion of demoralization and disaffection costs,[70] and is well-expressed by Calabresi:

> A decision which recognizes the values on the losing side as real and significant tends to keep us from becoming callous with respect to the moralisms and beliefs that lose out . . . it tells the loser that, though they lost, they and their values do carry weight and are recognized in our society, even when they don't win out.[71]

Comparative experience with labour market policies in various industrialized countries yields a very mixed record. Countries like the UK, France, Canada, the USA, and Australia have tended to favour a safety net approach, rather than proactive labour market policies. In contrast, Sweden, Japan, and to a lesser extent Germany, tend to favour much more proactive labour market policies that provide generous assistance to workers for training, retraining, and relocation. The empirical evidence generally suggests the superiority of the latter class of policies in terms of facilitating adjustment, although designing effective job training and retraining programmes, particularly for unemployed youths and older workers, has proven a demanding challenge for governments and empirical evidence on their efficacy is quite mixed.[72]

Another controversial issue relates to whether special labour market policies should be adopted in trade-impacted sectors. For example, the US Trade Expansion Act of 1962 and the 1974 Trade Act both sought to provide adjustment assistance to workers dislocated by import competition. The 1962 Act, with its very strict eligibility criteria (to be eligible for assistance it was necessary to demonstrate that imports were a more important factor than all others combined in causing injury and that tariff concessions and injury must have occurred simultaneously), was largely unsuccessful as an instrument of assistance. From 1962 to 1974, only 54,000 workers were certified for assistance involving total expenditures of $US85 million.[73] Adjustment assistance grew substantially under the 1974 Trade Act, under which the level of benefits was increased and the eligibility criteria were greatly relaxed. Between 1977 and 1981, 1.2 million workers received benefits. Spending on TAA in 1981 reached $US1.5 billion, although subsequently the programme budget was severely cut.[74] However, for the most part assistance under the Trade Act turned out to be an instrument of compensation for temporarily laid off workers rather than an instrument to promote adjustment out of declining industries.[75]

These are not arguments against trade-related adjustment assistance programmes *as such* – rather they suggest that policies should be designed to ensure that priority is placed on job losses that are likely to be permanent, and that eligibility criteria are not tilted in favour of sectors that are represented by powerful lobby groups.

A second, but related argument against linking adjustment assistance with trade liberalization is that singling out trade-displaced workers from other displaced workers is morally arbitrary and unfair. This kind of argument assumes that *only* trade-displaced workers are being offered assistance beyond that provided by the general social safety net (including unemployment insurance). However, when a variety of programmes exist that are targeted at specific groups of workers, and with a range of eligibility requirements, it is much less clear that providing a programme for trade-displaced workers is giving them an unfair advantage.

The logic of targeting or disaggregating adjustment assistance is that workers displaced for different reasons have different needs. Workers displaced by trade liberalization, for example, may be more likely to require retraining than those who lose their jobs due to cyclical downturns or the bankruptcy of a particular firm, since trade-induced dislocation may reflect a need to restructure an entire industry or sector in response to enhanced import competition. As Peter Morici suggests, in the wake of NAFTA:

> In the United States and Canada, jobs in low- and medium-technology activities must make way for jobs in high-technology activities. Generally this will entail the loss of low-skill/wage jobs in industries such as consumer electronics and the gain of high-skill/wage jobs in industries such as advanced telecommunications equipment.[76]

It might reasonably be argued that a *worker's* right to adjustment assistance in the case of trade induced displacement would, on both efficiency and ethical grounds, be a superior alternative to the right to safeguard relief presently accorded to *firms* under import pressure.[77] One of us has suggested that such a right to worker adjustment should be entrenched in a parallel accord to NAFTA.[78] The right could be satisfied by governments providing domestic adjustment assistance programmes that are generally available to all displaced workers (unemployment insurance, retraining and reskilling benefits, job counselling, etc.) or alternatively, by programmes more directly targeted at workers displaced by trade. Where workers believed that domestic policies of their own countries did not satisfy the right to adjustment they (or their representatives) would, on this scheme, be able to petition a Trinational Committee of Experts, which would examine and rule on the adequacy of the adjustment programmes in the country concerned. Ideally, once a right to adjustment was in place, a country would be permitted to invoke traditional safeguards only if it could show that domestic adjustment policies that satisfied the right to adjustment were nevertheless insufficient to cope with the nature or scale of the social and economic disruption caused by import surges.

Unfortunately, from a political perspective, incentives on the part of both demanders and suppliers of public policies tend in the direction of a complete inversion of the policy prescriptions implied by the analysis in this chapter. That is to say, in the face of trade-related adjustment pressures, politicians will face strong pressures to maintain or increase trade restrictions, in part because these entail off-budget expenditures and in part because they simultaneously buy off investor, worker, and other dependent interests. As a second-best policy, industrial subsidies will be favoured because while they, to a greater or lesser extent, involve on-budget expenditures, they are responsive to demands not only by workers but also by investors and other affected interests. As a distinctly third-best policy option, labour market adjustment policies may be favoured, but even then with a bias toward stay-oriented labour policies rather than exit-oriented labour policies. Most labour market policies involve on-budget expenditures and are responsive only to the demands of workers and not of investors and other affected interests; and stay (safety-net) oriented labour policies avoid an acknowledgement by government that the sector cannot or will not be preserved in its present form or on its current scale. The new constraints embodied in the GATT/WTO Safeguards Agreement discussed earlier in this chapter may help tilt domestic political forces more strongly in the direction of proactive labour market adjustment policies, enhancing simultaneously domestic and global economic welfare.

The interrelationship between trade and labour policies extends, however, far beyond the context of domestic adjustment assistance. Many critics of free trade have argued that it is unfair that producers and their workers in the developed industrial world should have to compete with imports from countries with very low wage rates and weak labour standards. This is a sufficiently important and contentious issue that we take it up in a separate chapter.

CONCLUSION

The new Uruguay Round Safeguards Agreement, if supplemented with further reforms to the regime along the lines discussed earlier in this chapter, and adequate domestic labour market adjustment policies, should adequately address the adjustment costs associated with trade liberalization or shifting patterns of comparative advantage. In particular, the normative case for retaining broadly-cast domestic antidumping and countervailing duty regimes, either to address the impact of growth of imports on domestic industries or to address claims of 'unfair trade', will have been substantially negated. Empirical evidence tends to suggest that rising levels of income inequality (particularly with respect to unskilled workers) in North America and high levels of unemployment in many European countries, while properly a matter of concern, are only attributable to a small extent to increased trade and are mainly attributable to other factors such as technological change.[79] Seeking trade-related responses to these problems is likely to aggravate rather than ameliorate them.

10 Trade in agriculture

INTRODUCTION

Over the last two decades, trade in agriculture has become one of the most prominent and acrimonious issues on the world trade agenda. A solution to some of these controversies, particularly those surrounding agricultural export subsidies and related domestic measures (such as price supports and production quotas) was crucial to the successful conclusion of the Uruguay Round of GATT negotiations. Protectionism has been pervasive in the agricultural sector in Canada, the United States, the EU and Japan. Prior to the Uruguay Round Final Act, the GATT itself placed fewer strictures on agricultural protection than was the case with most other sectors. Moreover, a number of the major exporting states had come close to ignoring GATT requirements altogether, even to the point of refusing to implement GATT panel decisions. The International Monetary Fund has estimated that the costs of agricultural protection to taxpayers and consumers in the OECD countries alone amounts to about $US300 billion each year. The IMF has also found that liberalization of this sector, involving both trade and domestic policy reforms in these countries, would result in gains to consumers and taxpayers far outweighing losses to agricultural producers.[1]

Despite the economic welfare case for liberalizing trade in agriculture, a number of rationales are still often invoked for treating the agricultural sector as a special case. These rationales include: supposedly exceptional price and income instability; the importance to national security of agricultural self-sufficiency; and the cultural and social value of preserving rural lifestyles. At the same time, liberalization – while leading to eventual substantial net gains in welfare, both global and domestic – poses significant adjustment and transitional equity issues.

In this chapter, we will consider the pre-Uruguay Round treatment of agriculture in trade law and practice; the extent to which it is justifiable to treat agriculture as a special case; and the liberalization achievements of the Uruguay Round Final Act, with particular attention to managing the challenge of adjustment.

The issue of health and safety standards in agricultural trade, including the Uruguay Round Sanitary and Phytosanitary Agreement, was considered in Chapter 6.

TRADE IN AGRICULTURE AND THE PRE-URUGUAY ROUND GATT

Historical origins of special treatment for agriculture

The special treatment of agriculture in the General Agreement was largely, if not exclusively, a reflection of the power and influence of the United States at the end of the Second World War. The negotiators of the GATT did not, generally speaking, see any need for a special regime for agriculture. Import quotas and export subsidies were, however, an integral feature of the American supply management system for agricultural products that existed at the time, and as Dam suggests, 'no treaty that impinged upon the U.S. Farm program could receive the constitutionally required senatorial approval'.[2] As will be discussed in detail below, the special treatment of agriculture contained in the General Agreement has led to a large number of disputes over the interpretation of the GATT. Moreover, in this area – more so than in any other – Contracting Parties found it impossible to live with GATT panel decisions limiting their capacity to engage in agricultural protection. Thus, for the United States, the special treatment it won under the General Agreement for import restrictions linked to domestic supply management proved insufficient, leading the US Administration to seek a waiver of Article XI GATT obligations as early as 1955, with respect to a variety of agricultural products, including sugar, peanuts and dairy products.[3] Similarly, the European Union has either blocked the adoption of, or refused to implement, panel decisions that threaten elements of its Common Agricultural Policy.

Quantitative restrictions

Article XI of the GATT prohibits quantitative restrictions on trade, subject to certain exceptions. Several of the exceptions are of particular relevance to trade in agriculture. First of all, Article XI:2(a) permits export 'prohibitions or restrictions' of a temporary nature in order to address critical food shortages in the exporting country. Second, XI:2(b) permits 'import and export restrictions'[4] necessary to the application of standards or regulations for the classification, grading or marketing of commodities in international trade. Third, and most importantly, XI:2(c) permits import restrictions on 'any agricultural or fisheries product' where necessary to enforce domestic restrictions on the marketing or production of a similar product or product substitute. Import restrictions are also permitted where necessary to remove a temporary surplus of a domestic like product or product substitute. Article XIII sets out detailed rules on the use of quantitative restrictions in cases where one or more of these exceptions apply.

In theory, at least, an important constraint on the protectionist impact of these exceptions to the ban on quantitative restrictions is that the import restrictions in question must be accompanied by like domestic measures. Foreigners cannot be singled out or targeted – hence, import restrictions must not reduce the total value of imports proportionate to domestic production below that 'which might reasonably be expected to rule between the two in the absence of restrictions' (Article XI:2). If this condition were applied rigorously, it would mean that domestic price supports could be operated in a manner consistent with comparative advantage. If, for example, a Contracting Party placed a quota of ten million chickens a year on domestic marketing of poultry, and chickens from another Contracting Party would have had a 60% market share under *unrestricted* market conditions, then the other Contracting Party would be entitled to a market share of six million chickens.

This, of course, involves a difficult counterfactual exercise – i.e. determining comparative advantage in agriculture absent the price distortions created by domestic price support policies in the import-restricting country. Nevertheless, in theory, it should make quantitative restrictions a rather unattractive instrument of agricultural protection, since foreigners end up with a market share equal to that which would exist in the absence of protection.

Perhaps for this very reason this condition on the use of quantitative restrictions was never effectively enforced. An attempt in the 1950s to enforce the even more general condition that import restrictions be 'necessary' to enforce domestic marketing and production limits resulted in a threat from the United States that it would leave the GATT. A GATT Working Party found that US import restrictions on dairy products were not accompanied by domestic restrictions on the production of the raw material for the products (milk), and retaliation was authorized under Article XXIII when the United States failed to remove the restrictions in question.[5] In the face of the threat of US withdrawal from GATT, the United States was granted a non-time-limited waiver from the strictures of Article XI with respect to agricultural products. This exemption for the United States may well have had the effect of dampening efforts to enforce strictly Article XI against other Contracting Parties – given that the United States was granted a waiver, it might have been difficult, on principled grounds, to have refused one to others.

Nevertheless, in several later panel decisions, a stricter view of the provisions of Article XI was taken. For instance, in ruling on an American complaint concerning Japanese quantitative restrictions on a wide variety of agricultural product groups, a GATT panel held that Article XI:2(c)(i) should be construed narrowly, and, in particular, that there was a burden of proof on the import-restricting state to show that it had granted to foreign producers the market share that would exist if there were no restrictions.[6] The panel decision did not, however, establish a methodology or detailed guidelines for making such a determination – the panel merely held that Japan had not attempted to discharge the burden of proof. In another case, which concerned import restrictions imposed by the European Union in the face of a surplus of apples, a panel held that the exemption in Article XI:2(c)(ii) did not apply, because the surplus was not temporary, but rather a chronic side-effect of the Union's own agricultural price support policies.[7] In a case that concerned Canadian quantitative restrictions on imports of yoghurt and ice cream from the United States, Canada argued before the panel that these restrictions were 'necessary' to render effective domestic production restrictions on milk, in the sense that the higher cost of milk generated by these restrictions made secondary products manufactured with the higher cost Canadian milk vulnerable to imports. Therefore, Canada claimed, the requirements of Article XI:2(c)(i) had been met. The panel took a narrow view of the word 'necessary', finding that it did not include import restrictions aimed at neutralizing the competitive disadvantage to other domestic industries of higher domestic prices for agricultural inputs. In effect, without the restrictions, Canada would still be able to enforce domestic restrictions on milk production and hence keep the price of milk high – albeit at some cost to Canadian yoghurt and ice cream makers. This ruling is arguably quite important, since it prevents Article XI:2(c)(i) from being used by Contracting Parties to shift the costs of their agricultural protectionism from their own agrifood industries on to foreign competitors in these industries.

Export subsidies

Article XVI of the General Agreement prohibits export subsidies, subject to an exception for 'primary products'. These are permitted, with the proviso that 'they shall not be applied in a manner which results in that Contracting Party having more than an equitable share of world export trade in that product'. In defining what constitutes an equitable share, 'shares of the contracting parties in such trade in the product in a previous representative period' are to be taken into account. This suggests that the essential issue is whether the export subsidy has caused an increase in market share over that which prevailed in the period before the subsidy was introduced. A 'primary product' is defined in an Interpretive Note to Article XVI as 'any product of farm, forest, or fishery at an early stage of processing'.

These provisions were incorporated into the Tokyo Round Subsidies Code (Article 10), with minor variations. In particular, the expression 'more than an equitable share of world trade' was defined to apply to those cases where 'the effect of an export subsidy granted by a signatory is to displace the exports of another signatory bearing in mind the developments on world markets' (Article 10(2)(a)). As well, the 'previous representative period' would normally be 'the three most recent calendar years in which normal market conditions existed' (Article 10(2)(c)).

Even with these criteria, it proved very difficult to interpret the concept of 'an equitable share of world trade'. In a 1958 case that concerned French subsidies on the export of wheat flour, the panel ruled that the subsidies did not comply with the GATT because France had attained more than an equitable share of the world market. Three considerations formed the basis of this finding: (1) France's exports of flour to the market in question (Southeast Asia) had increased over a previous period; (2) the complainant's (Australia's) exports to the same market declined; and (3) the subsidy was found to be a 'substantial cause' of the displacement.[8] In a more recent case,[9] however, a panel found that European Union subsidies on wheat flour were permissible under Article XVI, even though the Union's share of the world market had increased from 29% to 75% between 1962 and 1981, while the complainant (the United States) had seen its share over the comparable period decline from 25% to 9%. The panel noted the difficulty in determining whether, in fact, changes in market share could be attributable to a particular export subsidy, as opposed to other factors. It seemed to be suggesting that specific evidence of price undercutting in the market in question would be required to establish that export subsidies were unambiguously resulting in displacement – shifts in market share alone were insufficient, however dramatic.

The United States objected strongly to this approach, and vetoed adoption of the panel report. However, the report is defensible on at least two grounds: (1) As Jackson notes, the United States itself was selling its own wheat in the same market on non-commercial terms, through a food aid programme,[10] and therefore neither country's market share could be considered over the period in question to have been based on undistorted market conditions; and (2) although dramatic increases in market share had occurred, this had taken place over a period of twenty years, whereas the text of the Subsidies Code itself suggested that market share changes should be considered in terms of changes occurring within a threeyear representative period. More generally, by the time of this dispute world trade in agriculture had become so distorted by the domestic and export policies of the main producers that the panel's difficulty in finding a clear benchmark against which the distorting effect of one particular subsidy could be measured was entirely understandable.

In the *Pasta* case, the United States argued that subsidies paid by the European Community to exporters of pasta violated Article 9 of the GATT Subsidies Code, which prohibits export subsidies on 'non-primary' products.[11] The EU responded that the subsidy should be viewed as a subsidy on primary product inputs into pasta production, in particular European durum wheat. The effect of the subsidy, according to the EU, was simply to compensate EU pasta exporters for the higher than world prices of EU flour, thereby allowing them to be competitive on world markets despite purchasing wheat at higher prices than foreign competitors. This argument was rejected by a majority of the panel, which read Article 9 literally to include all subsidies *paid* to exporters of non-primary products, without regard to whether the intended or actual effect was to subsidize indirectly a primary product. One of the four panellists, however, wrote a dissenting opinion, taking the view that in negotiating the Tokyo Round Subsidies Code, governments had generally understood or assumed that subsidies on primary components of non-primary products would not be prohibited by Article 9.

The EU blocked adoption of the majority ruling by the Subsidies Committee and eventually reached a negotiated settlement with the United States of the dispute in question. But the ultimate consequence was continued uncertainty about the legality under GATT of one of the most pervasive and controversial features of the European Union's Common Agricultural Policy – export subsidies on products that use EU agricultural inputs.

Domestic subsidies and related domestic support measures

A more recent GATT ruling narrowed the scope for granting *domestic* subsidies to users of a product rather than its producers. As discussed in Chapter 8, domestic subsidies were not prohibited by the GATT, although, in accordance with the rules set out in the Subsidies Agreement, they might be countervailable. However, in the *Oilseeds*[12] case, a GATT panel found that a subsidy paid to European Union users of oilseeds violated Article III, the National Treatment principle of the GATT. Here, the panel took a quite literal approach to the wording of Article III, which only exempts subsidies from the National Treatment obligation if they are paid 'exclusively' to domestic producers of the subsidized product (Article III:8(b)). The EU revised the form of assistance so that it appeared to comply with the requirements of Article III. However, a subsequent panel found this new form of assistance still constituted non-violation nullification or impairment of a benefit that the United States could reasonably have expected from previous GATT concessions. Here, the United States was able to point to an early GATT tariff binding on oilseeds by the EU, which gave it reason to expect at least some level of access to the EU market.[13] Bilateral negotiations between the EU and the USA concerning implementation of the panel's ruling were initially unsuccessful; the dispute was finally resolved within the framework of a broader US/EU agreement on negotiating positions in the Uruguay Round (the Blair House Agreement, discussed in a later section of this chapter).

THE CANADA–US FREE TRADE AGREEMENT (FTA) AND THE NORTH AMERICAN FREE TRADE AGREEMENT (NAFTA)

Chapter Seven of the FTA deals with trade in agriculture. The main impact on agricultural trade is the phased-in reduction and eventual elimination of tariffs on many agricultural commodities. However, because the FTA contains few strictures with respect to domestic support measures, its overall liberalizing effect is quite modest. Article 701 does, however, prohibit export subsidies on agricultural goods moving from one FTA partner to the other. It should be noted that this does not prohibit the use of export subsidies when Canada and the USA are competing against each other in third-country markets. Instead, there is a weak obligation to take into account the harmful effects of such subsidies of exports to third countries on the other FTA partner (Article 701.4).

As well, although the FTA does not contain a general prohibition on non-tariff border measures, such as quotas imposed to implement supply management schemes, the United States was able to obtain from Canada minimum market access commitments under some of these schemes. For instance, with respect to chicken and chicken products, the United States is entitled to an import quota no less than 7.5% of the previous year's domestic production of chickens in Canada (Article 706). In addition, the Parties agree to work towards harmonizing technical standards, and a number of technical working groups are established for this purpose (Article 708).

In the case of NAFTA, there is, generally speaking, little substantial progress over the FTA with respect to trilateral trade liberalization, due largely to Canadian intransigence with respect to supply management schemes (which, of course, will now have to be modified in light of the Agreement on Agriculture in the Uruguay Round Final Act).[14] However, the NAFTA contains much more promising provisions with respect to US–Mexico agricultural trade, including a waiver of GATT rights with respect to imposition of quantitative restrictions connected to domestic supply management (Article XI:2(c) of GATT). There is a complicated scheme for tariff reductions, with tariffs on some commodities to be eliminated between all three countries immediately, whereas tariffs on other commodities are to be phased out in either a five, ten, or fifteen-year period, again depending upon the commitments each country has made with respect to that particular commodity. Canada insisted on excluding poultry, milk and eggs from these commitments. However, in some other areas, Canada has agreed to lift quantitative restrictions on imports from Mexico, including cereals, meats, and margarine (with respect to the United States, US rights of market access where Canada maintains quantitative restrictions remain governed by the provisions of the FTA which have been substantially incorporated into the NAFTA). NAFTA also contains provisions on technical barriers that resemble very closely those in the Uruguay Round Final Act (to be discussed later in this chapter).

An economic model of the effects of liberalization commitments in NAFTA with respect to agricultural products predicts that, when NAFTA is fully implemented, agricultural trade between the USA and Mexico will be 15% greater than it was in the 1988 base year.[15] US exports to Mexico are predicted to increase more rapidly than Mexican exports to the USA, in part because Mexico's pre-NAFTA level of border protection on these commodities was substantially higher than that of the USA.[16] A major shortcoming of this kind of model is, of course, the difficulty of predicting other factors such as exchange rate movements, changes in agricultural demand and supply in other countries, etc. that may affect the impact of the NAFTA. Significantly, Canada was not treated in the model as a NAFTA partner, because the impact of NAFTA on its agricultural trade was assumed to be minimal.

RATIONALES FOR DIFFERENTIAL TREATMENT OF THE AGRICULTURAL SECTOR: A CRITICAL OVERVIEW

Although much agricultural protectionism can be attributed to the influence of powerful farm lobbies in North America, Europe, and Japan, there are a number of long-standing rationales for the justification of protection that are specific to this sector.

Self-sufficiency/national security

In the most literal sense, a nation's survival can be said to depend upon access to food. Famines have appeared periodically throughout history, and continue to do so in much of the developing world, whether caused by war, pestilence, or drought. In times of shortage, access to food from foreign imports may well dry up, as countries impose export restrictions to ensure their own populace gets fed first. As we noted above, this kind of export control is in fact explicitly authorized by the GATT. Under these circumstances, it is not surprising that self-sufficiency is often cited as a rationale for agricultural protection, or more precisely, as a rationale for measures that maintain agricultural production in a country where it would be more efficient for most or all of its needs to be met from imports. A variant on the self-sufficiency argument is the purported advantage of not having to rely on foreigners who may be one's enemies in war (or potential enemies) for the supply of food.

Exceptional price instability

Agricultural commodities are subject to price fluctuations often considerably greater than many other goods that are traded, in significant part because supply is so susceptible to unpredictable factors such as weather. As a consequence, farmers' incomes are highly volatile. On the other hand, their costs (debt service on land, equipment, etc.) are likely to be fixed to a significant extent. In the end, it is argued, unless supply is restricted, or prices stabilized by other means, a single bad year may well result in many farmers being put out of business altogether, although in some sense they nevertheless have an on-going comparative advantage in producing food. Although much of the agricultural industry in developed countries is now constituted by large commercial producers, the image of the family losing its farm, and therewith a lifetime of work together, remains a powerful and poignant image in popular culture.

Preservation of the rural way of life/environment

Over the last few decades, efficiency of agricultural production has increased enormously in most developed countries. Therefore, even if a certain level of domestic food production could be seen as necessary for self-sufficiency reasons, or even if price stabilization could be justified as a means of making farm incomes less volatile, nevertheless there would still be a long-run shift of both land and people away from agricultural production – one can simply meet existing demand with less land and fewer people. Hence, in recent years an often heard argument for agricultural protection has been that keeping land and people in farming is a social good in itself. With respect to land, the implicit assumption is that, but for agricultural usages, the countryside would be much more heavily burdened with ugly, polluting industries, or simply replaced by industrial or commercial towns. A closely related argument is that agriculture sustains rural *communities*, which would either disappear or lose their distinctive character if economic activity in the countryside were shifted away from agricultural production.

Wilson and Finkle suggest, writing primarily of the Canadian context:

> Farmers enjoy an undercurrent of sympathy among urban voters which confers political power on them quite out of proportion to their numbers . . . most urbanites are attracted to the idealized image of the countryside: the hard

> working farm family, the noble virtues and traditional values which they imagine motivate their rustic compatriots. It is not a lifestyle most urbanites would care to live themselves but they are glad someone is doing it and they are willing to pay a bit to see it maintained.[17]

As well, Europeans in particular are fond of arguing that their countryside is a natural and cultural treasure that would be fundamentally threatened if land were taken out of agricultural production.

None of these three main kinds of rationales is entirely bogus, although assumptions that the agricultural industry is largely composed of needy farm families or that modern farming operations are more aesthetically or environmentally friendly than other kinds of contemporary economic activity deserve critical scrutiny. The more fundamental issue is whether any of these goals really necessitates measures that radically distort world trade and cost non-farm households more than a $1,000 per year in both higher food prices and in taxes that pay for farm subsidies. For example, with respect to the price instability of agricultural products, the real issue is the stability of farmer's incomes. Farmer's incomes could be stabilized directly, through income averaging techniques or income insurance, rather than distorting domestic prices and limiting foreign competition in order to maintain artificially high domestic prices. With respect to rural life-style values, careful regional development plans seem a more finely-tuned instrument than agricultural protection to ensure balanced economic activity in the countryside. As we shall argue below, much of the potential for reforming agricultural trade comes from this potential for 'decoupling' of policy goals such as income stabilization from trade distortive policies.

INSTRUMENTS OF AGRICULTURAL PROTECTION

Domestic price control and supply management systems and related trade measures

The European Union Common Agricultural Policy (CAP)

In theory, the Common Agricultural Policy (CAP) is based on the objectives in Article 39 of the Treaty of Rome, including market stabilization, increased agricultural productivity, and reasonable agricultural prices for consumers. During the 1960s and 1970s, the CAP developed into a complex web of price and sales guarantees, subsidies, and other support measures that largely insulated farmer's incomes from market forces. For most agricultural products, a minimum price was set to apply to all sales within the EU. In order not to undermine this price, it was essential that lower-priced imports be prohibited. This was achieved by a Variable Import Levy – a charge on imported goods equivalent to whatever difference exists at the time of entry between world price and the Union price. In effect, through the levy, the Union was able to neutralize whatever price advantage a foreign competitor might enjoy.

As Martin has remarked, 'European farmers have demonstrated beyond a shadow of a doubt that they are economically rational.'[18] Hence, in the face of guaranteed prices considerably above world prices and no production controls, they expanded production. It should be remembered that since the price was set so that the least efficient producers in Europe could make a profit, it offered significant rents or *supra*-normal profits to the more efficient producers. In addition, given that technological developments were increasing the efficiency of *all* farmers, it is not surprising that enormous surpluses soon developed. Since prices could not be lowered, there was no obvious way to dispose of the surplus in an orderly fashion. In consequence, the Union came to make undertakings to farmers to purchase their surplus at the high Union price. Enormous stockpiles of many commodities soon developed, and by the 1980s close to 80% of the Union budget was spent on agricultural programmes. Once again, farmers behaved entirely rationally, and now that they had not only prices but also sales guaranteed, further invested to expand production.

It is in the context of these pressures that the Union established a rebate on export sales, where in order to encourage disposal of the surpluses on world markets, the Union pays exporters the difference between the high Union price and the world price. Although these rebates have often been characterized, and condemned as export subsidies, in theory it should be noted that they do not actually undercut the world price. However, critics of the CAP have often charged that, in practice, rebates are given which exceed the difference between the Union and the world price, because the EU authorities tend systematically to underestimate world price in their calculation of the rebates. What is certainly true is that the CAP went from a programme that affected trade by keeping foreign producers out of the EU market to one that, at the same time, because of the massive surpluses being disposed of through the rebate scheme, made it increasingly difficult for foreign producers to sell their agricultural products in *third-country* markets.

North America

Although Americans have tended to single out the CAP as the main villain in the agricultural trade wars, it must be remembered that it was US agricultural protection that led to weak GATT rules in agriculture in the first place. These have included price support measures, coupled however with production restrictions. There is a legitimate argument that these measures were less harmful than the CAP price support mechanism – since production restrictions were in place, keeping prices high did not result in the generation of massive surpluses. Also, since the mid-1980s, the United States has attempted permanently to reduce production by paying farmers to take land out of service. As well, instead of keeping the market price artificially high, for some commodities the United States now pays to farmers the difference between the price they can get on the market and a target price based on a formula that reflects the revenue farmers need to break even. Although Americans often claim that US export subsidies are a competitive response to EU and other foreign programmes, in fact such subsidies long predate the CAP.

However, it is true that during the 1960s and 1970s the United States' use of export subsidies declined considerably, until in 1985 a new set of aggressive subsidies was introduced in response to the CAP.[19]

Canada maintains marketing and production restrictions on poultry and eggs, enforced through domestic and import quotas. These import quotas have been justified under Article XI:2(c) of the GATT, discussed earlier in this chapter.

In addition, Canada actively subsidizes the sale of wheat and other grains, often through concessional financing by the Canadian Wheat Board, which actively tries to undercut competitors' in many export markets. However, Canada tends to view these subsidies as a response to similar behaviour on the part of its competitors, particularly the European Union, where a grain industry would be largely non-existent but for the CAP. In addition, both Canada and the United States both provide a variety of forms of assistance to farmers that, arguably, do not directly distort world or domestic prices, such as crop insurance and low-interest loans and loan guarantees for purchase of land and equipment and generous tax write-offs (the latter, in the case of Canada, have created a new class of 'gentlemen-farmers'). The arguments concerning whether such subsidies are objectionable as leading to inefficient or unfair trade are much the same as for any other domestic subsidy.

Japan

Japan's domestic market for agricultural products is one of the most protected in the world, at least with respect to some commodities. A wide range of instruments is employed that includes price stabilization, control of supply by state or quasi-state monopolies, coupled with import quotas and extremely high tariffs. According to Gilson,[20] in 1988, the Japanese domestic price for wheat was eight times the world price. Rice is often estimated to cost ten or eleven times as much in Japan as on world markets and beef is heavily protected as well. Japan, however, is not a major exporter of agricultural products, and therefore does not participate in the export subsidy war between North America and the European Union.

Costs and benefits of agricultural protection

There have been many estimates in recent years of the costs and benefits of agricultural protection, using different methodologies and different definitions of what constitutes protection.[21] With respect to costs, these include the expense to the taxpayers of on-budget measures such as export and domestic subsidies, and commitments to purchase surpluses, costs to consumers of more expensive food, and allocative efficiency losses as resources are misdirected to agricultural production where no comparative advantage exists in the farm sector.

Figure 10.1, taken from a survey by *The Economist*[22] magazine, contains estimates of the per household per year costs of agricultural protection in the United States, Western Europe and Japan (including both higher taxes and higher food prices). These costs, which globally average around $1,400 per household per year for the countries concerned, represent a considerable welfare loss. To these costs must be

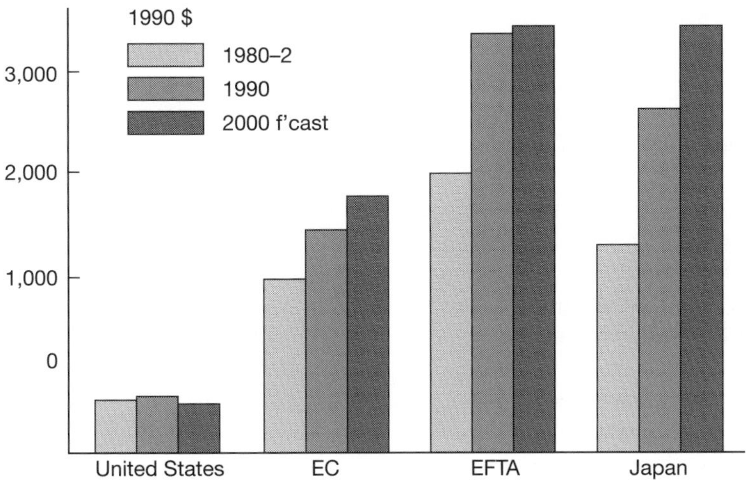

Figure 10.1 Cost of agricultural support per non-farm household
Source: Tyers and Anderson, *Disarray in World Food Markets*.

added the environmental costs of over-farming due to incentives to increase production in the European Union, and the deadweight loss of resources devoted to lobbying for protection. As well, the effect of protection in the developed countries is to shut out to a large extent the developing countries and the Newly Liberalizing Countries of Central and Eastern Europe from many agricultural markets, thereby further retarding growth and adjustment (although some developing countries may benefit, at least in the short run, from lower food prices due to subsidized food exports of developed countries).[23] As well, developed countries such as Australia and New Zealand, which have undertaken unilateral liberalization of their own agricultural support policies, see themselves as having much to gain from more open policies elsewhere, and have been leading forces behind the Cairns Group, which has pressed for comprehensive agreement on agriculture as part of the Uruguay Round.[24] The effects of protection on farmers' incomes in various countries, including industrialized and developing countries, are displayed in Figure 10.2.

The gains to farmers in the EU and Japan are clearly very large. As *The Economist* notes,[25] since the gains from protection are proportional to the amount produced, small or poor farmers receive a small percentage of these gains, and highly efficient, large 'industrial' farms capture the lion's share. These gains, however, do not easily translate into the purported rationales for or social benefits from agricultural protection discussed above. First of all, while prices have been supported domestically, protection has led to increased instability in world prices, as surpluses have rapidly developed in various commodities. This in turn has made domestic price support increasingly costly. Second, even very high levels of protection have not saved the family farm – the exodus to the cities continues,

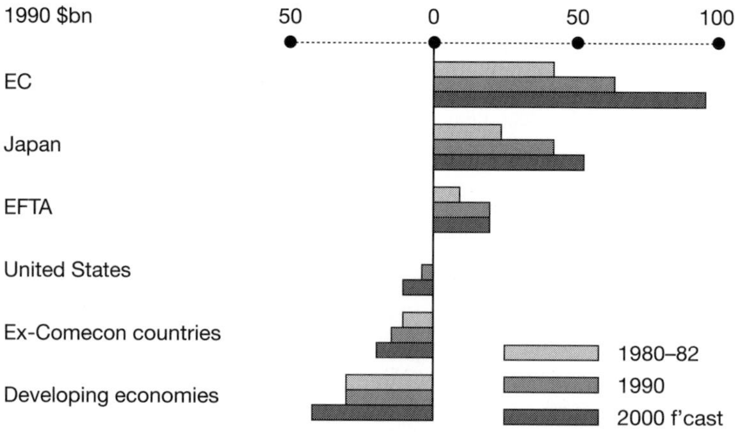

Figure 10.2 Effect on farmers' income of rich countries' policies
Source: *The Economist.*

because increased efficiency means that more can be produced with fewer farmers, and because small family farms often do not have access to the capital needed to invest in the expansion of production and particularly the technology that would allow them to capture major gains from protection. Finally, agricultural protection does not appear to have prevented environmental and aesthetic degradation in rural areas – indeed, as mentioned earlier, over-farming with intensive use of fertilizers and other chemicals has begun to contribute significantly to environmental degradation.

THE URUGUAY ROUND AGREEMENT ON AGRICULTURE

Given the extremely high costs and dubious benefits of agricultural protection – and particularly the increasing cost of beggar-thy-neighbour subsidy wars – the case for removing agricultural protection is a particularly strong one, and was accepted at the level of principle by both the United States[26] and the European Union as a basic goal of the Uruguay Round negotiations. Indeed, as early as 1982, the OECD Ministerial Council had adopted a declaration that 'agricultural trade should be more fully integrated into and within the open and multilateral trading system', also agreeing that multilateral negotiations should address 'adjustments in domestic policies'.[27] This ultimately resulted in a major initiative on agricultural policy reform in the OECD, which culminated in a 1987 ministerial agreement to undertake major reforms without delay. Such reforms were to include 'measures which, by reducing guaranteed prices and other types of production incentives, . . . will prevent an increase in excess supply'.[28] Ministers also undertook to 'refrain from confrontational and destabilising trade practices'.[29] Despite this apparent consensus within the OECD on the need for and the direction of reform, agricultural issues proved to be among the most contentious in the Round, and understanding the evolution of the bargaining positions of the major actors – the USA and the EU – is of considerable importance in appreciating the compromise on agriculture that finally permitted the Uruguay Round to close in mid-December 1993.

At one level, the problem was clearly political. Agricultural lobbies exercise enormous influence in the key countries concerned. This influence is usually quite disproportionate to the percentage of the population at large engaged in agricultural production. In some countries (Canada is an example) the boundaries of legislative districts have not changed in such a way as to reflect fully the shift in population from rural to urban areas, thereby resulting in the former being over-represented in legislatures. In some European countries, the electoral politics are such that forming a governing coalition may be difficult, if not impossible, if some rural-based Parties are not included. As well, in some countries, of which Germany is a prime example, the shift away from agricultural production to other economic activities as the major source of employment has not necessarily been accompanied by a population shift of comparable magnitude from the rural areas to the cities, and electoral boundaries are based on where people live not where they work. Philip notes: '[in the Western part of Germany] a majority of the population is still living in rural areas, even though they don't necessarily work there'.[30]

Just as the American agricultural lobby was adamant that US negotiators accept nothing less than radical reductions in EU export subsidies, the European (and especially the French) farm lobbies were equally adamant that the basic level of protection in the CAP be preserved. However, even where they had the political will to resist the most extreme demands of the farm lobbies, EU policy-makers had a series of legitimate concerns about adjustment and the management of transitional costs during the shift to a more liberal regime for agriculture.

Rapid removal of protection would lead to massive bankruptcies and significant job losses, as farm revenues plummeted in those countries with the highest costs of production. In addition, and perhaps most difficult of all, land values that now reflected rents from protection would decline dramatically[31] – as would the market value of quotas in supply management systems such as that of Canada. Here there would be a transitional gains trap[32] problem, because while older farmers who saw the value of their land go up as rents from protection increased arguably have done very well from protection over the years and may not be deserving of further compensation, there is a much greater difficulty in the case of those who acquired quotas or land more recently, paying a price that reflected an expected income stream based on the assumption of continued protection. The removal of protection in these instances might be viewed as a 'regulatory taking' and therefore require extremely costly compensation for the reduction in the value of land or quotas. Containment of transitional costs generally implies an incremental approach to the removal or at least restructuring of agricultural protection – a process that already had begun on a small scale in the mid- to late 1980s in the United States but has been overshadowed by subsidies wars that are a result of the excess capacity produced by past protectionist practices. An incremental approach, however, has its own drawbacks. First of all, a basic principle of equity suggests that each country should pull its own weight in the overall reduction in protection, but the setting of targets is made more difficult by the diversity of policy instruments employed by different countries. It is necessary to achieve consensus on a methodology for reducing the protectionist impact of these instruments to a common measure.[33] There are a variety of alternative techniques for doing this, each of which has its strengths and weaknesses.[34] A related requirement is effective monitoring of a complex variety of domestic policy changes to ensure that these changes are indeed being made in such a way as to reduce each country's common measure of protection by the targeted amount.

These are some of the transitional issues that set the scene for a dispute between the United States and the European Union over the approach to liberalization which lasted from the intensification of the Uruguay Round negotiations towards the end of the 1980s until the very last days of the Round in December 1993.

Although it showed rather early in the negotiations some flexibility with respect to its opening position that all protection (including domestic support) be eliminated within a ten-year period, the United States insisted that a major thrust of liberalization must be very substantial reductions in one particular instrument of protection, export subsidies, over a ten-year period. This intransigence was probably the result of a variety of factors, including scepticism concerning the ability to monitor more complex domestic policy shifts[35] and an increasing sense of frustration at European unwillingness to comply with existing GATT strictures (which reached a peak, as mentioned above, with the European refusal to implement the 1991 *Oilseeds* ruling). In addition some of the negotiating positions of the EU seemed almost calculated in their manner of presentation to raise the ire of the United States – for instance, at one point the EU, while offering to reduce domestic support by 30% over ten years (an apparently substantial concession) insisted that the offer be backdated to 1986, so the 30% target would be significantly met by reductions that had already occurred.[36]

The European Union, although prepared to make some concessions with respect to domestic support measures, insisted on the continuing capacity to subsidize exports, if only because as long as the other measures were to be phased out gradually, incentives to over-production would continue to exist, and there would be a continued need to use export subsidies to reduce surpluses. The European Union also insisted on the ability to pay income support to farmers as a substitute for protection.[37] From the European perspective any move away from price- and trade-distorting policies would necessarily require adjustment policies that would include a significant element of domestic support, even in the medium or long term.[38] The Union argued that adjustment-oriented measures such as income support were not trade-distorting and therefore ought not to be disciplined under GATT. The USA was sceptical; income support might nevertheless preserve incentives to farmers to continue overproduction, thereby perpetuating the pressure to resort to directly distortive measures, such as export subsidies, to reduce the resulting surpluses.

The 1991 'Dunkel Draft' of a possible Uruguay Round Agreement attempted to set forth a compromise aimed at breaking the impasse in negotiations between the USA and the EU. The Draft proposed: reduction of domestic support measured in terms of a common standard (the Aggregate Measure of Support or AMS) by 20% from 1993 to 1999 with credit to be given for reductions that occurred since 1986; tariffication of border measures other than tariffs (e.g. the import quotas used by Canada to sustain its supply-management system); and reduction in export subsidies by 36% between 1993 and 1999 in terms of outlays (aggregate expenditures) and by 24% in terms of quantities of output subsidized (Part B, para. 11). The Dunkel Draft was ambiguous as to whether income support payments to farmers, as conceived by the EU in the MacSharry Report on CAP Reform,[39] would be viewed as exempt from domestic support reduction commitments.

Negotiations based on the Dunkel Draft made limited headway until, after intense internal discussions, in May 1992, the European Council adopted a revised version of the plan for agricultural reform contained in the MacSharry Report. This entailed a substantial reduction in price support for cereals, accompanied by compensation in the form of income support to farmers, in most instances conditional upon their willingness to 'set aside', or take out of cereals production, a part of their land. In other areas, however (livestock and particularly dairy) the agreed reforms were much less significant – reflecting a difficult intra-European bargain (and above all, the compromises required to gain acceptance by France). In November 1992, the USA and the EU reached a bilateral agreement concerning the liberalization of agricultural trade, the so-called Blair House Agreement. Under the Blair House Agreement, the USA and EU agreed to support the following reductions as a basis for a Uruguay Round Agreement: a 20% reduction in domestic support in terms of the AMS, with 1986–8 as a base period; a 21% reduction in the volume of export subsidies and a 36% reduction in the cash amount of export subsidies, with the base period as defined in the Dunkel Draft; exemption of income support to farmers from domestic support reduction commitments provided that these payments are made on only a limited part of the total production of each farm (so as not to encourage future over-production).[40] These agreed terms for a Uruguay Round settlement on agriculture certainly represented very substantial concessions by the United States to the European Union, at least in terms of previous US negotiating positions. For instance, the USA ended up accepting a 1986 baseline for domestic support commitments – an element that it had rejected when it appeared in earlier EU negotiating positions. In return, however, the USA received satisfaction on a number of specific bilateral concerns, foremost among them the oilseeds controversy. Here, the EU agreed to reduce subsidies on oilseeds once oilseed acreage reached a certain trigger level. The EU also agreed to facilitate market access for US corn to Spain and Portugal. A mutually satisfactory resolution of bilateral disputes between the Parties with respect to corn gluten feed and malted barley sprouts was also achieved.

The Blair House Agreement represented an important breakthrough, but the future of the Uruguay Round was still clouded due to the unwillingness of the French to accept Blair House as a definitive basis for CAP reform. Finally, an adjustment of the Blair House Agreement was achieved through discussions between US Trade Representative Mickey Kantor and EU External Affairs Commissioner Leon Brittan at a meeting in Brussels on 7 December 1993 – just a week before the final deadline for the Uruguay Round negotiations. The major new US concession was to allow back-loading of commitments for reduction in export subsidies, so that smaller reductions would be possible in the first few years of the six-year transition period.[41] A new feature was, however, added to what had been agreed on at Blair House with respect to the basis for a Uruguay Round settlement on agriculture – a commitment to a minimum level of market access for foreign producers equivalent to 3% of domestic production, rising to 5% at the end of a six-year period.

Overview

In terms of general structure and basic principles, the key elements of the Agreement reflect, in the first instance, the Dunkel Draft. With respect to specific commitments, the Agreement is largely based upon the bilateral understandings between the United States and the EU in the Blair House Agreement, as modified by the 7 December Kantor/Brittan meeting (not surprisingly, some smaller countries, including developing countries, found it a source of irritation at the end of the Round that the final Agreement should be closely modelled on a bilateral deal between the USA and the EU). The key elements may be summarized as follows:

1 *Domestic support* is to be quantified in terms of a common metric, the Aggregate Measure of Support (AMS) (Article 1(a); Article 6; Annex 3) with mandatory minimum reductions amounting to 20% over a six-year period, with 1986–8 as the base period (i.e. at the end of six years from the entry into force of the Agreement on Agriculture domestic support must be 20% lower than it was in the 1986–8 base period). 'Direct' payments to farmers, when made under 'production-limiting programmes' are not subject to reduction commitments, provided the payments are based on fixed area and yields, or are made on 85% or less of the base level of production, or (in the case of livestock) on a fixed number of head (Article 6.5(a)(i)–(iii)). Where these payments also conform to the more specific exemption criteria contained in Annex 2, they are also *non-countervailable.*[42]
2 *Export subsidies* are to be reduced over a six-year period by 21% in terms of the volume of agricultural products that receive such subsidies and 36% in terms of total cash value. Except for certain permitted minor adjustments (Article 9.2), members undertake not to expand export subsidies beyond the levels reached after the achievement of their six-year reduction commitments. This in effect alters, with respect to agricultural products, the operation of Article XVI of the General Agreement, which permits export subsidies on primary products.
3 *Existing non-tariff border measures*, such as import quotas, VERs, and the EC Variable Import Levy are to be converted into tariffs (Article 4.2, footnote 1), and *new* measures of this kind are to be prohibited (Article 4.2). This modifies

Article XI:2(c) of the General Agreement, which permits quantitative restrictions on agricultural and fisheries products where necessary to the enforcement of the domestic marketing scheme. In addition, existing non-tariff border measures *must* be reduced to the extent required to allow foreign producers a minimum of 3% market access in terms of total domestic production of each product category, rising to 5% at the end of the six-year phase-in period.

4 *Tariffs* (including existing non-tariff border measures that have been converted to tariffs) are to be reduced by at least 36% overall by each Member over the six-year phase-in period, with a minimum 15% reduction on *each* product category.

Operationalizing the commitment to liberalization; other selected features of the Agreement on Agriculture

It is impossible in this chapter to do full justice to the complex definitional and methodological framework which the Agreement on Agriculture establishes for the operationalization of the reduction commitments sketched above. The Agreement contains finely-crafted provisions that set out basic rules for the calculation of Aggregate Measure of Support in the case of domestic support measures (Annex 3) and for the calculation of tariff equivalents in the case of non-tariff border measures (Attachment to Annex 5). For instance, with respect to domestic price support measures (characteristic of the CAP), these are included in the AMS by calculating the difference between a 'fixed external reference price' (i.e. a world price) and the higher administratively-set domestic price, and multiplying this difference by the volume of production to which the administered price applies (Annex 3, Article 8). Annex 2 of the Agreement provides a very detailed set of criteria for determining which domestic support measures are exempt from reduction commitments, including income support measures for farmers. To be exempt, domestic support measures must meet the 'fundamental' requirement that 'they have no, or at most minimal, trade distortion effects or effects on production' (Annex 2, Article 1). Measures are considered to have met this requirement where they conform to the following two criteria: (1) they are provided through a publicly-funded government programme that does not involve transfers from consumers; and (2) the measures in question do not have the effect of price support (Annex 2, Article 1). Several pages of much more specific criteria and examples of exempt measures follow, and these are based on the general concepts of Article 1 of the Annex. Some of the exempt measures include: research and training programmes; inspection services for health, safety, grading or standardization purposes; and various forms of adjustment assistance to farmers, including income support, where the measures meet very specific conditions aimed at ensuring that the effect is not to reward and thereby perpetuate current levels of production. Article 13 of the Agreement stipulates that domestic support measures that are exempt from reduction commitments by virtue of Annex 2, are to be non-countervailable (Article 13.1(a)). 'Due restraint' is also to be exercised in the initiation of countervail investigations of measures exempt from reduction commitments under Article 6.5 ('direct' payments to farmers in connection with a production-limiting programme).

There is a special safeguard provision in the Agreement on Agriculture, which permits imposition of an additional level of duty (but not reimposition of non-tariff measures) in the case where imports of a particular product exceed a trigger level in a given year or where the price of imports falls below a trigger price.

The trigger level for *volume* of imports varies between 125% and 105% as against the quantity imported over the last three years, depending on the level of existing market access opportunities for imports of the product in question. Thus, for example, where existing market access opportunities for imports amounted to 10% or less of domestic production, an additional 'safeguard' level of duty could only be imposed where imports of the product increased by 25% in the year in question over the average annual quantity imported for the previous three years. However, if existing market opportunities for imports were above 30% of domestic production, a safeguard could be imposed if the volume of imports of the product surged by only 5% over the average annual quantity imported over the previous three years. Where the volume of domestic consumption has changed, the volume of imports must exceed the sum of the trigger level *and* domestic changes in consumption. This reflects the fact that increases in domestic consumption are likely to mitigate the extent to which domestic producers are injured by import surges – there is a larger domestic market to absorb the additional imports. On the other hand, where imports surge at the same time as domestic consumption is decreasing, the injury to domestic producers is likely to be aggravated.

The trigger *price* level is set at an average 1986 to 1988 reference price. Varying levels of 'safeguard' duties may be imposed depending upon the extent to which the price in a given year falls below this trigger price level. For instance, where the price in a given year is 40% less than the trigger price level, a 10% duty would be permitted. If, on the other hand the price were 60% less than the trigger price level, a duty of 20% would be permitted. The formulae for calculating these various rates of safeguard duty are contained in Article 5.5(a)–(c) of the Agreement.

DISPUTE SETTLEMENT AND THE AGREEMENT ON AGRICULTURE

The Agreement on Agriculture, and related provisions of other WTO Agreements, have been considered by panels and/or the Appellate Body in several rulings, and in one case also by a NAFTA Chapter 20 Dispute Settlement panel.

In the *Desiccated Coconut* case, the panel considered the applicability of provisions of the Agreement on Agriculture countervailing duty investigations undertaken prior to entry into force of the WTO Agreements. Among the arguments of the complainant, the Philippines, was that pursuant to Article 13 of the Agreement on

Agriculture Brazil was prohibited from continuing countervailing duties against its exports of coconut, since the subsidies on coconut fully complied with provisions of the Agreement on Agriculture concerning reduction of domestic support measures.[43] The panel cited Note 4 to Article 13, which provides that the countervailing duties referred to in the Article are those covered by Article VI of GATT 1994 and Part V of the WTO Subsidies Agreement. Having already determined that these countervailing duties, by virtue of being imposed on the basis of an investigation prior to entry into force of the WTO Agreements, were not covered by Article VI or the Subsidies Agreement, the panel likewise found that Article 13 did not apply. The Philippines had argued that Article VI could apply independently of the Subsidies Agreement, and therefore that the phase-in provisions of the latter should not be used to exclude a claim exclusively based on Article VI – the panel noted that the reference to Article VI and the Subsidies Agreement together in Article 13 in fact reinforced its prior conclusion that an Article VI action was not available where the Subsidies Agreement itself did not apply, because the measures were based on an investigation that pre-dated the entry into force of the Agreement. The Philippines did not appeal the panel's interpretation of the Agreement on Agriculture, and the Appellate Body upheld the findings of the panel on the broader issue concerning applicability of Article VI and the Subsidies Agreement.

The *Bananas* case concerned the allocation of tariff quotas for bananas by the European Community pursuant to preferences granted under the Lomé Convention. Among the arguments of the complainants (several Central American countries and the United States) was that the allocation of tariff quota shares as between Members violated Article XIII of the GATT, which provides for non-discriminatory administration of quantitative restrictions. The EC had claimed that the Agreement on Agriculture had the effect of exempting tariff-quotas in its bound schedule from the requirements of Article XIII. In particular, the EC pointed to Article 4.1 of the Agreement on Agriculture which states that 'Market access concessions contained in Schedules relate to bindings and reductions of tariffs, and to other market access commitments as specified therein.' The Appellate Body rejected the view that, by virtue of this language, the concessions in the Schedules referred to was no longer subject to Article XIII disciplines. The AB noted a number of explicit limitations to the application of the GATT contained in the Agreement on Agriculture and concluded: 'the negotiators of the Agreement on Agriculture did not hesitate to specify such limitations elsewhere in that agreement; had they intended to do so with respect to Article XIII of the GATT 1994, they could, and presumably, would have done so.'[44] Another interesting feature of this case is that the AB took the view that provisions of the General Agreement on Trade in Services (GATS) could apply to the allocation of import licences to banana importers and distributors ('operators' within the meaning of the EC regulations). The AB held that the activities of these intermediaries came within the classification 'wholesale trade services' in respect of which the EC had taken a full commitment in its Schedule of Specific Commitments. Thus, discriminatory allocation of such licences was in violation not only of the GATS

MFN provision (Article II) but the National Treatment obligation as well (Article XVII), which applies only to activities bound in a Member's Schedule of Specific Commitments (paras 217–28). Where in fact wholesaling services have been bound in a member's schedule, this ruling may have significant implications for the operation of various kinds of marketing licence and quota allocation schemes that continue to characterize the agricultural sector in a number of countries.

Most recently, in the *Poultry* case, a panel had occasion to interpret the special safeguard regime in Article 5 of the Agreement on Agriculture. One of the claims of the complainant, Brazil, was that the EC had not followed the procedures set out in Article 5.1 in its imposition of a price-based special safeguards on imports of frozen meat. Article 5.1, as discussed above, provides that safeguard may be imposed if the price of imports falls below a certain trigger price, determined in relation to a 1986–8 reference price. The EC had calculated the price of imports without adding in the bound duty amount – Brazil argued that this was an incorrect application of Article 5.1. The panel referred to the fact that Article 5.1 stipulated that the price for purposes of comparison with the trigger price was that at which 'imports may enter the customs territory of the Member granting the concession'. Since imports cannot 'enter' without duty having been paid, the correct price for purposes of comparison with the trigger price would include the amount of duty to be paid.[45] The panel also noted that the 'terms of Article 5.1(b) should be construed narrowly, so as not to frustrate the attainment of the security and predictability in trade through the tariffs-only regime in Article 4.2 (para. 280).' One member of the panel dissented from this conclusion, suggesting that there was some evidence that the drafters had considered but rejected explicit language that would have referred to 'duty paid c.i.f. import price'. According to this panel member the fact that in several places Article 5 refers only to 'c.i.f. import price' without any qualification suggests an unambiguous rejection of the notion that the price should be calculated inclusive of duties. However, this might equally have been because negotiators considered the language 'may enter' made it sufficiently clear that the price would be one based on duty having been paid. The panel member made another, very obscure argument that including duty in the price could in some cases result in the impossibility of imposing a safeguard regardless of how low the pre-duty price had fallen, and that another result, presumably unacceptable, would be that in some cases imports with lower pre-duty prices but higher post-duty prices would not be eligible for safeguard protection, whereas some other imports with higher pre-duty prices (but lower duties) would be eligible. In our view, these results are not at all anomalous, but entirely consistent with the objective of creating a ceiling on the amount of protection that imports can enjoy – the higher the existing level of protection, the less room there should be for the imposition of additional safeguards. The main purpose of the safeguards is after all to provide some leeway where Members have taken a chance on reducing significantly their level of protection. On appeal, however, the AB adopted the view of the dissent, referring to 'customary usage in international trade' of the acronym 'C.I.F.' which did not include customs duties, an interpretation that ignores the context of this expression in 5.1(b). Nevertheless, the AB found a violation of

Art 5.5, which requires that only the C.I.F. price, and no other methodology, be used to calculate safeguard duties. The EU regulation had provided for an alternative method, where the importer did not require that the C.I.F. price be used or did not meet certain conditions.

In the *Agricultural Tariffication* case a NAFTA panel considered the relationship between Canada's tariffication of domestic support measures in its Schedule pursuant to the WTO Agreement on Agriculture and its tariff elimination obligations in the NAFTA.[46] The United States argued that by virtue of its obligation to eliminate tariffs on most of the products concerned in NAFTA, Canada was prohibited from applying its tariff equivalents for quantitative restrictions with respect to US imports. Canada argued that the WTO Agreement on Agriculture was an agreement later in time within the meaning of the *Vienna Convention* and therefore prevails over the conflicting NAFTA provisions. Canada also relied upon a provision of the FTA (Article 710), later incorporated into NAFTA, which stipulates 'the Parties retain their rights and obligations with respect to agricultural, food, beverage and certain related goods under the *General Agreement on Tariffs and Trade* (GATT) and agreements negotiated under the GATT, including their rights and obligations under GATT Article XI'. The United States' view was that this provision applied only to such agreements as were already in force at the time of the FTA, or alternatively, when this FTA provision was incorporated into NAFTA, which would thereby exclude the WTO Agreement on Agriculture – this view relied heavily on the use of the word 'retain' in the provision. The panel found that, despite the word 'retain', Article 710 referred to an evolving system of law, not a set of obligations frozen in the past. It noted that, elsewhere, when the Parties had sought to incorporate only pre-existing obligations or rights, they had used expressions such as 'existing provisions' or 'existing obligations'. Perhaps more fundamentally, the panel noted that a bizarre consequence would follow from the American interpretation of 710 as incorporated into NAFTA – the pre-Uruguay Round GATT right to adopt quantitative restrictions pursuant to Article XI(2)(c) would be incorporated into NAFTA, thereby creating with respect to Canada–US trade a less liberal regime (in as much as QRs are regarded as more distortive of or threatening to free trade than tariffs) than prevailed multilaterally. Thus, 'to adopt the approach of the United States would be to endorse an interpretation of Article 710 that does not further the NAFTA objective of trade liberalization' (para. 167).

There was a further issue of whether, even if Article 710 did apply prospectively, the WTO Agreement on Agriculture actually established tariffication as a 'right' or 'obligation' within the meaning of 710. As noted earlier in this chapter, the final text of the Agreement on Agriculture was produced following a last-minute compromise between the EU and the United States; this required frantic drafting exercises. In the *Agricultural Tariffication* case, the United States was able to show that, if one read the text of the Agreement very carefully, in fact there was no clear language that established tariffication as a right or obligation, despite the fact that (as noted above) tariffication of quantitative restrictions was a crucial element in the overall deal, including from the perspective of the United States itself! The panel made a careful examination of the *travaux preparatoires* for the Agreement on Agriculture, including the Dunkel Draft and the Modalities Document that had been the fundamental basis of negotiations, and came to the conclusion that

> the arrangement under which agricultural non-tariff barriers were eliminated rested on a simple bargain. States agreed to eliminate their non-tariff barriers as a *quid pro quo* for the right to replace them with 'tariff equivalents'. That is, they were replacing protection in the form of quotas or other non-tariff barriers with protection in the form of tariffs. This right to establish such tariffs was also subject to certain reduction and volume commitments, . . .' (para. 185).

In a related finding, the panel held that the schedules annexed to the Marrakesh Protocol 'crystallized the arrangement for eliminating non-tariff barriers' (para. 189) and that by accepting each others' schedules as part of the 'package' Members had essentially consented to the manner in which non-tariff barriers had been converted into tariffs by each country. Thus, the United States could not now claim that some of Canada's tariff equivalents were not in fact based on prior non-tariff measures but actually constituted new, additional protection. While there is no legal reason why a WTO panel would have to defer to this interpretation of the Agreement on Agriculture and related instruments, if such an approach *were* followed, it would effectively preclude any challenges to a Member's Members' tariffication as not properly based on methodologies agreed in the negotiations. This obviously has implications that go well beyond the interrelationship between NAFTA and the Agreement on Agriculture. We are not entirely certain of the soundness of such an approach, which implies that were a Member not to object to a Member's tariff equivalents between the publication of schedules in February 1994 and the signing of the Marrakesh Protocol two months later, it would forever be stopped from invoking dispute settlement, if it considered that a particular tariff equivalent did not reflect the terms of the fundamental tariffication bargain. The panel's position would have been stronger had it actually adduced evidence that Members were aware of the need to examine schedules of other Members for consistency with that bargain before the Protocol was signed, or at least before the coming into force of the WTO Agreement on 1 January 1995.

CONCLUSION

The Uruguay Round Agreement on Agriculture marks a vital turning point with respect to the regulation of trade in agricultural commodities. Implementing the Agreement, and particularly its complex disciplines on domestic policies, will be a major challenge for the WTO. It will be equally important, however, for political leaders to maintain the courageous stance that ultimately allowed them to sign the Final Act, and to win domestic legitimacy for freer trade in agriculture. This will entail carefully crafted adjustment policies for affected farmers and their communities, as permitted by the Agreement on Agriculture. It should also involve, however, a vigorous public defence of the justification for liberalizing agricultural trade, including a clear explanation of the gains to domestic and global economic welfare. Disappointingly, some governments have instead responded to the farm lobbies' predictable criticisms by pretending that little has changed.[47] The extent to which the Agreement realizes its promise, however, will be significantly affected by the capacity of governments to obtain public support for liberalization, thereby permitting specific commitments to liberalization that eventually exceed the rather modest minimum reductions required by the Agreement itself. Some trade diplomats and policy analysts place great hopes on the new institutional framework of the WTO as a means of sustaining and intensifying the liberalization commitments of the Uruguay Round.[48] Ultimately, however, the full potential of the Agreement will only be realized if citizens view the Uruguay Round liberalization of trade in agriculture, not as a damage control exercise or a concession to the unreasonable demands of others, but rather as a promising new beginning.

11 Trade in services

INTRODUCTION

In the developed industrial countries, services now account for 50% to 60% of GNP[1] and in North America in particular are at present the largest source of new jobs in the economy.[2] At the same time, trade in services is thought to account for only about 20% to 25% of world trade.[3] As comparative advantage in the production of many manufactured goods has shifted to the Newly Industrializing Countries (NICs), the developed industrial countries have become increasingly concerned with enhancement of trading opportunities in services, particularly in areas such as financial services, insurance, telecommunications, transportation, computer and professional services (e.g. architecture, engineering, law).

The pre-Uruguay Round GATT framework applies only to trade in goods, reflecting traditional assumptions that services are not easily tradeable. These assumptions have come into question for a variety of reasons. First of all, because of technological developments, it is possible to effect many services transactions without physical proximity between the provider and consumer of the service.[4] For example, many international banking or insurance transactions can be accomplished through electronic data transfers. Second, in almost all countries through most of the post-war period, many important service industries had been highly regulated, or maintained as state monopolies (telecommunications, transportation). The regulatory reform trend during the 1970s and 1980s resulted in a removal or loosening of prior substantial limits on domestic competition in these industries,[5] thereby focusing new attention on the possibilities of international competition. It is of significance that regulatory reform in a wide range of countries has led to (at least partial) liberalization of markets in service industries such as telecommunications and transportation that themselves provide the means to bring together providers and users of many *other* services; for example, in many countries on-line computer services have become both more feasible and less expensive as a result of regulatory reform in telecommunications.[6] Third, many services have traditionally been viewed as functions integral to the production of goods, e.g. storage of customer or other data or engineering designs. The 'splintering'[7] of services from goods, and the increasing use of external contracting to obtain service inputs into the production of goods (or, indeed, inputs into other services) have created new explicit markets. The logic of external contracting for services within a domestic economy (i.e. that better contract terms can be had outside the firm) seems equally applicable to external contracting with foreigners. Conversely, the globalization of production functions within the multinational corporation (discussed in Chapter 13 on trade and investment), can be extended to include international *intra*-firm trade in service inputs into production *either* of goods *or* of other services. Sauvant notes the example of an American insurance company that processes claims in Ireland: 'Insurance claims collected in the United States are shipped daily by air to Ireland, where they are processed. The claim information is then sent through transnational computer communication systems back to the United States, where checks are printed and explanations of benefits are mailed out.'[8]

In light of these various developments, all of which create increased potential for international trade in services, the reduction or elimination of barriers to services trade became a major priority of a number of developed countries in the Uruguay Round of GATT negotiations.

In this chapter we will consider the characteristics of traded services and the nature of the barriers to such trade. We will then examine provisions related to trade in services in a range of international agreements, including the Canada–US Free Trade Agreement, the North American Free Trade Agreement, the OECD Code on Invisibles and, most importantly, the Uruguay Round General Agreement on Trade in Services (GATS). The chapter will conclude with a consideration of the issues in trade in services in two sectors of particular importance to the global economy – financial services and telecommunications. Here, a major focus will be on the sector-specific provisions of the FTA, NAFTA, and GATS, as well as the future prospects for negotiation of further commitments to liberalization within the GATS/WTO framework.

THE NATURE OF SERVICES

There is a wide range of economic literature that attempts to define the nature of services, the intrinsic differences between goods and services, and how these differences affect (if at all) the application of the neo-classical theory of comparative advantage to trade in services.[9] At the level of general principle, there is no reason why the logic of gains from specialization and trade should not apply to services. Nevertheless, the factors that determine comparative advantage in services may often be rather different from those that determine comparative advantage with respect to goods. For instance, 'natural' factor endowments such as land and minerals will be of less importance than in the case of many goods, while 'man-made' factors such as knowledge and skill will be of paramount importance.[10] Nevertheless, one should be wary of exaggerating these differences – for example, countries with beautiful scenery may have an advantage in the export of tourist services.

Traditionally, economists have attempted to define services largely by contrast with goods. Therefore, definitions have emphasized the intangibility or invisibility of services, their supposedly non-durable or transitory character, or the notion that, unlike with goods, consumption and production occurs simultaneously.[11] It is, however, possible to find exceptions to each of these definitions. For example, is there anything intangible or invisible about an architect's drawing or a design for an integrated circuit? With respect to transitoriness, as Nicolaides notes, 'a lecture, or occasionally a bank transaction, is longer than the lifetime of an ice-cream'.[12] Also, with respect to some services (e.g. most television programmes) consumption and production are *not* simultaneous. Understandably, given these kinds of anomalies, none of these definitions has attracted any kind of consensus within the economic literature. It has sometimes been argued that services that are inputs in the production of *traded goods* should not be viewed as traded at all. The *real* trade transaction, it is claimed, occurs when the good itself, in which various service inputs are embodied, crosses national boundaries. This view was taken by the United States when it first sought to place the issue of services on the Uruguay Round agenda. The United States argued that the negotiations should be limited to trade in nonfactor services, i.e. services that could themselves be viewed as finished products, such as financial services, thereby excluding services that could be viewed solely as inputs into production (e.g. construction crews).[13] This distinction rather transparently served US self-interest: liberalization would occur with respect to knowledge- and technology-intensive services in which the USA had a comparative advantage, but would not occur with respect to labour-intensive services in which developing countries might have an advantage over the United States.[14]

It is not difficult to appreciate the artificiality of the distinction between services as final products and services as inputs. Most of the services often described as final products are also important inputs into the production, marketing and distribution of goods, including financial services that provide the capital required for production. At the same time, since *goods* that are primarily inputs into the production of other goods are governed by trade rules on goods, it seems illogical that services that are inputs into the production of goods (or indeed other services) would not also be governed by trade rules that apply to services.

A particular conceptual difficulty exists with respect to services that are embodied in goods as a *medium* for the delivery of the service. Literature and recorded music, for instance, could plausibly be considered as services that are embodied in or transmitted to the user through goods. However, trade in these services has been traditionally conceptualized as trade in the goods which embody them. Would it be more appropriate to subject the trade in question to rules on services?

These various definitional quagmires are largely avoidable, however, if instead of attempting an abstract definition, one looks to the purpose of creating trade rules on services in the first place. The purpose is to reduce or eliminate barriers to trade that are not caught by existing rules, since those rules have been designed largely with a view to liberalizing trade in goods. From the perspective of trade law and policy, what is most important is to be able to identify a set of barriers that should be reduced or removed to facilitate trade in services. Of course, the nature of these barriers arises from certain identifiable characteristics shared by a significant number of service industries (such as a high degree of domestic regulatory control or the importance of free movement of capital and labour to trading opportunities) but some non-service industries may also possess some of these characteristics. For this very reason, the knowledge of which traits of service industries are important from the point of view of trade liberalization may not generate a satisfactory abstract or conceptual definition of services, i.e. a definition that rigorously delineates goods from services in an essentialist manner.

BARRIERS TO TRADE IN SERVICES

Many barriers to trade in services relate to the modes of supply characteristic of service industries. Thus, in many cases a commercial presence may be necessary or highly desirable in order to provide services in another country – thus the liberalization of foreign direct investment is directly related to the liberalization of trade in services. Another way in which services are traded between providers of one country and consumers of another is through movement of people. Here, immigration restrictions that prevent temporary entry for purposes of providing a service, as well as restrictive licensing and certification requirements, may constitute barriers to trade in services. Services may also be traded through the movement of data and money across borders (insurance and accounting are examples) – thus, exchange and capital movement controls, as well as regulation or restriction of trans-boundary data flows may constitute barriers to trade in services. In other cases trade in services occurs through access of the provider and/or consumer to a network, either international or domestic or both – the terms of access or interconnection with such networks may constitute barriers to trade in services. Where the network is owned and operated by a dominant market player and/or former monopolist, competition policy issues become intertwined with the removal of barriers to trade in services (as is the case with telecommunications services).

The very fact that barriers to trade in services are so heterogeneous and difficult to quantify makes a comprehensive approach to their discipline extremely difficult to conceptualize. Some would clearly be caught by a National Treatment obligation, but many others would not. As well, and perhaps more fundamentally, many of the barriers (particularly those that are not discriminatory or directly targeted at foreign providers) relate to fundamental domestic regulatory choices (such as between regulated monopoly or competition in a particular sector) or quality regulation, for instance, requirements for training and certification of professionals that allow for limited recognition of foreign credentials but do not directly discriminate on the basis of the nationality of the *provider* as opposed to the source of her training.

Ultimately, removal of these barriers would require harmonization of domestic regulatory regimes or (as in the European Union blueprint for liberalization of financial services) home country regulation, whereby a service provider is given the right to enter a foreign market provided it complies with its home country's regulatory requirements. In the case of professional services, the equivalent to home country regulation is mutual recognition of qualifications or licences, whether in accounting, engineering, law or architecture (law is perhaps the most problematic of all these cases, since a country-specific knowledge base may often be seen as a legitimate pre-condition for professional competence).

Many advocates of liberalization of trade in services see the argument for free trade internationally as linked to the purported benefits of deregulation domestically.[15] Yet whether strict or liberal regulation (and these terms arguably conceal a much more subtle set of instrument choices)[16] maximizes *domestic* welfare depends on complex judgments about market failures, and the costs and benefits of a particular regulatory approach in light of the risk preferences of one's own citizens. Three important and related observations follow from this insight. First of all, the global gains from liberalization of trade in services should be conceptually separated from gains or losses to domestic welfare that may be entailed by the regulatory changes required to produce a level playing field to sustain liberalization. If we assume a beginning point where the regulatory choices of each member state represent a social optimum that maximizes domestic welfare within that state, then any changes in regulation needed to sustain liberalization in trade are likely to reduce domestic welfare – the global gains from trade that are yielded by liberalization must be then traded off against domestic welfare losses. Of course, if some countries' domestic regulatory regimes are sub-optimal from the perspective of domestic welfare, then liberalization may yield gains in excess of those from liberal trade itself.

On the other hand, in the absence of a high but level playing field, free trade in services may lead to spillovers that distort the global allocation of resources. For example, where lax regulation of a bank in one country results in failure of financial institutions or prejudice to depositors in another that have placed large deposits in that bank, significant costs will be incurred by the public authorities in that other country. The possibility of free trade in services allows countries to shift beyond their own borders some of the negative welfare effects of their regulatory approaches, thus driving a wedge between domestic and global welfare. Thus in the absence of agreed minimum regulatory standards, free trade in services may actually result in a net reduction in aggregate global economic welfare – i.e. the gains from free trade are more than outweighed by the reduction in global welfare due to the opportunities for externalizing the costs of domestic regulatory approaches abroad that are created by liberalization.

However, the existence of such spillovers has already led to considerable regulatory cooperation in a number of highly significant service sectors. The world's leading financial powers have accepted guidelines for capital adequacy of banks under their regulatory control (the Cooke Committee guidelines, negotiated under the auspices of the Bank for International Settlements in Basel (BIS) although the Asian Crisis showed the need to go much further in these respects);[17] cooperation between domestic securities regulators has become increasingly effective in containing contagion effects where instability or regulatory failure in one market undermines market confidence elsewhere;[18] and in telecommunications and aviation, coordination of a wide variety of domestic regulatory policies that have transboundary impacts occurs through a variety of bodies, including the

International Telecommunications Union (ITU) and the International Civil Aviation Organization (ICAO).

It would be wrong to suggest that any of these fora or processes is leading or can lead in the foreseeable future to a genuinely level playing field, or to a resolution of all important conflicts over differences in domestic regulatory philosophy or regulatory interests. At the same time, the evidence does indicate that, as markets in service sectors have become increasingly globalized, cooperative mechanisms have emerged to manage regulatory spillovers and constrain 'beggar-thy-neighbour' regulatory competition.

INTERNATIONAL AGREEMENTS FOR THE LIBERALIZATION OF TRADE IN SERVICES

The Canada–US Free Trade Agreement (FTA)

Article 1402.1 of the Canada–US FTA states a basic National Treatment obligation with respect to services: 'Each Party shall accord to persons of the other Party treatment no less favourable than that accorded in like circumstances to its persons.' This general obligation applies to a wide range of measures, including the right of establishment, access to domestic distribution systems, and generally any measure related to 'the production, distribution, sale, marketing and delivery of a covered service'. The National Treatment obligation applies to a limited number of sectors listed in an Annex to these provisions. The sectors range from construction to insurance to public relations.

The general National Treatment obligation is followed by a limitations clause, which permits deviation from national treatment, where 'the difference in treatment' is 'no greater than that necessary for prudential, fiduciary, health and safety, or consumer protection reasons' (Article 1402(3)(a)). Such deviations must be 'equivalent in effect to the treatment accorded by the Party to its persons for such reasons'. Suppose, for instance, a Canadian province was to require American construction service providers to post a bond to assure that funds were available to pay occupational health and safety or workers' compensation claims, but did not demand the same of local firms. The argument would first of all be made that the differential treatment of Americans is due to the fact that they are unlikely to have valuable assets in the jurisdiction that can readily be seized or attached in case of non-payment of these claims. Equivalence in effect would be established by showing that this required bond has much the same *regulatory impact* on American operators as provisions permitting seizure and attachment in the case of local providers. On the other hand, if it turned out that local laws did not provide means of securing judgment against local firms for such payments, the American firm could argue that the regulatory impact was not, indeed, equivalent in effect. Finally, prior notification of differential treatment must be provided to the other Party, and the Party imposing the differential treatment must bear the burden of justifying it.

The National Treatment obligation in the FTA is subject to grandfathering, i.e.

it does not apply to existing measures, or to continuation, 'prompt renewal', or amendment of existing measures. In the case of amendment, however, the effect must not be to *decrease* conformity with National Treatment. Obviously, the distinction between an amendment and a new measure is one that has no self-evident legal meaning. New comprehensive legislation would almost certainly be considered in the nature of a new measure, but the case of alterations that are more than caretaking amendments but less than a basic policy overhaul would be more difficult to classify.

The grandfathering provision may reflect in part expectations arising from the tendency toward deregulation and regulatory reform that was among the most prominent policy trends in both the United States and Canada – as well as in many other countries – during the late 1980s.[19] As these dynamics led to liberalizing reforms in both countries, the new measures, presumably more conducive to free trade in themselves, would then be caught by the FTA, which would prohibit a future retreat to more restrictive approaches.

It should be noted that the National Treatment obligation in the FTA is not accompanied by an MFN obligation. Therefore, a Party to the FTA is free to treat services provided by a third country more favourably or less favourably than those provided by the other FTA partner, where this treatment is also superior to that provided to its own nationals. Also, there is a provision that serves the same function as do rules of origin in the case of trade in goods. Hence, Article 1406.1 permits the other Party to deny the benefits of the National Treatment obligation with respect to services where it can be established that 'the covered service is indirectly provided by a person of a third country'. Clearly, this is a very rough rule of thumb – for instance, would a Japanese insurance company or architectural firm that provides services to the US market through a Toronto office where both Japanese and Canadian nationals are employed, be viewed as 'a person of a third country'? Or what of a Canadian engineering company that supplied advice on a particular project to an American client, but on the basis of groundwork done by a multinational team of mining engineers?

In addition to the general National Treatment obligation, sectorally specific treatment is given to telecommunications and financial services (to be discussed in detail in the final part of this chapter). As well, there are provisions that mandate in some instances, and encourage in others, the development of common standards in various professional disciplines, e.g. architecture – enabling mutual recognition of some professional qualifications and facilitating movement of some service providers (but not labour in general) across the Canada–US border.

The North American Free Trade Agreement (NAFTA)

The NAFTA takes an approach to liberalization of trade in services that is similar to that of the Canada–US FTA. However, one significant difference is that, unlike the FTA, the NAFTA contains an MFN obligation that applies with respect to both Parties and non-Parties (Article 1203). A second significant difference is that both the National Treatment (Article 1202) and MFN obligations in NAFTA are not limited to specific service sectors but are applicable to services generally.[20] Instead, a 'negative list' approach is adopted, whereby reservations are noted with respect to particular service sectors or particular measures within certain sectors to which a Party does not want these obligations to apply. The only service industries excluded altogether from coverage by the Services Chapter of NAFTA are those 'associated with energy and basic petrochemical goods and air services'. However, the reservations noted by Canada, the United States and particularly by Mexico in Annexes to the NAFTA apply to a wide range of measures in various service industries. Very extensive reservations apply for one or more of the NAFTA Parties with respect to transportation (especially maritime shipping) and some professional services (especially law). In addition, further Annexes are to contain reservations with respect to measures of sub-national governments. These lists may well be quite lengthy, as in both Canada and the United States provincial and state governments (respectively) are deeply involved in the regulation of many services, particularly professional services.

In contrast to the FTA, existing services measures are not grandfathered in the NAFTA, although there is to be a two-year delay with respect to state and provincial measures to allow these governments adequate time to elaborate satisfactory lists of reservations (Article 1206). As in the FTA, the communications and financial services sectors are dealt with in separate, sectorally-specific Chapters (Chapters 13 and 14), to be discussed in the final part of this chapter.

In addition to the National Treatment and MFN obligations, which address direct and facially discriminatory barriers to trade in services, the NAFTA provides a framework for removal of other classes of barriers. For instance with respect to direct but facially neutral barriers – defined in the NAFTA text as 'non-discriminatory measures relating to the cross-boundary provision of a service' (Article 1208) – Parties are invited to list specific commitments in Annex VI of the NAFTA (to date, very few such commitments have been made). As well, the NAFTA Parties are to engage in further negotiations with respect to temporary licensing of engineers on the basis of mutual recognition of professional credentials. These negotiations are to take place within a year of the entry into force of the NAFTA itself (Annex 1210 (Professional Services) Section C).

The OECD Invisibles Code

The Invisibles Code[21] requires OECD Members to eliminate between each other 'restrictions on current invisible operations' (Article 1). The expression 'current invisible operations' refers to a wide variety of transboundary service transactions, listed in Annex A of the Code. These include, *inter alia*, many forms of technical assistance to businesses, including training, market research, and provision of plans and blueprints, construction and maintenance services. As well, 'current invisibles operations' includes transactions that *facilitate* transboundary services provision. Thus, transboundary movement of the salaries and wages of non-resident workers is included in the list in Annex A.

Members are permitted to lodge reservations and (in some circumstances, such as a domestic economic or financial crisis) derogations from the basic obligation to remove restrictions on current invisible operations, but must indicate their reasons for doing so. These reasons are periodically scrutinized by the Committee on Capital Movements and Invisibles Transactions. The Committee may recommend to a Member that it remove a reservation, but these recommendations do not have binding legal force. Reservations appear to be lodged most frequently with respect to audio-visual, maritime transport and insurance services.[22]

The Invisibles Code contains a general limitation clause that allows Members to take measures that they consider necessary for reasons of public order, protection of public health morals and safety, or for reasons of domestic or international peace and security (Article 3).

The General Agreement on Trade in Services (Uruguay Round Final Act)

Background

It was largely due to the insistence of the United States that trade in services was placed on the Uruguay Round agenda.[23] This initiative generated much controversy and disagreement among other Contracting Parties, especially (but not exclusively) developing countries.[24] The reasons for this controversy can be traced to two interconnected factors. First of all, a major motivation for the United States' initiative was the belief that unlike many basic manufacturing sectors where it was losing global markets as well as part of its domestic market to NIC competitors, service sectors remained a strength of the United States, especially sectors like financial services and telecommunications, considered to be highly knowledge- and technology-intensive. Some developing countries responded to this logic, and drew the conclusion that liberalized trade in services would result in their domestic providers being out-competed by American firms. Moreover, most developing countries could see little benefit accruing to them through access to the services markets of other countries. It was argued that the comparative advantage that developed countries possessed with respect to services was due to their overall higher level of economic and technological development, and if liberalization of trade in services occurred under these conditions, developing country providers would lose their domestic services markets before even having had a chance to acquire comparative advantage in service sectors. This was, in essence, a variant of the infant industry argument for protection that had often been invoked by developing countries in previous GATT negotiations with respect to trade in goods.

Some economists, the most prominent among them Jagdish Bhagwati, challenged the notion that developing countries possessed no comparative advantage in service sectors.[25] They noted that a range of developing countries (e.g. India) possessed significant numbers of highly-trained professionals such as engineers and accountants who were typically paid far less than equivalent professionals in the developed industrial countries. Moreover, some services (such as construction) were labour intensive, thereby potentially conferring a comparative advantage on developing countries with abundant supplies of skilled or semi-skilled labour. Finally, the NICs, which had already acquired the capacity to manufacture medium- and some high-technology goods, could be expected to have some export potential with respect to related services, such as computer software.

In fact, these claims seem to be borne out by recent statistics. Between 1980 and 1987, a significant number of developing countries increased substantially the share of their total exports accounted for by services (including Egypt, Chile, and the Philippines).[26] Moreover, in at least a dozen developing countries, in 1987 the percentage of total exports accounted for by services approached, equalled or even exceeded that of many developed countries.[27]

Although at the level of general principle the United States espoused the idea that negotiations on services should have a comprehensive scope, the US position on the definition of services themselves had the effect of focusing the negotiations on those sectors of most export interest to the United States and other developed countries (e.g. cross-border transactions in sectors such as telecommunications and financial services), while excluding liberalization of factor movements, especially labour,[28] where developing countries might often have a comparative advantage (e.g. ship's crews, construction gangs, etc.).

A second, important concern shared by many countries as well was the aggressive 'market access' approach to an accord on services that appeared to be taken by the United States. The United States appeared interested not only in the extension of the National Treatment obligation to services, but also in negotiating whatever changes in countries' domestic regulatory structures might be necessary to allow market access by foreigners. Since, as we discussed in 'Barriers to trade in services' (this chapter) many of the barriers to trade in services do indeed result from fundamental choices of regulatory instrument by individual countries (e.g. state monopolies, licensing, or rate-setting), or from regulatory diversity itself, there was some substantive justification for a market access approach. However, the ultimate implications for domestic policy sovereignty would be profound. While all international trade obligations involve some surrender of domestic sovereignty, it was understandably far from clear to many Contracting Parties that the benefits of liberalization would outweigh the costs of substantially constraining or altering their domestic regulatory approaches. Since the Reagan Administration was firmly persuaded that the domestic changes required to meet its market access demands (e.g. privatization and deregulation) would also be of considerable benefit to the countries adopting these changes, it did not see any profound conflict of domestic and global interests in trade in services. Indeed, a range of countries (including some developing nations) had embarked unilaterally on ambitious programmes of deregulation and privatization and it could be argued that a GATT services agreement would be one means of attaining some reciprocal trade benefit from these policy shifts. Nevertheless, contrary to crude 'free market' rhetoric, deregulation and privatization entail complex transitional issues and formidable challenges of regulatory redesign.[29] It is not surprising, therefore, that even countries with short- or long-term intentions of liberalizing domestic competition in key service sectors did not want their room to manoeuvre fundamentally constrained or pre-empted by a multilateral market access agreement.[30] As well, negotiated reciprocal market access could easily turn into a market-sharing or managed trade arrangement, in tension with the general principles and philosophy of the GATT. This would be especially true if the position of some American experts were adopted[31] and these market access commitments were negotiated on a discriminatory non-MFN basis.

As the negotiations evolved, insistence on a non-MFN approach became an important means of the US backtracking from its original 'open borders' rhetoric, as many US providers became increasingly worried about having to compete with foreigners in their own market. Where domestic US service providers were opposed to more competition at home, it would always be possible to insist that commitments in the area in question should be negotiated on a reciprocal basis, on the grounds that other countries were not prepared to open up their markets sufficiently to justify free access for foreign producers to the US market. The large degree of indeterminacy in assessing how much other countries' specific commitments to liberalization were worth in terms of reciprocal access to one's own markets actually permitted a wide scope to the United States for justifying on reciprocity grounds its increasing refusal to make broad multilateral commitments to liberalize access to its own markets.

The negotiations, despite numerous impasses, were brought to at least a partial resolution (i.e. agreement on a framework with negotiations in some sectors to continue) on the basis of a number of carefully-negotiated compromises. First of all, it was agreed that liberalization of trade in services would be negotiated under the 'umbrella' of the Uruguay Round, but with a view to the conclusion of an accord that would be legally separate from the GATT itself, i.e. a General Agreement on Trade in Services (GATS). Since agreement was reached on the institutional framework for a World Trade Organization (WTO), it was possible to maintain GATS (as well as the Agreement on TRIPs) as separate from GATT, but to place GATS nevertheless within the overarching framework of the WTO. With respect to the debate over MFN, however, the United States insisted to the very end on being able to exclude almost entirely certain sectors (e.g. maritime services) from the general framework of the GATS, and also on being able to negotiate on a reciprocal basis market access commitments with specific countries, which would be excluded from MFN treatment. With respect to financial services (to be discussed in the final section of this chapter), it was necessary to provide a special accommodation for the United States with respect to MFN exemptions in order to allow the Round to close at the mid-December deadline.

Understanding the GATS

The GATS is a highly complex accord. The GATS contains an MFN obligation that applies to services generally, subject to reservations taken by individual members within some narrow exceptions. However, National Treatment and most other disciplines (including a prohibition on quantitative restrictions of various kinds, known as 'market access') apply only where Members have made specific commitments to such coverage in the Schedules – these commitments may be either general in scope with respect to a given mode of delivery for a service (e.g. local business presence) or they may apply to specific sectors; commitments for a mode of delivery also may contain certain qualifications on National Treatment and 'market access'. Thus, in a very real sense, the schedules of specific commitments constitute the pith and substance of the GATS.

Parts I and II of the GATS provide a set of general rules and principles with respect to liberalization of trade in services. Here, the GATS may be said to apply or adapt some of the key concepts and principles of the GATT to trade in services. Parts III and IV provide a framework for the negotiation of specific market access commitments to be bound in the schedules of individual Members. Part V contains provisions concerning dispute settlement and enforcement of obligations. Part VI deals with a variety of definitional issues in the application of the GATS. There follow a series of Annexes on exemption from MFN treatment, movement of persons, financial services, telecommunications, and air transport services. In addition, there is a series of eight Decisions concerning various aspects of implementation and interpretation of the GATS (ranging from financial services to dispute settlement).

The following discussion covers all of these various provisions and instruments, except those specifically addressed to the financial services and telecommunications sectors, which will be dealt with in the final part of this chapter.

Part I

The definitions in Part I evoke a very broad view of the meaning of trade in services, without thereby attempting to define services themselves. Along these lines, the GATS is to apply not only to 'supply of a service . . . from the territory of one Member into the territory of any other party' (I.2(a)), but also to such 'supply' 'in the territory of one Member to the service consumer of any other Member' (I.2(b)) and through 'the presence of service providing entities of one Party in the territory of any other Party' (I.2(c)), as well as 'by natural persons of one Party in the territory of any other party' (I.2(d)). Clearly, I.2(c) directly bears upon the treatment of foreign investment, including the right of establishment, and I.2(d) on the right to enter a state of which one is not a national. What kind of measure would involve a restriction on the supply of a service on the territory of one Party to the consumer of another may at first glance seem obscure. An example might be a requirement that nationals of country A engage in certain banking or securities transactions only within country A and not in other Contracting Parties. Here, what is being restricted is not the flow of other Contracting Parties' services into A but access of A's customers to services offered by providers of other Contracting Parties.

Article I.2(d), which refers to supply of services 'through presence of natural persons of a Member in the territory of any other Member', would seem to imply that the scope of the GATS extends to include liberalization of movement of persons. However, this is not an area where, pursuant to Parts III and IV of GATS, Members are under any obligation to negotiate specific commitments. This is reinforced by the Annex on Movement of Natural Persons Supplying Services Under the Agreement, which states that 'In accordance with Parts III and IV of the Agreement, Members *may* negotiate specific commitments with respect to movement of natural persons' (emphasis added). The Annex also states that the GATS does not apply in respect of 'measures affecting natural persons seeking access to the employment market of a Member, nor shall it apply to measures regarding citizenship, residence or employment on a permanent basis' (Article 2). However, a limited concession to the concern of developing countries that the GATS extend to movement of people is to be found in the Decision on Movement of Natural Persons, which provides that negotiations on movement of persons are to continue beyond the Uruguay Round through the establishment of a 'negotiating group on movement of natural persons'. The negotiating group is to conclude negotiations within six months of the entry into force of the Agreement establishing the WTO and to present a final report to the Council on Trade in Services at that time, when any commitments that result from the negotiations will be inscribed in Members' individual schedules.[32]

Article I.3 sets out the entities to which GATS strictures on services will apply. This includes not only three levels of government (described as 'central', 'regional', and 'local') but also 'non-governmental bodies in the exercise of powers delegated' by these three levels of government. This last inclusion represents an important departure from typical GATT practice of only seeking to bind governmental entities, whether directly in the case of Members' central governments or indirectly in the case of sub-national governments. The departure reflects the fact that in some countries, various professional services are often self-regulating in whole or in part (legal services, accounting, architecture and some health services are typical examples). A rather different kind of example would be the Canadian Radio and Television Commission – a public body created pursuant to statute but explicitly intended to exercise public authority independent from the government of the day. An important question will become whether a formal or functional definition of delegated powers is to be employed in the interpretation of this sub-section. Some self-regulating bodies (e.g. the Committee that promulgates the City rules that apply to London securities houses) do not exercise directly delegated powers, but could be argued to perform a function that in many other Contracting Parties would be given to a government agency (in this case a Securities Commission like the US SEC). The formal perspective would be more in keeping with the GATT tradition of relating disciplines only to direct government action, but could result in an arbitrary asymmetry of obligations, with Members that choose a self-regulating approach to certain sectors being subject to less discipline than those that adopt more direct regulatory instruments, or at least structure self-regulation as explicitly delegated regulatory power.

In any case *Members* (i.e. states) remain responsible for the compliance of these non-governmental entities with GATT provisions. One view of such an obligation, that would go hand in hand with a functional view of delegated powers, is that a positive obligation is imposed on governments to curb the practices of these entities that violate the GATS. The notion that the GATS – as a liberalizing agreement – could involve an obligation to regulate may seem, at first, odd. However, it should be noted that numerous provisions of the Agreement on TRIPs (Trade-Related Intellectual Property Measures) impose requirements of this kind with respect to protection of intellectual property rights.

Part II

MFN treatment

Article II:1 requires that MFN treatment be accorded 'immediately and unconditionally to services and service providers of any other country'. Article II:2 however, allows a Member to maintain exemptions to MFN treatment, provided that the Member lists the exempted measure in the Annex on Article II Exemptions, and provided that the conditions listed in that Annex are complied with. The conditions include: that exemptions granted for more than five years shall be reviewed by the Council for Trade in Services to determine 'whether the conditions which created the need for the exemptions still prevail' (Annex: Articles 3, 4(a)); that exemptions should not last for more than ten years and must be subject to negotiation in subsequent rounds of multilateral negotiations.

These provisions reflect a compromise between American insistence that, at least in many key sectors, the USA should not be required to open up its markets to countries not prepared to provide an adequate equivalent degree of market access, and the concerns of many other Members that the GATS do not evolve into a tangled web of bilateral sectoral deals, i.e. into a regime of sectoral managed trade at odds with basic GATT principles of rules-based multilateral liberalization. In essence, the USA and other countries that so wish are permitted to continue to pursue liberalization arrangements based on reciprocity, but the justification for refusing to extend these arrangements to other Members on an unconditional MFN basis is subject to ongoing scrutiny within the framework of the WTO.

Article II:3 exempts from the MFN requirement 'advantages' conferred on 'adjacent countries in order to facilitate exchanges limited to contiguous frontier zones of services that are both locally produced and consumed'. Part II contains a range of substantive obligations that are binding on all Members. Some of these obligations apply to trade in services generally, while others apply only where a Member has made specific commitments to market access in its schedule. Article III:1 requires prompt publication of 'all regulations of general application, which pertain to or affect the operation' of GATS, and Article III:3 requires, at a minimum, annual reporting to the Council for Trade in Services of any new measures 'which significantly affect trade in services' covered by specific commitments in a Member's schedule. Article VI:1 provides that in sectors where specific commitments are undertaken, each Member shall ensure that all measures of general application affecting trade in services are administered in a 'reasonable, objective and impartial manner' and Article VI:2 requires that administrative and/or judicial review of decisions that affect trade in services be available, subject to any constraints that may arise due to a Member's constitution or the nature of its legal system.

Among the most important substantive provisions of Part II is the framework for scrutiny of technical barriers to trade in services set out in Articles VI:4–5. The Council for Trade in Services is to develop a set of disciplines on these barriers (including 'qualification requirements and procedures, technical standards and licensing requirements') so as to ensure that these measures do not 'constitute unnecessary barriers to trade in services'. This work is to occur under 'appropriate bodies' established by the Council. The resultant disciplines will ensure that measures such as qualification requirements and technical standards are, inter alia: '(a) based on objective and transparent criteria, such as competence and the ability to supply the service; (b) not more burdensome than necessary to ensure the quality of the service; (c) in the case of licensing procedures, not in themselves a restriction on the supply of the service' (Article VI:4). The Decision Concerning Professional Services, which is part of the Uruguay Round Final Act provides that 'the work programme foreseen in Article V, paragraph 4 . . . should be put into effect immediately'. For these purposes a Working Party is to be established, which is to give priority to the elaboration of multilateral disciplines with respect to regulation of the accounting profession (Article VI:5(a) of GATS makes the criteria in Article VI:4 immediately and directly[33] applicable to domestic measures in a sector where a Member has already made specific commitments in its schedule, at least where there is a possibility that the measures in question may nullify or impair specific market access commitments in a Member's schedule).

Article VII is aimed at the multilateralization of existing arrangements for recognition of educational and other credentials in the licensing or certification of service providers. Whether such recognition is afforded to particular countries unilaterally or on the basis of negotiated reciprocity (i.e. mutual recognition), other Members must be given the opportunity of demonstrating that credentials, licensing or certification in their country are also worthy of recognition. Moreover, 'a member shall not accord recognition in a manner which would constitute a means of discrimination between countries in the application of its standards or criteria for the authorization, licensing or certification of service suppliers, or a disguised restriction on trade in services' (Article VII:3).

Articles VIII and IX concern monopolies and restrictive business practices. Article VIII requires that Members ensure that monopoly service suppliers act in a manner that is not 'inconsistent' with the Article II MFN obligation, or with specific commitments in the Member's schedule. Moreover, Members are required to prevent 'abuse' of monopoly position, where a domestic monopolist is competing in the supply of a service over which it does not have monopoly rights (Article VIII:2). An obvious example would be that of a telecommunications concern that has a monopoly over local service but competes with respect to long distance and other services. Article IX provides for mandatory consultations where a service provider is believed to be restricting competition through business practices other than those described in Article VIII.

Part II of the GATS contains safeguards provisions and a set of general exemptions to GATS obligations. Article X of GATS provides that a permanent safeguards provision shall be negotiated within a three-year period. In the interim,

Members are free to modify or withdraw specific commitments under the GATS provided that the Member justifies before the GATT Council that its measures are urgently needed and must be taken before the end of the three-year period contemplated for negotiation of a permanent safeguard instrument. There is an additional provision that permits the reimposition of restrictions on trade in services that would otherwise be inconsistent with a Member's specific commitments, where necessary to address serious balance-of-payments difficulties or other 'external financial difficulties' (Article XII). Such restrictions must, *inter alia*, be applied on a non-discriminatory basis and be consistent with the IMF Articles of Agreement.

Article XIII exempts government procurement from the MFN and National Treatment[34] obligation of the GATS, subject to a requirement that negotiations on government procurement of services take place within two years of the establishment of the WTO. Articles XIV and XIV *bis* contain general exceptions to GATS obligations, modelled respectively, on Articles XX and XXI of the GATT. Article XIV exempts from GATS discipline measures 'necessary to protect public morals or to maintain public order' as well as 'human, animal or plant life or health', provided these are not 'a means of arbitrary or unjustifiable discrimination between countries where like conditions prevail, or a disguised restriction on trade and services'. In addition to these exceptions, virtually identical to some of those in Article XX of the GATT, exceptions are also provided that reflect particular concerns with respect to service sectors, for example privacy concerns with respect to transborder data flow (Article XIV(c)(iii)). As well, Article XIV(d) exempts from the National Treatment obligation differential tax measures for foreign service providers, where these special measures are necessary, for example, to counter tax avoidance or evasion. Article XIV *bis* provides an exception for measures taken for the 'protection of essential security interests', and is for all relevant purposes, virtually identical to Article XXI of the GATT. Finally, Article XV requires Members to enter into negotiations with a view to multilateral disciplines on subsidies that affect trade in services, as well as on the issue of countervailablility of subsidies to service providers. Currently only subsidies on goods are countervailable under domestic trade remedy laws of the major trading states, and the GATT provisions on subsidies can be taken to authorize countervailing duty actions only with respect to trade in goods. Subject to the future negotiations contemplated by Article XV, GATS may be said to prohibit the imposition of countervailing duties in as much as these would violate the general MFN obligation in Article II of GATS. Article XV also provides that a Member that deems itself adversely affected by the subsidy of another Member may request consultations with the other Member. Such requests for consultations must be given sympathetic consideration.

Parts III and IV

Parts III and IV of the GATS apply with respect to specific market access commitments provided by Members in their schedules.

Scheduling of specific commitments

The methodology for scheduling of specific commitments is based on the four modes of supply identified in Part I of the GATS: cross-border supply, consumption abroad, commercial presence, and temporary entry of natural persons. With respect to each of these modes of supply, Parties have made either horizontal commitments (across all sectors) or specific commitments (with respect to a particular sector) or none (in which case the Member lists itself as 'unbound' with respect to that mode of supply). Either horizontal or specific commitments with respect to each mode of supply may be subject to conditions and limitations on market access or conditions and qualifications on national treatment. Market access refers to the obligations with respect to elimination of quantitative restrictions in Article XVI(2). Specific commitments have been scheduled based upon a classification of activities developed by the GATT Secretariat and based on the United Nations Central Product Classification. Nevertheless, there is no legal obligation that Member's use this list. Each country's schedule can be accessed through the WTO web site, which contains a useful guide as to how to read a schedule (www.wto.org).

It is difficult to estimate what degree of liberalization has actually been achieved by the specific commitments bound in the Uruguay Round. Hoekman[35] has attempted to measure these results in terms of the number of commitments bound, the number of sectors covered by each Member, and the extent to which restrictions have been placed on market access and National Treatment. With respect to the number of commitments bound the results are summarized in Table 11.1. With respect to sectoral coverage, weighted by the economic importance of the sector and the degree of restrictiveness (which determine together the liberalizing value of commitments in a given sector), Hoekman's findings are shown in Table 11.2. With respect to the magnitude of commitments where no conditions or qualifications are listed with respect to market access and/or National Treatment, Hoekman remarks: 'The figure for high income countries is 25 percent, for low- and middle-income countries 7 percent. These numbers vividly illustrate how far away GATS members are from attaining free trade in services, and the magnitude of the task that remains.'[36] Sauve suggests:

> Virtually all the commitments scheduled under the GATS – including by OECD countries – represent a binding of the *status quo* rather than a roll-back of existing restrictions to trade and investment in services. Such a regulatory freeze, which in many cases involves important qualifications and limitations (suggesting that some Members may, in fact, have offered less than the *status quo*) in effect establishes the liberalization frontier which successive rounds of negotiations will have as a central objective to push back [footnote omitted].[37]

Article XVI:1 reaffirms the application of the MFN principle to specific commitments. A footnote to this article also specifies that where a Member makes a

Table 11.1 GATS members: number of commitments scheduled

Developing countries			
Algeria	4	New Caledonia	24
Antigua and Barbuda	68	Nicaragua	196
Antilles (The Netherlands)	144	Niger	20
Argentina	208	Nigeria	96
Aruba	140	Pakistan	108
Bahrain	16	Paraguay	36
Bangladesh	4	Peru	96
Barbados	24	Philippines	160
Belize	8	Poland	212
Benin	44	Romania	176
Bolivia	24	St. Lucia	32
Brazil	156	St. Vincent and the Grenadines	32
Burkina Faso	8	Senegal	104
Cameroon	12	Slovak Republic	308
Chile	140	South Africa	288
China	196	Sri Lanka	8
Colombia	164	Suriname	16
Congo	16	Swaziland	36
Costa Rica	52	Tanzania	4
Côte d'Ivoire	56	Thailand	260
Cuba	120	Trinidad and Tobago	68
Czech Republic	304	Tunisia	52
Dominica	20	Turkey	276
Dominican Republic	264	Uganda	8
Egypt	104	Uruguay	96
El Salvador	92	Venezuela	156
Fiji Islands	4	Zambia	64
Gabon	44	Zimbabwe	72
Ghana	100		
Grenada	20	*High-income coutries*	
Guatemala	40	Australia	360
Guyana	72	Austria	412
Honduras	64	Brunei	76
Hungary	336	Canada	352
India	132	Cyprus	36
Indonesia	140	European Union	392
Jamaica	128	Finland	328
Kenya	84	Hong Kong	200
Korea	311	Iceland	372
Macao	76	Israel	180
Madagascar	8	Japan	408
Malaysia	256	Kuwait	176
Malta	28	New Zealand	276
Mauritius	43	Norway	360
Mexico	252	Singapore	232
Morocco	144	Sweden	320
Mozambique	48	Switzerland	400
Myanmar	12	Liechtenstein	312
Namibia	12	United States	384

Note: The maximum number of commitments is 620 – 155 activities multiplied by 4 modes of supply.

Table 11.2 Sectoral coverage of specific commitments (%)

	High-income countries	*Low- and middle-income countries*	*Large developing nations*
Market access			
Unweighted average count (sectors – modes listed as a share of maximum possible	47.3	16.2	38.6
Average coverage (sectors – modes listed as a share of maximum possible, weighted by openness or binding factors)	35.9	10.3	22.9
Coverage/count (average coverage as a share of the average count)	75.9	63.6	59.3
No restrictions as a share of total offer (unweighted count)	57.3	45.5	38.7
No restrictions as a share of maximum possible	27.1	7.3	14.9
National treatment			
Unweighted average count (sectors – modes listed as a share of maximum possible	47.3	16.2	38.8
Average coverage (sectors – modes listed as a share of maximum possible, weighted by openness or binding factors)	37.2	11.2	25.5
Coverage/count (average coverage as a share of average count)	78.6	69.1	66.1
No restrictions as a share of total offer (unweighted count)	65.1	58.0	52.3
No restrictions as a share of maximum possible	30.8	9.4	20.2
Memo item			
No restrictions on market access and national treatment as a share of maximum possible	24.8	6.9	14.3

Source: Author's calculations based on WTO and World Bank data.

particular market access commitment, and where 'cross-border movement of capital is an essential part of the service itself' the Member is thereby committed to liberalizing the movement of capital. Article XVI:2 prohibits the imposition of quantitative restrictions on trade in services with respect to those sectors where a Member has made specific commitments. The prohibited quantitative restrictions include limitations on the number of service providers, on the total value of service transactions, and limitations on the participation of foreign capital, either in terms of a percentage limit on foreign shareholding or on the total value of foreign investment, either in the aggregate or by a single entity.

Article XVII contains a National Treatment obligation with respect to sectors listed in a Member's schedule. 'Formally different treatment' of foreign suppliers may be consistent with the National Treatment obligation – provided of course that such formally different treatment nevertheless is 'no less favourable' in effect. However, this is very much a two-edged sword – for 'formally identical treatment' may be deemed to *violate* the National Treatment obligation where the measure in question nevertheless 'modifies the conditions of competition in favour of domestic service suppliers'. This approach to National Treatment, which goes beyond a ban on intentionally discriminatory measures, reflects the view that equal treatment implies adjustment of domestic regulatory regimes so that foreign suppliers have *substantively* equal competitive opportunities. Article XVIII states explicitly that Members may negotiate and bind within their schedules additional commitments beyond those that Articles XVI and XVII require with respect to any sector listed in a Member's schedule of specific commitments. Thus, a ban on quantitative restrictions (Article XVI) and National Treatment (Article XVII) may be said to constitute (subject to any reservations that are lodged; see below) the *minimum required content* of liberalization commitments with respect to any specific sector contained in a Member's schedule. However, it is anticipated that additional commitments to particular regulatory changes (e.g. 'qualifications, standards or licensing matters') will also occur with respect to those sectors on a Member's schedule.

Further negotiations

Article XIX commits Members to enter into 'successive rounds of negotiations . . . with a view to achieving a progressively higher level of liberalization'. Liberalization is to occur 'on a mutually advantageous basis' and should secure 'an overall balance of rights and obligations'. It is made explicit that what is involved is not merely the discipline of measures that discriminate against foreign suppliers directly or intentionally, but more generally 'the reduction or elimination' of measures which have '*adverse effects* on trade in services'. This legitimizes the notion that Members should be prepared to put on the bargaining table *any* domestic regulatory measure that has the effect of limiting market access. The far-reaching implications of this provision for domestic policy sovereignty are somewhat balanced by the statement in Article XIX:2 that 'the process of liberalization shall take place with due respect for national policy objectives and the level of development of individual Members, both overall and in individual sectors'.

Developing countries

Article XIX:2 further specifies that 'there shall be appropriate flexibility for individual developing countries for opening fewer sectors, liberalizing fewer types of transactions, progressively extending market access in line with their development situation and, when making access to their markets available to foreign service suppliers, attaching to it conditions aimed at achieving the objectives referred to in Article IV', which include *inter alia* the strengthening of developing countries' capacity in service sectors as well as liberalization in service sectors of export interest to these countries. Article XIX must be read in conjunction with the delicate compromise concerning the MFN obligation in Article II and in the Annex on Article II Exemptions. As discussed above, in light of US refusal to proceed with certain sectoral negotiations on an MFN basis it was necessary to allow for certain exemptions from MFN treatment for specific sectoral commitments. However, as also noted above, these exemptions will be subject to ongoing scrutiny by the Council for Trade in Services, which will 'examine whether the conditions which created the need for the exemptions still prevail' (Annex on Article II Exemptions). Arguably, Article XIX provides some significant guidelines to the Council in its examination of whether an exemption from MFN treatment is needed. Article XIX:2 may be said to set reasonable expectations with respect to the pace and extent of liberalization, particularly for developing countries. If, on the whole, the specific commitments of such countries are consistent with these reasonable expectations, an exemption from MFN treatment in the schedule of a developed country should not be justifiable on the basis that developing countries have not sufficiently opened up their own markets to allow for, in the words of Article XIX:1, 'an overall balance of rights and obligations'.

Safeguards

Article XXI provides that a Member may permanently withdraw or alter a specific commitment in its schedule at any time after three years following the entry into force of the Agreement. This is subject to a requirement of three years' advance notice, and to prior negotiation of a 'compensatory adjustment' where necessary. Such compensatory adjustments are to be made on an MFN basis, and are aimed at maintaining 'a general level of mutually advantageous commitments not less favourable to trade than that provided for in schedules of specific commitments prior to such negotiations' (Article XXI:2(a)). This provision makes it clear that modification or withdrawal of specific commitments by a particular country or countries is not to be used as a pretext for a broader move by other countries to narrow the scope of MFN-based liberalization. Where negotiations on compensation fail, binding arbitration under WTO auspices shall decide what compensatory adjustment, if any, is required.

The provisions of Article XXI clearly go beyond the traditional GATT 'safeguards' concept of temporary reneging on commitments. However, it should be emphasized that much of what Members will be binding in their schedules will consist of specific domestic regulations or regulatory changes. As technology, as well as social and economic conditions, evolve it is essential that Members have some scope for adjusting their domestic regulatory frameworks.

Dispute settlement and institutions

Part V contains provisions that relate to the institutional framework of the Services Agreement, and more specifically, to dispute settlement. The Council for Trade in Services is to have a very broad mandate for implementing the Agreement. It 'shall carry out such functions as may be assigned to it to facilitate the operation of [the] Agreement and further its objective'. The Council, and normally any subordinate body of the Council, is to be open to participation by all Members. This makes it clear that failure to provide a given level of specific liberalization commitments will not exclude any Member from participation in the decision-making of the Council (including decision-making about where exceptions to MFN treatment are justifiable). With respect to dispute settlement, the normal WTO procedures apply to GATS (these are outlined in the Understanding on Rules and Procedures Governing the Settlement of Disputes, which builds on Articles XXII and XXIII of the GATT). One difference, however, is that with respect to GATS, the Dispute Settlement Body (DSB) may only authorize suspension of concessions where 'it considers the circumstances are serious enough to justify such action' (Article XXIII:2). Moreover, it is only concessions under GATS that may be suspended – retaliation may not be authorized in the form of suspension of concessions under any other Agreement in the WTO. By virtue of Article XXIII:3 the concept of non-violation nullification or impairment is extended to GATS. The Decision on Certain Dispute Settlement Procedures for the General Agreement on Trade in Services provides that a special roster of panellists is to be established for purposes of settlement of disputes under GATS. These panellists are to have 'experience in issues related to the General Agreement on Trade in Services and/or trade in services, including associated regulatory matters' (Article 3). Moreover, 'panels for disputes regarding sectoral matters shall have the necessary expertise relevant to the specific service sectors which the dispute concerns' (Article 4).

Rules of origin

Part VI represents a very basic attempt to state rules of origin for services. Article XXVII specifies that a Member may deny the benefit of the Agreement, where it establishes that the 'service is supplied from the territory of a non-Member' or to a corporation that is not a 'service supplier' of another Member. Neither of these rules permits of straightforward application. With respect to the first, the concept of 'territory' is very difficult to apply in the case of multinational service provision. Take, for instance, the case of a multinational law firm that provides legal services to nationals of a GATS Member with respect to a business deal that involves a non-Member (e.g. Russia). Some of the work may be done in the firm's Moscow office, but many of the client contacts and even the negotiations may take place on the territory of GATS Members. How, then, can one decide whether the service in question is being provided from the territory of a non-Member? In the case of rules of origin for trade in goods, this is dealt with by specifying a threshold percentage of the value of the good that must be accounted for by economic activity within a Member country. With respect to the second rule, it depends upon the determination of corporate nationality, a very difficult issue in many service sectors where trade in services is dominated by multinational enterprises that have no unambiguous national identity (unless one invokes purely formal criteria such as the place of incorporation of the parent company, the head office location, etc.).

FINANCIAL SERVICES

The OECD Code on Liberalisation of Capital Movements

The Capital Movements Code[38] requires OECD Members to 'progressively abolish between one another, restrictions on movements of capital to the extent necessary for effective economic cooperation'(Article 1(a)). Annex D establishes a list of capital movements to which the Code applies. This includes a very wide range of transactions required for the transboundary supply of financial services, including banking, insurance, and securities. Members may lodge reservations and (in some circumstances) derogations with respect to the general obligation of progressive removal of restrictions. There is an MFN obligation with respect to domestic regulation that affects providers of financial services from other Member countries as well as an MFN obligation with respect to other OECD Members. However, the Code also encourages, without requiring, Members to extend the advantages of liberalizing provisions of the Codes to non-Members.

The European Union

Liberalization of trade in services within the European Union is stated as an objective in the Treaty of Rome, and is a major aspect of the Europe 1992 programme, reflected in the Single European Act (1986).[39] In the financial services sector,[40] the approach of the Union to liberalization of trade is based on the closely related principles of mutual recognition, home country rule, and minimum regulatory harmonization.[41] Mutual recognition entails the granting of market access to an institution from another EU Member State, based on the institution's compliance with regulatory requirements in its home country. The related principle of home country rule stipulates that the regulatory authorities in the home country retain responsibility for prudential supervision of the institution even where what is involved is activities in other EU states. Hence, market access is not granted on terms of compliance with the (non-discriminatory) regulation of the 'importing' country (as with National Treatment) but on condition that the entity meet relevant regulatory requirements in its own country.[42] Unlike National Treatment-based approaches, mutual recognition and home country rule, taken together, imply not only the elimination of direct and facially discriminatory barriers to service provision by foreigners but also the removal of those indirect and facially neutral barriers that exist where the foreign providers face costs in adapting products or operations so as to meet the distinctive regulatory requirements of the importing or host state.

However, since mutual recognition and home country rule necessarily entail reliance on another state's regulators and regulations to protect one's own citizens, an essential *quid pro quo* is a set of minimum standards sufficient to provide even the country with the strictest regulatory requirements the needed confidence in the regulatory regimes of the others. This is reflected in the third principle, minimum regulatory harmonization.

The minimum standards to which EU Member States' regulatory regimes must conform are set out in the 1989 Second Banking Directive.[43] As Kim notes, these standards cover a very wide range of regulatory requirements, including 'initial capital requirements, disclosure of a credit institution's major shareholders, limitations on the size of participation in nonfinancial undertakings, standard solvency ratios, and permissible activities'.[44] 'Minimum' regulatory harmonization thus entails, in fact, a very significant degree of harmonization.

It is important to note that the European Union has a strong, permanent institutional structure that allows for ongoing consultation and cooperation among the regulators of the various Member States, and for further harmonization. This allows for ongoing adjustment of common minimum standards in response to experience with liberalized trade in financial services, and allows adaptation of harmonized requirements to changes in the industry, such as the introduction of new products and the changing interrelationship between banking and other financial services. It may be difficult to extend the EU approach to bilateral or regional contexts where this kind of common institutional framework does not exist. As well, unless the minimum common standards are in fact set quite high, the EU approach may lead to 'unfair trade' complaints from domestic institutions who must now compete with foreign providers who have lower regulatory costs because their home country's regulatory standards are laxer. In such a situation, an EU-style approach could create downward pressures on the regulatory standards of the stricter countries. Where, however, it is the stricter countries that have the bargaining power to ensure that the common minimum standards remain high, or are moved upward, the end result may in fact be a higher standard. It should be noted that, within the European Union, the two major powers, France and Germany, have what are generally considered relatively strict, rather conservative approaches to regulation of financial services (in comparison, say to Italy or the UK). This may give an important clue as to why liberalization of trade in financial services has not led to downwards harmonization.

The Canada–US Free Trade Agreement (FTA)

The Canada–US FTA takes a National Treatment approach to liberalization of trade in financial services between the Parties. The failure to move to an approach based on regulatory harmonization or mutual recognition reflects significant assymmetries in domestic regulatory approaches in Canada and the United States prior to the FTA, especially with respect to banking.[45] In Canada, there are strict entry requirements for the banking sector, but once a bank is chartered or licensed, it can engage in banking business, as well as in securities business, throughout the country. The United States regime is characterized by ease of entry into the banking business, but by continued prohibition, under the Glass–Steagall Act, of bank participation in the securities business, as well as limits on inter-state banking. Prior to the FTA, Canadian banks had already obtained important exemptions from the limits on inter-state banking in domestic US regulation. Canadian banking laws prohibit concentrated ownership of banks – no one shareholder may own more than 10% of a Canadian chartered bank. In addition, strict limits are also imposed on foreign ownership – the aggregate of foreign-held shares in a chartered bank may not exceed 25%. Given these limitations, a foreign-owned bank that wishes access to the Canadian market must establish itself as a 'Schedule II' bank, with limited powers to engage in branch banking, and also limitations on assets. The aggregate assets of foreign 'Schedule II' banks may not constitute more than 16% of the total assets of the Canadian banking system.

Under Article 1703 of the FTA, the United States is exempt from the main limitations imposed on foreign 'Schedule II' banks in Canadian banking regulation, and from discriminatory treatment under federal laws that apply with respect to non-bank financial institutions such as trust companies (except the 10% limit on a single shareholder's stake). However, since most regulation in the non-bank financial sector in Canada is provincial, the commitments are of less significance than with respect to banking. Canada also makes a general commitment to go beyond National Treatment and to 'liberalize further the rules governing its markets' (Article 1703.4).

While US institutions thus gain considerably enhanced access to the Canadian market, Canadian institutions do not gain a comparable increase in access to the US market. Canadian banks do preserve some of their *existing* rights and privileges under US law, such as exemptions from restrictions on inter-state branching (1702.2) and the right to deal in government securities (1702.1). As well, Canadian institutions are promised National Treatment with respect to future changes to domestic US regulation, including the Glass–Steagall Act (1702.3). However, unlike Canada, which commits itself to liberalize further its domestic regulatory regime for financial institutions, the United States itself makes no such commitment. Instead, the preservation of Canada's *existing* access to the US market is premised on further Canadian *unilateral* liberalization of regulations (1702.4). In the FTA, the USA may thus be said to have succeeded in achieving a one-sided agreement on financial services – obtaining considerably greater market access in Canada, while yielding no immediate effective increase in access to its own markets. This success in the bilateral context may be one underlying reason why the United States, as will be discussed below, was so resistant to accepting a genuine multilateral approach to liberalization of trade in financial services within the GATS.

The North American Free Trade Agreement (NAFTA)

Unlike the FTA, the NAFTA contains general MFN (Article 1406) and National Treatment (1405) obligations with respect to financial services, as well as a Right of Establishment. The Right of Establishment is, however, recognized only as a 'principle' and this principle is subject to requirements that separate financial institutions deliver separate services (1403.2(a)), thereby protecting the provisions of the US Glass–Steagall Act from scrutiny under NAFTA. As well, although the Right of Establishment includes the right to 'expand geographically' within the territory of another Party (1403.2(b)), compliance with the principle of a Right of Establishment is only to be subject to review by the NAFTA Parties once the

United States has chosen of its own accord to lift domestic restrictions on interstate banking activity by foreign institutions (1403.3).

The National Treatment obligation in Article 1405 is based not upon the notion of facially non-discriminatory treatment, but rather of 'equal competitive opportunities'(Article 1405.5–7). This provides considerable scope for claims that neutral domestic regulation nevertheless does not create a level playing field for competition.

Article 1407.1 provides that 'each Party shall permit a financial institution of another Party to provide any new financial service of a type similar to those services that the Party permits its own financial institutions, in like circumstances, to provide under domestic law', subject to any non-discriminatory domestic regulatory control over the 'the institutional and juridical form through which the service shall be provided'. Article 1407.2 provides for free transboundary flow of data between NAFTA Parties in connection with the provision of financial services. Significantly, this is not subject to any obligations with respect to the protection of personal privacy or commercial confidentiality. Pursuant to Article 1408, Parties may make reservations with respect to their adhesion to the Right of Establishment, National Treatment, MFN and other obligations set out in Articles 1403–1407. Mexico, in particular, has filed a complex schedule for phasing in these obligations over a six-year period (1994–2000), as well as a safeguard provision to apply between 2000 and 2007 (Annex VII(B)-Mexico). The schedule entails an expanding set of limits on the aggregate market share of foreign institutions (whether from NAFTA Parties or non-Parties), as well as the individual market share of any one foreign institution. Separate limits apply with respect to each individual part of the financial services sector (banking, securities, insurance, etc.). For example, aggregate limits on banks will increase from 8–15% from 1994 to 2000, and may be frozen at 25% between 2000–7 under the safeguard provision. It should be noted that the safeguard provision applies only with respect to aggregate limits on market share; individual firm limits are to be phased out completely by the year 2000.[46]

Article 1410 exempts from the obligations contained in the NAFTA Chapter on Financial Services, 'reasonable measures [taken] for prudential reasons'. These will include measures taken to protect investors and other market participants, as well as for purposes of maintaining the 'safety, soundness, integrity or financial responsibility' of financial institutions, or to ensure 'the integrity and stability of a Party's financial system'. There are special provisions with respect to dispute settlement concerning the NAFTA financial services chapter. Members of dispute panels are to be chosen from a special roster of individuals with expertise in 'financial services law or practice, which may include the regulation of financial institutions'(Article 1414.3(a)).

The Uruguay Round Services Agreement (GATS)

The GATS contains two Annexes on Financial Services as well as an Understanding on Commitments in Financial Services and a Decision on Financial Services. These various instruments reflect the incompleteness of the negotiations on financial services at the closure of the Uruguay Round in December of 1993, as well as a compromise between different views as to how the negotiations should be completed. The United States took the view, during the final period of negotiations leading up to the December deadline, that other countries had not offered sufficient sectoral liberalization commitments in financial services to justify US adherence to a multilateral, MFN-based framework. The United States therefore stated its intent to take an MFN exemption with respect to its own commitments under a GATS agreement on financial services, and to proceed with bilateral and regional negotiations on liberalization of trade in financial services.[47] This would, in effect, amount to an opting out of the multilateral track towards liberalization. Through a mechanism described in more detail below, a compromise was reached whereby the United States would suspend its MFN exemption for a six-month period after the coming into force of the Final Act in 1995, during which period a further attempt would be made at multilateral negotiation of liberalization commitments within the GATS/WTO framework. If this attempt succeeded, the USA would permanently withdraw its MFN exception. If these further negotiations resulted in an impasse, the USA would be free to reinstate the exception and proceed along bilateral and regional lines.

The Annex on Financial Services does not contain any specific liberalization commitments with respect to trade in financial services, but rather concerns the application of the GATS to the financial services sector. Article 2.1, for example, provides an exemption from GATS strictures of measures taken 'for prudential reasons, including for the protection of investors, depositors, policy holders or persons to whom a fiduciary duty is owed by a financial service supplier, or to ensure the integrity and stability of the financial system'. This is, however, subject to the requirement that any such non-conforming measures not be used to circumvent GATS obligations. Article 3 permits either unilateral or mutual recognition of other countries' 'prudential measures'. This limited exception to the MFN principle is subject to the requirement that, where recognition is accorded through a negotiated agreement or arrangement, a Member must provide an opportunity for other Members to accede to the agreement, or to negotiate a comparable deal (Article 3.2).

In Article 5.1 of the Annex, the financial services sector is defined very broadly as including 'any service of a financial nature offered by a financial service supplier of a member'. This is followed by a lengthy list of services that fall within this general definition. The list includes a comprehensive range of insurance services, 'traditional' banking activities such as deposit-taking and lending, as well as underwriting of securities and trading in virtually every existing form of security or negotiable instrument. In addition, consulting and brokering services connected with these transactions are included within the ambit of financial services. As is suggested by the wide-ranging character of this summary of the list, the clear intent of Article 5.1 is to include as many activities as possible under the rubric of financial services.

The Second Annex on Financial Services allows Members a period of six months following the entry into force of the Agreement Establishing the WTO within which to 'improve, modify or withdraw' any specific commitments in their schedules with respect to financial services, and also to finalize any MFN exemptions in their schedules. The Decision on Financial Services stipulates that, until the expiration of this six-month period, Members shall suspend the *application* of any MFN exemption already filed in their schedules. These provisions were required in order to implement the crucial compromise discussed above, whereby the United States agreed to extend provisionally its participation in multilateral negotiations on financial services, without prejudice to its right to proceed on a bilateral or regional basis if the negotiations were not to succeed within the agreed time period.

The Understanding on Commitments in Financial Services outlines a framework for liberalization of trade in financial services which provides an alternative to that set out for services generally in Part III of the GATS. Members are free to choose to schedule specific commitments in the financial sector either in accordance with Part III or in accordance with the Understanding. The Understanding sets out a series of specific commitments that some, but not all Members, have inscribed in their individual schedules, *and which gain legal force not from their inclusion in the Understanding but from their presence in the schedules*. This contrasts with the approach in Part III of the GATS, where Members are *legally bound* to inscribe certain basic commitments within their schedules.

The commitments contained in the Understanding, taken together, represent a very extensive degree of liberalization. Members are obligated to list in their schedules monopoly rights with respect to financial services provision and to 'endeavour to eliminate them or reduce their scope' (Article 1). Both National Treatment and MFN obligations are to apply to government procurement of financial services (Article 2). Market access is to be conferred on non-resident suppliers on a National Treatment basis in the areas of marine, commercial aviation and space travel insurance (e.g. of satellites), as well as with respect to financial data processing and transmission. A Right of Establishment is provided in Articles 5 and 6, including a right to establish a commercial presence in the territory of another Member through acquisition of an existing enterprise. There is also a right of temporary entry for certain classes of personnel from the financial services providers of other Members, including senior management, specialists in financial services operations, and certain other technical specialists (e.g. computer services personnel) (Article 9). Article 10 of the Understanding entails a commitment to 'endeavour to remove' a wide range of *non-discriminatory* regulatory measures which are deemed to have an adverse effect on the market access of financial services suppliers from another Member. A notable instance is that of 'non-discriminatory measures that limit the expansion of the activities of financial services suppliers into the entire territory of the Member', which would apply to limits on inter-state branching in US domestic banking law. It is to be noted that the language 'endeavour to remove' stops short of formal legal commitment actually to eliminate the measures in question. Furthermore, a Member may, as an alternative to endeavouring to remove a measure, instead endeavour to limit its adverse effects on other Members (for example, by not applying the measure to service providers of other Members or applying it in a different manner). Finally, the Understanding requires that providers of other Members be given access, on a National Treatment basis, to 'payment and clearing systems operated by public entities, and to official funding and refinancing facilities available in the normal course of ordinary business', with the exception of 'lender of last resort' facilities. As well, the providers of other Members must be able to join any 'self-regulatory body, securities or futures exchange or market, clearing agency' in a Member's territory, on the same terms as the Member's own financial service providers. This applies whenever joining any such body or institution is a requirement for providing financial services in the Member's territory on a National Treatment basis (Article 11.2).

Negotiations on commitments in financial services were in fact concluded in 1995, although one month after the six-month period referred to in the Decision. Although 29 countries improved their schedule of commitments or reduced the scope of their MFN exemptions, the United States was dissatisfied with the results, and in the end chose to take a very broad MFN exemption for itself. In light of this outcome, it was decided to label the result of these negotiations an 'interim agreement', with further negotiations envisaged in 1997. These were concluded on 12 December 1997, agreement having been reached on an additional set of improved commitments. These were such that the US was finally able to withdraw its broad MFN exemption. The commitments are incorporated and bound in the Fifth Protocol of the GATS, and should enter into force by March 1999. The Schedules of Members can be accessed on the WTO web site, www.wto.org.

The WTO Secretariat summarizes the achievements of the 1997 negotiations with respect to specific commitments as follows:

> The new commitments contain *inter alia* significant improvements allowing commercial presence of foreign financial service suppliers by eliminating or relaxing limitations on foreign ownership of local financial institutions, limitations on the juridical form of commercial presence (branches, subsidiaries, agencies, representative offices, etc.) and limitations on the expansion of existing operations. Important progress was also made in 'grandfathering' existing branches and subsidiaries of foreign financial institutions that are wholly- or majority-owned by foreigners. Improvements were made in all of the three major financial service sectors – banking, securities and insurance, as well as in other services such as asset management and provision and transfer of financial information.[48]

The WTO has also published a country-by-country summary of the specific commitments agreed in December 1997.[49] A total of 102 WTO members will have made specific commitments on financial commitments once the Fifth Protocol comes into force in 1999.[50]

An important 1997 study by the WTO Secretariat identified the importance of appropriate domestic policies and regulations, if financial services liberalization is to be undertaken consistent with financial market stability, including stability-oriented monetary policies, sound fiscal and exchange rate policies, and measures related to the prudential regulation and supervision of financial institutions.[51] The

Asian financial markets crisis, which evolved in 1997 and was a direct product of financial market openness in these countries, illustrates the salience of such insights. In September 1997, the Basle Committee on Banking Supervision of the Bank of International Settlements (BIS) released the *Basle Core Principles for Effective Banking Supervision*: these 25 principles bear upon, *inter alia*, licensing, prudential regulations and requirements, methods of on-going bank supervision, and cross-border banking. The cross-border banking principles include the notion that banking supervisors must practice supervision over all aspects of the world-wide operations of their internationally active banking organizations, including contact and information exchange with host country supervisory authorities. In the wake of the Asian crisis, a number of ambitious proposals have developed for international surveillance of, and guidelines or rules on, the regulatory oversight of financial institutions.[52] At a meeting of G-8 finance ministers in early May 1998, Canadian finance minister Paul Martin Jr. put forth a plan for the creation of an international body for financial surveillance, which would, *inter alia*, 'provide a mechanism for peer review of financial sector regulatory and supervisory regimes' and 'form part of the crisis response team in responding to Asian-style crises'. The *Basle Core Principles* would inform the body's surveillance of financial sector regulation in member countries.[53]

TELECOMMUNICATIONS

The Canada–US FTA

The FTA provides for the liberalization of trade only with respect to what are termed in the Agreement as enhanced telecommunications services. The relevant provisions are contained in an annex to the Services Chapter of the FTA (Chapter 14), entitled 'Computer Services and Telecommunications-Network-Based Enhanced Services'. Each Party is required to maintain the existing access to the basic telecommunications network that it currently provides to the other Party (Article 4). Moreover, where a Party maintains a monopoly over basic services, it must insure that the monopoly does not abuse its power to compete unfairly in the area of enhanced services. This means, *inter alia*, that a Party's monopoly must provide access to its basic network on terms that do not discriminate against enhanced service suppliers of the other Party (Article 5).

As Globerman *et al.* observe, the significance of these provisions for liberalization of trade in telecommunications services depends on how 'basic' services are defined in contrast to 'enhanced' services.[54] The definitions in the Annex itself are of limited assistance. Basic telecommunications transport service 'means any service as defined and classified by measure of the regulator having jurisdiction that is limited to the offering of transmission capacity for the movement of information'. Enhanced service is defined as 'any service offering over the basic telecommunications transport network that is more than a basic telecommunications transport service as defined and classified by the regulator having jurisdiction'. It seems clear enough that local and long distance telephone services fall within the 'basic' category, and indeed at the time the FTA was negotiated these were largely subject to monopoly provision in Canada. With respect to many other services, however, it is unclear whether they should be viewed as offering 'transmission capacity for the movement of information' or as providing something more. For example, there are services that store or transform information, and thus from one perspective can be viewed as 'enhanced', but which do so primarily to *facilitate* its movement or transmission, rather than – as with computer services – to provide new or additional information (Store and Forward Telex and Pager Services are two examples).

NAFTA

Chapter 13 of NAFTA is devoted to telecommunications, and embodies a rather more extensive set of obligations than the FTA.

Article 1302 requires that a Party provide 'persons of another Party' access to its basic telecommunications network 'for the conduct of their business, on reasonable and non-discriminatory terms'. This refers to private communications and data networks maintained by firms for their internal use, and to the kind of enhanced services covered by the FTA. It does not imply a right to sell or resell telecommunications capacity itself. Thus Article 1301.3(c) states that nothing in Chapter 13 prevents a Party 'from prohibiting persons operating private networks from using their networks to provide public telecommunications transport networks or services to third persons'. Article 1302 contains a series of rather technical provisions that define many of the elements of the right of access to the basic network (for example, the right to attach one's own equipment to the basic network). The right of access may be limited where necessary, *inter alia*, to protect the privacy of basic network subscribers or to protect the technical integrity of the public telecommunications network (Articles 5–6).

Unlike the FTA, which refers to enhanced services, the NAFTA uses the expression 'enhanced and value-added services'. This expression is defined with some precision in Article 1310 as including services that 'act on' aspects of a customer's information, provide 'additional, different, or restructured information'; or 'involve customer interaction with stored information'. This is a very explicit and broad definition, which clearly encompasses most services beyond the basic local and long distance telephone service. There is a correspondingly narrow definition of public telecommunications transport service as a service 'required by a Party, explicitly or in effect, to be offered to the public generally, . . . that typically involves the real-time transmission of customer-supplied information between two or more points without *any* end-to-end change in the form or content of the customer's information'.

It should be noted that, unlike the FTA, the NAFTA confers on enhanced service providers something more than a right to non-discriminatory access to the public telecommunications network. Enhanced and value-added service suppliers are also to be exempt from requirements that they cost-justify their rates or that they provide enhanced services to the public generally (Article 1303.2(a)(b)). Finally, the NAFTA requires that the Parties 'consult with a view to determining the feasibility of further liberalizing trade in all telecommunications services, including public telecommunications transport networks and services' (Article 1309.2).

The Uruguay Round Services Agreement (GATS)

The GATS contains an Annex on Telecommunications, which is very similar in its substantive provisions and terminology to Chapter 13 of NAFTA. Thus, the Annex establishes a right of access for persons of another Party to a Party's public telecommunications transport networks and services on 'non-discriminatory and reasonable terms' (Article 5.1). However, the extent to which this right may be used by persons of a non-Party to supply telecommunications services to others (including, presumably, what are referred to in NAFTA as enhanced and value-added services) will depend on the specific commitments inscribed in the schedules of individual Members (Article 2.3.1).

In addition to the GATS Annex on Telecommunications, the Uruguay Round Final Act also contains the Decision on Negotiations on Basic Telecommunications. This Decision entails the conduct of future negotiations 'on a voluntary basis with a view to the progressive liberalization of trade in telecommunications transport networks and services within the framework of the General Agreement on Trade in Services' (Article 1). These negotiations are to be 'comprehensive in scope, with no basic telecommunications excluded *a priori*'. Although the negotiations are to be open to all Members, initially only twelve countries announced their intention to participate. Significantly all of these are developed countries, except Mexico (which is obligated by NAFTA to undertake 'consultations' of a similar nature in the NAFTA framework). The Decision provides for the establishment of a Negotiating Group on Basic Telecommunications, which must conclude its negotiations and make a final report by 30 April 1996.

Pursuant to the Decision, 69 countries eventually participated in the Negotiations on Basic Telecommunications. However, on the 30 April 1996 deadline, the United States walked out of the talks, dissatisfied with other countries' liberalization offers, and particularly concerned with respect to the treatment of satellite services and lack of discipline on anti-competitive practices.[55] The WTO Secretariat intervened and successfully proposed an extension of the deadline into early 1997. One issue that threatened the extended talks was the asymmetry between accounting pricing for telecommunication services to other countries provided from the United States and the international rates or accounting and settlement, which reflected inflated and unreal cost structures. Under these circumstances, if a US carrier wished to provide service to the US from another country it would typically have to price the service based on the international accounting and settlement practices; however, a foreign carrier could enter the US and use the resale market to provide international service to its home country at low US rates. Ultimately, a unilateral US regulatory solution was achieved – a foreign carrier could only enter the US resale market to provide service to its home country, if that carrier accepted a price cap on the accounting rates for US carriers providing such service.

Finally, in mid-February 1997 the negotiations reached a successful conclusion. In general, the United States was sufficiently satisfied with the offers of other countries that it was prepared to make MFN commitments in most areas; however, Canada's insistence on continued protection for Teleglobe, its satellite provider, coupled with Canadian refusal to lift foreign investment restrictions in the telecoms sector, may have contributed to a decision by the United States to take an MFN exception with respect to digital-audio satellite services.[56] Because of the nature of basic telecommunications, the most important commitments relate to market access (e.g. the number of service suppliers allowed), National Treatment with respect to operations (e.g. licensing and the conditions for service provision attached to licences or otherwise legally mandated) and foreign investment (obviously related to the local presence required to compete in most, although not all, sectors the basic telecoms market, for example as a primary long distance carrier for residential users).

Commitments achieved in the February deal in these and other areas are bound in Member's schedules, and constitute the Fourth Protocol to the GATS, which entered into force on January 1998. Bronckers and Larouche summarize the commitments as follows:

> [sixty-one countries made] commitments to liberalize the provision of voice telephony to some extent. Two countries only liberalize voice services to closed user groups [footnote omitted]. International voice services are liberalized in forty-two schedules (fifty-six countries), national long distance services in thirty-seven schedules (forty-one countries), and local services in forty-one schedules (fifty-five countries). A large number of commitments (for twenty-five countries), however, are phased-in beyond the entry into force of the Fourth Protocol . . . Forty-nine schedules (sixty-three countries) include commitments on data transmission services, forty-one schedules (fifty-five countries) on leased lines, forty-six schedules (sixty countries) on cellular/mobile telephony services, forty-five schedules (fifty-nine countries) on other types of mobile services (personal communication service (PCS), mobile data, paging), thirty-seven schedules (fifty-one countries) on mobile satellite services or transport capacity and thirty-six schedules (fifty countries) on fixed-satellite services or transport capacity . . . forty-two . . . contain a commitment to permit foreign ownership or control of all telecommunications services and facilities.[57]

In addition to these commitments, all but two countries (Ecuador and Tunisia) committed to follow the regulatory principles in a Reference Paper negotiated simultaneously with the other commitments. The Reference Paper requires the Members committed to it to establish 'appropriate measures' to prevent anti-competitive practices by major suppliers, which include 'cross-subsidization', 'using information obtained from competitors with anti-competitive results' and 'not making available to other services suppliers on a timely basis technical information about essential facilities and commercially relevant information which are necessary for them to provide services' (1.1, 1.2). Interconnection with a major supplier must be provided, *inter alia*, on a non-discriminatory basis (i.e. on as favourable terms as those provided for the major carrier's own like services and those non-affiliated or subsidiary suppliers) and in a timely fashion and on terms that are, *inter alia*, 'transparent' and 'reasonable' (2.2). There are a number of other provisions that relate to transparency and the existence of independent regulation (including dispute settlement by independent domestic regulatory tribunals with respect to interconnection).

After the Uruguay Round

With the completion of negotiations on Financial Services and Telecommunications under the GATS, an important, outstanding element in the Uruguay Round is now in place. In other areas, such as transportation, progress does not promise to be rapid, although the gains from liberalization promise to be significant, in part because transportation costs affect trade opportunities for many other sectors. Sauvé suggests:

> The search for a new negotiating paradigm for transportation in the WTO could usefully focus from a user perspective on the multi-modal, end-to-end, dimension of the industry. Recognising the infrastructural dimension of trade in transportation services, one idea could be to explore the degree to which a telecoms-like focus on conditions of access to and use of transport infrastructures might help identify a range of facilitation issues to which initial liberalisation efforts could be directed. Also, it should be possible to concentrate scarce negotiating attention to those market segments showing greater liberalisation prospects, e.g. courier services, air cargo services.[58]

With respect to professional services, in May 1997 the WTO Council for Trade in Services adopted guidelines to facilitate negotiation of Mutual Recognition Agreements among Members in the accountancy sector, pursuant to Article VII of the GATS.[59] Increasingly, electronic commerce is a means by which services are advertised, marketed, and sold in international trade. Access to the infrastructure for electronic commerce (including the Internet) and regulation of international transactions that occur in this medium. One significant issue is whether certain kinds of digitalized information flows on the Internet should be considered goods or services for purposes of determining which WTO Agreement applies, GATT or GATS. A recent study by the WTO Secretariat suggests:

> The goods approach might make sense when considering some of the products [footnote omitted] that are deliverable as digitalized information over the Internet, but which we are accustomed to thinking of as goods. An obvious example of this would be a book, a product which is clearly identified in the customs classification systems for goods. The contents of a book could be

> transmitted electronically from one jurisdiction to another and then transformed into a book in the normal physical sense . . . , but many digitalized information flows are not readily convertible into a physical format that is recognizable as a good.'[60]

The relationship between GATT and GATS has, in fact, been considered in the two cases in dispute settlement that have dealt with the GATS so far. In *Periodicals*, the United States complained, *inter alia*, about an 80% tax that Canada imposed on advertisements in split-run periodicals (which are periodicals with primarily foreign editorial content imported into Canada in versions with advertising directed at the Canadian market). The purpose of this tax was primarily to protect the advertising revenue of Canadian periodicals. Canada argued that this tax was a measure with respect to advertising, a service, and therefore that the provisions of the GATT did not apply. The panel noted that 'overlaps between the subject matter of disciplines in GATT 1994 and GATS are inevitable, and will further increase with the progress of technology and the globalization of economic activities. We do not consider that such overlaps will undermine the coherence of the WTO system.'[61] One may doubt whether, strictly speaking, in this case there was any overlap, since the tax did not discriminate against American providers of *advertising* services, but the panel was surely right that the GATT applied, since the tax in question resulted in (and indeed aimed to result in) a denial of equal competitive opportunities as between Canadian and foreign *periodicals*, which are a good. In the event, Canada did not seek to reverse this ruling in its appeal to the Appellate Body.

In *Bananas*, the AB considered the issue of whether the GATS applied to measures that purportedly discriminated against non EC and non-Lomé member country banana distributor/importers ('operators') with respect to the allocation of import licences. The EC claimed that the regulations in question were regulations with respect to the importation, sale, and distribution of bananas, a good, and therefore that the GATS did not apply. The AB noted the very broad language in Article I:1 of the GATS, stating that it applies to measures 'affecting' trade in services. Thus, there would be no reason to conclude that simply because a measure regulated trade in goods it should be excluded from GATS disciplines, provided it affected trade in services.[62] Further, the AB held that the GATT and the GATS were not mutually exclusive agreements:

> Certain measures could be found to fall exclusively within the scope of GATS when they affect trade in goods as goods. Certain measures could be found to fall exclusively within the scope of the GATT 1994, when they affect the supply of services as services. There is yet a third category of measures that could be found to fall within the scope of both the GATT 1994 and the GATS. These are measures that involve a service relating to a particular good or a service supplied in conjunction with a particular good. . . . However, while the same measure could be scrutinized under both agreements . . . [u]nder the GATT 1994, the focus is on how the measure affects the goods involved.

> Under the GATS, the focus is on how the measure affects the supply of the service or the service suppliers involved. Whether a certain measure affecting the supply of a service related to a particular good is scrutinized under the GATT 1994 or the GATS, or both, is a matter that can only be determined on a case-by-case basis. (para. 221).

The AB also held that the MFN obligation in the GATS applies to *de facto* as well as *de jure* discrimination.

CONCLUSION

Given the highly diverse nature of the barriers to trade in services, and the interconnection of many of these barriers with a wide range of complex domestic regulations and policies, liberalization of trade in services is not achievable through the general multilateral rules and negotiated removal of border measures that have characterized the GATT's approach to liberalization of trade in goods. While some barriers are caught by a National Treatment obligation, many others can only be addressed either through commitments to remove or alter non-discriminatory domestic regulations or to international regulatory harmonization (at least with respect to minimum standards or qualifications).

The attempt to insert a process for negotiation of specific commitments to regulatory change within a multilateral rule-based institutional and legal framework has been less than entirely successful – as witnessed by the severe tensions between different Members concerning the place of the MFN principle in this process. This has led to an incomplete result, disappointing to those who had expected more significant commitments to market access. There is a significant possibility that liberalization will in future be pursued further either through the elaboration of bilateral or regional accords that already deal with services (NAFTA and the OECD Codes, for instance), or through negotiations within the WTO framework on a basis which is, in fact, not genuinely universal or multilateral. The danger is that a set of liberalization commitments may emerge that closes off major markets for services from countries unwilling or unable to make particular kinds of commitments to deregulation of their own service industries. Of course, a convergence of approaches to regulation and deregulation among an increasingly wide range of countries would significantly attenuate this problem, and make a multilateral approach more feasible and attractive.

Such a convergence is arguably occurring, at least among a significant number of both developed and developing countries,[63] although not at a pace always satisfying those seeking the fullest possible liberalization. It is important nonetheless to recognize that, in theory and perhaps also in practice in at least some areas, important trade-offs may still exist between the gains from liberalized trade in services on the one hand and, on the other, the resultant sacrifice in regulatory diversity and innovation. Finally, if the initial, quite limited bargains within the WTO on services are to be sustained over the long term, it will be quite important that the WTO deliver on the promise of becoming a genuine supranational organization, capable of facilitating ongoing negotiation and adjustment of commitments with respect to trade in services, in light of technological and other changes that affect the covered sectors and that present new or renewed regulatory challenges.

12 Trade-related intellectual property (TRIPs)

INTRODUCTION

Over the last two decades, a number of the most economically advanced industrialized nations, including the United States and some members of the European Union, have faced increasing competition in manufactured exports from Newly Industrializing Countries (NICs) in Asia and Latin America. This increasing competition has focused attention on domestic policies of these nations that may adversely or (as is often claimed) even unfairly disadvantage American or European trading interests. It is in this manner that the issue of intellectual property rights has become a prominent item on the trade agenda, as reflected in the extensive provisions on intellectual property in both the Uruguay Round Final Act and the North American Free Trade Agreement.

Two main concerns have dominated the debate. The first is that many developing countries, including some NICs, have often afforded a shorter period of patent protection (and in some cases more narrowly defined protection) to products such as pharmaceuticals than do the United States and most European countries. The result is that domestic imitations of these products often dominate developing country markets, with a resultant loss of potential foreign sales by the original North American or European producer who financed the innovation in the first place. In addition, the patent-granting process and the enforcement of patent protection in many developing countries has been viewed as lacking in transparency and legal security and certainty. The second concern is the tolerance of some developing country governments (and lack of vigilance in some other states as well) with respect to the production and sale of pirate sound recordings and videos, as well as the 'theft' or appropriation of trade marks and symbols (like 'Rolex' or 'Pierre Cardin') and their attachment to cheap imitations that have no relationship to the original producer's own manufactures.

American business interests have estimated losses in the billions of dollars annually from these kinds of supposed inadequacies in intellectual property protection, primarily in developing countries. From a trade theory perspective, however, it is far from clear that all countries should be required to maintain the same level of intellectual property protection. Patent protection constitutes a form of monopoly rent to the innovator. This provides incentives for innovation, but also may entail at least short-term consumer welfare losses and may discourage imitation and adaptation by competitors, which themselves constitute valuable economic activities. The level of intellectual property protection each country decides to afford will thus be rationally related to whether its comparative advantage resides more in innovation or imitation and adaptation of innovations made elsewhere, and the relative weight it gives to the interests of consumers (including its own producers who are consumers of inputs), imitators, and innovators.

Two kinds of justification for the protection of intellectual property dominate the debate on TRIPs. The first centres on fairness or compensatory justice concerns, and the second on arguments about the relationship between protection of intellectual property and domestic and global economic welfare. The use of inventions or creative works of others without their permission is often labelled as piracy or theft. Of course, unless the act in question is defined in those terms in the positive law of the country concerned, or in international law, such a characterization merely states a normative conclusion that inventors and creators *should* have a proprietary entitlement to the fruits of their labour. One (Lockean) line of argument to support this view is that persons are naturally owners of the fruits of their own labour, and that the taking of these fruits represents an attack on the autonomy – or even the integrity – of the person.[1] Pushed to its limits, this view would point to a perspective that suggests that taxation – or any non-voluntary appropriation by society of some of the value of an individual's labour – is expropriation. While we cannot here explore all the theoretical difficulties with such an understanding of property,[2] it is worth mentioning one problem that presents particular complications with respect to intellectual property. Society provides the context in which creative activity takes place – few inventions or works of art or literature spring fully grown from the inventor's head. They usually depend on education within society, and build on the work of many others. There is thus a limit to the extent that creators can declare the work totally their own, and exclude any claim by society on some of that value.

In fact, despite the rhetoric of natural rights or proprietary entitlements that is often invoked to argue for strengthened protection of intellectual property, the debate centres around whether protection should be limited, say, to 15 years for patents or extended to 20 or 25 years. It is hard to imagine a natural right that miraculously disappears after 20 or 25 years! Once we have established that the issue is actually the *level* of compensation to which a creator is entitled, then it is clear that at least implicitly the creator's claims are being balanced against other social interests.

A complete absence of compensation, or a social expropriation of all the benefit of an individual's creativity would, essentially, amount to slavery (with the one significant difference being that the inventor or creator could presumably choose not to invent or create, whereas the slave must work for another's benefit). Proprietary entitlements over one's creative product are, however, not the only form in which such compensation may be provided. For instance, in many countries, a large percentage of inventors or creators work in government laboratories and universities, and even literary and artistic activity is subsidized by the state. Invention and creation may be regarded as a salaried occupation like any other.

Once we view the relevant normative concern as that of compensation, a wide variety of factors may well enter into the determination of what a fair level of intellectual property protection would be. Just as inadequate compensation for valuable inventions may constitute exploitation, so could profiteering on the monopoly control over, for instance, the formula for some life-saving drug.[3]

The economic argument for the protection of intellectual property rights is relatively straightforward – unless invention or creation is compensated at its full social value there will be sub-optimal incentives to undertake it. Central to this insight is the 'free-rider' problem – an individual or firm will be much less likely to make an investment if someone else (the free rider) can capture or appropriate at little or no cost a significant part of the economic returns from the investment in question. However, as is widely recognized in the economic literature,[4] this must be weighed against the economic effects of creating a monopoly on knowledge, namely higher cost products and the exclusion from the market of competitors who may be able to imitate or adapt the invention in such a way that its social value is increased.

To take a simple example, let us suppose that currently in a given country, 15 years of patent protection is extended to the development of new widget technologies. If protection is extended to 20 years, incentives for innovation are increased, and some new valuable widget technologies that otherwise might go undeveloped and unexploited would come into being. However, lower cost products based on competitors' imitations or adaptations of existing widget technologies will take longer to get to market. Extending protection from 15 to 20 years will *only* make sense if the welfare gain from the added incentive to innovation outweighs the welfare loss from deterring competition with respect to imitations of the technology. In the abstract, we cannot tell which is more important to a given country – cheaper widgets from existing technologies or more new widget technologies.

Before we introduce the implications of this basic insight for trade, it is important to note that rarely will a single level of protection for all technologies or sectors maximize domestic welfare. After all, the trade-off between the economic benefits of innovation and imitation will vary quite considerably depending, say, upon whether we are dealing with computer technologies or pharmaceuticals. Recent work in economics on patent protection suggests the possibility that very strict protection could result in wasteful outlays on research and development – due to the 'winner takes all' nature of such protection firms may compete to be the first past the post with a patent in hand. This 'patent racing' argument points to the social efficiency, in some contexts, of treating R&D as a public good.[5] Third, it should be noted that the gains from imitation and the corresponding losses from increased patent protection may be of two kinds – first, higher costs to consumers from the monopoly position that the patent confers on the holder and second, the loss with respect to imitation industries, where revenues and employment will decline.

Similarly, the overall trade-offs between innovation and imitation may well differ from country-to-country. A country where innovation is not a major source of economic activity and growth is likely to choose, on balance, a less stringent intellectual property regime than would a country whose economy is highly dependent on innovation. From this perspective, there is nothing suspect or unreasonable with the preference of many developing countries for a relatively lax system of intellectual property rights. These countries have much to gain, in terms of consumer welfare, from countenancing cheap domestic imitations of innovations made elsewhere, and perhaps little to lose if they are not at a stage of development that makes domestic research and development an important ingredient in domestic welfare. From the point of view of at least some developing countries, then, an agreement on TRIPs that raised intellectual property protection to developed-country levels could rightly be seen as a welfare-reducing or Pareto-inferior bargain.

Several arguments have nevertheless been advanced to show that such a bargain could be in the long-term self-interest of developing countries. The first is that these countries, like all others, benefit from innovation which occurs outside their own borders, and that the increased incentives to inventors due to increased global revenues from their innovations, will yield greater amounts of innovation, and therefore new benefits in which developing countries will share. Often, industry estimates of 'forgone' revenues from sub-standard intellectual property protection in developing countries assume that if proper protection were afforded, a quantity of original products would be consumed equal to that of the imitations now being purchased. This, as is widely noted in more recent economic literature,[6] may be quite misleading since original products (i.e. patent as opposed to generic drugs) would likely be much more expensive, one could expect a considerable decline in demand. Deardorff questions whether the marginal benefit of extra protection, in terms of products that would not have been invented but for the additional incentive from higher monopoly rents in developing countries, is likely to outweigh the reduction in consumer welfare due to higher prices.[7] It is also possible that the optimal level of innovation has already been achieved or exceeded in which case further protection of intellectual property might actually result in, or even intensify, a misallocation of productive resources to research and development. At the margin, would welfare be increased more by an extra dollar being spent on innovation or on applications of existing inventions and technologies?

Another line of argument is that developing countries will attract greater amounts of foreign investment and technology transfers if foreigners believe that products, processes, and trade secrets will be adequately protected. Empirical evidence that this is the case is, however, sketchy and anecdotal.[8] In addition, the appropriate response might be to negotiate specific guarantees with investors, rather than increasing intellectual property protection across the board.[9]

TRADE THEORY AND INTELLECTUAL PROPERTY RIGHTS

In terms of neo-classical trade theory, whether a particular country will want stronger or weaker intellectual property protection will depend on whether its comparative advantage lies more in innovation or in the imitation and adaptation of others' innovations. This is simply an extension of the argument concerning the allocation of resources domestically between imitation and innovation. More precisely still, a rational country would have different levels of protection for different industries, representing different trade-offs between innovation and imitation in each industry, depending upon where its comparative advantage lies.

The United States traditionally has been a country with a significant comparative advantage in innovation, reflected in the fact that a higher percentage of its exports contain domestically-generated technologies than those of any other country, far exceeding even Japan.[10] Under these circumstances, a high level of protection for intellectual property rights within the United States would seem to be well-justified. From the perspective of the *national* interest of countries that have a comparative advantage that lies more in imitative than innovative activity, however, a lower level of protection would likely be optimal. This argument, it should be stressed, does not apply only to developing countries. Much of Japan's dramatic economic growth in the 1960s and 1970s can be accounted for by its success at imitation and adaptation of innovations developed elsewhere, aided by a strategic use of intellectual property protection to stimulate imitation in some sectors and industries and innovation in others.[11] The strength of Canadian multinational enterprises has been linked to their capacity to find and adapt technology from elsewhere.[12] In sum, it is far from clear that increased intellectual property protection would benefit even developed countries with a strong advantage in imitation.

The conclusion that stronger intellectual property protection may benefit some countries but not others suggests a fundamental difference between the theoretical case for trade liberalization, as we developed it in Chapter 1, and the case for mandating high levels of intellectual property protection throughout the world. In the former instance, the neo-classical theory of trade suggests that further liberalization will, with certain defined exceptions, be *always* beneficial *both* to the domestic economic welfare of the liberalizing state, and to *global* economic welfare (defined in terms of global allocative efficiency and/or the aggregate of the domestic welfare of all Member States).

With respect to intellectual property protection, however, the case cannot be stated in these terms, for a requirement of strengthened protection, in the case of at least some sectors, could increase economic welfare in some countries, while reducing it in others. Mandated stronger protection for intellectual property rights is not necessarily, therefore, Pareto-superior and must be justified instead as a fair bargain or trade-off between the competing or conflicting economic interests of different states.

In addition, it is highly questionable whether increased protection is even Kaldor-Hicks efficient, i.e. whether the gains to economic welfare to countries who benefit from stricter protection outweigh the losses to those countries who lose by it. In a seminal and provocative article, Allan Deardorff has argued that global aggregate welfare may well be maximized if certain countries *are exempted completely* from requirements for intellectual property protection. The reason is that, with respect to these poorer countries, the marginal increased rents to the patent holder are unlikely to be substantial enough to constitute significant incentives to further innovation. However, the losses to developing countries from being forced out of imitation or buying imitations from elsewhere would probably be more substantial.[13] Additionally, if the effect of increased protection is to shift productive resources from an activity in which a country has a comparative advantage (imitation) to that in which it has less comparative advantage (innovation), then global allocative efficiency would be reduced by increased protection.

Deardorff's basic insight has been developed independently by Maskus as a formal model of the global welfare effects of IP protection. His empirical studies using this model, which are based upon United States International Trade Commission data with respect to impacts of lower IP protection in other countries, yielded the result that 'static global welfare would suffer from the extension of IP protection by information-importing countries' under most assumptions about elasticities of supply and demand.[14] Only under highly speculative dynamic assumptions (i.e. that increased protection would create enough incentives for technology transfer to, and new R&D within, developing countries to *create* a comparative advantage in innovation), could global welfare be predicted to rise. Work by Grossman and Helpman also suggests that global welfare may be reduced by higher levels of intellectual property protection in developing countries, since the effect may be to slow the process whereby products invented in the North come to be imitated and manufactured in the South at lower cost (i.e. more efficiently).[15]

THE PRE-URUGUAY ROUND INTERNATIONAL LEGAL FRAMEWORK

Having considered the case for strengthening of intellectual property rights from a number of perspectives, we now canvass the existing international rules on this subject. The international legal and institutional framework for cooperation in the protection of intellectual property rights that has emerged over the last hundred years, as we shall see, falls short of elaborating a set of universal, harmonized standards for intellectual property rights. Yet from the fairness, domestic and global welfare perspectives discussed above, the case for such harmonization is, as we have seen, far from compelling. At the same time, the existing framework reflects longstanding recognition by a wide range of states that intellectual property rights are a legitimate subject of international legal discipline.

The GATT

By virtue of Article XX of the General Agreement, intellectual property has been largely excluded from the ambit of GATT. Article XX states a number of exceptions to the basic obligations of the GATT with respect to trade, and these include 'measures . . . necessary to secure compliance with laws or regulations which are not inconsistent with the provisions of this Agreement, including those related to . . . the protection of patents, trade-marks and copyrights, and the prevention of deceptive practices' (Article XX(d)). However this exception, like all the others in Article XX, is subject to the following qualification: such measures must not be 'applied in a manner which would constitute a means of arbitrary or unjustifiable discrimination between countries where the same conditions prevail, or a disguised restriction on international trade'.

Students of the GATT have long been divided as to whether the meaning of this qualification is that the principle of National Treatment as defined in Article III nevertheless applies to Article XX exemptions, or whether the intent is to define an alternative, weaker, national treatment standard applicable only to the matters listed in Article XX (the standard would be weaker because of the qualifying words, 'between countries where the same conditions prevail', which imply a 'similarly situated' test).[16] To some extent, this issue has been resolved in favour of the latter view in a GATT panel decision on the GATT-consistency of s. 337 of the US Tariff Act.[17] In that case, the panel held that, in some circumstances, an Article XX(d) exception might be claimed for measures that, but for the exception, would be in violation of the Article III National Treatment obligation. This, of course, would be impossible if Article XX(d) itself were to imply the same National Treatment standard as Article III.

The Paris Convention

The Paris Convention[18] is the principal instrument of international law with respect to protection of patents and trademarks, described within the Convention by the general label 'industrial property'. The Convention was established in 1883 and has 98 signatories whose countries represented (in 1985) 88% of world trade in goods.[19]

The cornerstone of the Convention is the National Treatment principle, expressed in Article II(1), which provides that 'Nationals of any country of the Union shall, as regards the protection of industrial property, enjoy in all the other countries of the Union the advantages that their respective laws now grant, or may hereafter grant to nationals.'

In addition to the same substantive protections, Article II(1) also provides that nationals of other members of the Union shall have 'the same legal remedy against any infringement of their rights, provided that the conditions and formalities imposed upon nationals are complied with'. One important aspect of these obligations is that they apply to legal instruments defined as 'industrial property' in Article 1(2) including patents, trade marks, industrial designs and trade names. Thus, for instance, it is unclear whether the National Treatment obligation would apply to new *sui generis* forms of intellectual property rights. In the light of efforts by the United States to negotiate bilaterally with some countries special agreements for protection of the intellectual property of its nationals, it is also important to note that, on its face, the National Treatment obligation of the Paris Convention does not include a Most Favoured Nation requirement.[20] In addition to the National Treatment obligation, the Convention sets some minimum standards with respect to both patent and trademark protection. A priority registration system is created whereby if a patent is filed in one member country nothing which occurs within a 12-month period that runs from the first filing will affect the right to a patent in other Member countries (e.g. exploitation or use of the invention within that twelve-month period in a country where a patent has not yet been filed). The provision for trademarks is identical, except that the period is six months (Articles 4A–4B).

With respect to trademarks and trade names, there is a further set of much more rigorous obligations. Other countries are *required* to accept a trademark for registration and to protect it fully, once the mark has been properly registered according to the laws of the country of origin, subject to certain exceptions e.g. where third-party rights are violated or where the marks are 'contrary to morality or public order' (Article 6). In addition, Member States are obliged to seize, upon importation, all goods 'unlawfully bearing' a trademark or trade name entitled to legal protection in the importing country (Article 9).

National Treatment clearly prohibits one kind of national strategy for intellectual property that, as suggested above, may in fact be domestic welfare-maximizing for certain kinds of countries, e.g. extending generous intellectual property protection to domestic innovators (to provide an incentive for domestic innovation) while providing minimal protection to foreigners (so as to maximize consumer welfare and provide incentives for imitation and adaptation of foreign innovations). However, indirect pursuit of such a strategy is possible within a literal reading of the Convention.

For instance, as Lesser suggests, 'a member state may offer no patent protection for certain product groups, provided that the absence of protection applies equally to nationals and non-nationals'.[21] This permits very significant *de facto* discrimination against foreigners to occur through selection of product groups. Countries can (and do) exempt from protection products in whose innovation they themselves have no comparative advantage (e.g. pharmaceuticals in the case of many developing countries). *A fortiori*, a country would have little or no interest in protecting intellectual property rights in products of which it is solely an imitator and intends to remain so – here the national interest is above all consumer welfare, i.e. sourcing the product as cheaply as possible.

At what point differential protection for particular products, industries, or technologies becomes a *de facto* violation of National Treatment is of course very difficult to determine. Such differential treatment need not have a discriminatory intent; even assuming a country did not trade at all, it might well provide varying levels of protection depending upon the trade-offs between the benefits of encouraging innovation and those of encouraging imitation that existed in a particular sector. Here, the National Treatment principle itself, if it is to be effectively implemented, may point to some international minimum standards, i.e. to some kind of determination in international rules as to which balances between innovation and imitation are legitimate domestic policies and which constitute unfair trade practices.

An additional difficulty that arises with respect to National Treatment concerns rules or procedures that pertain to the granting and enforcement of intellectual property rights. Some legal systems place a premium on the exercise of administrative discretion in the determination of what intellectual property rights, if any, to grant to a particular innovation. Borrus notes with respect to Japan, for example,

> The exercise of discretion is enabled mightily by a lack of transparency in decision-making. The JPO (Japanese Patent Office) rarely documents its reasoning . . . when using the system to disadvantage foreign filings JPO examiners have been known to fail to communicate in a penetrable way. The resulting speculative interpretation of the examiner's intent leads to misinterpretation and instant justification for hindering or rejecting foreign filings.[22]

With respect to these kinds of complaints it is very difficult to know whether, in fact, discrimination against foreigners is actually occurring, or whether they simply find it burdensome working within a different legal and political environment. Despite the fact that foreigners may incur special costs in seeking intellectual property protection in another Member State (such as translation, hiring of local lawyers or patent experts able to guide them through the system), the Paris Convention clearly states that to avail themselves of National Treatment foreigners must 'observe the formalities and conditions imposed upon nationals' (Article 2(1)).

Related complaints concern the enforcement of intellectual property rights. Particularly with respect to developing countries, Primo Braga notes: 'Problems often mentioned include: the slowness of the enforcement process; discrimination against foreigners; biased court decisions; inadequate civil and or criminal remedies; and corruption.'[23] Not surprisingly, much of the evidence of these difficulties is anecdotal. It is probably true that foreigners are in some sense discriminated against in legal systems characterized by corruption and bias, inasmuch as locals are likely to have access to 'back channels' that foreigners lack. Yet these are symptoms of broader social and political issues that may be difficult to address in the rather specific context of international rules on intellectual property rights. As well, in some cases, foreigners may incorrectly assume that outcomes that appear unfamiliar, anomalous or unfavourable are the product of discrimination or improper dealing. Even if they are based on ignorance of law and institutions in other countries, such assumptions contribute powerfully to the notion that the National Treatment principle, as elaborated in the Paris Convention, is inadequate to discipline discriminatory practices.

The Berne Convention

The Berne Convention,[24] established in 1885, sets certain minimum standards with respect to authors' rights, and also contains a National Treatment and a Most Favoured Nation obligation.[25] In general, the required minimum length of protection is the author's life plus fifty years (Article 7(1)). During this period, authors (or their estate) 'enjoy the exclusive right of authorizing' any reproduction or communication of the works they have created (Articles 9–14). These minimum standards are subject to certain limitations or exceptions, such as for quotation and utilization of works in other publications or works (e.g. TV broadcasts). These are exceptions not only to the minimum standard itself, but also to National Treatment and MFN obligations; hence the Convention contemplates 'special agreements' on these matters between particular Member States of the Berne Union (Article 9(2)).

The Convention also contains special provisions applicable to developing countries, permitting them to substitute compulsory licensing for the minimum standards of the Convention. The (perhaps somewhat 'imperialistic') reasoning is that the dissemination of literary and artistic works from abroad is crucial to the development needs of these countries, and would often not be possible if the works had to be purchased as imports from the developed world, or reproduced on the basis of the kinds of royalties or fees that might be demanded in return for authorization by an author holding a copyright. The compulsory licensing provisions only apply where, after five years (or in certain cases three or seven years), the work has not been disseminated by the owner of the right of reproduction 'at a price reasonably related to that normally charged in the country for comparable works' (Appendix, Article III(2)). Thus the authors/owners retain the option of asserting their rights, if they are prepared to authorize reproduction at a price that is comparable to normal prices in the developing country in question. Moreover, for compulsory licensing to apply, the intent must be to disseminate the work 'for use in connection with systematic instructional activities' (Article III(2)(a)).

The language of the Convention clearly suggests an intent to cover virtually every kind of creative work.[26] However, with respect to certain kinds of scientific work or industrial and architectural design, the question arises of whether patent rather than copyright protection is more appropriate. This question has become of considerable importance as countries grapple with the appropriate means of protecting creative rights in computer software.[27]

The Berne Convention currently has more than 75 signatories. It is noteworthy that the United States only joined the Convention in 1988, having previously chosen to rely upon unilateral measures and bilateral reciprocity-based treaties to protect copyright.[28]

The World Intellectual Property Organization (WIPO)

WIPO was established in 1967[29] to administer multilateral agreements on intellectual property rights, including the Paris and Berne Conventions, and since 1974 has had the status of a specialized agency of the United Nations. WIPO does not embody a formal court-like mechanism for the resolution of disputes under these agreements, but regularly produces studies and reports on issues that arise in their implementation. As well, WIPO has been active in assisting developing countries in establishing their own systems of intellectual property protection, and has provided financial aid and technical advice for this purpose. At the outset of the Uruguay Round, it was the position of most developing countries that WIPO, not GATT, was the appropriate forum for evolving stronger international rules on the protection of intellectual property rights. This position was undoubtedly influenced by the perception that developing countries have traditionally had more influence in the UN system than in the GATT. It could also be defended on the basis that WIPO's accumulated expertise and experience in the intellectual property field make it a more appropriate forum for negotiations on TRIPs.[30]

After the Uruguay Round TRIPs Agreement, WIPO has moved to revitalize its central role in the internationalization of intellectual property protection. New treaty instruments were negotiated and adopted under WIPO on matters such as copyright and neighbouring rights, performance rights, and the harmonization of trademark law procedures and formalities. WIPO also adopted a dispute settlement mechanism. There is a cooperation agreement between WIPO and the WTO, providing for exchange of information and documents, but with little in the way of a formal legal structure for interaction of the two organizations on TRIPs matters.

Other international agreements

Besides the Paris and Berne Conventions, a number of other international agreements exist with respect to other forms of intellectual property rights, including the Rome Convention[31] (Performers' Rights), and the International Convention for the Protection of New Varieties of Plants (UPOV) (Plant Breeder's Rights),[32] and most recently (1989) the Washington Treaty (Integrated Circuits).[33] Although this last agreement addresses an increasingly important form of intellectual property, its significance is greatly circumscribed by the fact that the United States, Japan and the EU (i.e. the world's leading producers of these devices) have refused to sign the Treaty, apparently preferring to negotiate reciprocal accords among themselves rather than accept the general National Treatment approach embodied in the Treaty.[34]

In addition, agreements exist to facilitate cooperation between countries in the administration of patent laws (e.g. The Patent Cooperation Treaty) and trade mark law (the Madrid Agreement and Protocol). These agreements vary considerably in importance and in the number of countries that are signatories.[35]

AGGRESSIVE UNILATERALISM: US TRADE REMEDY LAW AND THE EU NEW TRADE POLICY INSTRUMENT

United States trade remedy law has long provided for unilateral retaliatory trade action against foreign products, based upon violations of intellectual property norms by the producing countries. Section 337 of the US Tariff Act of 1930 as amended applies to products imported into the United States, where the products in question have been produced in such a way as to violate intellectual property rights that American individuals or firms hold under domestic US law. There is no requirement of injury to the American producer, and a positive finding results in the complete exclusion of the product from the United States, unless the American holder of intellectual property rights and the foreign producer enter into a voluntary settlement (usually a licensing agreement). Conceptually, Section 337 can be considered either as a means of extra-territorial enforcement of domestic

American intellectual property or – more consistent with the overall framework of American trade law – as a counter to an unfair advantage acquired by a foreign producer in competition with domestic American producers for the American market. However, the remedy provided by s. 337, a ban on the imports in question rather than a duty aimed at neutralizing the supposed unfair advantage, comports more with the former interpretation than the latter. Nevertheless, the scope of s. 337 is limited to products imported in the United States, and does nothing to discourage use of American innovations in violation of domestic US law with respect to home market sales or exports to third countries.

Where a developing country is determined to have 'weak' intellectual property protection, tariff concessions extended to it under the Generalized System of Preferences can be withdrawn, which has apparently occurred in the case of Korea, Mexico, Brazil and Thailand. There is no requirement to prove injury to a particular American industry. Nor need it be shown that the intellectual property laws of the country concerned discriminate against American or other foreign holders of intellectual property rights or otherwise do not meet international norms as set out, for example, in the Berne or Paris Conventions. It should be noted that these provisions apply *only* to countries within the GSP; clearly, a discriminatory withdrawal of other tariff concessions provided to a WTO member would violate the MFN obligation of GATT and/or specific tariff bindings under the Agreement.

Broader in sweep still is the so-called Special 301 provision of the Omnibus Trade and Competitiveness Act of 1988, which provides that trade sanctions may be taken against countries named as engaging in 'unfair' trade practices.[36] Such sanctions would likely be contrary to the GATT MFN principle. To date, however, Special 301 has been used as a weapon to extract from named countries specific policy changes desired by US interests, or (it is also sometimes claimed) more sympathy for American positions in the Round negotiations, including on intellectual property.[37] The countries named to date under Special 301 have included Japan, Brazil and India. The aggressively extra-territorial dimension of Special 301 is highlighted by the fact that it does not refer to any set of norms or principles in order to define adequate intellectual property protection among US trade partners – the implicit assumption being that any level of protection inferior to that provided by US law is an unfair trade practice.

Section 337 of the Tariff Act has come under challenge in the GATT. A GATT panel held in 1989 that the Section violated the GATT National Treatment obligation, since it entailed a method of enforcement, through the office of the United States International Trade Commission (USITC), that provided weaker procedural protection to foreigners than that accorded to American firms and individuals accused of violating American intellectual property laws.[38] While (as mentioned earlier in this chapter) Article XX(d) provides, under certain circumstances, exception from GATT strictures for measures 'necessary' to the enforcement of domestic intellectual property laws, the panel found that measures provided in s. 337 were not 'necessary' in this sense, since other countries had found it possible to enforce adequately their intellectual property laws against foreign nationals by subjecting the foreigner to the same legal processes as applied to domestic actors.

A further provision of US law, contained in the Process Patents Amendment Act of 1988, may also be vulnerable to challenge under GATT rules: the provision makes importers or retailers who bring products made in violation of US intellectual property laws into domestic US commerce liable to civil suit by the US holders of the violated intellectual property rights.[39] Since importers and retailers will often not have the knowledge to determine whether a particular product has been made in contravention of intellectual property rights, the result is arguably a 'chilling' effect where buyers simply avoid products from countries with reputations for poor intellectual property protection, in order to obviate the risk of civil liability. In the result, arguably, the National Treatment principle of the GATT is violated since it is only to imported products that the risk of such liability is attached.

An instructive contrast with the American law is to be found in the approach of the EU. In 1984, the Union created what is called 'the new trade policy instrument'. The instrument allows the Union to engage in trade retaliation[40] against 'illicit commercial practices' of non-Union countries that affect EU economic interests. 'Illicit commercial practices' are defined as violations of 'international law or generally accepted rules'.[41] According to the European Commission *Green Paper* on copyright, 'in the field of intellectual property, and copyright in particular, the instrument could conceivably play a significant role in the future, particularly as regards countries which practise a policy of more or less active connivance in the pirating of goods and services developed elsewhere'.[42] In the intellectual property area, the instrument would be used primarily against countries in violation of existing treaty obligations, under both the Paris and the Berne Conventions. However, Brueckmann notes that pursuant to Article 113 of the Treaty of Rome, which gives the Union jurisdiction over a common commercial policy, bilateral action has also been taken (in particular against Korea) along the lines of the US Tariff Act, i.e. suspension of GSP concessions.[43] The background of this action was however rather unusual. Korea had agreed, as part of a negotiated settlement of action under s. 301 of the Tariff Act, to provide intellectual property protection for US innovations but did not extend such protection to other countries. The EU claimed at least as favourable treatment, hence – although from one perspective unilateralist – the Union's action countered a discriminatory arrangement arguably in violation of provisions of the Berne Convention requiring equally favourable treatment for all foreigners.

INTELLECTUAL PROPERTY PROVISIONS IN TRADE AGREEMENTS

The Canada–USA FTA

Apart from a general commitment of the Parties to 'cooperate in the Uruguay Round of multilateral trade negotiations and in other international forums to improve the protection of intellectual property' (Article 2004), the only provisions on intellectual property rights in the FTA concern retransmission of broadcasts.

This reflects a long-standing complaint of American broadcasters that Canadian cable companies rebroadcast their programming without any compensation, and moreover often remove the original advertising and replace it with advertising purchased from the Canadian cable company. Article 2006 of the FTA provides for a scheme whereby the holder of the programme copyright must be compensated for any retransmission. Furthermore, in the case of retransmission of pay TV programmes – i.e. those 'signals not intended in the original transmission for free, over-the-air receptions by the general public' – such retransmission must be with the permission of the original copyright holder. Finally, retransmission in altered form or non-simultaneous retransmission shall only be allowed where permitted by the original copyright holder. This last provision reflects the complaint that, where Canadian viewers are capable of receiving the American signal directly (the case for a large part of the population), Canadian cable companies are in direct competition with the American broadcasters for audience and hence for advertising. There is thus a danger that Canadian cable companies will rebroadcast at a time or in a format more congenial to Canadian viewers, and therefore take away audiences from the original transmission.

The Uruguay Round and intellectual property rights

Background

Not surprisingly, it was the United States that spearheaded the movement to have intellectual property rights included as an integral part of the Uruguay Round negotiations. The overall American goal was clear from the outset: to obtain a set of international rules that ensure that American innovators' intellectual property rights are as extensive and as effectively enforced abroad as in the United States itself. In general, Japan and the European Union were supportive of the American approach, although at first they required some prodding from high-technology industries and other domestic interests that stood to benefit from high international standards for IP protection.

Developing countries, however, generally opposed the negotiation of intellectual property rights within the GATT, arguing that WIPO was the more appropriate forum for these discussions. Underlying this concern about the institutional appropriateness of the GATT was, however, a more fundamental substantive concern that the American objectives, particularly with respect to patent protection and the curbing of compulsory licensing, were contrary to the economic interest of developing countries. As suggested by our analysis earlier in this chapter, this concern has a sound basis in economic theory.

The globalization of the American standard of patent protection was far from the only objective of the United States in the Uruguay Round negotiations. The United States, like some other developed countries, was also concerned that existing international obligations under the Berne and Paris Conventions, were not enforced adequately by many developing countries, and that WIPO did not provide a credible institutional framework for settlement of disputes under these agreements.[44] These were particularly acute concerns with respect to the Berne Convention, whose provisions the United States saw routinely ignored in a number of developing countries where piracy of American creative works was rampant. In the case of the Paris Convention, the United States had a related concern – the supposed difficulty that American patent-holders encountered in attempting to enforce their rights in foreign legal systems. Unlike the case with copyright, where the focus was on the lack of effective criminal or regulatory sanctions for piracy, in the patent context the emphasis was on the supposed lack of expeditious due process in the civil courts of other countries. This last concern, it should be noted, extended beyond the case of developing countries and encompassed complaints about several aspects of the patent registration and enforcement process in Japan. Developing countries, in particular, bristled at the notion that their domestic legal systems, and the level of scarce administrative and enforcement resources allocated to those systems, should have to pass muster according to American standards. There was considerable merit in the developing country position. Operating a truly effective patent system is a costly enterprise, given the high demand for patent registration, and the substantial component of technical expertise required to make such a system work properly.[45] As well, the problems of administration of justice complained of by the United States were often arguably of a general nature (slow courts, lack of written reasons for decisions,[46] and corruption) and not attributable either to an intention to disregard the intellectual property rights of foreigners or a reckless disregard for these rights. Perhaps, however, a 'win-win' or Pareto-optimal solution to this difference of perspectives would be to link expectations for improvements in patent registration, administration and enforcement in developing countries to the provision of technical assistance and funding to those countries so as to enable these improvements to be made.

A further dimension of the American position in the Uruguay Round negotiations was to ensure that developed country approaches to the provision of intellectual property protection to new, technology-based forms of innovation would set the international standard. In the biotechnology field, for instance, US industrial and scientific interests were concerned that, as these technologies took on increasing economic importance, they be fully protected by intellectual property rights.[47] For many countries, however, the patenting of life itself raises not only economic, but also important ethical issues.[48] The Biodiversity Convention, concluded at the Rio Environmental Summit, acknowledges the legitimacy of a country extending intellectual property protection at least to the genetic material of plants, but also states that individual countries have the sovereign right to determine on what terms and conditions private interests should have access to biological resources.[49]

The Uruguay Round Final Act

Despite these basic differences of perspective between the United States and some other developed countries, and most of the developing world, the Uruguay Round was successful in producing a comprehensive agreement on TRIPs. The TRIPs Agreement in the Uruguay Round Final Act represents a complex balance between conflicting national perspectives and interests with respect to the protection of intellectual property rights.

The Agreement consists of seven Parts: (1) a statement of general principles and of the interaction of the Agreement with the Paris and Berne Conventions; (2) substantive norms with respect to the protection of the various forms of intellectual property; (3) obligations with respect to the domestic enforcement of intellectual property rights; (4) obligations with respect to the facilitation in domestic legal systems of the acquisition and maintenance of intellectual property rights; (5) dispute settlement; (6) transitional arrangements; and (7) a WTO-based institutional framework for TRIPs.

General principles of intellectual property protection

Part I of the TRIPs Agreement sets out both National Treatment (Article 3) and MFN obligations (Article 4) with respect to Intellectual Property Rights. The National Treatment obligation is subject to the exceptions that already exist in the Paris, Berne and Rome Conventions and the Washington Treaty. The MFN obligation does not apply with respect to rights and privileges conferred on a reciprocal basis to certain GATT Members through bilateral or multilateral agreements in force prior to the Uruguay Round TRIPs Agreement. An example would be the bilateral accords for microchip (semi-conductor) protection in force between the USA, the EU and Japan. However, to be exempted from the MFN requirement these agreements must not operate so as to 'constitute an arbitrary or unjustifiable discrimination against other Members' (Article 4(d)). Similarly, where the WIPO strikes new multilateral agreements with respect to 'the acquisition or maintenance of intellectual property rights', the National Treatment and MFN obligations in the GATT Agreement will not apply (Article 5). This allows for the evolution of 'mutual recognition' type regimes for the filing and registration of claims for intellectual property protection.

Part I also contains a statement of principles, which acknowledges that a balance of legitimate (potentially competing interests) must be struck in determining the appropriate level and kind of intellectual property protection guaranteed by the GATT. According to Article 7, the protection and enforcement of intellectual property rights should contribute to the promotion of technological innovation and to the transfer and dissemination of technology, to the mutual advantage of producers and users of technological knowledge and in a manner conducive to social and economic welfare, and to a balance of rights and obligations.

Moreover, Article 8 states that 'appropriate measures, provided that they are consistent with the provisions of this Agreement, may be needed to prevent the abuse of intellectual property rights by right holders through the resort to practices which unreasonably restrain trade or adversely affect the international transfer of technology'.

A broad, purposive interpretation of Article 7 and Article 8 taken together would permit GATT Members considerable scope to impose competition policy or investment policy-related measures on foreign patent-holders, provided the level of intellectual property protection itself conforms to that provided in the TRIPs Agreement. It remains an open question whether, for instance, a foreign patent holder who refused to comply with policy measures aimed at facilitating technology transfer or preventing anti-competitive abuse of patent protection could be legally denied the level of protection specified in the TRIPs Agreement. In other words, are domestic policy measures that condition the granting of rights under the TRIPs Agreement on compliance with the kinds of measures contemplated in Articles 7 and 8 'consistent' with the TRIPs Agreement? A further interpretative issue is whether Articles 7 and 8 could be used as a 'shield' by developing or other countries against unilateral US action in response to policies in conformity with the Uruguay Round TRIPs Agreement but none the less considered 'unfair' by US trade authorities. Thus, arguably, in the presence of such unilateral action a WTO member could make a complaint in the WTO TRIPs dispute settlement forum that the United States was in violation of Article 7 and/or Article 8 in prejudicing its ability to implement the kinds of intellectual property-related domestic policies contemplated in these provisions. This would reinforce a more general complaint that unilateral action violated other GATT provisions, such as Articles II, III, or XI of the General Agreement itself (which would likely be the case if the action in question consisted in trade sanctions or discriminatory treatment of the Member's products under domestic US law (see the discussion of the s. 337 GATT panel above).

Standards concerning the availability, scope and use of Intellectual Property Rights

Copyright The basic obligations and rights contained in the Berne Convention[50] are incorporated into the TRIPs Agreement (Article 9). With respect to computer software, the Agreement clearly specifies that 'computer programs, whether in source or object code' shall be protected as 'literary works' under the Berne Convention (Article 10). This entrenches an approach to software protection long-favoured by the United States, and increasingly deployed in the developed world (despite initial interest by the EC and Japan in the development of a *sui generis* form of protection).[51] However, the extent of required copyright protection for software may be significantly affected by the general proviso in Article 9(2) that 'copyright protection shall extend to expressions and not to ideas, procedures, methods of operation or mathematical concepts as such'. Arguably, given this proviso, copyright will protect the originality of a computer programme as a whole, but will not extend to preventing use of ideas, functions, etc. in the development of new programmes. Clearly, interpreting such a distinction on a case-by-case basis may involve quite difficult technical judgments.

With respect to databases, if these merit the status of 'intellectual creations' by virtue of the 'selection or arrangement' of their contents, they are to be afforded copyright protection. However, this does not create any entitlement to the protection of the underlying data or material out of which the database was generated. Moreover, where a pre-existing copyright exists with respect to the data or material itself, any protection of the database as an intellectual protection 'shall be without prejudice' to the subsisting copyright on the material (Article 10(2)). With respect to rental of films and computer programmes, authors are to be provided with 'the right to authorize or to prohibit the commercial rental to the public of originals or copies of their copyright works' (Article 11). In the case of films, however, a Member may exempt itself from this requirement, provided that rentals have not resulted in widespread violation of authors' rights through copying.

Article 12 establishes that the minimum term for copyright protection is fifty years from the initial date of authorized publication, or alternately, fifty years from the making of the work.

Trademarks The Agreement states that

> the owner of a registered trademark shall have the exclusive right to prevent all third parties not having his consent from using in the course of trade identical or similar signs for goods or services which are identical or similar to those in respect of which the trademark is registered where such use would result in a likelihood of confusion (Article 16.1).

There is a requirement that all 'signs' with sufficient distinctiveness be accepted for registration by the Parties. This is, however, subject to the right of Parties to deny registration on other grounds (i.e. than lack of distinctiveness), provided that those grounds are consistent with the provisions of the Paris Convention. It should be recalled that the Paris Convention explicitly permits refusal to register, where the trademark is 'contrary to morality or public order' (Article VI),[52] where it is 'of such a nature as to deceive the public' or where the mark's use would constitute unfair competition.[53] A further exemption – specific to the TRIPS Agreement – applies to 'fair use of descriptive terms'. Thus, where a trademark becomes a common expression applied generically to a particular process of product (e.g. nylon), Parties may allow for its use by others without permission of the owner of the mark, 'provided that such exceptions take account of the legitimate interests of the owner of the trademark and of third parties'. Parties are permitted to provide for revocation of a registered trademark after an uninterrupted period of three years of non-use, unless non-use can be shown to be due to certain kinds of obstacles presented to the holder, e.g. import restrictions on the goods in question or other 'government requirements' that may impede their use in the country concerned (Article 19).

An extensive set of provisions with respect to sound performances and recordings places positive obligations on states to provide to performers the right to prevent unauthorized recording of their performances, unauthorized reproduction of authorized recordings, unauthorized broadcasting of any performance or recording, whether itself authorized or not. However, only 'broadcasts by wireless means' are included, which may indicate an intention to exclude cable re-broadcasts.[54] With respect to sound performances and recordings, the exemptions and limitations[55] contained in the Rome Convention are incorporated into the Agreement.

Patents The provisions with respect to patents reflect the largest modification of the existing international regime, in that a substantive standard of protection is required of all Members. That standard is twenty years from the filing date. Protection applies to both product and process patents. With respect to process patents, however, the obligation to protect from unauthorized use extends only to products 'obtained directly' from the patented process. This means that Members are not required to protect the rights of patent holders where a process they own is merely the basis for production, i.e. where significant alteration or innovation in a patented process is at issue as opposed to direct use (Article 28.1).

Furthermore, patent rights must be 'enjoyable without discrimination as to the place of invention, the field of technology and whether products are imported or locally produced' (Article 27(1)). At the same time, the Agreement acknowledges the concern of developing countries, and some developed countries, to protect the scope for legitimate domestic trade-offs of social and economic interests in the determination of patent rights. For instance, Members are permitted to exclude from patentability 'plants and animals other than microorganisms, and essentially biological processes for the production of plants or animals other than non-biological and microbiological processes' subject to providing some protection for plant varieties, either through patenting or a *sui generis* system (Article 27(3)(b)). However, this provision is to be reviewed every four years after the establishment of the WTO, and during this time the USA can be expected to exercise pressure (perhaps through unilateral trade instruments) for the inclusion of a requirement of patentability of life within the Agreement on TRIPs.

Most importantly, from the perspective of those countries with concerns about negative social and economic consequences from high levels of patent protection, the Agreement permits *compulsory licensing* during the period of required patent protection, provided certain conditions are fulfilled (Article 31). The proposed user must first have attempted to obtain explicit authorization for use from the patent holder on 'reasonable commercial terms' and have been refused. Once this condition is met, compulsory licensing is permitted. However, such licensing must be non-exclusive (i.e. anyone who applies must be granted a licence on similar terms and conditions); production under licensing must be intended primarily for the internal market of the licensing Party; and 'adequate remuneration' must be paid to the patent holder, taking into account the 'economic value' of the patent (Article 31(j)).

An important issue arises as to the role of WTO dispute settlement panels in considering whether compulsory licensing provisions of Members' domestic laws meet these various criteria. Many interpretations might be advanced as to the kind of methodology required to determine, for instance, 'reasonable commercial terms' and 'adequate remuneration'. In our view, some degree of deference is warranted to legitimate efforts by domestic policy-makers to incorporate these conceptions in the detail of their laws, balancing the competing policy interests at stake. Thus, it is not up to the panel to develop its own methodology that represents the ideal implementation of these requirements and judge domestic law accordingly. Rather, where the approach of a Member has been developed in an open policy process, in which all stakeholders could participate, and does not reflect an attempt to embed discrimination against other Members in its methodology, the main concern of the panel should be simply whether the methodology reflects adequately the various, diverse principles and public purposes reflected in the TRIPs Agreement itself. This is consistent with Article 1.1 of the Agreement, which states in part, '[m]embers shall be free to determine the appropriate *method* of implementing the provisions of this Agreement within their own legal system and practice' (emphasis added).

In interpreting the expressions 'reasonable commercial terms' and 'adequate remuneration', account should be taken not only of the claim of the patent holder to just compensation, but also of the various social and economic interests stated in Part I of the Agreement on TRIPs, including the 'transfer and dissemination of technology to the mutual advantage of producers and users of technological knowledge and in a manner conducive to social and economic welfare' (Article 7). In addition, the need 'to prevent abuse of intellectual property rights' (Article 8) should also be considered in interpreting the conditions of compulsory licensing in Article 31.

Other forms of intellectual property In addition to these three main types of intellectual property rights, the Agreement also contains provisions on Industrial Designs, Geographical Indications for Wines and Spirits, integrated circuits and protection of trade secrets. In the case of Industrial Designs, Members are required to provide a minimum of ten years protection to 'independently created industrial designs that are new or original', subject to the right of Members, if they so choose, to protect other designs (Articles 25; 26(3)). Furthermore, 'members may provide that such protection shall not extend to designs dictated essentially by technical or functional considerations' (Article 25). This last provision reflects a significant lobbying effort by US insurance companies, consumer groups, and replacement parts manufacturers, all of whom sought language on industrial designs that would not allow automobile manufacturers to protect the design of car parts, thereby threatening the 'generic' replacement parts and potentially raising the costs of replacement parts.[56]

The provisions on Geographical Indications, and particularly those that apply to Wines and Spirits, address long-standing European concerns about the use of labels to describe imitation products with no direct connection to the geographical area denoted by the label. The main operative provision, Article 23(1), requires each Member to 'provide the legal means for interested parties to prevent use of a geographical indication identifying wines for wines not originating in the place indicated by the geographical indication in question, . . . even where the true origin of the goods is indicated or the geographical indication is used in translation or accompanied by expressions such as "kind", "type", "style", "imitations" or the like'. This obligation applies identically to spirits. However, exceptions are provided with respect to geographical appellations in use for at least ten years preceding the conclusion of the Uruguay Round negotiations (Article 24(4)). In the case of geographical indications for products other than wines and spirits, protection need only be provided by Members against use of geographical indication 'which misleads the public as to the geographical origin of the good' (Article 22(2)(a)).

With respect to Lay-out Designs (Topographies) of Integrated Circuits, the required protection is more extensive than that provided in the Washington Treaty, to which, it will be recalled, most developed countries had refused to adhere. Hence, the term of protection is ten years as opposed to eight in the Washington Treaty, and compulsory licensing or governmental use can only occur under the same conditions as those set out for compulsory licensing in the TRIPs Agreement provisions on patents (Articles 38; 37(2)). It is significant that among the main reasons that the United States and Japan refused to sign the Washington Treaty was their opposition to the Treaty's provisions on compulsory licensing.[57] However, the applicable provisions on compulsory licensing in the TRIPs Agreement are, in the end, very similar to those contained in the Washington Treaty. This reflects at least some compromise with the concerns of developing countries.[58]

Enforcement, dispute settlement, and institutional design

Enforcement There is a wide range of obligations to provide other Members with access to appropriate mechanisms to enforce intellectual property rights. These provisions constitute a largely unprecedented degree of control by an international regime over domestic civil and administrative procedures. It is required that enforcement procedures 'not be unnecessarily complicated or costly, or entail unreasonable time-limits or unwarranted delays' (Article 41.2); decisions are 'preferably' to be in writing and to contain reasons; and a right of judicial review is to be provided in the case of administrative decisions, at least with respect to matters of law. These quite far-reaching obligations are balanced by the qualification that they create no 'obligation with respect to the distribution of resources as between enforcement of intellectual property rights and the enforcement of laws in general' (Article 41.5).

With respect to remedies, the TRIPs Agreement requires that 'judicial authorities' be empowered to issue injunctions (Article 44(1)); award damages and legal costs to successful right holders (Article 45); and to dispose of goods tainted by infringements of intellectual property rights 'outside the ordinary channels of commerce' (Article 46). In addition, the judicial authorities are to be authorized to grant interim or provisional injunctions, including in *ex parte* proceedings, 'where any delay is likely to cause irreparable harm to the right holder' (Article 50(3)).

These requirements would seem, at first glance, to be a massive intrusion into domestic legal systems, and especially the balance that those systems strike between the rights of defendants and those of plaintiffs. In some systems, for instance, there may be constitutional limitations on the capacity of courts to grant relief without hearing the other Party, even for certain kinds of interim relief. However, it is to be noted that where any of the remedies is 'inconsistent with domestic law', the domestic law is to prevail, subject to a requirement that 'declaratory judgments and adequate compensation' be available (Article 44(2)). It should also be noted that while the Agreement provides that judicial authorities be authorized to grant certain classes of remedies, the use of these remedies is not *mandated* by the GATT Agreement. Judicial authorities are, therefore, free to use their discretion to grant or deny a particular remedy, and to weigh plaintiffs' and defendants' rights in the exercise of that discretion.

A final important obligation with respect to enforcement relates to counterfeit or pirated goods. Rights holders are to have access to a procedure whereby customs authorities suspend 'the release into free circulation' of such goods, for example by seizure or by turning them back (Article 51). This is subject to the right of the importer that such suspension be promptly removed except where a judicial or administrative determination is made that, in fact, the goods are counterfeit. Moreover, Members who have eliminated border customs inspection as between themselves are not obligated to provide such a procedure (e.g. the case of the European Union).

Monitoring and dispute settlement A two-fold approach to monitoring and dispute settlement is set out in the TRIPs Agreement. First of all, a new institution is to be created, the Council on Trade Related Aspects of Intellectual Property Rights (TRIPs Council), charged with the monitoring of domestic compliance with the Agreement. Members are obliged to notify the Council of their domestic laws and regulations with respect to intellectual property protection (Article 63(2)). The Council may also provide a forum for consultations on intellectual property issues, and is 'to provide any assistance requested by them in the context of dispute settlement procedures' (Article 68). This might include, for example, a kind of mediation or the provision of advisory opinions concerning Members' interpretations of the Agreement. Nevertheless, no special dispute settlement process is established in connection with the Council instead the general GATT procedures are to apply (Article 64).

With respect to settlement of disputes under the TRIPs Agreement the provisions in Articles XXII and XXIII of the GATT are to apply, subject to suspension of the operation of dispute settlement under Articles XIII:1(b) and XXIII:1(c) of the GATT for the period of five years. This refers to complaints of non-violation nullification or impairment, which are to be referred to the TRIPs Council and the Ministerial Conference during the five-year period.

Developing countries

As discussed in an earlier section of this chapter, one of the main aims of the United States in placing TRIPs on the Uruguay Round agenda was to address what it considered ineffective protection of intellectual property rights in developing countries. It is not surprising, therefore, that developing countries do not enjoy many special exemptions from these obligations. They are entitled to a one-year delay with respect to implementing most of the obligations of the Agreement and a further four-year delay upon application to the Council. The further four-year delay does not apply, however, to the general requirements of National Treatment and MFN treatment in Part I. A further five-year delay applies, where a particular area of technology is currently unprotectable under the domestic law of a developing country. This reflects the fact that extension of protection may result in loss of entire industries in some developing countries (e.g. pharmaceuticals), with attendant adjustment costs.[59] Finally, *least*-developed countries are exempted entirely from the Agreement.

The North American Free Trade Agreement (NAFTA)

The provisions on intellectual property rights in the NAFTA are, in most important respects, largely identical to those in the Uruguay Round Agreement, discussed in detail in the previous section. Unlike the Uruguay Round Agreement, the NAFTA does not contain substantive provisions on performers' rights. Performers' rights would seem to be covered by the National Treatment obligation with respect to intellectual property rights. An exception to National Treatment is, however, that 'a Party may limit rights of performers of another Party in respect of secondary uses of sound recordings to those rights its nationals are accorded in the territory of such other Party' (Article 1703.1).

The NAFTA also contains a provision on the decoding of encrypted satellite signals that is not present in the Uruguay Round TRIPs Agreement. Under this provision each Party would be required to make it a criminal offence to manufacture or sell any device used for the purpose of decoding encrypted satellite signals, and a civil offence to decode or improperly receive these signals. These provisions would appear to be primarily aimed at protecting the rights of Pay-TV broadcasters. Finally, unlike the Uruguay Round TRIPs Agreement, the NAFTA does not contain any special provisions on dispute resolution with respect to intellectual property rights, suggesting that the general dispute resolution mechanism in the NAFTA will apply to disputes under the intellectual property provisions of the NAFTA.

The NAFTA represents a major victory for mostly US based multinational pharmaceutical companies. Canada had a significantly shorter period of patent protection for pharmaceuticals (ten years) after which compulsory licensing was provided under Canadian law.[60] The consequence was a wealth of low-cost generic drugs, with major cost savings to consumers, as well as to government programmes that provide free or subsidized medications to the elderly and the poor. In order to comply with NAFTA and a possible Uruguay Round Agreement on TRIPs the previous Government in Canada changed the law to provide 20 years of patent protection to patent pharmaceutical producers. However, under the letter of both NAFTA and the Uruguay Round Agreement on TRIPs, compulsory licensing is still permissible, provided reasonable compensation is offered to the patent-holder and some other conditions are met. This suggests that there was some kind of informal understanding between Canadian and American authorities that Canada's approach to pharmaceuticals must be dismantled if the spirit of NAFTA is to be respected. Perhaps also influential with the Canadian authorities was a massive, high-profile lobbying effort on the part of patent drug manufacturers stressing the amount of new R&D activity that would occur in Canada with the adoption of these changes. In any case, despite these major changes in the Canadian domestic regulatory regime to the advantage of American proprietary drug interests, Canada failed completely to win any insulation from US aggressive unilateralism, including actions under s. 337 of the Tariff Act.[61] The current government in Canada is apparently considering the reintroduction of measures to provide for the compulsory licensing of pharmaceuticals, on terms consistent with NAFTA and the Uruguay Round TRIPs Agreement.

POST-URUGUAY ROUND DEVELOPMENTS

Implementation of the WTO TRIPs Agreement

Perhaps more than any other trade agreement in history, the WTO TRIPs Agreement requires extensive changes to, and in the case of many countries additions to, domestic law and regulations. Pursuant to its mandate under the Agreement, the WTO TRIPs Council has established procedures for notification[62] and examination[63] of Member's domestic intellectual property laws and regulations. The review of national implementing legislation is now largely complete, with the exception of newly acceding Members and several Members who joined the review process late.[64] Pursuant to Article 67 of the TRIPs Agreement, which contains an obligation that developed-country Members provide technical assistance to developing countries with respect to the establishment and reform of intellectual property regimes, as well as enforcement issues, the TRIPs Council has received numerous notifications of their technical cooperation programmes from developed countries. The WTO Secretariat has also begun to provide technical assistance to developing countries, in some instances in cooperation with WIPO (such as joint workshops on institutional capacity and other issues for developing countries).

To date, there have been only two decided dispute settlement cases based on the TRIPs Agreement, the *Indian Patents* case and a related EU complaint. The United States complained that India had not conformed with the transitional provisions of Article 70.8 of the TRIPs Agreement, which require that where a developing country Member exercises its right to delay full application of the Agreement with respect to patents on pharmaceutical and agricultural chemical products, it must nevertheless make available a means for the filing of patent applications and ensure that rights are not compromised, so that they can be effectively exercised at the end of the transition period. As well, the United States claimed that Article 70.9 of the Agreement, which deals with exclusive marketing rights, required that a mechanism to provide such rights be in place from the date of entry into force of the TRIPs Agreement. With respect to filing, the central issue became whether certain 'administrative instructions' to the Indian Patent Office by the government were sufficient to provide 'a sound legal basis to preserve both the novelty of the inventions and the priority of the applications as of the relevant filing and priority dates'.[65] India had initially sought to establish the filing system through a legislative amendment, which was subject to considerable delays in its parliament. A temporary presidential ordinance was issued in lieu of legislation but this expired, resulting in the resort to administrative instructions. This suggested to the panel that in fact the Indian government itself initially viewed legislative action as necessary to provide an adequate legal basis for the filing, and protection of priority, of patent applications; as well, on the panel's interpretation the administrative orders contradicted certain mandatory provisions of the Patents Act, thereby suggesting that the orders might be effectively challenged in court on administrative law grounds. India argued in the Appellate Body that the panel should have been more deferential to India's own view of its legal system, and the effectiveness of administrative action to provide the required legal security to patent holders. The Appellate Body, however, held that where provisions of a WTO agreement required a determination of the compliance of a Member's domestic law with that agreement, a panel can appropriately engage in a detailed examination of the domestic law in question.

In itself, this ruling seems appropriate, especially given the character of the TRIPs agreement, which imposes very detailed requirements on domestic law and regulations. At the same time, it is questionable whether the panel and AB should have interpreted Indian law as if they were interpreting a WTO Agreement – i.e. without any real analysis or consideration of expert views on the relationship between administrative orders and legislation in the Indian constitutional and administrative law system. This is especially troubling in light of Article 1.1 of the TRIPs Agreement, which provides, *inter alia* that 'Members shall be free to determine the appropriate method of implementing the provisions of this Agreement within their own legal system and practice.' At a minimum, this should mean that there is if anything more than the normal burden of proof on the complainant to show that the means chosen by a Member are inadequate for purposes of implementing the TRIPs provisions in question. However, the Appellate Body seemed to consider it India's responsibility to make a persuasive case that its administrative instructions were an adequate means of implementing its obligations in Article 70.8, once the United States had put forth 'evidence and arguments' concerning the inadequacy of the administrative instructions (para. 74). In fact, the United States did not go much further than simply suggesting that the fact that India initially proceeded with legislation and a presidential ordinance in lieu of legislation, proved that the Indian government itself must have thought that legislative action was necessary. However, some legal systems are very tolerant of administrative action, even where in similar circumstances the matter might have been addressed by legislation; the United States did not make out even a *prima facie* case that Indian administrative or constitutional law were such as not to tolerate an administrative approach to this problem, even if legislation would have been a neater solution. With respect to exclusive marketing rights, as required by Article 70.9, the AB held that 70.8 and 70.9 operated in tandem, so that India was obligated to have in place upon the coming into force of the TRIPs Agreement a mechanism for the granting of such rights, even if it could delay making the rights effective until the end of the transition period (para. 82).

The United States also lodged a complaint against Pakistan concerning its compliance with the same provisions that were at issue in the Indian case. The matter was settled prior to panel proceedings, however, when Pakistan adopted in February 1997 an ordinance on filing and exclusive rights with respect to pharmaceutical and agricultural chemical products that was to the satisfaction of the US.[66] There is a recent challenge by the European Union to provisions of Canada's pharmaceutical patent law which allow manufacture and stockpile of patented products by a non-patent holder for a period of up to six months before expiry of a patent for sale after the patent expires.[67] The EU is also challenging a related provision that permits experimentation and testing before the expiry of a patent so that marketing approval can be obtained for an innovative medicine for market access immediately after expiry. The EU's argument is that these provisions violate Article 28 of the TRIPs Agreement, which provide that a patent must confer a right on the patent holder to prevent third parties from, *inter alia*, making and using the patented product during the lifetime of the patent. In the recent *Indonesian Autos* case, discussed in the next chapter on Trade and Investment, the United States claimed that a measure requiring that trade marks acquired in respect of autos eligible for certain government incentives must be acquired by an Indonesian company violated various provisions of the TRIPs Agreement. The panel found that the United States had not demonstrated discriminatory treatment within the various relevant senses provided in the TRIPs Agreement as it applies to trademarks. The panel declined to apply a broad de facto discrimination concept in interpreting the TRIPs Agreement.

WIPO treaties on copyright and performance rights

The 1996 WIPO Copyright Treaty[68] has as its main thrust the updating of the Berne Convention in light of information technology and communications developments. Article 4 of the Treaty mirrors Article 10 of the TRIPs Agreement in establishing that computer programs are to be protected as literary works within the meaning of the Berne Convention. Article 11 confers on authors the right to control the dissemination of their works through electronic means such as the Internet. The Treaty also requires Member States to establish effective legal remedies against tampering with encoded information that allows authors to track and control the making and distribution of digital copies of their works. At the WIPO diplomatic conference at which the Copyright Treaty was negotiated an initiative was put forward to provide intellectual property rights protection with respect to data.[69] This was rejected, although further examination of the issue of protecting databases (as opposed to 'raw' data) was agreed. The notion of proprietizing facts raises serious issues of individual freedom of expression, as well as the possibility of seriously undermining the civic, democratic and educational potential of the Internet. Boyle notes that the proposed

> right would have been effectively permanent and would not have been restrained by the traditional limitations of copyright law, such as fair use. This proposal, with its potentially devastating effects on research and free speech, and its offer of a potent new tool of private censorship, drew fire from the research establishment, civil liberties groups and even – embarrassingly for its proponents – the database industry it was designed to protect [footnote omitted].[70]

The WIPO Performances and Phonograms Treaty[71] updates, in light of new (including digital) technologies, the Rome Convention provisions on copyright protection to be afforded with respect to performance of sound recordings, including for broadcast. The Treaty also grants performers moral rights of attribution and integrity (Article 5.1). Rights to royalties for performance of recordings are, however, subject to a reciprocity provision; this provision is necessary because the United States only has very limited performance rights in its domestic law (i.e. for digital performances only) and other Member States could not accept a reservation by the US to the treaty provisions on these rights, unless they were free to derogate from these provisions in respect of the rights of American performers.[72] According to a study by the WTO Secretariat, the WIPO Copyright and Performances and Phonograms Treaty, taken together, 'will greatly facilitate the creation of a secure and predictable legal environment that will foster the development of electronic commerce involving on line distribution of protected materials'.[73]

Emerging issues

There are several important emerging issues that will likely need to be addressed in the near future, either through dispute settlement under TRIPs or relevant WIPO conventions, or through the creation of new laws. One issue is the continuing use by the United States of unilateral trade action, particularly under s. 301 and Super 301, to deal with complaints about inadequate protection of intellectual property rights in developing countries, in some instances simultaneously with the pursuit of dispute settlement in the WTO. It is arguable that even if unilateral action does not violate any specific provision of the GATT or the TRIPs Agreement (as it would not for instance in the case of withdrawal of voluntary GSP preferences as was recently done in the case of Honduras),[74] it may be in contravention of Article 23 of the WTO Dispute Settlement Understanding. Article 23 provides that Members 'shall have recourse to the rules and procedures of this Understanding', when they seek redress of violations of WTO Agreements. The Article further provides that a Member shall not 'make a determination that a violation has occurred, that benefits have been nullified or impaired or that the attainment of any objective of the covered agreements has been impeded' except through recourse to WTO dispute settlement. This would seem to preclude unilateral action without reference to WTO dispute settlement, where the subject matter is covered by the TRIPs Agreement.[75] Another emerging issue of importance is the relationship between trademarks and domain names on the Internet (domain names constitute an essential part of a web address). As a study by the WTO Secretariat notes,

> [o]ne of the questions that has arisen is under what circumstances and under which jurisdiction(s) the use of a domain name that is identical to or similar to a trademark may constitute a trademark infringement, and what remedies should be available for the trademark holder. Further consideration is needed to determine whether the above mentioned problems call for adaptations to the international protection of trademarks.[76]

A third issue arises from the interaction of the emerging international environmental law with respect to biodiversity and international intellectual property law. One dimension of this issue that is not yet explicitly addressed by international legal rules is the use of patentable technology that exploits genetic resources found in nature in developing countries; there is a concern that these resources themselves be protected as intellectual property, so that the contribution of farmers and local communities to their conservation can be compensated. A report of the WTO Trade and Environment Committee appears to take the view that nothing in the TRIPs Agreement would prevent a Member from requiring that a user of these resources provide compensation for their use.[77] Thus, while a Member would normally have to grant a patent on an innovation based on use of genetic resources in nature, it could decide to restrict access to the resources themselves in its domestic law. Yet it is foreseeable that some kinds of restrictions (particularly onerous ones) might be seen as a circumvention of TRIPs rights with respect to patent protection itself. In general, however, we tend to support the Trade and Environmental Committee's reading of the TRIPs Agreement – a right to unrestricted access to genetic resources in nature would amount to a claim to be able to patent, and use exclusively, the resources themselves, which is clearly not provided under the TRIPs criteria for patentability.

CONCLUSION

While trade theory provides little basis for mandating uniform standards of intellectual property protection across all countries, intellectual property rights is an issue that is here to stay on the international trade agenda. The Uruguay Round TRIPs Agreement, while at the level of general principle promoting a uniform approach, in fact allows for a balance to be struck between countries' legitimate interests in limiting intellectual property rights for consumer welfare and economic and social development reasons, and the interests of their trading partners in sustaining adequate incentives for innovation. Maintaining this balance through monitoring and dispute settlement will be a major challenge for the World Trade Organization.

13 Trade and investment

INTRODUCTION

The last decade has seen a dramatic increase in foreign direct investment (FDI), defined as ownership and (normally) control of a business or part of a business in another country. Foreign direct investment is usually distinguished from portfolio investment, where a foreign actor purchases securities in a domestic company solely to earn a financial return, without any intent to own, control or manage the domestic firm.[1] Foreign direct investment generally takes one of 'three forms: an infusion of new equity capital such as a new plant or joint venture; reinvested corporate earnings; and net borrowing through the parent company or affiliates'.[2]

According to UNCTAD,

> The global FDI stock, a measure of the investment underlying international production increased fourfold between 1982 and 1994; over the same period it doubled as a percentage of world gross domestic product to 9 per cent. In 1996, the global FDI stock was valued at $3.2 trillion. Its rate of growth over the past decade (1986–96) was more than twice that of fixed capital formation, indicating an increasing internationalization of production systems. The worldwide assets of foreign affiliates, valued at $8.4 trillion in 1994 also increased more rapidly than world gross fixed capital formation. . . . Unlike the two previous investment booms in 1979–81 and 1987–90 (the first one being led by petroleum investments in oil producing countries and the second one being concentrated in the developed world) the current boom is characterized by considerable developing-country participation on the inflow side, although it is driven primarily by investments originating in just two countries – the United States and the United Kingdom.
>
> (Investment Report, 1998)

While many developing countries have come in recent years to take a more positive view of foreign investment and have moved to dismantle many explicit barriers and disincentives (such as limits on the percentage of an enterprise that can be foreign-owned and on repatriation of profits), ownership by foreigners has become of increasing concern in certain industrialized countries, particularly the United

States, that traditionally complained about illiberal attitudes elsewhere towards foreign investment.[3] As well, increased interest in foreign investment in Japan by nationals of other major industrialized countries, especially the United States, has focused attention on a range of domestic policies and practices in Japan that (including competition policies that provide few constraints on domestic cross-ownership of enterprises) supposedly create obstacles to foreigners wishing to acquire business assets there.[4]

The issue of foreign investment is closely linked to the role of multinational corporations in the global political economy. Some see such corporations as powers unto themselves, capable of buying or intimidating governments, or at least with the capacity to spread production and other functions around the globe so as to exploit regulatory differences between states – taking advantage of one country's cheap labour, another's tax haven, and yet another's favourable rules on intellectual property, and perhaps creating a race to the bottom.[5] Others view the multinational corporation as a logical and desirable extension of the inherent logic of comparative advantage, combining the benefits of organizing production within a single firm with the gains from free trade.[6]

Much of the contemporary controversy over foreign investment has surrounded measures that aim not to exclude investment but to direct it in a manner that benefits the economic development of the host country. In fact, measures aimed at channelling foreign investment to benefit the economies of host countries actually challenge two of the major assumptions that have traditionally underpinned hostility to foreign investment and the multinational firm: first and most obviously that foreign ownership is necessarily harmful to development; and second, that developing countries are powerless to determine the way in which foreign firms exploit their productive resources.[7] Also of significance are incentives to attract foreign investment, such as tax holidays or subsidies.[8] Indeed, incentives are often used in conjunction with export performance or local sourcing requirements, and may have the effect of offsetting some or all of the disincentive effects of such restrictions or conditions on foreign investment.[9]

As will be described in the next section, in a world completely free of restrictions on the movement of goods, services, and capital, any measure that distorts the global allocation of productive resources would be world-welfare reducing from the perspective of neo-classical economic theory.[10] However, within the GATT, the focus of attention has been on investment measures that have direct effects on trade in goods, such as measures that require or encourage foreign-owned firms to discriminate between domestically produced and imported inputs in production in the host country (local content requirements), as well as measures that require that a certain percentage of the foreign firm's output be exported.[11] The investment provisions of the Uruguay Round Final Act would subject some investment measures with direct effects on trade to more explicit scrutiny against existing GATT norms. These are relatively modest disciplines on investment disincentives and incentives in comparison with those found in the Canada–US FTA and the NAFTA, both of which include a National Treatment obligation with respect to foreign investors, as well as a general right to invest (right of establishment) subject to certain limitations and exceptions. Finally, the equivalent of a right to establishment is also entrenched in the OECD Code of Liberalisation of Capital Movements (1991) and a National Treatment obligation with respect to foreign investors is contained in the OECD 1976 Declaration on International Investment and Multinational Enterprises.

FOREIGN INVESTMENT AND TRADE THEORY

The theory of comparative advantage outlined in Chapter 1 shows the gains to both domestic *and* global economic welfare from specialization of each country in the production of those goods in which it has a comparative advantage. However, most goods – including Ricardo's classic examples of wine and cloth – can be understood as composites of other goods and services. It is unlikely that a country that has an overall comparative advantage in the production of a particular good also has a comparative advantage with respect to all the inputs required to produce the good in question. To return to Ricardo's example, England's comparative advantage in cloth may arise from the skill of its weavers, and in fact Portugal may have a comparative advantage in the production of wool or cotton; similarly, Portugal's comparative advantage in wine may arise from the quality of its grapes, and would not exclude English comparative advantage in the production of wine-making technology. In such a case, it may still make sense for Portugal to make wine and trade it for English-produced cloth, but it will also make sense for Portugal to export its cotton or wool to England and for England to export wine-making technology to Portugal.

Such an outcome need not, of course, lead to any foreign investment. Wholly Portuguese companies may make wine with technology produced by wholly British companies. However, just as it may make sense to produce domestically a good through internalizing different activities required for production within a given firm, rather than through contracts between discrete individuals or firms, so too it could make sense for Portuguese vineyard-owners to purchase British producers of wine technology, or for the British producers to buy Portuguese vineyards. According to the modern theory of the firm, production will be organized within a given firm where the agency costs of internal contracting between the firm's owners, agents, and employees are lower than the costs of external contracting between independent producers or providers of each component or element required to make the final product.[12] The rapid growth in intra-firm trade over the last few decades testifies to the economic logic of transboundary internal contracting.[13]

Increasingly, the production of complex goods may entail both cross-boundary internal and external contracting. For instance, many of the activities required to produce an automobile may be subsumed within a given auto-maker, which in turn will locate production facilities globally in order to maximize comparative advantage, but other important components will be obtained through external contracting with both domestic and foreign firms.[14]

Nicolaides suggests that there may be some archetypal cases where cross-boundary internal contracting will occur, rather than or in addition to external cross-boundary contracting (trade): the multinational company (MNC) exists precisely because it is not easy to trade intangible assets in open markets. It is difficult, for example, to write contracts for experience and newly-developed technology which is in the process of being adapted for commercial applications. The reasons that encourage corporate integration are that production costs are reduced, information flows faster and actions of individual units are more effectively coordinated.[15] Some of the reasons for engaging in foreign investment as opposed to or in addition to external contracting may be endemic to, or particularly salient to, the international context. For instance, the greater difficulty in enforcing external contracts across borders may lead to increased agency costs of contracting.[16] As well, intellectual property and related laws in other countries may provide inadequate protection of firm-specific innovations or knowledge, leading to a reluctance to transfer these to domestic firms through arms-length external contracts (e.g. licensing arrangements or direct sale of technology or processes).[17]

Dunning has analysed a vast literature on the theory of the multinational firm and the globalization of production, and has developed what he calls an 'eclectic' theory, which emphasizes a wide range of factors, including transportation and wage costs, greater suitability of internal contracting to the development and dissemination of firm-specific technology and processes, and hedging of the political risk of locating in a single country in a volatile world environment.[18] In many respects, this pluralistic approach is quite consistent with contemporary views on the nature of comparative advantage in trade, which take into account a wide variety of factors that may determine the comparative advantage or disadvantage of a particular country, including dynamic factors that change with changes in governments' domestic policies, technologies, consumer preferences and other rapidly evolving domestic and international realities.

ECONOMIC RATIONALES FOR GOVERNMENT INCENTIVES AND DISINCENTIVES TO FOREIGN INVESTMENT

Do the combined insights of the neo-classical theory of free trade and the modern theory of the firm suggest that economic welfare could actually be increased by government incentives or disincentives with respect to foreign investment? In a world where (apart from background rules of contracting) government action does not influence the allocation of productive resources, markets themselves should generate optimal levels of foreign investment. In such a world, government intervention would, almost by definition, distort the allocation of productive resources, inasmuch as disincentives reduced the level of investment below the market optimum, or incentives increased the level above that optimum.

A number of important qualifications to this view have been proposed by trade scholars and merit serious examination.

For example, according to one prominent theory of industrial competitiveness – that of Michael Porter and his associates – much economic development is attributable to the creation of 'clusters' of industries in a given country or region. Clusters are groups of industries that are interdependent or complementary.[19] According to Porter, many industries develop in response to the needs of other industries within a particular region or country. Most firms form part of an industry cluster in their home base – they have developed over time a complex web of relationships with suppliers and customers, including suppliers who have incurred sunk costs in developing or adapting products and services to the needs of the particular firm. When a firm establishes operations abroad, it or its foreign subsidiary, is likely to continue to source many inputs from the firm's 'home base', thus failing to help build a cluster in the host country. On this view, local content or sourcing requirements may have desirable domestic welfare effects, if they can effectively counter the 'home base' bias identified by Porter, and lead to the development of functioning clusters in the host country.

In addition, host-country local content requirements, or local hiring and manufacturing requirements, may offset the cumulative effects of subsidies or other governmental measures in the 'home base' of the investing firm. The pressures to source in the 'home base' may come less from the market than from government. These pressures may be informal, as well as formal. Formal pressures would include subsidies linked to job creation in the domestic economy and local content requirements in 'home base' government procurement contracts. More informally, the perception that a firm is a good local 'corporate citizen' may be viewed as important in effectively lobbying 'home base' governments on a wide variety of regulatory matters of concern to the firm, whether environmental standards, labour policies, or taxation issues. Often, the treatment a firm receives from its 'home base' government may be linked to the perception and reality that the firm really 'belongs' to that country.

Finally, it may make sense to impose special burdens or requirements on foreign firms where these firms are able to elude more general or neutral forms of redistributive regulation. For instance, multinational corporations, especially those characterized by high levels of intra-firm trade, may find it easy to manipulate transfer pricing[20] so as to avoid taxation on actual earnings in a foreign country. Many developing countries, in particular, do not have the sophistication in the design and enforcement of corporate tax regimes required to counter effectively this kind of conduct. As well, manipulation of transfer pricing may allow a multinational corporation to 'cheat' on tariff restrictions by significantly underpricing imports of inputs. Seen as a response to this kind of behaviour, local content or sourcing requirements may be viewed as a substitute for ineffective tariff protection.

These various considerations do not, admittedly, add up to a decisive argument in favour of local content and related requirements, which may have negative consumer welfare and allocative efficiency effects within the host country. This does, however, weigh against any kind of general assumption that trade would be undistorted, or less distorted, in the absence of such requirements.

Investment and trade protection

There is a complex interaction between foreign investment and trade protection. First of all, foreign investment may occur as a means of jumping tariff walls or avoiding harassment of imports under the trade remedy laws of the host country (so-called 'cooperative protectionism'). If much of its comparative advantage is portable, consisting of know-how, processes and technology, a company may avoid border restrictions simply by manufacturing within the domestic market. Enhanced access to host country markets generally ranks high among the factors that industries cite as reasons for foreign investment.[21]

Protection-avoiding foreign investment has both opportunities and risks attached to it. One such opportunity is the strategic use of tariffs or, more likely, administered protection, to encourage foreign investment. Where a tariff (or other trade protection) induces a foreign producer to relocate production facilities to the protecting state, new jobs in that state are created, and in fact there is a possibility of shifting some of the foreign firm's comparative advantage itself to the host country. For instance, when Honda or Toyota sets up production in Canada or the United States, it brings with it the processes, know-how, and so forth, that arguably constitute much of its comparative advantage.

It is important, however, to note that in one important sense consumers in the protecting state will still be worse off than under conditions of liberal trade, because the foreign firm that does relocate will be able to price up to tariff or other trade barriers (e.g. VERs), thereby still charging consumers prices higher than would be the case without trade restrictions.

A simple example will illustrate this point. A and B are both foreign car manufacturers who have been exporting cars into C. A and B both produce a mid-sized car that would sell, in the absence of protection, for £6,000 and C's consumers are indifferent as between the car produced by A and that produced by B. Assume that a tariff of 30% is imposed on imports and an elasticity of demand for this kind of car that results in two-thirds of the tariff being passed on to the consumer in higher prices. If A and B both export their cars to C, C's consumers will pay £7,200 per car. If A starts to produce the car in C, and comes inside the tariff wall it *may* be able to underprice B while still earning more than the non-tariff price per car. As long as consumers are indifferent between A's car and B's, A will be able to outcompete B at any price below £7,200. The end result will be somewhat less of a consumer welfare loss than if both A and B's cars are imported and subject to tariffs, but consumers will still be somewhat worse off than they would be if there were no protection.

At the same time, because *some* of the rents of protection have been shifted from domestic firms to the foreign firm producing domestically, this may compensate in whole or in part for additional costs incurred in shifting some production to the importing country, including compliance with export performance, technology transfer or other requirements imposed by the host-country government. A disturbing implication, especially for consumer welfare, is that the higher the amount of protection, the more attractive the shift of production is, because the rents from protection that accrue to the domestically-producing foreign firm are correspondingly higher.[22]

The dynamic effects of foreign investment in protected markets

In reality, when foreign firms have come within a tariff wall, they have often found it to be something less than a safe haven. Domestic firms are apt to petition government for relief from the increased competition, frequently arguing that the foreign plants are little more than screwdriver operations aimed at circumventing tariffs or other border restrictions, and that they create less employment per car sold, for instance, than domestic firms, which source domestically to a greater degree and thus create jobs in a wider range of sectors that produce inputs. As a consequence, once inside the tariff wall, foreign firms may well find themselves confronted with new obstacles to exploitation of the domestic market. A prominent example of this has been the effort of the European Union to limit the market share of cars manufactured by Japanese producers within Europe, claiming that these are not really European automobiles.[23] Quite commonly, local content requirements are imposed upon the foreign firm.

At one level, such *ex post* adjustments of the 'bargain' between the protecting country and the foreign firm could be viewed as opportunism – once it has sunk substantial costs in the creation of factories or other production facilities, the foreign firm may have little choice but to stay. On the other hand, it is arguable that domestic welfare is improved by such measures – some of the rents from protection against competing foreign firms that accrue to the investing firm are clawed back in the form of boosted sales for domestic providers of inputs.

In theory, there are losses in allocative efficiency since otherwise uncompetitive manufacturers of inputs are being kept in business. However, in the case of inputs for some complex products, arguably the effect is to transfer comparative advantage to input providers as well. Where a firm is unhappy with the quality of domestic inputs but must use them to circumvent the tariff wall through foreign investment, it may still be in the firm's interest to produce locally but also to work with domestic input providers on quality control, making their products genuinely competitive with imported inputs.

Alternatively (or additionally), the host country may find a way of increasing the rents from protection to compensate the investing firm for the costs of complying with new local content or local sourcing requirements. Quotas and VERs, because of their discriminatory potential, are a simple way of increasing such rents. In return for local content requirements, for instance, a foreign car manufacturer producing domestically could be offered larger quotas on models that it continues to produce offshore. Consumers will benefit from the increased quota (a larger supply will result in somewhat lower costs), but will of course not benefit as much as when quotas on all imported cars in a similar category or competing for the same market are increased or at the limit eliminated. Conversely, the foreign firm with the increased quota benefits from greater sales, but at the same time loses fewer of the scarcity rents than it would if the supply of its foreign competitors' comparable products were also increased.

The dynamics of the relationship between trade protection and foreign investment described above have broader implications that should dampen the enthusiasm of advocates of strategic protection. First of all, a clear consequence is to reinforce the dominant position of the strongest firms in a given industry, thereby reducing global competition. In order to play the game, a firm must be large enough and have sufficient resources to expand production globally, investing large amounts of capital in new production facilities. Second, in the host country, a whole new set of jobs is created that, in effect, depends upon continued protection. If comparative advantage has genuinely been transferred to the host country, of course it may still make sense to continue production even after the removal, or reduction, of protection. But the closing of American branch plants in Canada, and their relocation to the United States, that has occurred in the wake of the Canada–US Free Trade Agreement, is a powerful reminder that jumping the tariff wall may remain a decisive consideration in a plant's continuing operation in the host country. Arguably, as well, this suggests that if protection is to be used to induce foreign investment, then it is important to attach conditions that actually assure a real transfer of comparative advantage (such as requirements for reinvestment and renewal of the plant, training of workers, and technology transfer).[24]

NON-ECONOMIC RATIONALES AND EFFECTS OF INVESTMENT POLICIES: SOVEREIGNTY AND THE FOREIGN FIRM

The discussion so far has focused exclusively on economic and trade policy dimensions of foreign investment measures. Traditionally, however many of the reasons for which states have imposed restrictions on foreign investment have been connected with political arguments about sovereignty. These arguments concern a wide range of specific harms that are believed to flow from ownership of a country's productive resources by foreigners. They include national security and defence considerations; the supposed difficulty of subjecting foreign or multinational firms to domestic jurisdiction; concerns that foreign investors or foreign firms will become a vehicle for inappropriate influence by their home governments on politics and society within the host country; and concerns about the protection of cultural autonomy or distinctiveness.[25] We will briefly consider several of these preoccupations with the potential drawbacks of foreign investment.

Defence and national security

A traditional dictum of security policy, at least since Machiavelli,[26] is that no state should rely on others to furnish the weapons needed for its own defence. Nevertheless, the global arms trade flourishes, and only a handful of relatively industrially advanced nations are capable of manufacturing sophisticated weapons systems in any quantity.

The concern about having one's own arms often extends to autarchy with respect to the inputs necessary to produce those arms, whether steel or computer chips. For instance, as Japan and some European countries have become world leaders in the development and manufacture of products and technologies considered to have critical defence applications, the United States has become increasingly concerned that it may be placing its vital security interests in the hands of foreigners. This concern has been deployed as a rationale for trade protection to sustain uncompetitive national industries considered vital to the security of the United States. It has also resulted in measures intended to control foreign ownership of productive assets in the United States. The United States has justified prohibitions or restrictions on foreign investment in many sectors on national security or related grounds (i.e. vital national interest). These sectors include: air transportation, coastal shipping, commercial fisheries, communications, energy resources, and real property.[27]

In 1988, an amendment was added to the Omnibus Trade and Competitiveness Act (the Exon–Florio Amendment, named after the US legislators who proposed the bill) providing the President of the United States with the authority to block mergers or acquisitions involving foreign firms on grounds that US national security interests would be impaired by the resulting foreign ownership.[28] The Committee on Foreign Investment in the United States (made up of representatives of various agencies in the US government, including the State Department, the Defense Department, the Commerce Department and the office of the United States Trade Representative) is given the authority to conduct investigations of mergers, acquisitions and takeovers that may threaten US national security. On the basis of these investigations, the Committee makes recommendations to the President as to whether national security interests justify blocking a transaction or altering its terms. Until recently, at least, there have been few investigations, and even fewer instances where the result has been Presidential intervention in a transaction.[29] Nevertheless, the need to avert the threat of such intervention may, in a wider range of cases, lead to various 'voluntary' undertakings by the potential investor, making the terms of the investment more favourable to American interests.[30] However, as Graham and Ebert note,[31] there is strong pressure in Congress to make investigation of proposed investments mandatory, at least with respect to some sectors.

Does foreign ownership of strategically-sensitive enterprises really jeopardize security? First of all, if in fact foreign producers do have a monopoly over products or processes that are vital to a country's security interests, the country in question is certainly better off having those products or processes developed within its borders. Dependency on imports is much riskier since a foreign government can, in effect, control the export of the needed materials. In a national emergency, by contrast, domestic production facilities (even though foreign-owned) could be commandeered by the government, or made directly subject to its orders.

What, however, of the case where there currently exist two suppliers of a given technology or product, one domestic and one foreign, and where the foreign supplier chooses to buy out the domestic supplier? Here, the acquisition may be motivated by the desire to obtain a monopoly, and in fact could result in *all* production, or much of it, being moved offshore. In such an instance, it may be quite justifiable to weigh carefully national security implications within any overall review of the impact of such an acquisition.

In addition, foreign firms in the defence sector are likely to have particularly close relationships with their home-country government – often reflected in the presence of former politicians and senior bureaucrats on their board of directors, government subsidies, procurement and R&D contracts, or partial government ownership. Where this is the case, some concern that foreign powers will be able to exercise influence or control over the firm's strategy, and have privileged access to its products or research, may be warranted. Again, however, this concern would be justified mainly where a merger or acquisition results in a monopoly in a particular product or process.

In the instances just discussed, national security concerns may in fact be warranted with respect to foreign investment. However, in the United States in particular, the national security argument has been extended far beyond the case of very sensitive defence industries to sectors that produce a wide variety of inputs into military products, or whose production facilities might, in war time, need to be converted to military uses (steel, cars, civil aircraft). In most of these instances, a variety of producers, domestic and foreign, currently exist. Taken to its logical conclusion the argument would end up justifying something close to complete autarchy, since there are few sectors of civilian production that do not contribute something of importance to the materiel needed, in the broadest sense, to sustain an all-out war effort.

Furthermore, blocking a foreign takeover or merger will itself far from guarantee either the continuation of a domestic source of supply for the products in question or protection against foreign influence. For example, where the merger or acquisition is required to rescue the domestic firm, or to ensure its continuing viability, the alternative may well be bankruptcy, with the result that the foreign firm becomes the monopolist anyway but produces abroad, and hence the source of supply becomes even more insecure. Hence, in a number of instances, one suspects that national security arguments against *foreign* acquisitions are disguised attempts to attract a government supported bail-out at home, or more protection. Once the firm is considered a domestic producer vital to national security, the logical consequence is not just that foreigners should be prevented from acquiring it, but that its survival as a domestic firm should be guaranteed by the state.

Inadequate regulatory or political control over the foreign investor

The multinational firm is often described as a kind of power unto itself, able to slip through the normal control of national jurisdictions through the global diffusion of its activities. There are few inherent legal constraints on the application of domestic jurisdiction to the activities that multinational corporations engage in within a particular country; however, there may be significant practical constraints, where the bulk of the firm's assets and much of the information about its activities and decision-making are located abroad. Of course, while it is true that offshore activities and decisions of a foreign multinational may affect the regulatory interests of its host country, so may the foreign activities and interests of the host country's *own* firms. Thus, the problem concerns both inward and outward foreign investment.

In some sectors the regulatory issues may be particularly acute. In the case of financial services, for instance, regulators may be concerned with the overall stability of an institution, the quality of its investments, etc. Ultimately, domestic deposit holders are dependent upon the stability of the overall institution, including the soundness of its lending practices and other activities abroad. As is illustrated by the Bhopal disaster, regulatory issues may also arise where multinationals are engaged in high-risk activities in a host country, but where they retain elsewhere the assets necessary to satisfy potential liabilities for these risks, or information about the risks.

These kinds of regulatory issues may justify some kinds of differential treatment of foreign investors – the requirement to carry liability insurance, to maintain a minimum level of assets within the host country, or to post a bond or a deposit to guarantee regulatory compliance.

Extraterritoriality

Another set of concerns about foreign investment may be considered the 'mirror image' of the concern about lack of domestic control of the foreign-owned company or subsidiary, that is, the possibility that foreign ownership will result in the extraterritorial application of the laws and regulatory authority of the firm's home country to its activities in the host country.[32] Extraterritoriality has been particularly a concern raised by the explicit extraterritorial sweep of a number of US regulatory regimes. One important example is export controls. The United States has sought to prevent foreign subsidiaries of American firms from exporting products to countries that are embargoed by United States law, such as Cuba.[33] From the perspective of the law of the GATT, this can rightly be seen as an interference with the trade relations of another Contracting Party. However, export controls based upon national security considerations are explicitly exempted from normal GATT rules by Article XXI,[34] although, it is highly questionable whether even Article XXI provides scope for a Contracting Party to interfere with exports and imports flowing between another Contracting Party and a third state.

It bears emphasis that extraterritoriality is not a problem that is limited to the context of foreign investment. Ownership by nationals is but one basis among many that the United States, for instance, uses as a grounds for exercising jurisdiction beyond its borders. For instance, US antitrust law is applied extraterritorially not just to American-owned companies, but to any activity that materially affects United States commerce, including for example participation of foreign-owned firms in cartels with US firms that restrict competition in the US market.[35]

The most promising avenue for resolving problems of extraterritoriality is not restrictions on investment, but the evolution of multilateral processes to deal with particular cases of conflicting exercise of jurisdiction, and eventually to evolve a set of detailed principles or guidelines broadly consistent with international law norms on state sovereignty. In this regard, it should be noted that a 1991 Decision of the OECD Council allows any Member State of the OECD to refer to the Committee on International Investment 'any problem arising from the fact that multinational enterprises are made subject to conflicting requirements'.[36] With respect to extraterritorial application of antitrust laws, the OECD has developed a separate process intended to address directly issues of restrictive business practices and the multinational enterprise.[37] A number of constructive approaches to inter-jurisdictional conflict have been suggested, including harmonization of domestic competition laws and designation of a lead jurisdiction for review of international mergers.[38]

In addition to the matters discussed above, developing countries have traditionally had an additional (although often overlapping) range of concerns about foreign investment, which have been used to justify severe restrictions on the activity of foreign firms. These have included concerns that foreign investors often will deploy technologies that are inappropriate for exploitation of and development of local skills for best advantage, that may aggravate or create balance of payments problems by heavy reliance on imported inputs in the production process; and that foreign investors will perpetuate existing patterns of Southern dependency in exploiting cheap, unskilled labour in developing countries without transferring the skills and technologies required for economic development.[39]

On balance, the recent empirical evidence seems to suggest that foreign direct investment has had a positive impact on growth and development in LDCs.[40] In addition, it appears that on a comparative basis developing countries with relatively restrictive policies towards foreign investment have experienced much lower rates of economic growth over the last 30 years than those (e.g. Malaysia) with relatively open policies.[41] However, it may be that what distinguishes, at least in part, the countries with more open policies, is that instead of placing general (and severe) restrictions on, for example, repatriation of earnings or the right of establishment as such, these countries negotiated specific agreements on issues like technology transfer and local employment with individual firms. Thus, instead of adopting either a generally negative stance towards FDI, or a completely open attitude, they proceeded in a more selective fashion to impose requirements or conditions on some foreign investors, where it was believed this would serve the interests of domestic economic development. This case-by-case approach, however, is more transaction-cost intensive and heightens the risk of corruption in the administration of foreign investment policies.

This being said, in the aftermath of the LDC debt crisis (which has resulted in substantial reduction of new debt financing available to many developing countries) and given what many observers consider to be a world shortage of capital (considering, for instance, the substantial needs of the Newly Liberalizing Countries in Central and Eastern Europe), many developing countries have adopted a much more liberal attitude towards foreign investment, and see the issue for governmental policy much more as that of attracting foreign investment rather than restricting or limiting it. This led *The Economist* magazine to remark, in a recent survey of multinationals, that

> too many governments see foreign investment as a shortcut to prosperity, bringing in skills, capital and technology to push their countries rapidly from the 1950s to the 1990s. . . . Those governments that rely too heavily on multinationals are likely to look for a foreign scapegoat when inflation heads for triple figures, unemployment fails to drop and demonstrators surround the ministry.[42]

The impact of the Mexican Peso crisis of 1994–5 and the crisis in Asian capital markets in 1997 on FDI suggests that this prediction of *The Economist* was overly pessimistic. These crises involved massive outflows of *portfolio* equity investment, but neither crisis has led to a devastating impact on FDI flows or the FDI climate in the affected countries. A joint report of the International Chamber of Commerce and UNCTAD notes: 'total portfolio investment flows to Mexico fell from $12 billion in 1994 to $7.5 billion, with portfolio equity investment flows falling from $4.5 billion to $0.5 billion in 1995. FDI inflows, in contrast, which had more than doubled in 1994, fell by only 13% in 1995.'[43] With respect to the Asian crisis, the report notes: 'The financial crisis in East and South-East Asia has involved a sharp decrease in private external capital flow to some developing countries in the region. . . . FDI flows in 1997 to the five most affected Asian countries as a group, however, are estimated to have remained close to the level attained in 1996.'[44] The report entailed a survey of almost 200 major transnational corporations operating in the region concerning how the crisis would affect their future plans; the vast majority responded that their confidence in the region as an investment destination had remained unchanged. One concern, however, is that in the wake of the crisis some countries might impose restrictions on the ability of investors to purchase domestic company assets at 'fire sale' prices. In general, however, the crisis has not resulted in a reversal or rethinking of the trend towards liberalizing FDI regimes. In fact, in dramatically illustrating the dangers of reliance on external bank lending and portfolio equity investment to finance economic growth, the crisis may actually reinforce positive attitudes towards FDI.

ALTERNATIVE APPROACHES TO INTERNATIONAL DISCIPLINE OF FOREIGN INVESTMENT MEASURES

The pre-Uruguay GATT

Investment measures and the General Agreement: an overview

Our discussion in 'Foreign investment and trade theory' and 'Economic rationales' (this chapter) has emphasized the complexity of the relationship between foreign investment measures, liberal trade and protectionism. The dramatic expansion in foreign investment in recent years has depended heavily on liberal rules governing trade in goods, yet this expansion has also provided new opportunities and incentives to exploit the rents from protection, thus leading to new kinds of protectionist pressures. At the same time, the interdependencies created by the globalization of production have brought into being new interests that would lose enormously from a fundamental unravelling of the liberal trading order.

As a matter of law, only a few of the investment measures that can be deployed strategically along with trade protection arguably fall within the ambit of the GATT. The most clear-cut example is that of local content or sourcing requirements, which explicitly discriminate against imports and in favour of like domestic products, hence violating the National Treatment obligation of the GATT (Article III:4). Export requirements are a somewhat more complicated case. As will be discussed below, a GATT panel decision with respect to Canadian foreign investment measures held that export requirements did not *per se* violate any provision of the General Agreement. However, as we will argue, export requirements linked with a subsidy to the foreign investor may in some circumstances constitute an export subsidy, the only kind of subsidy explicitly banned in the General Agreement (Article XVI). Export requirements may also lead to dumping, inasmuch as they lead to the product being exported below cost or at a price lower than that which applies in the domestic market.

In addition to local content and export requirements, the law of the GATT may be violated by trade balancing requirements, which typically limit the value of what a foreign investor is allowed to import into the host country to the value of exports. Here, two sets of provisions in the GATT are relevant. First of all, the limitation on imports might be considered, like a domestic sourcing requirement, as a form of discrimination against imported goods. However, it might be argued that this need not be the result, since with a trade balancing requirement (unlike a direct local sourcing requirement) a foreign firm wishing to import more inputs will be permitted to do so if this is balanced by an increase in exports of finished products (and, as we have just mentioned, *export* requirements are not as such illegal under GATT). A stronger case can be made that trade balancing restrictions violate the Article XI ban on quantitative restrictions, as they place (albeit variable) quantitative limits on imports. Because Article XI bans restrictions on exports as well as imports, a *prima facie* violation of Article XI might also occur where the host country places limits on the percentage or amount of production that it can export, i.e. requiring that a portion of the production be set aside for the domestic market. Such a requirement might be imposed where, perhaps for technology transfer reasons, a country wishes domestic users to have access to what is being produced by the foreign firm. The requirement might go hand in hand with an additional provision that the percentage of production in question be made available to domestic users for local currency or at a lower than world market price.

Additional investment measures that implicate GATT law are requirements that foreign investors re-invest a percentage of earnings within the host country and, conversely, limitations on the repatriation of profits in convertible currency. In the former communist countries (of which several were long-standing GATT Members) such requirements were commonplace, and they still exist today in many developing countries. Arguably, both re-investment requirements and limitations on the repatriation of profits could constitute violations of Article XV of the GATT, which requires Contracting Parties to adhere to IMF rules with respect to balance of payments and exchange arrangements. However, as has been discussed in detail in Chapter 3, these rules allow considerable scope for developing countries to restrict foreign exchange, including exchange of local earnings into foreign currency. In addition, it should be noted that trade-balancing requirements or other investment measures that would otherwise be in violation of Article XI of the GATT may nevertheless be saved by Article XII, which permits some, mainly non-discriminatory, quantitative restrictions where necessary to address a balance of payments crisis. Although the drafters clearly had temporary measures in mind, Article XII has been used to sustain much longer-term restrictions. In addition, Article XVIIIB: 9 explicitly authorizes a broader range of quantitative restrictions – including discriminatory quantitative restrictions – where these are measures undertaken by developing countries to protect or enhance their balance of payments.

The *FIRA* Panel Decision

The *FIRA* Panel Decision[45] represents the only case where foreign investment measures were the central focus of a panel prior to the WTO, and therefore deserves detailed analysis. At issue were various undertakings obtained from foreign investors pursuant to Canada's Foreign Investment Review Act. The Act established a governmental agency, the Foreign Investment Review Agency, to screen investment proposals by foreign interests. The Agency was to review the proposals and either accept, reject, or modify them. The essential criterion was whether the investment would be of significant benefit to Canada, significant benefit being defined to include increases in employment and exports, technology transfer, and advancement of 'national industrial and economic policies'. Under the Act, foreign investor applicants were able to make undertakings with respect to any aspect of the operation of their business in Canada, with a view to more favourable treatment of their application. Such undertakings were not, however, mandatory or a formal prerequisite for the success of an application. Once an investment application was approved, however, the undertakings were legally enforceable.

The United States argued that three kinds of undertakings violated provisions in the GATT: local content, local manufacturing, and minimum export.

Local content and local manufacturing requirements

With respect to local content requirements, the main argument was that these undertakings violated Article III:4 of the General Agreement (National Treatment). Given that the undertakings were not formally *required* by the Canadian law, a threshold issue was whether they could be considered, for purposes of Article

III, as 'laws, regulations, or requirements'. The United States argued that such undertakings could not be viewed as simply voluntary, since no firm would make them unless it would gain some advantage or avoid some penalty by doing so. The panel, however, sidestepped the issue of voluntariness, simply stating that 'private contractual obligations entered into by investors should not affect the rights which contracting parties, including contracting parties not involved in the dispute, possess under Article III:4'.

A second issue was raised by the Canadian argument that these undertakings merely constituted predictions of what foreign investors intended to do based upon commercial considerations.

The panel rejected this argument, pointing out that the specific content of some of the undertakings showed that firms were expected to act in a manner not consistent with commercial considerations or in explicitly discriminatory terms, for instance binding themselves always to purchase a Canadian product when available on similar terms to an import. The panel's approach seems justified in light of the economic analysis developed earlier in this chapter. Because the foreign firm producing domestically can capture rents from protection by pricing up to the tariff, there are good reasons to believe that commitments investors make about how much local sourcing they will undertake are not simply in the order of a prediction about how they will behave in future in accordance with market forces, but also reflect a 'price' investors are willing to pay to capture some of the rents of protection.

A further important issue raised by the economic effects of local content or local manufacturing undertakings is that of injury. The panel chose to sidestep this issue, noting that 'under standing GATT practice, a breach of a rule is presumed to have an adverse impact on other contracting parties' (para. 6.4). It is not obvious that foreign investors who make undertakings are worse off under a scheme for screening foreign investment than under circumstances where investment is unimpeded. As discussed earlier, the rents from protection that a foreign investor gains from coming within the tariff wall (i.e. from being able to price up to the tariff) may be substantial, and may more than compensate for the costs of compliance with domestic content or other performance requirements. Also, such requirements may in some situations be balanced with explicit subsidies or other incentives to investment (such as tax holidays). There is clearly, however, a trade-related injury from local content and local manufacturing requirements that is borne by producers and suppliers of imported goods that would otherwise compete favourably with locally produced imports. These producers *may*, of course, include the foreign investor itself, or other firms from its 'home base' country – but they may be entirely from other countries.

Thus, it is incorrect to conceive of the debate over the trade effects of these measures as simply a conflict between host country and home country interests. Even though developed countries are more likely to be home than host countries, developing countries or other countries that are not major sources of foreign investment still can lose significantly from investment restrictions in the nature of local content requirements, if the result is discrimination against their exports.

Export performance requirements

The FIRA panel also considered the legality of export performance requirements under the GATT. The United States had argued that these requirements violated the obligation in Article XVII:1 of the GATT for certain enterprises to act 'in accordance with commercial considerations'. The panel found that this obligation only applied to state-trading enterprises as defined in the general provisions of Article XVII, and therefore was not relevant to foreign investors. However, the panel also found that 'there is no provision in the General Agreement which forbids requirements to sell goods in foreign markets in preference to domestic markets. In particular, the General Agreement does not impose on contracting parties the obligation to prevent enterprises from dumping' (para 5.18).

Here, the panel seems to have overlooked the spirit (although perhaps not the strict letter) of the prohibition of export subsidies in Article XVI:2 B of the General Agreement. The panel's general position – that undertakings are not made gratuitously but in exchange for a benefit that flows from the host country government to investor – would argue in favour of the view that in fact export undertakings are likely to be subsidized, at the very least by the rents from protection that the host government 'grants' to the investor in authorizing the investment. Article XVI:4 B, furthermore, prohibits Contracting Parties from granting 'directly or indirectly any form of subsidy' on exports, at least where the result is a lower price for exports than the domestic price of the product.

The case for deeming export performance requirements as equivalent to an export subsidy is, of course, particularly strong where an investor is attracted to the host country by explicit financial incentives to establish operations there. However, at the same time, the GATT rules on subsidies do not refer explicitly to investment incentives as such. Some such incentives may constitute countervailable subsidies under the WTO Subsidies Agreement, but only because domestic *products* are being subsidized, not because of the impact of such subsidies on the location decisions of foreign firms.

The evolution of the GATT rules: TRIMs and the Uruguay Round

Clearly, the GATT rules extend only to a relatively narrow range of investment measures with direct and immediately identifiable impacts on trade. In the Uruguay Round of GATT negotiations, the United States in particular sought a much more comprehensive GATT code on investment based upon the principle of free access to foreign markets. On this free access approach, the investment measures disciplined by the GATT would no longer be limited to measures such as local content requirements that discriminate against imported products, but would extend to a potentially vast range of domestic policies of Contracting Parties that create barriers to in-bound foreign investment regardless of whether specific trade impacts are present. The free access approach, it should be noted, gains some normative weight from the allocative efficiency arguments for liberal investment policies explored in 'Foreign investment and trade theory' (earlier in this chapter). These imply that, in principle, almost any incentive or disincentive to investment can be regarded as a distortion of the optimal global allocation of productive resources. However, under real world conditions of imperfect competition and tariff and other trade restrictions, important qualifications exist on these allocative efficiency arguments – qualifications explored earlier in this chapter. In addition, the free access approach provides no obvious means of weighing against allocative efficiency considerations the non-economic rationales for investment restrictions discussed above in 'Non-economic rationales' (this chapter).

Unlike the United States, most other Contracting Parties were sceptical of the free access approach, and saw the task of the Uruguay Round negotiations on TRIMs as that of developing more detailed and explicit rules with respect to measures that appear inconsistent with well-established GATT principles, such as National Treatment with respect to products. This suggests a cautious extension of the kind of analysis undertaken by the FIRA panel to a somewhat broader set of measures (such as trade balancing requirements or export performance requirements) that directly affect trade flows. A concrete example will elucidate how the much more comprehensive US view of what is trade-distorting conflicts with the more text-bound view of other Contracting Parties. The US views technology transfer requirements as distorting trade, in that a possible result is to transfer to the host country the capacity to develop products and processes that it would otherwise have to import from the home country.[46] Other countries question whether this impact is very well established: it might be the case, for instance, that absent such a transfer, some developing countries would not be able to afford such products and processes at all, and therefore that imports would be negligible.[47]

The Uruguay Round Final Act reflects a rather subtle compromise between these differing perspectives.[48] On the one hand, there is a binding obligation not to apply any investment measures 'inconsistent with the provisions of Article III or Article XI of the General Agreement' (Article 2(1)). There is thus a clear re-affirmation of the principle that existing GATT provisions do apply to some investment policies. Moreover, an 'illustrative list' of such measures is provided, which includes local content, sourcing, and some trade balancing requirements (which violate National Treatment) and import and export restrictions (which violate the ban on Quantitative Restrictions, in Article XI of the General Agreement).

On the other hand, the illustrative list does not contain any of the measures with more indirect or questionable effects on trade for which United States negotiators had been seeking explicit disciplines, such as technology transfer requirements. In addition, the existing exceptions with respect to Article XI that apply to developing countries are re-affirmed (Article 4). As well, developing countries are provided with substantial transition periods (five years and seven years in the case of the least-developed countries) for elimination of TRIMs that offend Article III and/or Article XI (Article 5).

However, it should also be noted that the illustrative list is just that – the text leaves it open for GATT panels to find that measures not on the list violate the GATT, and in addition, the fact that no list of 'green light' or explicitly non-GATTable measures is provided, means that no further protection is extended to Contracting Parties against unilateral retaliatory action by the United States on the basis of its market access approach. Indeed, additional legitimacy could well be conferred on the US approach in that the Final Act provides for a five-year review of the provisions on TRIMs, possibly with a view to including new provisions on 'investment policy and competition policy' (Article 9). The Final Act Agreement on Trade Related Investment Measures also calls for the creation of a Committee on TRIMs whose functions are, *inter alia*, to 'monitor the operation and implementation of' the Agreement. In the *Indonesian Autos* case (not appealed), the panel held that the TRIMs Agreement has 'an autonomous legal existence' from the GATT (para. 14,62). It also held that the Agreement could apply to performance requirements that were a condition for receipt of subsidies, even if the subsidy measures themselves might be covered by the Agreement on Subsidies and Countervailing Measures – (paras. 14.47–14.55). The panel further found that the local content requirements could be covered by the TRIMs Agreement, even if these requirements, or the advantages conditioned upon meeting them, were not targeted at foreign investors, but rather generally applicable to enterprises, whether domestically or foreign-owned (para. 14.73).

The NAFTA

Articles 1102 and 1103 of NAFTA, respectively, establish National Treatment and MFN obligations with respect to investors *and* investments of other NAFTA Parties. National Treatment is required with respect to establishment, acquisition, expansion, management, conduct, operation, and sale or other disposition of investments. Thus, in effect, the National Treatment obligation embodies a right of establishment. These obligations may be subject to various reservations and exceptions, listed in various Annexes to the NAFTA (especially Annexes I–III) and in the case of Mexico include measures related to the following sectors: transportation, telecommunications, petrochemicals, the postal service, professional services, and social services. Canada and the United States, however, have also included reservations with respect to some of these sectors in Annex II, in some cases out of specific policy concerns and in others simply to preserve reciprocity or symmetry between the obligations of Mexico and its NAFTA partners.[49] Where not reserved, existing non-conforming measures must be eliminated within ten years.

In addition, there is a general provision in the introductory section of Chapter 11 stating that nothing in this Chapter shall be construed to prevent a Party from providing a service or performing a function such as law enforcement, correctional services, income security or insurance, social welfare, public education, public training, health and child care in a manner that is not inconsistent with this Chapter (Article 1101.4). This reflects Canadian as well as Mexican concerns that some provisions of the Investment Chapter, particularly the right of establishment, could be interpreted as providing to private investors of other NAFTA partners a right to compete in areas that are characterized by complete or substantial public sector provision in Mexico and Canada, but where some or all of delivery is provided by the private sector in the United States. One may question, however, the legal significance of this clause, since it protects only those measures that are *in any case* 'not inconsistent' with the provisions of Chapter 11, and thus does not override the application of Chapter 11 to public provision of essential services. In addition, on its terms, the clause only seems to apply to direct governmental provision: thus, once a government begins contracting out some of these functions, even to the non-profit sector, it might be required to permit a direct business presence in that sector by private interests in other NAFTA countries, on a National Treatment basis. The effect may be to deter governments from innovative experiments with delivery through non-governmental actors such as non-profit community groups, for fear of losing adequate scope for regulatory control or being required to allow competition on essentially commercial criteria.[50]

The NAFTA prohibits various kinds of performance requirements, including minimum export, domestic content, domestic purchasing, and technology transfer requirements (Article 1106(1)). The prohibition on technology transfer requirements is somewhat qualified by the fact that requirements for the domestic conduct of Research and Development and training of workers are explicitly permitted (1106(4)). The NAFTA does not discipline investment *incentives*. From an allocative efficiency perspective, it is just as undesirable to encourage a higher level of investment than would occur on the basis of market forces alone, as to discourage investment that would occur on the basic of such forces alone – thus the failure to discipline incentives is a major defect of the NAFTA Investment Chapter. However, Article 1106(3) provides that some of the requirements listed in Article 1106(1) cannot be stipulated as *conditions* for the receipt of subsidies, which may discourage to some extent the use of investment incentives.

The NAFTA provides some protection for investors from non-NAFTA countries who already have substantial business activities in the territory of one of the NAFTA Parties. These investors from non-NAFTA Parties are to enjoy the full rights of NAFTA country investors if they choose to expand their activities into the territory of another NAFTA Party (Article 1113.2). Thus, for example, a German-owned company operating in Canada that wishes to engage in business activities in the United States would be entitled to the same benefits of the NAFTA as would be a Canadian-owned company operating in the United States.

Article 1110 of NAFTA prohibits 'direct or indirect' expropriation of an investment unless certain criteria are met. These are: that the expropriation be for a public purpose; undertaken on a non-discriminatory basis; in accordance with due process; and with payment of full compensation at market value. As Jon Johnson notes, the NAFTA lacks a definition of 'expropriation'.[51] The American view of the meaning of expropriation is deeply influenced by the 'regulatory takings' doctrine in US domestic law, under which, in some circumstances, changes in general laws and regulations that affect the value of property may be considered as 'expropriation', thus triggering some right of compensation, even if title to property is in fact not taken.[52] While as Johnson correctly notes, in interpreting this Article of NAFTA 'the relevant body of law is international law and not the domestic law of any Party',[53] he also acknowledges that 'international jurisprudence on the subject of taking versus regulation is not nearly as well developed as

Canadian or U.S. jurisprudence.'[54] In 1997, a challenge to a Canadian environmental law was launched by a US investor under Article 1110 of NAFTA, claiming that a ban on the importation and inter-provincial transport of a gasoline additive which is a neurotoxin and also interferes with anti-pollution devices in automobiles (MMT). The investor, the Ethyl Corporation, which manufactures MMT, claimed that the ban amounted to an 'expropriation' and sought $350 million in damages but eventually settled the case for a lower amount.[55]

Ethyl was able to take the Canadian government to arbitration due to what is arguably the most innovative feature of the NAFTA investment provisions – the establishment of investor-state dispute settlement processes based on arbitration according to international arbitral rules, in particular those of ICSID, the International Convention on the Settlement of Investment Disputes. The NAFTA Parties consent to submission to arbitration of investment disputes under Chapter 11, at the request of the private investor itself. This makes NAFTA the first comprehensive international trade treaty[56] to provide to private parties direct access to dispute settlement as of right.

The Codes of Conduct approach: negotiating the rights and responsibilities of multinationals and sharing the costs and benefits of foreign investment

A third approach to international discipline of foreign investment measures is embodied in the various multilateral and bilateral Codes of Conduct that have been negotiated between states as well as between states and multinational firms themselves. The Codes of Conduct generally aim at striking an explicit balance between concerns of investors (compensation for expropriation, repatriation of earnings) and concerns of host countries about the conduct of foreign firms (whether corruption and bribery, avoidance of domestic regulatory and tax regimes, or unfair labour practices). In return for commitments of 'fair treatment' from the host country the firm commits itself to behave there as a good corporate citizen. Reflective of this approach are the 1976 OECD Guidelines for Multinational Enterprises[57] and the United Nations Draft Code on Transnational Corporations, as well as Guidelines for Investment developed by international business groups such as the International Chamber of Commerce for inclusion in negotiated agreements between multinational enterprises and individual countries.[58]

One attractive feature of the Codes and Guidelines is their inherently pluralistic character, involving an explicit balance of economic and a variety of political, ethical, and social concerns in the regulation of foreign investment. Another, often cited advantage with respect to some Codes and Guidelines is that they result from a multilateral process where there is a relative equality of bargaining power between large and small countries, and between the developed and developing world. This is particularly true of instruments developed within the UN system, including the UN Draft Code on Transnational Corporations.

Often, however, the language of these instruments reflects a high level of generality and diplomatic vagueness. They therefore often provide very limited guidance for the resolution of specific disputes or conflicts. For instance, an obligation to abstain from bribery is specific enough, but what of the obligation on multinationals by the OECD Guidelines 'To take fully into account established general policy objectives of the Member States in which they operate'? How would one go about determining whether this vague obligation had been sufficiently complied with by a particular foreign investor? Despite their voluntary character, and the vagueness of many of their prescriptions, the Guidelines have been credited with improving channels of communication between multinational corporations and host country governments (as well as local trade unions) in OECD countries. Implementation of the Guidelines is monitored by the OECD Committee on Investment and Multinational Enterprises (CIME), which however does not serve the function of settling specific disputes between multinationals and host governments. The CIME does issue 'clarifications' of the Guidelines, and these 'clarifications' are usually triggered by specific disputes which involve disagreement about the meaning of the Guidelines.[59]

In contrast to the Guidelines, two other OECD instruments contain strict substantive commitments by OECD Member States with respect to liberalization of investment measures. The OECD Code of Liberalisation of Capital Movements and the Code of Liberalisation of Current Invisibles contain specific disciplines on measures that impede the flow of capital between OECD Member States.[60] Cumulatively, these disciplines are viewed by the OECD as the equivalent of a right of establishment.[61] The Codes of Conduct are legally binding on OECD members. A commitment to National Treatment of foreign investors is contained in Article II of the OECD Declaration on International Investment and Multinational Enterprises (1976). Unlike the Codes, the Declaration is not binding in international law. Subsequent Decisions of the OECD Council (which *are* binding) have, however, required that Member States lodge with the OECD any exceptions to National Treatment in their national policies. Such exceptions are to be examined by the CIME at regular intervals (at least once every three years) with a view to 'making suitable proposals designed to assist Members to withdraw their exceptions'.[62] In addition, any member country 'which considers that its interests may be adversely affected by significant official incentives and disincentives to international direct investment' by another member country may demand consultations in the CIME 'to examine the possibility of reducing such effects to a minimum'.[63] The National Treatment commitment in the Declaration is subject to 'needs [of member states] to maintain public order, to protect their essential security interests and to fulfil commitments relating to international peace and security'.[64] Member States are, nevertheless, required, for transparency purposes, to notify to the OECD measures that may be justified on these terms.

In contrast to these OECD instruments, most multilateral investment codes, especially those concerned with investment relations between developed and developing countries, only become effective through explicit or implicit understandings between host countries and individual multinational corporations. This is the case for example, with the UN Draft Code on Transnational Corporations. Here, all the inherent difficulties of inequality of bargaining power between developing and developed countries – supposedly redressed in part through multilaterally-developed Codes – return as countries and firms bargain as to what sub-set of rights and obligations will be adopted and complied with in these explicit or implicit bilateral understandings.[65] At the same time, some observers have noted that the Codes of Conduct have succeeded in influencing the settlement of some investment disputes through private litigation, due to the willingness of judges and arbitrators to invoke them as interpretative aids or sources of guidance on matters of international economic policy.[66]

An attempt to remedy the problem of inequality of bargaining power, at least in part, is reflected in the Convention on the Settlement of Investment Disputes Between States and Nationals of Other States (ICSID).[67] ICSID provides a vehicle by which host countries, home countries and multinationals can agree to submit investment disputes to third-Party arbitration. ICSID responds both to the concerns of developed country foreign investors that they may not be fairly treated in the domestic legal processes of host countries and to the parallel concerns of the developing countries about investment disputes being adjudicated in, for example, American or British courts (as would often be provided in the choice of forum clause of an investment agreement, at the insistence of the developed country investor). While a variety of bilateral investment treaties and agreements between host countries and multinationals provide for arbitration through the ICSID process, it has rarely been resorted to in order to resolve investment disputes, for reasons that are not entirely clear.[68] ICSID's future may now, however, be somewhat brighter by virtue of the incorporation of the ICSID arbitration process into the dispute resolution provisions of the NAFTA Chapter on investment. Finally, inasmuch as principles in the codes end up being part of bilateral, reciprocal bargains that strike a balance of interests between investors and host countries, they present the same kind of danger as any managed trade, bilateral reciprocity-based approach to liberalization. The balance of interests struck may ignore effects of investment measures on third countries (e.g. import substitution effects) with a global welfare perspective being lost sight of entirely.

At the same time, these dangers may be somewhat attenuated through the development of general norms of international law with respect to compensation for the expropriation of the property of foreign nationals and extraterritoriality, as well as more specific regimes that deal with inter-jurisdictional dimensions of corporate taxation or antitrust policies. As discussed earlier in the chapter, these are matters that loom large in investment relations between states, but overlap with other international and domestic regimes not specific to the foreign investment context.

THE MULTILATERAL AGREEMENT ON INVESTMENT (MAI)[69]

Background

As noted earlier in this chapter, negotiations on investment in the Uruguay Round failed to yield a result even approaching a comprehensive set of rules on foreign direct investment, the Uruguay Round TRIMs Agreement being little more than an affirmation and modest strengthening of the status quo of the 1947 GATT, particularly as interpreted in the FIRA panel ruling. This failure of the Uruguay Round (at least from liberal trade perspective) was often attributed to the recalcitrance of developing countries. Not long after the completion of the Round, thinking in Western trade policy circles began to turn to alternative venues and mechanisms for achieving a set of comprehensive liberalizing commitments on investment. This thinking suggested that among an increasing number of countries there was (in the words of one advocate) 'a convergence of attitudes'[70] about the relationship of investment policy to the interests of the regulatory state, i.e. in the direction of economic liberalism. Among this expanding group of like-minded countries it would be easier to achieve agreement on far-reaching investment rules, beginning with already developed countries and soon extending to Newly Industrializing Countries, and then to others competing for foreign investment, which would not be able to afford not to go along. In 1995, thinking along these lines was reflected in an OECD Report to Ministers, which proposed the negotiation of a Multilateral Agreement on Investment within the OECD forum, but open to accession to non-OECD countries prepared to accept its strictures.[71] The timing and venue could partly be justified on the rather benign grounds that the existing OECD Liberalisation Codes (discussed earlier in this chapter) required renewal, and one could build from these existing instruments towards a comprehensive agreement. Various drafts were produced from 1996 through April 1997, all of them reflecting a general architecture (including National Treatment, MFN, and Dispute Settlement) but all of them also with gaps and alternative texts indicating important areas where consensus was elusive. We have chosen to base our analytical overview of the initiative on the last draft text, indicating its relationship to some of the earlier versions, and also where agreement remains elusive, and so the text is bracketed or alternative wording are presented, neither or none of which has yet attained a consensus. In early December 1998, the MAI negotiations were formally halted.

An Introduction to the draft MAI text

The draft Multilateral Agreement on Investment[72] has at its core the principle that governments must not discriminate against, or among, foreign investors from countries that have signed the Agreement – the obligations of National Treatment and Most Favoured Nation, respectively (Article III, 1–3). These obligations are subject to certain general exceptions, as well as reservations to be filed by individual signatories, which are in turn governed by the principles of standstill and (possibly) rollback. Standstill signifies the notion that any measures reserved may not be more restrictive of investment than existing measures. Rollback connotes the idea that, over time, countries' reservations will be subject to an on-going process of scrutiny, and (hopefully) negotiated removal.

The rules on performance requirements in the draft MAI are quite similar to those in NAFTA – minimum export, domestic content, and domestic sourcing requirements are all prohibited (it will be recalled that these last two kinds of requirements were already found to violate the GATT by the FIRA panel, an approach reinforced by the illustrative list in the Uruguay Round TRIMs Agreement). More controversially, especially in light of the potential adoption of this text by developing countries, the draft MAI contains a prohibition on technology transfer requirements as well, except as a competition law remedy. Initially, it was intended that the MAI would also cover, in addition to requirements, investment *incentives*, which would have been a major advance over NAFTA. However, disagreement on how to do this proved intractable, with some Parties objecting to any meaningful disciplines. Therefore, the draft MAI text is silent on these measures.

In some areas, such as movement of key personnel, the MAI goes appreciably beyond NAFTA in securing a liberal investment regime. In other areas, such as protection of investments against 'expropriation' and dispute settlement, there are important issues to resolve, issues which however are already present in the NAFTA in a not dissimilar form. Finally, the interface between MAI obligations and legitimate domestic policies in areas such as environment and culture – and the relationship between liberal investment and labour rights – was not resolved.

The movement of key personnel

One of the areas in which the MAI has made significant progress is with the movement of key personnel. To support the globalization of production, it is important for multinational enterprises be able freely to exchange managers and specialists between entities in different countries for efficient deployment of human capital. While the notion of key personnel is not always precisely defined, most OECD countries have national laws that contain special provisions relating to the temporary entry of this category of foreign personnel. Regulations affecting visas, residence and work permits remain part of the country's immigration policy, which is strongly influenced by the country's national political and economic considerations. However, a recent OECD survey points out that despite any potential immigration problems that may arise, most members recognize that the 'ability to quickly and easily move key personnel between countries is an important element of investment decisions, technology transfers as well as research and development activities of MNCs'.[73] Nevertheless, key employees are still put through tests and procedures which may adversely affect firms' competitiveness or investment flows. There have been some attempts – in other investment instruments – to address the issue of key personnel. For example, the NAFTA sets out commitments by its three members to facilitate on a reciprocal basis, temporary entry into their respective territories of business persons who are citizens of Canada, Mexico or the United States. As noted elsewhere in this book, each NAFTA country maintains its rights to protect the permanent employment base of its domestic labour force, to implement its own immigration policies and to protect the security of its own borders.[74] The NAFTA categories are rather broad – business visitors, traders, intra-company transferees and certain categories of professionals – which provides

NAFTA members with a great degree of flexibility. Thus, NAFTA has in many ways been able to strike the difficult balance of broadening the category of key personnel while maintaining sovereignty in the area of immigration. For example, the United States and Mexico have agreed to an annual numerical limit of 5,500 Mexican professionals being allowed to enter the United States.[75] While the provisions of this agreement are quite innovative and far reaching, the obvious limitation of this treaty is the number of its members. In devising the MAI, the OECD has borrowed ideas from this treaty and extended its breadth to encompass all of its members.

The MAI reflects a 'wider' and 'deeper' conception of the notion of key personnel. First, this agreement will apply to all of the Contracting Parties of the MAI.[76] Although, each Contracting Party has made a number of reservations,[77] there is an overall consensus on the importance and necessity of such a provision in the treaty. The agreement demonstrates respect for state sovereignty in that the key personnel provisions remain subject to 'the application of Contracting Parties' national laws, regulations and procedures affecting the entry, stay and work of natural persons'.[78] At the same, time, however, this agreement has broad application, with its scope extending to groups such as investors seeking to provide essential technical services to the operation of an enterprise to which the investor has committed,[79] employees working in the capacity of an executive, manger or specialist,[80] and spouses and minor children of these 'key personnel'.[81]

Investment protection

The OECD subcommittee studying the broad issue of investment protection, concluded quite early on in the negotiating process, that additional protection under an MAI may be of limited interest to MNCs unless it goes beyond the parameters established in existing instruments and domestic laws.[82] This includes finding a definition of investment expropriation that is as broad as possible, namely, 'all measures adopted by a state whether direct or indirect that have the effect of depriving the investor of its investment'.[83]

A major concern with this broad approach to expropriation is that it could conceivably lead to investor claims against signatory states where regulatory changes, whether in environment, safety, other areas, negatively affect the value of the investment. This could make regulatory reform extremely costly, but is an interpretation of the meaning of expropriation quite common in US domestic takings jurisprudence. As noted above, under a similar provision in NAFTA, a US investor obtained a multi-million dollar damages on the grounds that a ban on international and interprovincial trade in a substance that it produces in Canada constitutes 'expropriation'.[84] Language was apparently agreed, subsequent to the publication of the most recent working draft, to deal with this issue. Thus, it was proposed to include the following qualification in the Investor Protection provisions of the MAI: 'the MAI will not inhibit the exercise of the normal regulatory powers of government and the exercise of such powers will not amount to expropriation.'

Dispute settlement

The 24 April 1998 Draft of the MAI contains provisions on both state-to-state and investor-state dispute settlement (earlier versions had dealt only with investor-state processes).

In the case of state-to-state dispute settlement, the procedures are clearly modelled on the kind of dispute settlement reflected in trade agreements such as the WTO and NAFTA. If a Party has failed to resolve its dispute with another Party by consultations, after a 60-day period it may request the establishment of an arbitral panel, which is to be appointed by agreement between the Parties to the dispute within 30 days of a request for consultations. In the absence of agreement between the Parties, the Secretary General of the OECD may intervene to name the panellists. Other Member States ('third Parties') may make oral or written submissions to the panel, and are entitled to access to documents pertaining to the proceedings, with the exception of designated 'confidential and proprietary information'. The panels may also consult technical and scientific experts. Unlike the case with the WTO, arbitral panels are to be given explicit authority to grant pecuniary compensation or even restitution in kind (this last remedy being subject to the consent of the Party against which it is made). A right of appeal to another panel is also contemplated, on grounds such as corruption, that the panel manifestly exceeded its jurisdiction, or that 'the award has failed to state the reasons on which it is based'.

With respect to investor-state dispute settlement, MAI provides investors with a right to arbitration in accordance with various international commercial arbitration regimes, including ICSID (on which NAFTA investor-state dispute settlement is based), UNCITRAL, and the International Chamber of Commerce rules.

The arbitration rules that apply to investor-state dispute settlement under the MAI contemplate a secret process, where neither the pleadings, nor the hearing before the arbitrator, nor the reasons for decision are public unless permitted by both Parties. This practice might be entirely appropriate in the kind of commercial disputes between private Parties for which arbitration was originally designed, or even in investor-state contexts where what is at issue is, for example, the interpretation of a contract between the state and an enterprise. None the less, it seems highly questionable where arbitration is being used to interpret public international law, in whose meaning many Parties have a stake. Also, many of the issues surrounding interpretation of the MAI are likely to pertain to the relationship of investor rights to domestic public policies – thus there are important democratic concerns about the absence of publicity and transparency. The 24 April draft attempts to address this in several ways. First of all, third Party rights of intervention are created for investor-state dispute settlement – the arbitral tribunal is required to notify the Parties Group (the institution overseeing the MAI compromised of all its Member States) of its formation, and 'may give to any Contracting Party requesting it an opportunity to submit written views on the legal issues in dispute, provided that the proceedings are not unduly delayed thereby'. This being said, there is no requirement that such an opportunity be provided, and the Parties

Group take into account the views of the Parties to the dispute in deciding whether to grant it. Second, the arbitral award itself (which must contain reasons) is to be a publicly available document.

With respect to environmental and labour standards, the 24 April version of the MAI contains several alternative NAFTA-like provisions, both of which would commit the Parties to the MAI not to lower or derogate from environmental or labour standards in order to attract or retain foreign investment. The weakest versions would state the commitment in less than legally imperative language ('should' rather than 'shall') and would limit remedial action to consultations, as opposed to binding dispute settlement.

The General Exceptions are limited to national security and to monetary and foreign exchange policy-related measures. As will be discussed below, the fact that there is no general exception for legitimate health, safety, and environmental measures has been an important basis of the criticism of the draft MAI by various groups. In the 24 April draft, there is, however, with respect to the constraints on performance requirements, an environmental and health and safety exception modelled on Article XX(b) and (g) of the GATT (the text of these GATT provisions and the interpretation of them in dispute settlement is extensively discussed in Chapter 15 on trade and the environment). Finally, there is a limited Exception for taxation measures.

Public controversy over the MAI and the fate of the negotiations

On 28 April 1998, a decision was taken at the OECD Ministerial to suspend efforts to conclude the MAI as a binding investment treaty within a specific time frame: instead, OECD Ministers called for a period 'of assessment and further consultation between the negotiating Parties and with interested parts of their societies'.[85] For many observers, this signified the death of the MAI initiative, particularly given that May 1998 had been often cited as a target for actual approval by Ministers of a final text. It was decided subsequently to terminate negotiations and pursue the issue in the WTO forum.

By May 1997, agreement had been reached between the negotiators on many elements of the basic architecture of the MAI, including MFN and National Treatment. However, important differences of view between countries were surfacing with respect to the relationship of the MAI to environmental and labour standards and cultural policies.[86] As well, considerable disagreement existed concerning whether and how investment incentives should be disciplined (as noted above, the result is that incentives are simply not dealt with in the 24 April draft). At the same time, however, a vigorous public debate was beginning in OECD countries such as Canada, the United States and Australia concerning the impact of the MAI on the democratic regulatory state in general, and on environment, labour rights, and cultural protection more specifically. Canadian activist groups were at the forefront of bringing the MAI negotiations into public view. In January 1997, when no public version of the negotiating text was available, Canadian activists obtained a confidential version, and began circulating it to like-minded groups, using the Internet as an effective dissemination tool. In April 1997, accounts of the MAI began to appear in the popular press, and governments were placed on the defensive to justify their negotiating positions to the public at large.[87] Some of the groups in question had unsuccessfully challenged the Canada–US FTA and the NAFTA, often making grossly exaggerated and hypothetical claims about the damage likely to flow from these agreements to the social welfare state. With the MAI, their approach was shrewder and more careful. They linked a more general critique of globalization driven by corporate interests with a highly plausible analysis of specific provisions of the draft MAI, or omissions from it, as well as a critique of the way it was negotiated. While many groups took different and overlapping positions, the thrust of the overall attack is well expressed by Tony Clarke and Maude Barlow:

> We do not wish to leave the impression that we reject the idea of a global investment treaty. We are well aware that transnational investment flows have been accelerating at a rapid pace and that there is a need to establish some global rules. But the basic premise on which the draft versions of the MAI have been crafted is, in our view, largely flawed and one-sided. It expands the rights and powers of transnational corporations without imposing any corresponding obligations. Instead, the draft treaty places obligations squarely on the shoulders of governments, . . . Meanwhile the MAI says nothing about the rules that transnational corporations must follow to respect the economic, social, cultural, and environmental rights of citizens.[88]

However much the rhetorical tone of this attack may reflect an unjustified conspiratorial or even paranoid view of transnational corporations, its substance could be defended on the basis of concrete features of the negotiating texts (especially the earlier versions). While, as discussed in an earlier part of this chapter, the OECD had promulgated voluntary guidelines for the conduct of multinational enterprises, the MAI allowed such enterprises to sue governments, but not to be sued in kind based upon the breach of behavioural norms contained in the Guidelines. The secrecy surrounding the negotiations and the usual cloak and dagger behaviour by foreign ministries when faced by early enquiries about the course of the negotiations, gave prima-facie credence to a conspiratorial view of the whole undertaking. The fact, noted above, that the draft MAI did not contain an environmental or health and safety exception even comparable to that existing in the 1947 GATT lent credibility to the notion that only the interests of capital were reflected in the Agreement. With respect to the provisions on investor protection, a powerful legal case could be made that the definition of expropriation might extend to regulatory changes that affected the value of an investor's assets, thereby holding legitimate regulatory activity of national governments hostage to huge compensation payments to foreign investors.[89] The fact, noted above, that just such a claim had been made in the *Ethyl* case with respect to environmental regulations under a comparable provision of the Investment Chapter of NAFTA, lent an air of reality to this legal interpretation. The secrecy of investor-state dispute settlement (partly addressed, as noted above, in the very latest draft), combined with the secrecy of the process itself and the failure to provide any democratic control on corporate activity to make the case that there was a serious democratic deficit.

In the wake of this public controversy, a number of governments responded by indicating that their final approval of any MAI text would be conditional on the Agreement addressing concerns of this nature. In a valiant effort to preserve or regain momentum in the negotiations, the Chair of the negotiating group succeeded in putting together a package of proposed amendments on labour and environment, which has been annexed to the 24 April draft.[90] It is claimed that a 'large majority' of the negotiating Parties 'expressed support for the overall approach and believed that it could be a basis for future work' (footnote 1). Among the proposals is a provision that states: 'A Contracting Party may adopt, maintain or enforce any measure that it considers appropriate to ensure that investment activity is undertaken in a manner sensitive to health, safety or environmental concerns, provided such measures are consistent with this agreement' (Para. 3). This is a highly unsatisfactory provision, since the main issue is in fact that of exempting measures that *would otherwise be* in*consistent with the Agreement* – it is useless to state that Parties may take environmental measures consistent with the Agreement, since any measure consistent with the Agreement is in any case *ipso facto* permissible. A similar proposal with respect to labour rights or standards suffers from the same fundamental defect. With respect to expropriation, the language is slightly more satisfactory, stating that the MAI does not establish 'a new requirement that Parties pay compensation for losses which an investor or investment may incur through regulation, revenue-raising and normal activity in the public interest undertaken by governments' (para. 5). Even here, however, the qualification 'new' creates a difficulty – it refers to the existing international law baseline concerning expropriation, which is far from clear, and therefore does not shut the door to arguments that existing international law requires compensation for 'regulatory takings'.

While activist groups have recently been given credit or blamed (depending on the perspective of the observer) for 'killing' the MAI, informed sources close to the negotiations had been predicting failure long before a public debate on the draft MAI was provoked. As noted, the initiative to proceed with evolving investment rules in the OECD was based on the premise (often unstated) that developing countries had been the main obstacle to the achievement of a comprehensive TRIMs agreement in the Uruguay Round, and that without them consensus would be much easier to reach. In fact, before public controversy became intense, differences of views among OECD countries about culture and labour rights were already surfacing. As well, concern about the Helms–Burton legislation, led to a number of proposals concerning extraterritoriality and conflicting requirements, which would have surely met with total rejection by the United States. Further, the removal of investment incentives from the coverage of the Agreement represented a major disappointment for some negotiating Parties. The MAI negotiations are, in fact, an illustration of the fallacy that agreement is likely to be easier when negotiations are limited to a smaller group of countries, with supposedly more comparable economic systems, discussed in Chapter 5 of this book.

Of course part of the MAI strategy – an essential part – was that developing countries would be invited to accede to the MAI, and that those who were seeking to attract FDI would find themselves unable to afford not to. However, the rapid growth in FDI, including and especially inflows to developing countries, cited earlier in this chapter shows that investor confidence is not dependent upon adhesion to this kind of agreement. Moreover, the notion of simply signing up these countries betrays a naïve view of the accession process, as is well illustrated by attempts to 'extend' NAFTA to other countries in Central and Latin America. In any Agreement such as the MAI, any accession is likely to involve country-specific reservations, that will potentially change the balance of concessions in the overall agreement. Also, the proposed accession of a country to this kind of agreement is unlikely to take place without affected economic and other interests raising issues about the commercial policy as well as environmental and labour rights performance of the country in question.

Another major difficulty with the MAI as a self-standing treaty, noted even by some of the more insightful and cautious supporters of global investment rules, such as Pierre Sauve and Ed Graham, is the relationship of such a Treaty to overlapping existing multilateral rules as reflected in the GATT, and the WTO TRIMs, Services, and Intellectual Property Agreements. This raises serious issues concerning the respective jurisdiction of MAI and WTO (and perhaps NAFTA) dispute-settlement bodies, in addition to substantive and temporal issues with respect to the applicability of provisions of the various Agreements and their interaction. Effort is made in the draft MAI text to be sensitive to these problems, but they are far from being resolved. In fact, at the outset an MAI separate from multilateral rules would create considerable uncertainty.

Against the drawbacks of the MAI, supporting governments have had few decisive arguments to make on the positive side. First of all, in an environment where, as already noted, FDI is growing at a rapid pace (much more rapidly than average global economic growth generally) the idea that the gains from FDI crucially depend on a new agreement would seem hard to sustain. Second, since most of the OECD countries already conform in large measure to the main disciplines of the MAI (and since in sensitive areas they will continue to reserve many measures) the specific market-opening benefits of the Agreement, absent developing countries accession, are quite limited. Those developing countries likely to accede have already significantly liberalized their investment regimes, at least to the extent necessary to attract investment and/or satisfy the demands of the IMF and World Bank.

CONCLUSION

In light of all these considerations, in our view, it makes sense to place the evolution of investment rules squarely in the WTO forum, as an issue for the next negotiating 'round'. The MAI text can be simply regarded as useful preliminary work for a genuinely multilateral negotiation – here, as noted in Chapters 10 and 11 on these subjects in this book, agriculture and services are precedents to bear in mind; in both cases much preliminary conceptual and technical work was done at the OECD, which then was channelled into the Uruguay Round negotiations. We think that the starting point for such negotiations might be agreement on the following:

1 The basic architecture of an investment agreement must include MFN, National Treatment, and Transparency obligations (the MAI process produced a broad consensus on this), subject to appropriate exceptions and limitations to protect legitimate regulatory interests, including labour and the environment.
2 Disciplines on incentives as well as performance requirements should be subject to negotiation, but the aim should be a balanced set of constraints, that reflects legitimate arguments that some kinds of measures may be appropriate for the situations of some countries, including measures to promote technology transfer.
3 As among the OECD countries, those provisions of the draft MAI text that have now attracted consensus should be applied as 'soft law', the equivalent of a non-binding code (as Daniel Schwanen of Canada's C.D. Howe Institute has recently suggested).
4 In any future agreement, if private investors are to have the benefit of dispute settlement through binding arbitration, they should have to agree to abide by the investor conduct rules of the OECD Guidelines on Multinational Enterprises or some other instrument of this character; this reflects the principle of reciprocal rights and responsibilities for transnational corporations of so much concern to critics of the MAI. On the other hand, a corporation would remain free not to accept these responsibilities, as long as it did not wish a direct right of action, and was willing to rely on traditional state-to-state dispute settlement to protect its interests under a WTO investment agreement.

It is inevitable that differences between nations will remain about the balance between values of economic efficiency, and competing or sometimes competing, considerations in some sensitive sectors, like cultural industries. A policy dialogue should begin now, before any negotiations, on the alternatives to investment restrictions that are available to governments to vindicate these considerations, and the relative desirability of various policy instruments. In the end, some countries may still consider it necessary to reserve investment measures in this area, but a sense that there are often better ways of achieving these legitimate public goals could better inform debate on these issues in many countries.

14 Trade and developing countries

INTRODUCTION

Developing countries[1] currently account for about a quarter of world exports, and about the same percentage of world imports.[2] Although some developing countries were included within GATT from the outset,[3] they had a marginal influence on the original Bretton Woods negotiations.[4] By the 1960s, developing countries had come to predominate numerically in the GATT, and during the 1960s and 1970s their share of world trade, and particularly of exports grew rapidly, although in this respect the performance of some developing countries was vastly superior to that of others.[5] Indeed, there is substantial heterogeneity amongst developing countries including differences in size, levels of development, levels of indebtedness, composition of trade, degree of concentration of trading relationships, etc.[6] Throughout this period, developing countries complained that their influence on the design and functioning of the GATT rules remained marginal, and increasingly pressed demands for more preferential treatment within GATT, as well as attempting to evolve other fora for the creation of rules on trade (particularly, UNCTAD – the United Nations Conference on Trade and Development) where they could wield greater influence.

While some developing countries continued through the 1970s to experience considerable growth, particularly those with more open or outward-oriented trade policies, the strategy that was adopted by most LDCs and that predominated in the development literature at the time – import substitution and protection of infant industries – yielded disappointing results.[7] The conclusion most often drawn was that the rules of the game of international trade and finance were so heavily skewed to the disadvantage of the LDCs that a radically new strategy was necessary, based upon a fundamental redistribution of wealth and opportunities between North and South. Developed in UN fora such as UNCTAD, the strategy was termed the New International Economic Order (NIEO).[8] While the NIEO remained at the level of ideology or at most the 'soft law' of UN resolutions, the developed countries did, at a practical level, respond to these pressures by granting further tariff preferences to developing countries on a non-reciprocal but also a non-binding basis (the Generalized System of Preferences). At the same time the availability of recycled petrodollars promised to give the strategy of protected, state-assisted rapid industrialization a new lease on life.

The further failure of this strategy, combined with the second oil shock and recession in the developed world (which produced high interest rates and low demand for developing country exports), led to the debt crisis of the early 1980s. The rescheduling of loans to developing countries was premised upon the undertaking of domestic reforms, including price liberalization, movement towards convertible currency, and unilateral trade liberalization. Thus, many developing countries moved towards an outward-oriented, export-driven approach to development and growth.[9] While these policy shifts can be in part understood as imposed from the outside through institutions like the IMF as a price for cooperation by the North in solving the debt crisis, they also reflect increasing recognition of the extraordinary success enjoyed by the Asian NICs (newly industrializing countries) through an export-oriented, as opposed to import-substitution-based, strategy for growth. They also may reflect, or at least be reinforced by, the intellectual and political decline of Marxism, which in its Leninist/centralist and neo-Marxist variants was an important ideological source of resistance to economic liberalism.[10]

The treatment of developing countries in the GATT that emerged during the first few decades after the General Agreement came into force reflects what Bela Balassa has aptly termed a 'Faustian bargain' between the North and the South.[11] On the one hand, developing countries were granted significant exemptions from GATT disciplines, so as to allow them considerable scope to adopt import-substitution, infant-industry-protection strategies of development. Eventually, as well, developing countries were granted preferential tariff concessions or complete removal of tariffs on a non-binding basis, with respect particularly to raw materials. On the other hand, with respect to exports that could immediately figure in an export-led growth strategy, such as textiles, light manufactures, and processed agricultural products, developed countries maintained extremely high trade barriers, including high tariff rates, and also in the case of textiles, quantitative restrictions under a special GATT-exempt arrangement that came to be known as the Multi-Fibre Arrangement. Thus, although it is fashionable to blame leftist theories of development economics and the influence of Soviet bloc central planning approaches for the protectionist follies of the developing world in this epoch, the treatment of developing countries in the Western-dominated global trading order made inward-oriented policies easy, while it set up obstacles to export-led growth.

We now proceed to examine in some detail the nature of this treatment.

THE LEGAL AND INSTITUTIONAL FRAMEWORK FOR DEVELOPING COUNTRY TRADE

The pre-Uruguay Round GATT

Article I

Article I, which establishes the MFN (Most Favoured Nation) principle, nevertheless allows for the *continuation* of preferential tariff rates – i.e. tariffs below the bound MFN rate negotiated within the framework of the GATT – between countries that shared a common sovereignty before the Second World War, and also between countries that formed part of the Ottoman Empire until the settlement at Versailles that ended the First World War. Under the first category, preferences given by (ex-colonial) powers such as Britain, France, and Spain to their former colonies are permitted, and this would have included a substantial part of trade between developed and developing countries at the time the GATT was created. The margin of preference, however, cannot exceed that which existed between the MFN rates and the preferential rates in question at the time of entry into force of the GATT (1947). Thus, further preferential treatment has required an explicit GATT waiver from the MFN obligations of Article I.

Quantitative restrictions (Articles XI, XII, XIII, XVIII)

As discussed in earlier chapters, Article XI of the General Agreement contains a general prohibition on quantitative restrictions on imports and exports, subject to a range of exceptions. The balance of payments exceptions defined in Articles XII and XIII were not especially aimed at the needs of developing countries – at the beginning of the post-war era, very few of the *developed* countries possessed stable, or even convertible currencies.[12] Nevertheless, Article XII does contemplate that a Contracting Party may assert an exception to Article XI on balance of payments grounds, where its balance of payments difficulties are due to 'domestic policies directed towards the achievement and maintenance of full and productive employment or towards the development of economic resources' (XII:3(d)). This has the effect of immunizing a developing country from the claim that, since its balance of payments crisis is induced or prolonged by its own illiberal or distortive domestic policies, the appropriate solution is to change those policies rather than to increase trade protection.

Article XVIII, in the form that emerged after the 1954–5 review of the General Agreement, contains much more explicit recognition for development-based exceptions from GATT strictures. Article XVIII begins with a lengthy preamble that states the agreement of the Contracting Parties that developing countries[13]

> should enjoy additional facilities to enable them (a) to maintain sufficient flexibility in their tariff structure to be able to grant the tariff protection required for the establishment of a particular industry and (b) to apply quantitative restrictions for balance of payments purposes which take full account of the continued high level of demand for imports likely to be generated by their programmes of economic development' (XVIII:2).

This statement is notable for its incorporation within the terms of the GATT itself of the infant industry protection view of economic development – the notion that the goal of 'establishment of a particular industry' is an appropriate rationale for protection where pursued by a developing country.

The preamble to Article XVIII is followed by Sections A, B and C, which set out the specifics of the 'additional facilities' to be granted to developing countries. Section A provides that a developing country may, where it wishes 'to promote the establishment of a particular industry', reopen negotiations on bound tariffs with any Contracting Party 'with which such concession was initially negotiated' (A 7(a)). It is foreseen that the developing country would offer compensation for the withdrawal or modification of a concession, perhaps in the form of a reduction of tariffs on other products. If, despite an offer of adequate compensation, the developed Contracting Party or Parties in question refuse(s) to allow the concession to be withdrawn or modified, the developing country can apply to the GATT Council for the right to proceed unilaterally. Section B reiterates but also expands the balance of payments exceptions to Article XI strictures already contained in Article XII. For instance, developing countries may impose quantitative restrictions for balance of payments purposes on a discriminatory basis, i.e. 'in such a way as to give priority to the importation of those products which are more essential in the light of its policy of economic development' (XVIII(B):10).

Section C applies where a developing country 'finds that governmental assistance is required to promote the establishment of a particular industry with a view to raising the standard of living of its people' (XVIII(C):13). If the developing country is experiencing difficulties in the achievement of this goal, it may notify the GATT Council of the difficulties and any GATT-inconsistent measure with respect to imports that may be indicated. Upon notification, the GATT Council may, within 30 days, either request consultations with the developing country in question, or allow it to proceed with measures that would otherwise be in contravention of provisions of the General Agreement. There are two limits on this relief from GATT strictures: first, where the measures in question affect products for which there are already tariff bindings, the developing country must first consult with, and seek the consent of, the Contracting Party with whom the initial concession was negotiated; second, no deviation from Articles I, II and XIII of the General Agreement is permitted under Section C. Hence, whatever import-restricting measures are adopted pursuant to Section C must be implemented on a non-discriminatory basis.

In practice, as is described in detail by Hudec,[14] Article XVIII provided a basis for the granting of sweeping exemptions from GATT strictures to many developing countries, usually with a view to import substitution and protection of infant industries. The GATT Council routinely accepted such deviations from the general provisions of the GATT, and without insisting on the consultation requirements and other formal criteria embodied in Article XVIII. The explanation for this laxity is to be found less in development theory than in the fact that developed countries simply did not feel threatened by infant industries in developing countries. These industries posed little threat to developed country dominance in the sectors concerned, both in home markets and third-country markets. In more recent years, there has been increased pressure for scrutiny of developing country trade practices, in part because a number of the larger and relatively more prosperous developing countries have come to be seen as significant potential markets for developed country exports, whether goods, services, or technology. This has been reflected to a large extent in US pressure to include disciplines on services and intellectual property in the Uruguay Round (the implications for developing countries are discussed below) but also in demands that developing countries' Article XVIII exemptions be re-examined and eliminated wherever not justified, or no longer justified, by the wording of the GATT.[15]

Part IV

Part IV of the General Agreement, entitled 'Trade and Development', was added in 1965, in response to the increasingly insistent demands of developing countries as they emerged through UNCTAD, which had been formally established in 1964.[16] Unlike Article XVIII, which had as its focus the relaxation of GATT strictures to enable developing countries to pursue inward-looking growth policies based on protection and promotion of infant industries, Part IV concerns the access of developing countries to developed country markets, and therefore appears to at least implicitly endorse the theory of export-led growth. Hence, the preambular section of Part IV states (in part): 'the export earnings of the less-developed contracting parties can play a vital part in their economic development' (Part IV: Article XXXVI:1(b)).

Nevertheless, the persistence of the inward-looking approach is reflected in the statement that 'the developed contracting parties do not expect reciprocity for commitments made by them in trade negotiations to reduce or remove tariffs and other barriers to the trade of less-developed countries' (Part IV: Article XXXVI:8). This principle of non-reciprocity, along with special dispensations for import substitution policies, are often referred to as 'special and differential status' for developing countries. The clear implication is that export-led growth is consistent with, and indeed should go hand in hand with, protection of developing countries' domestic markets – a mercantilist view in profound tension with the neo-classical perspective that protectionism which distorts domestic price mechanisms and insulates industries from international competition is likely to frustrate the development of viable export industries.[17]

A pervasive characteristic of the substantive provisions of Part IV is that they lack the clearly binding or obligatory character of most provisions of the General Agreement. Thus the developed countries 'shall to the fullest extent possible – that is, except when compelling reasons, which may include legal reasons, make it impossible – give effect' to commitments to reduce and eliminate trade barriers with respect to 'products currently or potentially of particular export interest to less-developed countries' (Part IV: Article XXXVII:1(a)). In other instances, developed countries are 'to make every effort' to, *inter alia*, 'give active consideration to the adoption of other measures designed to provide greater scope for the development of imports from less-developed countries' (Part IV: Article XXXVII:3(b)). The only remedy specified in Part IV where developed countries are not living up to these loosely-worded commitments is the possibility of a developing country requesting consultations either with individual developed countries or in the GATT Council (Part IV: Article XXXVII:2).

Other GATT provisions

The Tokyo Round Codes

Serious tensions arose between developed and developing countries in the GATT due to the refusal of the United States to grant the benefit of the Tokyo Round GATT Subsidies and Antidumping Codes to countries that had not signed the Codes, which included most developing countries. In the 1960s, India had obtained a legal ruling from the GATT Secretariat that MFN obligations applied to the Kennedy Round Antidumping Code, thereby obliging the United States to provide the benefits of the Code to non-signatories.[18] In the Tokyo Round, the United States pressed for an explicit conditional MFN approach to the revised Antidumping Code and the new Subsidies Code. The resultant Codes, on their face, required that benefits only be extended to signatories. However, the Codes did provide some special treatment for developing countries. In the case of the Antidumping Code this only amounted to a general provision (Article 13) requiring Parties to explore 'possibilities of constructive remedies provided for by this Code [i.e. price undertakings]' before 'applying antidumping duties where they would affect the essential interests of developing countries'. This supposed special consideration for developing countries has not been translated into concrete provisions in the domestic trade remedy law of major developed nations. In the case of the Subsidies Code, developing countries were exempted from the general ban on export subsidies, provided that these subsidies are not 'used in a manner which causes serious prejudice to the trade or production of another signatory' (Part III: Article 14(2)(3)). It was, however, an open legal question whether this exemption only applied to the export subsidies provisions of the Code (Article 9) itself, or whether it extended by implication to the restrictions on export subsidies in Article XVI of the General Agreement. The latter view seems to be more plausible, since the entire Subsidies Code could be seen as an elaboration and detailed application of the subsidies provisions of the General Agreement.

In addition, the Code stated that with respect to *any* subsidy granted by a developing country signatory (i.e. either export or domestic) no action may be taken under the dispute resolution provisions of the Code, unless the subsidy had nullified or impaired a tariff concession 'or other obligations under the General Agreement' (Article 14(7)). Nullification and impairment was defined narrowly as displacement of imports into the subsidizing country or 'injury to domestic industry in the importing market of a signatory'. However, this provision was of little practical significance, since it only applied to subsidies actions under the multilateral dispute resolution process provided for in the Code, and did not constrain the unilateral application of countervailing duties.

Dispute settlement

The dispute settlement procedures of the GATT have rarely been invoked either by or against developing countries. From 1947 to 1986 only 12.5% of GATT complaints were initiated by LDCs and LDCs were respondents in only 15% of the cases.[19] One reason for this state of affairs may be the consequences (perceived or real) of power imbalances between developed and developing countries. The GATT enforcement mechanism is ultimately based on retaliation as the sanction of last resort – a sanction that most developing countries would be hard-put to apply to developed countries. Since few developing countries represent, individually, major export markets for developed countries, withdrawal of concessions would not normally be a very powerful sanction. On the other hand, where developed countries wish to induce developing countries to comply with trade rules, they possess very effective leverage, including development aid and GSP preferences. In addition, because of the power imbalance, unilateral measures can often be applied to developing countries with relative impunity. Significantly, as developing countries acquire greater political and economic power and influence they do tend increasingly to be taken to the GATT; hence, in the last few years NICs such as Korea and Chile have been the subject of GATT complaints.[20]

The Generalized System of Preferences and the Lomé Convention

Despite the absence of self-contained and self-activating 'hard' legal obligations in Part IV, it set the scene for the granting of non-reciprocal trade preferences to developing countries through mechanisms outside the GATT. The two main mechanisms are the Generalized System of Preferences and the Lomé Convention. The GSP was initiated under the auspices of UNCTAD in 1968. The intent was to build on existing colonial preferences which (as discussed above) had been grandfathered in the GATT MFN requirement – no longer would only the ex-colonial powers grant such preferences and the ex-colonies be their only recipients (hence the expression 'generalized'). Each developed country would be free to grant or not grant such preferences as it chose. And the preferences are not 'bound' in the GATT – therefore they may be removed or modified at any time. A 'waiver' – pursuant to Article XXV of the GATT – was granted in 1971 to permit the derogation from Article 1 MFN obligations that would be needed to introduce new preferences. However, the GATT waiver did require that each Contracting Party's GSP programme benefit developing countries generally – a potential constraint on open-ended discrimination between developing countries and the use of the GSP to strike bilateral side-deals with particular developing countries.[21]

In the case of the European Union, preferences have been embodied in the Lomé Convention which first came into force in 1975, and has been renewed and revised several times since.[22] While containing non-reciprocal tariff preferences, these agreements also deal with a wide-ranging agenda for commercial cooperation between the EU and some 65 developing countries (almost all of them ex-colonies of Britain or France).[23] Since the preferences contained therein do not benefit all developing countries, it might be argued that in principle they do not conform with the terms of the GATT waiver. However, it has been suggested that the Lomé system could be viewed as a free trade area or customs union, and therefore consistent with the GATT even absent a waiver, provided that it conforms to the provisions of Article XXIV:5.

A recent WTO Appellate Body decision 'dealt a severe blow to the European Union's system for regulating the import of bananas in a way that restricts access for Latin American bananas in favour of fruit from its Member States' former colonies'.[24] The complaint, initiated by a coalition of Latin American countries and the United States, alleged that the EU's regime for the import, sale and distribution of bananas was inconsistent with a number of GATT provisions, as well as the Import Licensing Agreement, the Agreement on Agriculture, the TRIMs Agreement and the GATS.[25] In May 1997 the panel ruled in favour of the coalition, finding aspects of the EU regime inconsistent with the GATT. The EU subsequently appealed the decision. The Appellate Body largely upheld the findings of the panel, but tightened 'the original ruling in … ways that strengthened the hand of the opponents of the EU regime.'[26] The Appellate Body found that the Lomé waiver did not allow the EU to derogate from its obligations of non-discrimination in the administration of quantitative restrictions under Article XIII or to expand historical deviations from Article I (MFN) obligations. Thus, in the case of bananas at least, the Lomé waiver had limited protective effect on the EU's preferential trading arrangements.

In contrast to the European Union, the United States and other developed countries such as Canada and Australia have embodied trade preferences for developing countries in domestic customs legislation rather than in agreements with the developing countries themselves. Given the importance of the United States as a market for developing country exports, the American GSP system has loomed large in debates about the desirability of the GSP approach to promoting export-led growth in developing countries. The United States initially opposed the granting of preferences to developing countries, but finally established its own GSP system in the mid-1970s.[27]

The present version of this system is found in the Trade Act of 1974, as amended in 1984. The Act contains a number of provisions that open the door to discrimination between different developing countries, and to use of the threat of withdrawing GSP status as a political and economic weapon. For instance, the Act gives the US President authority to waive GSP status if the country in question fails to provide 'reasonable access to its markets and to its commodities' and if it does not afford 'adequate and effective protection of intellectual property rights'.[28] In addition, the Act provides for 'graduation' of developing countries from GSP status once they reach a certain level of per capita GDP ($US8,500 in 1984, indexed to a formula based on half the annual US growth rate).[29] This threshold is relatively high, but some of the most prosperous NICs are now beginning to pass it.[30] As well, detailed rules exist for removal of preferences on particular products, even where a country does not meet the threshold for complete graduation. A preference will be removed when a developing country has become a major world exporter of a product – arguably a highly perverse approach that punishes the most successful LDC exporters (i.e. those who are most competitive in developed country markets).[31] This partial graduation has occurred with respect to particular exports of more than a dozen LDCs.

Aside from the issue of graduation, and the obvious drawbacks of trade preferences that are non-binding and that can be used as political and commercial leverage by developed countries, there is a more general question to be raised about whether, in fact, the kinds of preferences actually granted have done much to assist export growth in the developing world. As Balassa suggests, the GSP itself excludes 'product groups of principal interest to developing countries such as steel, textiles,[32] clothing, and shoes'.[33] In addition, trade remedy laws (countervail and antidumping) have frequently been used against developing countries, thereby clawing back much (and in some cases, all) of the benefits provided by tariff preferences – in recent years, for instance, the number of antidumping cases initiated by the United States and the European Union against developing countries has often equalled or even exceeded the number of cases against developed country exporters.[34]

Furthermore, preferences do not appear to have responded adequately to developing countries' concerns about 'tariff escalation'. Tariff escalation denotes the tendency for developed countries to impose very low tariffs on imports of raw materials and much higher tariff rates on processed or finished products that are made from those raw materials. This practice makes it very easy for developing countries to export raw materials in an unprocessed state and much more difficult to export products that have a significant value-added component. The escalation effect occurs because while developed country producers of the processed or finished products have access to raw materials at almost the same price as developing country producers (due to the low tariffs on the raw materials), they also have a protected market against the developing country producers by virtue of the significant tariff imposed on the processed or finished products in question. The end result is to discourage export-driven strategies of moving up the value chain from the extraction of raw materials to increasingly sophisticated processing industries. Balassa found that, even on the basis of GSP and Lomé preferences, effective protection afforded against higher value-added products from developing countries due to tariff escalation ranged from three to almost nine times the applicable nominal tariffs.[35]

More generally, as MFN tariff rates have fallen in successive rounds of GATT negotiations the value of the GSP to developing countries has inevitably eroded. As well, GSP arrangements have often contained 'safeguard' provisions, allowing re-imposition of higher tariffs or other import restrictions where a surge of developing country imports threatens developed-country domestic producers.

The Multi-Fibre Arrangement (MFA)

The MFA is an agreement between nine importing developed country signatories (including the EU) and 31 exporting developing countries. It provides a framework for Voluntary Export Restraints (VERs), primarily quotas, limiting developing country exports of textiles and clothing to the nine developed country signatories. The MFA was formally established in 1974. It superseded two earlier agreements, the Short- and Long-term Arrangements, that applied to a far narrower range of developing country exports.[36]

The Short-term Arrangement on cotton textiles was in force from 1961 to 1962, and had been negotiated at the initiative of the Kennedy Administration. It was replaced in 1962 with the Long-term Arrangement Regarding International Trade in Cotton Textiles. It is important to note that these Arrangements did not initiate restrictive trade practices with respect to these sectors, which had existed since the end of the Second World War, particularly in the Western European countries.[37] Indeed, at the beginning these Arrangements held the promise of an orderly codification of restrictions with a view to their eventual phase-out, as developed country producers adjusted to new competitive realities through technological innovation and gradual labour shedding.[38]

In the 1970s, however, competitive pressure from the NICs in particular became much more intense than had previously been experienced, and the MFA became a convenient vehicle to respond to these pressures through further restricting trade in these sectors with the use of special safeguards, VERs and quotas.[39] In addition, the incorporation of protectionism in a formal interstate agreement disguised to some extent the GATT-inconsistency of most of the measures in question, which were discriminatory quantitative restrictions, in violation of both Articles I and XI of the General Agreement. Jackson goes so far as to suggest that 'the countries who have accepted the textile or multifibre arrangements have arguably partially "waived" their GATT rights'.[40] In our view, this claim is highly suspect, because (as Jackson himself acknowledges) developing countries have accepted these arrangements only under the threat of even more restrictive GATT-inconsistent measures.

It is sometimes argued that developing countries are nevertheless protected by the MFA because the right to impose import restrictions is limited to cases where 'real risks of market disruption' exist in the import-restricting country (Article 4), and also because the MFA provides for gradual expansion of quotas, as well as exemptions for new entrants in the market and small suppliers. However, as Dao remarks, despite the existence of a monitoring mechanism (the Textiles Surveillance Body or TSB), 'importing countries are reluctant to adhere to the Arrangement and often take additional restrictive measures beyond the Arrangement'.[41]

The fundamental reality is that developing countries suffer very large losses from import restrictions imposed by developed countries in these sectors. It has been estimated that if *all* trade restrictions on LDC textile and clothing imports were lifted by the EU, Japan and the United States, the gains to LDCs 'would be no less than 50.8 per cent of total possible gains related to all trade'.[42] It has been further estimated that if all import restrictions were removed, developing country textile exports would increase by about 50% and clothing exports by 128.9%.[43]

The last extension of the MFA, which occurred in 1986, further sanctified the increasing restrictiveness of developing country measures. Thus, coverage was extended to include new types of fibres and developed countries gained new rights to take unilateral measures against developing country imports. Developing countries gained very little, save a statement that the final objective of the Parties was eventual submission of trade in textiles to GATT strictures and some strengthening of the (in any case little used and little heeded) TSB.[44]

The Uruguay Round Final Act contains an ambitious plan for sweeping reform and the eventual phasing out of the MFA, which is described in detail in a later section of this chapter.

UNCTAD (The United Nations Conference on Trade and Development)

UNCTAD was founded in 1964 as a periodic conference of all UN members, with an ongoing institutional framework (the Secretariat). The intent was to establish a forum on trade where developing countries would find themselves less marginalized in the decision-making process than was thought to be the case with the GATT.[45] Under the stewardship of Raoul Prebisch, an Argentinian economist, UNCTAD became a leading forum for the elaboration of the 'import-substitution', protectionist view of economic development in the Third World.

According to Krueger,[46] this view of development was predicated on the following premises: First, developing economies production structures were heavily oriented towards primary commodity production and many observers attributed the low living standards in developing countries to dependence on primary commodity production and export. Second, if developing countries were to adopt policies of free trade, their comparative advantage would forever lie in primary commodity production. Third, both the global income and price elasticities of demand for primary commodities was low, so that expansion of primary commodity production would simply depress prices ('immiserizing growth'). Fourth, the labour force in developing countries, predominantly engaged in agricultural activities, had a marginal product of labour that was negligible, zero, or even negative. Thus, it was explicitly or implicitly assumed that labour was a free good while capital was the scarce factor of production. Fifth, capital accumulation was crucial for growth and in early stages of development this occurs only with the importation of capital goods. Since it was expected that the demand for capital goods imports and imports of other products used in the production process would grow rapidly while foreign exchange earnings would not, it appeared that growth could follow only if domestic production of import-competing goods could expand rapidly. Sixth, there was very little response to price incentives in developing countries, especially in the agricultural sector: peasants were traditional in their behaviour and there were structural problems within the economy. Thus, most developing countries chose to maintain high fixed nominal exchange rates which reflected the perception that there was little response to prices and that maintaining such exchange rates taxed agricultural exports while simultaneously subsidizing capital goods imports.

At times, the developing countries appeared to be prepared to withdraw from

GATT and to utilize UNCTAD as a forum for evolving an alternative legal order for world trade.[47] However, this threat never materialized, and instead UNCTAD became an instrument for applying pressure on developed countries to liberalize trade unilaterally with developing countries (while permitting developing countries themselves wide exemptions from GATT strictures in order to sustain import-substitution-based growth policies, such as protection of infant industries). The main product of UNCTAD has been the non-law or at most 'soft law' of UN Resolutions. In the 1970s and early 1980s, UNCTAD sought to develop a New International Economic Order, a grandiose project aimed at a fundamental restructuring of North–South relations. In fact, the NIEO was largely a recasting of the old demands for unilateral developed country trade liberalization in a new ideological language – that of the moral imperative of redistribution of wealth from developed to developing countries.[48]

The Global System of Trade Preferences

A much more concrete initiative of UNCTAD is the Global System of Trade Preferences (GSTP). Unlike the GSP, this is a system of preferences negotiated between, and applicable to, trade among developing countries themselves. It reflects UNCTAD's enthusiasm for the promotion of South–South trade as a response to supposed developed country domination of the rules and terms of North–South trade. In fact, however, South–South trade continues to account for a very small percentage of world trade (about 7%, holding constant through much of the 1980s).[49]

The GSTP developed from the 1971 GATT 'Protocol Relating to Trade Negotiations Among Developing Countries', which obtained an explicit Article XXV waiver to allow preferences in contravention of the Article I MFN requirement.[50] Despite official UNCTAD ideology that South–South preferences should reflect the relative economic development needs of the various developing countries, it appears that GATT-type reciprocity or trading of concessions on the basis of mutual self-interest dominated the most recent (1988) negotiations on GSTP preferences. The resulting agreement embodies 1,300 tariff concessions, and has been signed by 46 developing countries.[51]

With some exceptions, the GSTP provides for an MFN principle to apply with respect to concessions negotiated between the signatories. It appears, however, that the legal text of the GSTP permits the signatories, if they so desire, to confer the same preferences, or even more preferential treatment on *non-signatories*, even where this may erode the value of concessions to signatories. This latitude was made necessary by the overlapping of the GSTP with various South–South regional trade agreements and customs unions.[52]

The GSTP contains a provision that obligates signatories not to undermine concessions negotiated in the GSTP through the application of any charge or measure restricting commerce other than those existing prior thereto, with exceptions for countervailing and antidumping duties, border tax adjustments, and balance of payments measures (Article 10).

International Commodity Agreements and export earnings stabilization

Given the prominence of concerns about deteriorating terms of trade (particularly as related to primary commodities) in the UNCTAD view of trade and development, it is not surprising that a major thrust of UNCTAD's work has been in the area of commodity price stabilization. Under the auspices of UNCTAD's Integrated Programme for Commodities, established in 1976, numerous International Commodity Agreements (ICAs) were struck, including cocoa, coffee, copper, cotton, and tin, among other commodities. These Agreements are in essence producers' cartels. Each producer country that is a member of the Agreement is assigned an export quota, with the global total of such quotas determined in such a way as to sustain world prices at a level acceptable to the membership. Some of the ICAs also provide for Stabilization Funds that purchase surplus production at times of oversupply with a view to selling when there are shortages.

The ICAs have not been particularly successful at sustaining commodity prices at the desired levels. The core difficulty is that which is endemic to many forms of cartelization: the tendency of individual members to 'cheat' on the supply constraints.[53] As well, a cartel can only function effectively if all or almost all the producers of the commodity in question are members, and this has not been the case with a number of the ICAs.[54]

In addition to ICAs, UNCTAD has also sought to establish a system of export earnings compensation, which would involve loans or grants to developing countries when their export earnings decline below a certain level due to supply and price fluctuations with respect to primary commodities. A limited facility for export earnings compensation, called the STABEX, exists under the Lomé Convention but applies only to exports of a limited number of agricultural commodities to the EU.

The UNCTAD scheme involved the creation of a Common Fund that would apparently finance both the Stabilization Funds of individual ICAs (i.e. funds for purchase of buffer stocks or surpluses) as well as export earnings compensation. However, although first proposed in 1976, the Common Fund has yet to become a reality. The United States has consistently refused to participate, and a number of other developed countries (while agreed in principle on the idea) have failed to ratify the Agreement to create the Fund.[55]

TRADE AND DEVELOPMENT: THEORY AND POLICY

Having reviewed the legal rules and institutions that apply to developing country trade we now proceed to examine the evolving theoretical and policy stances with respect to the relationship between trade and development that have influenced the evolution of these rules and institutions over the last 40 years.

The theory of comparative advantage and economic development: the limits of neo-classical theory

Despite the intense interest of their eighteenth- and nineteenth-century predecessors – particularly Smith, Hume, and Mill – in the causes of wealth and poverty among nations, modern neo-classical trade economists have until recently not devoted a great deal of attention to articulating a rigorous theory of the linkage between trade and economic development.[56] As discussed in Chapter 1, neo-classical theory can explain why a country will experience welfare gains when it specializes in those products in which, given existing factor endowments, it possesses a comparative advantage. Comparative advantage has often taken to be *revealed* comparative advantage, leading to a static perspective that largely ignores the issue of how nations actually come to acquire comparative advantage in particular products in the first place. Today, of course, it is widely recognized that much more goes into the determination of comparative advantage than fixed, 'natural' factors like endowments of natural resources, and there is an important and expanding economic literature on the causes of and constraints on economic growth and development.[57]

Quite early in the post-war period, however, the creation of comparative advantage became a persistent concern of development theory and for a quite straightforward reason – the existing specialization of economic activity in developing countries seemed to provide no guarantee of generating sustained economic growth. On the basis of the example of the developed world (and the early experience of Soviet Bloc industrialization), specialization in large-scale manufacturing industries was viewed as the key to growth. In addition, the existing specialization patterns of many developing countries could with justification be viewed as the historically contingent product of colonialism – developing countries served as ready sources of raw materials on the one hand, and as markets for the finished products of the colonial powers, on the other. This suggested not only the artificiality of existing comparative advantage in developing countries, but also its foundation in fundamentally unjust power relationships.[58]

Trade and development in the import-substitution theories of the 1950s and 1960s

Although sometimes its intellectual success is blamed on the popularity of Marxist or neo-Marxist views of political economy, import-substitution-based development theory rapidly gained acceptance as an orthodox policy prescription for developing countries even among the developed, 'capitalist' countries and among liberal policy analysts. The simple fact is that neo-classical liberal economists did not possess an alternative theory of growth and development, based on liberal trade, with which to launch an effective response.

Perhaps the one significant exception was Raymond Vernon's 'product cycle' theory.[59] Vernon's key argument is well-summarized by Grossman and Helpman:

> Most new goods . . . are developed in the industrialized North and manufactured there until their designs have been perfected and production techniques standardized. Then the innovating firms move the locus of production to the less developed South where wage rates and perhaps materials prices are lower. In a final stage of the product's life, new and superior goods may impinge upon this market share and ultimately render it obsolete.[60]

Vernon's approach did provide a plausible strategy for developing countries to acquire comparative advantage in increasingly sophisticated manufactured products through foreign investment-based technology transfer. However, from the developing country perspective, the theory had a number of unattractive features. First of all, it supposed, and accepted, that developing countries would never actually 'catch up' with the North, but would always remain a stage or two behind in the product cycle. Second, it was premised upon the acceptability of foreign ownership and investment, and was therefore susceptible to the critique that developing countries themselves (as opposed to foreign investors and multinational corporations) would realize few of the gains from their place in the product cycle, and would become subject to a new kind of economic colonialism.

In any event, the predominance of the import-substitution view is reflected in the wide range of exemptions from GATT strictures afforded to developing countries, which we have outlined above, as well as the approaches and initiatives of UNCTAD. The many developing countries that adopted import-substitution policies typically erected extremely high tariff and non-tariff barriers to imports, maintained artificially high exchange rates and stringent exchange controls, and in many cases domestic price controls (for instance, the prices of agricultural products were often controlled in order to contain the cost of living of industrial workers in the cities).[61]

Dependency theory and the beginnings of a neo-classical response to import-substitution approaches

It quickly became apparent that import-substitution policies were producing disappointing, or even disastrous, results in the many developing countries that had attempted them. According to Krueger,[62] once the easy opportunities for import substitution were largely exhausted, the new candidates normally had higher capital to labour ratios than the old, while many of the goods were items demanded by only the few in the upper income groups in poor countries. This meant that higher capital labour ratios required a higher rate of saving and investment to maintain the rate of economic growth while for those industries with fixed costs and a minimum efficient scale of production the cost disadvantages of producing in developing countries with small domestic markets were significant. Moreover, domestic import substituting producers were provided with monopoly positions in the sheltered domestic market and the incentives were such that few producers found it worthwhile to enter markets, particularly export markets, in which they were likely to face competition. Moreover, periodic balance of payments crises arose in reaction to over-valued exchange rates, increased indebtedness, and the failure of export earnings to grow, leading to stop-go policy cycles.

These policy failures yielded two diametrically opposed responses in development theory. Many of those who advocated import-substitution approaches turned to dependency theory to explain the continued failure to generate adequate economic growth in developing countries. According to dependency theory, these countries remained economically and socially backward due to complicity between the local power élites and the forces of developed-country capitalism. Early efforts at industrialization could easily be exploited by multinational corporations, who – with the support of corrupt and avaricious local élites – would build branch plant facilities in developing countries, but without contributing to development through significant technology transfer or training of local workforces.[63] The policy implications were a general continuation of import-substitution policies but with a new emphasis on control of the multinational corporation, support for democratization movements, and guarantees that developed countries would not interfere with the sovereignty of developing nations.[64]

While many of those who had from the beginning supported import-substitution approaches resorted to dependency theory to explain the early failure of these approaches, neo-classical trade economists began to reflect on the interesting fact that those few developing countries, mainly in East Asia, that had eschewed import-substitution for outward-oriented strategies were experiencing high levels of economic growth.[65] According to Balassa, the share of Korea, Singapore and Taiwan in total LDC manufactured exports increased from 6% in 1963 to 42% in 1984. Over the same period, per capita real incomes quadrupled in these three countries, while they increased at a much slower pace in inward-oriented LDCs such as India, Argentina, and Mexico.[66]

In reflecting on the empirical evidence of export-led growth, some neo-classical economists began to sketch a liberal alternative to import-substitution-oriented development theory. The flavour of this alternative is captured by the following passage from an essay by Bela Belassa, one of the leading exponents of liberal development theory:

> At the early stages of development, countries will generally benefit from specializing in natural resource products. In the process of industrialization, it will be advantageous to concentrate first on products utilizing mainly unskilled labour, with subsequent upgrading in the product composition of exports as the country accumulates physical and human capital.[67]

The theory thus emphasizes how developing countries can move up the 'value chain' beginning from a pre-existing comparative advantage in the least value-added exports (unprocessed raw materials). It thereby directly counters the claims of the import-substitution-oriented theorists that absent the creation of protected industries by the state, developing countries will be fated to remain 'hewers of wood and drawers of water' under constantly deteriorating terms of trade.

A further focus of the liberal theory is the negative consequence for economic growth of 'the chaotic nature of differential incentives among diverse activities in IS (import substitution) regimes'.[68] The effect of this chaos is largely to destroy the market signals that would normally lead to efficient resource allocation. In addition, the pervasive government 'rigging' of economic activity diverts considerable resources to 'directly unproductive profit-seeking activities', i.e. rent seeking, bribery of government officials, corruption, etc.[69] Finally, a liberal import policy can provide a substitute for domestic rivals which may be few or non-existent in many developing countries, thereby inducing competitive pressures to increase productivity.[70]

The direct policy implications of the liberal theory of trade and development are the liberalization of *both* developed *and* developing country trade policies. Liberalization of the former gives developing countries new opportunities to achieve growth through export expansion, allowing these countries to move their exports up the 'value chain'. And liberalization of developing country trade policies bring the gains from more efficient resource allocation that we have just described, with a corresponding increase in the competitiveness of developing country products on world markets.

However attractive to proponents of liberal trade (such as ourselves), the theory and evidence of export-led growth still leave much to be explained and debated concerning the relationship between trade liberalization and development. It has been pointed out that those developing countries characterized by significant export-led growth did not simply replace import-restrictive policies with a *laissez-faire* approach. While reducing tariffs and other barriers to trade and reforming exchange rate regimes, these countries also initiated or activated a wide range of alternative government policies aimed at encouraging exports, including significant subsidies and loans to export-oriented industries.[71] A study by the World Bank of growth in East Asian economies concluded that while targeted industrial policies (e.g. subsidies to specific firms) made little positive contribution to the so-called Asian economic miracle, more generally available export subsidies and other export incentives had a modest but significant impact on the extraordinary economic success of these countries.[72] Moreover, the economic difficulties that are currently being experienced by a number of the East Asian economies suggest that a number of firms may have over-expanded capacity through access to cheap debt capital provided in part by domestic financial institutions subject to weak capital market disciplines and excessive political interference in capital allocation decisions ('crony capitalism'). Thus, even in its own terms, there remain unresolved questions as to the sustainability of the East Asian successes. In addition, there are further questions as to the generalizability of the East Asian experience to other contexts, such as whether the dynamic Asian economies display certain 'exceptionalist' institutional, social, or cultural characteristics that explain in large part the success of the export-led model of development, including: a relatively pragmatic, 'this-worldly' orientation in the mainstream culture; superior human resources (higher education levels among the general population); high savings rates; and a bureaucracy that is meritocratic and relatively 'autonomous' from patrimonial politics.

The LDC debt crisis

The debt crisis arguably marks a crucial watershed in the evolution of approaches to LDC economic development. Owing to the Petrodollar surplus of the 1970s, major American, European and Japanese commercial banks found themselves with unprecedented amounts of money to lend on world markets. The banks became increasingly interested in lending to developing country governments. They often presumed that since a sovereign could not go bankrupt, the very fact that the debtor was a government would provide adequate security for the loans. For developing country governments, these loans represented an opportunity for another attempt at import-substitution-based industrial development. The loans were particularly attractive since they offered the capital needed for industrialization, but without the strings attached to foreign direct investment or multinational corporate activities. Developing country governments would have direct control of the money, and full rights to distribute or reinvest domestically the profits from successful investments. In the event, commercial banks lent to developing country sovereigns an average of over $US40 billion per year between 1977 and 1982.[73]

By the early 1980s, a number of developing country debtors were having increasing difficulty in paying off these loans. First of all, once again import-substitution-based industrialization failed to yield high rates of growth. Second, the recession in the developed world had considerably dampened demand for developing country exports, while at the same time leading to increased protection against those exports even where demand continued to be strong. At the same time, interest rates increased as the United States and other Western countries adopted an anti-inflationary monetary policy. Since the developing country loans were based on floating rates, this meant that just at a time when their foreign currency earnings from exports were declining, developing country debtors were faced with very substantial increases in the cost of servicing their loans.[74] Finally, in 1982 Mexico announced that it could not continue to pay its creditors according to schedule, and a number of other LDC debtors soon followed suit.[75]

The initial response of the creditor nations was that of debt rescheduling. Repayment of loans would be stretched out over a much longer period, without any debt reduction. The debtors would be required to have the rescheduling backed by an IMF stand-by credit, which in turn would be conditional on domestic policy reforms to provide some assurance that the countries in question would attain the balance of payments stability required to repay on the rescheduled terms. The reforms in question included anti-inflationary policies, currency devaluation, and also liberalization of prices and (to some extent) foreign trade. Not only did some of the policy conditions of rescheduling cause severe human hardship in LDCs (for instance rapid increases in food costs due to removal of price controls) but frequently, at the outset, the policy prescriptions were internally contradictory (for instance, tight money policies to fight inflation alongside inflation-inducing currency devaluations and price liberalization), although eventually IMF officials paid greater attention to the interaction and sequencing of the various policy reforms.

During the 1970s, even despite the disappointing results from import-substitution policies, many of these LDCs nevertheless continued to experience strong, albeit far from adequate, export growth, and increases in GDP. The effect of the debt crisis was to halt this growth almost entirely, as the debtor countries' foreign exchange earnings were eaten up by debt servicing requirements and they were unable to make investments in industrial production. In consequence, developing country imports from the developed world declined significantly, further worsening the recession. This led to the fundamental recognition by the Reagan Administration of the dependency of world economic recovery on the renewal of growth in developing countries, and a sense of urgency to finding a solution to the LDC debt crisis that would permit such a renewal of growth.

The Baker Plan (named after the then US Treasury Secretary, James Baker) was the first such effort. Launched in 1985, it involved a proposal that commercial banks loan fresh money for investment in economic renewal to a select group of LDC debtors who were prepared to make major structural economic reforms, to be backed by structural adjustment lending by the World Bank and the IMF.[76] While it appears that some new loans were made pursuant to this Plan, the overall level of lending by commercial banks to LDC debtors actually declined from 1985 to 1987, and per capita income in debtor countries continued to fall.[77]

While the Baker Plan did not provide for debt reduction, some LDC debtors were, towards the end of the 1980s, beginning to have some success with debt reduction, through repurchase of debt on the secondary market at discounted rates and also through debt/equity swaps. The swaps were most successful in the case of countries such as Chile and Mexico, who eventually were able to make credible commitments to provide an attractive climate for foreign investment to be purchased with debt. At the same time, in part due to pressure from domestic regulatory authorities, many developed country creditor banks were increasing reserves on LDC loans, and their ability to do so lessened the sense of fear or panic that eventual debtor default could bring down the international financial system.

It was in this context that the United States proposed the Brady Plan in 1989. It would involve the commercial banks for the first time accepting debt reduction, but in return for a degree of backing for repayment of the remaining debt through various kinds of securities, with active participation in this backing by the US Treasury. After an (albeit somewhat shaky) beginning in Mexico the Brady approach came to play an important role in debt restructuring in the Philippines, Venezuela, Uruguay, Costa Rica and Nigeria.[78] Mexico, Chile and the Philippines in particular have recognized the potential for credible domestic policy reforms to induce significant influxes of capital, both foreign investment and (often more importantly) funds taken out of the country by its own nationals in order to avoid onerous taxation.

Trade policy reform at the end of the 1980s

The lessons that have emerged from the debt crisis, along with the collapse of central planning in the Soviet Bloc, and the general decline of Marxist-inspired development ideology, as well as the dramatic successes of more liberal trade policies in the Asian NICs, have led a variety of developing countries to move towards liberalization of their trade and related domestic policies even without the pressure of strict IMF conditionality. It has been estimated that, since the mid-1980s some 36 LDCs have undertaken significant trade policy reforms, and 17 of these have undertaken comprehensive reforms of distortionary policies, including exchange rate, price and wage policies.[79] Frequently, these reforms have been supported by lending facilities from the World Bank and the IMF.

Two issues that loom large with respect to these reforms are *adjustment* and *sequencing*. Lifting of trade restrictions can lead to the rapid decline of protected industries that would never have existed but for government intervention and isolation from global competitive forces. The result is often widespread labour dislocation, because of a lag before the positive growth effects of more liberal policies are felt. Moreover, because liberalization is unilateral, increased competition from abroad is not immediately offset by greater access for developing country products in global markets. While they have undertaken very substantial lending to assist in the stabilization of the balance of payments during macroeconomic and related reforms, the international financial institutions have been very reluctant to engage in lending to facilitate labour adjustment. Worker adjustment is narrowly conceptualized as a distributional issue, and there is often suspicion that displaced workers may not be the most deserving beneficiaries of assistance. A World Bank paper suggests, for instance, that 'workers displaced from protected industries are not among the poorest groups in society'.[80] This is arguably a short-sighted view, as unemployment among relatively advantaged segments of the population gluts the labour market in general and reduces consumer demand, therefore indirectly inflicting hardship on other, possibly less-advantaged segments of the population.[81] A further difficulty is that, in some developing countries, particularly those with poor tax collection systems, tariff revenues may constitute an important source of revenue, and removal of tariffs therefore actually reduces the income stream which the government has at its disposal to fund labour adjustment programmes.

A second issue is that of sequencing: should import controls be removed before macroeconomic and other domestic reforms are already in place? There is a strong argument that until distortions in domestic prices and wages (inputs into production) are removed, and exchange rates become more realistic, it is unlikely that import competition will send the appropriate signals to domestic producers. It has been found that trade policy reforms can be effective when introduced either simultaneously with other reforms or shortly thereafter.[82]

POLICY OPTIONS AND PROSPECTS FOR THE FUTURE

Unilateral trade liberalization

This option, which has just been described from the perspective of structural policy reform, has the obvious limitation that the adjustment process is not facilitated through any additional access to developed country markets. However, in many developing countries the costs of distortive policies to productivity and growth may have become so high as to justify not delaying liberalization until reciprocal trade liberalization can take place. Balassa suggests that in these instances developing countries should proceed with liberalization, and that in eventual negotiations on the basis of reciprocity they can credibly demand concessions for making liberalization that has already taken place binding and irreversible.[83] This depends on the credibility of the implicit threat that such liberalization would be reversed in the future – the fact that many of the original protectionist policies are now seen as fundamentally pernicious to the developing countries themselves reduces the credibility of the threat considerably.

South–South trade liberalization

Despite the increasing activity with respect to South–South trading arrangements, and the implementation of the GSTP, South–South trade remains, as we have noted, a very small percentage of global trade. However, in the wake of structural domestic reforms, particularly those directed towards currency convertibility, this may change somewhat. In the past, trade between developing countries rarely took place in convertible currency and therefore was less attractive than trade with developed countries. Moreover a pattern is already discernible whereby the more developed LDCs, particularly the Asian NICs, relocate some of the production processes for their exports to lesser-developed LDCs with lower wages and less skilled workforces.

Regional trading arrangements between developed and developing countries

This option is most clearly reflected in the possibility of a North American Free Trade Agreement encompassing Canada, the United States and Mexico, with future extension to other Latin American LDCs. Unlike multilateral liberalization, liberalization through a regional arrangement may bring with it adjustment and technical assistance from the more developed members of the grouping. On the other hand, there is the possibility that the developed country or countries in the grouping will exercise overwhelming power and influence over the way in which the arrangement is implemented.

Multilateral liberalization: developing countries and the Uruguay Round result

The Uruguay Round provides a number of attractive trade-offs for (at least some) developing countries. On the one hand, many developing countries have been (particularly at the outset of the negotiations) resistant to American demands that their domestic policies with respect to regulation of service industries, foreign investment, and intellectual property become subjects of negotiation in the GATT. On the other hand, the prospect of substantial reduction in agricultural protection and the phasing out of a significant part of textiles and clothing protection offers the prospect of real gains for many developing countries. In previous chapters on trade in services, intellectual property and investment, we have discussed in greater detail the issues that these Uruguay Round agenda items raised for many LDCs. However, as we note in these chapters, the Uruguay Round Final Act reflects a number of compromises between developed country demands and the concerns of developing countries. For instance, in the case of TRIPs, compulsory licensing of patented inventions is permitted subject to certain conditions being met, including compensation to the patent holder. This reflects a significant compromise of the American view, shared to a large extent by the EU and Japan, that no compulsory licensing should be permitted within the twenty-year period of required patent protection. In the case of TRIMs, the Final Act stops short of characterizing, for instance, technology transfer requirements as violations of trade rules, and leaves considerable scope for investment measures aimed at ensuring that foreign enterprises further the developing goals of host countries – again, the United States in particular, had pushed hard for a much more restrictive approach to investment measures.

While the general provisions of the Final Act thus reflect developing country concerns in a number of areas, the tendency has not been to grant developing countries broad exceptions to compliance with GATT rules. In some instances, developing countries may be given a somewhat longer period of time to phase in domestic compliance with the new rules, but the Uruguay Round result reflects, in large measure, a rejection of the view that developing countries should not be required to make reciprocal commitments to trade liberalization. The following brief survey of the Final Act canvasses many of the specific references to developing countries as well as issues such as the MFA of direct, specific relevance to developing country trade. It is intended to be illustrative, not exhaustive.[84]

Manufactureds Trade Liberalization

Significant tariff reductions on manufactured imports were achieved in the Round. Developing countries actively participated in these negotiations and bindings on imported industrial products rose from 13 to 61%. While developed countries' tariffs on imports from other developed countries were reduced by an average of 40%, tariffs on imports from developing countries were reduced by only 28%. Cuts by LDCs in protection of mechanized trade are estimated to increase real incomes in developing countries between US$60 and $100 billion at 1992 prices, despite cautious commitments made by many developing countries.[85]

Understanding on the Balance of Payments Provisions of the GATT

This Understanding, discussed in detail in Chapter 4, reflects concern by the United States and some other developed countries about insufficiently rigorous application of the conditions or criteria established in Articles XII and XVIII:B of the GATT to justify trade measures taken for balance-of-payments reasons. This mostly concerns, in contemporary circumstances, measures taken by developing countries.

Agreement on Agriculture

The Agreement allows developing countries the flexibility to implement their commitments to reduction of protection and domestic support over a ten-year period (Article 15; the normal implementation period for developed countries is six years). The least-developed country Members are not required to make reduction commitments.

The existing system of agricultural support in developed countries is widely viewed as having depressed world prices for temperate zone agricultural commodities.[86] The effects on developing countries of the liberalization process set out in the Agreement on Agriculture are, therefore, mixed. As Winters suggests: 'Exporters of the temperate products whose prices are most affected by agricultural liberalisation – for example, Argentina and Thailand – have strong and direct interests in the dismantling of protection; their revenues and income would increase significantly. On the other hand chronic food importers – for example, Bangladesh – would undoubtedly suffer.'[87] The fact that developed country liberalization of trade in agriculture may harm this latter group of countries is taken into account in the Decision on Measures Concerning the Possible Negative Effects of the Reform Programme on Least-Developed and Net Food-Importing Developing Countries.

The Decision commits Trade Ministers of GATT Members to review levels of food aid provided to developing countries to ensure that they are sufficient to meet the legitimate needs of developing countries during the reform programme (Article 3(i)); to increase the proportion of food aid provided to developing countries as aid or on concessional terms (Article 3(ii)); and to give 'full consideration' to developing country requests for technical assistance to develop their domestic agricultural sectors (Article 3(iii)). As well, it is accepted that difficulties in financing imports of food on commercial terms may be a basis for assistance from international financial institutions (Article 5).

Agreement on Textiles and Clothing

Of major importance to many developing countries will be the gradual liberalization of protection pursuant to the MFA, as provided for in the Uruguay Round Agreement on Textiles and Clothing.[88] Under the Agreement, all restrictions provided for in bilateral agreements and under the MFA are to be notified to the Textiles Monitoring Body (TMB), and removed according to a graduated schedule. Thus, upon entry into force of the Agreement, Members are to remove all MFA-based or bilaterally-agreed restrictions on products accounting for at least 16% of the total volume of their imports in 1990 in the following product groups: tops and yarns, fabrics, made-up textile products, and clothing (a detailed annex listing the individual product classes according to the Harmonized System of Classification is attached to the Agreement on Textiles and Clothing). With respect to restrictions that remain after this initial phase of liberalization, within three years, members must remove restrictions on products accounting for a further 17% of the total volume of imports in 1990 terms. Removal of restrictions on products accounting for at least another 18% of import volume is required after seven years. All further restrictions are to be eliminated within ten years of the entry into force of the Agreement. During the transition period, quotas are to be expanded on imports that have not yet been completely derestricted.

It is to be emphasized that the above liberalization commitments apply only to restrictions imposed based upon the MFA or bilateral agreements outside the GATT legal framework. In the case of many of the products in question, the bound MFN tariff rates remain quite high, and are in themselves unaffected by these liberalization commitments. Tariff reductions achieved in the Uruguay Round, while substantial, will nevertheless leave in place tariffs on many textile and apparel items that are much higher than the average for industrial products generally.

It should be noted, as well, that special safeguard provisions apply with respect to the liberalization of MFA-based and bilaterally-negotiated restrictions. A Member may take safeguard action when ‘it is demonstrated that a particular product is being imported into its territory in such increased quantities as to cause serious damage, or actual threat thereof, to the domestic industry producing like and/or directly competitive products’ (Article 6(2)). It is specified that ‘serious damage or actual threat thereof must demonstrably be caused by such increased quantities in total imports [of the product in question] and not by such other factors as technological changes or changes in consumer preference’. Safeguard protection is to be temporary (a maximum of three years with no right of renewal) and must in any event cease when, pursuant to the liberalization commitments discussed above, all past MFA-based or bilaterally-based restrictions are to have been removed from the product. The level of restraint under the safeguard ‘shall be fixed at a level not lower than the actual level of exports or imports from the Member concerned during the twelve-month period terminating two months preceding’ the request for safeguard protection (Article 6(8)). An importing Member seeking to take safeguard action must first attempt a voluntary agreement with the exporting Member before acting unilaterally. However, any such voluntary agreement must be reported to the TMB, which is to determine its consistency with the safeguard provisions of the Agreement on Textiles and Clothing. Finally, safeguards are to be applied on a Member-by-Member basis, rather than to all Members exporting the product in question. Therefore, a determination must be made that serious damage or threat thereof is attributable to *each* Member to whom safeguard action is to be applied (Article 6(4)).

Fearing serious damage to its domestic underwear industry, the United States relied on the Agreement on Textiles and Clothing to restrict Costa Rican imports of underwear. Costa Rica challenged this measure, alleging that it violated a number of provisions of the Agreement on Textiles and Clothing. In November 1996, a panel ruled largely in favour of Costa Rica, because, *inter alia*, the United States had not ‘demonstrated that serious damage or actual threat thereof was caused by such imports to the United States’ domestic industry.’[89] Costa Rica appealed, however, on a technical point regarding the legality of the retroactive application of apparel quotas which it had lost. This appeal was allowed, thereby strengthening Costa Rica's victory. A similar case involved the consideration of US restrictions on imported wool shirts and blouses from India.[90] The primary issue was whether the TMB is required to endorse safeguard actions taken by Members. India argued that TMB endorsement was necessary, while the United States argued that there was no such requirement. Here the panel found a middle ground, ruling that 'members imposing safeguards are required to refer the matter to the TMB and then endeavour to accept'[91] the resulting recommendations of the TMB. Thus the US restrictions were found to be in violation of the Agreement. India appealed the ruling on a number of technical points regarding the burden of proof, the findings on the TMB and the panel's use of judicial economy.[92] The Appellate Body did not accept India's arguments and left the original panel decision intact.

Finally, Article 8 of the Agreement on Textiles and Clothing sets out the procedures for establishment and operation of the TMB. The TMB is to consist of a Chairman and ten Members. The membership 'shall be balanced and broadly representative of the Members and provide for rotation of its Members at appropriate intervals' (Article 8(1)). The membership of the TMB is to be selected by Members of the WTO designated by the Council for Trade in Goods to serve on the TMB, voting in their personal capacity and not as representatives of their governments. The TMB is charged with a range of monitoring functions, including a major review of the liberalization process, to be conducted after the end of each of the stages (i.e. 3, 6 and 10 years).

Agreement on Technical Barriers to Trade

The Agreement stipulates that developing country Members shall be provided, upon request, with technical assistance and advice from other Members in order to facilitate the process of standardizing technical requirements both through national standardizing bodies, and participation in international standardization exercises (Articles 11(2), 11(4), 11(5)). Such assistance and advice is to occur on 'mutually agreed terms and conditions'. Generally speaking, Article 12, although entitled Special and Differential Treatment of Developing Country Members, does not exempt developing countries from the obligations of the Technical Barriers Agreement with respect to harmonization, standardization, or mutual recognition of technical requirements. Rather, most of the provisions of Article 12 merely require that various special needs of developing countries be taken into account in the interpretation and implementation of the Agreement. However, Article 12(4) seems to go further towards an actual modification (or at least, a qualification) of substantive obligations, in stipulating that 'developing country Members should not be expected to use international standards as a basis for their technical regulations or standards, including test methods, which are not appropriate to their development, financial and trade needs'.

Agreement on Implementation of Article VI of the GATT (Dumping)

Article 15 states that 'special regard' is to be given by developed country Members to the 'special situation' of developing countries when considering the imposition of antidumping duties. Members are required to explore the possibility of constructive remedies (i.e. price undertakings) before imposing duties where these would 'affect the essential interests of developing country members'. This provision is essentially identical to Article 13 of the Tokyo Round Dumping Code.

Agreement on Subsidies and Countervailing Measures

The ban on export subsidies in Article 3(1)(a) in Article 3 does not apply to least-developed country Members, and will apply to other developing country Members only after a transition period of eight years (Article 27(1)). The ban on subsidies 'contingent . . . upon the use of domestic over imported goods' shall not apply to developed countries in general for five years and to the less-developed countries for eight years (Article 27(2)). However, once a developing country has achieved 'export competitiveness' in a given product, it is required to phase out export subsidies over a period of two years (Article 27(4)), unless it is one of a listed group of least-developed countries, in which case the phase-out period is extended to eight years (Article 27(4)). 'Export competitiveness' is deemed to have been achieved where the exports of the developing country in question have reached at least 3.25% of world trade for two consecutive years (Article 27(5)). Finally, the Agreement on Subsidies and Countervailing Measures contains special *de minimis* exemptions from countervailability for developing countries. Thus a countervailing duty investigation is to be terminated when it is determined that a subsidy accounts for less than 2% of value on a per-unit basis or where the *volume* of subsidized imports accounts for less than 4% of the total imports of like products (unless imports of like products from developing countries, taken together, amount to more than 9% of total imports of like products into the importing country) (Article 27(9)).

Understanding on Rules and Procedures Governing the Settlement of Disputes

The Dispute Settlement Understanding contains several provisions that arguably seek to address long-standing complaints that developing countries have been marginalized or disadvantaged in the GATT dispute settlement process. Article 8(2) includes 'a sufficiently diverse background' as one of the criteria for composition of dispute panels, and – much more specifically – Article 8(10) stipulates that 'when a dispute is between a developing country Member and a developed country Member the panel shall, if the developing country Member so requests, include at least one panellist from a developing country Member'. Within the general time limits established by the Dispute Settlement Understanding, a panel examining a complaint against a developing country Member is to 'accord sufficient time for the developing country Member to prepare and present its argumentation' (Article 12(10)). Furthermore, where a developing country Member is Party to a dispute, the panel must explicitly address in its report the applicability of any special GATT provisions with respect to developing countries, where these provisions have been invoked by the developing country Member that is a Party to the dispute (Article 12(10)).

In the case of least-developed country Members, particular consideration is to be given to the 'special situation' of these Members throughout the dispute settlement process. Members are required to 'exercise due restraint' in making complaints against least-developed country Members under the WTO dispute settlement procedures. A special role is contemplated for the Director-General of the WTO or the Chairman of the Dispute Settlement Body (DSB) with respect to facilitating consultations in the event of a dispute involving a least-developed country Member (Article 24(1), 24(2)). Finally, the Secretariat of the WTO is charged with the provision of legal advice and assistance to developing country Members with respect to dispute settlement (Article 27(2)).

Decision on Measures in Favour of Least-developed Countries

The Decision reflects what remains of the non-reciprocal approach to trade liberalization with developing countries, applied *only* to the least developed countries 'as long as they remain in that category'. With respect to specific commitments and concessions as opposed to compliance with the general rules of the Final Act and its various agreements, least-developed country Members will 'only be required to undertake commitments and concessions to the extent consistent with their individual development, financial and trade needs, or their administrative and institutional capabilities' (Article 1). Thus MFN tariff and non-tariff concessions 'on products of export interest to the least-developed countries may be implemented autonomously, in advance and without staging' – i.e. without being tied to reciprocal concessions from these countries.

The above survey of the provisions of the Final Act and related Agreements and Decisions that apply to developing countries clearly suggests that the overall approach is one of full integration of all but the least-developed countries into the GATT/WTO, with some special allowance made for special difficulties that developing countries may experience with respect to full integration, e.g. through longer phase-in periods for compliance with GATT/WTO obligations. Even with respect to the least-developed countries, 'special and differential treatment' falls far short of outright exemption from the main general rules of the GATT/WTO. Overall, the Uruguay Round outcome represents a wager by developing countries in favour of an approach to trade and development premised upon openness and export-led growth. Whether this wager will be won depends significantly on the will of developed countries to offer tariff concession on products of export interest to developing countries. It also depends on the willingness to prevent (sometimes legitimate) concerns about 'fair trade' – e.g. labour and environmental standards – from releasing a new wave of protectionism against developing countries.[93]

CONCLUSION

The empirical evidence to date suggests that liberal trade policies are more conducive to economic development than import-substitution policies. However, at least three caveats are in order. First, liberal trade policies may be a necessary condition for economic development but they are far from a sufficient condition. Domestic policies relating to investments in education, infrastructure, health care, and the quality of a country's legal system and bureaucracy clearly also matter. More generally, the quality of a country's institutional capital seems to be an important determinant of development.[94] While economic liberalization tends to advance the long-term process of political liberalization and democratization, some authoritarian political regimes have co-existed with market economies for long periods of time, in limiting cases pursuing predatory and welfare-reducing policies towards their citizenry. Second, while it has become conventional wisdom amongst trade economists to be critical of the import-substitution policies pursued by many developing countries in the post-war decades, it is important that this criticism be tempered with an acknowledgment that many developed countries also pursued such policies for extended periods of time earlier in their development, e.g. the US, Canada, Germany, and arguably more recently Japan, raising questions as to whether these policies were equally mistaken, or whether the circumstances of these countries were different in some relevant respects from those of more recent developing countries. Third, there remain unresolved questions as to whether a state-promoted export-led growth strategy is a superior strategy for developing countries, given questions about the sustainability and generalizability of the East Asian experience and severe limits on institutional capacity in many developing countries. This might argue instead for agnosticism on the part of the state to any particular industrial or trade strategy leaving sectoral judgments (other than reciprocal trade liberalization) to competitive private capital markets and instead focusing collective resources more sharply on developing general background endowments such as human capital, infrastructure, health care, law and order, and well-functioning legal and public sector institutions. Multilateral and bilateral foreign aid policies might focus on a similar set of priorities.

15 Trade and the environment

INTRODUCTION

In the last three decades, we have witnessed a remarkable increase in support for environmentalism among citizens of liberal democratic regimes throughout the world. Environmentalism is a very broad concept, extending from concern about traditional forms of pollution, such as emissions of dangerous substances into the air and the water, to the protection of endangered species and the aesthetic purity and integrity of natural landscapes. It has been increasingly recognized that environmental problems cross national boundaries, and that many of the most pressing challenges cannot be addressed adequately without international cooperation and international rules – saving the world's ozone layer from further damage is an obvious and important example.

The relationship between international trade and the environment has only recently attained a prominent place on the trade agenda, although it has been a concern of environmentalists for some time. Much of the debate on this issue is highly emotive and polarized. Often, environmentalists tend to identify liberal trade with environmentally-destructive unrestrained economic growth. Many free traders, on the other hand, are largely dismissive of the environmentalists' concerns as either disguised protectionism or irrational fanaticism.[1]

The links between trade and environment are complex and multi-faceted. In this chapter, we attempt to clearly separate and define the issues, examine existing international trade law that affects environmental concerns, and explore prospects for reform.

In our view there are several crucial distinctions that must be made in order to clarify and better focus the debate. The first is between the use of trade restrictions to protect the domestic environment of the importing state and the use of such restrictions as a response to the environmental policies of *other* states. However, within this second category, several further distinctions must be drawn. Among the most important is between environmental and competitiveness aims of environmentally-based trade restrictions.

Some international environmental treaties, such as the Convention on International Traffic in Endangered Species (CITES), use control of trade as a direct means of achieving an environmental purpose. Even where there is no such direct relationship between trade restrictions and environmental regulation, environmentalists may view trade restrictions as appropriate *sanctions* for non-compliance with international environmental standards, as a means of imposing such standards where there are none, or a response to the failure of particular nations to engage in negotiations to develop or adopt such standards. Whether trade measures are an appropriate or effective means of achieving these ends raises a wide variety of normative and empirical issues. Environmentalists, in addition to this concern about international standards, are also concerned about the so-called 'race to the bottom' – the possibility that, in response to the competitive advantage that is gained from lower environmental standards in some industries, a greater share of jobs and trade in those industries will shift to countries with lower domestic environmental standards. This, it is feared, will put downward pressure on environmental standards in countries that presently have higher levels of protection. Here, environmentalists are not necessarily seeking adoption by all countries of the same domestic environmental standards but are simply concerned that such standards continue to be sustainable in countries that have already decided to adopt them. Although some free traders are largely dismissive of the problem posed by the 'race to the bottom', our own view is that this problem is real but that there will usually be a better alternative response to increased competitive pressures than the lowering of environmental standards – including better instrument choices in environmental regulation that achieve the same or improved results while imposing lower costs on industrial production, investment in technologies that promise to reduce the cost of complying with higher environmental standards, and adoption of adjustment and exit-oriented measures that shift resources from sectors where comparative advantage continues to depend on lower environmental standards to those where it does not.

By contrast with environmentalists, 'fair traders' are concerned with the impact on trade, not on the environment as such, of other countries' lower environmental standards. They consider it 'unfair' that a country can gain an advantage in trade from lower environmental standards. Unlike the claims of environmentalists, we view these claims of fair traders with great scepticism. First of all, the claims implicitly assume that the importing state's environmental standards are optimal from both a domestic and a global perspective. But absent some defensible international norm or benchmark for environmental standards, this assumption merely reflects the bias of the importing country towards its own regulatory approach. Second, higher environmental standards may actually *confer* a competitive advantage in some sectors, where these standards may create incentives for the development of environmental technologies that can then be exported to other countries as their demand for environmental protection increases. Third, environmental standards and costs must be distinguished. 'Fair traders' are really concerned with differential costs to industry of environmental standards, yet even if standards *were* harmonized, different countries for technological, climatic, other geographical and demographic reasons, could still face vastly different costs of meeting these harmonized standards. Here the arguments of fair traders exhibit the same kind of incoherence that is evident with respect to countervailing duty law, which we have discussed at length in

Chapter 8. Briefly, for unfairness to have a normatively defensible meaning it must entail the violation of some neutral, objective baseline for the balance of benefits and burdens that governments create for industries.

In this chapter, we review the existing trade law and jurisprudence that affects environmentally-based trade measures, and attempt a clarification of the concepts and arguments at stake in the trade and environment debate. We pay particular attention to jurisprudence of the GATT and the FTA that has applied a number of key legal norms and principles of international trade law in environmentally-related contexts. As well, we consider the environmental provisions of the NAFTA, including the environmental side-agreement.[2]

THE GATT

The General Agreement (especially Articles I, II, and XI) prohibits border restrictions on the exportation and importation of goods, subject to a narrow range of exceptions. In addition, the GATT prohibits certain internal measures that discriminate against foreign imports (Article III). Clearly, the vast majority of domestic environmental policies fall into neither of these categories, and hence no potential or real conflict with the GATT is likely to emerge except in a relatively small number of cases.[3] Nevertheless, the number and importance of these cases is growing as many Contracting Parties place increasing priority on protection of the environment. In the case of the FTA, the relevant provisions are closely similar or identical to those of the GATT, including the provisions on National Treatment with respect to trade in goods and the prohibition of quantitative restrictions.

Article XX: a GATT environmental charter?

Given that many of the border measures connected with environmental goals are on their face violations of Article XI, much of the jurisprudence has centred on whether such measures can be saved by virtue of any of the exceptions listed in Article XX of the GATT. Article XX exempts certain classes of measures from the strictures of other GATT articles, provided that 'such measures are not applied in a manner which would constitute a means of arbitrary or unjustifiable discrimination between countries where the same conditions prevail, or a disguised restriction on international trade'. Among the classes of measures listed are those 'necessary to protect human, animal or plant life or health' (XX(b)); and 'relating to the conservation of exhaustible natural resources if such measures are made effective in conjunction with restrictions on domestic production or consumption' (XX(g)).

The word 'environment' is not mentioned explicitly in either paragraph. Commentators are divided on whether, nevertheless, these provisions were intended by the drafters to apply to the environment in the broadest sense (including moral and aesthetic concerns) or, alternatively, to a much narrower range of policy concerns. Shrybman, for instance, argues for the latter point of view.[4] It is possible to understand Article XX(b), for example, as intended to cover measures designed either to protect public health against diseases (e.g. from contaminated meat) or to protect animal or health life for commercial reasons (e.g. the economic consequences of crop pestilences). With respect to Article XX(g), its purpose might be to allow a country to protect 'exhaustible natural resources' such as minerals or petroleum that are considered as essential to its economic well-being. In a detailed analysis of the negotiations that produced the General Agreement, Charnovitz has shown, however, that the drafters had at least conservation goals in mind, as well as economic or public health and safety concerns. He argues that the drafters were aware of existing international conventions on conservation, and probably did not include a more explicit environmental exemption precisely because they thought that Articles XX(b) and (g) would suffice for this purpose and the *Turtles* appeal to the AB found that Art. XX(g) could encompass measures to protect living resources, in this case endangered species. This ruling was based on a consideration of developments in international environmental law and policy subsequent to the 1947 GATT, thus employing methods of treaty interpretation required under Art. 31 of the Vienna Convention, as well as a reading of the preamble to the WTO Agreement.[5]

Throughout much of the history of the GATT, the main issues raised by Article XX concerned the potential for protectionism to be disguised as measures taken for health and other goals stated in the Article. For example, phytosanitary measures with respect to livestock were often cited as indirect protectionist measures, as well as other technical barriers such as idiosyncratic product standards or inspection requirements. The explicit language of Article XX presupposes that it is possible to detect instances where measures are in fact 'disguised restrictions on trade'. In practice this has proven far from straightforward in the presence of conflicting scientific evidence as to the non-protectionist justification of particular measures, and also due to the fact that much of the claimed protectionism might be embedded in the manner in which a measure that did have a genuine non-protectionist basis was administered.

The WTO Agreement on Technical Barriers to Trade and Sanitory and Phytosanitary Agreement attempt to address the task of distinguishing genuine non-protectionist measures from disguised trade protection through a multi-faceted approach, including the encouragement of the use of international standards. These agreements are discussed in detail in Chapter 6, on health and safety standards. Significantly, the Agreement on Technical Barriers to Trade permits 'technical regulations and standards' which are 'for the protection of human health or safety, animal or plant life or health or the environment' (Article 2(2)). Here the addition of 'the environment' to language that otherwise duplicates the wording of Article XX(b), may suggest an explicit acknowledgement that the Article XX exemptions are to be interpreted broadly to include measures taken for environmental purposes.[6]

The jurisprudence of the GATT (including interpretation of GATT provisions by Canada–USA FTA panels)

In several GATT/WTO and FTA panel decisions during the 1980s and 1990s, and in one WTO Appelate Body decision, the consistency of environmental measures with Articles III and XI of the GATT was addressed, as well as the application of Article XX to the environment.

Herring and Salmon

The application of Article XX to trade restricting measures to protect the restricting country's own environment was addressed in the *Herring and Salmon* case.[7] Here, the United States was the complainant, arguing that Canadian requirements that salmon and herring caught in Canadian waters be processed in Canada before export violated Article XI of the GATT. Among Canada's arguments in response was that these restrictions were an integral part of its overall scheme for management of West Coast fisheries resources, and therefore 'related to' the 'conservation of exhaustible natural resources' within the meaning of Article XX(g).[8] According to Canada, the export restrictions functioned in the following two ways to support its conservation scheme. First of all, the vulnerability of the species required an extremely accurate catch control system, and the only way of having precise data on the catch was to limit its destination to Canadian fish plants, which were subject to rigorous reporting requirements. Second, because of the cyclical nature of the catch for both species, making the unprocessed fish available exclusively to Canadian plants was the only means of balancing the conservation objective with the goal of sustaining a viable domestic fish processing industry. The implication of this latter claim was that unless Canadian fish plants were assured of the entire Canadian catch, the Canadian government would be faced with the choice of either accepting the demise of the industry or permitting overfishing when the catch was good.

The United States replied that the Canadian requirements were 'neither necessary nor particularly useful' for the purpose of ensuring an accurate estimate of the Canadian catch, since in the case where unprocessed fish was exported to the United States, 'United States authorities routinely provided to Canada, upon request and for use in the Canadian conservation programme, full data on United States landings of unprocessed fish'.[9] The United States also objected to the broad view of 'conservation' suggested by the notion that conservation measures included measures that balanced conservation goals with socioeconomic concerns such as the preservation of a domestic processing industry – in any case, Canada's domestic processing industry would have access to fish imports to make up any shortfall resulting from the combined impact of conservation measures and the cyclical nature of the industry.

Finally, the United States presented evidence that the Canadian government itself had described the export ban as a means of protecting Canadian jobs in its own official literature, and therefore that the measure should be viewed as a disguised restriction on trade.

The GATT panel interpreted the Article XX(g) requirement that measures be 'related to' conservation of exhaustible natural resources as meaning 'primarily aimed at' such conservation,[10] but it viewed this as weaker than the requirement of 'necessity' imposed by Article XX(b). Among the main factors that led the panel to find that the Canadian export ban was not 'primarily aimed' at conservation was that accurate statistical data could be collected without such a ban, as was done for other species that were subject to conservation measures but whose export in an unprocessed state was not banned. The panel thus adopted an objective test to determine primary intent, i.e. instead of examining the legislative history of the measure to determine whether its primary aim was protection of the domestic Canadian processing industry, it considered whether other means less restrictive of trade could equally serve the stated conservation purpose. An important clarification of the meaning of 'necessary' in Article XX(b) occurred in the non-environmental *Thai Cigarette* case.[11] In that case, the United States challenged a ban on imports of cigarettes into Thailand as a violation of Article XI of the GATT. Thailand defended the ban, under Article XX(b), as 'necessary' for the protection of public health. While no comparable ban existed on domestic Thai cigarettes, the Thai government claimed that American imports were more likely to induce women and young persons to take up smoking, because of sophisticated advertising directed at these groups. Thailand also argued that American cigarettes were somehow more addictive or more likely to be consumed in larger quantities than comparable Thai cigarettes, due to their chemical composition (this claim was largely unsupported, however, by scientific evidence). The panel ruled that an import ban would only be 'necessary' for public health reasons, within the meaning of Article XX(b), if alternative non-trade restricting measures could not be used to achieve the public health objectives in question. The panel considered that restrictions or bans on advertising and labelling and content requirements that applied on a non-discriminatory basis to both domestic cigarettes and imports would be satisfactory alternatives to an import ban, and therefore the ban could not be justified under Article XX(b) as 'necessary' for reasons of public health. In coming to this decision, the panel simply ignored the possibility that the alternative measures might involve high regulatory and compliance costs, or might be impracticable to implement effectively in a developing country.

Salmon and Herring Landing Requirements

In the *Salmon and Herring Landing Requirements*[12] case, an FTA panel considered the scope of the Article XX(g) exception with respect to measures 'primarily aimed at conservation of an exhaustible natural resource'. In that case, the United States challenged provisions of a Canadian law that required that salmon and herring caught on Canada's West Coast be landed and unloaded in Canada before processing. The landing requirement was imposed after Canada's domestic *processing* requirement had been found in violation of Article XI by a GATT panel, as discussed above.[13] Unlike the measure impugned in the earlier case, the landing requirement did not explicitly prohibit or restrict exports of the unprocessed fish. Nevertheless, its *effect* was to disadvantage American processors, because in the case of fish destined to US processing plants, they would have to be both landed and unloaded in Canada (due to the law) and then repacked, and unloaded again in the United States before processing. The United States claimed that the measure was, in effect, a restriction on 'exportation or sale for export' (i.e. of unprocessed Canadian fish to the United States) and therefore in violation of Article XI of the GATT. Canada argued that even if the landing requirements were in violation of Article XI, the Article XX(g) exception applied, because landing of the fish was necessary for accurate monitoring of the catch pursuant to Canadian conservation programmes. The panel found that other means less restrictive of trade existed to achieve Canada's objectives of monitoring and compliance with its conservation schemes, including cooperation with US authorities and on-board inspection of catches and cargo, and that (at least implicitly) Canada had adopted more restrictive means for protectionist reasons. The panel was also prepared to accept that landing of part of the catch might be necessary for sampling in order to achieve Canadian monitoring and compliance objectives, but considered that a requirement that 100% of the catch be landed went farther than was reasonably necessary for these purposes. In consequence, conservation could not be considered the 'primary purpose' of the landing requirements and therefore Article XX(g) did not apply.

In our view, where a panel employs a least-restrictive means test in its application of Article XX, it should do so in a manner that reflects sensitivity to the fact that environmental policy-makers have limited resources, and often operate under broad background constraints imposed by the political and legal system in their country. The availability of a hypothetically less restrictive means of achieving the same goals should not necessarily mean that the measures under scrutiny fail the least-restrictive means test. The panel should be open to arguments that the hypothetical alternative is not truly available at a reasonable cost to the Contracting Party that has enacted the trade-restricting environmental measure. For instance, in some countries with weakly developed regulatory and legal systems, border controls may be among the few effective ways of addressing some environmental hazards, even if they seem a rather blunt or crude instrument from the perspective of 'state of the art' regulatory theory and practice. To return to the *Thai Cigarette* case, in the abstract, it would have undoubtedly have been possible for the Thai government to have adopted some of the alternative, less trade-restricting means suggested by the panel, such as consumer warnings, public information campaigns, and so forth. But this simply ignores the issue of whether the kinds of sophisticated techniques of persuasion and psychological manipulation employed by Western cigarette manufacturers could be matched, at reasonable cost (or any cost), by the informational resources available to a developing country government. In the environmental area, a more contextually sensitive application of the least-restrictive means test would arguably require panels to draw upon evidence from the broader environmental policy community as to the available regulatory alternatives and their strengths and limitations in a given set of circumstances. Here again, the *Thai Cigarette* decision sets a bad precedent – the panel simply chose to ignore a report of the World Health Organization suggesting that the Thai government's approach was a reasonable instrument choice under the circumstances.

In its recent ruling in *Reformulated Gasoline*, discussed below at pp. 413–16, the WTO Appellate Body rejected the view that the apparently less stringent language of XX(g), referring to measures 'relating to' the conservation of exhaustible natural resources, should be interpreted in the the same way as the expression 'necessary to' in Article XX(b), contrary to the approach taken by the FTA panel in *Salmon and Herring Landing Requirements*. Significantly, in *Reformulated Gasoline*, the Appellate Body breathed life into the criteria in the 'chapeau' of Article XX as a means of preventing protectionist misuse of the exceptions in the Article – thus, the AB considered it an important dimension of any Article XX analysis to enquire into whether measures are 'a disguised restriction on international trade' or 'a means of arbitary or unjustifiable discrimination between countries'. The meaning given by the AB to these provisions will be discussed later in this chapter; it is appropriate to note at this juncture that, to the extent that the 'chapeau' provides a set of legal tests to weed out protectionist misuse, a more contextually sensitive and flexible interpretation of 'necessary' in XX(b) and, *a fortiori*, 'relating to' in XX(g) may be possible without major risk to the integrity of the multilateral trading order.

Lobsters

The *Lobsters* case raised a vexing issue, on which the GATT jurisprudence is far from clear: how to distinguish between border bans that are part of an internal regulatory scheme aimed at both domestic and imported products (permitted by GATT subject only to the Article III National Treatment obligation) and prohibitions or restrictions on imports within the meaning of Article XI (banned by GATT unless strictly justified under Article XX). In the *Lobsters* case,[14] a Canada–US FTA panel considered whether application of a domestic US minimum size requirement to imports of Canadian lobster should be considered as an Article XI prohibition on imports (i.e. the effect of the measure being the exclusion of all Canadian lobsters beneath a certain size) or as part of an internal regulatory scheme within the meaning of Article III.

The minimum size requirement, as it applied to American lobster, was unquestionably a reasonable conservation measure: the intent was to conserve the stock by ensuring that young lobster would not be taken before they could breed. However, because Canada has colder waters, its mature lobster are in general of smaller size, and accordingly Canada had a lower minimum size requirement, which arguably served in the Canadian context the conservation objective as well as did the higher American size requirement in the US context.

The evidence suggests that imposition of the same minimum size requirement on imports of Canadian lobster was largely in response to complaints by American fishermen that the domestic US requirement put them at a competitive disadvantage with Canadian fishermen. In its argument to the panel, however, the US government attempted to justify the application of its minimum-size requirement to Canadian lobster as necessary to the enforcement of the requirement with respect to American lobster. Since lobsters do not carry passports, it would be costly to determine whether a given lobster was Canadian or American once it had entered the stream of commerce. This difficulty was entirely obviated through application of the size requirement to *all* lobster in the market, whether Canadian or American.

In considering whether to view the extension of the size requirement to Canadian lobster as the application at the border of an internal US regulation, or as a prohibition or restriction on imports within the meaning of Article XI, the majority panel judgment reviewed a variety of GATT panel decisions. The majority rejected the view that trade-restricting impacts should be the decisive consideration in classifying a measure as an Article XI measure. This seems in direct contradiction with another FTA panel's ruling in the *Salmon and Herring Landing Requirement* case, where (as discussed above) the panel found that the measure in question, while not taking the legal form of a prohibition or restriction on exports or sale for export, had this effect, and should therefore be considered a prima-facie violation of Article XI.[15] Nor did the *Lobster* panel consider it of paramount importance whether the measure was to be enforced at the border by customs officials or through internal inspections once the product entered the domestic stream of commerce. Instead, the panel's majority decision seems to rest upon its acceptance of the United States's position that the import ban was genuinely an integral part of an internal regulatory regime applicable to both foreign and domestic product. As pointed out in the vigorous dissenting judgment by one expert on the panel, this was precisely how Canada had characterized its landing requirement measure in the *Salmon and Herring Landing Requirement* case, i.e. as connected to the monitoring requirements of its internal conservation regime, and yet in *Salmon and Herring Landing Requirement* the measures were nevertheless categorized as Article XI restrictions or prohibitions on exports.[16] In *Lobsters* the panel did not go on to consider whether, in fact, the scheme violated Art. III, since this issue had been excluded from its terms of reference.

Of course, even where the measures in question are classified as internal regulations under Article III, complex issues may be implicated in determining whether in fact foreign products are being treated equally. A particularly difficult issue is whether only facially discriminatory measures should be considered in violation of Article III, or whether measures with a 'disparate impact' on foreign producers also, in some circumstances, violate the National Treatment obligation. For instance, a country may impose on both domestic products and imports a requirement of environmentally-safe (e.g. biodegradable) packaging, in circumstances where most domestic producers are already using such packaging. Foreign producers, unlike their domestic equivalents, would be required at considerable cost to change packaging methods and materials in order to sell their goods within one particular foreign market. The more specific and idiosyncratic the requirements, the more likely that any foreign producer who does not possess a large market share in the country concerned will simply find that the costs of adapting the product are prohibitive, and will effectively be excluded from the market. Situations of this kind have led to considerable trade frictions within the European Union, despite the existence of institutional mechanisms for harmonization of national environmental standards.

The issue was addressed somewhat indirectly by a GATT panel considering the application of Article III to a variety of measures affecting the importation of beer into several Canadian provinces.[17] Among these measures was a tax on beer containers applied to both domestic and imported beer. However, the tax was refundable where a system of collection of the containers for re-bottling and recycling was used. Such a system was readily available to domestic beer producers, as they were permitted to sell their beer through privately owned retail stores that had such a system in place. Imported beer, by contrast, could only be sold at provincial monopoly liquor outlets where no such system for return of containers was in place. As a result, the only way a foreign producer could comply with the conditions for refund of the tax was to set up its own independent system for collection, re-bottling and recycling of beer containers, which would involve considerable if not prohibitive expense. Since the tax applied equally on its face to both domestic and imported beer, the United States argument amounted to a claim that disparate impact of a facially neutral internal measure could constitute a violation of Article III. The panel found that the container tax as it applied to imported beer did not violate Article III. In significant part, its reasoning was that the disparate impact in question was really due to another, *explicitly* discriminatory practice that was in itself a violation of Article III, i.e. the effective prohibition of foreign beer producers from sale of their beer through private retail outlets.[18] At a minimum, this finding may be interpreted to mean that a mere disparate impact on imports does not render facially neutral internal environmental measures in contravention of the GATT.

Superfund

The *Superfund* case concerned US taxes on imports of certain petroleum and chemical products, the revenues from which were to go to a fund dedicated to environmental protection purposes.[19] In the case of petroleum products, an excise tax for environmental purposes was applied to both domestic and foreign petroleum. The tax on imports was, however, higher than that on domestic products (11.7 cents as opposed to 8.2 cents per barrel). The United States gave no justification for this discrimination, other than that there was no 'nullification and impairment' of a GATT concession because the difference was so small as not to create a competitive disadvantage for foreign suppliers. The panel had little difficulty concluding that there was nevertheless a prima-facie nullification and impairment, and that the discriminatory tax violated the National Treatment obligation of Article III.

The panel treated quite differently, however, the tax on imported chemicals. The United States argued that this tax was no greater than the tax that would be levied on similar substances when used by American producers to make the same chemicals. Therefore, the USA claimed, the tax met the conditions for an exemption from the National Treatment obligation in Article II:2(a), being 'equivalent to an internal tax . . . in respect of an article from which the imported product has been manufactured in whole or in part'.

The panel accepted this claim despite the complainants' objection that the environmental harm from the use of the substances in question in the production of *imported* chemicals occurred not in the United States but in the jurisdiction of manufacture, and thus that the tax represented a United States tax on pollution that was occurring outside its borders. The panel responded to this objection by stating that the General Agreement provisions on tax adjustment 'do not distinguish between taxes for different policy purposes'.[20] This outcome suggests that one clear means by which Contracting Parties can sanction environmentally harmful conduct outside their borders is through environmental taxes that apply to imported products – provided, of course, that equivalent taxes also apply domestically.

Canadian Tuna

The 1979 *Canadian Tuna* case concerned an American import ban on Canadian tuna, imposed under the US Fishery Conservation and Management Act. The ban followed the seizure by Canadian authorities of 19 US fishing boats within the Canadian 200 mile territorial limit. The United States argued that, although in violation of Article XI of the GATT, the tuna ban represented an essential element of the American approach to the conservation of the species. The interests of conservation required that Canada stop unilaterally enforcing its territorial limit against American fishermen and instead negotiate with the United States jointly-agreed catch limits on this essentially shared fisheries resource: 'it was fruitless [according to the American representative] for one coastal state to limit the catch when a school of tuna was in its waters, if the school would be overfished in another State's waters or the high seas'.[21] The tuna ban was a sanction aimed at inducing Canada to end its unilateral actions against American fishermen and instead to accept a cooperative approach to management of the resource, and therefore could be justified on the basis of Article XX(g) as 'related to the conservation of an exhaustible natural resource'. In reply, Canada claimed that the American action was a direct retaliation for the act of seizure and not a response to more general concerns about Canadian non-acceptance of US approaches to management of tuna stocks. The United States did not deny this, but argued that the wording 'related to' in Article XX(g) did not require conservation objectives to be the sole or even primary cause of the measure in question.[22] A final issue related to the requirement of Article XX(g) that the measures in question be 'made effective in conjunction with domestic restrictions on consumption and production'. Although the United States had domestic production quotas with respect to tuna, these did not apply to at least one of the specific species whose importation from Canada had been banned (i.e. albacore tuna). In its decision, the panel began by considering an additional argument, i.e. that the import ban might be justified under Article XI:2, which permits quantitative restrictions where necessary to sustain a system of domestic supply management for primary products (the intent of this provision was arguably to exempt from GATT strictures the border measures required to enforce price and quantity restrictions in domestic agricultural marketing schemes).[23]

The panel rejected the application of Article XI:2 on two largely technical grounds: (1) domestic restrictions were not consistently in force with respect to species covered by the import ban; (2) the language of Article XI:2(c) was explicitly limited to 'restrictions' on imports and therefore this sub-paragraph could not be used as a basis for a total ban.

With respect to Article XX(g), the panel found that this exception did not apply, also for the rather narrow, technical reason that some species of tuna covered by the import ban were not covered by the domestic US restrictions on production. The panel sidestepped entirely the two extremely fundamental jurisprudential issues raised by the case: first, in what circumstances can unilateral action aimed at inducing another state to accept one's own approach to management of a joint resource be considered a GATT-consistent conservation measure; and second, how closely connected to the purpose of conservation the specific measure adopted must be for Article XX(g) to apply. (The panel did note that inasmuch as the American action was solely a retaliation for the seizure of American ships, it would not be covered by Article XX, but failed to comment on the application of this observation to the facts at hand.) Moreover, the panel did find that the import ban on Canadian tuna was not a 'disguised restriction on international trade' within the meaning of Article XX, because it 'had been taken as a trade measure and publicly announced as such'.[24] This interpretation of 'disguised restriction' must now be reconsidered in light of the more complex meaning given to this notion by the Appellate Body in *Reformulated Gasoline*, as discussed below at pp. 413–16.

Tuna/Dolphin I

In the *Tuna/Dolphin* case,[25] Mexico complained that an American embargo of its tuna exports violated, *inter alia*, Article XI of the GATT. The embargo was imposed because Mexico had failed to satisfy US authorities that its tuna was caught in a manner that did not risk the destruction of dolphins. The United States argued that because its restrictions on the manner in which tuna was caught applied to American tuna as well, the import ban should be treated as the enforcement of 'laws, regulations and requirements affecting (the) internal sale, offering for sale, purchase, transportation, distribution or use' of imported products within the meaning of Article III, and not as quantitative trade restrictions. Here, the United States relied specifically on an Interpretive Note annexed to Article III, which states that 'any internal law, regulation or requirement of the kind referred to in [Article III:1] which applies to an imported product and the like domestic product and is collected or enforced in the case of the imported product at the time or point of importation' nevertheless is to be treated as an internal measure within the meaning of Article III:1. As discussed earlier in this chapter, the view of Article III suggested by this Interpretative Note has led to considerable disagreement on whether a given measure should be classified as a restriction or prohibition on imports and exports within the meaning of Article XI, or as an internal measure merely enforced through a border ban (in which case the Article III National Treatment obligation alone would apply, and if non-discriminatory the measure would be found to be GATT-consistent).

Here, the panel rejected the view that Article III, rather than Article XI was applicable, on the grounds that what was being regulated was not the actual imported product (tuna) but the manner in which it had been produced, and that Article III concerned measures that applied to and affected the nature of products themselves. The panel suggested: 'Regulations governing the taking of dolphins incidental to the taking of tuna could not possibly affect tuna as a product.'[26] The panel thus went on to characterize the import ban as a quantitative restriction within the meaning of Article XI, the issue thus becoming whether either Article XX(b) or Article XX(g) could apply to exempt the ban from Article XI strictures. With respect to Article XX(b), the panel simply excluded the possibility that it could apply to the protection of animal life outside the jurisdiction of the Contracting Party taking the measure. Two grounds were provided for this interpretation, neither of which has any textual basis in the General Agreement itself. The first was that the drafting history of Article XX(b) suggested that the essential purpose was to permit sanitary measures to protect human animal and plant health in the importing country. The second ground was that if the broader interpretation of Article XX(b) were accepted, each Contracting Party could unilaterally determine the life or health protection policies from which other Contracting Parties could not deviate without jeopardizing their legal rights under the General Agreement. The General Agreement would then no longer constitute a multilateral framework for trade among all Contracting Parties but would provide legal security only in respect of trade between a limited number of Contracting Parties with identical internal regulations.[27]

Although this finding itself sufficed to make Article XX(b) inapplicable to the US import ban, the panel went out of its way to further narrow the Article's scope. The panel claimed that the language of 'necessity' in Article XX(b) meant the United States would have to show that it had exhausted all options less restrictive of trade before resorting to import restrictions. The panel noted that the possibility of international cooperation with respect to dolphin conservation was an option that the United States had not exhausted.

With respect to Article XX(g), the panel suggested that, like Article XX(b), it could only be invoked to justify measures aimed at protecting the trade-restricting state's own environment. The panel based this view, in part, on the notion that Article XX(g) requires that import restrictions be imposed in tandem with internal measures to control production or consumption of the resource. The panel noted: 'a country can effectively control the production or consumption of an exhaustible natural resource only to the extent that the production or consumption is under its jurisdiction'.

The panel also suggested that since, at a given moment, Mexico could not know how many dolphins had been killed by American fishermen, it could not know whether it was complying with American law, and therefore whether it could avoid an export ban. In the panel's view, 'a limitation on trade based on such unpredictable conditions could not be regarded as primarily aimed at conservation.'

The panel also considered a quite different American measure concerned with the protection of dolphins, the Dolphin Protection Consumer Information Act, which permitted producers to market tuna in the United States with a 'Dolphin-Safe' label, provided US authorities could be satisfied that the tuna were indeed caught in a manner that did not unnecessarily endanger the lives of dolphins. Mexico argued that this law violated Article I:1 of the GATT, the Most Favoured

Nation provision, since documentary evidence on the manner in which tuna were harvested was only required when the tuna came from the Eastern Tropical Pacific; thus, less than the full benefit of the label was conferred on tuna producers from countries such as Mexico that fished in the Eastern Tropical Pacific. The panel rejected this argument, finding that the requirement of documentation would apply equally to any country that wished to fish in the Eastern Tropical Pacific.

The *Tuna/Dolphin* decision has been widely criticized by environmentalists, but vigorously defended by the GATT Secretariat[28] and some trade lawyers.[29] There are many aspects of the decision that are difficult to justify – including the notion that measures that apply to the production process for a product cannot be regarded as internal measures for the purposes of Article III, which would mean that measures that apply equally to domestic products and imports would nevertheless be GATT-illegal, being considered as quantitative restrictions under Article XI.

The forced reading of the General Agreement that characterizes some aspects of the panel's decision must be considered, however, in light of its overall interpretation of the normative structure of the GATT, and it is this interpretation that must be the basis of any fundamental critique of the decision. The panel's view of the GATT is revealed most clearly in the concluding remarks of the panel:

> The panel wished to note the fact, made evident during its consideration of this case, that the provisions of the General Agreement impose few constraints on a Contracting Party's implementation of domestic environmental policies. . . . As a corollary to these rights, a Contracting Party may not restrict imports of a product merely because it originates in a country with environmental policies different from its own. It seemed evident to the panel that, if the CONTRACTING PARTIES were to permit import restrictions in response to differences in environmental policies under the General Agreement, they would need to impose limits on the range of policy differences justifying such responses and to develop criteria so as to prevent abuse.[30]

The fundamental dividing line that the panel sees is between environmental policies for the sake of protecting one's own environment, and policies that somehow dictate to another Contracting Party how it should protect its own environment. This seems a mischaracterization of the problem. First of all, the United States was not aiming paternalistically, as it were, to dictate to Mexico how it should regulate a purely domestic environmental problem. The measure was aimed at the preservation of dolphins as a species surviving in the world's oceans, i.e. of the global environmental commons. There was no domestic Mexican jurisdiction over dolphins that was being encroached upon. Second, the American legislation was not interfering with any specific obligations or rights assigned to Mexican fishermen under Mexican law. Despite the adoption of extraterritoriality language by the panel, the American dolphin protection measures did not impose any obligations on Mexican fishermen that were in actual conflict with environmental laws or policies of the Mexican government. The Mexican government did not have an environmental policy forcing Mexican consumers to eat dolphin-destructive tuna, for instance, or enjoining Mexican fishermen to kill dolphins when fishing for tuna. Nor was the lifting of the import ban on the tuna necessarily conditional upon the Mexican government adopting identical legislation to the American dolphin protection legislation. Mexico was free to permit access to its own market for dolphin-destructive tuna, whether caught by Mexican or foreign fishermen. As long as Mexican fishermen did not use fishing technology that threatened the lives of dolphins, their tuna was free to enter the United States. It is true that in order for Mexican fishermen to use dolphin-threatening technology *and* for their tuna nevertheless to be admitted to the United States, the Mexican government would be required to adopt similar rules to those in force in the United States. But this is far from the massive intrusion on Mexican legal sovereignty evoked by the panel's suggestion that the American measures virtually forced the Mexicans either to adopt identical environmental protection laws to those of the United States or give up their legal rights under the GATT.

By making access to the US market depend upon either an American-like regulatory scheme or adoption of different technology by Mexican fishermen, the US measures did place a commercial disadvantage or burden on Mexican fishermen, in that if their government failed to act the only way they could get access to the US market was to acquire and use a different fishing technology, presumably less efficient or in any event more costly.

However, the panel also was prepared to accept that these kinds of commercial disadvantages might be permissible under Article XX(b) if 'necessary' to protect the United States' own environment. What is most questionable is the panel's view that where the preferences of the trade-restricting state are for protection of the global commons rather than for protection of its own domestic environment, Articles XX(b) and XX(g) can *never* be relied on.

This view seems based upon several different arguments, some of which are more explicit than others in the panel's reasoning. The first is that the drafting history suggests that Article XX(b) was only intended to apply to protection of animal or plant life or health within one's own boundaries. This view of the drafting history is contradicted by evidence that the drafters were likely aware that at the time the GATT was negotiated there were various international conventions and agreements as well as some unilateral legislation that involved import and export restrictions linked to global conservation goals (e.g. for endangered species).[31] In not restricting the wording of XX(b) explicitly to domestic animal and plant life, the drafters may well have intended to make room in the GATT for these pre-existing conservation-related restrictions.

Moreover, other provisions of Article XX suggest that its purpose was not to be limited to exempting measures to protect domestic interests within the trade-restricting state. The clearest example is the exemption for products made with prison labour – clearly what is at issue here is preferences concerning the morality of prison labour in the *exporting* country, not simply in one's own country. Similarly, the general view of Article XX(f) which refers to the 'protection of national treasures of artistic, historic or archaeological value' is that it permits not only restrictions on the export of a Contracting Party's own national treasures, but import and export restrictions on national treasures of *other* Contracting Parties as well.[32] A final view, also implicit in the panel's report, reads into the legal order of the GATT a prohibition on unilateral action to protect the environment beyond one's borders. Undoubtedly, certain kinds of unilateral action that are extraterritorial violate particular rules of international law, both treaty law (e.g. the Law of the Sea Convention) and customary international law.[33] These include direct assertion of control over activity in international waters through the use or threat of military force. Yet apart from the risk described above of increased cheating on trade concessions, it is hard to understand why a *sui generis* rule on non-intervention for environmental purposes should be read into an international regime concerned with preserving and enhancing international commercial exchanges. There is a considerable body of public international law on the issues of non-intervention and the use of economic sanctions against other states. But – at least in its current form – the GATT dispute settlement mechanism has, arguably, neither the institutional competence nor the legitimacy, to interpret and develop these public international law rules. In any event, there is no general public international rule against unilateral action to protect the environment as long as such action does not result in illegal assertion of jurisdiction over international waters or territory or usurpation of the territorial jurisdiction of another state.[34] Clearly, it would be inappropriate to be simply dismissive of the important sovereignty concerns that underpin the panel's ruling. In our estimation, however, these concerns were more appropriately addressed in the panel's observation that the United States had not pursued with sufficient vigour international cooperation as a means of protecting the dolphin population (either bilaterally with Mexico or on a multilateral basis), and therefore that the adoption of unilateral trade restrictions was precipitous and hence not clearly 'necessary' within the meaning of Article XX(b).

The *Tuna/Dolphin I* ruling was never adopted by the GATT Council, Mexico and the United States having agreed to resolve the dispute through diplomatic negotiation. This ultimately led to the conclusion of a *multilateral* agreement on the protection of dolphins in the Eastern Tropical Pacific Ocean – the *Agreement for the Reduction of Dolphin Mortality in the Eastern Pacific Ocean*, which took effect in January 1993, and to which nine countries including Mexico are signatories.[35] However, even as amended in 1992, the US legislation did not fully exempt from the embargo countries that had signed the *Agreement*, although it did provide for a 'fast track' avenue for getting an exemption, if one accepted monitoring under the *Agreement* of one's commitment to reduce dolphin mortality rates.

Tuna/Dolphin II

In *Tuna/Dolphin II*,[36] the European Union challenged provisions for a secondary embargo in the US tuna legislation. Ostensibly aimed at 'leakage' from the primary embargo by transhipment of dolphin-unfriendly tuna through a third country, these provisions were, however, interpreted by a US court to extend to all cases where the exporting country did not have a primary embargo of its own, regardless of whether the tuna it was exporting to the United States had in fact been caught in a dolphin-unfriendly manner. Interpreted in this way, the secondary embargo clearly went beyond what was necessary to prevent circumvention of the primary embargo through shipment of dolphin-unfriendly tuna through third countries.

In considering the EU complaint that the measures violated Article XI of the GATT and could not be saved by any of the exceptions in Article XX, the panel reconsidered the approach of the *Tuna/Dolphin I* panel to Article XX. It forcefully rejected the view expressed in *Tuna/Dolphin I* that Articles XX(b) and (g) could apply only to save environmental measures taken to protect the domestic environment. The panel noted that neither the GATT nor 'general international law' prohibits in principle measures related to things or matters located outside a country's own territory. Moreover, in addressing itself to the original intent argument of the *Tuna/Dolphin I* panel, the *Tuna/Dolphin II* panel, pursuant to the relevant *Vienna Convention* provisions, considered evidence from the *travaux preparatoires* of the 1947 GATT, coming to the conclusion that it was far from clear that the framers had intended to exclude global environmental measures from the Ambit of Articles XX(b) and (g).

The *Tuna/Dolphin II* panel went on, however, to invent a new kind of limit on the scope of XX(b) and (g). It suggested that the exemptions stated in these paragraphs could not be applied to measures the *sole* environmental impact of which is through inducing other countries to change their policies. The panel stated: 'If . . . Article XX were interpreted to permit Contracting Parties to take trade measures so as to force other Contracting Parties to change their policies within their jurisdiction, including their conservation policies, the balance of rights among Contracting Parties, in particular the right of access to markets, would be seriously impaired' (para. 5.26). This reasoning seems based on a misunderstanding of Article XX – this Article does not create or destroy any acquired, legal rights of Contracting Parties, but rather permits on a case-by-case basis exemptions from other GATT strictures, if a set of strict criteria are met. In order for Contracting Parties to have a 'right' not to have their market access disrupted by sanctions-type measures even where such measures could be justified under Article XX, this 'right' must be embodied in a legal rule or norm. No such legal rule or norm exists in the text of the GATT itself. And, as the ICJ held in the *Nicaragua* case[37] there is no general customary rule of international law that prohibits economic sanctions.

In *dicta*, the *Tuna/Dolphin II* panel took the view that not only the secondary embargo, but the primary embargo, could not be justified under Article XX, suggesting that it viewed the environmental impact of the primary embargo *as well* solely in terms of inducing policy changes in other countries. This assumption reveals an ignorance of economics. Quite aside from its impact on policies abroad, the embargo has the direct result of eliminating demand for dolphin-unfriendly tuna in the US; all things being equal, if fewer dolphin-unfriendly tuna are demanded, fewer such tuna will be caught, and fewer dolphins will be killed.[38] Thus, there will be an environmental impact, irrespective of any changes to other countries' policies. Moreover, apart from whatever impact it might have on the policies of any foreign government, the primary embargo places incentives on tuna fishers to adopt the methods necessary to avoid killing excessive quantities of dolphins.

Taxes on Automobiles

In *Taxes on Automobiles*,[39] the European Community challenged, under Article III of the GATT, taxes and related measures of the United States, some of which were aimed at reducing air pollution caused by automobile emissions. The 'gas guzzler' tax, enacted by Congress in 1978 and doubled in 1990, was imposed on the sale of automobiles that did not meet mandated fuel economy requirements. The EC argued that the tax violated the National Treatment requirement with respect to domestic taxation in Article III(2). Much along the lines of the view taken by the panels in *Tuna/Dolphin I* and *II* concerning the National Treatment requirement in Article III(4), the EC claimed that distinctions based on other than physical characteristics of a product (in this case its fuel economy) could not satisfy the National Treatment standard. Thus, domestic automobiles meeting the fuel economy standard, were for Article III purposes, to be regarded as identical *products* to imported automobiles not meeting the standard. In deciding this issue the panel in *Taxes on Automobiles* took a very different approach from the *Tuna/Dolphin* panels. It held that the distinction in question had a legitimate non-protectionist objective – the conservation of fossil fuels – and therefore that imported cars that did not meet the standard did not have to be treated as 'like products' to domestic cars that did; distinctions, if non-protectionist, did not necessarily have to be based on physical characteristics of a product, as long as they were based on objective criteria related to a genuine non-protectionist policy objective. The panel also noted that the fuel economy threshold itself had been set at a level such that many domestic as well as imported vehicles did not meet it at present, therefore suggesting the scheme had not been designed in a protectionist fashion.

The EC also argued that the Corporate Average Fuel Economy (CAFE) provisions violated Article III. CAFE stipulated that for purposes of determining whether the vehicle of a particular manufacturer met the fuel economy threshold, an average would be used that would allow manufacturers to offset large low-fuel economy vehicles against *domestically-produced* small high-fuel economy vehicles (the major policy goal here being to encourage domestic manufacturers to produce more small cars). The panel held that this measure fell within Article III (4), which applies to laws, regulations, and requirements, even though it was related to the taxation measures already discussed. The panel did not see the distinction in question – between cars whose manufacturers have achieved a given overall level of fuel economy in their fleets and those that have not – as inherently discriminatory, even though the distinction did not apply to the individual *products* as such but rather to the behaviour of their manufacturers. It did, however, find an element of discrimination, because foreign manufacturers were less likely to have domestic production against which to offset the lower fuel economy of their imported products.[40]

Clearly, in *Taxes on Automobiles* the panel did not accept the idea developed in the *Tuna/Dolphin* cases that measures on products as such are to be sharply distinguished from other measures, such as Production and Process Methods (PPMs). If products can be distinguished on the basis of how well their manufacturers perform in advancing the objective of fuel conservation, then they can equally well be distinguished on how well their producers achieve the equally legitimate policy objective of dolphin conservation. Yet despite the divergent approaches of these unadopted panels, the trade policy elite has simply accepted the notion of a sharp divergence between measures on products and PPMs as if such a distinction had been written into the GATT all along and not simply invented in the *Tuna/Dolphin* case.

The matter has been further confused by the introduction into the WTO Technical Barriers Agreement of the concept of product-related PPMs. Thus in Annex 1 of the TBT Agreement, a technical regulation is defined as a 'document that lays down product characteristics or their related processes and production methods'. Here, the mainstream interpretation would be that this excludes those PPMs that go to aspects of processes and production methods that have effects aside from those on physical characteristics of a product, such as the import ban on dolphin-unfriendly tuna.[41] However, the language of the TBT Agreement simply begs the question of what can, or cannot, be considered a characteristic of a product. Along the lines of the *Taxes on Automobiles* panel, we believe that relevant characteristics must be determined in light of the regulatory context of the measure in question, and need not be limited to physical characteristics. This is consistent with the view of the Appellate Body in the *Japanese Alcoholic Beverages* case, which with respect to the interpretation of the expression 'like' products for purposes of Article III(2), affirmed the appropriateness of a case-by-case approach, which may employ criteria for likeness that fit the particular regulatory context, including criteria both related and unrelated to physical product characteristics.[42] The Appellate Body noted that the concept of 'like' products should be 'construed narrowly so as not to condemn measures that its strict terms are not meant to condemn'.[43] Of course the structure of Article III(2) is not the same as that of III(4), in that III(2) requires not only similar treatment of like products but of the more expansive category of 'directly competitive' products. However, this does not render a similar logic applicable to the interpretation of characteristics of a product for purposes of determining likeness under Article III(4).

Reformulated Gasoline

In *Reformulated Gasoline*,[44] Brazil and Venezuela challenged requirements of US environmental legislation that conventional and reformulated gasoline sold in the United States conform to a minimum level of 'cleanness', set in terms of a 1990 baseline for emissions. This baseline was determined either on a refinery-specific, 'individual' basis, or on the basis of average 1990 US gasoline quality. Which kind of baseline would apply depended upon whether an entity was a domestic refiner, importer or foreign refiner. While individual baselines (with some qualifications) were used for domestic refiners and importers, calculated on the gasoline actually sold or imported by the entity in question in 1990, foreign refiners were regulated exclusively on the basis of the constructed (average 1990 US quality) baseline. The panel accepted the arguments of Venezuela and Brazil that this differential treatment constituted a violation of the National Treatment obligation in Article III(4). The panel then considered the US claim that, even if a violation of III(4), the differential treatment was justified as a measure 'necessary' to protect life and health under XX(b) or as 'relating to' the conservation of natural resources under Article XX(g). With respect to XX(b), the panel found that the United States had not demonstrated that the method of calculation imposed on foreign producers was the least-trade-restrictive means of achieving its environmental objectives. Thus, the panel rejected US arguments that verification and compliance would be very difficult to execute with respect to individual baselines for foreign refineries, given the way that gasoline is shipped as a fungible commodity, and the lack of US regulatory control over foreign refineries. Also, the US could have achieved its clean air goals equally well by simply applying the statutory or constructed baseline to *both* domestic *and* imported gasoline. In the case of XX(g). While accepting that clean air was an 'exhaustible natural resource' for purposes of this provision, the panel applied a stringent interpretation of 'relating to', much along the lines of the *Herring and Salmon* case, as meaning 'primarily aimed at'. Then, in the manner of *Salmon and Herring Landing Requirements*, it viewed this meaning as implying a least-restrictive means test, and came to the conclusion that the measures in question were not 'primarily aimed at' conservation of exhaustible natural resources because there were many options available to the United States for attaining the desired air quality without discriminating against imported gasoline.

Having found that the US measures could satisfy the requirements of neither XX(b) nor XX(g), the panel considered it unnecessary to examine whether, under the 'chapeau', the measures constituted 'a disguised restriction on trade' or 'a means of arbitrary and unjustifiable discrimination between countries'.

The Appellate Body rejected the reading of a least-restrictive means test into Article XX(g), finding that the panel had failed to interpret the provision in question in accordance with *Vienna Convention* rules for the interpretation of treaties, which required that the 'ordinary meaning' be given to the words of a treaty. The expressions 'necessary to' and 'relating to' on their ordinary meaning did not imply the 'same kind or degree of connection between the measure under appraisal and the state interest or policy to be promoted or realized' (p. 17). However, given that none of the Parties in the appeal had challenged the notion that 'relating to' implied the idea of being 'primarily aimed at' the AB refused explicitly to overrule the *Herring and Salmon* panel on this occasion. It did, note, none the less: '"primarily aimed at" is not itself treaty language and was not designed as a simple litmus test for inclusion or exclusion from Article XX(g)' (p. 18). In any case, the AB – having rejected a least-restrictive-means approach to XX(g) – found that the measures in question were indeed, in the relevant sense, primarily aimed at conservation of exhaustible natural resources:

> The baseline establishment rules, whether individual or statutory, were designed to permit scrutiny and monitoring of the level of compliance of refiners, importers and blenders with the 'non-degradation' requirements. Without baselines of some kind, such scrutiny would not be possible and the Gasoline Rule's objective of stabilizing and preventing further deterioration of the level of air pollution prevailing in 1990, would be substantially frustrated (p. 19).

It is important to note that, unlike the panel, the AB found that in applying XX(g) it was important to consider whether the measures as a whole, and not simply the otherwise GATT-illegal (in this case discriminatory) element, are aimed at conservation.

The AB went on, however, to make a very significant finding concerning the importance of the 'chapeau' (preambular paragraph) of Article XX in a determination of whether otherwise GATT-illegal measures can be justified under the Article. Thus, Article XX analysis must proceed in two steps: (1) provisional characterization of the measure as falling within one (or more) of the specific exceptions in paragraphs XX(a)–(j); (2) 'further appraisal of the same measure' under the criteria of the 'chapeau' (p. 22).

The AB interpreted the 'chapeau' as being aimed at the prevention of protectionist 'abuse' of the exceptions in Article XX:

> The chapeau is animated by the principle that while the exceptions of Article XX may be invoked as a matter of legal right, they should not be applied so as to frustrate or defeat the legal obligations of the holder of the right under the substantive rules of the General Agreement. If those exceptions are not to be abused or misused, in other words, the measures falling within the particular exceptions must be applied reasonably, with due regard both to the legal duties of the party claiming the exception and the legal rights of the other parties concerned (p. 22).

The AB chose to read the three concepts in the 'chapeau' together, such that 'arbitrary discrimination', 'unjustifiable discrimination' and 'disguised restriction' all went in interrelated and overlapping ways to the question of whether there was 'abuse or illegitimate use' of the exceptions available in Article XX. It held that the United States had not explained why its concerns about verification and compliance in the case of foreign refineries could not be resolved by cooperation with foreign authorities, and that the record had not included any evidence that the United States had attempted to enter into such cooperation. Also, in imposing the statutory requirement on imported gasoline, the US had not attempted to obviate imposing costs on foreign refiners that it had clearly thought important to relieve in the case of domestic entities. The first omission of the United States, its non-pursuit of cooperation, showed that the discrimination was 'unjustified'; the second omission, a willingness to alleviate certain costs for domestic but not foreign entities, pointed to a 'disguised restriction on international trade'.

The Appellate Body ruling in *Reformulated Gasoline* is an important advance towards the development of a principled jurisprudence on environmentally-based trade measures. The AB found in the text of Article XX itself a mechanism for ensuring that the exceptions in XX(b) and (g) do not lead to protectionist abuse and therewith pose a threat to the integrity of the trading system; it therefore pointed to at least one way in which this latter goal could be furthered without the results-based manipulation involved in the *Tuna/Dolphin* panels, where an admittedly genuine concern for the avoidance of abuse and the integrity of the system led to the invention of legal distinctions without a textual basis, and the resultant removal of entire classes of measures from possible justification under Article XX. In the subsequent *Turtles* case, a WTO panel misapplied (or wilfully ignored) these jurisprudential advances, producing a decision as defective and disingenuous as the *Tuna/Dolphin* rulings. (As this book went to press, the AB reversed several major elements in the panel's legal reasoning, however.)

Turtles

In *Turtles*,[45] several Asian Members challenged a trade embargo pursuant to a domestic US scheme aimed at preventing shrimp fishing techniques that produce high mortality rates of sea-turtles, an endangered species included in Annex I of the CITES. The scheme permitted unrestricted entry into the United States of shrimp from any country, provided that it was not harvested with technology that endangered sea-turtles. However, where foreign shrimpers chose to employ methods that could endanger the turtles, the access of their shrimp to the United States would depend upon the harvesting country having a regulatory programme similar to that of the United States, aimed at controlling incidental turtle deaths, or a determination that the harvesting environment of the country was such as not to pose any concern about incidental sea-turtle deaths. Pursuant to State Department guidelines, where shrimpers used Turtle Excluding Devices (TED) of the kind required in the United States, they were eligible to export their shrimp to the United States, even if their home government did not have in place a regulatory programme requiring the regulation of shrimping for turtle protection purposes. However, a decision of the US Court of International Trade interpreted the legislation as requiring that the ban be extended to all shrimp imported from countries without the requisite regulatory programmes, even if caught with TED-equipped trawlers.

The complainants, basing their claims on the approach of the *Tuna/Dolphin* panels, argued that the ban was a violation of Article XI, even if part of a scheme that imposed similar turtle conservation methods on US shrimpers. Interestingly, the United States chose not to 'dispute" the claim of an Article XI violation; the panel made a finding of Article XI violation which it said was independent of whether this statement by the US amounted in legal terms to a concession. The panel came to this conclusion in a summary and unreasoned fashion, pointing to the word 'prohibited' in the legislation, and previous panel reports, presumably the unadopted *Tuna/Dolphin* reports. However, the fact that a measure is worded in terms of a prohibition on trade is in itself no proof that, taken in its overall regulatory context, it should be regarded as an Article XI measure and not simply a means of enforcing at the border a domestic regulatory scheme and therefore be considered under Article III (recall the discussion of *Lobsters* above). As for previous panel decisions, the *Turtles* panel did not even bother to consider whether the treatment of Article III in the *Japanese Alcoholic Beverages* and *Periodicals* cases[46] might alter the weight to be attached to the exclusion of so-called PPMs from consideration as measures on 'products' within the meaning of Article III on grounds that they do not go to physical characteristics of the products themselves. (Indeed there would be no reason not to give equal weight to the interpretation of 'like' products in the unadopted *Taxes on Automobiles* panel as to the invention of PPMs in the also unadopted *Tuna/Dolphin* panels.)

The most serious defect in the panel ruling, however, is its approach to Article XX. Apparently relying on the emphasis on the 'chapeau' in Article XX in the *Reformulated Gasoline* AB decision, the panel held that measures such as the shrimp embargo were as such outside of the ambit of Article XX by virtue of the general risk they posed to the integrity of the multilateral trading order. The panel never even considered whether the measures might fall within (b) or XX(g), holding them to be simply excluded in light of the overall purpose and intent disclosed in the 'chapeau' of preventing damage to the integrity of the trading system.

According to the panel,

> In our view, if an interpretation of the chapeau of Article XX were followed which would allow a Member to adopt measures conditioning access to its market for a given product upon the adoption by exporting Members of certain policies, including conservation policies, GATT 1994 and the WTO Agreement could no longer serve as a multilateral framework for trade among Members as security and predictability of trade relations under those Agreements would be threatened. This follows because if one WTO Member were allowed to adopt such measures, then other Members would also have the right to adopt similar measures on the same subject but with differing, or even conflicting, policy requirements. Indeed, as each of these requirements would necessitate the adoption of a policy applicable not only to export production . . . but also domestic production, it would be impossible for a country to adopt one of those policies without the risk of breaching other Members' conflicting policy requirements for the same product and being refused access to these other markets (para. 7.44).

In this discussion, we can only briefly note the numerous jurisprudential errors that the Panel made in its approach to Article XX. First of all, whereas the AB in *Reformulated Gasoline* had stated that the application of Article XX is a two-step process, involving first of all a determination of whether the measures fall within a particular exception, and second, whether they meet the criteria in the chapeau, the panel instead began with the chapeau and never in fact got to the issue of whether the measures fell within XX(b) or (g). Second, and relatedly, in *Reformulated*

Gasoline, the AB had distinguished between the first step, the determination of whether a measure falls within a particular exception, and the second step, that of ascertaining whether the *manner of application* (p. 22) of measures is reasonable or abusive; the panel in *Turtles,* however, got this backwards – it invoked the chapeau not to examine the manner of application of the US measures, but rather to exclude an entire general class of measures from Article XX justification altogether. Fourth, in *Reformulated Gasoline* and also in *Japanese Alcoholic Beverages* and *Beef Hormones*, the AB underlined that a purposive interpretation of an agreement as a whole cannot be a basis for ignoring or not applying its explicit language to the case at hand. Yet the *Turtles* panel used an emphasis on general purposes to ignore the actual legal tests in the chapeau with respect to 'arbitrary' and 'unjustified' discrimination and 'disguised restriction of international trade'. In suggesting that measures that discriminate on the basis of the country of origin of products are inherently unjustifiable under Article XX given the purposes of the Article and the GATT as a whole, the panel essentially rendered meaningless the words 'arbitrary' and 'unjustifiable'. If it had been the intent to render all measures that discriminate 'between countries where the same conditions prevail' unsustainable under Article XX, then the qualifiers 'arbitrary' and 'unjustifiable' would have been entirely superfluous. Indeed, the panel's approach also has the implication of rendering the language 'where the same conditions prevail' superfluous, as it suggests that, on the basis of general purposes of the GATT, measures may not be justified under Article XX regardless of any consideration as to whether the discrimination is in fact due to the same conditions *not* prevailing in the Members subject to differential treatment (as the US claimed in this case). As the AB held in *Reformulated Gasoline*, 'interpretation must give meaning and effect to all the terms of a treaty. An interpreter is not free to adopt a reading that would result in reducing whole clauses or paragraphs of a treaty to a nullity' (p. 23).

Further, there is nothing in the chapeau that suggests the notion that an entire class of measures is simply excluded from possible justification under Article XX, regardless of whether, in the particular case at hand, they are found to constitute 'arbitrary' or 'unjustified discrimination' or a 'disguised restriction on international trade'. In fact, far from viewing Article XX as operating to exclude in principle general classes of measures, in *Reformulated Gasoline*, the AB made the significant observation that 'The relationship between the affirmative commitments set out in, e.g., Articles I, III, and XI can be given meaning within the framework of the General Agreement and its object and purpose by a treaty interpreter only on a case-to-case basis, by careful scrutiny of the factual and legal context in a given dispute, without disregarding the words actually used by the WTO Members to express their intent and purpose' (p. 18). The *Turtles* panel did just the opposite: it failed to apply the words of the 'chapeau', while at the same time substituting a case-specific analysis with the judgment that 'we must determine not only whether the measure *on its own* undermines the WTO multilateral trading system, but also whether such type of measure, if it were to be adopted by other Members, would threaten the security and predictability of the multilateral trading system' (para. 7.43).

This approach, aside from ignoring the characterization of Article XX analysis as a case-by-case determination, applying the specific wording of the Article including the 'chapeau' may actually be in serious tension with the role of a panel under the Dispute Settlement Understanding. As the AB emphasized in *Japanese Alcoholic Beverages*, whatever the precedential value panel rulings may have in subsequent disputes, the central role of the panel is to decide the dispute between the Parties, not to establish an 'authoritative interpretation' of the GATT; in considering whether other, similar measures adopted by other Members not Parties to the dispute would threaten the integrity of the multilateral trading system, the *Turtles* panel purported to affect the future legal rights and obligations of other Members in respect of measures, which were not only not the subject of a complaint pursuant to the DSU, but largely not yet in existence.

Despite all these errors, it is important also to consider the central claim of the panel that measures such as the shrimp embargo do in fact have the impact of imposing conflicting requirements of a kind inherently in tension with the multilateral trading order. The notion that the shrimp regime would result in conflicting requirements seems far-fetched – this would only be the case if foreign shrimpers were required by some other legal system to use a technology that actually did result in harm to turtles, or were prohibited from using devices aimed at conserving them.

This being said, there is a sense in which the possibility of conflicting requirements is inherent in the balance between guarantees of market access and respect for regulatory diversity embodied in the existing multilateral trading system.

While intended to encourage increasing use of and compliance with international standards, the Technical Barriers Agreement and the SPS Agreement clearly affirm the right of Members to maintain differential levels of protection, including for environmental purposes, subject to various justificatory requirements. This deference to diverse regulatory approaches entails the possibility that a producer in country A will find themselves having to satisfy quite different technical regulations when exporting to country B than domestically, and even as between country B and country C to which they may also be exporting. The need to satisfy multiple and diverse requirements imposed by different Members undoubtedly imposes a cost on Members seeking to exercise their trading rights in these circumstances, but this is a necessary cost if regulatory diversity is to be preserved to the extent permitted under the current multilateral system. It is simply arbitrary to associate this kind of cost with measures aimed at protecting the global environment, rather than a Member's domestic environment, or measures that go to processes and production methods, as opposed to physical characteristics of products.

Of course, if one were to properly apply the chapeau, i.e. in accordance with the approach in *Reformulated Gasoline*, discrimination on the basis of processes or production methods might still be found 'unjustifiable', if *in the circumstances* it was not apparently necessary in order to achieve the environmental objectives in question. Thus, for example, if foreign shrimpers had found a technology other than TEDs that produced as good or better an environmental performance, and yet use of TEDs remained a precondition for exemption from the ban, then the PPM in question might well constitute 'unjustified discrimination'. If the TED requirement also favoured shrimpers in the United States, who had already adopted this particular technology due to domestic requirements, then it could be considered as well 'a disguised restriction on international trade'. This is one illustration of why the appropriate route to preventing abuse of Article XX that threatens the multilateral trading system is through careful case-by-case application of its language, not through arbitrary and textually unfounded distinctions between entire classes of measures, as were drawn in the *Tuna/Dolphin* rulings and, now, in the *Turtle* ruling as well. In *Turtles*, upon appeal, the AB rejected the panel's approach to the chapeau as inconsistent with the two-step test in *Reformulated Gasoline.* The AB made the important ruling that '[i]t is not necessary to assume that requiring from exporting countries compliance with, or adopting certain policies (although covered in principle by one or other of the exceptions) prescribed by the importing country, renders a measure *a priori* incapable of justification under Article XX. Such an interpretation renders most, if not all, of the specific exceptions of Article XX inutile, a result abhorrent to the principles we are bound to apply' (para. 121). The AB found the US scheme justified under Art. XX(9), but held there were elements of unjustified and arbitrary discrimination in the manner in which it was applied. For instance the US had not made the same offer for a negotiated agreement to the appellees as it had made to some other countries, and had only allowed imports where countries had adopted policies identical to those of the US, regardless of their different circumstances. (The scheme itself allowed flexibility in this regard.)

The WTO Trade and Environment Committee

It was in part dissatisfaction with the pre-Uruguay Round treatment of trade and environment issues in dispute settlement that led to insistence by some Members, particularly the United States, that trade and environment be recognized as an official part of the WTO agenda. This resulted in the Marrakesh Decision on Trade and Environment, directing the establishment of a WTO Trade and Environment Committee. The Committee is charged with examining, *inter alia*, trade measures for environmental purposes including those taken pursuant to multilateral agreements, the relationship between multilateral trading norms and environmental taxes and charges, ecolabelling, and exports of domestically prohibited goods. In its first two years of work, a number of promising proposals were put before the Committee, including several (by the EC, New Zealand, and Switzerland) that relate to the negotiation of an Understanding that would clarify the relationship of the GATT Article XX to trade measures taken pursuant to the multilateral environmental agreements. The EC proposal, in its most far-reaching form, is for an Understanding that would explicitly permit under Article XX measures taken pursuant to a multilateral environmental agreement, either where specifically mandated by the agreement or where otherwise necessary to protect the environment, provided the criteria in the 'chapeau' of Article XX are met. 'The WTO would not judge the legitimacy of the environmental objectives or the necessity of the measures taken to achieve these objective because the multilateral character of the trade measures would be the best guarantee against abuse'[47] provided that the multilateral agreement was 'open to participation by all parties concerned with the environmental objectives of the MEA, and reflected through adequate participation, their interests, including significant trade and economic interests'. Another proposal, by New Zealand, would explicitly legalize measures taken pursuant to a multilateral environmental agreement against parties to the agreement, even when not specifically mandated by the text, as well as mandated measures against non-parties provided the agreement reflected a genuine multilateral consensus. A WTO panel would determine the existence of such a consensus on the basis of the following conditions: ' (i) negotiation of and participation in an MEA to be open on equitable terms to all interested countries; (ii) broad participation of interested countries in both geographical terms and representing varying levels of development; and (iii) adequate representation of consumer and producer nations of the products covered by the MEA.'[48] In addition, the trade measures would have to meet a proportionality and least-restrictive means test.

Proposals of this kind, and on other issues that are controversial (such as ecolabelling), have failed to advance beyond the discussion stage in the Trade and Environment Committee, a reflection of basic lack of consensus within the Committee.

Managing the risks of environmental protectionism

To us, this lack of consensus is hardly surprising, given the incoherence of the jurisprudence and the lack of analytical clarity in much of the general debate on trade and environment. As we have seen, the panels merely assert that global environment-based trade measures are in tension with liberal trade policy, without any kind of analytical inquiry into the grounds or welfare effects of such measures. However important it is to point out the defects in the jurisprudence in these cases, the future treatment of global environmental measures in international trade law and policy can only be adequately debated on the basis of an analytical enquiry into the rationales and costs and benefits, both domestic and global, of environmentally-based trade measures.

The question is whether there is some reason, intrinsic to the GATT, for viewing preferences for protection of one's domestic environment as a superior justification for limits on GATT strictures to preferences for global environmental protection.

In understanding this issue, it is crucial to draw a distinction between claims that trade measures should be used to attain a specific non-trade goal or vindicate a specific non-trade value, and arguments for a 'level' competitive playing field, evening the odds, or establishing 'fair' rules of the game that are internal to the trading system. The first kind of claim relates to the measures such as the trade sanctions at issue in cases like *Tuna/Dolphin*; the second produces demands for countervailing duty-type measures aimed at protecting domestic producers against the supposed advantage that foreigner producers possess due to lower environmental standards in their home countries.

Environmentally-based trade sanctions

With respect to the first kind of claim, there are important and legitimate policy rationales for why countries may have to intervene with respect to the policies and practices of other countries that affect the environment. These are:

Externalities

In certain circumstances, a country may be able to externalize some of the environmental costs of economic activity within its borders to the nationals of other countries. The classic example is pollution which flows from country A into the territory of country B through common air or water bodies. These spillovers can be of major significance – for example, a significant portion of the acid rain that affects Canada can be attributed to emissions in the United States.

The global environmental commons

The commons may be defined as 'physical or biological systems that lie wholly or largely outside the jurisdiction of any of the individual members of society but that are valued resources for many members of society. International commons of current interest include Antarctica, the high seas, deep seabed minerals, the electromagnetic spectrum, the geostationary orbit, the stratospheric ozone layer, the global climate system and outer space.'[49] Protection of endangered species might be added to this list. Where unconstrained and uncoordinated, exploitation of these physical and biological systems by nationals of each individual jurisdiction may produce what is widely referred to as the 'tragedy of the commons'.[50]

Shared natural resources

'Shared natural resources are physical or biological systems that extend into or across the jurisdictions of two or more members of international society. They may involve non-renewable resources (for example, pools of oil that underlie areas subject to the jurisdiction of adjacent or opposite states), renewable resources (for example, straddling stocks of fish or migratory stocks of wild animals), or complex ecosystems that transcend the boundaries of national jurisdiction.'[51] Property rights to these shared resources cannot easily be assigned on a purely territorial basis, and therefore each sharing state has an interest in the practices and policies of each other sharing state with respect to these resources.

There is not much evidence on the effectiveness of environmental trade sanctions in particular, to achieve these rationales; however empirical work has been undertaken with a view to measuring the impact of economic sanctions more generally on state behaviour. To our knowledge, the most comprehensive work on this question remains the study by Hufbauer, Schott and Elliott,[52] which examines 115 instances of the use of economic sanctions over a period of about 40 years. The authors conclude that these sanctions had an overall success rate of about 34% in achieving an alteration of the conduct of the targeting country in the desired direction.[53] Not surprisingly, they found sanctions were more likely to succeed in changing behaviour where the policy changes in question were relatively modest, and where the sanctions-imposing country was larger and more powerful than the targeted country.[54] Another important observation in this study is that sanctions are least likely to succeed against intransigent, hostile regimes as opposed to countries that are relatively friendly to the sanctions-imposing state.

Relative to many of the sanctions studied by Hufbauer, Schott and Elliott, most environmental trade sanctions would certainly count as aimed at only modest policy changes,[55] in comparison with sanctions that seek to topple an entire regime, or the removal of a pervasive form of social ordering (e.g. apartheid in South Africa). Moreover, Hufbauer, Schott and Elliott's general observations on the importance of the relative size of the sanction-imposing and the targeted country, and about friends and enemies, seem consonant with recent evidence about the effectiveness of some environmental and labour rights sanctions. The threat of trade sanctions by the United States has, for instance, been credited with altering fishing practices that harmed endangered species in countries such as Japan, South Korea, Chile, Taiwan and Peru – all of which could be described as relatively 'friendly' states from the US point of view, and all (with the possible exception of Japan) significantly smaller and less powerful than the US.[56] By contrast, US threats to deny MFN status to China, a totalitarian quasi-superpower with a hostile ideological system, has made little impact in terms of human rights, including labour rights compliance.

Overall, the evidence suggests that trade sanctions are of limited but real effectiveness, and in this respect they are no different from other, more extreme forms of coercive action such as military force where the record of effectiveness is also extremely mixed (e.g. Lebanon, Bosnia, Somalia, Rwanda, Haiti and Vietnam). On the other hand, a systematic strategy of isolationism, appeasement, or acquiescence would largely resign us to accept grotesque human rights abuses or indeed attempted genocide without external opposition.

An issue closely related to the effectiveness of economic sanctions is the relative desirability of sanctions as opposed to other instruments for influencing the behaviour of other countries and their producers. For instance, the GATT Secretariat advocated the use of financial inducements as an alternative means to sanctions for influencing countries to adopt higher environmental standards.[57] This proposal has the virtue of attaching a price to the invocation of such sanctions and thus providing some assurance that these higher standards are truly valued for their own sake in the country desiring the changes, especially in cases of ostensible *ad hoc* paternalism or altruism, while trade sanctions, lacking such an explicit price (beyond price effects on consumers), may be easily subverted by protectionists. Chang argues, however, that subsidies, as opposed to sanctions, create a perverse incentive for foreign countries to engage in, or intensify, the offensive behaviour (or make credible threats to this effect) in order to maximize the payments being offered.[58]

A recent study of the effects of both carrots and sticks on political change in South Africa supports Chang's scepticism about carrots; it concludes that 'political strategies that rely on inducements rather than commands are limited in what they can accomplish'.[59] Moreover, in cases of transboundary externalities, the global environmental commons, and shared natural resources (in contrast to exchanges of tariff concessions), a principle that victims (or their supporters) should always pay ('bribe') violators to achieve compliance would seem impossible to defend either ethically or politically. However, in some cases financial assistance to enable poor Third World countries to meet higher environmental standards may be warranted on distributive justice grounds.

Another alternative[60] to trade restrictions is environmental labelling (so called ecolabelling), which allows individuals as consumers to express their moral preferences for environmental protection.[61] Products that are produced in a manner that meets a given set of environmental standards would be entitled to bear a distinctive logo or statement that informs consumers of this fact. While labelling may enable individual consumers to avoid the moral 'taint' of consuming the product in question themselves, if most consumers have a preference for terminating production altogether (rather than merely reducing consumption and production) by changing a foreign country's domestic policies, then a collective action problem arises as in any approach to influencing behaviour that depends upon coordinating action among large numbers of agents. Unless she can be sure that most other consumers will do likewise, the individual consumer may well not consider it rational to avoid buying the product in question.[62]

In sum, neither financial inducements nor labelling programmes are self-evidently superior policy instruments to sanctions for influencing other countries' environmental practices. Each has its own drawbacks. However, it must be admitted that little concrete empirical evidence exists that would allow a rigorous comparison of these alternative instruments with sanctions. In addition, the greatest effectiveness might actually be achieved by a combination of more than one of these instruments. Again, in the absence of empirical work, it is difficult to make out a clear-cut case for excluding the use of trade sanctions as an instrument for influencing.

Competitiveness-based environmental trade measures

Unlike the arguments for trade restrictions on environmental grounds that we have been discussing up to this point, which have a normative reference point external to the trading system itself, competitiveness-based 'fair-trade' claims focus largely on the effects on domestic producers and workers of other countries' environmental policies and not *per se* on the effects of those policies on the environment and on workers elsewhere. Competitiveness claims are, in principle, indifferent to the improvement of environmental practices in other countries. Hence, in the case of competitiveness claims, trade measures that protect the domestic market or 'equalize' comparative advantage related to environmental standards are a completely acceptable *substitute* for other countries raising their standards.

Competitiveness claims usually refer to one of two kinds of supposed unfairness (and, it is often argued as well, welfare losses) that stem from trade competition with countries that have lower environmental standards:

1 It is unfair (and/or inefficient) that our own firms and workers should bear the 'costs' of higher environmental standards through loss of market share to foreign producers who have lower costs due to laxer environmental standards in their own country.
2 It is unfair that downward pressure should be placed on our own environmental standards through trading with countries that have lower standards.

Both these arguments are, in our view, largely incoherent and in fact in tension with the basic theory of comparative advantage in trade. Assuming there is nothing wrongful with another country's environmental policies along the lines discussed in the first part of this chapter, then why should a cost advantage attributable to these divergent policies not be treated like any other cost advantage, i.e. as part and parcel of comparative advantage? In fact, even if all countries had the same level of environmental consciousness, or even the same general environmental standards, approaches to instrument choice as well as the choice of risks on which to concentrate would still differ widely, due to differing climatic and other geographical or demographic conditions. For these reasons, even in a world where all citizens shared the same environmental preferences, environmental laws and regulations would still be likely to differ substantially between countries, and even where they were the same, the costs to industry of complying with those laws and regulations would still likely differ substantially from country to country.

Precisely because the implicit benchmark of fairness is so illusory, i.e. a world where governmentally-imposed environmental protection costs are completely equalized among producers of like products in all countries, trade measures based upon this kind of fairness claim are likely to be highly manipulable by protectionist interests. Since, of course, protectionists are really interested in obtaining trade protection, not in promoting environmental standards, the fact that the competitive fairness claim in question does not generate a viable and principled benchmark for alteration of other countries' policies is a strength not a weakness – for it virtually guarantees that justifications for protection will always be available, even if the targeted country improves its environmental standards.

As for the argument concerning downward pressure on one's own standards, shifting the competitiveness costs of these standards to workers in other countries seems distributively *perverse*. No matter how high an intrinsic or instrumentalist value we may wish to put on high environmental standards in our own country, there is simply an unsupportable leap of logic in the conclusion that someone else should be paying the price for them. First of all, workers in other countries do not even usually directly benefit from these higher standards, whereas workers in one's own country do. Second, most competitiveness-based fair trade claims are targeted against countries which are poorer than the trade-restricting country, often with lower *per capita* incomes, higher levels of unemployment, and weaker social welfare nets (in some instances, the revenue from trading products may be essential to obtaining foreign exchange to buy essential goods such as medicines and foods). Moreover, we do not believe that, generally speaking, lowering environmental standards is an appropriate response to competitive pressures. There is, in fact, a wide range of alternatives, such as better regulation which reduces compliance costs without lowering standards[63] and investment in technologies that are likely to reduce the costs of compliance with environmental standards.

Of course, it is arguable (although there is not much hard empirical evidence on the matter) that governments and/or firms are in fact responding by lowering standards, rather than through these arguably superior policy alternatives. However, these sub-optimal policy responses surely represent a political and social problem within countries that are lowering standards in response to competitive pressures. Again, it seems hardly fair that workers (or firms for that matter) in other countries should bear the burden of avoiding choices in another country that are ultimately attributable to a flawed policy process in that country.

A variation of the claim about the effect of competitiveness pressures on domestic environmental standards suggests the possibility of a form of beggar-thy-neighbour behaviour that may, admittedly, leave all countries worse off. This is the 'race to the bottom', whereby countries competitively lower their environmental standards in an effort to capture a relatively greater share of a fixed volume of trade or investment.[64] Much like the beggar-thy-neighbour subsidies wars that characterized agricultural trade among the Canada, the US and the EU and other countries during the 1980s, it is not difficult, using the model of a Prisoner's Dilemma game, to show that competitive reduction in environmental standards will typically result in a negative sum outcome,[65] as long as one assumes that before entering the race each country's environmental standards represent an optimal domestic policy outcome for that country.

The 'race to the bottom' claim has a different normative basis from the other competitiveness-based claims discussed above. Those claims relate to the proper distribution of the competitiveness costs of maintaining higher environmental standards than one's trading partners. The normative basis for concern over the race to the bottom, by contrast, sounds in the language of efficiency: the race ends, literally, at the bottom, with each country adopting sub-optimal domestic policies, but no country in the end capturing a larger share of the gains from trade.

Frequently, beggar-thy-neighbour regulatory competition is able to flourish much more easily where it is possible to reduce on a selective basis environmental standards to attract a particular investment or support a particular industry or firm. It is more difficult and more costly to engage in these activities where the formal statutory framework of environmental regulation must be altered across-the-board.

Accepting, however, that cooperation is the ultimate solution to the 'race to the bottom', a further difficult question remains as to the appropriateness of trade restrictions as a sanction to induce a cooperative outcome. Here, there is important further work to be done in applying the insights of game theory to beggar-thy-neighbour trade conflicts such as, for instance, the agricultural subsidies wars: did trade retaliation facilitate or frustrate a cooperative solution, i.e. the Uruguay Round Agreement on Agriculture? The role of unilateral sanctions in inducing rules-based, cooperative solutions to conflict is a complex one. Sophisticated advocates of unilateralism or aggressive reciprocity, such as Laura Tyson[66] and Carolyn Rhodes,[67] argue for trade measures as a means of inducing a rules-based cooperative equilibrium, not as a long-term strategy of non-cooperative behaviour. The problem, as has been articulated by Bhagwati and others, is that these trade restrictions usually constitute deviations from *existing cooperative outcomes (pre-existing multilateral rules)*. Therefore, depending on one's standpoint such restrictions may resemble cheating on an existing cooperative equilibrium, rather than inducement to create a new one. One response of the unilateralists and reciprocitarians might be that the 'race to the bottom' or 'beggar-thy-neighbour' conduct of one's trading partners has, in fact, already put in danger the pre-existing cooperative equilibrium, and that no return to a rules-based approach is possible unless new rules are adopted to deal with the 'race to the bottom'. However, free traders might well respond that an approach to inducing a new equilibrium based upon the use of technically illegal trade measures as a sanction to bring about negotiation of new rules is likely to undermine countries' overall confidence in the rule of law, and therefore actually to complicate the future prospects for rules-based solutions to trade conflict.

In the GATT, there is arguably already a kind of implicit response to this dilemma, to be found in the concept of non-violation nullification and impairment in Article XXIII. In some circumstances, a GATT panel may find that a Contracting Party's practices, even if not in technical violation of the General Agreement, nevertheless undermine reasonable expectations of another Party as to the benefit that it would receive from GATT concessions. In this situation, trade sanctions may ultimately be authorized, even if the targeted country did not engage in a technical violation of the GATT rules. Where a Contracting Party views the 'beggar-thy-neighbour' but technically GATT-legal conduct of another Party as undermining the existing cooperative equilibrium of GATT rules and concessions, it may seek GATT approval of ultimate recourse to unilateral trade measures through making a case that non-violation nullification or impairment has occurred. This procedure prevents each Party being judge in its own cause, and thereby obviates the consequent potentially negative implications for overall confidence in the rule of law. Through this means, trade sanctions or the threat of sanctions, may be used as a legitimate instrument for inducing one's trading partners to bargain towards new or reformed rules to end a 'race to the bottom'. Thus, even where it could be shown that trade restrictions are appropriate as a means of inducing a cooperative solution, we do not see a justification for taking such measures outside the existing jurisprudential framework of the WTO, or for making the framework more amenable to unilateral actions in which Members are judges in their own cause as to whether the existing cooperative equilibrium has been undermined by purported 'beggar-thy-neighbour' conduct of other

Members.

The 'systemic threat' argument

Even in the presence of indeterminate welfare effects, free traders might still reject environmental trade measures on the basis that such measures, if widely permitted or entertained, would significantly erode the coherence and sustainability of rule-based liberal trade. We ourselves, in earlier chapters, have argued that competitiveness-based or level playing field 'fair trade' measures, such as countervailing and antidumping duties, already pose such a threat. This is based on the notion that the legal order of international trade is best understood as a set of rules and norms aimed at sustaining a long-term cooperative equilibrium, in the face of on-going pressures to cheat on this equilibrium, given that the short-term political pay-offs from cheating may be quite high (depending, of course, on the character and influence of protectionist interests within a particular country, the availability of alternative policies to deal with adjustment costs etc.).[68] In the presence of fundamental normative dissensus as to what constitutes 'cheating' on the one hand, and the punishment of others' cheating on the other, confidence in the rules themselves could be fundamentally undermined, and the system destabilized.

With respect to the systemic threat from environmental trade measures, it is important to distinguish between purely unilateral measures, and those that have a multilateral dimension. The former measures are based upon an environmental or labour-rights concern or norm that is specific to the sanctioning country or countries. Here, there is a real risk of dissolving a clear distinction between protectionist 'cheating' and genuine sanctions to further non-trade values – the sanctioning country may well be able to define or redefine its environmental causes so as to serve protectionist interests. Measures with a multilateral dimension, by contrast, will be based upon the targeted country's violation of some multilateral or internationally recognized norm, principle, or agreement – for instance, a provision in an accord to protect endangered species. These norms, principles, or agreements are typically not the product of protectionist forces in particular countries, nor are they easily captured by such forces (although the example of the Multi-Fibre Arrangement suggests that this is not invariably the case). It is a similar logic that informs the favourable view of technical requirements based on international standards in the WTO Technical Barriers Code.

It should be possible to build into Article XX of the GATT a series of limits or criteria that are likely to minimize the protectionist abuse of environmental rights[69] trade sanctions, and the corresponding risk of a loss of coherence and integrity in the GATT legal framework. In developing such criteria, we believe it is important to distinguish four contexts in which environmental trade sanctions may be employed: (1) where trade measures are explicitly contemplated in an international treaty that establishes environmental standards; (2) where trade measures are not contemplated in the treaty or agreement, but where an independent body, such as a supranational dispute settlement panel, commission, or monitoring authority, has found the targeted country in violation of international environmental standards; (3) where the sanctions-imposing country or countries themselves have determined that the targeted country is in violation of an international norm or standard, in the absence of an independent ruling by a neutral third-party (e.g. international institution); (4) where the sanctions-imposing country merely asserts a norm or standard of environmental protection as appropriate, in the absence of an internationally recognized norm or standard. Obviously, trade sanctions involved to promote environmental protection are much more readily justified in categories (1) and (2) than categories (3) and (4).

We now consider how an Article XX analysis in dispute settlement might adequately address the 'systemic threat' potentially present in the use of each of these classes of measures.

Earlier in this chapter, we alluded to the existence of international environmental agreements that explicitly provide for trade restrictions as a means of enforcing the agreement or of achieving its environmental objectives. The most obvious example is the CITES Convention,[70] restricting trade in endangered species. Lucrative export markets are often a major incentive for hunters to violate domestic regulations with respect to the protection of endangered species. Domestic monitoring and enforcement of limits or prohibitions on the killing of such species are often of limited effectiveness. Effective border measures may well be an attractive alternative or supplement.[71] Here, the environmental agreement itself embodies an explicit choice for trade restrictions as an instrument of environmental regulation (not merely a sanction). The agreement does not merely permit, but *requires* such restrictions. Such is the case, as well, with the Basel Hazardous Wastes Convention and the Nuclear Non-Proliferation Treaty.

In these kinds of instances, trade measures taken against *signatories* of the international environmental agreement posed no real legal issue for the GATT 1947, since most such agreements came into force subsequent to the relevant GATT provisions. This is due to the public international law principle that, in the event of a conflict, the provisions of a later treaty take precedence over those of an earlier one.[72] However, the GATT 1994 is legally distinct from the GATT 1947,[73] and therefore for purposes of the relevant *Vienna Convention* provisions, most of these environmental agreements would no longer be treaties later in time with respect to the GATT 1947 obligations incorporated into the GATT 1994. Hudec suggests, that none the less, as between signatories of both the GATT 1994 and the environmental agreements, the latter may take precedence on *lex specialis* grounds: 'environmental agreeements are clearly more specific than GATT in terms of their subject matter. Under the principle of *lex specialis*, it is normally presumed that the more specific of two agreements is meant to control, even when the more general agreement happens to be later in time.'[74] However, the concept of *lex specialis* more ordinarily applies where the more specific agreement is an elaboration of the more general one, rather than in the case of two independent legal regimes.

With respect to trade measures taken against non-signatories of the environmental agreement who are Members of GATT/WTO, a legal issue does arise. Even if the Members are non-signatories of the environmental agreement, we see no compelling reason why such measures should not be justified under Article XX.

There is a lesser risk of countries actually negotiating international environmental agreements for the purpose of cheating on their trade commitments, and so here the concern with protectionist 'cheating' does not justify particularly rigorous scrutiny of the trade measures in question. As well, the trade measures are closely bound up with the structure and purpose of the agreements themselves; the closeness of the interrelationship will, in these instances, often reflect important rationales for choosing trade controls as an environmental instrument, thereby addressing the concern that trade not be unnecessarily or gratuitously restricted for environmental purposes. There is a more general international law issue of whether the use of trade measures against a country based on an agreement that it has not signed represents an unwarranted interference with that state's sovereignty. However, the bounds of state sovereignty (and the very meaning of the concept) are in flux in a number of areas of international law.[75]

Even where an international environmental agreement or an international legal norm does not justify or require trade measures for its enforcement, a country may decide to use trade measures as a sanction against another country or countries that it deems in violation of the agreement or norm. Here, serious risks of cheating on trade liberalization commitments do in fact exist. This is especially true where trade measures are imposed based on a unilateral determination that some relatively general or even controversial norm of international environmental law has been violated. As well, there is a genuine concern that trade restrictions do not become the instrument of choice for dealing with disputes about international environmental law, just because they constitute a relatively easy and certainly in many instances a visceral response to such disputes. For both these reasons, such measures should only be exempted from GATT strictures where they pass a rigorous 'screen' for protectionism. As discussed above, in *Reformulated Gasoline* and *Turtles* the Appellate Body determined that, with respect to how a scheme is *applied*, the appropriate vehicle for such scrutiny was the 'chapeau' or Article XX, with the Member invoking Article XX having the burden showing that the application of the measure in question does not constitute 'arbitrary' or 'unjustifiable' discrimination, or a 'disguised restriction on international trade'.[76] In addition, under Art. XX(b), measures must be 'necessary', which has been interpreted to mean the least trade-restrictive available to achieve the goal in question. Art. XX(g) has its own 'screen' for protectionism – the measures must have been taken in conjunction with constraints on domestic production or consumption. Under XX(b), it will be important to enquire whether alternative avenues of dispute settlement exist, either under international agreements or within international environmental institutions, whether an attempt has been made to resolve the disagreement through consultations or arbitration aided by international environmental institutions, and whether it is the view of international environmental institutions or authorities[77] that a violation of an international agreement or norm has, indeed, occurred. To facilitate a determination on this last point, panels should bear in mind Article 13.2 of the Dispute Settlement Understanding, which gives panels the right to consult experts, and obtain 'an advisory report in writing from an expert review group'. This clearly permits consultation with international environmental institutions or authorities.

While such consultation should generally concern factual issues, with respect to the determination of whether a measure constitutes a disguised restriction on international trade, whether in truth an international norm or environmental agreement has been violated *is* a factual issue, which goes to the probability that the trade measure constitutes protectionism as opposed to legitimate (albeit unilateral) enforcement of environmental norms.

A final case is that of trade measures that are taken against a country in the absence of any alleged violation of an international agreement or norm, merely on the basis that the citizens of the country in question find the environmental practices or policies of the affected state to be repugnant and/or they seek to change those policies. Here, trade measures are being used in the first instance as sanctions to support the domestic values of the trade-restricting state. Since there is no external benchmark of any kind to assist in distinguishing, on an objective basis, these sanctions from disguised 'cheating' on trade liberalization commitments, the scrutiny of these measures should entail special vigilance in the application of the least-restrictive means test. There are a number of factors that a dispute panel should consider in determining whether an environmental exemption from GATT strictures is warranted. Foremost among these is why a multilateral approach has not succeeded in the evolution of international agreements or norms. Have attempts at international cooperation been defeated by free-rider problems? Is the state against which the trade restricting measures are directed a hold-out that is frustrating bona fide attempts by other states, including the trade-restricting state, to secure a multilateral solution? Here it is important to consider the extent to which the non-adherence of some states to a multilateral approach will undermine the efforts of others to address a global environmental problem.[78] A second factor that should, arguably, always be taken into account is whether the trade-restricting state has exhausted all avenues of bilateral negotiation and cooperation as a solution to the problem. In the *Reformulated Gasoline* case, it will be recalled, the Appellate Body considered that the enforcement and verification issues that the US had cited in justification of not permitting foreign refiners to use individual baselines could have been solved by cooperation with authorities of gasoline-exporting states, and it viewed the measure in question as unjustifiable discrimination in large part because the US had not made a serious attempt at a solution based on cooperation, or had not shown evidence of such an attempt. Of course, it is fundamental to a determination as to whether all reasonable efforts have been made for an international cooperative solution – either bilateral or multilateral – to know whether the trade restricting state's *terms* for such a settlement are themselves reasonable. This goes to one of the main concerns of developing countries with respect to international environmental law – the costs to these countries of international solutions to global environmental problems. Here (as the AB would suggest in *Turtles*), international environmental agreements that contain obligations that are variable according to the circumstances of individual countries[79] may provide a benchmark for determining the reasonableness of the terms on offer for a cooperative solution. This is certainly a matter on which it would be appropriate for a GATT/WTO dispute panel to seek an advisory opinion from international environmental institutions and authorities, as well as international institutions and authorities concerned with the situation of developing countries. In some circumstances, a reasonable offer for a cooperative solution may be deemed to include economic assistance to defray some of the costs of implementing domestically such a solution. Again, to return to the AB ruling in *Reformulated Gasoline*, where a measure imposes differentially greater costs on foreign producers, and the Member taking the measure has *not* made reasonable efforts to mitigate these costs in a manner consistent with its regulatory objectives, a conclusion may well be possible that the measure is a 'disguised restriction on international trade'.

THE NORTH AMERICAN FREE TRADE AGREEMENT

The North American Free Trade Agreement (NAFTA) is the first comprehensive trade treaty that deals explicitly with the relationship between trade and environmental protection. Nevertheless, the key NAFTA provisions on environment are unlikely to play any significant role in sustaining or enhancing levels of environmental protection in the Member countries, and in the case of the provisions on technical standards, may actually threaten high environmental standards. The NAFTA environmental side-agreement, the North American Agreement on Environmental Cooperation, does not establish any substantive transnational environmental norms or standards. However, it does establish an institutional framework from which such norms or standards may eventually emerge. As well, the side-agreement binds the Parties to effective enforcement of their own domestic environmental laws, and provides for dispute settlement and, ultimately, sanctions where a NAFTA Party persistently fails to enforce these laws.

Article 104: Environmental and Conservation Agreements

Article 104 states that in the event of an 'inconsistency' between the NAFTA and the trade provisions of several major environmental treaties, including the Convention on International Trade and Endangered Species (CITES), the provisions of the environmental treaty shall prevail 'to the extent of the inconsistency'. The kinds of trade obligations in question are, generally speaking, export and/or import bans, which would normally run afoul of Article 309 of the NAFTA. Article 309 incorporates into the NAFTA the GATT Article XI prohibition on both export and import restrictions and prohibitions.

Since any measure saved by Article 104 is, therefore, likely also to constitute a violation of Article XI of the GATT, will Article 104 have any real significance in enabling the implementation of environmental treaties? This will depend on whether Article 104 applies to the Parties' pre-existing GATT obligations as well as to the provisions of NAFTA. Article 103(1) of the NAFTA states that 'The Parties affirm their existing rights and obligations with respect to each other under the *General Agreement on Tariffs and Trade* and other agreements to which the Parties are party'. Article 103(2) then goes on to state: 'In the event of any inconsistency between the provisions of this Agreement and such other agreements, the provisions of this Agreement shall prevail to the extent of the inconsistency, except if otherwise provided in this Agreement'.

Does the expression 'other agreements' in 103(2) mean any agreement besides the NAFTA to which the Parties are signatories, including GATT, or does it refer to 'other agreements' as defined in Article 103(1) – i.e. agreements other than the GATT and NAFTA? If the second interpretation is correct (i.e. that NAFTA does not take precedence over GATT although it does over agreements other than GATT), then Article 104 is likely to have very little effect. The one case where Article 104 would still have an impact is if, in the future, an otherwise GATT-inconsistent environmental treaty received a waiver under Article XXV:5 of the General Agreement. In that case, while the treaty would no longer entail violation of the NAFTA Parties' GATT obligations (i.e. due to the waiver), it could still be in violation of their NAFTA obligations. Here, Article 104 *would* apply to resolve the inconsistency in favour of the environmental treaty. Finally, it is to be noted that any dispute between NAFTA Members concerning a treaty listed under Article 104 is to be referred to the NAFTA dispute settlement process rather than to the GATT (Article 2005.3).

Article 1114: Environmental Measures

Article 1114(2) states in part that 'The Parties recognize that it is inappropriate to encourage investment by relaxing domestic health, safety, or environmental measures. Accordingly, a Party should not waive or otherwise derogate from, or offer to waive or otherwise derogate from, such measures as an encouragement for the establishment, acquisition, expansion, or retention in its territory of an investor'. This provision is the most innovative of the NAFTA provisions on environment, in that it does recognize explicitly the danger of an environmental 'race to the bottom', where investors are attracted to the NAFTA jurisdiction with the lowest environmental standards – thereby possibly exerting downward pressure on standards elsewhere as the Parties compete for the jobs that come with investment. However, the actual provisions of Article 1114 may be inadequate to its purpose. First of all, and of greatest significance, the language 'a Party should not waive' connotes something less than a full legal obligation – generally, NAFTA obligations are expressed by the more clearly imperative word 'shall'.

One drawback in adopting existing environmental measures as the baseline is that removal or relaxation of some existing environmental measures may actually be justified, from an environmentalist perspective, in light of changes in technology as well as shifts in the choice of environmental instrument, for instance from 'command and control' type regulations to taxes and charges. For example, if Canada implements a new reforestation management system that results in much more rapid reforestation, why should Canada not be able to exploit any competitive advantage that comes from being able to provide producers located in Canada with more liberal quotas for timber than a less effective conservation system in the

United States would permit?

Finally, the proposed dispute settlement process with respect to Article 1114(2) does not appear to lend itself to the kind of in-depth investigation that would be required to determine if a Party was under-enforcing its own laws in order to encourage investment. Thus, Article 1114(2) states: 'If a Party considers that another Party has offered such an encouragement, it may request consultations with the other Party and the two Parties shall consult with a view to avoiding any such encouragement'. Is this process of 'consultations' intended to exclude further recourse to the normal NAFTA dispute resolution mechanism that allows for in-depth investigation and the assessment of expert opinion? While the normal dispute resolution mechanism applies to all the provisions of NAFTA, it does so '(e)xcept as otherwise provided in this Agreement' (Article 2004). It is unclear whether the provision for consultations in Article 1114 would constitute one of these exceptions to the application of the Chapter Twenty dispute settlement mechanism. It could be argued that the Chapter Twenty mechanism still applies, since elsewhere in the NAFTA when the Parties have wished to exclude recourse to Chapter Twenty procedures, they have done so through an explicit exclusionary clause (see Annex 1137.2 Exclusions from Dispute Settlement).

The NAFTA provisions on environment fall far short of an effective environmental charter, especially if one balances the strict scrutiny of a Party's differentially higher trade-impacting environmental standards provided for in Chapter Nine against the rather weak limits on investment-impacting downward movement in a Party's standards stipulated in Article 1114(2). It is perhaps not surprising, therefore, that the Clinton Administration would insist on the negotiation of supplemental provisions in a parallel accord. It is to this side-agreement that we shall now turn our attention.

The North American Agreement on Environmental Cooperation

The NAAEC, often referred to as the NAFTA environmental side-agreement, states a set of general objectives that include fostering 'the protection and improvement of the environment in the territories of the Parties', increased 'cooperation . . . to better conserve, protect and enhance the environment' and the avoidance of 'trade distortions and new trade barriers' (Article I). The NAAEC also contains a set of 'general commitments', which include public reporting and education about environmental matters, assessment of environmental impacts where appropriate, and the promotion of economic instruments of environmental regulation (Article II). In addition, Article III stipulates that 'each Party shall ensure that its laws and regulations provide for high levels of environmental protection and shall strive to continue to improve those laws and regulations'. However, Article III also recognizes 'the right of each Party to establish its own levels of domestic environmental protection'. It is difficult, but not impossible to reconcile these two aspects of Article III. One approach would be to argue that Article III permits a Party to set its own levels of protection, as long as those levels are 'high' by some objective standard. An alternative interpretation, which would greatly attenuate the significance of Article III, is that each Party must set a level of environmental protection that is 'high', but that the meaning of a 'high' level of environmental protection is to be determined by each Party's domestic values and priorities.

Article 5 requires that 'each Party shall effectively enforce its environmental laws and regulations through appropriate government action' and gives a list of examples of such actions, ranging from the use of licences and permits to contractual and voluntary arrangements for environmental compliance. Article 6 requires that 'interested persons' be able to request a Party's regulatory authorities to investigate possible violations of domestic environmental laws and regulations. Since the NAAEC does not contain a definition of 'interested persons', whether this includes, for example, environmental NGOs will depend on the standing rules in each Party's domestic legal system.

Of all these obligations, *only* a Party's obligation to enforce effectively its own environmental law can be regarded as 'hard' trade law, for only this obligation carries with it the possibility of binding dispute settlement and, ultimately, sanctions for non-compliance. Thus, where there is a complaint that 'there has been a persistent pattern of failure [of a NAFTA Party] to enforce its environmental law', Part V of the NAAEC provides for a dispute settlement process that closely parallels the general NAFTA dispute settlement process set out in Chapter 20. A rather significant difference is that a request for a panel must be approved by a two-thirds vote of the Parties. This means that where, for instance, Canada requested a panel to investigate an alleged persistent failure of Mexico to enforce its environmental laws, it would have to obtain the agreement of either Mexico or the United States in order for dispute settlement to proceed (Article 24(1)).

If, in its final report, a panel concludes that in fact, a persistent failure of enforcement has occurred, the Parties to the dispute 'may agree on a mutually satisfactory action plan, which normally shall conform with the determinations and recommendations of the panel' (Article 33). If no such action plan is agreed upon, then, after 60 days (but within 120 days) of the final report, the complaining Party may request that the panel reconvene and determine an appropriate action plan and/or a monetary assessment against the offending Party. If the panel subsequently determines that an action plan (either mutually agreed upon or stipulated by the panel itself) is not being implemented it may impose monetary assessments against the offending Party (Article 34(5)(b)). Where the offending Party fails to pay a monetary assessment within 180 days after it is imposed, the complaining Party may suspend concessions under the NAFTA itself 'in an amount no greater than that sufficient to collect the monetary enforcement assessment'. Annex 34 states, *inter alia*, the limits on monetary assessments 'For the first year after entry into force of the NAAEC, these shall not exceed $20 million US. Thereafter, an assessment may not exceed 0.007% of total trade in goods between the Parties during the most recent year for which data are available' (Annex 34, Article 1). Here, 'between the Parties' most logically refers to the total trade between all three NAFTA Parties, not that between the two Parties to the dispute.[80] The latter interpretation would create the arbitrary result that a monetary assessment arising out of exactly the same violation would vary enormously depending, for instance, on whether Canada or the United States was the complainant. Here, it should be stressed that monetary assessments are not intended as compensation for injury to the complaining Party's trade from persistent violation of the Agreement, but rather as an enforcement measure or sanction – they are not paid to the complaining Party but rather are paid into a fund to be spent at the direction of the NAFTA Parties for improving or enhancing environmental protection in the territory of the offending Party (Annex 34, Article 3). In the case of a monetary assessment against Canada, a rather disingenuous procedure replaces withdrawal of trade concessions as the sanction of last resort where the assessment remains unpaid. The panel decision imposing the monetary assessment is to be registered in a domestic Canadian court and to be subject to an enforcement order of that court, just as a foreign civil judgment might be enforced according to principles of conflict of laws (private international law). The ultimate effect is really the same as with the withdrawal of trade concessions, but the insertion of this separate procedure allowed the Canadian government of the day to make the (rather empty if literally true) public claim that it had succeeded in adhering to its position that no trade sanctions should be attached to the violation of environmental obligations.

If only Article 5 obligations are genuinely enforceable through dispute settlement and sanctions, what is the real significance of the various other, more general obligations and commitments in the NAAEC? The answer to this question will lie in the effectiveness of the institutional mechanisms that are aimed at fulfilling the broader promise of the NAAEC through on-going cooperative efforts concerning environmental regulation and standards.

The NAAEC provides for the estabishment of four institutions for environmental cooperation: the Commission, the Council, the Secretariat, and the Joint Public Advisory Committee. The Commission is the umbrella organization that encompasses the other three institutions (Article 8). The Council comprises ministerial-level representatives of the Parties who are required to meet at least once a year. The Council may make recommendations with respect to a wide variety of environmental matters, including 'transboundary and border environmental issues, such as the long-range transport of air and marine pollutants' and the 'protection of endangered and threatened species' and 'eco-labelling'. Perhaps most significantly, the Council, 'without reducing levels of environmental protection', may establish a process for developing recommendations on the 'greater compatibility of environmental technical regulations, standards and conformity assessment procedures'. This, in effect, gives the Council a mandate for the development of harmonized minimum environmental standards. In carrying out these various responsibilities the Council may establish committees, working groups or expert groups, and seek the advice of NGOs (Article 5). It should be noted that recommendations of the Council are to be made by consensus (Article 6), and that a Contracting Party's obligation is merely to 'consider' such recommendations, not to implement them.

The Secretariat consists of a permanent professional staff which provides administrative and technical support to the Council, headed by an Executive Director appointed for a (once renewable) three-year term (Article 11(1)). In addition to this general support function, the Secretariat is charged with preparing an annual report of the Commission, based upon instructions from the Council (Article 12(1)). The report is to contain, *inter alia*, data on each Party's compliance with its obligations under the agreement (Article 12(2)(c)) and 'relevant views and information submitted by non-governmental organizations and persons' (Article 12(2)(d)).

Finally, Articles 14 and 15 establish a procedure where a non-governmental organization may bring a submission before the Secretariat asserting that a Party is failing to enforce effectively its own environmental law. Upon approval by a two-thirds vote of the Council (i.e. by two of the three Parties) the Secretariat may prepare a 'factual record' concerning the NGO's claims, based upon the NGO's submissions as well as any 'relevant technical, scientific or other information', including submissions by the Party that is the object of the complaint. The Council may decide, by a two-thirds vote, to make the factual record public. It is to be emphasized that no formal dispute settlement or sanctions ensue in consequence of an adverse factual record. However, such a record would provide a strong evidentiary basis for a complaint against the offending Party should either of the other Parties choose to lodge one in accordance with the separate Part V dispute settlement procedures. Once made public, an adverse factual record would also assist environmental NGOs in bringing public pressure to bear upon the other NAFTA Parties to lodge such a complaint.

The Joint Public Advisory Committee consists of 15 members, 5 of which are appointed by each Party (Article 16(91)). The Committee may participate in the process of developing a factual record in accordance with Article 15. The Secretariat must also provide the Committee, *inter alia*, with the draft annual report, presumably for comment before its final adoption.

In assessing the significance of the NAAEC, at least as much emphasis should be placed on the broader institutional framework it establishes as on the rather limited enforceable legal obligations that it contains. This framework holds the promise of setting in motion a process for the evolution of genuine regional environmental norms, linked (albeit indirectly) to evolution of deeper economic integration among the NAFTA Parties. Although the NAAEC does not, by any means, transcend the state-centric paradigm of traditional international law[81] (i.e. only Parties have direct access to dispute settlement), it does acknowledge in important ways the legitimate stake that NGOs have in the process of monitoring and enforcing NAAEC legal obligations, i.e. that environmental protection is not just a matter between governments, but is of direct concern to individuals throughout the NAFTA region. Although there is yet to be a formal complaint or dispute panel under the legal obligations established by NAAEC, it does seem to have given birth to a set of active, if only partly effective, institutions. The Secretariat has, for example, developed a concrete work programme of cooperation in areas such as ecological mapping to determine pollution flows across North America, the development of consistent laboratory procedures for assessing environmental risk, assessment of environmental training needs, and cooperation in conservation of biodiversity and forest ecosystems.[82] These kinds of initiatives represent forms of win-win cooperation that raise few of the sovereignty concerns entailed in enforcing the legal obligations of the NAAEC. However, this being said, the work programme of the Secretariat is badly underfunded.[83] The Commission now proposes to create a North American Environmental Fund, that would provide grants to NGOs to pursue environmental projects related to the NAAEC, but the total proposed funding for this is US$2 million.[84] Another achievement of the Commission is an agreement on the phase-out or reduction of certain toxic substances throughout North America – PCBs, DDT, clordane and mercury. However, specific action plans on these substances are yet to be developed, so the agreement is really a resolution or agreement in principle.[85]

At the time this book went to press (late 1998) the Secretariat had received 15 submissions from NGOs concerning possible violations of the obligation of a NAFTA Party to enforce its own environmental laws. A number of the early submissions were rejected as falling outside the terms of the NAAEC. The first submission, filed in June 1995, by among other NGOs the Biodiversity Legal Foundation, alleged that fiscal restraint legislation in the US that prohibited the Fish and Wildlife Service from making final determinations for species or critical habitat designations for the remainder of fiscal year 1995 and cutting its budget had the effect of a failure to enforce the US Endangered Species Act.[86] In its reply to this submission, the Secretariat refused to take the matter further, finding that 'the alleged failure to enforce environmental law results from competing legislative mandates, and not from other action or inaction taken by agencies or officials'.[87] This establishes a fundamental limitation on the obligation of each country to enforce its own environmental law – such an obligation does not extend to a requirement that non-environmental legislation not frustrate such enforcement. Other submissions have not been taken further by the Secretariat because they complained of non-enforcement that had occurred in the past (an environmental assessment on a particular project) or because parallel actions were being pursued in domestic courts, therefore making a judgment that a country was not enforcing its own laws premature. One complaint made to the Commission, by the Sierra Club, concerned a 'rider' on a US budget-cutting statute that essentially eliminated the possibility of review of salvage timber sales for environmental effects.[88] This complaint was not taken further by the Secretariat on the same basis as it invoked with respect to the first complaint, i.e. that 'The Secretariat cannot . . . characterize the application of a new legal regime as a failure to enforce an old one.'[89] In this second determination the Secretariat also stressed the importance of a factual record showing that non-enforcement was actually occurring, thereby suggesting that even if the 'rider' had been in regulation not legislation, it would have been essential to show that it resulted in an actual pattern of non-enforcement of the relevant environmental framework law.

The first (and only) submission so far to give rise to a determination by the Secretariat that a full factual record should be developed was filed by Mexican

NGOs with respect to non-enforcement of Mexican environmental law.[90] This complaint alleged that during the evaluation of a project for a cruise terminal on Cozumel Island a range of Mexican environmental laws had not been effectively enforced, and that two coral reefs were being endangered by the project. A Factual Record was prepared and submitted to the Council in April 1997, and a final version publicly released later that year.[91] It is clear from the Record that the Mexican government vigorously and completely denied the claims of the petitioners. The Factual Record presents intricate and arcane arguments on both sides concerning whether extensions of environmental authorizations were granted in accordance with Mexican law, and whether and for what elements of the project a comprehensive *de novo* environmental assessment might have been required, as well as the applicability of various wildlife preservation provisions in respect of the location of the pier in proximity to coral reefs. However, while the dispute was being dealt with by the NAAEC Secretariat and before the Factual Record was provided to the Council, the Mexican authorities appear to have placed a number of conditions on the donation of federal lands required to realize the project.[92] One may speculate that the prospect of a full Factual Record being published thus had some impact on the Mexican government, despite its complete rejection of the claim that it had not previously been enforcing its own environmental laws.

Finally, under the NAAEC NGOs may also make submissions on matters not directly related to the issue of a NAFTA Party's enforcement of its environmental law. One such submission has actually become the subject of a Secretariat Report. The submission concerned the death of migratory birds at the Silva Reservoir in Mexico. The Secretariat struck a panel of scientific experts to investigate the matter, which found that the death of the birds was related to high levels of toxins in the area.[93] The Secretariat suggested a number of options for dealing with the problem, including that the reservoir be monitored for waterbird mortality, that the reservoir be drained if there is evidence of a waterbird mortality problem, that birds be kept off the reservoir, or that the topography of the reservoir be altered to make it less susceptible to these problems. However, in terms of formal recommendations that the Council would make to Mexico, these were limited essentially to the recommendation that the Mexican government conduct a comprehensive evaluation of the problem and the possible solutions to it. The panel of scientific experts had, by contrast, some very specific suggestions as to the environmental measures needed to remedy the route source of the problem, including proper treatment of raw-discharge municipal wastes, and large industrial waste sources. These suggestions are now being pursued with the support of the Secretariat.

The positive results attained by the NAAEC and its institutions belie the scepticism of many environmentalists about the significance of the side-agreement. However, there is an issue as to the extent to which this activism was due to the leadership of the first director of the Commission for Environmental Cooperation, the Mexican Victor Lichtinger. Lichtinger's forced resignation from this position in February 1998 has been linked by informed observers to NAFTA government dissatisfaction with the Commission's activist role.[94] Thus, the future effectiveness of NAFTA's environmental institutions remains in question.

CONCLUSION

The existing jurisprudence on trade and environment in the GATT displays a lack of coherence and consistency. Especially given the increasing number of trade conflicts related to environmental matters, the present state of GATT law as just described is far from satisfactory. The uncertainty and incoherence that characterize the existing jurisprudence only serve to undermine the legitimacy of GATT strictures that affect environmental protection, thereby fuelling increased demands for aggressive unilateralism. As the very limited progress of the WTO Trade and Environment Committee suggests, addressing this situation through new rules or understandings agreed among Members is likely to be an insurmountable task, at least before a new 'round'. However, the creation of an Appellate Body, and the determination of this body, quite evident in its first rulings, to bring greater order and coherence to the jurisprudence, suggest that much can be done even without formal changes to the WTO Agreements, or other new legal instruments. In the *Reformulated Gasoline* case, the Appellate Body went some distance in demonstrating how a careful, textually-orientated application of the existing GATT text can address in a legitimate and principled manner the trade/environment interface. As the *Turtles* appeal decision illustrates, this approach can easily be applied in the case of disputes concerning *global* environmental measures, the prejudice of the trade policy establishment that such measures are inherently at odds with a liberal trading order, or threatening to its integrity, needs to be reversed. In this chapter we have attempted to show how a conceptual clarification and global and domestic welfare analysis of trade and environment claims can help reverse the prejudice.

16 Trade and labour rights

INTRODUCTION

The interrelationship between trade policy and labour rights is among the most contentious issues that the world trading system faces today. Many critics of free trade have argued that it is unfair that producers in the developed industrial world should have to compete with imports from countries with very low wage rates and poor labour standards. Advocates of free trade, by contrast, often view differences in countries' labour standards as a legitimate source of comparative advantage or disadvantage. They argue that low-wage competition benefits workers in developing countries themselves, and is in many instances an important element in the economic growth that is needed to improve living standards and ultimately distributive justice in those countries. Concern about labour policies in other countries, particularly developing countries, has also been characterized as inappropriately paternalistic or culturally patronising. At the same time, increasing international attention has been focused on the challenge of obtaining compliance with certain minimum labour standards, so-called 'core' labour rights, which reflect widely-accepted international human rights norms. In these instances, where what is at issue is violent suppression of collective bargaining, gender discrimination, forced or slave labour, or exploitative child labour, trade measures appear less like a protectionist attempt to level the playing field, and resemble the kinds of sanctions against gross human rights violations that have been imposed by the world community (or at least the major Western powers) in cases such as South Africa under apartheid and, more recently, Serbia. At the same time, resistance within the World Trade Organization to any real linkage between trade and core international labour rights remains powerful, as is reflected in the declaration on this issue that emerged from the 1996 Singapore ministerial, suggesting that this issue is a matter, above all, for the International Labour Organization (ILO). Where some progress has been made, due to the profile of this issue, is in creating greater focus within the ILO itself on the central challenge of compliance with core standards, including the adoption in June 1998 of an ILO Declaration on fundamental labour rights. As well, the OECD – an organization with an institutional orientation towards economic liberalism – has shown greater openness and subtlety in its approach to the debate concerning trade and labour rights, suggesting in a recent study that non-compliance with core labour standards is unlikely to be beneficial, and may actual be harmful, to a country's overall economic growth and development prospects. The NAFTA labour side-agreement, the North American Agreement on Labour Cooperation (NAALC), has produced some limited but useful transnational dialogue about the enforcement of labour rights in North America and, despite its weak institutional structure, has proven somewhat effective in creating pressure, through publicity, to resolve some especially egregious cases of non-enforcement.

This chapter considers these various trends, on the basis of a conceptual framework for understanding the debate over trade and labour rights which attempts to take into account in a more subtle way than the typical 'equity vs. efficiency' notion both the economic welfare and human rights dimensions of this issue (and the relationship between the two).

A CONCEPTUAL FRAMEWORK FOR UNDERSTANDING THE TRADE AND LABOUR RIGHTS DEBATE[1]

Sanctions as a means of inducing other states to alter their labour practices

Trade sanctions may be advocated as a means of inducing recalcitrant governments and/or firms to meet a given set of labour standards.[2] This may involve trade restrictions being imposed in the case of a country violating labour agreements that it has already signed (such as conventions of the International Labour Organization), or to induce a country to adopt a standard or norm that it has not yet accepted as binding, even in principle. As we suggested in our discussion of environmentally-based sanctions in Chapter 15 on trade and the environment, in this sense the trade measures at issue are little different from the kind of response that states have had to practices such as apartheid in South Africa and genocide in the former Yugoslavia. The embargo of Iraq is a further recent example of the use of economic sanctions in support of non-trade policy goals.

The non-trade related rationales for labour sanctions

An initial issue is whether the ultimate goals of such sanctions can be justified. Here it is useful to identify the main reasons why concerns about labour laws and practices may legitimately extend beyond national borders.

Human rights

Human rights are frequently and increasingly regarded as inalienable rights that belong to individuals regardless of their national affiliation, simply by virtue of being human. Such an understanding of rights is implicit in the Kantian understanding of human autonomy that has profoundly influenced contemporary liberal theory. Certain labour rights or standards have come to be widely regarded as basic human rights with a universal character. These include: the right to collective bargaining and freedom of association; the right not to be enslaved; the abolition of child labour; and equality of opportunity in employment for men and women.[3] These rights are reflected in the Conventions of the International Labour Organization (ILO). Some of the Conventions have been ratified by a large number of countries; others by far fewer countries. They are also now affirmed in the June 1998 ILO Declaration on fundamental labour rights.

While labour rights are conceived of as universal in the ILO Conventions, they are not viewed as absolute. Thus, for example, in the case of the prohibition on child labour, the minimum age of 15 years applies in most circumstances, but in many developing country contexts, the applicable age may be 12 years; as well, child labour in agricultural contexts is generally permitted.[4] Respect for the universal normative content of international labour rights does not usually entail *identical labour policies or standards*. Precisely because universal human rights have important contextual dimensions, even these labour rights elicit quite different views as to their exact scope and meaning. For example, the extent to which collective bargaining and freedom of association rights should entail a right to strike, and in what circumstances, may be a matter of considerable controversy even among individuals who have a strong commitment to the idea of rights. At the same time, there are certain practices that would be unacceptable on any reasonable interpretation of such rights, whatever the balance between negative and positive liberty one happens to subscribe to – for instance, the use of violence and intimidation to prevent workers from organizing into an independent trade union. The fact that existing international labour law has been drafted such that these practices are not singled out and proscribed as 'obvious' violations of rights may be a reason why some of the Labour Conventions of the ILO have not been ratified by a much larger group of countries; in other words, this uneven ratification record may understate the degree of existing or emerging normative consensus in the international community concerning a core minimum content or scope to core labour rights.[5]

International political and economic spillovers

Some human rights abuses and some labour practices, particularly violent suppression of workers' rights to organize or associate, may lead to the kind of acute social conflict that gives rise to general political and economic instability. Such instability may spill over national boundaries, and affect global security. Increasingly (as the cases of the former Yugoslavia, Rwanda and Somalia illustrate), 'internal' conflicts are capable of raising regional or global security, economic or social (e.g. immigration and refugee) issues.

Altruistic or paternalistic concerns

Even if they are not directly affected in any of the ways described above, citizens of one country may find the purely domestic labour practices or policies of another country to be misguided or morally wrong. Similarly, citizens of one country may believe that workers in another country would be better off if protected by higher labour standards. Such a belief may or may not be warranted. For instance, higher minimum wages or other improvements in standards that raise labour costs, may in some circumstances do more harm than good, if the result is a significant increase in unemployment. Proponents of external intervention make the strong assumption that citizens in one country are better able to make these welfare judgments than governments in another country, which seems unlikely to be systematically true, even where the government in the latter country is not democratically elected or accountable. However, the provision of foreign aid, often with major conditions attached as to recipients' domestic policies, by international agencies such as the World Bank and the IMF, suggests that a welfare presumption against paternalism should be rebuttable. One version of the anti-paternalism argument draws on the notions of cultural relativism or cultural autonomy. Thus, for instance, Bhagwati suggests that the 'equation between culture-specific labour standards and universal human rights cannot survive deeper scrutiny'.[6] This, on its own terms, however, is a very selective kind of argument for cultural autonomy, since it entails an admission that *some* rights *are* genuinely universal, but just not labour rights. Yet Bhagwati gives no rigorous explanation of why labour rights in particular lie on one side of the line between the universal and the culturally specific (the idea that, for instance minimum wages are appropriately set relative to a country's level of wealth and economic development has nothing to do with *cultural* specificity; it emanates from a perspective on economic regulation that is purportedly universal). Martha Nussbaum has criticized the simplistic and opportunistic manner in which the idea of cultural determinism or autonomy has been invoked to force closure on transcultural dialogue about the relationship between the universal and contextual dimensions of rights.[7] Another fallacious but frequently heard notion is that rights are a luxury good, in which poor people in developing countries themselves have little interest: however, examining human rights struggles in a number of poor Asian nations, Amartya Sen concludes: 'To the extent that there has been any testing of the proposition that the poor Asians do not care about civil and political rights, the evidence is entirely against that claim.'[8]

Given that there are several legitimate rationales for making the compliance with core labour rights a matter for international concern and action, trade sanctions are one instrument among many that may be used to advance this goal. Although the strongest rationales for protecting core labour rights may be grounded deontologically in a conception of autonomy, and do not necessarily sound in claims about welfare, this need not be a reason to be indifferent to the welfare effects of alternative instruments for vindicating these rationales. Of course, there is a coherent, if limited point of view that suggests that once we characterize the practices in questions as violations of human rights any truck or trade with the products or services produced through such violations is intrinsically immoral – from this perspective, sanctions are an indicated policy, regardless of their welfare impacts more generally, or even whether as an empirical matter they are likely or unlikely to result in reduction or elimination of the offending practices. Thus, on this understanding, for example, even if it were provable that sanctions against child labour actually made the children in question worse off, reducing them to starvation or illegal activity, the moral imperative to maintain sanctions would be unaffected. In practice, however, this sort of extreme, results-blind moralism is rare – international human rights activists usually are concerned about the real world situation of those whom rights are meant to protect, and even if the foundation of rights is not welfarist, their effective realization implies a concern with the actual conditions of people. Thus, if it were systematically true, as many free traders tend to suggest or assume, that trade sanctions for labour rights non-compliance reduce global or domestic welfare (in the sanctioned state), this should not be a matter of indifference to rights activists in the real world, even it might be for some Kantian ethicists. Thus, from the perspective of the debate on the relationship between labour rights and trade policy, it is important to clarify the welfare effects that are at issue. In the following discussion we attempt to identify the kinds of potential welfare effects, both positive and negative, that would need to be considered in any analysis of labour-rights based trade sanctions.

Scenario #1: trade sanctions or the threat of sanctions succeed in inducing higher labour standards

The first scenario is that the country or countries targeted by sanctions, or at least some firms within those countries, change their domestic practices and adhere to or accept the minimum standards.

Welfare effects in targeted country

With respect to the *domestic welfare of the country or countries that change policies*, if the status quo prior to the alteration of the policies is welfare-maximizing (either in the Pareto or Kaldor-Hicks sense) then conforming to higher standards will reduce domestic welfare.

With respect to labour rights abuses, some of the practices that have been singled out as justifying trade sanctions – slave labour camps in China, for instance – would be difficult to characterize as the product of political or regulatory processes likely to maximize welfare based on the revealed preferences of individuals. Since the countries concerned are not genuine democracies, the domestic political process is simply not designed to take into account the preferences of all citizens. Indeed, in a Marxist totalitarian state like China, individual preferences – except for those of the ruling elites – may well count for very little. In the end, to know whether higher labour standards will result in an improvement in domestic welfare, defined either in Pareto or Kaldor-Hicks terms, would entail judgments and analysis that go far beyond the disciplinary expertise of trade economists and trade policy experts.[9]

In general, the domestic welfare gains from improved labour standards are most likely to exist where, in the first place, there is a strong case for regulation to correct specific instances of market failure[10] (e.g. information asymmetries in the case of occupational health and safety[11]), or where markets fail more radically due, for instance, to the presence of coercion (slave labour, child labour, the use of violence to intimidate workers, etc.). Some recent empirical studies suggest that domestic welfare gains may well result from the enforcement of core labour rights, especially in a context where trade liberalization and improved labour rights performance occur simultaneously. For example a recent OECD study came to the conclusion that 'the clearest and most reliable finding is in favour of a mutually supportive relationship between successfully sustained trade reforms and improvements in association and bargaining rights'.[12] This particular finding has special significance for the trade and labour rights debate, since it tends to refute the notion that non-compliance with core labour rights is an important source of comparative advantage for poorer countries.

In understanding the welfare impacts of compliance with core labour standards it is important to bear in mind a fundamental distortion in world labour markets – restrictive immigration policies that prevent most people from moving to locations where employment conditions and related government labour policies maximize their preferences.[13] In a world where labour was as mobile a factor of production as capital or technology, regulatory competition between jurisdictions might well ensure a close to optimal domestic policy equilibrium with respect to labour rights, given that transboundary externalities are not nearly as pervasive in this area as for example is the case with the environment. Where workers cannot move, however, and where they are disempowered domestically as well, labour rights policy outcomes may well not accurately reflect their preferences.[14]

Welfare effects in sanction-imposing country

Depending on elasticities of supply and demand, where foreign producers are faced with higher costs due to higher labour standards, they may be able to pass on some of these costs to consumers in the country that imposed the trade sanctions. However, it may be the case that compliance with core labour rights will not result in significantly higher prices to consumers, where *some* producers in the targeted country are *already* in compliance within existing cost structures. Where, for instance, a producer is located in a part of the country where political and social conditions have allowed trade unions to survive, it may already have had to measure up to basic levels of labour rights protection. Such a producer may have learned to be competitive with other producers who have not been meeting minimum standards, through increasing the productivity of labour, better employment of technology, etc.[15] In fact, there is empirical evidence that many of the more successful export-oriented developing country enterprises do comply with core labour rights.[16] However, it must be acknowledged that, making the conventional economic assumption that supply curves are never infinitely elastic, some adverse price effects on consumers in the sanction-imposing country seem likely, although in many cases these may be small.

In very many instances, the next-lowest-cost producer complying with minimum labour standards is likely not to be a domestic firm in the sanctions-imposing country, but a firm in another country. For this reason, compliance with core labour rights will often not confer substantial benefits on producer interests in the country which has imposed sanctions, although there are always likely to be some protective price effects (depending on supply elasticities).

Scenario #2: the case where trade sanctions fail to induce higher standards

Welfare effects in the targeted country

There are several studies that have attempted to model the economic impacts of trade sanctions against states that are not enforcing compliance with core labour standards. These suggest the complexity of the possible welfare effects from sanctions, particularly where these do not lead to the desired behavioural changes in either firms or governments. In the case of child labour for example an impact of a sanction (a tariff in this case) imposed on a particular import produced with child labour may be to increase the supply of child labour to sectors producing goods for domestic consumption, where output cannot be affected by sanctions. As Maskus notes, depending on elasticities of supply and demand and certain other assumptions, the impact could be an actual increase in the number of children working under-age, and perhaps also a decline in the wages of the children actually working.[17] In the case of gender discrimination, according to Maskus, the effects on women of a sanction against the exports of a particular country, in the absence of any policy change being induced, will differ depending on whether the export sector is male- or female-labour intensive relative to the import-competing sector:

> In the case where exports are intensive in female labor, [women workers] would be harmed by reducing wages even further [than has already occurred due to discrimination] and exacerbating the output effects. In the case where exports are intensive in male labor, the tariff would raise demand for female labor, causing female wages to place upward pressure on the female maximum wage. In this case, firms might prefer to relax the discrimination to some degree.[18]

This effect occurs on the assumption that, with the decline in export competitiveness due to the tariff sanction, productive resources will be shifted from the export sector to the import-competitive sector, with demand for labour shifting as well. Maskus's overall conclusion is that 'the impacts of trade restrictions taken by foreign countries depend on the circumstances. . . . Much depends on issues such as whether the sector with weak rights is labour-intensive, whether it is the exportable sector, and what linkages there are to the informal or residual employment sectors.'[19]

Global welfare effects

Even where sanctions fail to induce any policy change in the targeted country, there may be some positive effect on global welfare where sanctions result in a decline in the global sales of products that are manufactured in a fashion that entail labour rights abuses. If the country imposing the sanctions, or the group of countries imposing them, constitute a major market for the products in question, then global demand will now be met through production that complies with the standards in question. But for this to happen, sanctions should be imposed *consistently*, i.e. against all producers or countries world-wide that do not comply with the rights in question. Otherwise, production may simply be shifted from one firm that is responsible for abuses in question to another.

Just as with domestic welfare, trade sanctions that are not carefully targeted against only those industries, sectors or (ideally) firms that actually do not comply with core labour rights, in theory, could result in significant global welfare losses, shifting production away from least-cost producers in the targeted country to higher-cost producers elsewhere. However, many product areas are characterized by the existence of a variety of rival producers in different countries, often with closely comparable cost structures. In such a case, and assuming that some of these companies will be in compliance with the labour rights in question, global welfare losses may not in the end be significant. Rivals in compliance with international minimum standards will simply expand their market share. However, there are likely to be some price increases, assuming supply is not infinitely elastic.

With respect to the welfare effects of sanctions that fail to change government policy on those with pro-labour rights preferences, these are still likely to be positive for three reasons. Two of the reasons will be evident from the above analysis. First, if the sanctions are properly targeted at *firms* they may induce higher levels of labour rights protection even in the absence of a change in government policy. Second, sanctions, because they reduce world demand for products made in ways that abuse workers' rights, will reduce the levels of these harmful activities. Third, sanctions will provide the moral satisfaction of resisting government policies or practices that violate human rights norms, even if the government does not change its policies. However, even those with pro-labour rights preferences may have some of these utility gains offset from utility losses due to the knowledge that sanctions may well cause harm to 'innocent' victims of the government's intransigence in the face of sanctions, i.e. workers who lose their jobs, persons who suffer from a country's reduced ability to purchase essential supplies given a reduction in its convertible currency earnings, etc.

Finally, there may be possible longer-term impacts of the reduction in oppressive labour practices that would have positive impacts on global welfare, and which are hard to quantify or study through the examination of short-term impact. These might include accelerated political liberalization as workers become less intimidated, better organized, and generally more capable of asserting their rights.[20] Increasing liberalization of domestic political regimes was linked early on by the philosopher Immanuel Kant[21] and much more recently in empirical work by Michael Doyle,[22] to a reduced threat of global conflict, including a reduced likelihood of war. Resort to practices such as forced labour, child labour (which often amounts to the same thing since generally children in such regimes have little say in whether they work or not), and violent suppression of independent trade unions (e.g. the Solidarity movement in Poland) provides a means of resistance to pressures for political and economic reforms – reforms which, it has been suggested, may well in the medium or longer run produce regimes that are significantly less likely to threaten international peace and security.

Welfare effects in the sanctions-imposing country

Welfare effects on consumers and producers in the sanctions-imposing country are likely to be similar to those in Scenario 1.

Summary

The above analysis has taken into account, for the most part, only the static effects of sanctions. A dynamic perspective could alter the analysis significantly. Restrictions on the use of child labour may, as with the *Factory Acts* enacted in Britain in the first half of the nineteenth century, lead to political demands for enhanced access to public education, in which case the possible short-term negative impact of higher standards – greater impoverishment of some children – may be offset by the longer-term dynamic impact.

The very general analysis of labour rights-based trade sanctions outlined above suggests that little can be said, in the abstract, about the likely effects of such sanctions on aggregate domestic welfare in either the targeting or sanction-imposing country, or on global welfare. This clearly distinguishes trade measures of this kind from conventional protectionist trade restrictions, where formal analysis suggests overall net welfare losses, both domestic and global, when one considers the welfare effects of trade restrictions on consumers as well as workers and firms.[23]

When are sanctions likely to be effective?

Clearly, as the above analysis suggests, the welfare effects of sanctions will differ considerably depending on whether or not sanctions are actually able to change policies or practices in the targeted country. This underscores the importance of examining whether and when sanctions are likely to be effective in achieving such policy changes.

There is limited formal evidence on the effectiveness of labour rights trade sanctions in particular. Dufour suggests there is some evidence that withdrawal of GSP trade preferences by the United States, or the threat thereof, has led to changes in labour law in Malaysia and Chile.[24] A similar threat, combined with activism by indigenous labour rights groups may have led to the lifting of legal restrictions on collective bargaining in the Dominican Republic.[25] The OECD suggests that in most cases where a petition was made under US trade law for withdrawal of GSP preferences on grounds of non-compliance with international labour rights, '[p]rogress in raising core standards has been made'.[26] Moreover, the threat of withdrawal of preferences was usually sufficient to procure the result, without sanctions having to be put in place (which means that the gains in compliance were not mitigated by the kinds of negative welfare effects from the actual implementation of sanctions discussed above). As the OECD also suggests, 'its effectiveness is clearly related to the fact that the US market is the largest for most of the GSP beneficiaries.' As noted in Chapter 15 on trade and the environment, significant empirical work has been undertaken with a view to measuring the impact of economic sanctions more generally on state behaviour. As we noted in that chapter, the most comprehensive work on this question remains the study by Hufbauer, Schott and Elliott,[27] which examines 115 instances of the use of economic sanctions over a period of about 40 years. The authors conclude that these sanctions had an overall success rate of about 34% in achieving an alteration of the conduct of the targeting country in the desired direction.[28]

An issue closely related to the effectiveness of economic sanctions is the relative desirability of sanctions as opposed to other instruments for influencing the behaviour of other countries and their producers. Several economic studies of the issue have advocated the use of financial compensation as an alternative to trade sanctions.[29] This proposal has the virtue of attaching a price to the invocation of such sanctions and thus providing some assurance that these higher standards are truly valued for their own sake in the country desiring the changes, especially in cases of ostensible *ad hoc* paternalism or altruism, while trade sanctions, lacking such an explicit price (beyond price effects on consumers), may be easily subverted by protectionists. Compensation-based approaches have, however, their own complexities and drawbacks. Maskus, for example, who considers the use of compensation in the case of child labour as 'in principle an effective route to reducing child labor employment', notes that there may be difficulty in raising the funds for compensation in developed countries because

> consumers in both the exporter and [the rest of the world] are likely to free ride on these gains [from higher labour standards], suggesting that revealing their preferences for higher standards could be problematic. Thus, extracting these compensatory taxes could be impossible. Moreover, costless transfer of the payments may not be possible; political failures and transactions costs in both countries could inefficiently absorb some or all of the revenues, with little impact on labor demands.[30]

Discussing the issue of carrots vs. sticks in the environmental context, Chang argues that subsidies, as opposed to sanctions, create a perverse incentive for foreign countries to engage in, or intensify, the offensive behaviour (or make credible threats to this effect) in order to maximize the payments being offered.[31]

From a deontological perspective on core labour rights, a principle that victims (or their supporters) should always pay ('bribe') violators to achieve compliance would seem impossible to defend either ethically or politically. However, in some cases financial assistance to enable poor Third World countries to meet higher labour standards may be warranted on distributive justice grounds. It is sometimes suggested that aid transfers, for instance, could alleviate the poverty that is supposed to be the root cause of non-compliance with core labour rights.[32] Certainly, in the case of child labour, poverty is a crucial part of the picture in explaining why very young children go to work. But not all poor countries lack protections against exploitation of child labour,[33] and not all poor countries are in violation of core labour rights. Again, this is consistent with the OECD conclusions cited above that not only can poor countries 'afford' compliance with core labour rights, but that such compliance interacts positively with a trade-driven open market-based growth strategy.

A further alternative[34] to trade restrictions is social labelling, which allows individuals as consumers to express their moral preferences for labour rights protection.[35] Products that are produced in a manner that meet core labour standards would be entitled to bear a distinctive logo or statement that informs consumers of this fact. While labelling may enable individual consumers to avoid the moral 'taint' of consuming the product in question themselves, if most consumers have a preference for terminating production altogether (rather than merely reducing consumption and production) by changing a foreign country's domestic policies, then a collective action problem arises as in any approach to influencing behaviour that depends upon coordinating action among large numbers of agents. Unless he or she can be sure that most other consumers will do likewise, the individual consumer may well not consider it rational to avoid buying the product in question.[36] A key issue with respect to labelling programmes is that of credible monitoring to ensure that claims made in association with the label are not fraudulent. This problem is acute with respect to self-labelling by multinational corporations who have made public undertakings to abide by voluntary codes of conduct. One promising development in this respect is the possibility that, with the consent of the regimes in question, the ILO itself would play a role in monitoring the credibility of social labelling. Thus, the 1997 ILO Director General's Report makes the following suggestion (which, however, has subsequently not attracted substantial support from the membership):

> As far as the ILO is concerned, labelling should . . . aim . . . at promoting law and practice which meets the demands of fundamental standards (thus also benefiting workers whose products are not identifiable or exported). . . . But if these labels are to have any credibility at all, they must guarantee that legislation has been complied with in actual practice. However, neither spontaneous initiatives nor the present procedures of the ILO can provide such a guarantee because there is no way of carrying out an international inspection on the spot which is reliable and legally independent. But it would be perfectly feasible to provide for such a system of inspection under an international labour Convention which, because of its voluntary nature, would allow each State to decide freely whether to give an overall social label to all goods produced on its territory – provided that it accepts the obligations inherent in the Convention and agrees to have monitoring on the spot.[37]

In sum, neither financial inducements nor labelling programmes are self-evidently superior policy instruments to sanctions for influencing other countries' environmental and labour practices. Each has its own drawbacks. However, it must be admitted that little concrete empirical evidence exists that would allow a rigorous comparison of these alternative instruments with sanctions. In addition, the greatest effectiveness might actually be achieved by a combination of more than one of these instruments. At a minimum, and given the apparently positive results of the threat of unilateral sanctions (withdrawal of GSP preferences) by the United States, it is difficult to make out a clear-cut case for excluding the use of trade sanctions as an instrument for influencing the behaviour of other countries' governments or firms.

The 'systemic' threat to a liberal trading order

Even in the presence of indeterminate welfare effects many free traders have still rejected labour rights-based trade measures on the basis that such measures, if widely permitted or entertained, would significantly erode the coherence and sustainability of rule-based liberal trade. We ourselves, in earlier work, have argued that competitiveness-based or level playing field 'fair trade' measures, such as countervailing and antidumping duties, already pose such a threat. This is based on the notion that the legal order of international trade is best understood as a set of rules and norms aimed at sustaining a long-term cooperative equilibrium, in the face of on-going pressures to cheat on this equilibrium, given that the short-term political pay-offs from cheating may be quite high (depending, of course, on the character and influence of protectionist interests within a particular country, the availability of alternative policies to deal with adjustment costs, etc.).[38] In the presence of fundamental normative dissensus as to what constitutes 'cheating' on the one hand, and the punishment of others' cheating on the other, confidence in the rules themselves could be fundamentally undermined, and the system destabilized.

With respect to the systemic threat from labour rights-related trade measures, it is important to distinguish between purely unilateral measures, and those that have a multilateral dimension. The former measures are based upon a labour rights concern or norm that is specific to the sanctioning country or countries. Here, there is a real risk of dissolving a clear distinction between protectionist 'cheating' and genuine sanctions to further non-trade values – the sanctioning country may well be able to define its labour rights causes so as to serve protectionist interests. Measures with a multilateral dimension, by contrast, will be based upon the targeted country's violation of some multilateral or internationally recognized norm, principle, or agreement – which is clearly the case with respect to core labour rights in general. It is true that protectionist interests will always be attracted by the possibility of sanctions for non-trade purposes – self-interested lobbying that invokes high-minded purposes is an endemic feature of any vigorous liberal democratic polity. As Langille observes: 'Self-interested and opportunistic behaviour will colour all arguments where a question of distribution between capital and labour is involved.'[39] But the real issue is whether such behaviour will necessarily *subvert* the integrity of the sanctions decision-making process. In this respect, it should be recalled from the welfare effects analysis above that very often the next least-cost producer will be another low-wage country not subject to sanctions, rather than a producer from the sanctions-imposing country; therefore apart from perhaps some scarcity rents due to the temporary contraction of overall supply, domestic interests will often have little to gain from such sanctions.

If, for example, Article XX of the GATT 1994 were interpreted[40] to include violations of labour rights as a basis for 'saving' otherwise GATT inconsistent measures, the sanctions imposing country would nevertheless still bear the burden of showing that the sanctions were undertaken in a manner consistent with the requirements of the 'chapeau' in Article XX, i.e. that they do not constitute 'arbitrary' or 'unjustified' discrimination, or a 'disguised restriction on international trade'.[41]

A number of factors could be relevant to a determination as to whether the requirements of the 'chapeau' have been met. Alternatively, these factors could be incorporated into a new provision of Article XX that deals explicitly with labour rights. Among the factors relevant would be: (1) the extent of international consensus on the unacceptability of the practices, as evidenced by international agreements, conventions, and customary international law; (2) the extent to which the sanctions-imposing country is consistent in its application of sanctions to all countries that engage in a similar scale of violations of core labour rights; (3) the extent to which the country concerned has been identified as a violator by independent international organs; (4) the extent to which attempts at solving the problem through cooperation, either bilateral, or through the International Labour Organization or regional institutions such as the North American Agreement on Labour Cooperation have been made and have failed. The fact that the ILO is now coming to grips with the task of identifying a broad overlapping consensus on certain core labour rights, and monitoring and reporting with respect to these,[42] weakens the force of criticisms that the notion of core labour rights is so manipulable and debatable as to preclude objective benchmarks that allow for screening against protectionist abuse.

Competitiveness-based arguments for labour rights-based trade measures

Unlike the arguments for trade restrictions on labour rights grounds that we have been discussing up to this point, which have a normative reference point external to the trading system itself, competitiveness-based 'fair-trade' claims focus largely on the effects on domestic producers and workers of other countries' labour policies, and not *per se* on the effects of those policies on workers elsewhere. Competitiveness claims are, in principle, indifferent to the improvement of labour practices in other countries, and extend to differences in competitive conditions, such as wage rates, that do not reflect violations of widely-recognized core labour rights. Hence, in the case of competitiveness claims, trade measures that protect the domestic market or 'equalize' comparative advantage related to labour standards are a completely acceptable *substitute* for other countries raising their standards.

Competitiveness claims usually refer to one of two kinds of supposed unfairness (and, it is often argued as well, welfare losses) that stem from trade competition with countries that have lower labour standards:

1. It is unfair (and/or inefficient) that *our* firms and workers should bear the 'costs' of higher labour standards through loss of market share to foreign producers who have lower costs due to laxer labour standards in their own country.
2. It is unfair that downward pressure should be placed on *our* labour standards by virtue of the impact of trade competition with countries with lower standards.

Competitive fairness claim #1

The first kind of claim is, in our view, largely incoherent and in fact in tension with the basic theory of comparative advantage in trade. Assuming there is nothing wrongful with another country's labour policies along the lines discussed in the first part of this chapter, then why should a cost advantage attributable to these divergent policies not be treated like any other cost advantage, i.e. as part and parcel of comparative advantage?

Precisely because the implicit benchmark of fairness is so illusory, i.e. a world where governmentally-imposed labour protection costs are completely equalized among producers of like products in all countries, trade measures based upon this kind of fairness claim are likely to be highly manipulable by protectionist interests. Since, of course, protectionists are really interested in obtaining trade protection, not in promoting labour rights, the fact that the competitive fairness claim in question does not generate a viable and principled benchmark for alteration of other countries' policies is a strength not a weakness – for it virtually guarantees that justifications for protection will always be available, even if the targeted country improves its environmental or labour standards.

Welfare effects of trade restrictions aimed at equalizing comparative advantage

Trade restrictions will lead to reduced exports, with consequent welfare losses to firms and workers in the targeted country. Since *every* foreign producer whose labour rights compliance costs are less than those of domestic producers will be vulnerable to trade action, trade restrictions based on equalization of comparative advantage are likely to affect imports, potentially quite dramatically, from a wide range of countries. Firms and workers engaged in the manufacture of like products to those imports targeted by trade restrictions will benefit where the restrictions in question make imports relatively more expensive than domestic substitutes, thereby shifting demand from imports to domestic production. Consumers will pay more, probably substantially more, as domestic producers will price up to the duty imposed by the trade restriction. Here, the welfare effects essentially resemble those from the imposition of a tariff or countervailing duty. Inasmuch as production is shifted from lower to higher cost producers, there is also some loss of global allocative efficiency.

Clearly, overall, these welfare effects entail a shift in wealth to firms and workers in the trade-restricting country from firms and workers in the targeted country as well as consumers in the trade-restricting country. In our view, it is difficult to construct a theory of distributive justice to support the fairness of these transfers.

Competitive fairness claim #2

Whereas competitiveness claim #1 presumes that governments will not respond to the competitive implications of higher labour standards, and simply allow domestic firms to become uncompetitive, the second competitive fairness claim assumes just the opposite – that governments will respond by lowering domestic standards below the optimal level.

We do not believe that, generally speaking, lowering labour standards is an appropriate response to competitive pressures. There is, in fact, a wide range of alternatives – such as better regulation which reduces compliance costs without lowering standards, or investment in training, technology, etc. to increase the productivity of labour.[43]

Where governments and/or firms *are* in fact responding by lowering standards, rather than through these arguably superior policy alternatives, these sub-optimal policy responses may represent a political and social problem within countries that are lowering standards in response to competitive pressures.

A variation of the claim about the effect of competitiveness pressures on domestic labour standards suggests the possibility of a form of beggar-thy-neighbour behaviour that may, admittedly, leave all countries worse off. This is the 'race to the bottom', whereby countries competitively lower their labour standards, in an effort to capture a relatively greater share of a fixed volume of trade or investment.[44] Much like the beggar-thy-neighbour subsidies wars that characterized agricultural trade among the Canada, the US and the EU and other countries during the 1980s, it is not difficult, using the model of a Prisoner's Dilemma game, to show that competitive reduction in environmental or labour standards will typically result in a negative sum outcome,[45] as long as one assumes that before entering the race each country's labour standards represent an optimal domestic policy outcome for that country.

The 'race to the bottom' claim has a different normative basis from the other competitiveness-based claims discussed above. Those claims relate to the proper distribution of the competitiveness costs of maintaining higher labour standards than one's trading partners. The normative basis for concern over the race to the bottom, by contrast, sounds in the language of Pareto efficiency: the race ends, literally, at the bottom, with each country adopting sub-optimal domestic policies, but no country in the end capturing a larger share of the gains from trade.

Frequently, beggar-thy-neighbour regulatory competition is able to flourish much more easily where it is possible to reduce on a selective basis labour standards to attract a particular investment or support a particular industry or firm. It is more difficult and more costly to engage in these activities where the formal statutory framework of labour regulation must be altered across-the-board. Here, some of the provisions in the NAFTA Labour Side Agreement may create disincentives to beggar-thy-neighbour competition in as much as they oblige the signatories to enforce effectively those labour rights laws that are formally on the books. At the same time, it must be acknowledged that effectively monitoring whether a country is fully enforcing its own laws is not an easy task, especially for outsiders.

Finally, it is possible simply to ban by international agreement beggar-thy-neighbour competition. As noted in Chapter 13 on trade and investment the draft Multilateral Agreement on Investment is intended to contain a provision that would commit Member States not to reduce or abrogate labour rights protections in order to attract or retain foreign investment.

THE EXISTING AND EVOLVING LEGAL AND INSTITUTIONAL FRAMEWORK

The World Trade Organization

In the Havana Charter, which was to be the blueprint for the failed International Trade Organization (ITO), there was a stipulation that Members were to take measures against 'unfair labour conditions'.[46] The GATT contains no explicit provision either permitting or requiring trade action against labour rights violations. Article XX(e), however, permits otherwise GATT-inconsistent measures 'relating to the products of prison labour'. The possibility has been raised that that Article XX(a), which permits otherwise GATT-inconsistent measures 'necessary to protect public morals', might be invoked to justify trade sanctions against products that involve the use of child labour or the denial or basic workers' rights.[47] There is no GATT or WTO jurisprudence on the interpretation of XX(a), and the reference to prison labour in XX(e), as well as the fact that explicit language on labour rights was in the failed Havana Charter, arguably suggests that if the GATT Article XX had been designed to encompass sanctions with respect to labour rights, explicit language would have been used to articulate such an exception. This being said, the interpretation of public morals should not be frozen in time, and with the evolution of human rights as a core element in public morality in many post-war societies and at the international level the content of public morals should extend to universal human rights, including labour rights. This is consistent with a dynamic interpretation of Art. XX of the kind which the AB gave to Art. XX(g) in the *Turtles* case, discussed earlier in the Trade and Environment chapter. Feddersen has suggested that provisions of Article XX, other than XX(e), do not encompass measures with respect to process and production methods (PPMs): 'the fact that Article XX(e) is the only provision explicitly addressing production methods strongly indicates that the other Article XX sections were not intended to include measures based on production methods.'[48] This reasoning is obscure if not perverse – the fact that XX(e) was included leads to just the opposite inference, i.e. that there is nothing about the basic purpose or structure of Article XX that renders it inapplicable to PPMs, provided the PPMs in question fall under one of the heads, such as 'public morals'. Again, as discussed in the Trade and Environment chapter, the AB in *Turtles* held that the exceptions in Art. XX could include measures that condition imports on the policies adopted by the exporting country.

Insistence by the United States that the possibility of a WTO 'social clause' be put on the post-Uruguay Round multilateral trade agenda led to an extremely tense Singapore WTO Ministerial in December 1996. In a notorious incident, an invitation to the Director-General of the ILO to address the Ministerial was withdrawn by the WTO, in response to pressure from developing countries.[49] The communique which issued from the meeting reflected some abatement of the visceral hostility in the WTO even to engaging in discourse on the link between trade and labour rights. Thus, according to the Ministerial Declaration, Ministers 'renew [their] commitment to the observance of internationally recognized core labor standards'. At the same time, the ILO 'is the competent body to set and deal with these standards'. The use of labour standards for 'protectionist purposes' is rejected, which implies some openness to trade measures that are demonstrated to have non-protectionist purposes, i.e. not aimed at neutralizing the comparative advantage of developing countries, but rather at insuring compliance with core standards. There is also a statement that suggests the WTO and ILO Secretariats should 'continue their existing collaboration'. The incident at Singapore, however, suggests that what would be needed is not a continuation of existing collaboration, but far stronger and more cooperative relations.

In discussions concerning a possible role for the WTO in addressing the links between trade and labour rights there is frequently considerable confusion or uncertainty about exactly what kind of role is at issue. One possibility would be for the WTO, through a discrete legal instrument or possibly an amendment to the GATT and/or GATS, to involve itself in the taking of multilateral sanctions where a Member has failed to comply with core labour rights. Such action might be made contingent on a judgment of the ILO that a Member that is also a signatory to some relevant ILO instrument or Convention is in non-conformity or has refused to cooperate with ILO organs in addressing the problem.[50] One difficulty that we see with options that entail the taking of sanctions, or other action, by the WTO itself in connection with labour rights violations, is that the fundamental legal mandate of the WTO is to police trade; such an approach might then give rise to the implication that the practices in question are somehow unfair trade practices, a claim that we reject and as argued above has real potential to lead to protectionist abuse. The more coherent approach would be to envisage the role of the WTO as vetting for protectionism trade sanctions imposed by Members, either unilaterally or multilaterally. Thus, Article XX of the GATT, or other relevant provisions, would be amended or made subject to an interpretative understanding that would allow trade sanctions where necessary for purposes of addressing non-compliance with core labour rights, subject – at a minimum – to the requirements of the chapeau of Article XX, i.e. the measures in question must not constitute 'arbitrary' or 'unjustified' discrimination, or a 'disguised restriction on international trade'. We have suggested above, in the discussion concerning the 'systemic threat', what factors might be taken into consideration in applying the requirements of the chapeau to measures related to labour rights compliance. A possibility consistent with such a reform of the WTO system would be that the ILO would become implicated in the authorization and indeed the mandating of trade sanctions for violations of core labour rights, as suggested by Charnovitz.[51] Such an approach would certainly be diametrically opposed to the ILO tradition, which emphasizes diplomacy and consensualism, and in fact does not even encompass binding dispute settlement, let alone enforcement action. A recent report by ILO research staff notes that discussions in the ILO Working Party on social dimensions of world trade indicate very strong resistance to any approach that contemplates the possibility of trade sanctions to enforce compliance with core labour rights, with the Workers' group of the Governing body having chosen to 'suspend' its demand for an approach that includes sanctions.[52] One alternative approach that has been suggested, including within the ILO, would be to make compliance with a set of core labour rights a condition of membership, and subject to enhanced surveillance. This would almost certainly require amendments to the Conventions, or new legal instruments, as the existing Conventions that articulate core rights have features that make them inconsistent with the labour law even of some countries that generally respect workers' basic rights (for example many liberal democracies place limits on the right to strike of certain essential workers). As well, for some countries such as Canada, there have been some difficulties in ratifying Conventions that relate to the internal division of powers (with sub-national governments having primary jurisdiction over labour matters). The 1998 ILO Convention on labour rights is an important step towards a solution to this problem. Alternatively, as our colleague Brian Langille has sometimes suggested, a list could be created of practices which all members of the ILO must prohibit, representing an overlapping consensus of the irreducible minimum content of core workers' rights.

Internal trade law of the United States and the European Union

US trade law provides for withdrawal of trade concessions with respect to countries that fail to respect international workers' rights. For example, s. 301 of the US Trade and Tariff Act of 1974 as amended in 1988,[53] provides the United States Trade Representative (USTR) with discretionary authority to recommend a wide variety of trade sanctions against countries which, *inter alia*, engage in acts, policies, and practices that 'constitute a persistent pattern of conduct denying internationally recognized worker rights'.[54] In addition, with respect to developing countries in particular, trade preferences granted under the GSP[55] are denied to a country that is determined not to be 'taking steps' to implement internationally recognized workers' rights.[56] These are defined as: the right of association; the right to organize and bargain collectively; freedom from any kind of forced or compulsory labour; a minimum age for the employment of children; and acceptable conditions of employment with respect to minimum wages, hours of work, and occupational safety and health.[57] Although application of trade sanctions against unfair labour practices involves a unilateral judgment by the US authorities about the domestic policies of other countries, the language of the US statute does suggest as a reference point certain widely accepted international norms, as reflected in the Conventions of the International Labour Organization.[58] In other words, although the process is unilateral, it refers to rights recognized in international instruments. Because, as is explained in greater detail in Chapter 14 on trade and development, the GSP preferences are voluntary commitments, and not bound in any trade agreement, they may freely be withdrawn without provoking any violation of international law. S. 301 measures, however, could include withdrawal of trade concessions bound in WTO schedules, and would therefore result in a conflict with WTO obligations as they currently stand (subject to justification under Article XX(a), which as discussed above would entail the rather difficult claim that the measures are necessary to protect 'public morals').

In fact, while GSP preferences have been withdrawn numerous times, s. 301 action has yet to be taken on the basis of consistent non-compliance with international labour rights. The relevant legislation with respect to GSP preferences allows interested parties to bring a petition before the GSP Subcommittee, an interagency group of US trade officials, requesting review of the labour rights performance of a country with, or seeking, GSP status. The review may result in a recommendation to the President that a country's GSP status be withdrawn. The OECD notes:

> In reviewing workers' rights petitions, the GSP Subcommittee undertakes a thorough investigation in order to obtain a balanced view using information from a variety of sources. The Subcommittee looks in particular for evidence of progress in the country's legislation and in its practices, and relies on ILO Conventions and Recommendations as benchmarks for interpreting progress.[59]

The OECD further notes that the pressure created by public exposure and scrutiny of labour practices in such reviews may have an impact on performance, even apart from the threat of actual sanctions through GSP withdrawal. According to the OECD as well, '[from] 1984 through 1995, 40 countries have been named in petitions citing labour rights abuses according to GSP law', with fewer than half these cases being pursued by the Subcommittee to the stage of a formal review.[60] According to Dufour, among the countries that have had their GSP status withdrawn by virtue of a recommendation of the Subcommittee are: the Central African Republic, Chile, Liberia, Myanmar, Nicaragua, Paraguay, Romania and the Sudan.[61]

Finally, there is now legislation pending in the United States that would prohibit importation of products produced with child labour (the draft *Child Labor Deterrence Act*); in mid-1997 the proposed bill was referred to committees of the House of Representatives and Senate for comment.

In 1995, the European Union amended its GSP programme so as to condition the granting of a margin of preferentiality in excess of a base rate upon, *inter alia*, respect for certain core labour rights; the relevant EU regulations refer explicitly to the ILO Conventions concerning freedom of association and collective bargaining, as well as child labour. This provision came into force in 1998. In addition, GSP status may be withdrawn altogether where a country permits any form of slavery or the exportation of products made with prison labour.[62]

NAFTA and the North American Agreement on Labor Cooperation (NAALC)

In the context of NAFTA, US concerns in particular about Mexican labour practices led to the negotiation of a parallel accord on labour standards. Mexican labour laws do provide for most of the workers rights contained in the ILO Conventions, but are widely believed to be un- or under-enforced.[63] Some proponents of NAFTA attribute this un- or under-enforcement to a shortage of labour inspectors.[64] However, the problem is likely much more deeply rooted reflecting widespread corruption of politicians or public officials (especially at the regional or local level), and the use of intimidation and violence to keep workers from organizing in some parts of Mexico, such as the economically important *Maquiladora* zone. Furthermore, as Morici suggests, there may be collusion between the Mexican government and the official Mexican trade union movement to keep workers unorganized in the *Maquiladoras* so as to attract more foreign investment into Mexico.[65]

The North American Agreement on Labor Cooperation, usually referred to as the NAFTA Labor Side-Agreement or side-deal, has two major components. The first is a hard legal obligation on the part of NAFTA Parties to enforce adequately their own domestic labour laws, particularly with respect to occupational safety and health, child labour and minimum wage standards (Articles 3, 27). This obligation may be described as hard, in that a binding dispute settlement process may, where there is 'persistent failure' to enforce these labour laws, lead to a monetary judgment against the offending Party. In the case of a successful action against Canada, the monetary judgment can be enforced through an order of a Canadian domestic court; in the case of the US and Mexico, it may be enforced through withdrawal of concessions under NAFTA. Another substantive obligation of the Side-Agreement is that 'each Party shall ensure that its labor laws and regulations provide for high labor standards consistent with high quality and productivity workforces, and shall continue to strive to improve those standards in that light' (Article 2). However, this obligation is hedged by the qualifying language that it is subject to 'the right of each Party to establish its own domestic labor standards', and – unlike the Article 3 obligation – no means of legal enforcement is contemplated for this obligation.

A Commission for Labor Cooperation is provided for, comprised of a Council and a Secretariat (Article 8), charged with, *inter alia*, promoting the collection and dissemination of data on labour issues, the production and publication of reports and studies, and the facilitation of consultation between the Parties on labour matters (Article 10). Article 11 provides a list of specific matters regarding which the Council 'shall promote cooperative activities between the Parties, as appropriate'. NAALC Annex 1 states that the Parties are 'committed to promote' a range of labour principles, including freedom of association and the right to organize, prohibition of forced labour, 'labor protections for children and young persons', and elimination of employment discrimination (the commitment to these and the other principles is subject to the important qualification that no minimum standards are being set for domestic law).

The primary avenue for complaints by interested Parties that a NAFTA Party is not enforcing its labour laws is through the National Administrative Office of one of the other two NAFTA Parties. Thus, the US National Administrative Office (NAO) typically receives complaints about under-enforcement, or non-enforcement of Mexican labour law. The NAO may accept or reject the complaint for review, and in the case of rejection must furnish written reasons to the complainant. Such a review produces a report, which may or may not recommend ministerial consultations. The sole avenue through which enforcement action may eventually be taken against a NAFTA Party is, however, through panel dispute settlement, and two of the three NAFTA Parties must consent to the striking of a panel. To date, 12 complaints have been accepted for review by NAOs, with Mexico named as the offending Party in all but one (which complained of US practices). Several of the submissions have resulted in Ministerial Consultations. In almost all cases, the complaints have concerned failure to enforce the right of free association and the right to organize. An important exception is a recent complaint concerning pregnancy-based discrimination by Maquiladora employers (submission US 9701). It has been claimed that the publicity effects of these complaints, and the reports and consultations in which they have resulted, have led to some positive adjustments in labour law enforcement;[66] however the Mexican and in one case the United States authorities have not surprisingly left unacknowledged the role of the NAALC in altering their dispositions on the matters at issue. Many of the cases have involved anti-union activity by major multinational corporations or their local affiliates, including General Electric, Honeywell and Sprint: in these kinds of cases, an NAO report may have a positive impact on the practices of the corporation, even if it does not result in the government itself improving its enforcement of labour laws. In no case has a matter been taken to an arbitral panel. Because of the role of the provinces in labour matters under the Canadian constitution, Canada's full participation in the NAALC process was subject to a minimum threshold of voluntary provincial involvement. In 1997 the threshold specified in the NAALC was crossed, with the federal government and three provinces (Manitoba, Quebec and Alberta) having decided to participate. Finally, there is an additional mechanism in the NAALC, as yet unused, which contemplates the striking of Evaluation Committees of Experts, which may be requested by a Party under certain conditions: a Committee may deal with 'technical standards' in eight areas, which include, *inter alia*, prohibition of forced labour, labour protection for children and young persons, and elimination of employment discrimination.

CONCLUSION

Increasingly, discussion in the international policy community on the relationship between liberal trade and labour rights has focused on the issue of compliance with core universal rights, which have a close relationship to the rights contained in general international human rights instruments such as the UN Declaration and the UN Covenant on Civil and Political Rights. Competitiveness-based claims about 'social dumping' have become less prominent, and the notion that the objective should be to obtain some kind of 'level playing field' between developed and developing countries is now less and less heard, even from labour rights advocates on the left of the political spectrum. Complaints under the NAFTA labour side-agreement, as well as cases where GSP preferences have been unilaterally withdrawn, or threatened to be withdrawn by the United States, are all cases where the labour practices or policies have amounted to documented, egregious violations of human rights, often involving the use of intimidation and violence to impede freedom of association, or even explicit legal restrictions on the right to organize. In some instances, one may suspect that the motivations for such practices are the perpetuation of social and political oppression as opposed to any strategy to promote competitiveness through keeping wage costs low. In sum, contrary to the picture still painted by some free traders, the claim for a trade and labour rights link is not some fanatical or protectionist adventure to attempt harmonization of conditions of work across the world, regardless of different economic and cultural conditions.

Of course, the overall effects of globalization on the fate of workers continue to be a subject of intense debate and controversy – in particular, there is the issue of whether freer trade, along with liberalization of investment and capital flows, has led to greater income inequality and more precarious conditions of work in the developed world, an issue closely related to the concerns with respect to adjustment and adjustment policies that we have discussed in Chapter 9 on safeguards and adjustment and some of the more general critiques of globalization that we will address in the Conclusion.

Such empirical evidence as is available suggests little relationship between comparative advantage and compliance with core labour rights. Insistence on compliance with these rights is thus unlikely to damage the trade prospects of developing countries, and may have positive dynamic effects, supporting political and social evolution that leads to the kinds of institutions able to sustain economic growth over time, as well as a more productive workforce.

The use of trade sanctions to address non-compliance with core labour rights remains highly controversial, even if there is much greater understanding of what these rights are, and renewed impetus at the ILO to define more precisely their irreducible content (as reflected in the June 1998 ILO Declaration), as well as more effective mechanisms for monitoring and reporting. The main impact of this lack of agreement is that some of the most powerful developed countries will continue to impose their own sanctions through the withdrawal of GSP preferences – measures that are perfectly legal under existing multilateral trading rules.

By failing to respond to the demand for a social clause within the WTO, the Organization has simply created an incentive for developed countries to make fewer offers for tariff cuts on an MFN basis in future rounds of negotiations (especially on products of interest to developing countries), so as to preserve the impact that comes from being able to grant – and withdraw – GSP treatment. This is a consequence that free traders who are dogmatic opponents of a place within the WTO for permissible trade sanctions should consider more carefully.

17 Trade and competition policy

THE BASIC ECONOMIC FUNCTION OF COMPETITION LAWS

In exploring the relationship between trade policy and competition policy, it is useful at the outset to review briefly the underlying economic theory on the welfare implications of monopoly, so that similarities and differences in the welfare frameworks that conventionally animate both trade policy and competition policy can be clearly kept in focus.[1] The concept of 'market power' or 'monopoly power' – these terms will be used interchangeably – drives most aspects of modern competition laws. Whether one is concerned with a single firm monopoly, competitors colluding with a view to acting as if they were a monopoly, a firm seeking to predate on existing or potential rivals in order to exclude them from the market, restrictive vertical distribution arrangements, or a merger that may lead to a dominant position, in every case the focus is on the social welfare implications of excessive market power. In economic terms, market power basically means the ability to increase prices profitably above (or reduce non-price dimensions of competition below) competitive levels by a non-trivial amount for an extended period of time. In order to establish whether any of the foregoing arrangements involve excessive market power, it is obviously necessary to define one or more relevant product and geographic markets in which the firms in question are alleged to be exercising market power, which largely turns on demand-side and supply-side substitution possibilities – an exercise that is central and problematic in most antitrust cases.[2] Whether market power in a market, once defined, can in fact be effectively exercised turns on factors such as whether incumbents' market shares indicate a likelihood of unilateral abuse of dominance or explicit or tacit collusion and the scale of barriers to entry (including regulatory barriers, trade barriers, incumbents' intellectual property rights, minimum viable scale of entry and the extent of entrants' sunk costs, access to critical inputs and distribution channels, and customers' switching costs).

The traditional economic analysis of monopoly has a structural and static focus. It examines the welfare implications of a firm *being* a monopolist. Although most laws relating to monopolization or abuse of dominant position deal with *conduct* entailed in attempting to acquire, defend or enlarge a monopoly position, the static analysis provides the foundation for legal concerns that have a more dynamic or conduct-oriented focus. Thus, we begin with this conventional static analysis, which is shown in Figure 17.1.

In a 'perfectly competitive' market, firms would price at PC (where the marginal cost curve intersects the industry demand curve), and would produce QC of output. Aside from transitory effects, there are no 'economic profits' to be made. The monopolist, in contrast, will maximize its profits by restricting output to QM – the point at which its marginal cost and marginal revenue curves intersect.[3] It therefore prices at PM.[4]

As can be observed from Figure 17.1, there are several undesirable consequences of monopoly relative to a competitive market. First, quantity is lower (by QC-QM). Second, price is higher (by PM-PC). Third, consumers on the demand curve between PC and PM are priced out of the market even though the resource costs entailed in serving them (as represented by MC_1) are lower than the prices that they are willing to pay. Compelling them to reallocate their expenditures to less preferred forms of consumption creates the so-called 'dead-weight-loss' triangle designated as DWL in the diagram (allocative inefficiency). Fourth, consumers who remain in the market (i.e. those consumers on the demand curve above PM) are required to transfer part of the 'consumer surplus' that they would have realized under competitive conditions (with price at PC) to the monopolist (as reflected in the hatched rectangle). Although such wealth transfers in themselves have purely distributional effects and are not a misallocation of resources, political opposition to monopolies often focuses on this factor. Moreover, it may often be the case that the lure of monopoly profits will induce socially wasteful investments in rent-seeking activities, rendering at least part of the rectangle indirectly an additional measure of resource misallocation.[5] Finally, some lines of objection to monopoly are non-economic in nature, such as populist concerns that large concentrations of economic power carry the potential for undue political influence.[6]

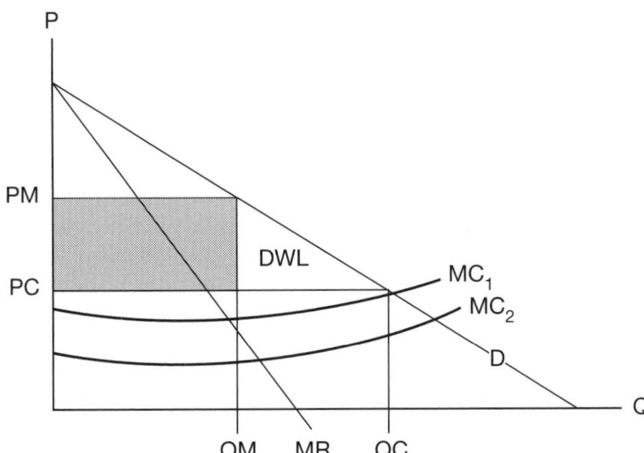

Figure 17.1 Welfare effects of monopoly

The model of monopoly depicted in Figure 17.1 assumes a single monopoly price. However, a monopolist may be able to do even better than this if it is able to price discriminate by raising the price to highly inelastic customers on the demand curve above PM and/or lowering the price to more elastic customers on the demand curve between PM and PC. At the limit, a perfectly discriminating monopolist would charge every consumer on the demand curve his or her reservation price and appropriate the entire consumer surplus under the demand curve and above PC. While this strategy would exacerbate the wealth transfer implications of monopoly noted above, it would also raise the monopolist's output to the competitive level (QC) by ensuring that all consumers prepared to pay more than the resource costs of producing a unit of output are in fact served, thus eliminating the dead-weight-loss triangle (or allocative inefficiency). In the real world, however, perfect price discrimination is almost never feasible because it would entail a monopolist having both perfect information about each customer's reservation price (i.e. elasticity of demand) and the ability to prevent arbitrage between low price and high price purchasers. Thus, one is more likely to observe attempts to segment customers into several broad groups (e.g. business and leisure travellers, adult and children cinema-goers, etc.), who are charged different prices reflecting general differences in their elasticities of demand. In such cases it is not possible, as a matter of a priori analysis, to deduce whether total industry output is likely to rise or fall relative to the single monopoly price scenario (although typically it will rise).[7]

There is an important additional implication of monopoly to be noted from Figure 17.1. Suppose that in moving from a competitive to a monopolized industry the monopolist is able to reduce its cost of production from MC_1 to MC_2 through various economies of scale and/or scope, thus releasing resources for more productive use elsewhere in the economy. Two opposing welfare (as opposed to distributional) effects result. The negative welfare (i.e. misallocation) implications of the dead-weight-loss associated with monopoly remain, but there are now also productive efficiency gains from the savings in resources. As Williamson demonstrated in a seminal article with respect to mergers, depending on the elasticity of demand (and therefore the size of the dead-weight-loss triangle), if monopoly results in a reduction in average costs in the order of 5–10%, the merger must give rise to price increases in excess of 20% (with an elasticity of 0.2) and in excess of 40% (with an elasticity of 0.05) for the net allocative effects to be negative.[8] This raises difficult questions as to whether some form of efficiency defence should be available to firms achieving monopoly power.[9] In effect, this would entail the adoption of a total welfare rather than consumer welfare criterion, i.e. maximization of the sum of producer and consumer surplus.

It should be noted that some analysts worry about the opposite phenomenon. Undisciplined by competition, a monopolist may be able to enjoy 'the quiet life' which, through excessive management perks and general organizational slack, results in its costs rising above or rates of innovation falling below the level which would prevail in a competitive market ('X or dynamic inefficiency'). Other commentators discount this possibility by arguing that even monopolists (or their shareholders) have an incentive to maximize rather than dissipate monopoly rents (although this may not be as likely in the case of state-owned monopolies where monitoring incentives are often weak).

An important point to emphasize from this brief review of the basic economics of monopoly is that economic concerns over the effects of monopoly (or market power) focus primarily on its adverse effects on consumers. Competition policy is thus primarily concerned with protecting *consumer welfare*, not preserving some given state of competition or number of competitors. Conceived of as consumer protection legislation, competition laws should not be encumbered with other policy objectives such as protecting small businesses, or industrial policy concerns such as promoting 'national champions', or populist political objectives. This view of the purposes of competition policy has now won wide acceptance amongst antitrust scholars and enforcement authorities in the United States, Canada, the EU and many other industrialized countries (while recognizing that this still leaves room for much debate as to the effects on consumer welfare of particular practices in particular cases). This has been an important advance over earlier and widely divergent understandings as to the purposes of competition policy. It also provides a normative framework consistent with liberal trade policies for assessing the global welfare effects of both public and private restrictions on competition.

INTERNATIONAL DIMENSIONS OF COMPETITION LAWS[10]

The nature of the concerns

The US and Canada have possessed domestic competition laws for more than a century. For many other industrialized countries and the European Union, competition laws are a much more recent phenomenon (mostly adopted after the Second World War). Almost half the members of the GATT/WTO have no competition laws at all and may, in many cases, lack the institutional capacity to implement and administer an effective domestic competition law regime. Amongst Member countries with such laws, there are significant substantive, institutional and procedural differences.[11] These differences or divergences in domestic antitrust or competition regimes have led to increasing calls for harmonization or integration much like the impetus for harmonizing domestic Intellectual Property regimes that led to the Uruguay Round TRIPS agreement. Dr Sylvia Ostry argues[12] that, as tariffs and other border measures have been eliminated or reduced, the new arena for international policy cooperation is moving beyond the border to domestic policies. The basic reason for this shift lies in changes in the extent and nature of the international linkages among countries, which have produced a new type of friction which she calls 'system friction'. Ostry argues that a globalizing world has a low tolerance for system divergence. In particular, different traditions of government involvement in domestic economies and different industrial organization traditions have rendered increasingly contentious public–private distinctions in international trade law where trade regimes have traditionally focused on governmentally-induced impediments to trade but not private restrictions on competition (including foreign competition). This view often argues for broad international commitments to ensuring effective market access or contestability, whatever the source of existing constraints thereon.

In this chapter we ask how domestic competition policies (or their absence or ineffective or selective enforcement of them) may improperly constrain international trade and investment.[13] It is now widely argued that as firms attempt to improve or maintain their competitive position in an increasingly more open economic environment, they may take actions aimed at effectively locking competing imports or foreign investors out of their domestic market. A dominant firm or a colluding group may engage in predatory behaviour, such as price cutting, to fend off the efforts of a foreign rival trying to get access to its market. Some forms of price discrimination, such as loyalty bonuses, rebates and discounts accorded to local purchasers may deter them from dealing with foreign firms. A group of firms may engage in horizontal exclusionary behaviour by collectively practising predatory pricing or by collectively boycotting distributors who deal with foreign firms seeking to gain access or suppliers who deal with foreign firms trying to establish a presence. Import cartels may seek to exercise monopsony power against foreign suppliers. The operation of trade associations may also be anti-competitive if they provide a forum to organize industry cartels with exclusionary effects on foreign competitors or are used to discriminate against foreign controlled domestic companies by limiting their rights to participate in association activities, including access to product or service certification regimes, thus impairing their competitiveness. Vertical restraints may also be a vehicle to impede market access and presence. If incumbent manufacturers have tied up all distributors or retailers through exclusive dealing arrangements or through full vertical integration, a foreign entrant will have to overcome barriers created by the larger amount of capital required and risks entailed in setting up its own distribution network. Alternatively, a producer which controls all distribution outlets may charge foreign rivals a higher price in order to allow access to the market, thus limiting their competitiveness. Global rationalization through mergers and acquisitions can promote monopoly, oligopoly or oligopsony in domestic markets. Strategic alliances, which are becoming increasingly common in high technology sectors where R&D costs are often substantial, may be efficiency enhancing but may also provide a vehicle to segment markets or to achieve a dominant position.[14] State-owned or protected monopolies may foreclose competitive foreign entry and distort competitive conditions in upstream or downstream competitive markets in which these domestic entities are also active. Firms given protected home market positions may be able to use their supracompetitive profits to engage in 'strategic' (predatory) dumping in export markets. Alternatively, monopolies or mergers leading to dominant positions may be permitted by domestic antitrust authorities if most of their output is sold in foreign markets where rents can be realized by supracompetitive prices at the expense of reductions in foreign consumer welfare; similarly, in the case of export cartels or domestic cartels that sell most of their output in foreign markets.

Past efforts at international coordination of domestic competition policies

This section provides a brief historical review of efforts at international coordination of domestic competition policies.

Multilateral fora

In the 1940s the precursor to the GATT – the Havana Charter and the International Trade Organization that it contemplated – envisaged multilateral regulation and review of restrictive business practices (Chapter V). These provisions would have obliged the Members of the proposed ITO to take appropriate measures to prevent private commercial enterprises that had effective control of trade from restraining competition, limiting access to markets, or fostering monopolistic control in international trade. Member nations would have been entitled to complain about prohibited restraints to the ITO. The ITO would have been authorized to investigate and to demand information in the course of its investigation, and to recommend remedial action to the governments of Member nations. Upon finding a complaint valid, the ITO would have been required to publish its findings and request full reports from the offending Member State about the progress of its remedial measures. However, the Charter could not withstand opposition in the US Congress motivated by concerns over institutional incursions into US domestic political sovereignty.[15]

In 1953 the United States, Canada and others, through the Economic and Social Council of the United Nations, prepared a draft agreement envisaging the formation of an international coordinating agency which would receive, investigate and recommend remedial action relating to complaints about restrictive business practices in international trade. Five years later, at the instance of Norway, the GATT struck a committee to study the extent to which, and how, the GATT should undertake to deal with such practices. These early attempts to reach international agreements yielded no practical results: differences in national policies at the time were too great to move beyond general recommendations.[16]

In 1980, the United Nations Conference on Trade and Development (UNCTAD) adopted a Code on Restrictive Business Practices.[17] However, the Code takes the form of recommendations which lack binding legal force, and it has had negligible impact. Similarly, the UN Commission on Transnational Corporations has encountered severe difficulties in attracting legal endorsement by industrialized countries of a proposed Code of Conduct for TNCs, which would include provisions on restrictive business practices similar to those contained in the UNCTAD Code.[18] In both cases, developing countries promoted provisions designed to control and regulate the conduct of multinational enterprises that were widely perceived in less-developed countries as abusive and rapacious, while developed countries sought to apply strong competition principles to state-owned as well as private enterprises. These differences in perspective resulted in often vague and largely exhortatory provisions.[19] The OECD Agreement on Restrictive

Practices Affecting International Trade of 1986 (which has a lineage dating back to more modest OECD initiatives beginning in 1959) is endorsed by all OECD Members but imposes only modest obligations, i.e. Member States commit themselves to notifying other Member States where enforcement action is contemplated that may affect important interests of the latter and to providing an opportunity for consultations.[20] Conciliation provisions, including use of the good offices of the OECD Committee on Competition Law and Policy, in the event of Members being unable to resolve conflicts, have rarely – if ever – been invoked.

An important recent development has been the incorporation of competition-related provisions in various GATT/WTO Agreements.[21] These include:

1 The Agreement on Technical Barriers to Trade contains detailed rules regulating the adoption of technical regulations and conformity assessment procedures by non-governmental bodies to ensure that they are not more trade restrictive than necessary.
2 The Understanding on the Interpretation of Articles XVII of the GATT provides for increased surveillance of state trading enterprises.
3 The Agreement on Safeguards requires Member States not to encourage or support the adoption or maintenance by public and private enterprises of equivalent non-governmental measures to voluntary exports restraints.
4 The General Agreement on Trade in Services includes rules designed to ensure that monopolies and exclusive service suppliers do not nullify or impair obligations and commitments under the GATS, particularly where monopolies are also active in related competitive market segments. The 1997 Plurilateral Agreement on Basic Telecommunications Service incorporates regulatory principles aimed at preventing anti-competitive practices by major suppliers (such as anti-competitive cross-subsidization, use of information obtained from competitors, and withholding technical and commercial information) and ensuring that the interconnection practices of such suppliers do not impede market access and meet non-discrimination requirements.
5 The TRIPS Agreement permits the application of competition policy to abuse of intellectual property rights, including compulsory licensing.
6 The Agreement on Government Procurement regulates tendering procedures so as to ensure optimum effective international competition and addresses certain competition problems such as collusive tendering.
7 The TRIMS Agreement requires the WTO Council on Trade in Goods to consider whether the Agreement should be complemented with provisions on investment policy and competition policy.
8 The Draft Multilateral Agreement on Investment being negotiated under the auspices of the OECD also contemplates the possibility of including commitments to prevent abuses of dominant position by public or private monopolies.
9 At the first WTO Ministerial in December 1996 in Singapore, Members agreed to constitute a WTO Working Group to study more broadly the interaction between trade policy and competition policy.

Bilateral agreements[22]

The United States has negotiated formal, bilateral, competition-law enforcement Protocols with Canada[23] (recently re-negotiated and expanded),[24] Australia,[25] Germany,[26] and the EU.[27] While important variations exist among these Protocols, all are roughly patterned on a model of cooperation recommended by the OECD and now promoted by the US *International Antitrust Enforcement Assistance Act* of 1994.[28] They do not extend, for the most part, beyond requiring the Parties to notify each other of pending enforcement actions that may have an impact on important interests of the other Party, and to take account of the views of the latter in deciding whether to proceed.[29] The Canada–US Mutual Legal Assistance Treaty goes somewhat further in requiring assistance from the Parties in criminal matters (including criminal aspects of competition policy), extending to the use of formal investigative powers where suspected criminal conduct has occurred in one country but the Parties involved in the conduct reside in the other country. The recent US–EU Protocol and the renegotiated Canada–US Agreement go somewhat further again in identifying a set of both negative and positive comity principles by which the Parties will be guided in deciding whether to forgo or exercise jurisdiction. Positive comity principles require a country to give sympathetic consideration to taking enforcement action against conduct on its territory that is allegedly causing harm to interests in another country. Negative comity principles, in contrast, require a country not to take enforcement action that may affect another country's nationals before consulting the latter country's government.

Regional trading blocs

Under Articles 85 and 86 of the Treaty of Rome, the EU has been successful in adopting a unified competition policy for all Member States with respect to transactions that have a Community dimension. Moreover, with respect to transactions covered by the Treaty, enforcement is unified in the European Commission, and ultimate adjudicative authority resides with the European Court of Justice.[30]

NAFTA contains a short chapter (Chapter 15) on Competition Policy, Monopolies and State Enterprises. Under this chapter, each Party commits itself to adopting and maintaining measures to proscribe anti-competitive business conduct and to take appropriate action with respect thereto. Pursuant to this commitment, Mexico recently enacted a comprehensive competition law.[31] The Parties also commit themselves to cooperating on issues of competition-law enforcement policy, including mutual legal assistance, notification, consultation and exchange of information relating to the enforcement of competition laws in the free trade area. However, no Party may have recourse to dispute settlement under the Agreement in the foregoing matters. In the case of monopolies and state enterprises, each Party commits itself to ensuring that state-sanctioned monopolies will minimize or eliminate any nullification or impairment of benefits anticipated under the Agreement. Moreover, in the case of both privately owned and government-owned monopolies, they are committed to act solely in accordance with commercial considerations in the purchase or sale of goods or services in the relevant market, and to provide non-discriminatory treatment to investments of investors, and to goods and service providers, of another Party.[32] With respect to services generally, Article 1201 contains several obligations aimed at ensuring that licensing and certification measures of Parties do not 'constitute an unnecessary barrier to trade'. The telecommunications chapter (Chapter 13) provides that where a monopolist competes in a segment of the market that is open to competition, a Party must ensure 'that the monopoly does not use its monopoly to engage in anti-competitive conduct', including discriminatory network access requirements. Under the intellectual property chapter (Chapter 17), Parties may limit the intellectual property rights they are otherwise obligated to recognize where licensing practices or conditions 'constitute abuses of intellectual property rights having an adverse effect on competition in the relevant market'. In the case of patents, compulsory licensing is explicitly contemplated as a potential remedy.

This brief historical sketch of efforts to date, either to harmonize domestic competition laws or to create some form of supranational review process for anti-competitive or restrictive business practices, suggests modest progress over the past four decades (with the notable exception of the European Union).

A framework for evaluating future international initiatives

In considering future reform strategies, the 'system frictions' thesis advanced by Ostry is not especially helpful as an analytical guide. In a world of nation states, system frictions are everywhere. If the whole world spoke the same language, there would be fewer system frictions (e.g. in facilitating foreign investment). If everybody in the world drove on the same side of the road, there would again be fewer system frictions (e.g. in exporting automobiles). If preferences and priorities regarding education and credentialling policies, labour policies, environmental policies, culture, health care, law and order and the rule of law, property rights, and almost every other area of domestic policymaking one could identify were the same the world over, there would be fewer system frictions. However, in her otherwise magisterial Handler Lecture on the evolution of competition policy, Professor Eleanor Fox speaks repeatedly of her vision of 'one world' and the inspiration afforded to the rest of the world in this context by the evolution of the European Union.[33]

Reflecting this perspective, the Draft International Antitrust Code[34] (the Munich Code) published by the International Antitrust Working Group (primarily a group of German competition scholars), proposes a complete mandatory World Competition Code. This Code sets out minimum standards to be incorporated into the GATT, and enforceable in domestic jurisdictions by an International Antitrust Authority operating under the auspices of the new World Trade Organization (WTO), with disputes being adjudicated by a permanent International Antitrust Panel operating as part of the new GATT dispute resolution regime.[35] In some respects, this proposal is a more ambitious form of the Uruguay Round GATT

Agreement on Intellectual Property, which provides for common minimum substantive and procedural standards to be applied by domestic administrative and judicial authorities, subject to international dispute resolution mechanisms. The difficulties and controversies engendered in negotiating this more modest multilateral harmonization regime should be salutary.[36]

This general captivation with the European Union model seems to be seriously misguided in the present context. In few, if any, other parts of the world do the special geo-political circumstances which led to the evolution of the European Union exist, and the prospects for creating the supranational institutions which have been central to the integration project of the European Union are close to non-existent. In a multilateral context such as the GATT/WTO, agreement amongst the more than 130 Member States on both the substance and enforcement of domestic competition laws would seem remote.

In our view, it is difficult to approach the case for harmonizing domestic competition laws in a substantially different way from that of harmonizing any number of other domestic laws or policies that may create 'system frictions'. In thinking about harmonization issues generally, and competition policy issues specifically, in either a regional or multilateral context, it is useful to bear in mind the distinction often drawn in the economic integration literature between negative and positive integration.[37] Negative integration essentially tells countries what policies they may *not* adopt, while positive integration tells countries which policies they *must* adopt. It is obviously true that harmonized domestic laws and policies are likely to reduce the administrative (compliance) costs of firms operating across a wide range of jurisdictions, which would have to undertake compliance with only one set of rules. In this respect, harmonization can facilitate freer movement of goods, services and capital. Second, differential or distinctive regulatory requirements can constitute a barrier to entry to a foreign market, where a foreign producer is required to adapt its products to distinctive requirements of the importing jurisdiction. Third, common regulatory standards across a range of jurisdictions may enable economies of scale in production and distribution to be realized. However, as David Leebron suggests, 'if the optimal policies for national populations do differ, then harmonization requires that some measure of local welfare be sacrificed.'[38] These welfare losses are unlikely to be completely captured in measured income estimates. It is true that in many contexts, domestic policies may not reflect the true preferences of a majority of the population, perhaps because the government is undemocratic or even predatory. In other cases, policy differences may largely reflect the contingencies of history and no longer reflect current social objectives or at least the most appropriate means of realizing them (but rather simply policy inertia). In these cases, policy harmonization carries few, if any, costs, and potentially significant benefits. But in a wide range of other cases Leebron's observation presumably holds true. Indeed, many pro-free trade economists, who have generally supported harmonization efforts within the European Union and elsewhere, have at least implicitly recognized this in their rejection of fair trade and related harmonization claims in the labour and environmental areas.[39]

Professor Fox herself, in a paper with Professor Ordover, recognizes these considerations in identifying as 'the aspiration and guiding light world welfare, appropriate sovereignty, and national autonomy', or 'the one-world-with-appropriate-autonomy vision',[40] but rather like Ostry's 'system friction' thesis, this 'guiding light' provides very little purchase, in itself (like the elusive concept of 'subsidiarity' in the EU), on how to strike the appropriate balance. In other papers,[41] she spells out in more detail this more cautious vision – what she describes as 'a targeted constitutional approach', in contrast to a 'comprehensive' approach, on the one hand, or a 'minimalist' approach, on the other. A somewhat similar approach has recently been proposed by an EC Expert Group[42] in the form of a plurilateral agreement containing (1) procedural rules relating to notification, cooperation, and negative and positive comity obligations; (2) minimum substantive rules for cross-border cases to be embodied in domestic competition laws of signatories; and (3) an international institutional structure to perform monitoring and dispute resolution functions.

We believe that a cautious approach is warranted to proposals for radical harmonization of domestic laws and policies, including competition policies. In adopting this more cautious approach, we return to the negative and positive integration distinction noted above. International trade treaties such as the GATT have traditionally emphasized negative integration, i.e. what kinds of policies countries may not adopt, and in particular, have prohibited the adoption of domestic policies that either explicitly or implicitly discriminate either between foreign trading powers (the Most Favoured Nation principle) or that discriminate between domestic producers and foreign producers (the National Treatment principle), at least beyond certain clearly identified exceptions such as bound tariffs and health and safety and related exceptions set out in Article XX of the GATT, and national security exceptions set out in Article XXI of the GATT. In a competition policy context, Bacchetta, Horn and Mavroidis[43] usefully distinguish between 'spillovers' and 'distortions' from domestic competition policy. A negative spillover may occur where a competition policy decision taken in one country has adverse effects on Parties in another. For example, an efficiency enhancing merger permitted in country A may disadvantage competitors in country B, or a price fixing prosecution in country A may disadvantage conspirators located in country B but trading into country A's market, but in neither case is there necessarily a distortion from a global perspective. This would entail evaluating whether the decision reduces global welfare, defined as the maximization of global consumer and producer surplus. Only when a domestic competition policy decision, while perhaps maximizing domestic welfare, reduces global welfare is there presumptively the kind of distortion that causes a tension in the interface between competition policy and trade policy.

APPLICATION OF FRAMEWORK TO SPECIFIC ASPECTS OF COMPETITION POLICY

In developing a tractable agenda for reconciling domestic competition policies and international trade policies, this approach enables us to develop a useful purchase on a number of problems. First, exemption from, or non-enforcement of, competition laws for export or import cartels are clearly discriminatory, in that they explicitly treat either domestic producers or domestic consumers differently from foreign producers or foreign consumers.[44] While dispensations for export or import cartels may enhance national income (at least in the case of export cartels) in the short run, they are myopic in that they encourage a downward spiral or beggar-thy-neighbour dynamic through reciprocal measures that in the long run reduce both national and global welfare (much as with reciprocal tariffs).[45] These are easy cases. These dispensations should be removed and appropriate procedural mechanisms adopted for ensuring non-discriminatory enforcement of anti-collusion laws. With respect to these procedural mechanisms, Professor Fox has developed some useful proposals. She suggests that, at least with respect to export market access, the home (importing) nation where the internal market conduct has occurred should have the primary right to take enforcement measures. A harmed nation may request a home nation to take enforcement action against an apparent violation, and the home nation should be obliged to give sympathetic regard to this request. If recourse cannot be had through action by home nation authorities or otherwise in home nation courts, the harmed nation should be entitled to assert enforcement jurisdiction over the subject matter of the controversy, but at the option of the defendant the court should apply the substantive principles of the defendant nation's law.[46] Assertion of jurisdiction by the harmed nation will, of course, be of little value if the injurers maintain no presence in the form of personnel or assets in the harmed country's territory. Thus, an additional step would be to build on the Chapter 19 binational panel experience under the FTA and NAFTA, relating to the application of domestic trade remedy laws,[47] by providing a WTO or NAFTA panel procedure whereby aggrieved foreign Parties (states or firms) could complain to a supranational panel in cases where it is alleged that Member States are not faithfully interpreting or enforcing *their own* domestic competition laws in a non-discriminatory manner.

There also appear to be easy cases at the other end of the spectrum. Foreign producers trading into the United States market who collude to fix prices in the United States market should not be permitted to complain of the relatively stringent United States price fixing laws, on the grounds that in their home jurisdiction price fixing laws are lax or non-existent. Thus, we see no objection to the United States asserting jurisdiction in such cases, as the majority of the United States Supreme Court held in *Hartford Fire Insurance Co. v. California*.[48] In *Hartford*, where United States insurers were alleged to have conspired with UK re-insurers to curtail the availability of certain forms of liability insurance coverage in the United States market, to have treated local insurers as subject to domestic price fixing laws while exempting foreign re-insurers on grounds of extraterritoriality would have entailed discrimination in favour of foreign firms relative to domestic firms. On the other hand, to the extent that domestic insurers were able to claim the insurance exemption under the *McCarran–Ferguson Act* from United States antitrust laws, then to hold the foreign re-insurers liable would have entailed discrimination against them relative to domestic insurers.

Conversely, United States producers trading into or investing in jurisdictions with lax or non-existent anti-collusion laws (that for example may affect the price or supply of inputs) equally have no basis for complaint, provided that these policies are applied in a non-discriminatory manner. This observation would extend to permissive provisions on joint research and production ventures, research consortia and other forms of strategic alliances, provided again that the provisions are not framed or applied in a discriminatory manner. We are thus sceptical of the case for the United States asserting jurisdiction against *Pilkington Glass*[49] in a recent suit, alleging restrictive distribution arrangements impeding effective market access by United States competitors to other markets around the world.[50] Equally, United States or other producers trading into or operating in the European market have no basis for complaint because the abuse of dominant position provisions of Article 86 of the Treaty of Rome are applied somewhat more stringently than the monopolization provisions in Section 2 of the Sherman Act. Similarly, if the European Union should choose to take account of industrial policy considerations, and not only consumer welfare considerations, in the administration of its merger law, or conversely some other country should apply its merger law in a more populist fashion designed to prevent concentrations of economic power, foreign firms operating in these markets, notwithstanding sharp differences from competition laws obtaining in their home market, should accept the local rules of the game (whether perceived to be well-conceived or not), *provided* that these rules are applied in a non-discriminatory fashion to both domestic and foreign firms. Again, if one country chooses to create or maintain state-owned or sanctioned monopolies in some sectors, foreign producers should have no right of complaint about being excluded from these markets, given that other domestic producers face similar exclusion, although discrimination by such monopolies in sales or purchasing decisions against foreign firms would be objectionable (as both the GATT and NAFTA presently provide).[51]

Other cases are admittedly more difficult. One controversial case relates to the relatively quiescent state of Japanese competition law as it applies to both vertical and horizontal *keiretsu*. Vertical production and distribution *keiretsu* and other exclusive dealing arrangements are often alleged to prevent foreign firms from gaining ready access to Japanese manufacturing, retail and distribution networks. These issues figured prominently in an important (1998) GATT/WTO panel proceeding involving a complaint by the US on behalf of Eastman Kodak that Fuji, with government support enjoyed access to an exclusive wholesale and retail distribution system in Japan for consumer film to which Kodak (and other foreign film producers) could not gain access.[52] The US alleged under Article XXIII(1)(b) of the GATT that various Japanese government measures constituted non-violation nullification and impairment of benefits reasonably anticipated by the US under tariff concessions on consumer film made by Japan during the Kennedy, Tokyo and Uruguay Rounds. These measures covered (1) distribution measures which allegedly encouraged and facilitated the creation of a market structure in consumer film in which imports are excluded from traditional distribution channels; (2) restrictions on large retail stores, which allegedly restrict the growth of an alternative distribution channel for imported film; and (3) promotion restrictions which allegedly disadvantage imports by restricting the use of sales promotion techniques that foreign suppliers might wish to deploy in expanding their presence in the Japanese market. In the alternative, the US argued that many of these practices were a violation of the National Treatment principle contained in Article III(4) of the GATT.

The WTO panel rejected all of the US allegations. As to non-violation nullification and impairment, the panel held that the US bore the burden of adducing 'a detailed justification' for its allegations, recognizing the exceptional nature of this ground of complaint. This justification would need to address three issues: (1) whether the practices in question were government 'measures'; (2) if so, whether the measure in question related to a benefit reasonably anticipated to accrue from prior tariff concessions by upsetting the competitive relationship between imports and domestic products; and (3) whether the benefit accruing to the complainant state had in fact been nullified or impaired by the measure in question (causality).

The panel affirmed that purely private rather than governmental measures were not reviewable under the GATT, and that purely advisory reports or recommendations to government by specialist committees and task forces were not government measures, unless clearly adopted or acted on by government. However, the panel was prepared to accept that many traditional forms of 'administrative guidance' engaged in by the Japanese government constituted government measures, even though informal and lacking explicit sanctions, provided that such guidance entailed implicit incentives or disincentives to comply.

With respect to the requirement that a challenged measure relate to a reasonably anticipated benefit from prior tariff concessions, the panel held that many of the disputed measures were in force prior to the concessions in question and imputed knowledge of them to the US government, rejecting the latter's claim of opaqueness or unpredictability in administration.

With respect to the requirement that the measures in question cause the nullification or impairment of a benefit reasonably anticipated from the prior tariff concessions, the panel found that none of the measures were *de jure* or *de facto* discriminatory and applied equally to domestic and foreign suppliers. For similar reasons, the panel rejected US claims of violation of the National Treatment principle.

In the wake of this decision, the US government announced an inter-agency monitoring committee whereby Japanese government assurances to the WTO panel on non-discriminatory access to Japan's distribution channels, on large retail stores and on non-restrictive application of promotions laws, so as to permit free competition with respect to pricing and quality, are viewed as 'commitments' potentially attracting s. 301 trade sanctions if not lived up to.

Horizontal *keiretsu*, because of the prominent role played by lead banks and because of cross-shareholdings, are alleged to prevent foreign investors from readily acquiring Japanese firms as a means of lower cost and more efficient entry into the Japanese market than greenfield entry. Data indicate a dramatically lower level of foreign investment stock in Japan than most other industrialized economies, and notwithstanding the major growth in foreign direct investment flows in the 1980s, dramatically lower levels of inflows into Japan.[53] It is true, of course, that Japanese competition laws on these matters are facially neutral as between the ability of domestic and foreign firms to challenge these arrangements, although one should not be so naïve as to terminate the analysis there. If, as in the case of import cartels, the evidence disclosed discrimination in the application and enforcement of these laws depending on whether the complainant was a domestic firm or a foreign firm, this would constitute a form of discrimination for our purposes. Moreover, even if the laws were both framed and enforced in a neutral fashion, one would still want to ask (as many GATT decisions under Article III (National Treatment) and Article XX (exceptions to GATT obligations)) have done, whether these laws are a form of disguised protectionism or discrimination. This question is not always easily answered, because it may be the case that Japanese competition laws do have a disparate impact on foreign exporters or investors relative to domestic producers. However, this is equally true (as argued above) of different language laws, driving laws, etc., so that mere demonstration of disparate impact is not sufficient unless disparate impact is also indicative of a disguised attempt at discrimination. In the case of the Japanese *keiretsu*, given the central role that they have traditionally played in corporate governance and organizational structures in Japan,[54] it is difficult to believe that the primary purpose for their adoption has been to differentially disadvantage foreign producers, even though that may be a consequence. An ironic feature of current United States concerns over Japanese vertical arrangements and lack of antitrust scrutiny of them is that much recent thinking amongst United States antitrust scholars (reflected increasingly in United States case-law) has rejected sinister (anti-competitive) explanations of vertical restraints and views many such restraints as benign (efficiency-enhancing).[55]

Even if domestic competition policy is not applied in a discriminatory fashion to private restrictions, more fundamental objections to such restrictions, and indeed other domestic policies of foreign countries, such as the maintenance of state-owned or sanctioned monopolies in given sectors, invoke instead a notion of *reciprocity*. Here the argument is made that even if these restrictions or policies satisfy the National Treatment Principle, if one country has adopted much more liberal policies in these respects while another country has adopted much more restrictive policies, for example if the United States has adopted much more assertive antitrust policies on vertical restraints and has privatized and/or deregulated state-owned or sanctioned monopolies, while Japan has adopted much more permissive policies on vertical restraints and allows much greater scope for state-owned or sanctioned monopolies, Japanese firms have much more favourable access to United States markets, both as exporters and investors, than United States exporters and investors with respect to Japanese markets. This claim may well be true. It is also true that the notion of reciprocity has long played a central role in international trade policy, for example, in tariff negotiations under the GATT and various regional trading arrangements. However, if this broad notion of reciprocity, or functional *equality of access*, were to become the normative touchstone rather than the National Treatment Principle in addressing divergences in domestic competition and related policies, the ability of countries to maintain any diversity or distinctiveness in a whole range of domestic policies would largely be forfeited, with serious implications for notions of political sovereignty. Countries which have chosen unilaterally to adopt more assertive domestic antitrust policies, for example with respect to vertical restrictions, or have chosen to privatize and/or deregulate state-owned or sanctioned monopolies, have presumably done so for what were conceived to be good domestic reasons, taking fully into account the implications for foreign trade and investment *inter alia*. That other countries have chosen to pursue different policies in this respect, provided that they are non-discriminatory, should provide no basis for complaint by the first country, otherwise the latter would be in a position to 'export' its domestic policies to every foreign market in which it has present or prospective trade or investment interests, dramatically expanding notions of extraterritoriality beyond any scope hitherto considered defensible. This is not, of course, to foreclose the possibility of international negotiations over such policies (by way of analogy with tariff negotiations), but it is to argue for a highly restrained role for *unilateral* action by one country with respect to another country's domestic policies, or indeed agreements on modifications to these policies extracted under threat of unilateral action.

Another problematic case is transnational mergers.[56] Some cases are easier than others. If two firms which are based in country A but sell most of their output in country B, merge and acquire a dominant position in country B's market, monopoly rents will be realized in country A but consumer welfare losses will be sustained primarily in country B. This may induce the competition authorities in country A to approve the merger. In our view, this is a form of disguised discrimination against consumers in country B. The competition authorities in country A would have reached a different and adverse conclusion if all the affected producers and consumers had been located within their own jurisdiction. In other words, this is to discriminate against consumers in country B and, as with export cartels or tariffs, is myopic in the longer run.[57] Thus, in our view, competition authorities in country B are entitled to object to this merger, as the US Federal Trade Commission did in the *Institut Merieux/Connaught* case,[58] despite being widely criticized for doing so. This kind of case is not conceptually different from the export cartel case, except that the discrimination is implicit.

Other cases are not so straightforward. One such example is the widely discussed decision of the European Commission[59] prohibiting the acquisition of de Havilland, a Canadian-based commuter aircraft producer (owned by an American firm, Boeing) by a European joint venture, ATR (whose parents were, respectively, owned by French and Italian interests), on the grounds that the merger would give the merged entity excessive market power in the European (and global) market (ATR was the leading producer of commuter aircraft in the EU and global markets), despite the fact that the merger was not opposed by the Canadian competition authorities. On a charitable view of the facts, we assume that the Canadian competition authorities had approved the merger pursuant to the efficiencies defence under section 96 of the Canadian *Competition Act* (a provision unique to Canadian competition law), despite some enhanced ability of the merged entity to raise prices in its output markets (primarily outside of Canada), and not simply because of a desire to save Canadian jobs or to appropriate monopoly rents from foreigners. In this case, we may have a genuine problem of interjurisdictional conflict. That is to say, assuming the Canadian authorities would have made the same decision if all of the merged entities' output had been sold in the Canadian market, it would no longer be possible to impute discrimination against foreign customers, but rather the source of the conflicting determinations would genuinely reside in differences in the domestic competition law regimes applied to the transaction. Conversely, of course, one would want to be reassured that the EU competition authorities would have reached the same decision had the acquired firm been located not in Canada but in the EU, and the claimed efficiency gains from the merger would have been fully realized within the EU and not Canada.[60] Given any reasonable understanding of the 'effects' test adopted in the US and the EU for exercising extraterritorial jurisdiction, both jurisdictions could legitimately lay claim to jurisdiction in this case, and on the facts assumed neither could be shown to have discriminated either against foreign producers or foreign consumers. The EU could claim that the consumer welfare test that it applied enjoys wide currency in other countries' competition law regimes (in particular the United States) and in much respected academic literature. On the other hand, the Canadian authorities could reasonably claim that the total welfare test applied by them, while perhaps less justiciable and more speculative, actually accords better with pure economic theory. Short of a meta-choice, presumably through international agreement, by affected jurisdictions between these two welfare tests in this class of case, such cases of interjurisdictional conflict are not easily resolved. In making such a meta-choice, on balance the consumer welfare test is probably to be preferred, in part because it reflects the predominant test applied in United States and EU competition law and in part because it is more straightforwardly reflective of the consumer (rather than the producer) protection rationale for competition law.[61]

Another difficult case is one where two firms merge and the relevant geographic market is either the global market or at least a regional market (e.g. North America). The recent merger between Boeing and McDonnell Douglas presented this scenario in the global large passenger aircraft manufacturing market, leading to conflicts between US and EU competition authorities that were finally resolved by an undertaking by Boeing to restrict its use of long-term exclusive supply contracts with major airlines. In such cases, in principle even applying a consumer and not a total welfare test, in the first case every competition authority in the world could legitimately assert jurisdiction, invoking a reasonable interpretation of the 'effects' test, and in the second case every competition authority within the regional market could properly assert jurisdiction. In some cases, the merger may be able to be addressed by requiring divestiture of subsidiaries or assets in particular submarkets within the regional market, but in other cases the entire market may be served by single companies. It may be possible to envisage negotiating an international agreement by which a lead jurisdiction is designated by reference to a 'primary effects' test, perhaps operationalized by identifying the market where the largest percentage of the merged entity's output is likely to be sold.[62] In a regional context, this will mostly be the United States, and this will also often be the case in global markets, given the size of the United States economy. In addition, one might need to contemplate the creation of a supranational authority in which jurisdiction is vested to determine the lead jurisdiction in the event of disputes over whether the relevant market is supranational or where the largest proportion of the merged entity's output is likely to be sold.[63] It should be emphasized that in these last two examples the problem is not necessarily a problem of discrimination but rather a problem of conflict of laws where a choice of law (and forum) rule is required in order to resolve the potential for interjurisdictional conflict. It should also be acknowledged that these problems of interjurisdictional conflict would obviously be drastically reduced or eliminated if all countries could agree on a common set of competition laws and credibly commit to a consistent enforcement policy, but for reasons noted above this would forfeit the value of policy diversity for both purely domestic and supranational transactions while agreement on a choice of law and forum rule would much more narrowly target the area of required agreement on the latter class of cases only.

Beyond these difficult substantive issues, a range of procedural harmonization measures are much more likely to be resolved in that they appear to represent positive-sum strategies for most countries and their constituents. In this respect, the American Bar Association's NAFTA Task Force offers a number of extremely useful suggestions for enhancing cooperation between domestic competition authorities, and thus minimizing duplicate investigative efforts (public transaction costs), and for minimizing the direct transaction costs faced by private parties in meeting divergent information requirements and decision timetables under existing domestic competition law regimes.[64] Bilateral agreements between the United States and the EU, the United States and Canada, the United States and Australia, and New Zealand and Australia, already go some distance towards providing for inter-agency cooperation in competition law enforcement (but could be usefully expanded).[65]

TRADE POLICY IMPLICATIONS

In contrast to 'one world' (or 'flat earth') visions of competition as a global organizing economic principle, 'system frictions', or inappropriate EU analogies applied to the multilateral or trilateral context, which are politically quite unrealistic and indeed at the limit normatively uncongenial in their implications for political sovereignty and democratic accountability (concerns that are increasingly manifest even in Europe over more ambitious integration proposals), a series of more modest multilateral or regional initiatives might usefully be contemplated. These initiatives would focus on several distinct problems: (a) minimizing the scope for explicit or implicit discrimination in the formulation or enforcement of domestic competition laws; (b) minimizing the potential for interjurisdictional conflict and hence risk and uncertainty in transactions affecting supranational geographic markets through international agreements on choice of law and forum rules and supranational mechanisms to oversee their application; (c) minimizing public and private transaction costs in the administration of competition laws through harmonized information requirements, decision timetables, and exchange of information and cooperation amongst enforcement authorities; (d) maximizing transparency in the administration of domestic competition law regimes and hence minimizing the arbitrary and non-accountable exercise of administrative discretion (and unpredictability).

To advance these objectives, Member States of the new World Trade Organization (or NAFTA) should agree to ensure that their domestic competition laws adopt prohibitions against both export and import cartels and adopt complementary procedural mechanisms to ensure effective enforcement. With respect to merger law as this might impact on international mergers, various forms of procedural harmonization might be contemplated pertaining to information requirements, decision timetables, and information sharing among competition authorities. With respect to substantive harmonization, Member States with merger laws might commit themselves, in the interests of transparency, to publishing a set of non-binding merger enforcement guidelines that indicate how these merger laws are likely to be enforced with respect to a common checklist of issues that the guidelines would be required to address (but without a commitment to a common position on these issues). In the case of transnational mergers impacting on supranational geographic markets, international negotiations need to be contemplated over choice of law and forum rules such as a 'primary effects' test designed to identify a lead jurisdiction for evaluating such mergers with a possible role for a supranational authority to resolve disputed issues of jurisdiction. With respect to the contentious issue of vertical foreclosure of effective access to foreign markets, controversy here is likely to be particularly intense given widely differing industrial organization and antitrust traditions in different countries, and substantial theoretical controversies as to the appropriate form that laws should take with respect to vertical restrictions.[66] In this area, it is difficult to contemplate ready multilateral consensus on an appropriate set of legal norms. Perhaps the most that might be hoped for is that member countries would agree that, as a baseline, vertical restrictions should be included in domestic competition laws as discrete reviewable practices or as reviewable practices within a more general abuse of dominant position provision, without sectoral or similar exemptions, but without any common commitment to the legal norms governing the review process.[67] Again, as with merger review, it may be possible to reach agreement on a commitment for each member state to publish a set of non-binding vertical restraint enforcement guidelines that address a common checklist of issues. By way of analogy with the Chapter 19 binational dispute resolution panels provided for under NAFTA in domestic antidumping or countervailing duty determinations, one might go further by providing a WTO or NAFTA panel procedure whereby aggrieved foreign parties (states or firms) could complain to a supranational panel in cases where it is alleged that Member States are not faithfully interpreting or enforcing *their own* domestic competition laws in a non-discriminatory manner. Providing a broader mandate for multilateral or supranational adjudication of competition law issues is likely to raise a host of difficult institutional and procedural issues relating to standing, information-gathering, expertise, and remedies.[68]

It may also be useful for the OECD Competition Law and Policy Committee to convene a group of internationally recognized apolitical competition law experts to work on a non-binding model competition code[69] that, over time, may exert an exemplary or exhortatory influence over the evolution of domestic competition law regimes (rather like the United States *Restatements*).[70] This might usefully build on the Report of the OECD Committee on Competition Law and Policy, 'Interim Report on Convergence of Competition Policies'.[71]

Beyond these competition policy innovations, we should return to the historical origins of the tension between competition law and international trade policy in North America that consigned the former to a deep second-best policy role and attend to the remaining protectionist elements in international trade policy, particularly trade remedy regimes such as antidumping and countervailing duty regimes (residual elements of the 'political fraud' that is sometimes alleged to have characterized the initial enactment of competition laws in North America at the same time as the adoption of high tariffs),[72] and set seriously about the task of exorcising these elements of mercantilism that constrain the operation of international competitive forces far more than do any aspect of current domestic competition policy regimes.[73] Because trade remedy laws apply pricing constraints to foreign firms that do not apply to domestic firms, they are inherently discriminatory (and are inconsistent with the National Treatment principle). In this respect, the outlines of a political deal may be discernible: in return for LDCs and NICs adopting basic competition law measures of the kind outlined above, industrialized countries would agree to substantial curtailment of their trade remedy laws and some supranational oversight in their application – a deal which Mexico in effect accepted under NAFTA by agreeing to enact an effective domestic competition law regime. As outlined in Chapter 7 on antidumping laws, more radical proposals, which we favour, would entail the complete repeal of antidumping laws and their replacement with non-discriminatory harmonized cross-border predatory pricing laws, along the lines of the regime adopted by Australia and New Zealand in 1990 under ANZCERTA.[74] This distinctive role for harmonized competition laws surely warrants a high priority.

18 The international movement of people[1]

INTRODUCTION

Classical free trade theory assumed that goods could often readily be traded across national borders but that the factors of production employed to produce those goods (land, capital and labour) were fixed and immobile. In the contemporary world, largely due to technological changes, this has become dramatically untrue of capital, and much less true of labour. However, the frequent political resistance to international mobility of goods is often dramatically intensified in the case of the international mobility of people. Here we move from the domain of international trade policy to the domain of immigration policy. The most critical linkage between the two relates to international trade in services, especially services which require physical proximity between service supplier and service user. As international trade in services of various kinds continues to grow, the line between trade in services and migration of people becomes increasingly blurred.[2] Of the economic integration regimes reviewed in this book, only the EU to date has committed itself to free internal movement of people, subject to substantial efforts at harmonization of minimum professional and vocational qualifications and without any automatic entitlement to national citizenship of Member States. NAFTA (Chapter 16) contains a much more limited set of provisions for issuance of temporary entry visas for business, professional and technical personnel in connection with international business activities.

This chapter addresses a question that has confronted all individuals and groups of individuals who, throughout history, have chosen to live in a state of civil society with one another and for whom social, political, and economic relationships are integral to the self-definition of each individual in the community of which they are a part. How does one define and justify the conditions of membership in the community? In the context of the modern nation state, this primarily directs our attention to the substance and procedures of our immigration policies; who may become citizens and who must remain strangers, for nations imply boundaries and boundaries at some point imply closure.

As of the late 1980s, approximately 100 million people were resident outside their nations of current citizenship. Roughly 35 million were in sub-Saharan Africa alone and approximately 13–15 million each in the prosperous regions of

Western Europe and North America. Another 15 million or so were in the Middle East or Asia.[3] The United Nations estimates that over 60 million people, or 1.2% of the world's population, now reside in a country where they were not born.[4] Although most immigrants choose a traditional destination (over one-half go to the United States, Canada or Australia), many other countries are also receiving relatively large immigrant flows, including Germany, Switzerland, France and the United Kingdom. Of the total number of immigrants, as of 1993, about 18 million were refugees, most of whom were located in Africa and Asia, up from 8 million in 1980 and 2.5 million in 1970.[5] Table 18.1 describes immigrants as a percentage of the population for most OECD countries in 1981 and 1991.

Table 18.1 Immigrants as a percentage of the total population

	1981	*1991*
Australia	20.6	22.7
Austria	3.9	6.6
Belgium	9.0	9.2
Canada	16.1	15.6
Denmark	2.0	3.3
Finland	0.3	0.7
France	6.8	6.3
West Germany	7.5	8.2
Italy	0.6	1.5
Luxembourg	26.1	28.4
The Netherlands	3.8	4.8
Norway	2.1	3.5
Spain	0.5	0.9
Sweden	5.0	5.7
Switzerland	14.3	17.1
United Kingdom	2.8	3.1
United States	6.2	7.9

Source: OECD (1994).

Table 18.1 obscures locational concentrations of immigrants within countries: for example, 21.7% of the population of California is foreign-born;[6] almost one-quarter of the populations of Ontario and British Columbia in 1991 were immigrants, including 38% of the population of Toronto and 30% of the population of Vancouver.[7]

A number of features of contemporary immigration trends have precipitated major political controversies in host countries around the world, including the US, Canada, Australia, New Zealand, and Western Europe. These features include the sheer scale of immigration; the changing composition of source countries; and the dramatic increase in the number of refugees, all of which have focused attention in receiving countries on the impact of immigrants on native participants in domestic labour markets, the impact on social programme expenditures, and the impact on social and cultural homogeneity and cohesiveness.

IMMIGRATION POLICY IN HISTORICAL PERSPECTIVE

In the US, the first great migration wave occurred between 1881 and 1924 when almost 26 million people entered the country. Reacting to the increase in immigration and to the widespread perception that the new immigrants differed from the old, Congress closed the floodgates in the 1920s by enacting the National Origins Quota System that allocated entry visas according to the ethnic composition of the US population in the 1920s. During the 1930s, only 0.5 million immigrants entered the US. Since then, the number of legal immigrants has increased at about the rate of one million per decade and by 1993, nearly 800,000 people were being admitted annually.[8] The number of illegal immigrants has also steadily increased and is now estimated at between 200,000–300,000 per year. The illegal immigrant population was estimated at around 3.4 million in 1992 (equal to 1.3% of the US population). About 40% of the illegal immigrants have come to the US from Mexico.[9] Amendments in 1965 to the *Immigration and Nationality Act* repealed the national origins restrictions and made family ties to US residents the key factor that determines whether immigrants are admitted into the country. Partly as a result of these changes, the composition of source countries of immigrants to the US has changed dramatically in recent decades. In the 1950s over half of all immigrants to the US came from Europe. Currently fewer than one in five immigrants is European. Almost 40% of recent immigrants are from Asia (especially South East Asia) and a roughly equal number originate in Mexico, the Caribbean and Latin America.[10]

Canadian immigration policy for much of the past century has been similar to that of the US: a major influx of immigrants between 1890 and the late 1920s, minimal immigration through the depression and Second World War years, and a steady increase in immigration levels thereafter, with current levels running at about 200,000 per year. For much of this period, Canada explicitly excluded most immigrants from non-European source countries. Beginning in 1963 and formalized through the adoption of a point system in 1967, Canada abandoned selection criteria based on country of origin and admitted immigrants on the basis of family ties and in the case of independent immigrants assessments of various factors, including education and occupational skills considered likely to influence the ability of immigrants to resettle successfully in Canada. Initially the point system applied to about 50% of immigrants. Since the 1980s the family sponsorship class has come to dominate independent entrants assessed under the point system.[11] A total of 90% of immigrants who arrived in Canada before 1961 were born in Europe. This proportion fell to 69% for those who arrived between 1961 and 1970; 36% for those who immigrated between 1971 and 1980; and one-quarter for those who arrived between 1981 and 1991. At the same time the proportion of immigrants born in Asia and other non-European countries has increased. People born in Asia and the Middle East made up almost one-half of immigrants who came to Canada between 1981 and 1991, but only 3% of those who came before 1961.[12]

European immigration since the Second World War falls into four phases.[13]

The period of war adjustment and decolonization covers the period between 1945 until the early 1960s. The number of people displaced by the war was estimated at about 20 million. For instance, 12 million Germans had to leave Eastern Europe by 1950 with about 8 million going to West Germany. Great Britain, France, Belgium and The Netherlands were affected by return migration of European colonists and the inflow from workers from former overseas territories. The second period – 1955 to 1973 – reflected considerable labour migration. Labour shortages in some countries induced openness and sometimes active recruitment policies. Germany and some other Western European countries established guest worker systems. Net immigration to the north from the Mediterranean countries was about 5 million. The third period – from 1974 to 1988 – was one of restrained immigration throughout Western Europe reflecting recessionary conditions after the first oil price shock. Labour recruitment ceased, although it proved difficult to induce return migration by foreign workers. Family and political migration dominated migration patterns during this period. The last period from 1988 to the present day reflect the dissolution of Communist and Socialist regimes in Eastern and Central Europe which has dramatically increased the flow of east–west immigrants, predominantly to Germany. The migration potential from Eastern Europe is estimated in the range of 5–50 million, mostly over a period of 10–15 years. One estimate suggests a potential immigration flow of 3% of the current population size in Eastern Europe for the next 15 years, which implies a migration inflow of about 3 million ethnic Germans and 10 million others.[14] Additional immigration pressures are likely to be caused by south–north migration, particularly from Turkey, Egypt, and other countries in Northern Africa.[15]

THE VALUES

Liberty

At the heart of debates in all Western democracies over immigration policy now, and in the past, lie two core values which stand in some irreducible degree in opposition to one another: liberty and community. Theories of liberty and community each present themselves with almost endless variations, but for our purposes, the essence of the two values, in the context of immigration policy, can be fairly readily captured. As Carens points out:

> [All liberal] theories begin with some kind of assumption about the equal moral worth of individuals. In one way or another, all treat the individual as prior to the community. Such foundations provide little basis for drawing fundamental distinctions between citizens and aliens who seek to become citizens.[16]

Carens goes on to review three contemporary approaches to liberal theory: libertarianism, social contractarianism, and utilitarianism. From the libertarian perspective, exemplified by scholars such as Nozick, individual property rights play a central role.[17] In a state of nature, individuals have rights to acquire and use property and to alienate it voluntarily. The existence of the state is only justified to the extent that it is required to protect property rights and facilitate their voluntary transfer. On this view, if aliens wish to move to Canada or the USA they should be free to do so, provided they do not violate anyone else's rights. To the extent that citizens choose to enter into contracts of employment with them, or sell them land, homes, or businesses, the rights of both citizens and aliens would be violated by externally imposed constraints thereon. From a social contractarian perspective, as exemplified most prominently by the writings of John Rawls,[18] an ideal social constitution would be constructed behind a veil of ignorance, where individuals know nothing about their own particularities such as class, race, sex, natural talents, religious beliefs, individuals goals, values and talents, etc. The purpose of the veil of ignorance is 'to nullify the effect of specific contingencies which put men at odds', because natural and social contingencies are 'arbitrary from a moral point of view', and therefore are factors which ought not to influence the choice of principles of justice.

As Carens points out, whether one is a citizen of a rich nation or a poor nation, whether one is already a citizen of a particular state or an alien who wishes to become a citizen, are the kinds of specific contingencies that could set people at odds, and a fair procedure for choosing principles of justice should therefore exclude knowledge of these circumstances, just as it excludes knowledge of one's race, sex or social class. We should therefore take a global, not a national, view of the original position (the 'universal brotherhood of man').[19] Behind this global veil of ignorance, and considering possible restrictions on freedom, we should adopt the perspective of those who would be most disadvantaged by the restrictions, in this case often the perspective of the alien who wants to immigrate. From this perspective, very few restrictions on immigration can be morally justified. Rawls would recognize that liberty may be restricted for the sake of liberty, in the sense that all liberties depend on the existence of public order and security. To cite a metaphor used by Carens, it does no one any good to take so many people into a lifeboat that it is swamped and everyone drowns.[20] But short of a reasonable, as opposed to a hypothetical expectation of this prospect, largely unconstrained immigration would seem implied by Rawls' social contract theory.

From a utilitarian perspective, the utilities or disutilities experienced by both aliens and citizens would be entered in the utilitarian calculus.[21] Some citizens would gain from being able to enter into contractual relationships with immigrants; others might lose if wages are depressed through the additional competition they bring to labour markets; taxpayers may lose if they are required to support financially dependent immigrants; yet other citizens as consumers might benefit from access to cheaper goods or services. Against these costs and benefits accruing to citizens must be set whatever costs and benefits accrue to aliens by being permitted entry – in most cases one assumes that the benefits substantially outweigh the costs otherwise they would presumably not have chosen to resettle in another land. Moreover, to the extent that many aliens will have made the wrenching decision to resettle because of economic privation or religious or political oppression or persecution in their homelands, the gains to them from being permitted to join a new and more congenial community may be very substantial. Thus, from a utilitarian perspective, while perhaps providing more scope for restrictions on immigration than either the libertarian or social contractarian perspective, relatively open borders would in general be dictated.

Community

In opposition to these liberal values stand the core values of community. Here, it is asserted, in the context of immigration policy, that control over who may enter is a powerful expression of a nation's identity and autonomy – in other words its sovereignty. Sovereignty entails the unlimited power of a nation, like that of a free individual, to decide whether, under what conditions, and with what effect it will consent to enter into a relationship with a stranger.[22] One of the most prominent contemporary proponents of this view is Michael Walzer.[23] In justifying this view, he draws analogies between neighbourhoods, clubs, and families. While it is true that in the case of neighbourhoods, people are free, in general, to enter and exit as they please, he argues that to analogize nations to neighbourhoods, permitting unconstrained entry by aliens in any number from anywhere in the world would destroy the concept of neighbourhood. He argues that it is only the nationalization of welfare (or the nationalization of culture and politics) that opens the neighbourhood communities to whoever chooses to come in. Neighbourhoods can be open only if countries are at least potentially closed. Only if the state makes a selection among would-be members and guarantees the loyalty, security, and welfare of the individuals it selects, can local communities take shape as 'different' associations determined solely by personal preference and market capacity. Walzer claims that if states ever become large neighbourhoods, it is likely that neighbourhoods would become little states. Their members would organize to defend the local politics and culture against strangers. Historically, it is claimed, neighbourhoods have turned into closed or parochial communities whenever the state was open. Thus, Walzer rejects the analogy of states to neighbourhoods and rather analogizes states with clubs and families, where members are free to determine the conditions of membership. Walzer concludes:

> The distribution of membership is not pervasively subject to the constraints of justice. Across a considerable range of the decisions that are made, states are simply free to take in strangers (or not) – much as they are free, leaving aside the claims of the needy, to share their wealth with foreign friends, to honor the achievements of foreign artists, scholars, and scientists, to choose their trading partners, and to enter into collective security arrangements with foreign states. But the right to choose an admissions policy is more basic than any of these, for it is not merely a matter of acting in the world, exercising sovereignty, and pursuing national interests. At stake here is the shape of the community that acts in the world, exercises sovereignty, and so on. Admission and exclusion are at the core of communal independence. They suggest the deepest meaning of

> self-determination. Without them, there could not be *communities of character*, historically stable, ongoing associations of men and women with some special commitment to one another and some special sense of their common life.[24]

Unlike the liberal theories, which imply no or very few limitations on entry, Walzer's theory, at least without further qualification, appears to permit almost any limitations on entry that a state should choose to impose, including admission policies that are overtly racist. Two controversial features of his theory are the notion that political sovereignty is a near-absolute value – a view increasingly challenged by the evolution of international human rights norms – and that the only communities of character are those that reflect ethnic, religious or cultural commonalities – a view many liberals would challenge on the grounds that common commitments to liberal civic institutions and mutual tolerance of intermediate sub-communities of interest can sustain communities of character. In any event, these two core values of liberty and community clearly frame the major issues that must be confronted in the design of any country's immigration policies.

The issue of the size of the intake of immigrants cannot readily be separated from the composition of the intake, in terms of deducing what kinds of demands the immigrants are likely to make on our community. However, to the extent that the two issues can be separated, regardless of the composition of the intake, it can probably be accepted that no country could accept and absorb millions of immigrants a year without critical features of infrastructure collapsing and congestion externalities being created on all sides. One might, of course, argue that a natural equilibrium is likely to establish itself before this happens – if the intake threatens these conditions, some would-be immigrants will abandon an interest in resettling. However, collective action problems may prevent such an equilibrium emerging at all or at any event quickly or smoothly, and it is not obvious that Rawls' 'public order' qualification on the right of entry tells us anything very helpful about when congestion externalities have reached the point where the lifeboat metaphor can appropriately be invoked. This concern is somewhat reminiscent of the concerns raised by Thomas Malthus in 1798 in his famous essay on the *Principle of Population as it Affects the Future Improvement of Society*. As Heilbroner states the Malthusian thesis:

> [The essay on population claimed] that there was a tendency in nature for population to outstrip all possible means of subsistence. Far from ascending to an ever higher level, society was caught in a hopeless trap in which the human reproductive urge would inevitably shove humanity to the sheer brink of the precipice of existence. Instead of being headed for Utopia, the human lot was forever condemned to a losing struggle between ravenous and multiplying mouths and the eternally insufficient stock of Nature's cupboard, however diligently that cupboard might be searched.[25]

In Malthus' view, land, unlike people, cannot be multiplied – land does not breed. Malthus' fears were subsequently proven to be greatly exaggerated, and most dramatically refuted by the settlement of the New World, where increased population through immigration, in terms of increased labour and capital on the supply-side and increased aggregate demand on the demand-side, made possible the realization of enormous economies of scale and the technological advances that accompanied them. However, as birth rates and destitution levels in many impoverished Third World countries exemplify today, Malthus' concerns were not entirely without foundation, and a totally unrestricted immigration policy may legitimately implicate those concerns. Once some restriction on total intake is recognized as necessary, then the composition of that restricted intake must be addressed.

In particular selection policies will need to address the following classes of immigrants:

1 Claimants who pose a national security risk or who have past histories of criminality or suspected criminality, associations with illiberal or oppressive political regimes, or a personal history of illness or disability;
2 refugee or asylum claimants;
3 economically necessitous aliens;
4 family members;
5 culturally homogeneous aliens;
6 better-endowed and less well-endowed aliens;
7 guest workers;
8 illegal immigrants.

While the welfare effects of immigration policy have not traditionally received anything like the attention that has been devoted to other aspects of international economics, fortunately recent theoretical and empirical work[26] has begun to yield a fairly clear consensus on the effects of immigration, despite the fact that this consensus is sharply at variance, in many respects, with widely held popular perceptions.

THE WELFARE IMPLICATIONS OF IMMIGRATION

The welfare implications of immigration pose many complex issues. One threshold issue is the perspective to be adopted in evaluating these implications, particularly whether the perspective should focus only on the impact of immigration on domestic welfare in a receiving country; or whether a more global perspective should be adopted including the impact of immigration on the welfare of immigrants themselves; and the impact of immigration on the welfare of residents of sending countries who remain behind. Another threshold question is whether a narrowly economic conception of welfare should be adopted or whether the welfare calculus should include non-economic factors such as humanitarian, social, cultural, and distributional concerns.

From the perspective of immigrants themselves, it seems obvious that in most cases immigration is likely to enhance their welfare, either economically or psychically (in cases where they are escaping political, religious, or ethnic persecution in their home countries), otherwise they are unlikely to incur the economic and emotional costs of uprooting themselves and moving to a foreign country. From a global economic perspective, it seems equally clear, applying standard international trade theory paradigms, that global welfare is enhanced by relatively unrestricted migration. For example, Hamilton and Whalley provide estimates from 1977 that the gains from removing all restrictions on international immigration could exceed world-wide GNP in that year. More qualified estimates would still yield gains constituting a significant proportion of world GNP and exceeding gains from removing all trade restrictions.[27] The premise behind these estimates is that open immigration encourages human resources to move to their most productive uses, whatever the localized impact in countries of emigration or immigration. The most important qualification to this proposition is fiscally induced migration driven by a desire to access non-contributory entitlement systems such as social welfare and public health care systems in other countries. Obviously, migration undertaken for these reasons may not entail a redeployment or relocation of human resources to more productive uses.[28]

The effects of emigration on the welfare of citizens in sending countries is far from clear. Arguably, owners of capital receive a reduced return (and consumers may pay higher prices) if wage rates among workers who remain increase (although these workers are to that extent better off). Negative externalities from population density may be reduced, but some advantages from population density and size (e.g. ease of communication and transportation) may also be reduced. While the brain drain from source countries has often elicited concern, this requires the assumption that highly skilled professionals, business people, or workers are not capturing in their returns the full value of their marginal product, but are creating positive externalities that will be lost when they leave (e.g. imparting skills or knowledge to younger individuals). To the extent that their education has been financed by their home governments, their departure may entail a loss of this investment, but on the other hand taxes paid by parents, may, on average, reflect these costs. To the extent that emigrants are younger and more productive than the home population on average, the sending country loses their taxes with which to finance social programmes for older citizens and children.[29] Largely mitigating or even offsetting many of these costs to sending countries are substantial remittances sent home by immigrants – estimated at about US 66 billion dollars world-wide in 1989.[30]

Most of the theoretical and empirical research undertaken to date on the welfare implications of immigration has focused on the impact of immigration on the welfare of the native population in receiving countries. This research has focused principally on economic impacts. An assessment that included non-economic impacts of immigration would need to take account of, on the one hand, humanitarian considerations that may favour generous family reunification and refugee policies, and on the other hand, concerns over erosion of cultural and social homogeneity and cohesiveness.[31] The principal findings of research that has focused on the economic impacts of immigration on the welfare of native populations in receiving countries is briefly reviewed below.

Economic research in the early 1980s reached highly optimistic findings regarding the impact of immigration on native economic welfare. For example, Chiswick in an analysis of the 1970 census found that at the time of arrival, immigrants earn about 17% less than the natives. However, immigrant earnings overtake native earnings within 15 years after arrival. After 30 years in the US the typical immigrant earned about 11% more than the comparable native workers.[32] Simon's influential book, *The Economic Consequences of Immigration*[33] substantially extended these findings, and not only concluded that immigrants out-perform comparable native workers in the long run but that immigrants have little or no effect on wage and employment levels of the native population, including unskilled native workers, and that they contribute substantially more in taxes than the costs they impose on social programmes (and indeed that their net fiscal contribution on average was greater than the native population). The 'catch-up' and overtaking effect was largely attributed to initial challenges in overcoming language and skill deficits and the greater drive and ambition of immigrants who had decided to incur the wrenching costs of leaving their home countries and re-settling in a foreign country (a self-selection effect).

While Borjas in a 1990 book reached many similar findings, he also found that recent immigrants were under-performing previous generations of immigrants and in some cases the native population.[34] In subsequent writings, he has elaborated on this theme.[35] For example, in 1970, the typical immigrant who had just arrived in the US had 11.1 years of schooling, as compared to 11.5 years for the typical native worker. By 1990, the typical immigrant who had just arrived in the US had 11.9 years of schooling, as compared to 13.2 years for natives. The most recent arrivals enumerated in the 1970 census earned 16.6% less than natives. By 1990, the wage disadvantage between the most recent immigrant wave and natives had grown to 31.7 percent. In 1970 immigrants were less likely than natives to receive public assistance. By 1990, the welfare participation rate of immigration households had risen to 9.1 percent, or 1.7 percentage points higher than the participation rate for native households.[36] According to Borjas, the changing national origin mix of immigrants explains over 90% of the decline in educational attainment and relative wages across successive waves of immigrants between 1960 and 1980.[37]

In evaluating the impact of immigrants on native participants in US labour markets, Borjas estimates the impact of immigrant workers on native worker wage levels and compares this loss to gains by employers and indirectly consumers from lower input costs. He estimates that currently native workers lose about 1.9% of GDP, or $133 billion in a $7 trillion economy, while native employers and consumers gain about 2% of GDP, or $140 billion, yielding an immigration surplus of $7 billion. This implies a sizable redistribution of wealth from native workers to the users of immigrant labour, and implies in turn that debates in receiving countries over immigration policy are likely to focus more on these distributional impacts than on the relatively small efficiency gains entailed.[38] Borjas, analogizing to theories of the effects of international trade liberalization, argues that 'no pain, no gain', so that studies that find no or minimal impacts of immigrants on labour markets in receiving countries imply that immigrants capture all the returns from immigration and the native population in receiving countries none. This in fact would not be true if immigrants are pure complements to the native labour force. Borjas argues that greater selectivity in immigration that focuses on screening out unskilled immigrants and admitting mostly skilled immigrants would raise the immigration surplus substantially, reflecting the fact that factor prices for skilled labour appear to be more elastic than for unskilled labour and that complementarities between skilled labour and capital in production are greater than complementarities between skilled and unskilled labour or between unskilled labour and capital, particularly in an advanced economy like that of the US. With respect to the fiscal impacts of immigration in the US (sometimes discussed in terms of the dependency ratio), estimates vary dramatically, with some estimates reporting net annual fiscal benefits from immigration of $27 billion and other estimates reporting fiscal losses of over $40 billion. These estimates are highly speculative, because beyond estimating the impact of immigrants on social welfare programmes, it is difficult to estimate the marginal impact on the vast array of other public services that they utilize.[39] Again, skilled immigrants are less likely to be unemployed than unskilled immigrants and hence are less likely to become dependent on social welfare programmes.

Despite these recent research findings on the deteriorating performance of recent waves of immigrants to the US, the consensus position among researchers remains that the impact of immigration on the labour market outcomes of natives is small, both in terms of employment and wage levels.[40] Evidence from other receiving countries supports this view. Canadian researchers have concluded that immigrants have a minimal impact on employment or wage levels of native workers[41] and that immigrant households, including recent immigrants, pay more in taxes than they receive in benefits and that their contribution exceeds the average Canadian-born household lifetime contribution[42], although the net fiscal contributions of recent immigrants, while still positive, have been declining significantly.

As to whether the performance of more recent immigrants to Canada has deteriorated more generally relative to earlier immigrants and relative to the native born population of Canada, an extensive analysis by the Economic Council of Canada reaches cautious conclusions.[43] The proportion of persons with only elementary education has slightly increased amongst recent immigrants, but the latter also include a higher proportion of university-educated persons than the native population. Knowledge of the English language has also declined with recent waves of immigrants. The Council found no evidence that immigrants from the new source countries have consistently lower labour force participation rates than those from traditional source countries, although there has been a decline in the general participation rate for immigrants arriving in the 1980s. While unemployment rates are generally lower for immigrants than natives (8.2% compared to 10.8%), for immigrants arriving between 1978 and 1983 the rate has been slightly higher: 11.2% compared to 10.8% for natives, and for immigrants arriving in the period 1983 to 1986, the unemployment rate was 16%. However, the Council was unable to find any significant changes in the characteristics of the most recent immigrants relative to those who had arrived between 1978 and 1982, and was therefore not prepared to attribute changes in labour force participation rates to changing immigrant characteristics. With respect to participation in welfare programmes, 12.5% of immigrants who came during the period 1981 to 1986 received welfare compared to 1.7% of immigrants who came between 1976 and 1980 and 13.8% of the native born population. Contrary to Borjas' findings in the US, refugees do not seem to perform markedly less well than other immigrants or the native born population.

A recent study by Statistics Canada[44] analysing data from the 1991 Census largely confirms the Economic Council's findings. In 1991, the overall dependency ratio for immigrants was 29.8 while that for the Canadian-born was 52.9; thus immigrants have a higher proportion of people of working age than do the Canadian-born. Immigrants were also more likely to have higher levels of education than the Canadian-born – about 16% of immigrants aged 15 and over had university degrees compared to 11% of the Canadian-born, although a higher proportion of immigrants (19%) than the Canadian-born (13%) had less than Grade 9 education. Of immigrants who came between 1981 and 1991, 17% had a university degree, compared with 9% of immigrants who arrived before 1961. For those aged 25 and over, the difference is even more pronounced: 21% of recent immigrants had a university education, compared with 9% of immigrants who came before 1961. In 1991, the overall labour force participation rate of immigrants was 65.2%, slightly higher than in 1984 (64.7%) and only slightly lower than the Canadian-born (68.7%). However, 71% of immigrants who came to Canada between 1981 and 1991 reported a mother tongue other than English or French, compared with 59% of those who came before 1961.

With respect to the European experience, research on the impact of immigration on native participants in labour markets in receiving countries seems broadly consistent with the US and Canadian evidence, finding minimal impact on wage and employment levels, despite higher unemployment levels in Europe and less flexible labour markets (often reflecting the role of centralized unions and more generous social safety nets).[45]

It should be noted with respect to most of the foregoing studies on the impacts of immigration on native workers in labour markets in receiving countries that they assume constant returns to scale. It might be argued that countries with a larger and more rapidly growing population will be able to sustain some industries and some social infrastructure which would not be viable at smaller population sizes. Apart from scale effects *per se*, dynamic effects, such as broader diffusion of technological and other ideas, and greater possibilities for learning by doing, may generate significant positive effects on average native incomes from a larger population.[46] These arguments are not especially convincing, particularly in a country the size of the US, or even in the case of smaller countries, given a liberal international economic environment where scale effects, especially in capital rather than labour intensive industries, can often be captured by trading into foreign markets and do not require a large local employment or consumer base.[47]

IMPLICATIONS FOR IMMIGRATION POLICY

Commentators concerned with the deteriorating performance of recent immigrants to receiving countries and the diminishing domestic returns to immigration associated therewith typically argue that immigration policy should focus more on screening for skilled immigrants.[48] This proposed policy reorientation raises a number of difficult issues. With respect to refugee claimants, most receiving countries are signatories to the UN Convention on Refugees, which entails commitments to admit refugees who satisfy the UN Convention definition. While there appears to be high variability from one country to the other in how this commitment is interpreted and applied, it nevertheless implies a limited latitude to alter radically refugee intake policies, at least with respect to inland refugee claimants, although a good deal more latitude with respect to admission or sponsorship of off-shore refugees. With respect to the family sponsorship category, proposals to limit entry in this category entail either narrowing the class of eligible relatives to immediate family members; treating this category as the residual category within overall immigration quotas after independent immigrants have been screened for skills; or requiring family sponsors to assume financial responsibility for sponsored relatives by for example purchasing surety bonds against the risk of sponsored relatives becoming dependent on social welfare programmes.[49] None of these measures is likely to prove uncontentious in receiving countries. With respect to independent immigrants who are screened for skills, two problems arise. The first is that receiving countries do not unilaterally determine the skill set of immigrants seeking entry. This is in significant part determined by conditions in sending countries. Both 'push' and 'pull' factors are relevant. Sending countries that are generally impoverished are likely to send mostly unskilled immigrants. Sending countries with high degrees of inequality of wealth are again likely to send mostly unskilled immigrants, with skilled residents for the most part facing few inducements to emigrate. Only skilled workers from countries that 'tax' directly or indirectly the earnings and opportunities of high performing skilled workers, where receiving countries permit higher dispersions in returns to human capital, are likely to find it attractive to emigrate. This may be a relatively small applicant pool. If receiving countries were to confine themselves exclusively or almost exclusively to this pool, this may entail substantial curtailment of total current levels of immigration.

A second problem relates to how skilled workers are selected by receiving countries. Even assuming a substantial skilled applicant pool, presumably not all skills are in equal demand in receiving countries. The challenge then becomes of screening amongst various classes of skilled prospective immigrants. The Canadian experience with the point system that was implemented in 1967 suggests that attempts at fine-tuning screening criteria by occupation or class of skill imply an accuracy in manpower forecasting that is mostly unwarranted, and they have been of limited efficacy.[50] Screening on some very basic variables such as age, health, language skills, and level of education may be as far as screening criteria can usefully go.

In response to the limitations and deficiencies of bureaucratically administered entry policies, many economists see virtues in an auction system for quotas, assuming entry is to be limited.[51] It is argued that the immigrants who purchase these quotas will be those who value the opportunity to emigrate most highly, principally because they are confident that the employment or business opportunities available to them in the country of immigration will warrant the investment in the quota, reflecting the higher value that residents place on their potential contributions. One can also view an auction system as a means of extracting monopsony rents from immigrants analogous to the optimal tariff in trade theory.[52] However, there seem compelling reasons in principle why an auctioned quota system cannot be assigned a central role in allocating entry positions to immigrants. Assuming that there are good humanitarian and compassionate reasons for preserving a significant role for family reunification policies, there would seem to be no role here for an auctioned quota system. Equally, it is obviously untenable to screen refugees on this basis. With respect to independent immigrants, an auction system seems both inefficient and unfair: inefficient because given the well-known difficulties of borrowing money against future employment income or human capital (which is the rationale for most student assistance programmes, for example), many efficient relocation decisions may not be made; and unfair simply because it penalizes those with few present resources, whatever the future contributions they may make to the country of immigration. Business or investor-class immigrants may be more amenable to an auctioned quota system. At present, Canada admits a small number of immigrants in this category (about 2 to 3% of the annual immigration flow) by requiring as a condition of entry the investment of several hundred thousand dollars in approved Canadian projects, which resembles an auctioned quota system.[53]

The category of temporary workers warrants brief comment. Here there is a compelling argument that foreign students in receiving countries on student visas, on successful completion of their studies, should be entitled to apply for permanent residence status, fairly much of right.[54] This would clearly seem to be in the domestic interest of the receiving country. Whether it is welfare enhancing from the global perspective entails the somewhat indeterminate debates about the effect of the brain drain on developing countries. But given that this is also entailed in a number of the other long established immigrant categories, it is not clear why this is a particular objection to providing successful students with the opportunity to become permanent residents. To the extent that they receive financial assistance with their studies from their countries of origin, presumably these countries can demand bonds or security from the student or his or her family to ensure reimbursement of this assistance. With respect to other temporary workers, there are serious difficulties in designing and administering programmes providing for legal, unskilled, temporary immigrants. While it is true that temporary workers often contribute positively to the dependency ratio, partly because of their age, and partly because they are often not entitled to non-contributory forms of public assistance, the European experience suggests that it is very difficult to send these people home if they have been temporary workers for a number of years and they and their families have established roots in the community. Simon suggests various financial bonding arrangements to ensure departure on the expiration of temporary work visas,[55] and Sykes sees such a programme as a strong substitute for illegal or undocumented immigration.[56] However, many temporary workers may simply go 'underground' upon the expiration of their visas and become illegal or undocumented aliens. With a transient population such as is often involved with unskilled guest worker programmes, it is not clear how easy it would be to design and enforce the bonding arrangements that Simon proposes. In any event, both efficiency and humanitarian considerations seem to dictate that if a guest worker has worked productively in the country of immigration for any significant period of time, he or she should be entitled to apply for permanent resident status, treating his or her work experience as a substitute for other forms of education, training, or financial assets.

One last aspect of immigration policy requires comment. In making initial eligibility determinations (health, criminality, national security risk), inland refugee determinations, family sponsorship entitlements, and deportation decisions, designing legal processes that, on the one hand, accord immigrants some basic measure of due process, and, on the other hand, avoid miring the administration of immigration policy in costly and protracted legal processes has proved a daunting challenge for many countries, with the appropriate balance between the two sets of considerations often the subject of on-going and unresolved debates.

CONCLUSION

In moderating the strains currently being experienced by immigration policy in many countries, it is crucial to identify key linkages between immigration policies and other classes of international and domestic policies and in so doing not to impose on immigration policies and the social and political consensus surrounding them more weight than they can reasonably bear. In this respect, it is clear that the level of demand for resettlement would be substantially diminished if developed countries, through appropriate forms of international cooperation, took stronger and more effective policy stances towards human rights violations and political or religious oppression in many countries of origin. In addition, much more liberal trade policies towards developing country exports, the provision of more generous foreign aid in cases of natural disasters, and more effective developmental aid in forms, or with conditions attached, designed to address (and, if necessary) discipline governmental incompetence and corruption that is often pervasive in many developing and former command economies, are clearly important substitutes for immigration. For foreign aid to be fully effective, developing and former command economies need to be encouraged to adopt domestic policies that promote high levels of economic growth at home. A key element in such policies is outward-looking trade policies that assign substantial weight to export-led growth, and concomitant reduction in reliance on trade and currency restrictions designed to foster often inefficient import-substituting domestic industries. Unfortunately, in this respect, reflecting a massive exercise in hypocrisy on the part of many Western countries, the costs of protectionist policies imposed by developed countries on developing countries exports currently exceed the entire value of foreign aid provided to these countries.[57]

In short, all other things being equal, it seems clear that most refugees or displaced persons would prefer to return to their homelands, but the policies of most developed countries do not reflect this priority. Instead, the consequences of displacement are seen primarily as an immigration problem, where effective policy responses are highly circumscribed or at any event intensely controversial. It needs to be added that while growth-oriented development policies are likely to reduce migration rates over the long term, evidence suggests that in the shorter term, the disruptive impacts of rapid development on traditional social and economic structures in developing countries (e.g. rural–urban migration and saturated urban labour markets) may actually increase international migration.[58] This said, however, the insights from recent empirical work on immigration tell us that, perhaps within some broad parameters that most developed countries presently seem well inside, they could benefit modestly and potential immigrants very substantially from a much higher level of immigration than most developed countries are presently committed to. Just as with trade policy, the facts (as opposed to the prejudices) suggest that national and cosmopolitan perspectives on immigration policy do not diverge as sharply as is often supposed.

19 Conclusion

The future of the global trading system

INTRODUCTION

In this concluding chapter, we discuss several of the most pressing challenges facing the world trading system. In our judgment, these challenges create a formidable, but not unmanageable, post-Uruguay Round agenda for students and practitioners of the law and policy of international trade. The three major challenges are: (1) managing the interface between trade liberalization and the domestic regulatory state; (2) strengthening the legal and institutional foundations of open markets in developing countries; and (3) addressing the dangers that regionalism poses to the coherence and sustainability of the global trading order.

TRADE LIBERALIZATION AND THE REGULATORY STATE: MANAGING THE INTERFACE[1]

There has been a dramatic expansion over the past three decades or so of domestic regulations pertaining to health, safety, consumer protection, the environment and labour markets. As trade liberalization, at least with respect to border measures, has continued to advance, these 'within the border' regulatory measures are increasingly seen by many liberal trade proponents as the most prominent and arguably the most costly form of non-tariff barriers to trade (NTBs), requiring new disciplines under international trade rules, particularly in a globalizing economy which, it is argued, has a low tolerance for 'system frictions'.[2] As Miles Kahler puts it: 'The decades-long process of lowering trade barriers resembles the draining of a lake that reveals mountain peaks formerly concealed or (more pessimistically) the peeling of an onion that reveals innumerable layers of barriers.'[3]

The relatively recent focus on these forms of domestic regulation as potential NTBs has substantially heightened both domestic and international political conflicts as trade policy linkages have increasingly been drawn with broad sweeps of domestic policy domains previously largely thought to lie outside the arena of trade policy. As Vogel notes,

> Free trade advocates want to limit the use of regulations as barriers to trade, while environmentalists and consumer advocates want to prevent trade agreements from serving as barriers to regulation. While the trade community worries about an upsurge of 'eco-protectionism' – the justification of trade barriers on environmental grounds – consumer and environmental organizations fear that trade liberalization will weaken both their own country's regulatory standards and those of their nation's trading partners.'[4]

Vogel well describes the implications for international trade of these two positions, at least if taken to extremes:

> If all regulations that disadvantaged importers were classified as non-tariff barriers, then virtually all regulations could be considered protectionist. For example, the United States could not require that all product labels be printed in English, since this requirement clearly imposes additional costs upon foreign producers (or at least those from non-English speaking countries). Likewise, Singapore would be forced to rescind its ban on the sale of chewing gum, since this regulation clearly serves as a barrier to the import of Wrigley's products. In short, defining NTBs very broadly would have the effect of subjecting virtually all national regulatory standards to those of the least stringent exporting country. At the same time, it would probably significantly expand international trade.
>
> The consequences of defining non-tariff barriers very narrowly are equally significant. A nation could demand that all imported products be produced according to the same standards to which domestic producers are required to adhere. Thus the United States could refuse to permit the imports of any cars, steel, or chemicals produced in facilities that violated American standards for factory emissions, land-use controls, or, for that matter, family-leave policies. If such a regulation was *not* considered a non-tariff barrier, and was widely adopted, international trade would decline significantly.[5]

These conflicts over NTBs have drawn new domestic political constituencies into debates over trade policies in the form of consumer and environmental groups or other non-governmental organizations (NGOs) who seek to resist the imposition of constraints on domestic political sovereignty by international trade agreements.

In responding to these diverse pressures, Alan Sykes (amongst others) notes that a wide array of remedial options is available.[6] At one end of the continuum lies complete deference to national sovereigns. At the other end of the continuum lies total harmonization. In between the extremes lie many alternatives that impose greater or fewer constraints on national sovereigns while still affording some opportunity for variations across nations. Many of these alternatives involve 'policed decentralization', whereby national authorities are largely free to pursue their own policy objectives but must do so subject to a set of broadly applicable legal constraints. The options here include non-discrimination principles, the sham principle, transparency requirements, generality requirements, presumptive deference to negotiated international standards with specified procedures for deviation, mutual recognition, and benefit/burden balancing tests.

As is reflected in the chapters in this book on matters such as trade related intellectual property rights, services, environment and labour rights we often are sceptical of the case for domestic policy harmonization or convergence and thus for a position closer to the first end of Sykes' spectrum. This general orientation is influenced by at least four basic premises. First, as Sykes also notes, the analysis of regulatory barriers to trade is complicated by both theoretical and empirical uncertainty in many cases about their effects on social welfare (given the wide array of values and concerns that domestic policies are designed to serve) and in this respect stand in sharp contrast to traditional impediments to trade, such as tariffs and quotas, which can be shown both theoretically and empirically to be welfare-reducing in almost all cases from both a global and domestic perspective.[7] Thus, it is emphatically not the case that international harmonization of domestic policies will always increase domestic and global welfare – indeed often, depending upon how harmonization is induced, it will have the opposite effect.[8]

Second, we believe that proponents of more sweeping or extreme forms of international harmonization in domestic policies in the interests of creating more open and competitive international markets in goods and services severely discount the importance of what our colleague at the University of Toronto, Albert Breton, calls in an important book 'competitive governments'.[9] In contrast to a view of government as a monolith or monopoly, whose policies are typically viewed by Public Choice theorists as the product of rent-seeking behaviour by special interest groups that have captured Leviathan, Breton argues that governments in most democracies are intensely competitive in a wide variety of dimensions: opposing parties compete for political office (competition for the market in Demsetz' terms),[10] agencies within government compete with each other over policy priorities and claims on resources; lower houses compete with upper houses and both compete with constitutional courts; central governments compete with subnational levels of government and with non-profit organizations; subnational levels of government compete amongst each other; and national governments compete with other national governments. In Breton's thesis, these competitive features of government serve a crucial demand revelation function, and yield a more benign view of public or collective provision of goods, services or public policies than that taken by Public Choice theorists by establishing linkages between revenue and expenditure decisions of the kind that economists like Wicksell and Lindahl earlier in this century viewed as a precondition to efficient public policies.[11] A final premise that motivates our relatively conservative orientation to the trade policy-based case for international harmonization is that whatever view one takes of the European experience, the crucial shift that occurred in Europe with the enactment of the *Single European Act* of 1986 from an emphasis on negative integration (rules proscribing what domestic policy measures countries may *not* adopt) to positive integration (supranational regulations and directives prescribing what domestic policies Member States *must* adopt) is simply not feasible in most other institutional contexts. As we have argued earlier in this book,[12] deep economic integration amongst nation states is typically predicated either on the existence of a hegemonic power with the ability to impress its will on other smaller and weaker states (the US in the immediate post-war years), or willingness amongst Member States to cede substantial aspects of their domestic political sovereignty to supranational political institutions – a willingness that for the most part is likely to be conditional on a reasonably egalitarian distribution of political influence and a common interest in overarching political objectives (in the case of Europe, the mitigation of conflicts that had devastated the continent militarily and economically over the first half of this century). Neither of these conditions is likely to apply in the foreseeable future outside of the European context either with respect to other regional trading blocs or with respect to the multilateral system at large. For example, under NAFTA, it is inconceivable that Canada and Mexico would be prepared to cede to the US a major hegemonic role in imposing its own domestic macro-economic and micro-economic policies on them. Conversely, it is equally inconceivable that the US would accept the creation of supranational political institutions with substantial legislative authority over major aspects of macro- and micro-economic policies in the three countries, on the basis of a relatively egalitarian sharing of political influence in these institutions. These impediments to deep economic integration are likely to be compounded several times over at the multilateral level. Thus, it is not surprising, as we have suggested elsewhere,[13] that despite a dazzling range of harmonization-related norms and initiatives contained in the FTA and especially in the NAFTA, in areas as diverse as competition policy, environment and trucking regulation very little harmonizing activity has in fact resulted.

This suggests to us that in these other institutional contexts the focus of attention on domestic policies that may constitute non-tariff barriers to trade should relate principally to two objectives: first, elaborating on the principles of negative integration that have historically characterized the approach of the GATT to these issues, i.e. the application of the National Treatment principle in Article III of the GATT to domestic policy measures of Member States (requiring that products of foreign countries receive no less favourable treatment than that accorded to like products of national origin), and elaborating the criteria presently contained in Article XX of the GATT that justify exceptions to this basic obligation of non-discrimination and the constraints thereon, in particular constraints on disguised or unjustified forms of discrimination (the sham principle and the least trade-restrictive means or proportionality principle); and second, to structure the ground rules pursuant to which mutually beneficial agreements between Member States can be reached over policy harmonization or convergence that are both non-coercive and non-discriminatory *vis-à-vis* other trading partners (i.e. respect the Most Favoured Nation principle). In short, we would be in much less haste than other commentators[14] to abandon well-established principles of non-discrimination in international trade law as the primary analytical concept for addressing the consequences for international trade of domestic regulatory diversity.

Having said this, we do not want to be understood as being opposed to consensual forms of harmonization where mutual benefits are to be derived from policy convergence by reducing these costs of divergence.[15] However, it is worthwhile emphasizing the ways in which these specialized harmonization processes preserve, unlike trade law prescriptions for uniformity, significant elements of desirable regulatory competition. First of all, where such processes are driven not by trade diplomacy but by experts and affected interests, they can engender a lively competition among different national regulators as to which country or countries' regulatory approach will become the model for international standards or regulatory norms. While government or industry representatives may well argue for the adoption of a given approach for strategic reasons such as that their own national producers gain an advantage from their products or services already conforming to that standard, the net effect is to increase scrutiny and debate as well as information about national regulatory approaches. Second, the fact that regulatory norms or standards have had to be accepted in a multilateral process, implicating coalitions of interests from a wide range of countries, may act as a counterweight to the tendency of many purely domestic regulations to reflect the interests of narrow concentrated constituencies, or rent seeking and rent provision by government. Third, competition may exist between international voluntary standards bodies and intergovernmental organizations for predominance in international standard and norm-setting. For example, ISO, a non-governmental organization, may end up competing with the ILO in terms of the setting of certain international norms in areas of worker protection, such as occupational health and safety. Fourth, effective regulatory competition implies the possibility of informed evaluation of different approaches to regulation; inasmuch as multilateral processes increase such knowledge, by requiring transparency with respect to regulation, or through the establishment of general principles concerning regulatory inputs,[16] such as that regulation must be based upon the analysis of certain kinds of factors,[17] they may lead to more real regulatory competition at both the domestic and international level. Moreover, a consensual approach to regulatory harmonization can have significant room for regulatory competition, by focusing primarily on regulatory ends, leaving scope for diversity in regulatory means. As John Braithwaite argues, in evoking a concept of regulatory cooperation consistent with efficient regulatory competition, 'Consumers need to be provided with the resources to watch out for their collective interests and call regulators to account when they are captured by producer interests.'[18] Fifth, voluntary international approaches may facilitate a genuinely competitive consumer market in standards – consumers can decide whether to buy products, manufactured goods or services with the ISO label, or in the case of environmental protection, whether they are willing to pay more or go out of their way to find tuna labelled as dolphin-friendly. The ILO is now considering the potential for labelling in the labour rights context.[19] And in this last case, the ILO will find itself competing with various NGOs who have sought to negotiate codes of conduct on labour practices directly with multinational corporations, resulting in labelling based upon a purely non-governmental process. Finally, an aspect of many of these processes or institutions is technical assistance or support for the improvement of regulatory capacity, particularly in developing countries, including the training of regulatory decision-makers and the dissemination of appropriate scientific knowledge and techniques as well as best regulatory practices.

This, if anything, generates more not less regulatory competition, because it promises to put more countries in the game, so to speak. This is not an unimportant point – a significant amount of regulatory diversity, including the kind of diversity that leads to trade complaints, may in fact be generated by inadequate or corrupt legal and regulatory infrastructures in poorer countries. Dealing with these kinds of shortcomings directly has the advantage, unlike the use of the trade 'club', of potentially increasing, and at a minimum, not reducing regulatory competition.

Much regulatory harmonization is likely to occur as a result of private initiatives either at the firm or industry level. Firms have private incentives in many contexts to minimize product incompatibilities if they wish to maximize access to export markets. Private or public – private standardizing organizations, national and international, can often promote standards that avoid pointless incompatibilities. However, in some cases, incompatibilities are an unavoidable, indeed desirable, by-product of product innovation and differentiation. In other cases, both firms and national governments may face incentives to promote strategic standard-setting, e.g. technical interfaces in network industries, in order to realize first-mover advantages and possibly monopoly profits, in which cases international standardizing bodies are likely to encounter difficulties in achieving a voluntary consensus on appropriate standards.[20]

However, even inter-governmental harmonization efforts, outside the context of the EU, must necessarily be consensual in nature. Evidence from the early history of the EU and elsewhere suggests that such state-to-state negotiations will often be slow and limited, at least where they occur between countries with roughly symmetric bargaining power. Negotiations pursuant to the new General Agreement on Trade in Services (GATS) will provide a further important test of the scope and limits of multilateral negotiations over NTBs and the extent to which the Most-Favoured Nation Principle will be respected in these negotiations.[21] More generally, the relationship between harmonization initiatives undertaken within regional trading blocs and the multilateral system creates additional tensions in that arrangements concluded within the former are almost necessarily discriminatory *vis-à-vis* non-Member States. Nevertheless, it is important to recall that it was the concept of reciprocity – carrots, not sticks – that facilitated tariff reductions (the GATT's greatest achievement) by changing the domestic political dynamics surrounding trade protectionism and more closely aligning them with the economics of trade liberalization by enlisting a new political constituency in favour of trade liberalization (exporters).[22] Tariff reductions were not achieved, by and large, by legal fiat or by threats of unilateral trade sanctions but by providing acceptable *quid pro quos* for other countries' tariff concessions. In the NTB context, countries may well be prepared to make similar concessions to reduce the costs to them of policy divergences, increase competition and innovation in their domestic markets and increase access to foreign markets, even if these gains require some compromise of legitimate policy objectives previously served by the policy measures being modified. Within the EU this bargaining has been facilitated through EU supranational institutions and the adoption of qualified majority rules that mitigate the strategic hold-out problem while still respecting reasonable equality of influence of Member States. Outside the EU, in the absence of supranational institutions with paramount legislative authority, a more purely consensual approach is likely to dominate, although to the extent that greater reliance is placed on standards generated by international standard setting bodies like ISO and the Codex Commission the decision-making processes of these institutions, which often do not involve direct government-to-government negotiations, will attract greater scrutiny in terms of the relative influence of various stake-holders, public transparency and democratic legitimacy.

Where negotiations over alleged NTBs occur between countries with asymmetric bargaining power, as arguably exemplified by the Strategic Impediments Initiative between the US and Japan, they carry the serious risk of gross over-reaching into the domestic policy affairs of one country by another (e.g. domestic savings rates, public investment policy, land costs), and moreover are likely to result in managed trade arrangements that are antithetical to a non-discriminatory multilateral trading system. Out of frustration with the prospects of achieving extensive harmonization, some commentators (principally so-called American revisionists) argue for 'black boxing' domestic systems by relying on managed trade (results-oriented or 'crowbar' based trade policy) to achieve more balanced economic relations, even at the risk of some international disintegration.[23] However, this both flatly denies fundamental elements of the theory of comparative advantage and often constitutes a gross interference in the domestic affairs of countries who are parties to such arrangements, whose governments are required to orchestrate domestic economic activities in extraordinary detail in order to meet these targets, while at the same time typically discriminating against other Member States (as exemplified by the Semi-Conductor Agreement between Japan and the US). On the other hand, liberal traders who find themselves unattracted by the concept of managed trade and who feel frustrated at the likely pace of international policy harmonization and who propose instead that a central role be assigned to a relatively unqualified principle of Mutual Recognition[24] (at least where not complemented by negotiated harmonization of minimum standards) fail to acknowledge that such a principle would confer major forms of extraterritorial jurisdiction on countries of origin in exporting goods or services (and their policies with them) to other countries which may well have legitimate reasons for maintaining distinctive policies of their own, provided that they meet basic principles of non-discrimination.[25]

Thus, at the end of the day we believe that trade regimes and institutions should largely confine themselves to a more fully elaborated principle of non-discrimination with well-defined exceptions thereto – that is, a concept of negative rather than positive integration.[26] The principle of effective equality of opportunity (not outcome) lies at the heart of the National Treatment principle, and exceptions to it should require a demonstration that policy measures that have a substantial disparate impact on foreign trade (a) genuinely serve some legitimate (non-trade related) domestic policy objective and are not merely a disguised form of discrimination (the sham principle) and (b) are not an unjustified means of attaining those objectives (the least trade restrictive or proportionality principle). Thus, the policy objective should be genuine and the means of attaining it proportionate. These principles have the additional virtue of enjoying wide familiarity in many domestic constitutional contexts and in EU constitutional law with respect to the protection of human and other constitutional rights from state encroachment.

In designing institutional processes in an international context in which these concepts can be rendered justiciable and operational, more attention needs to be given than hitherto to relative burdens of proof. As a tentative proposition, we would argue that a complainant should bear the burden of proving that a domestic policy measure of another country has a disparate and substantial impact on international trade. If this can be proven, it seems to us that the burden of proof should then shift to the respondent country to demonstrate that notwithstanding this, the policy measure both genuinely engages a legitimate policy objective – the sham principle (and here we would contemplate a much longer list of legitimate policy objectives than is presently embodied in Article XX, reflecting in part, for example, the legitimate policy objectives for domestic subsidies formerly contained in Article 11 of the Tokyo Round Subsidies Code) – and that the discriminatory trade effects of the policy instrument are closely related to vindicating the objectives in question – here, some combination of juridical techniques such as proportionality and least-restrictive means tests may be appropriate. This is much along the lines of the approach of the Appellate Body to Article XX in the *Reformulated Gasoline* case (discussed in Chapter 15 on trade and the environment) in applying the requirements of the chapeau of Article XX that measures justified under the Article not constitute 'arbitrary' or 'unjustified' 'discrimination' and not be a 'disguised restriction on international trade'.

However, as to what constitutes adequate discharge of the burden of proof on these latter issues, there is an important consequential issue of the standard of judicial or panel review to be applied. This has been a bitterly contentious issue in a somewhat analogous context with respect to FTA and NAFTA binational panel reviews of ITA and ITC determinations in the US in antidumping and countervailing duty cases.[27] One view (reflecting a 'correctness' standard) would require that the respondent country bear the burden of adducing substantial evidence on the record that the challenged policy is necessary for the attainment of a legitimate policy objective and that no less trade restrictive means is available to achieve this purpose (arguably a difficult negative to prove). An alternative view (reflecting a 'patently unreasonable' standard) would be substantially more deferential to the country whose domestic policies are under challenge and would simply require that the evidence adduced be sufficient to suggest that the policy choice is not patently unreasonable or a grossly disproportionate adaptation of means to ends, or put otherwise is a plausible means of attempting to achieve the legitimate policy objective in question, even if the reviewing body could itself imagine superior instruments. We favour something close to the latter approach (perhaps a 'clearly unreasonable' standard) because it seems to us more respectful of domestic political sovereignty and policy autonomy than the former view which invites supranational panels to second-guess the domestic policy choices of democratically elected, accountable, and competitive governments by applying a strict *de novo* cost-benefit analysis of their own. Moreover, by substantially limiting the ability of one country to challenge the domestic policy choices of another in quasi-judicial fora, the 'threat point' of the former in political negotiations over possible policy convergence is sharply reduced, thus also reducing the risk of coerced forms of harmonization reflecting asymmetric bargaining power, or worse, coerced forms of discriminatory managed trade arrangements.

In adopting approaches that rely upon negative Commerce Clause type jurisprudence in the United States, or European Court jurisprudence, trade panels must remember a key difference between the WTO and these regimes – the latter provide institutional mechanisms for positive harmonization which can be availed of where negative integration through judicial or quasi-judicial enforcement proves inadequate, or does undue damage to non-trade policy objectives. There are no equivalent political or regulatory institutions available to provide a safety valve within the WTO. This may suggest, on the basis of institutional considerations, a greater degree of deference to domestic policy outcomes. For example, regulatory options less restrictive of trade that may be available to developed countries with sophisticated regulatory systems, may not be currently available to developing countries, who rely heavily on border controls or inspections. In designing a regulatory measure, a country may need to attract the support of a variety of diverse constituencies – what if the less restrictive alternative measure is unable to command such a consensus in a particular political or cultural context? Or consider the case where there is a divergence of technical or scientific opinion, with some experts believing a less-restrictive measure is possible while others question its feasibility in practice. The attitude of trade panels to these problems so far is not encouraging, a prime example being the *Thai Cigarette* ruling,[28] where the panel relied entirely on its own axiomatic reasoning that alternatives less restrictive than banning imported cigarettes would be available to achieve the health objectives of the Thai government, without considering the various constraints, including institutional and fiscal, on implementation of the less restrictive alternatives, such as regulation of advertising and marketing.

Finally, the issue of the use of trade sanctions to promote non-trade goals such as environmental protection and respect for core labour rights have often been misstated in terms of the issue of harmonization of domestic policies, including by GATT and WTO panels in cases such as the recent *Turtles* case. These are instances, where, however, the existence of important externalities (environment) or the salience of widely-recognized international human rights norms, raise quite specific arguments about justified constraints on the domestic policy autonomy of states. At the same time, these arguments – if made with precision – do not amount to a case for eliminating regulatory diversity as such, but rather for observance of some kind of minimum standards that relate to the transnational dimension of the issue.

These considerations also suggest that, to the extent to which harmonization is justified or inevitable, it is crucial to address the consequences for democracy of domestic policy outcomes being significantly determined, or pre-empted, by transnational processes. As Anne-Marie Slaughter argues, the strength of transnational policy networks and institutions

> as a world order ideal will ultimately depend on their accountability to the world's peoples. To many, the prospect of transnational government by judges and bureaucrats looks more like technocracy than democracy. Critics content that government institutions engaged in policy coordination with their foreign counterparts will be barely visible, still less accountable to voters still largely tied to national territory.[29]

World democracy is, of course, a practical impossibility, and the effort to create a transnational representative democracy in Europe, through the European Parliament, has generally not been viewed as successful in dealing with the democratic deficit even within Europe.

We believe a different approach is necessary, which reflects the increasing recognition of the role of global civil society – non-governmental organizations and associations of various kinds and even transnational networks of interested individuals linked by the Internet and email – in mediating between the supranational level and domestic and local polities.[30] As Kingsbury suggests:

> The system of rule-making and dispute settlement by narrowly-based state representatives – who may have more in common with each other than with many of the societal interests they 'represent' is increasingly controversial. . . . The insufficient involvement of interest groups, civic organizations, legislatures, and other elements outside the executive branch – the 'democratic deficit' – has been a difficult problem for most international organizations. . . . Much of the WTO dispute-settlement process remains closed to non-state involvement and secretive n hearings and documentation – . . . In extreme cases, these and other problems of representation and accountability in rule-making and dispute settlement may lead in the long run to the marginalization of international institutions.[31]

This approach would emphasize much greater avenues for participation of such stakeholders in international regulatory processes, as well as international trade dispute settlement where it relates to domestic and global non-trade policy outcomes. This entails an attitudinal change in organizations that have traditionally identified populism with protectionism, and have been steeped in traditions of cloak and dagger diplomacy where anything other than a press release was typically given a restricted security classification. Some of the measures that are required include:

1 extensive derestriction of classified documents, so that stakeholders can follow directly supranational policy processes that affect their interests;
2 to the extent practicable, NGO participation in meetings and conferences of international regulatory organizations and regimes, and the WTO;

3 the right for NGOs to participate in dispute settlement at the WTO through intervention briefs;
4 availability on the Internet of important documents and proposals that relate to transnational regulation and trade policies and laws that affect domestic regulation. Some progress has already been made on certain of these fronts. At the WTO, under pressure from the United States, a decision has been taken to unrestrict substantial numbers of documents, many of which are now instantly accessible on the Internet. Other organizations such as the World Intellectual Property Organization have developed extensive web sites, with detailed accounts of their meetings and conferences. The NAFTA environmental side-agreement institutions are an excellent example of extensive NGO participation in the study and investigation of North American environmental problems. As with the side-agreement on Labour as well, NGOs can actually petition at least for a study or report behaviour they believe violates these agreements. Secrecy surrounding the negotiations was a major element in the widespread opposition by grassroots groups to the Multilateral Agreement on Investment, negotiated at the OECD. Having learnt from this lesson (although perhaps a little too late), the OECD is now placing on its web site the current negotiating draft of the MAI, as well as background papers that explain the underlying reasoning and positions on which many aspects of the draft Agreement are based. This being said, in many respects the WTO remains one of the most closed organizations to meaningful NGO involvement, despite some experiments with greater participation in the Trade and Environment Committee. For instance, the recent *Turtles* panel summarily refused even to examine NGO submissions on the environmental measures at issue, despite no textual basis in WTO dispute settlement rules and procedures for this rejection.

An aspect of the debate about harmonization, which – like the issue of sanctions for non-trade purposes – is not really about the relationship between harmonization and the overall welfare effects of trade, is that of the role of reciprocity and balanced concessions in trading relations. Many 'fair trade' advocates are perfectly prepared to accept domestic regulatory diversity, provided that it does not create undue asymmetries in the extent to which different countries can benefit from liberal trading rules. This is a concern about dividing the pie globally, not the size of the pie.

Reciprocity and the gains from trade

In its broadest sense, the principle of reciprocity has pervaded both multilateral and regional efforts at trade liberalization in the post-war period, even though – as we have discussed at various points in this book – it is at odds with the logic of the economic theory of the gains from trade, which suggests the rationality of unilateral liberalization, i.e. the removal of trade barriers even in the absence of reciprocal concessions by trading partners. Nevertheless, reciprocity is in a certain sense rational, for it may be entirely rational to insist on being paid for doing something that it is in one's own interests to do anyhow.

However, the reciprocity demanded by 'fair traders' amounts to requiring concessions that have in fact *never* been negotiated for. There is nothing wrong with the USA demanding negotiations on, say, Japanese competition policies – what is wrong is to require these concessions on the threat of reneging on existing concessions for which the Japanese have already 'paid'.

Once trade agreements are conceptualized as mutually advantageous exchanges, then it is inevitable that issues of fairness or morality of exchange enter the picture. In fact, contract theorists have long struggled with the difficulties presented by situations where, due to changes in circumstances, one of the parties to a long-term contract or bargain no longer benefits from it. In such cases, should modifications in the terms in the initial bargain be enforceable, even where the modification has been exacted by one party's implicit or explicit threat to renege on the initial bargain if the revised terms are not accepted? Making such modifications enforceable where no additional advantage or payment accrues to the Party made worse off by the change in terms may well imply acceptance of the legitimacy in some circumstances of exacting more advantageous contractual terms through exercising commercial pressure on the other Party or Parties to a bargain.[32] The fact is, however, that the United States, by any meaningful measure, *has* benefited enormously from liberalized trade, even if it no longer enjoys the predominance that it did in global markets at the outset of the GATT era.[33]

Diffuse reciprocity

For this reason, the more sophisticated reciprocity-based 'fair trade' claims focus on how the gains from liberalized trade are shared or divided, rather than on the argument that the liberal multilateral trade order has actually become a Pareto-inferior bargain, at least from the perspective of some countries. This variant in the argument is concerned with relative gains from, or equality in, exchange. Proponents of the realist school of international relations theory identify the concern with relative gains as at its core a concern about power – each state is not only concerned with whether a change in its relationship with other states will increase its domestic welfare, but also about the effects of this change on its relative power *vis-à-vis* other states. This leads to a fundamental disagreement between realists and neo-liberals or liberal internationalists. Neo-liberals believe that Pareto-superior bargains or agreements between states can be struck and sustained in the long run provided transaction costs can be managed and appropriate institutions and rules put into place to constrain cheating (the latter exercise may require, at the outset, a hegemon with strong interests in the creation of such institutions and rules).[34] Realists are sceptical of the capacity of states either to create or sustain international agreements or rules for international cooperation, because they believe that states will never voluntarily agree to, or at least continue to adhere to, rules that result in their relative power in the international system being weakened, even if in domestic welfare terms, they benefit from the agreements or rules in question.[35] If the realist interpretation of the concern with relative gains is correct, then the increasing sense that the United States faces a relative loss of power from open rules of trade bodes ill indeed for the sustainability of a liberal trading order in the long run. The realist view, in fact, strikes at the very heart of liberal political economy, for it suggests that enlightened economic self-interest remains secondary in international economic relations to the primordial struggle for relative power among nations.

An alternative interpretation, however, is possible of the concern about relative gains from exchange. This alternative interpretation is based in a normative theory of fairness or equality in exchange, rather than a power-based understanding of state behaviour. On this view, the long-term legitimacy and indeed sustainability of an exchange depends upon the maintenance of a fair distribution of benefits and burdens among the Parties. Pareto-superiority, on this view, is a necessary but not sufficient criterion for the fairness of an exchange or bargain.[36] Unlike pre-liberal 'just price' theorists, contemporary advocates of equality in exchange tend to emphasize the importance of balance and the avoidance of one-sidedness in contractual obligations, rather than the imposition of a requirement of strict equivalence in values exchanged (which would constitute a paternalistic destruction of the freedom of contract ideal). Unlike the power-based perspective of the realists, this perspective suggests that long-term bargains between countries can be sustained much like long-term contracts between individuals, provided that the agreements themselves contain the flexibility required to prevent one-sidedness or imbalance as circumstances change, or alternatively as long as there is a set of general or meta-norms that permit Parties to insist on occasional readjustment of the initial bargain in order to correct emerging imbalances or inequities in rights and responsibilities.

It is important to note that the post-war economic order, of which the GATT is an integral part, contained a mechanism for precisely such rebalancing. The mechanism in question was the Bretton Woods system of exchange rates and payments, characterized by fixed exchange rates backed by gold. If a country's exports substantially exceeded its imports, eventually demand for its currency would exceed its gold reserves. Its currency would then need to be revalued in order to reflect this scarcity. The revaluation would increase imports and reduce exports, thereby correcting the trade imbalance. Similarly, where a country was unable to cover the foreign currency needed to pay for imports with foreign currency it received for its exports, it would have to sell gold to make up the difference. Where its gold reserves began to run out, the country would have to devalue its currency (to increase exports and reduce imports) and maintain its liquidity and convertibility obligations under the IMF Articles. The Bretton Woods system also entailed both explicit and implicit responsibilities of countries to adopt or alter domestic policies so as to avoid payments problems and thereby obviate the need for frequent changes in exchange rates, which would undermine a system of fixed rates by creating constant speculation on markets as to when revaluations and devaluations would occur. In a previous chapter we have described the breakdown of the Bretton Woods system of exchange rates and payments and the largely unsuccessful effort to attempt rebalancing under floating rates through macroeconomic policy coordination among the major economic powers.

Under the rebalancing through the exchange rates and payment systems envisaged by Bretton Woods, a supranational authority, the IMF, was to bear the primary responsibility for determining which countries' domestic policies required what adjustments in order to preserve exchange rate stability and to clear trade and payments imbalances – on the basis, of course, of the Keynesian policy science of macroeconomics. But under contemporary circumstances, there is no supranational authority with the normative legitimacy to decide which, for example, American and/or Japanese policies should change in order to achieve rebalancing through *trade*. Unlike the realists, we believe that rebalancing can, in theory, be accommodated within long-term bargains and actually serve the goal of sustaining those bargains as circumstances change over time. But there is an important concern that the existing institutions and normative framework of the GATT – built on the assumption that rebalancing would occur through another part of the system – are not adequate to the task of adjudicating or arbitrating claims for rebalancing, and particularly of distinguishing legitimate claims from unjustified cheating, or strategic games of 'up the ante'. A sustained dissensus about what is cheating and what is not could pose a significant long-run threat to the sustainability of the liberal trading system, at least on a neo-liberal or liberal internationalist perspective that views the sustainability of a cooperative equilibrium as dependent on effective means of identifying and sanctioning defection. However, in the short run, the most effective avenue for addressing diffuse reciprocity concerns may be through increasing the range of issues subject to *future* multilateral negotiations. The Uruguay Round itself is an example of this approach, with the addition of services, investment, and intellectual property rights reflecting, in part, a concession to the American concern about rebalancing of benefits and burdens within the liberal multilateral trading order.

Specific reciprocity

The diffuse reciprocity concerns described above usually do not stand on their own but go hand in hand with concerns about reciprocity within specific sectors or with respect to particular products. While the Bretton Woods system as originally conceived seemed to encompass a concept of rebalancing that corresponds to concerns about diffuse reciprocity, it certainly did not contemplate any mechanism for balancing or rebalancing trade within specific sectors or in specific products. Indeed, this would seem tantamount to attempting to suppress comparative advantage itself.

The counterargument from fair traders is that domestic policies in certain highly competitive sectors, like microelectronics, can fundamentally distort comparative advantage or rig the competitive game. Where both global and domestic market share are crucial to survival, if I can arrange my domestic policies (e.g. competition rules, technical standards) in such a way that your producers have little access to my domestic market, while my producers have largely unimpeded access to yours, I may be able to force you out of business. Free trade advocates are likely to reply that most of the domestic policies in question are not intended to rig the game, but are general 'background' policies that should be considered as a normal part of comparative advantage, rather than a distortion of it. Nevertheless, at the limit, some range of domestic policies may be correctly characterized as targeted efforts at capturing market share from foreign competitors – subsidies in the case of civil aircraft are a case in point. As well, while some policies may constitute an integral part of a country's underlying social and economic arrangements, and thus are unlikely to be adaptable to meet fair trade concerns, others may indeed be alterable, at least with respect to their application to specific sectors.

While the demand for sectoral reciprocity, or reciprocal market access in particular sectors, runs the risk of generating a thicket of discriminatory managed trade arrangements in the absence of complete harmonization of domestic policies (a highly unrealistic possibility), in one sense the demand for sectoral reciprocity is more manageable than that for diffuse reciprocity. Because one is dealing with a limited number of domestic policies of a few countries that are major players in specific sectors it is possible to engage in some kind of focused dialogue about the effects of domestic policies on trade reciprocity. Concerns of diffuse reciprocity are more difficult to handle, absent a supranational authority or judge, simply because the value judgments are so open-ended. The Japanese argue that the US budget deficit and debt is the problem, driving up interest rates and the value of the US dollar. Some fair traders will reply that the size of the US debt and deficit are partially attributable to America's global defence responsibilities, from which Japan has actually benefited substantially.

In the case of specific reciprocity, a range of trade-offs concerning domestic policy constraints may be possible by applying certain normative criteria or tests to a limited number of policies. For example, Bhagwati has suggested that principles of proportionality, intentionality, selectivity and proximity can be invoked to evaluate claims that particular domestic policies distort trade unfairly within a specific sector. The proportionality principle would eliminate from scrutiny domestic policies determined to have a minimal impact on trade. The intentionality principle would limit offensive domestic policies to those intended to rig the game. The selectivity principle would limit scrutiny of domestic policies to those targeted to the specific sectors in question. Finally, the proximity principle would limit fair trade claims to those domestic policies that directly affect comparative advantage.[37] Bhagwati himself characterizes these principles as 'pragmatic' in the sense that the distinctions they draw between distortive and non-distortive domestic policies have no real basis in the theory of liberal trade. Applied by domestic trade authorities and tribunals with respect to an indeterminate range of foreigners' policies in the context of unilateral trade actions driven by protectionist demands, these kinds of principles would prove highly manipulable (consider the fate of the injury and specificity tests with respect to countervailing duty actions under domestic US trade law). By contrast, they might function quite well as *lignes directrices* for a structured multilateral negotiation on trade-impacting domestic policies within certain sectors.

These kinds of principles, as well, are not without some normative foundation even within the pre-Uruguay Round GATT. First of all, the jurisprudence of the GATT suggests a willingness to submit to scrutiny domestic policies that may have discriminatory or harmful impacts on trade even where on their face the domestic policies in question do not single out imported products for discriminatory treatment. GATT panels as well as FTA panels interpreting the GATT have been prepared to consider the possibility that facially neutral policies mask a discriminatory protectionist intent, or even to take an effects-based approach to key GATT provisions such as Articles III and XI,[38] subjecting to GATT scrutiny some measures that while not forming barriers to trade in products or discriminatory domestic policies, nevertheless appear to have a particularly harmful impact on trade and whose domestic benefits seem disproportionately small relative to the harm they do to the interests of trading partners. Along similar lines, the WTO Technical Barriers Agreement places Contracting Parties under a general obligation to minimize the negative trade effects of distinctive national standards or regulatory requirements with respect to trade in goods, and to adopt internationally recognized standards or norms wherever available and not prejudicial to domestic interests. Finally, supported by some GATT jurisprudence, there is plausibility to the view that, on its terms, Article XXIII of the General Agreement includes a right to relief from 'nullification and impairment' of GATT concessions, even where the actions leading to nullification and impairment do not involve a formal violation of GATT rules.

There thus seems to be some (albeit rather general) normative basis for multilateral sectoral bargaining on trade-impacting domestic policies. This, combined with sound empirical work on the trade impacts of domestic policies, the domestic goals and functions of the policies, and possible alternative policies with fewer negative trade impacts, may allow for sectoral agreements that are widely viewed as legitimate rather than simply as a capitulation to unilateralism. Such agreements are certainly vastly superior to achieving specific reciprocity through discriminatory managed trade arrangements, such as bilateral VERs, the Auto Pact, the Multi-Fibre Arrangement (MFA), and the US–Japan Semi-Conductor Agreement. In this sense, the demand that trade-impacting domestic policies be put on the bargaining table may be inherently less threatening to the normative order of the GATT than traditional managed trade arrangements, which the GATT has been rather ineffective in preventing in the past (witness the tremendous expansion of managed trade in textiles from the 1960s to the 1970s and of VERs in steel and autos during the late 1970s and 1980s[39]), as long as claims of unfairness can be defined, evaluated and constrained within an appropriate normative and institutional framework.

In our view, it would be appropriate to encourage sectoral bargaining with respect to domestic policies in sensitive industries under the auspices of the WTO, along the lines (broadly speaking) of the Civil Aircraft Code, and to establish certain rules for such bargaining. These might involve an obligation to include in negotiations all countries involved in global competition in the sector; a prohibition on explicit agreements with respect to quotas and market shares (i.e. an anti-cartelization rule); a requirement that all market access commitments in the form of adjustment of domestic policies as they apply to foreign producers be offered to all countries party to the agreement (conditional MFN); a general proviso that the agreements not be more restrictive of trade than existing rules; and an obligation to consider interests of non-signatories (both consumer interests and those of *potential* entrants to the market).

STRENGTHENING THE LEGAL AND INSTITUTIONAL FOUNDATIONS OF OPEN MARKETS[40]

The Asian crisis of 1997–8, in both its economic and political dimensions, offers a dramatic illustration that durable outward-oriented development strategies depend on more than free trade or the right economic formulas for domestic policy. The crisis, and other events in Russia and elsewhere, should teach economic liberals, and especially free traders, that the values they endorse also depend on political liberalism, including the rule of law and democracy. Particularly with the collapse of communism, as well as the fashionability (now tarnished) of the thesis of an authoritarian Asian alternative to Western political liberalism (compatible with and indeed supportive of free markets), some economists saw a rapid route to economic liberalization that did not pass through the messy process of indigenously-driven political, social and legal development. In fact, although this simplistic approach has led to criticisms of the 'ideology' of free trade as such, it must be remembered that the classical political economists, from Smith through Ricardo and Hume to J.S. Mill, regarded the political, legal and indeed moral conditions for liberal trade as of singular intellectual interest, as well as cardinal policy importance. We must seek to recover something of the broadness of their vision. In the contemporary language this often expresses itself as a call for a focus on governance. According to Leila Frischtak, governance has become the key variable in explaining the adjustment performance of developing countries during the 1980s and early 1990s.[41] Governance is defined expansively by the World Bank in its 1992 *Report on Governance and Development* as 'the manner in which power is exercised in the management of a country's economic and social resources for development'.[42] After surveying more than 100 years of comparative development experience in 40 LDCs, Reynolds concludes that 'the single most important explanatory variable is political organization and the administrative competence of government'.[43] According to Arturo Talavera, a distinguished Chilean political philosopher, 'Good institutions are the best capital that a society can have, and they are precisely what most poor countries lack.'[44] An important empirical study by Barro of around 100 countries from 1960–90 finds that for a starting level of real per capita GDP, the economic growth rate is enhanced by higher school and life expectancy, lower fertility, lower government consumption, better maintenance of the rule of law and improvements in the terms of trade.[45]

As Naim points out:

> Discovering the market and abandoning over-reliance on the state has done wonders for Latin America. But the discovery of the market will soon force Latin American countries to re-discover the state . . . the process of dismantling the state and limiting its scope of intervention is still far from finished. At the same time, however, the more difficult task of creating or rehabilitating indispensable public sector institutions lags far behind the requirements of a new economic strategy. Bringing the state back in ways that support and reinforce recent progress – without restoring the state's previously displayed penchant for inflicting economic, social and moral havoc – will be the central challenge facing governments throughout the region.[46]

Robert Putnam's celebrated study of civic traditions in modern Italy demonstrates that civic organizations play an important role in ensuring the accountability of public sector organizations and often appear to promote economic growth.[47] According to Naim, Latin America's real public sector wages fell 30 percent between 1980 and 1989, more than triple the drop experienced in the private sector. Peruvian teachers lost 75 percent of their real wages between 1980 and 1989 causing trained instructors to flee the field for less hard hit sectors. As a result, the proportion of uncertified teachers doubled to 50 percent by 1990.[48] Reorienting the public sector so that it employs far fewer people in aggregate, reducing employment in activities where the state has no comparative advantage, perhaps increasing employment in sectors (such as education, agricultural extension, and health care) where it has a comparative advantage, and much more generously compensating those that it does employ are widely identified by development analysts as crucial priorities. Sectors such as education, health, and agricultural support services, are particularly relevant to the alleviation of poverty and to rural development. These sectors have typically attracted fewer, less well qualified and less well remunerated personnel than high specificity, highly competitive sectors (e.g. engineering functions), where employee performance can be more readily measured and where both employees and recipients of the services may have readier alternatives.

While decentralization of personnel and other functions to departments or agencies within one level of government or more fundamentally to lower levels of government may make sense in principle, given the scarcity of managerial capacity in most developing countries there are also serious risks that, at least in the short run, more delegation and decentralization may in fact impair the quality and integrity of public sector management. According to the World Bank's Report on *Governance and Development*, micro-level accountability has become more important as the role of the state has expanded and made it impossible to apply broad accountability norms to all the myriad actions of modern government. However, the effectiveness of local voice will often turn on the existence of intermediate organizations that provide a means of mobilizing local constituents or clients and many authoritarian regimes have been hostile to encouraging the emergence of such intermediate organizations because of a fear that they may become countervailing political centres of power or threats to the incumbent regime.[49] Even where these mobilization problems can be overcome, there is then a risk that agencies will become captive to parochial interests and lose sight of a broader set of public interests. Intermediate organizations are not necessarily conducive to economic development if they reinforce sectional, ethnic or religious differences or reflect narrow special interests. More broadly based civic organizations or other organizations with substantial overlapping memberships may be more conducive to broader perspectives on economic development.

As with the relationship between bureaucracy and development, the relationship between legal systems and development has been less extensively analyzed and empirically studied than the relationship between democracy and development. However, Barro in his recent empirical study finds that better maintenance of the rule of law significantly influences growth rates.[50] In the Bank's *Governance and Development* study, serious deficiencies are reported to afflict the legal systems in many developing countries, all of which in one respect or another increase transaction and information costs and levels of risk and uncertainty. These deficiencies afflict the law-making process, the public administration and enforcement of laws, and the judicial interpretation and enforcement of laws. First, laws and regulations that are enacted or promulgated are often not published – indeed in a number of countries the World Bank notes that public gazetting of laws was running several years behind their enactment – and in any event often were not widely accessible or intelligible to the general public. Second, laws and regulations are often unstable, and changed or replaced frequently, engendering high levels of uncertainty for private economic agents contemplating long-term investment decisions in part in reliance on the stability of these laws. Third, even when new laws or regulations are enacted or promulgated, often they are not followed and applied by other agencies or levels of government – a particularly acute problem in a number of the former communist countries in Eastern and Central Europe. More generally, the application and enforcement of the laws is often highly inconsistent or non-existent, i.e. they are only laws on the books – often state-of-the-art laws – but they have little or no effect on actual behaviour. Fourth, laws or regulatory regimes are often adopted without any serious attention given to alternative and more efficient ways of achieving the policy objective in question (through a fuller canvassing of alternative governing instruments). Many new laws and regulations are adopted with minimal public or political debate or scrutiny so that information and feedback loops on possible policy errors are highly attenuated, exacerbating problems of non-transparency in the legislative process. Fifth, inadequate attention is typically devoted to designing public administration systems that will ensure that the laws are competently and efficiently administered.[51] Deficiencies in a country's legal capital are likely to become even more of a constraint on development with greater reliance on the private sector and markets as a major driving force in economic development.

The paramount institutional challenge with respect to bureaucratic and legal reform seems to require much more imaginative thinking on the relationship between institutional autonomy and accountability. It is simply neither possible nor desirable to completely 'neuter' politics by taking all important public functions out of the political domain – otherwise the case for democratic political regimes would be at an end and the case for authoritarianism substantially strengthened. Thus, at the limit, in the case of incorrigibly predatory rather than developmental states, it is difficult to be optimistic about the prospects of significantly enhancing the institutional performance of the bureaucracy and legal system. However, short of these limiting cases, striking a new balance between institutional autonomy and accountability represents a major new policy challenge. In particular, devising accountability mechanisms (to whom? for what?) that do not run directly to the political regime, and either stop there or run on weakly and in a diffused way to an often ill-informed and unorganized general public, but rather entail wider participation in more open decision-making processes by intermediate organizations or communities of interest to which these public sector agencies or institutions are accountable on a meritocratic basis for their performance, or in some cases supra-majority bipartisan legislative approval of key public sector appointments, seems to be a productive area of further research calling for much more imagination than the existing literature reflects. To emphasize institutional insulation and autonomy exclusively is unlikely to be an appropriate long-term prescription, because without some set of effective mechanisms for accountability, most of these institutions in the long run are likely to degenerate into autocratic fiefdoms in their own right. This seems a worthy and realistic long-term aspiration.

MULTILATERALISM VERSUS REGIONALISM

As discussed earlier in this book,[52] the rise of regional trading blocs poses a special challenge to the multilateral system. The principle of non-discrimination that lies at the heart of the multilateral system is potentially put at serious risk by regional trading blocs which, by definition, extend more favourable trading rules to members than non-members. The principle of non-discrimination enshrined in the GATT (in the form of the Most Favoured Nation and National Treatment principles) has important economic and political rationales. From an economic perspective, regional trading blocs always entail some degree of trade diversion as well as trade expansion and thus carry the potential for distorting global trade and reducing global economic welfare. From a political perspective, the principle of non-discrimination is designed to discourage countries from playing favourites with other countries, and inducing the kind of mutually self-destructive forms of factionalism that led to the collapse of the open trading system in the inter-war years.

We believe that both the economic and political rationales for the principle of non-discrimination seen as central to the GATT by its founders remain of paramount importance. In order to preserve these values, consideration should be given to tightening the conditions under which free trade areas or customs unions can be authorized under the GATT. More specifically, several key conditions contained in Article XXIV need to be interpreted and applied more stringently than they often have been in the past. First, the requirement that when a free trade or customs union is formed, substantially all trade between or among Member countries must be liberalized should be interpreted to mean exactly what it says, so as to exclude various kinds of bilateral, sectoral, managed trade arrangements. While sectoral agreements with reciprocal market access commitments *may* be liberalizing (e.g. the chapter on financial services in the NAFTA), these agreements also have considerable potential to reinforce restrictive managed trade arrangements, whether directly through measures such as quotas or indirectly, for example, through complex re-adjustment of the rules of origin for particular products or sectors. In sensitive sectors such as textiles, autos and agriculture, the NAFTA seems to take on the character of a managed trade arrangement rather than a free trade arrangement.

Second, the requirement that external duties imposed by Member countries of free trade areas or customs unions should not be higher on average than those prevailing before the formation of such an arrangement should be amended to require that such external duties imposed following the formation of regional trading arrangements should not exceed the *lowest* external duties imposed by any Member country prior to the formation of the arrangement, thus minimizing the amount of trade diversion likely to be induced. Such a requirement would also reduce the need for complex rules of origin.

To ensure that trade diversion is minimized, it is not sufficient to scrutinize only the external duties imposed following the establishment of regional arrangements. Rules of origin and rules with respect to the extent to which partially or wholly foreign-owned or controlled firms operating within the free trade area can benefit from liberalization commitments on investment or services also have a considerable impact on the extent to which regional arrangements are trade diverting. In the case of rules of origin, the trade diverting effects may be quite dramatic. The rules determine, with respect to each product grouping, what percentage of value of the finished product must have been added within the free trade area in order to qualify for preferential or duty-free admission into other countries within the area. They can easily be fine-tuned so as to affect significantly the market share of non-Members of the free trade area for certain products. To take a hypothetical example, suppose that prior to the existence of a free trade area, producers of widgets in country A have been using an input manufactured in Japan that constitutes 40% of the value of the finished product. If the rule of origin is now set at over 60%, in order to be able to export duty-free the finished product within the free trade area, the producer will have to substitute for the Japanese input one produced within the area. Therefore, assuming that the price advantage of the Japanese input is less than the advantage in terms of lower duties that comes from meeting the rules of origin by selecting an input manufactured within the free trade area, Japanese producers will lose market share. In sum, there is a clear need for scrutiny of the effects of a range of rules in regional arrangements on the trade of non-Members.

Mutual Recognition Agreements with respect to product and service standards, such as the MRA recently concluded between the United States and the European Union, raise important trade diversion issues when they are negotiated on a regional or plurilateral basis; the consistency of such agreements with MFN obligations should be closely scrutinized at the WTO.[53] The recent promulgation by WTO of guidelines for MRAs with respect to accountancy (mentioned in Chapter 11 on trade in services) suggests a salutary awareness of the stake that the multilateral trading system has in ensuring that these arrangements do not create closed trading blocks, discriminating against non-Members.

Third, there is also much to be said for the view that in order for regional trading arrangements to be authorized under the GATT an additional condition should be satisfied – that membership of such an arrangement is open to any country prepared to accept the obligations to which existing Members have committed themselves. That is to say, these arrangements should be required to be open to application by new Members, through an obligatory accession provision, along the lines of the accession provisions in the GATT (Article XXXIII), and building on the accession provisions contained in NAFTA (Article 2205). Even where (because of particular characteristics of the country concerned or its stage of social and economic development) a country may not be prepared automatically to accept all the obligations of the existing arrangement, there should be a duty at least to enter into negotiations in good faith with a view to admission on terms and conditions that are mutually acceptable. As well, in specific areas such as services, investment and intellectual property rights, Members of a regional arrangement should be encouraged to extend the rights provided by the arrangement to non-Members who are prepared to accept regional obligations in these areas even if they are not Members of the region itself, or if for other reasons it would be inappropriate for them to become full Members of the regional arrangement. Here, a precedent exists with respect to the agreements that existed between the EFTA countries and the European Union prior to their decision to join the EU. While both WTO and NAFTA accession provisions contemplate a process of negotiation and approval by existing Members, where a country seeking membership of a regional trading arrangement is able to demonstrate a willingness to accept all the obligations that existing Members are subject to, some right of review by a WTO Working Group or Committee of a negative decision by Members would seem to be an important check on arbitrary or discriminatory exclusions. While the findings and recommendations of such a Working Group might not realistically bind existing Members, they would improve the transparency and legitimacy of the decision-making process, and provide applicants for membership in regional trading arrangements with additional political leverage.

Quite apart from the potential for increasing the tendency towards managed trade and discrimination, a proliferation of regional arrangements and regional dispute settlement processes for trade disagreements poses a threat to clarity and certainty in trade rules. Overlap between WTO and regional obligations, the latter often stated in similar but not identical terms to those in the WTO, can create confusion with respect to the appropriate interpretation of both sets of rules. Furthermore, free trade areas (as opposed to customs unions, where matters are simplified by a common external policy) increase the regulatory knowledge and burden that trading partners require to engage in effective commercial relations – they must still take account of the trade policies of each individual country and the WTO rules, while also being aware of the meaning and implications of the regional rules as well, and the evolving jurisprudence surrounding those rules. In the pre-Uruguay Round environment, the problem was less pronounced because regional arrangements built on the GATT, and created rules in areas such as intellectual property, services and investment, where the GATT had few or none. However, there are now both WTO and overlapping regional rules in all these areas. Cowhey and Aronson, who are favourably disposed towards regional arrangements, nevertheless see a need eventually to 'multilateralize' these arrangements.[54] In our view, multilateralization would ideally implicate a Working Group of the WTO in the task of harmonizing regional and multilateral rules to the extent possible, as well as addressing on an *ad hoc* basis conflicts that occur with respect to the interaction of regional and multilateral rules, or important divergences in the jurisprudential approaches of different dispute settlement fora.

In sum, in order to minimize the potential threat that regional trading blocs pose to the multilateral system, we consider that some significant rethinking and reworking of the conditions for approval of such arrangements under Article XXIV of the GATT should be an important priority on the future international trade policy agenda.

Notes

Preface

1 E.U. Petersmann, 'Strengthening GATT Procedures for Settling Trade Disputes', *World Economy*, March 1988, pp. 55–6.

1 The evolution of international trade theory and policy

1 This section draws heavily on several widely accessible accounts of the evolution of international trade theory: Douglas Irwin, *Against The Tide: An Intellectual History of Free Trade* (Princeton NJ: Princeton University Press, 1996); Richard G. Harris, *Trade, Industrial Policy and International Competition* (Research Study No. 13, Macdonald Royal Commission and the Economic Union and Development Prospects for Canada, University of Toronto Press, 1985); Peter B. Kenen, *The International Economy* (Cambridge UK: Cambridge University Press, 3rd ed., 1994); and Richard Caves and Ronald Jones, *World Trade and Payments: An Introduction* (Boston: Little Brown, 4th ed., 1985).

2 Irwin, *op. cit.*

3 For a recent attempt to revive a natural rights justification for free trade, see Robert McGee, *A Trade Policy for a Free Society: The Case Against Protectionism* (Westport CT: Quorum Books, 1994); McGee, 'The Moral Case for Free Trade' (1995) 29 *J. of World Trade* 69.

4 See Paul Krugman and Maurice Obstfeld, *International Economics: Theory and Policy* (Reading MA: Addison-Wesley, 4th ed., 1997) pp. 541–2.

5 Adam Smith, *The Wealth of Nations* (1776; New York: Modern Library Edition, 1937) p. 424.

6 Taken from P. Samuelson and A. Scott, *Economics* (Toronto: McGraw-Hill, 1980) p. 807; for a recent review of the theory of comparative advantage, see Alan Sykes, 'Comparative Advantage and the Normative Economics of International Trade Policy', (1988) *J.J. of International Economic Law* 49.

7 See Herbert G. Grubel and P.J. Lloyd, *Intra-Industry Trade: The Theory and Measurement of Trade in Differentiated Products* (London: Macmillan, 1975).

8 See e.g. Raymond Vernon, 'International Investment and International Trade in the Product Cycle' (1966) 80 *Quarterly J. of Econs* 190; Vernon, 'The Product Cycle Hypothesis in a New International Economic Environment' (1979) 41 *Oxford Bulletin of Economic Statistics* 255.

9 See Krugman and Obstfeld, *op. cit.*

10 See William R. Cline, '"Reciprocity": A New Approach to World Trade Policy', in W.R. Cline (ed.) *Trade Policy in the 1980s* (Washington DC: Institute for International Economics, 1983) p. 152.

11 See Cline, *op. cit.*

12 See Beth and Robert Yarborough, 'Reciprocity, Bilateralism and Economic "Hostages": Self-enforcing Agreements in International Trade' (1986) 30 *International Studies Quarterly* 7; Alan O. Sykes, 'Mandatory Retaliation for Breach of Trade Agreements: Some Thoughts on the Strategic Design of Section 301' (1990) 8 *Boston University International Law Journal* 301.
13 See R. Axelrod and R. Keohane, 'Achieving Co-operation Under Anarchy' in K. Oye (ed.) *Co-operation Under Anarchy* (Princeton NJ: Princeton University Press, 1985).
14 Adam Smith, *op. cit.*, pp. 434–5.
15 See Jagdish Bhagwati and Hugh Patrick (eds) *Aggressive Unilateralism* (Ann Arbor: University of Michigan Press, 1992).
16 See Carolyn Rhodes, 'Reciprocity in Trade: The Utility of a Bargaining Strategy' (1989) 43 *International Organization* 273.
17 See Yarborough and Yarborough, *op. cit.*; Laura Tyson, 'Managed Trade: Making the Best of the Second Best', and Rudiger Dornbusch, 'Policy Options for Free Trade: The Case for Bilateralism', in R. Lawrence and C. Schultz (eds) *An American Trade Strategy: Options for the 1990s* (Washington DC: Brookings Institution, 1990).
18 See Irwin, *op. cit.*, ch. 8.
19 John Stuart Mill, *Principles of Political Economy* (London: Longman, Greene & Co., 1848) p. 922.
20 See Robert Baldwin, 'The Case Against Infant Industry Protection' (1969) 77 *Journal of Political Economy* 295.
21 See e.g. Paul Krugman (ed.) *Strategic Trade Policy and the New International Economics* (Cambridge MA: MIT Press, 1986); Elhonan Helpman and Paul Krugman, *Trade Policy and Market Structure* (Cambridge MA: MIT Press, 1989); J. David Richardson, 'The Political Economy of Strategic Trade Policy' (1990) 44 *International Organization* 107; Irwin, *op. cit.*, ch. 14.
22 Irwin *op. cit.*, ch. 14.
23 See Chapter 9 below.
24 Gary Hufbauer and Jeffrey Schott *NAFTA: An Assessment* (Washington DC: Institute for International Economics, 1993) pp. 12, 13.
25 Richard Freeman, 'Are Your Wages Set in Beijing?' (1995) 9 *J. of Economic Perspectives* 15; William Cline, *Trade and Economic Distribution* (Washington DC: Institute for International Economics, 1997).
26 See Chapter 16.
27 See Chapter 15.
28 Francis Fukuyama, 'The End of History', *The National Interest* (Summer, 1989) p. 3; Fukuyama, *The End of History and the Last Man* (New York: Free Press, 1991).
29 George Grant, *Lament for a Nation: The Defeat of Canadian Nationalism* (Toronto: Anansi, 1967).
30 See Michael Trebilcock and Robert Howse 'Trade Liberalization and Regulatory Diversity: Reconciling Competitive Markets with Competitive Politics', (1998) 6 *European J. of Law & Economics* 5.
31 A. Downs, *An Economic Theory of Democracy* (New York: Harper, 1957).
32 M. Olson, *The Logic of Collective Action* (New York: Schoken, 1965).
33 I.M. Destler and J. Odell, *Anti-Protection: Changing Forces in United States Trade Politics* (Washington DC: Institute for International Economics, 1987).
34 H. Milner, 'Trading Places: Industries for Free Trade', *World Politics* XL, 3 (April 1988) pp. 350–76.
35 H. Milner and D. Yoffie, 'Between Free Trade and Protectionism: Strategic Trade Policy and a Theory of Corporate Demands' (1989) 43 *International Organization* 239.
36 Robert Baldwin, *The Political Economy of Import Policy* (Cambridge MA: MIT Press, 1985) ch. 1.
37 This evidence is reviewed in M. Trebilcock, M. Chandler and R. Howse, *Trade and Transitions* (London: Routledge, 1990) pp. 178–80.

38 Baldwin, *op. cit.*, p. 180.
39 See Gilbert Winham, *The Evolution of International Trade Agreements* (University of Toronto Press, 1992) ch. 1.
40 S.B. Clough and C.W. Cole, *Economic History of Europe* (Boston MA: D.C. Heath, 1941) p. 458.
41 Charles P. Kindleberger, 'The Rise of Free Trade in Western Europe, 1820–1874' (1975) 35 *J. of Economic History* 20 at p. 23, and Clough and Cole, *op. cit.*, pp. 456–8. See also A.G. Kenwood and A.L. Lougheed, *The Growth of the International Economy* (London: Allen & Unwin, 1971) p. 73. In this respect, the situation in the German states around 1815 is especially striking – 8,000km of borders divided the twenty-eight German-speaking states; heavy transit tolls substantially impeded trade.
42 Clough and Cole, *op. cit.*, p. 473. James Foreman-Peck, *A History of the World Economy* (Ottawa: Barnes & Noble, 1983) p. 56 also emphasizes that Britain was fiscally more able to reduce tariffs than most at this time because of the substantial size of her commerce with respect to the economy as a whole, and the relative absence of government debt.

In Prussia, the Junkers, for the most part large exporters of wheat, favoured free trade. Their dominance of national institutions helped solidify support for the policy in Germany until the 1870s. Then a more cohesive manufacturing sector, and stiff competition from overseas wheat, helped turn the political tide against free trade. See Kindleberger, *op. cit.*, p. 42.
43 Clough and Cole, *op. cit.*, pp. 469ff. Such trade treaties actually had their genesis in the late eighteenth century – Britain and France signed a treaty on trade just before the Revolution. The latter saw the renunciation of the treaty almost directly the King was removed from power.
44 Kenwood and Lougheed, *op. cit.*, p. 77; and P. Bairoch, 'European Trade Policy, 1815–1914', in P. Matthias and S. Pollard (eds) *The Cambridge Economic History of Europe*, vol. 8 (Cambridge MA: Cambridge University Press, 1989) 1 at p. 36.
45 Kenwood and Lougheed, *op. cit.*, p. 78; Clough and Cole, *op. cit.*, pp. 608–9; and Kenen, *op. cit.*
46 Kenwood and Lougheed, *op. cit.*, p. 78.
47 P. Bairoch, 'European Trade Policy, 1815–1914', in Matthias and Pollard (eds) *op. cit.*, p. 101.
48 Kenen, *op. cit.*, p. 213, and P. Bairoch, 'European Trade Policy, 1815–1914', in Matthias and Pollard (eds) *op. cit.*, 1 at pp. 51–2.
49 Foreman-Peck, *op. cit.*, p. 57, and Kindleberger, *op. cit.*, p. 45.
50 Foreman-Peck, *op. cit.*, p. 57. Kindleberger, *op. cit.*, p. 33, points out that some English industrialists supported free trade in the 1840s as a means of slowing down European industrialization.
51 Clough and Cole, *op. cit.*, p. 477.
52 P. Bairoch, 'European Trade Policy, 1815–1914', in Matthias and Pollard (eds) *op. cit.*, 1 at pp. 51–2. For a description of the 'colonial pact' see P. Bairoch, 'European Trade Policy, 1815–1914', in Matthias and Pollard (eds) *op. cit.*, 1 at p. 103. It should be noted that colonial policy was not a constant. Britain's stance in this respect was largely dictated by protection on the Continent: in mid-century she was dismantling imperial preference (for a description, see Clough and Cole, *op. cit.*, p. 466), and it was only after the return of protection in the 1880s that the idea of imperial preference regained any real legitimacy. See Kenwood and Lougheed, *op. cit.*, p. 79, and Clough and Cole, *op. cit.*, p. 476. Moreover, colonies were not acquired for economic reasons only; nationalism played an important role as well.
53 Kenwood and Lougheed, *op. cit.*, p. 186.
54 Foreman-Peck, *op. cit.*, pp. 215–16.
55 Kenen, *op. cit.*, p. 216.
56 J.H. Jackson, W.J. Davey and Alan O. Sykes, Jr., *Legal Problems of International Economic*

Relations, 3rd ed. (St. Paul: West, 1995) at ch. 5. R.E. Hudec, *The GATT Legal System and World Trade Diplomacy*, 2nd ed. (St. Paul: Butterworth, 1990) Part I, contains a detailed description of the negotiations.

57 For excellent treatments of the evolution of the GATT, see Judith Goldstein, 'Creating the GATT Rules: Politics, Institutions and American Policy', in J. Ruggie (ed.) *Multilateralism Matters: The Theory and Praxis of an Institutional Forum* (New York: Columbia University Press, 1993), ch. 6; Anne-Marie Burley-Slaughter, 'Regulating the World: Multilateralism, International Law, and the Projection of the New Deal Regulatory State', in Ruggie *ibid*, ch. 4

58 Jackson, Davey and Sykes, *op. cit.*, p. 295. See also Hudec, *op. cit.*, at ch. 6.

59 Jackson, Davey and Sykes, *op. cit.*, pp. 294ff.; J.H. Jackson, *The World Trading System* (Cambridge MA: MIT Press, 1979, 2nd ed.) at ch. 2; and Hudec, *op. cit.*, ch. 7. See also *Review of the Effectiveness of Trade Dispute Settlement Under the GATT and the Tokyo Round Agreements: Report to the Committee on Finance, U.S. Senate* (Washington DC: U.S. International Trade Commission, 1985) pp. 11–12 [hereinafter *ITC Report*]; Hudec, *Enforcing International Trade Law: The Evolution of the Modern GATT Legal System* (Salem NH: Butterworths 1993).

60 Jackson, Davey and Sykes, *op. cit.*, at s. 6.2.

61 Jackson, Davey and Sykes, *op. cit.*, p. 314; K.W. Dam, *The GATT: Law and International Economic Organization* (Chicago: University of Chicago Press, 1970) at ch. 5; and Jackson, *op. cit.*, pp. 52–7.

62 Dam, *op. cit.*, at ch. 14. See also R.E. Hudec, *Developing Countries in the GATT Legal System* (London: Gower, 1987); and Jackson, *op. cit.*, at ch. 12.

63 For a very useful review of recent developments in international trade policy, see Margaret Kelly and Anne Kenny McGuirk, *Issues and Developments in International Trade Policy* (Washington DC: International Monetary Fund, August 1992).

64 Sylvia Ostry, *The Post Cold War Trading System: Who's On First?* (Chicago: University of Chicago Press, 1997).

65 Jackson, Davey and Sykes, *op. cit.*, at s. 4.2 provide useful citations to sources for EU history.

66 See Chapter 5.

2 The basic elements of the GATT/WTO, the North American Free Trade Agreement, and the European Union

1 For introductory treatments of the GATT, see Olivier Long, *Law and Its Limitations in the GATT Multilateral Trade System* (London: Graham & Trotman, 1987); Frank Stone, *Canada, the GATT and the International Trade System* (Montreal: The Institute for Research on Public Policy, 1984); Michael Hart, *Trade – Why Bother?* (Ottawa: Centre for Trade Policy and Law, Carleton University and University of Ottawa, 1992); Alan Oxley, *The Challenge of Free Trade* (London: Harvester Wheatsheaf, 1990). For more extensive treatments, see Kenneth W. Dam, *The GATT: Law and International Economic Organization* (Chicago: University of Chicago Press, 1970); Robert E. Hudec, *The GATT Legal System and World Trade Diplomacy* (2nd ed. Salem NH: Butterworth Legal Publishers, 1990) and John Jackson *The World Trading System: Law and Policy of International Economic Relations* (Cambridge MA: MIT Press, 1997, 2nd ed.); Michael Hart, *Fifty Years of Canadian Tradecraft: Canada and the GATT 1947–1997* (Ottawa: Centre for Trade Policy and Law, 1998).

2 For a comprehensive review of international codes and agreements dealing with trade and government procurement, see Arie Reich, *Towards Free Trade in the Public Sector: A Comparative Study of International Agreements on Government Procurement* (S.J.D. thesis, University of Toronto Faculty of Law, 1993).

3 J. Bhagwati, 'Fair Trade, Reciprocity and Harmonization: The New Challenge to the Theory and Policy of Free Trade', in A. Deardorff and R. Stern (eds) *Analytical and*

Negotiating Issues in the Global Trading System (Ann Arbor: University of Michigan Press, 1993).

4 See, in general, L. Haus, *Globalizing the GATT: the Soviet Union's Successor States, Eastern Europe, and the International Trading System* (Washington DC: Brookings Institution, 1992).

5 See Chapter 14.

6 The relationship between trade and the environment is discussed in detail in Chapter 15.

7 See Michael J. Hahn, 'Vital Interests and the Law in GATT: An Analysis of GATT's Security Exceptions' (1991) 12 *Michigan J. of International Law* 588.

8 See Shelley Kierstead, 'An International Bind: Article XXIV(12) of GATT and Canada' (1993) 25 *Ottawa L. Rev.* 315.

9 *Assessing the Effects of the Uruguay Round*, OECD, Paris, 1993. More generally, see Jeffrey Schott, *The Uruguay Round* (Washington DC: Institute for International Economics, 1994).

10 For treatments of the Canada–USA Free Trade Agreement, see Debra P. Steger *et al.*, *A Concise Guide to the Canada–United States Free Trade Agreement* (Toronto: Carswell, 1988); Jon Johnson and Joel Schacter, *The Free Trade Agreement: A Comprehensive Guide* (Toronto: Canada Law Book, 1988); John D. Richard and Richard G. Dearden, *The Canada–U.S. Free Trade Agreement: Final Text and Analysis* (Toronto: CCH Canadian Ltd., 1988); Peter Morici, *Making Free Trade Work: The Canada–U.S. Agreement* (New York and London: Council of Foreign Relations Press, 1990); *The Free Trade Law Reporter* (Toronto: CCH Canadian Ltd., 1989) (Looseleaf); Duncan Cameron and Ed Finn (eds) *The Facts on Free Trade* (Toronto: James Lorimer, 1988); John Crispo (ed.) *Free Trade: The Real Story* (Toronto: Gage Educational Publishing Co., 1988); Marc Gold and David Leyton-Brown (eds) *Trade-Offs on Free Trade: The Canada–U.S. Free Trade Agreement* (Toronto: Carswell, 1988); and Bruce Doern and Brian Tomlin, *Faith and Fear: The Free Trade Story* (Toronto: Stoddart Publishing Co. Ltd, 1991).

11 For the complete legal text of the NAFTA, see NAFTA Text (CCH Inc., 1994). For discussions of the provisions of NAFTA, see S. Globerman and M. Walker (eds) *Assessing NAFTA: A Trinational Analysis* (Vancouver: The Fraser Institute, 1993); G.C. Hufbauer and J.J. Schott, *NAFTA: An Assessment* (Washington DC: Institute for International Economics, 1993); J. Lemco and W.B.P. Robson (eds) *Ties Beyond Trade: Labor and Environmental Issues Under the NAFTA* (Canadian–American Committee) (Toronto: C.D. Howe Institute, 1993); A.R. Riggs and Tom Welk, *Beyond NAFTA: An Economic Political and Sociological Perspective* (Vancouver: The Fraser Institute, 1993); Government of Canada, *NAFTA: What's It All About?* (Ottawa: External Affairs and International Trade Canada, September 1993); R. Lipsey, D. Schwanen and R. Wennacott, *The NAFTA* (Toronto: C.D. Howe Institute, 1994); Jon Johnson, *The North American Free Trade Agreement: A Comprehensive Guide* (Toronto: Canada Law Book Co., 1994).

12 This discussion relies, to a significant extent, on the following sources: F.G. Jacobs and K.L. Karst, 'The "Federal" Legal Order: The U.S.A. and Europe Compared: A Juridical Perspective', in M. Cappelletti, M. Seccombe and J. Weiler (eds) *Political Organizations, Integration Techniques, and Judicial Process: Methods, Tools and Institutions*, vol. 1 (Berlin: W. De Gruyter, 1986 [hereinafter, *Integration Through Law*]); T. Heller and J. Pelkmans, 'The Federal Economy: Law and Economic Integration and the Positive State – The U.S.A. and Europe Compared in an Economic Perspective', in *Integration Through Law*; M. Brealey and C. Quigley's 'Introduction', in *Completing the Internal Market of the European Community: 1992 Handbook* (London: Graham and Trotman, 1989); G. Hufbauer 'An Overview', in G. Hufbauer (ed.) *Europe 1992: An American Perspective* (Washington DC: Brookings Institution, 1990); D. Swann, *Competition and Industrial Policy in the European Community* (London: Methuen, 1990, chs 1 and 2); P. Leslie, *The European Community: A Political Model for Canada?* (Ottawa: Supply & Services, 1991); and P. Monahan, *Political and Economic Integration: The European Experience and Lessons for Canada* (Toronto: York University Centre for Public Law and Public Policy, 1992).

13 *Treaty Establishing the European Economic Community*, 25 March 1957, 298 UNTS 11 (hereinafter Treaty of Rome).

14 At the outset, direct enforceability was controversial, as some states adhered to the narrower view of the Treaty as a 'normal' interstate agreement. Early decisions of the Court were of decisive importance in establishing a 'constitutional' status for the Treaty, and in moving the Community towards genuine integration. See *Van Gend en Loos v. Nederlandse Administratie der Belastingen*, Case 26/62 [1963] E.C.R. 1125, and the discussion of this and subsequent cases in D. Wyatt and A. Dashwood, 'The Community Legal Order', in W. Wyatt (ed.) *The Substantive Law of the EEC*, 2nd ed. (London: Sweet and Maxwell, 1990).
15 Brealey and Quigley, *op. cit.*, p. xxii.
16 See Brealey and Quigley, *op. cit.*, p. xxvi.
17 On the importance of the abandonment of the unanimity requirement to the realization of Europe, 1992, see for example, L. Bergeron, 'L'integration européenne', ch. 2, in Commission sur l'avenir politique et constitutionelle du Québec, *Eléments d'analyse institutionelle, juridique, et demolinguistique pertinent à la révision due status politique et constitutionelle du Québec*, Document du travail, numero 2, Québec City 1991, at 116; see also Tarullo, 'Can the European "social market" survive?', *American Prospect*, Spring 1991; Brealey and Quigley, *op. cit.*, p. xii.
18 The Article reads as follows: 'The provisions of Articles 30 to 34 shall not preclude prohibitions or restrictions on imports, exports or goods in transit justified on grounds of public morality, public policy or public security; the protection of health and life of humans, animals and plants; the protection of national treasures possessing artistic, historic or archaeological value; or the protection of industrial and commercial property. Such prohibitions or restrictions shall not, however, constitute a means of arbitrary discrimination or a disguised restriction on trade between member states.'
19 *Rewe-Zentral AG v. Bundesmonopoverwaltung für Branntwein, E.C.J.* 120/78.
20 The notion of mandatory requirements suggests that the measures in question must be pursuant to a mandatory legislative scheme and not a mere exercise of executive or administrative discretion.
21 Case 178/84 (1988) 1 CMLR 780.
22 See Articles 92(1) and 92 of the Treaty.
23 Hufbauer, 'An Overview', *op. cit.*, p. 9.
24 Europe, Documents No. 1759/60, February 1992.
25 For a discussion in greater depth of some of these institutional changes, see P. Ludlow, 'The Maastricht Treaty and the Future of Europe', *Washington Quarterly*, Autumn 1992, pp. 127–9.
26 Discussed in Chapter 4, on trade, exchange rates, and the balance of payments.
27 See, for a discussion of these issues, R. Portes, 'EMS and EMU After the Fall', 16 *World Economy*, January 1993, pp. 1–15. See also, for a background to some of the tensions among EC Member Countries with respect to macroeconomic policy, L. Pauly, 'The Politics of European Monetary Union: National Strategies, International Implications' (1992) 27 *International Journal* 93.
28 See A. Hartley, 'Europe's New Populism', *National Interest*, Winter 1992/93, pp. 37–40.
29 On the seriousness of the immigration issue, see Hartley, *ibid.*, pp. 39–40.

3 Dispute settlement

1 See J.H. Jackson and W.J. Davey, *Legal Problems of International Economic Relations* (St. Paul: West Publications, 1986) pp. 294–5; see also United States, International Trade Commission, *Review of the Effectiveness of Trade Dispute Settlement under the GATT and the Tokyo Round Agreements* (Washington DC: USITC, 1985) p. 2 [hereinafter *ITC Report*].
2 R.E. Hudec, *The GATT Legal System and World Trade Diplomacy* (Salem NH: Butterworths, 1990) p. 68 and *ITC Report, op. cit.*, p. 11; Hudec, *Enforcing International Trade Law: The Evolution of the Modern GATT Legal System* (Salem NH: Butterworths, 1993).
3 *ITC Report, op. cit.*, p. 8.

4 See Hudec (1990) *op. cit.*, p. 77. See also *ITC Report, op. cit.*, p. 11. The Netherlands complained that Cuba's consular taxes were a violation of Article I (MFN). The matter was referred to the Chairman, who ruled against Cuba which complied with the finding a few months later.

5 *ITC Report, op. cit.*, p. 13.
It should be noted that in recent years the E.C.J. has veered towards a more deferential approach, distinguishing between product regulations and 'selling arrangements' – the latter will not be found in violation of Art. 30 to the extent that they are not explicitly discriminatory. See Heck and xxxxx [1993] ECRI–6097.

6 *ITC Report, op. cit.*, p. 14.

7 The *ITC Report, op. cit.*, p. 47 states that between 1975 and 1985 85% of the disputes dealt with by the Contracting Parties went to panels and 15% went to working groups.

8 *ITC Report, op. cit.*, pp. 15–17. The panel procedures adopted during the Seventh Session are basically the same as those used by panels today, although it was not until the Ninth Session that the practice began of appointing panel members in their individual capacity rather than as representatives of their countries. It should be noted that the use of working Parties continued at the Seventh Session. Working Parties continue to be used from time to time.

9 *ITC Report, op. cit.*, p. 17.

10 Rosine Plank, 'An Unofficial Description of How a GATT Panel Works and Does Not' (1987) 4:4 *J. of Int'l. Arbitration* 53, p. 55.

11 *ITC Report, op. cit.*, p. 20, and J.H. Bello and A.F. Holmer, 'Settling Disputes in the GATT: the Past, Present, and Future' (1990) 24 *The Int'l Lawyer* 519, p. 521.

12 See the *ITC Report, op. cit.*, p. 20; Robert Hudec, Daniel Kennedy and Mark Sgarbossa, 'A Statistical Profile of GATT Dispute Settlement Cases; 1948–1989' (1993) 2 *Minnesota Journal of Global Trade* 1, p. 18; Hudec (1993) *op. cit.*

13 Perhaps there are cultural reasons for this aversion to legalism – the Japanese have been conspicuous in their absence from participation in GATT dispute resolution processes, at least as complainants. This reluctance to resort to the GATT is often ascribed to Japanese aversion to confrontation. EC trade officials, as well, are fond of explaining EC–USA clashes over the meaning of dispute resolution as reflecting differences in legal culture. The Europeans are said not to share the American fascination with the vindication of rights through legal processes.

14 The ITC cites the textile agreement of 1962, and the steel export restraints of 1968 as examples. See the *ITC Report, op. cit.*, p. 20.

15 *ITC Report, op. cit.*, p. 23. The *ITC Report* attributes the aggression to American concerns about declining influence within the GATT, and Congressional concerns about declining exports and growing imports.

16 The 'codification' is the *Understanding Regarding Notification, Consultation, Dispute Settlement, and Surveillance*, GATT BISD (1979), 26th Supp., p. 210 [hereinafter *1979 Understanding*].

17 *ITC Report, op. cit.*, p. 29. Because of the overall similarity between the Tokyo Codes' dispute resolution mechanisms and the general GATT mechanism, this chapter will make no special attempt to describe ways in which the mechanisms do differ. In any case, few countries have resorted to dispute resolution under the Code mechanisms. Jackson counts only nine disputes between 1979 and 1988 where resort was had to the Code provisions (see J.H. Jackson, *Restructuring the GATT* (London: Pinter, 1990) p. 66; and *ITC Report, op. cit.*, p. 55. Descriptions of the Code provisions on dispute resolution can be found in J.H. Jackson, *The World Trading System* (Cambridge MA: MIT Press, 1997, 2nd ed.) chap. 4; and in the *ITC Report*, pp. 33–4.

18 Jackson, *World Trading System, op. cit.*, p. 116. Jackson blames the EC for blocking US efforts in this direction.

19 R.E. Hudec (1980) 13 *Cornell International Law Journal* 145, reprinted in R. Howse (ed.) *The World Trading System: Critical Perspectives on the World Economy*, vol. II (London and New York: Routledge, 1998), p.125.

20 *Uruguay Round Understanding on Rules and Procedures Governing the Settlement of Disputes*, December 1993 [hereinafter *Uruguay Round Understanding*].

21 Of course, cheating is attractive not because it will maximize short-term aggregate domestic welfare in the cheating state, but because the government may be able to make political gains from the rents that flow to a pro-protection constituency within the state. See the discussion of the political economy of free trade and protection in Ch. 2.

22 G.R. Shell, 'Trade Legalism and International Relations Theory: An Analysis of the World Trade Organization' (1995) *Duke Law Journal* 829, reprinted in R. Howse (ed.) *op. cit.*, pp. 333–416.

23 This follows from the analysis in Ch. I, which indicates how *domestic welfare* can always be increased by unilateral, and even more so, by reciprocal trade liberalization, because the interests of those constituencies that 'lose' from liberalization can always be vindicated through alternative policies that are less welfare-reducing than trade restrictions. In new areas, like intellectual property rights, however, where trade liberalization is linked with prescription or constraint of domestic policy outcomes that may in itself be domestic (or even global) welfare reducing, each individual state's commitment to a liberal cooperative equilibrium will depend on the perception of the balance between gains from trade and possible welfare losses from being required to adopt less than optimal domestic regulatory outcomes. This is developed at length in Chapter 12 in this book on TRIPs.

24 Shell, in Howse (ed.) *op. cit.*, p. 372.

25 Of course, dispute rulings always did indirectly affect domestic distributive outcomes, but did not entail constraint of (non-discriminatory) domestic policy instruments. Governments were left free to adopt any non-protectionist policy response of their choice, and as noted could always in principle find a less welfare-reducing instrument than trade restrictions to vindicate the interests of negatively affected constituencies.

26 Shell, in Howse (ed.) *op. cit.*, p. 372.

27 An interesting insight into the hesitant course of progress can be culled from the diplomatic language introducing each of the *1979 Understanding*, *op. cit.*, and the 1989 *Dispute Settlement Procedures Improvements*, BISD 36S/61 (1990).

28 *ITC Report, op. cit.*, pp. 69 and 79.

29 The following figures are taken from the *ITC Report, op. cit.*, pp. 50–64, supplemented by Jackson, *The World Trading System, op. cit.*, p. 120. The ITC study examines 84 cases referred by the Contracting Parties to working Parties or panels under Article XXIII:2 or the MTN Codes. Cases settled by consultation are not included because of a paucity of data. The ITC estimates that a much larger number of cases never reach the panel stage; consultations are enough to settle the dispute or the case is simply dropped.

30 The 'DISC' case; see *ITC Report, op. cit.*, Appendix I.

31 Hudec, Kennedy and Sgarbossa, *op. cit.*; Hudec (1993) *op. cit.*

32 R. Plank, 'An Unofficial Description of how a GATT Panel Works and Does Not' (1987) 4 *International Journal of Arbitration* 53, reprinted in Howse (ed.) *op. cit.*, pp. 60–105.

33 *Ibid.*

34 *United States–Restrictions on Imports of Cotton and Man-made Fibre Underwear*, Report of the Appellate Body, WT/DS24/AB/R (10 February 1997).

35 *United States–Imposition of Import Duties on Automobiles from Japan Under Sections 301 and 304 of the Trade Act of 1974*, Request for Consultations by Japan, WT/DS6/1 (22 May 1995).

36 *European Communities–Regime for the Importation, Sale and Distribution of Bananas*, Report of the Appellate Body, WT/DS27/AB/R (9 September 1997), para. 133 [hereinafter in this chapter, *Bananas*].

37 *Brazil–Measures Affecting Desiccated Coconut*, Report of the Appellate Body, WT/DS22/AB/R (21 February 1997).

38 *India–Patent Protection for Pharmaceutical and Agricultural Chemical Products*, Report of the Appellate Body, WT/DS50/AB/R (19 December 1997), para. 92.

39 *EC Measures Concerning Meat and Meat Products*, Report of the Appellate Body, WT/DS26 and 48/AB/R (16 January 1988), para. 156 [hereinafter in this chapter, *Hormones*].

40 *United States–Measures Affecting Imports of Woven Wool Shirts and Blouses from India*, Report of the Appellate Body, WT/DS33/AB/R (23 May 1997), [hereinafter in this chapter, *Shirts and Blouses*].
41 *United States–Standards for Reformulated and Conventional Gasoline*, Report of the Panel, WT/DS2/R (29 January 1996), paras. 1.1–1.5.
42 'Confidential Findings Section of WTO Panel Report on Shrimp-Turtle Case', *Inside U.S. Trade*, March 1998, paras. 7.7–7.8.
United States – Import Prohibition of certain Shrimp and Shrimp Products, Report of the Panel, WT/DS 58/R, 15 May 1998. Upon appeal the AB held that the panel erred in finding that it was *prohibited* from recovering non-requested briefs, from non-governmental persons, while emphasizing that the panel has wide discretion as to what weight to give to such material. *United States – Imports Prohibition of Certain Shrimp and Shrimp Products*. Report of the Appellate Body, WT/DS 58/AB/R, 12 October 1998 [hereinafter *Turtles*].
43 E.-U. Petersmann, 'How to Promote the International Rule of Law? Contributions by the World Trade Organization Appellate Review System' (1998) 1 *Journal of International Economic Law* 25.
44 D. Palmeter and P.C. Mavroidis, 'The WTO Legal System: Sources of Law', July 1998, 92 *American Journal of International Law*, p. 4. The following discussion owes much to this seminal article.
45 *Japan–Taxes on Alcoholic Beverages*, Report of the Appellate Body, WT/DS8, 10–11/AB./R (4 October 1996), AB-1996-2.
46 23 May 1969, 1155 *U.N.T.S.* 331, 8 *International Legal Materials* 679 [hereinafter in this chapter, *Vienna Convention*].
47 Indeed, one could argue that the expression 'customary rules of interpretation in public international law' would be superfluous if it only referred to rules that now constitute customary law in themselves – since these rules are binding by virtue of their status as custom.
48 *United States–Restrictions on Imports of Tuna*, Report of the Panel, *S29/R* (16 June 1994), para. 5.19.
49 Palmeter and Mavroidis, *op. cit.*, p. 34.
50 *Rules of Conduct for the Understanding on Rules and Procedures Governing the Settlement of Disputes*, WT/DSB/RC/1 (11 December 1996).
51 WT/L/160/Rev. 1 (26 July 1996).
52 'TRANSPARENCY AND DERESTRICTION: Communication from the United States', WT/GC/W/77 (9 February 1998).
53 E.-U. Petersmann, 'The Dispute Settlement System of the World Trade Organization and the Evolution of the GATT Dispute Settlement System Since 1948' (1994) 31 *Common Market Law Review* 1157, reprinted in Howse (ed.) *op. cit.*, pp. 278–80.
54 WT/AB/WP/3 (28 February 1997).
55 E.-U. Petersmann, 'How to Promote the International Rule of Law? Contributions by the World Trade Organization Appellate Review System', *op. cit.*, p. 39.
56 See the discussion of the NAFTA *Agricultural Tariffication* panel in chapter 10 on agriculture.
57 *EEC–Oilseeds*, BISD 37S/86, para. 144. This statement was cited and applied by the *Kodak* panel, discussed in Chapter 17 on trade and competition.
58 In particular, the FTA is very explicit about setting out detailed schedules for the panel review process.
59 Canada, Department of External Affairs, *The Canada–US Free Trade Agreement* (Ottawa: Minister of Supply and Services, 1988) at Article 1801:1 [hereinafter *FTA*]. Article 1801:2 provides that trade disputes between the two countries can be resolved *via* either the FTA or the GATT if both Agreements are applicable; but these avenues of redress are mutually exclusive according to Article 1801:3.
60 *FTA*, Article 1802:1.

61 *FTA*, Article 1803.
62 *FTA*, Article 1804.
63 *FTA*, Article 1805:1. Article 1805:2 permits the Commission to consult whatever technical advisers it deems necessary, and it allows for the use of mutually acceptable mediators to assist in resolving disputes.
64 If the matter involves an action taken under Chapter II.
65 *FTA*, Article 1806:1.
66 *FTA*, Article 1807:2.
67 *FTA*, Article 1807:1.
68 *FTA*, Article 1807:4. GATT panels are not restricted to the Parties' submissions in reaching their 'verdicts'; their procedures can be much more inquisitorial.
69 *FTA*, Article 1807:8.
70 *FTA*, Article 1807:8.
71 *FTA*, Articles 1806:3 and 1807:9. Article 1807:9 requires the Party suspending benefits to consider that its fundamental rights or benefits under the Agreement are or would be impaired by the measure or proposed measure. There is no such stipulation in 1806:3. Article 1807:9 also provides for the termination of such suspension when the offending measure is removed. Again, 1806:3 has no comparable provision.
72 See Canada, Department of External Affairs, *Canadian Trade Negotiations* (Ottawa: Supply and Services Canada, 1986).
73 In order for countervailing duties to be applied there must be a finding that a subsidy in the relevant legal sense exists as well as material injury. In order for antidumping duties to be applied, there must be a finding of dumping (usually selling at a lower cost in the importing country market than the exporting country market, or selling below cost) as well as of material injury. The ITA determines the existence of subsidies in the countervail cases and of dumping in antidumping cases, while the ITC makes determinations of injury in both kinds of cases. A similar bifurcation of function exists in Canada as between Minister of National Revenue and the Canadian International Trade Tribunal.
74 This is obviously only a brief summary of the procedure
75 A good, brief discussion of the standard of review is to be found in C.M. Gastle and J.-G. Castel, 'Should the North American Free Trade Agreement Dispute Settlement Mechanism in Anti-Dumping and Countervailing Duty Cases be Reformed in Light of *Softwood Lumber III*?' (1995) 26 *Law and Policy in International Business* 821.
76 M.J. Trebilcock and T.M. Boddez, *Unfinished Business: Reforming Trade Remedy Laws in North America* (Toronto: C.D. Howe Institute, 1993) p. 153.
77 See, for example, G.N. Horlick and F.A. DeBusk, 'The Functioning of FTA Dispute Resolution Panels' in L. Waverman (ed.) *Negotiating and Implementing a North American Free Trade Agreement* (Vancouver: Fraser Institute, 1992).
78 J.M. Mercury, 'Chapter 19 of the United States–Canada Free Trade Agreement 1989–1995: A Check on Administered Protection' (1995) 15 *Northwestern Journal of International Law & Business* 525.
79 *Ibid.*, p. 529.
80 M.P. Ryan, 'Court of International Trade Judges, Binational Panellists, and Judicial Review of U.S. Antidumping and Countervailing Duty Policies' (1996) 30 *Journal of World Trade* 103, p. 119.
81 Nevertheless, in the more routine cases there is clearly a substantiated savings of time over the CIT. See W.J. Davey, *Pine and Swine* (Ottawa: Carleton University Centre for Trade Policy and Law, 1996) p. 297.
82 See Gastle and Castel, *op. cit.*, pp. 837–46.
83 *National Corn Growers Ass'n.* v. *Canada (Import Tribunal)* [1990] 2 S.C.R. 1320; *Bell Canada* v. *Canada* (C.R.T.C.) [1989] 1 S.C.R. 1722.

84 *North American Free Trade Agreement*, Annex 1904.13.
85 NAFTA Implementation Act, H.R. Rep. No. 361, 103d Cong., 1st Sess. 75–76 (1993), as quoted in Gastle and Castel, *op. cit.*, p. 838.
86 As Davey notes, 'The principal explanation for the favourable reviews of the panel process, and, in particular, the high quality of the panel opinions, is that the panels were composed largely of active international trade law experts. While it may be helpful to expand the use of non trade law practitioners, it would likely be a mistake to severely curtail the use of trade law practitioners as panellists.' *Pine and Swine*, *op. cit.*, p. 279.
87 *In re Certain Softwood Lumber Products from Canada*, No. ECC-94-1904-01USA, 1994 FTAPD LEXIS 11 (Binational Review) (3 August 1994), 177–8.
88 See Gastle and Castel, *op. cit.*, pp. 878–81.
89 Davey, *Pine and Swine*, *op. cit.*

4 Trade, exchange rates, and the balance of payments

1 See R. Gilpin, *The Political Economy of International Relations* (Princeton NJ: Princeton University Press, 1987) p. 121.
2 This is an extremely simplified presentation of the understanding in contemporary finance theory of equilibrium exchange rates. For a clear elaboration of the complexities, see C. Fred Bergsten and John Williamson, 'Exchange Rates and Trade Policy', in C. Fred Bergsten and William R. Cline (eds) *Trade Policy in the 1980s* (Washington DC: Institute for International Economics, 1983).
3 J.E. Spero, *The Politics of International Economic Relations* (New York: St. Martin's Press, 1990) pp. 33–4.
4 These arrangements are usefully summarized in S. Fischer, 'International Macroeconomic Policy Coordination', in M. Feldstein (ed.) *International Economic Cooperation* (Chicago: University of Chicago Press, 1988) pp. 25–7. See also, R. Solomon, *The International Monetary System, 1945–1981* (New York: Harper & Row, 1982) and P.B. Kenen, *The International Economy* 3rd ed. (Cambridge: Cambridge University Press, 1994) ch. 19, 'Evolution of the Monetary System'.
5 P. Volcker, *Changing Fortunes: The World's Money and the Threat to American Leadership* (New York: Times Books, 1992) p. 20.
6 For a helpful discussion of the evolution of the international monetary system during this period, see J.C. Pool, *International Economic Policy* (New York: Lexington, 1989) pp. 4–22.
7 Fischer, *op. cit.*, p. 15.
8 Kenen, *op. cit.*, p. 3.
9 V. Riches, 'Quarante-cinq ans de commerce mondial; régionalisation ou globalisation?', in J. Doyère and S. Marti (eds) *Bilan économique et social 1993* (Paris: Le Monde Dossiers et Documents, 1994) p. 45.
10 See, particularly, S. Strange, *Casino Capitalism* (Oxford: Basil Blackwell, 1984) ch. 1.
11 Pool, *op. cit.*, pp. 17–18.
12 See W.J. McKibbin and J.D. Sachs, *Global Linkages: Macroeconomic Interdependence and Cooperation in the World Economy* (Washington DC: Brookings Institution, 1991).
13 For instances of their use, see R. Roessler, 'Selective Balance-of-Payments Adjustment Measures Affecting Trade: The Roles of the GATT and the IMF' (1975) 9 *J. of World Trade Law* 238.
14 See, for example, *United Kingdom Temporary Import Charges: Report of the Working Party adopted on 17 November 1966*, L/2675, BISD 15th Supp. (1967) p. 113.
15 BISD, 26th Supp. (1980) p. 205.
16 E.-U. Petersmann, 'Trade Restrictions for Balance-of-Payments Purposes and the GATT Strengthening of the Soft International Law of Balance-of-Payments Adjustment Measures', in D.C. Dicke (ed.) *Foreign Debts in the Present and a New International Economic Order* (Fribourg: University Press, 1986).

17 On the LDC debt crisis and its general impact on trade, see Chapter 14.
18 *Republic of Korea – Restrictions on Imports of Beef – Complaint of the United States*, BISD, 36th Supp., p. 268.
19 'WTO Committee on Balance-of-Payments Restrictions', WT/L/45, 23 February 1995.
20 The following summary is based on *Report (1995) of The Committee on Balance-of-Payments Restrictions*, WT/BOP/R/10 (4 December 1995); *Report (1996) of the Committee on Balance-of-Payments Restrictions*, WT/BOP/R/19 (5 November 1996); *Report (1997) of the Committee on Balance-of-Payments Restrictions*, WT/BOP/R/37 (12 November 1997).
21 See, for an excellent account of exchange controls and restrictions in OECD countries from the post-war period to the present, OECD (Centre for Co-operation with the European Economies in Transition) *Exchange Control Policy* (Paris: OECD, 1993) Part I, 'Experience of OECD Countries with Exchange Controls'.
22 See J. Gold, 'Convertibility', in *Legal and Institutional Aspects of the International Monetary System: Selected Essays*, vol. II (Washington DC: International Monetary Fund, 1984).
23 GATT doc. L/88, 1 May 1953.
24 Roessler, *op. cit.*, p. 39.
25 *Ibid.*
26 See *Liberalization of Capital Movements and Financial Services in the OECD Area* (Paris: OECD, 1990).
27 See Bergsten and Williamson, *op. cit.*, note 2.
28 See Strange, *op. cit.*, note 10; see also Gilpin, *op. cit.*, note 1.
29 Spero, *op. cit.*, note 3, p. 50.
30 This is the position of Deborah Coyne. See D. Coyne, 'Canada in an Interdependent World', unpublished manuscript, Toronto, Ont., 1992, ch. 3.
31 Marston, surveying the empirical evidence available as of 1988, suggests 'despite strong evidence that exchange rate volatility is much greater under flexible than under fixed rates, it has been difficult to establish statistically that this increase in volatility has seriously affected international trade'. R.C. Marston, 'Exchange Rate Policy Reconsidered', in M. Feldstein (ed.) *International Economic Cooperation* (Chicago: University of Chicago Press, 1988) p. 87.
32 Coyne, *op. cit.*, advocates such a tax, as does J. Tobin, 'A Proposal for International Monetary Reform', in *Essays in Economics* (Cambridge MA: MIT Press, 1982).
33 As is suggested by R. Cooper, 'What Future for the International Monetary System?', in *International Financial Policy: Essays in Honour of Jacques Polak*, J. Frankel and M. Goldstein (eds) (Washington DC: IMF 1991) pp. 140–1.
34 See J. Williamson and M.H. Miller, *Targets and Indicators; A Blueprint for the International Coordination of Economic Policy*, Policy Analysis in International Economics No. 22 (Washington DC: Institute for International Economics, 1983). A succinct discussion and critique of the technical aspects of Williamson's proposal can be found in Kenen, *The International Economy*, *op. cit.*, pp. 557–8.
35 In Williamson's proposal, the commitment to intervene once a target zone was exceeded would not be absolute or unconditional. Instead, movement of a currency outside the zone would signal the possibility of intervention.
36 Cooper, *op. cit.*, note 31, p. 142.
37 See, generally, B. DeLong, C. DeLong and S. Robinson, 'The Mexican Peso Crisis: In Defense of U.S. Policy Toward Mexico', *Foreign Affairs*, March 1996.
38 By capital, Bhagwati means flows of portfolio equity and debt investment; he would obviously recognize that free trade in goods and services itself demands liberalization of the current account transactions required to sustain this trade.
39 J. Bhagwati, 'The Capital Myth', *Foreign Affairs*, May/June 1998.
40 'The IMF's Response to the Asian Crisis', International Monetary Fund, April 1998, p. 1.
41 R. Haas and R. Litan, 'Globalization and its Discontents', *Foreign Affairs*, May/June 1998, p. 5.

42 Our discussion of the breakdown of the EMS in September 1992 owes much to R. Portes, 'EMS and EMU After the Fall', 16 *World Economy*, January 1993, pp. 2–15, as well as to coverage of these events throughout the Fall of 1992 and Winter of 1992/3 in *The Economist* magazine.

43 This brief and simplified account owes much to the following more detailed discussions of the EMS crisis: Kenen, *op. cit.*, pp. 546–67; M. Kaelberer, 'Money and Power in Europe: The Political Economy of European Monetary Cooperation', paper presented at the Annual Meeting of the American Political Science Association, 2–5 September 1993, Washington DC; Portes, *op. cit.*

44 Here it should be recalled that when capital flows into a country, that country's currency is purchased and the currency in which the capital was originally held is sold, placing downward pressure on the latter. However, when, say, German imports increase and exports decrease, there is the opposite effect on other currencies – since relatively more Deutschmarks are sold for other currencies (i.e. to purchase imports from abroad) than are bought by foreigners to pay for German exports, other currencies rise in value as against the Deutschmark.

45 Kaelberer, *op. cit.*, p. 24.

46 Kenen, *op. cit.*, p. 553.

47 IMF, *World Economic Outlook*, April 1998, 'Appendix: Countdown to EMU: Progress Toward Convergence and Challenges Remaining'.

48 C. Whitney, '11 Countries Move Ahead With Changeover to Euro', *The New York Times*, 3 May, 1998, 1/17.

49 'Fanfare for the euro', *The Economist*, 2 May 1998, p. 45.

50 See Timothy Garton Ash, 'Europe, Unified Against Itself', *New York Times*, 3 May, 1998, 4/17.

5 Tariffs, the MFN principle, and regional trading blocs

1 Roy J. Ruffin and Paul R. Gregory, *Principles of Economics* (Glenview IL: Scott Foresman and Company, 1983) pp. 350–1.

2 See J.M. Finger, 'Trade Liberalization: A Public Choice Perspective', in R. Amacher, G. Haberler and T. Willett (eds) *Challenges to a Liberal International Order* (Washington DC: American Institute Enterprise, 1979); see also Richard Snyder, *The Most Favoured Nation Clause* (New York: Columbia University Press, 1948); Warren Schwartz and Alan Sykes, 'Towards a Positive Theory of the Most Favoured Nation Obligation and its Exceptions in the WTO/GATT System' (1996) 16 *International Review of Law and Economics* 27.

3 Schwartz and Sykes, *op. cit.*

4 Finger, *op. cit.*

5 We explore these issues more fully in Chapter 14.

6 Samuel Laird and Alexander Yeats, 'Tariff Cutting Formulas – and Complications', in J.M. Finger and Andruzej Olechavski (eds) *The Uruguay Round: a Handbook on Multilateral Trade Negotiations* (Washington DC: The World Bank, 1987) p. 89.

7 For an excellent review of the Uruguay Round tariff negotiations and outcomes, see Maarten Smeets, 'Tariff Issues in the Uruguay Round' (1995) 29 *J. of World Trade* 91, from which the following highlights are taken.

8 Quoted by J. Quinn and T. Slayton, 'The GATT and the Deep Structure of Customs Administration', in Quinn and Slayton (eds) *Non-Tariff Barriers After the Tokyo Round* (Montreal: Institute for Research on Public Policy, 1982) p. 237.

9 For a detailed description of current and past valuation systems see M. Irish, *Customs Valuation in Canada* (Montreal: CCH, 1985).

10 J.H. Jackson, *The World Trading System* (Cambridge MA: MIT Press, 1997, 2nd ed.) p. 151.

11 Canadian Tariff Board, *The GATT Agreement on Customs Valuation*, Part One: Proposed Amendments to the Customs Act (1981) p. 6.

12 Jackson, *op. cit.*, p. 152.
13 BISD, 26 Supp. 116 (1980).
14 M. Stark, 'Valuation Principles: Canadian Customs Duties and Sales Tax' (1988) 36 *Canadian Tax J.* 1261, p. 1262.
15 Agreement on Implementation of Article VII of the GATT, 15 December 1993.
16 Article VII:2 (a).
17 Under the BDV, value was based on a notional concept of valuation, that is, a price at which goods *ought* to be sold under a specified set of circumstances. Because it was not based on any real price it did not achieve a truly uniform valuation standard (G. Winham, *International Trade and the Tokyo Round Negotiations*, Princeton NJ: Princeton University Press, 1986) p. 179.
18 55 UNTS 308 (1947).
19 R.E. Smith, *Customs Valuation in the United States: A Study in Tariff Administration* (Chicago: University of Chicago Press, 1948) p. 141. The ASP provided for the assessment of duty based on the value of 'like or similar goods' produced domestically. This made it possible for domestic producers to inflate their prices and thereby relieve import pressure on a wide range of functionally related products (Winham, *op. cit.*, pp. 67–8). The ASP was only applied to a few imports but its impact on those exporters was substantial. According to W.M. Snyder 'the ASP . . . led to protection equal to more than a 100% rate of duty' ('Customs Valuation in the European Economic Community' (1981) 11 Georgia. *J. of International Company Law* 79 p. 83).
20 Winham, *op. cit.*, pp. 180–1.
21 Two aspects of the Canadian system were considered inconsistent with these GATT rules: value was based on 'fair market value' in the country of export; and value could be established by ministerial prescription when fair market value could not be determined. These rules directly conflict with the GATT Article VII which states: 'value for customs purposes . . . should not be based on the value of merchandise of national origin or on arbitrary or fictitious values'. See G.E. Salembier, A.R. Moroz and F. Stone, *The Canadian Import File: Trade, Protection and Adjustment* (Montreal: The Institute for Research on Public Policy, 1987) ch. 5, 103 pp. 111–12 [hereinafter *Canadian Import File*].
22 An attempt was made during the Kennedy Round to abolish the ASP and adopt more uniform standards but the US Congress refused to ratify the agreement.
23 There were many difficulties with the BDV. Even in countries that applied the system in a non-protectionist manner there were large variations in the value assigned to a particular good (Winham, *op. cit.*, p. 179).
24 Twenty-eight countries (including the EC as one) have accepted the code, including five developing countries. Developing countries were of the view that the Code would make unreasonable demands on their administration systems. As a result, a Protocol was added making allowances for special treatment of developing countries (GATT BISD, 26 Supp. 151 (1980)). There are also quite extensive interpretive notes with the Code making it more precise than other GATT codes.
25 The effective date of the EC legislation was 1 July 1980 and the legislation is in the Council Regulation 1224/80 of 28 May 1980, 23 *O.J. Eur. Comm.* (no. L134) 1 (1980); the USA implemented the Code on 1 July 1980, the current legislation is the Trade Agreements Act of 1979, Pub.L. 96–39, 93 U.S. Statutes at Large 144 – 19 USC s. 1401a; in Canada the Code became law on 1 January 1985 and is found in Part III (ss 44–53) of the Customs Act, SC 1986, ch. 1.
26 For detailed descriptions of the provisions of the Tokyo Round Code see: S.L. Sherman and H. Glashoff, *Customs Valuation: Commentary on the GATT Customs Valuation Code* (Deventer: Kluwer, 1988) and D.A. Wyslobicky and J.H. Warnock, 'Customs Valuation: Overview and Problem Areas in Determining Transaction Value', in *Customs and Trade Law Development* (Toronto: Canadian Institute of International Affairs, 1989).
27 Article 1.1(a) of the Uruguay Round Customs Valuation Agreement.

28 Article 1.2. 'Related persons' are defined in Article 15.4.
29 The order of the last two methods may be reversed by the importing country.
30 The last proscription is aimed primarily at the ASP (Snyder, *op. cit.*, note 19, p. 82). The Canadian legislation does not prohibit any methods of valuation.
31 Jackson cites the example of the 1904 Swiss–German Treaty reducing German Tariffs on the imports of '. . . large dapple mountain cattle or brown cattle reared at a spot at least 300 meters above sea level and having at least one month's grazing each year at a spot at least 800 meters above sea level . . .' (footnote omitted) (*op. cit.*, p. 127).
32 *Canadian Import File*, *op. cit.*, p. 115.
33 The system became law in Canada on 1 January 1988 and in the USA in September of that year. In addition to Canada and the USA, there are over 50 signatories to the System including the EC and Japan. In addition, nearly 30 other countries use the system but have not signed the convention. See Maureen Irish, *The Harmonized System and Tariff Classification in Canada* (D.C.L. thesis, McGill Law School, 1992).
34 The details of the system are drawn from T. Lindsay, *Outline of Customs in Canada*, 8th ed. (Calgary: Erin, 1991) [unpublished].
35 *Canadian Import File*, *op. cit.*, p. 114.
36 The seventh and eighth are a tariff classification, and the ninth and tenth are statistical.
37 This provision applies to all rules of origin used in non-preferential commercial policy instruments including application of: MFN treatment, antidumping and countervailing duties, safeguard measures, origin marking requirements and any discriminatory quantitative restrictions.
38 A Technical Committee was established to develop a definition of this and other terms.
39 See Jon Johnson, 'What Is a North American Good? The NAFTA Rules of Origin' (C.D. Howe Institute Commentary (Toronto: 1993).
40 Kenneth Dam, *The GATT: Law and International Economic Organization* (Chicago: University of Chicago Press, 1970) p. 183.
41 Dam, *op. cit.*, p. 181. A recent example of such a fee is discussed by P.G. Justice in 'Customs User Fee: A Survey of Recent Developments' (1987) 17 Georgia. *J. of International and Company Law* 507.
42 See R. Lawrence and R. Litan, 'The World Trading System After the Uruguay Round' (1990) 8 *Boston University International Law Journal* 247.
43 See e.g. Jagdish Bhagwati, *Protectionism* (Cambridge MA: MIT Press, 1988); Jackson, *op. cit.*
44 See e.g. R.O. Keohane, *After Hegemony* (New York: Princeton Press, 1985); R. Axelrod and R. Keohane, 'Achieving Co-operation Under Anarchy', in K. Oye (ed.) *Co-operation Under Anarchy* (Princeton NJ: Princeton University Press, 1985); I. Ikenbarry, 'The State and Strategies of International Adjustment' (1986) 39 *World Politics* 53; C. Lipson, 'International Co-operation in Economic and Security Affairs' (1984) 37 *World Politics* 1.
45 Axelrod and Keohane, *op. cit.*; Alan O. Sykes, 'Mandating Retaliation for Breach of Trade Agreements: Some Thoughts on Strategic Design of Section 301' (1980) 8 *Boston University International Law Journal* 301; Michael J. Trebilcock, Marsha A. Chandler and Robert Howse *Trade and Transitions* (London: Routledge, 1990) pp. 211–23.
46 Kenichi Ohmae, *The Borderless World: Power and Strategy in the International Economy* (New York: Harper Business, 1990).
47 Peter Drucker, *Frontiers of Management* (New York: Harper & Row, 1987) p. 65.
48 See Peter J. Lloyd, *Regionalization and World Trade* (OECD Economic Studies no. 18, Spring 1992); Jagdish Bhagwati 'Regionalism versus Multilateralism', *World Economy*, September 1992.
49 See Andrew Faye, 'APEC and the New Regionalism' (1996) 28 *Law and Policy in International Business* 175.
50 See Richard Bernal, 'Regional Trade Agreements and the Establishment of a Free Trade Area of the Americas' (1996) 27 *Law and Policy in International Business* 945.
51 See Horst Siebert, Rolf Langhammer and Daniel Piazolo, 'The Transatlantic Free

Trade Area: Fuelling Trade Discrimination or Global Liberalization?' (1996) 30 *J. of World Trade* 45.

52 See e.g. Dam, *op. cit.* ch. 16; Anne O. Krueger, 'Free Trade is the Best Policy' in Robert Lawrence and Charles Schultze (eds) *An American Trade Strategy: Options for the 1990s* (Washington DC: Brookings Institution, 1990); Jeffrey J. Schott, *More Free Trade Areas?* (Washington DC: Institute for International Economics, 1989); Michael Aho and Sylvia Ostry, 'Regional Trading Blocks: Pragmatic or Problematic Policy', in William Brock and Robert K. Hormats (eds) *The Global Economy: America's Role in the Decade Ahead* (New York: American Assembly, 1990); Andrew Stoeckel, David Pearce and Gary Banks, *Western Trade Blocks: Game, Set or Match for Asia Pacific and the World Economy?* (Centre for International Economics, Canberra, Australia, 1990) p. 7.

53 Jacob Viner, *The Customs Union Issue* (New York: Carnegie Endowment for International Peace, 1950).

54 See e.g. Rudiger Dornbusch, 'Policy Options for Free Trade: The Case for Bilateralism', in Lawrence and Schultze (eds) *op. cit.*

55 Lawrence and Litan, *op. cit.*

56 See Paul Krugman, 'Regional Blocs: The Good, The Bad and The Ugly' (1991) *International Economy* (Nov.–Dec.) 54.

57 For a generally positive recent view of regional trading arrangements as complementary to the multilateral system, see World Trade Organization, *Regionalism and the World Trading System* (Geneva: 1995).

58 Stoeckel *et al.*, *op. cit.*, p. 7.

59 *Ibid.*, p. xi.

60 *Ibid.*, p. 39.

61 *Ibid.*, p. 18.

62 Jagdish Bhagwati, 'Fast Track to Nowhere', *The Economist*, 18 October, 1997, 21–23.

63 Bernal, *op. cit.*, p. 949.

64 See Stephen D. Krasner, 'State Power and the Structure of International Trade', in R. Art and R. Jervis (eds) *International Politics: Anarchy, Force, Political Economy* and *Decision-Making* (Boston: Little, Brown, 1985).

65 Paul Wonnacott and Mark Lutz, 'Is There A Case for More Free Trade Areas?', in Jeffrey J. Schott (ed.) *Free Trade Areas and U.S. Trade Policy* (Washington DC: Institute for International Economics, 1989).

66 Bhagwati, *op. cit.*

67 See Sylvia Ostry, *Governments and Corporations in a Shrinking World* (New York: Council on Foreign Relations, 1990) ch. 2.

68 See e.g. Schott, *op. cit.*, p. 25.

69 See R.J. Wonnacott, 'U.S. Hub-and-Spoke Bilaterals and the Multilateral Trading System' (C.D. Howe Institute Commentary, no. 23, October, 1990, Toronto).

6 Trade policy and domestic health and safety standards

1 Jagdish N. Bhagwati and Robert E. Hudec (eds), *Fair Trade and Harmonization: Prerequisites for Free Trade?, Volume 2: Legal Analysis* (Cambridge MA: MIT Press, 1996).

2 Alan M. Rugman, John Kirton and Julie A. Soloway, 'NAFTA, Environmental Regulations and Canadian Competitiveness' (1997) 31 *Journal of World Trade* 4.

3 Miles Kahler, 'Trade and Domestic Differences' in Suzanne Berger and Ronald Dore (eds) *National Diversity and Global Capitalism* (New York: Cornell University, 1996) p. 299.

4 See Sylvia Ostry, 'Beyond the Border: The New International Policy Arena', in E. Kantzenbach, H. Sharrer and L. Waverman (eds) *Competition Policy in an Interdependent World Economy* (Baden-Baden: Nomos, 1993) p. 261.

5 David Vogel, *Trading Up: Consumer and Environmental Regulation in a Global Economy* (Cambridge MA: Harvard University Press, 1995) p. 3.

6 See Vogel, *op. cit.*; Kym Anderson, 'Environmental Standards and International Trade',

in Michael Bruno and Bruno Pleskovic (eds) *Annual World Bank Conference on Development Economics 1996* (Washington DC: World Bank 1997) p. 317; see also Chapter 13 of this book.

7 See Chapter 1.

8 Robert M. Millimet, 'The Impact of the Uruguay Round and the New Agreement on Sanitary and Phytosanitary Measures' (1995) 5 *Transnational Law & Contemporary Problems* 443.

9 Barry N. Rosen, 'Environmental Product Standards, Trade and European Consumer Goods Marketing: Processes, Threats and Opportunities' (1995) 30 *Columbia Journal of World Business* 1, 74.

10 Peter W.B. Phillips, 'Biotechnology, the Consumer and the Marketplace: The Role of Labeling in the Canola Industry', *Policy Commentary 3*, Department of Agriculture, University of Saskatchewan, July 1997.

11 National Research Council, International Standards, Conformity Assessment and U.S. Trade Policy Project Committee, *Standards, Conformity Assessment and Trade: Into the 21st Century* (Washington DC: National Academy Press, 1995) p. 111 [hereafter *Standards, Conformity Assessment and Trade*].

12 U.S. Department of Agriculture, *SPS Accomplishments Report: Fiscal Year 1996* (Washington DC: APHIS, 1997).

13 General Agreement on Tariffs and Trade, Oct. 30, 1947, 61 Stat. A3, 55 U.N.T.S. 188, reprinted in GATT, *Basic Instruments and Selected Documents*, 4th Supp. 1 (1969) [hereinafter GATT].

14 Edmond McGovern, *International Trade Regulation* (Exeter: Globefield Press, 1995) Issue 3, §8.212.

15 See John J. Barceló III, 'Product Standards to Protect the Local Environment – the GATT and the Uruguay Round Sanitary and Phytosanitary Agreement (1994) 27 *Cornell Int'l L.J.* 755 citing GATT panel decisions in support of this proposition, e.g., *Canada – Import, Distribution and Sale of Alcoholic Drinks by Canadian Provincial Marketing Agencies*, GATT Doc. L/6304 (22 March 1988), BISD GATT, 35th Supp. para. 4.24 and Canada – Administration of the Foreign Investment Review Act, GATT Doc. L/5504 (7 February 1984), BISD GATT, 30th Supp. para 5.14.

16 See McGovern, *op. cit.*, Issue 3, §8.211 citing *Report of panel on US imports of certain automotive spring assemblies*, BISD 30S/107 (1984); *Report of the panel on United States – measures affecting alcoholic and malt beverages*, BISD 39S/206 (1993), para. 5.2; *Report of panel on United States – standards for reformulated and conventional gasoline*, WT/DS2/R, 1996, para. 6.17.

17 McGovern, *op. cit.*, Issue 2, §13.111 citing *Report of panel on United States – standards for reformulated and conventional gasoline*, WT/DS2/R, 1996, sec. III.B.

18 Former U.S. Senate Finance Committee Chairman Lloyd Bentsen once criticized the limited scope of the Article XX exceptions by commenting that it was only designed to deal with 'rabid dogs and sick plants', illustrating that such narrow language remains unhelpful for policies that embrace a 'precautionary' approach to environmental protection. See Dan Esty, *Greening the GATT* (Washington DC: Institute for International Economics, 1994) p. 48 and more generally Robert Housman and Durwood Zaelke 'Trade, Environment and Sustainable Development: A Primer' (1992) 15 *Hastings International and Comparative Law Review* pp. 535–612.

19 Esty, *op. cit.*, p. 48.

20 Esty, *op. cit.*, p. 48, citing Steve Charnovitz 'Exploring the Environmental Exceptions to GATT Article XX' (1991) 25 *Journal of World Trade* 5.

21 David A. Wirth, 'The Role of Science in the Uruguay Round and NAFTA Trade Disciplines' (1994) 27 *Cornell Int'l L.J.* 817.

22 Agreement on Technical Barriers to Trade, 12 April 1979, 1186 U.N.T.S. 276, GATT, BISD, 26th Supp. 8 (1980) [hereinafter *Standards Code*]. Earlier works on the Standards Code include Nusbaumer, 'The GATT Standards Code in Operation' (1984) 18 *J. World*

Trade L. 542 and R.W. Middleton, 'The GATT Standards Code' (1980) 14 *J. World Trade L.* 201 and J. Bourgeois, 'The Tokyo Round Agreement on Technical Barriers and on Government Procurement in International and EEC Law' (1982) 19 *Comm. Mkt. L.Rev.* 5 as noted in John H. Jackson and William J. Davey, *Legal Problems of International Economic Relations*, 2nd ed. (St Paul MN.: West Publishing Co., 1986) p. 534.

23 Wirth, *op. cit.*

24 *Standards Code*, Article 1.

25 *Standards Code*, Article 2.

26 *Standards Code*, Article 2.3.

27 *Standards Code*, Article 2.2.

28 *Standards Code*, Article 2.4.

29 Suppose country A is a large producer of lawnmowers and would like to protect its market from cheaper, foreign made imports. Standards relating to the lawnmower's maximum allowable noise level in decibels differ from standards which mandate exact technological specifications of how that lawnmower must achieve the reduced noise level. One could imagine a situation where country A could draft such regulations to favour a specific domestically patented technology in noise reduction, thereby favouring its own producers.

30 *Standards Code*, Article 2.5.

31 *Standards Code*, Article 5.

32 *Standards Code*, Article 5.2.

33 R.W. Middleton, 'The GATT Standards Code' (1980) 14 *J. World Trade L.* 201, p. 206.

34 *Agreement on the Application of Sanitary and Phytosanitary Measures*, GATT Doc. MTN/FA II-A1A-4 (15 December 1993) [hereinafter the SPS Agreement] in *Final Act Embodying the Results of the Uruguay Round of Multilateral Trade Negotiations* [hereinafter the Uruguay Round], GATT Doc. MTN/FA (15 December 1993), 33 I.L.M. 9 (1994).

35 *Agreement on Technical Barriers to Trade*, GATT Doc. MTN/FA II-AIA–6 (15 December 1993) [hereinafter TBT Agreement] in *Uruguay Round, ibid.*

36 As noted in Chapter 2 of this book, the Uruguay Round eliminated for the most part the 'a la carte' style of picking and choosing which agreements to adopt. For a comprehensive list of the precise obligations of Members, see McGovern, *op. cit.*, Issue 1, §1.121.

37 *Standards, Conformity Assessment and Trade, op. cit.*, p. 113. See also note 27 stating the calculation was made using 1991 World Bank and IMF data on imports, total signatories to the Tokyo Standards Code and new Signatories to the Uruguay Round Agreement.

38 *Standards, Conformity Assessment and Trade, op. cit.*, p. 108.

39 *Ibid.*

40 TBT Agreement, Article 1.

41 The definitions are quite broad and read,

1 *Technical regulation*: Document which lays down product characteristics or their related processes and production methods, including the applicable administrative provisions, with which compliance *is mandatory*. It may also include or deal exclusively with terminology, symbols, packaging, marking or labeling requirements as they apply to a product, process or production method.

2 *Standard*: Document approved by a recognized body, that provides, for common and repeated use, rules, guidelines or characteristics for products or related processes and production methods, with which compliance *is not mandatory*. It may also include or deal exclusively with terminology, symbols, packaging, marking or labeling requirements as they apply to a product, process or production method.

3 *Conformity Assessment Procedure*: Any procedure used, directly or indirectly, to determine that relevant requirements in technical regulations or standards are fulfilled.

42 The relevant portion of the preamble reads,

> *Recognizing* that no country should be prevented from taking measures necessary to ensure the quality of its exports, or for the protection of human, animal, plant life

or health, of the environment, or for the prevention of deceptive practices, at the levels it considers appropriate, subject to the requirement that they are not applied in a manner which would constitute a means of arbitrary or unjustifiable discrimination between countries where the same conditions prevail or a disguised restriction on international trade and are otherwise in accordance with the provisions of this Agreement [.]

43 This view is supported in McGovern, *op. cit.,* Issue 2, §7.2421.
44 TBT Agreement, Article 2.4.
45 TBT Agreement, Article 2.5.
46 TBT Agreement, Articles 2.5, 2.9.
47 TBT Agreement, Article 2.12.
48 TBT Agreement, Annex 1 definition of 'conformity assessment procedures'.
49 The U.S. National Research Council estimates the revenues of independent testing industry to be approximately $10 billion in 1993, with growth rates averaging 13.5% per annum. *Standards, Conformity Assessment and Trade, op. cit.*, p. 118.
50 One such example can be found in United States Trade Representative (USTR) *1996 U.S. Foreign Trade Barriers Report* (Washington DC: USTR, 1996) at p. 261 where Mexico rules governing conformity assessment have been particularly onerous. For example, under Mexican law, only facilities based in Mexico can apply for recognition as competent bodies to test products in order to determine whether they comply with technical regulations, i.e., conduct conformity assessments. This has resulted in increased costs and uncertainty for US suppliers and has 'proven particularly difficult in sectors where technical capability is non-existent or insufficient to meet the demand, or resides solely in the laboratories of competing manufacturers'. The report lists this as a trade barrier inconsistent with the international disciplines on technical barriers.
51 *Standards, Conformity Assessment and Trade, op. cit.,* p. 121.
52 See generally, Esty, *op. cit.*
53 Michael Trebilcock and Robert Howse 'Trade Liberalization and Regulatory Diversity: Reconciling Competitive Markets with Competitive Politics' (1998) 6 *European Journal of Law and Economics* 5.
54 Michael J. Trebilcock and Robert Howse, *Reconceiving the Canadian Standards System: A Study for the Canadian Standards Association*, Final Draft, 3 January 1995, Canadian Standards Association, Toronto, p. 5.
55 *Ibid.*
56 *Ibid.*, p. 8.
57 Barrie McKenna, 'Health Rules Replace Tariffs in Food Trade' *The Globe and Mail,* 2 March 1998, p. B1.
58 *From the GATT to the WTO: Prospects for Agriculture*, Conference Proceedings, 26–28 October 1997.
59 One commentator suggested that the SPS Agreement was motivated in part by the US–EU dispute regarding the safety of hormone-treated beef (addressed later in this chapter). Wirth, *op. cit.*; see also Donna Roberts, 'Preliminary Assessment of the WTO Agreement on Sanitary and Phytosanitary Regulations' (1998) I.J. of International Economic Law 377.
60 Annex A, SPS Agreement.
61 Wirth, *op. cit.*
62 *Ibid.*, p. 827.
63 For a concise formulation of the precautionary principle in the context of trade, see Richard Blackhurst *et al.*, *Trade and Sustainable Development: Principles* (Winnipeg, Canada: International Institute for Sustainable Development, 1994).
64 'Coping with BSE', *The Economist*, 14 March 1998 at p. 15.
65 See generally on this issue Robert W. Hahn (ed.) *Risks, Costs* and *Lives Saved: Getting Better Results from Regulation* (Washington DC: AEI Press, 1996).

66 For a thorough exploration of these ideas, see Jeremy Fraiberg and Michael J. Trebilcock, 'Risk Regulation: Technocratic and Democratic Tools for Regulatory Reform', *McGill Law Journal* (forthcoming).

67 See Esty, *op. cit.*, pp. 172–6; see also Alan Rugman and John Kirton (eds) with Julie Soloway, 'Introduction' in *Trade and the Environment: Economic, Legal and Policy Perspectives* (Cheltenham UK: Edward Elgar, 1998).

68 Vogel, *op. cit.*, pp. 5–8.

69 Esty, *op. cit.*, p. 173.

70 *Ibid.*

71 For an argument in favour of these approaches, see A.O. Sykes, 'The Economics of Regulatory Protectionism and Its Implications for Trade Regulation: The WTO and Other Systems' (unpublished manuscript, U. of Chicago Law School, 1997).

72 This was due to the fact that the Agreements were negotiated virtually at the same time with many of less powerful nations in the case of NAFTA and perhaps the same players. For example, the same Canadian government negotiators responsible for the SPS Agreement under the WTO were at the table for NAFTA's SPS provisions. See John Kirton and Julie Soloway, 'Assessing NAFTA's Environmental Effects: Dimensions of a Framework and the NAFTA Regime', *Trade and Environment Working Paper Series No. 1*, North American Commission for Environmental Cooperation, Montreal, 1996.

73 See Kirton and Soloway, *op. cit.*

74 Pierre Marc Johnson and André Beaulieu, *The Environment and NAFTA* (Washington DC: Island Press, 1996).

75 Jon R. Johnson, *The North American Free Trade Agreement: A Comprehensive Guide* (Aurora ON: Canada Law Book, 1994) p. 245.

76 TBT Agreement, Article 2.5. See also Johnson, *op. cit.*, p. 246.

77 Tuna-Dolphin case.

78 In 1994, the United States exported over $3.1 billion in agricultural products to Mexico and imported over $2.8 billion of agricultural products from Mexico. In the same year, the United States exported $5.1 billion of agricultural products to Canada and imported about $5.3 billion from Canada. Canada–Mexico trade was significantly smaller, Canadian agricultural exports to Mexico in 1994 were about $157 million and Canadian imports from Mexico were roughly $159 million.

79 Johnson, *op. cit.*, p. 238.

80 J. Kirton and R. Fernandez, 'NAFTA's Institutions: The Environmental Potential and Performance of the NAFTA Free Trade Commission and Related Bodies', *Environment and Trade Series* 5 (Montreal: North American Commission for Environmental Cooperation, 1997).

81 *Procureur du Roi* v. *Dassonville et al.*, Case 8/74 [1974] E.C.R. 837.

82 See Case 120/78 *Rewe-Zentral AG* v. *Bundesmonopolverwaltung für Branntwein* [1979] E.C.R. 649 ('*Cassis de Dijon*') which allows for the possibility of extending the list of exceptions enumerated in Article 36 and Case 240/83 *Procureur de la République* v. *Association de Défense des Brûleurs d'Huiles Usagées* [1984] E.C.R. 531 ('*Waste Oils*') which allows an environmental exception to be read into Article 36, cited in Damien Gerardin and Raoul Stewardson, 'Trade and Environment: Some Lessons from *Castlemaine Tooheys* (Australia) and *Danish Bottles* (European Community)' (1995) 44 *International and Comparative Law Quarterly*, 41–71.

83 Gerardin and Stewardson, *op. cit.*, p. 56.

84 *Ibid.*, pp. 53–4.

85 *Cassis de Dijon* E.C.J. 120/78.

86 Case 178/84 (1988) 1 CMLR 780.

87 ISO website <www.iso.ch>

88 McGovern, *op. cit.*, Issue 2, §7.23.

89 John Audley, *Green Politics and Global Trade: NAFTA and the Future of Environmental Politics* (Washington DC: Georgetown University Press, 1997) p. 131.

90 *Ibid.*
91 Conference Proceedings from Trilateral Meeting, ISO 14000 (Montreal: Commission for Environmental Cooperation, 1998).
92 *Ibid.*, p. 23.
93 *Ibid.*, p. 21.
94 Jeffrey Atik, 'Science and International Regulatory Convergence' (1996–97) 17 *Northwestern Journal of International Law and Business* 736.
95 FAO website <www.fao.org>
96 See Chapter 5, 'Regulatory Reform in the Agro-Food Sector,' in OECD, *The OECD Report on Regulatory Reform, Volume I: Sectoral Studies* (Paris: OECD 1997) p. 251.
97 Patti Goldman and Richard Wiles, *Trading Away Food Safety*, Occasional Report (Washington DC: Public Citizen, 1994) cited in Esty, *op. cit.*, p. 173.
98 Wirth, *op. cit.*, p. 825 citing Roger W. Miller, *This Is Codex Alimentarius* (1993).
99 Steve Charnovitz, 'The World Trade Organization, Meat Hormones and Food Safety', *International Trade Reporter*, 15 October 1997.
100 *Thailand – Restrictions on Importation of and Internal Taxes on Cigarettes*, GATT BISD, 37th Supp. 200 (1991).
101 Case 302/86, *Commission of the European Communities v. Kingdom of Denmark* [1988] E.C.R. 4607.
102 Gerardin and Stewardson, *op. cit.*, pp. 41–71.
103 *Ibid.*, p. 59.
104 *Ibid.*, pp. 41–71.
105 *Ibid.*
106 EC Complaint Against Canada, GATT Panel Decision, 5 February 1988; U.S. Complaint Against Canada, GATT Panel Decision, 16 October 1991.
107 See Michael Hare and Don Dewees, 'Packaging Waste Reduction in Canada: An Assessment of Policies, Markets and Myths', Working Paper, *Centre for the Study of State and Market*, University of Toronto Faculty of Law, 17 December 1996.
108 David Vogel, 'Social Regulations as Trade Barriers' in Pietro Nivola (ed.) *Comparative Disadvantages? Social Regulations and the Global Economy* (Washington DC: Brookings Institution Press, 1997).
109 *Ibid.*
110 See A. Dick, 'The EC Hormone Ban Dispute and the Application of the Dispute Settlement Provisions of the Standards Code' (1989) 10 *Michigan J. of International Law* 872; Vogel, *Trading Up*, *op. cit.*, pp. 154–71.
111 WTO Panel Decision, *EC Measures Concerning Meat and Meat Products (Hormones)*, Complaint of the United States, WT/DS26/R/USA, August 1997.
112 This summary is taken from Steve Charnovitz, 'The World Trade Organization, Meat Hormones and Food Safety', *International Trade Reporter*, 15 October 1997.
113 *Ibid.*
114 'WTO Backs Key Finding on Hormones, But Could Make SPS Cases Harder', *Inside US Trade*, vol.16, no. 2, 16 January 1998.
115 Charnovitz, *op. cit.*
116 Paragraph 187 of Appellate Body Report.
117 WT/DS26/AB/R, para. 248. Many of the issues in *Beef Hormones* were considered subsequently by the Appellate Body in a dispute involving an Australian prohibition on imports of Canadian salmon for reasons of alleged infectious disease. Further to a Canadian challenge of the prohibition, a WTO panel ruled that Australia had violated its obligations under the WTO by maintaining a sanitary measure not based on a risk assessment; by adopting arbitrary or unjustifiable distinctions in levels of protection; and by maintaining a sanitary measure more restrictive than necessary. On appeal, the WTO Appellate Body reaffirmed for the most part the panel decision, but for slightly different reasons, and was unable to reach a conclusion on the key issue of whether the measure was more trade-restrictive than necessary. See

Australia – Measures Affecting Importation of Salmon, AB-1998-5, WT/DS18/AB/R, October 1998.

118 Wirth, *op. cit.*, p. 842.

119 *In the Matter of: Puerto Rico Regulations on the Import, Distribution and Sale of U.H.T. Milk from Quebec*, USA-93-1807-01, 3 June 1993. Ultra high temperature [hereinafter UHT] milk is produced by heating milk to 138 degrees Celsius for a minimum of two seconds. The milk is then cooled and packaged in hermetically sealed boxes. UHT milk has a shelf life of between six and twelve months at room temperature.

120 William J. Davey, *Pine and Swine, Canada–United States Trade Dispute Settlement: The FTA Experience and NAFTA Prospect* (Ottawa ON: Carleton University Centre Trade Policy and Law, 1996) p. 58.

121 Canada found it impossible to comply with the regulations because (a) the regulations required an FDA-certified inspection but the FDA refused to certify any Canadian or Quebec inspectors carrying out such inspections; (b) the regulations required not equivalency, but an identical regime to that found in the PMO; and (c) the regulations required that Canada join the NCIMS. §4.9

122 §4.7, 4.8.

123 §4.20 and on.

124 Armand de Mestral, 'Dispute Avoidance: Weighing the Values of Trade and the Environment Under the NAFTA and the NAAEC' *Environment and Trade Series* 3 (Montreal, Commission for Environmental Cooperation, 1996) p. 16.

125 *Ibid.*

126 OECD, *The OECD Report on Regulatory Reform, Volume I: Sectoral Studies* (Paris: OECD, 1997) and OECD, *The OECD Report on Regulatory Reform, Volume II: Thematic Studies* (Paris: OECD, 1997).

127 OECD, *The OECD Report on Regulatory Reform, Volume I: Sectoral Studies, op. cit.*, p. 3.

128 *Ibid.*, see Chapter 6, 'Product Standards, Conformity Assessment and Regulatory Reform', pp. 275–328.

129 *Ibid.*, p. 285.

130 Alan O. Sykes, *Product Standards for Internationally Integrated Goods Markets* (Washington DC: The Brookings Institution, 1995) p. 117.

131 There is some evidence that this process has begun in Canada. A meeting of selected Canadian business leaders and Ambassador John Weekes, Canadian Permanent Representative to the WTO, was held at the Faculty of Management, University of Toronto in March 1998. At that meeting, Ambassador Weekes emphasized the need for greater private sector participation in all WTO processes, beyond periodic negotiating rounds.

132 OECD, *The OECD Report on Regulatory Reform, Volume I: Sectoral Studies, op. cit.*, p. 21.

133 *Ibid.*, Chapter 6, 'Product Standards, Conformity Assessment and Regulatory Reform', see Box 1, p. 292.

134 *Ibid.*, pp. 289–91.

135 *Ibid.*

136 See *Agreement on Mutual Recognition Between the United States of America and the European Community.*

137 See Chapter 6, 'Product Standards, Conformity Assessment and Regulatory Reform', in OECD, *The OECD Report on Regulatory Reform, Volume I: Sectoral Studies, op. cit.*, pp. 289–91.

138 See Alan M. Rugman and Julie A. Soloway (1997) 'An Environmental Agenda for APEC: Lessons from NAFTA' in *The International Executive* 39(6) 735–44. Chapter 6, 'Product Standards, Conformity Assessment and Regulatory Reform', in OECD, *The OECD Report on Regulatory Reform, Volume I: Sectoral Studies, op. cit.*, pp. 289–91.

139 See Chapter 6, 'Product Standards, Conformity Assessment and Regulatory Reform', in OECD, *The OECD Report on Regulatory Reform, Volume I: Sectoral Studies, op. cit.*, pp. 289–91.

140 *Ibid.*, p. 291.
141 *Ibid.*, p. 292.
142 *Thailand: Restrictions on Importations of and Internal Taxes on Cigarette*, BISD 37th. Supp. (1990).
143 See the Canada – US *Softwood Lumber* Case, *op. cit.*
144 This observation is based upon interviews by one of the authors with officials of ISO, FAO and the WTO in the summer of 1996. Significantly, while officials of the specialized organizations saw the need to develop such links as important, WTO staff did not express particular interest in this objective.

7 Antidumping laws

1 Sylvia Ostry, 'Antidumping: The Tip of the Iceberg', in M.J. Trebilcock and R.C. York (eds) *Fair Exchange: Reforming Trade Remedy Laws* (Toronto: C.D. Howe Institute, 1990) 3 p. 17.
2 GATT, Basic Instruments and Selected Documents, Thirty-sixth through Forty-fourth Session (Geneva: GATT, March 1981–June 1989) Appendix Tables; Summary of Antidumping Actions and Countervailing Duty Actions; reported in A. Anderson and A. Rugman, 'Country Factor Bias in the Administration of Anti-Dumping and Countervailing Duty Cases', in Trebilcock and York, *op. cit.*, p. 152.
3 See Jorge Mirandes, Raul Torres and Mario Ruiz, 'The International Use of Antidumping 1987–1997', (1998) 32 *Journal of World Trade* 5.
4 In the alternative, according to Article VI, the normal value can be based on either the highest comparable price for the like product for export to any third country in the course of trade, or the cost of production of the product in the country of origin plus a reasonable addition for the selling cost and profit.
5 Both countries used the grandfather clause, contained in the Provincial Protocol of Application governing accessions of countries to membership of the GATT, to retain their own legislation with respect to these duties. For more details on this and other aspects of the development of the GATT antidumping regime, see J.F. Beseler and A.N. Williams, *Antidumping and Antisubsidy Law: The European Communities* (London: Sweet and Maxwell, 1986) p. 3.
6 The actual status of the code, both then and as revised, is more substantive than merely interpretive. See R.M. Bierwagen, *GATT Article VI and the Protectionist Bias in Antidumping Law* (Deventer: Kluwer, 1990) p. 23.
7 Article 8(a).
8 Article 3(a).
9 This Act requires 'a causation link but . . . not . . . that dumped imports must be a principal cause, or a major cause, or a substantial cause of injury caused by all factors contributing to overall injury to an industry' (S. Rep. No. 1298, 93rd Cong., 2nd Sess. 180 (1974), brackets omitted).
10 USC. §160 note (1970).
11 See Beseler and Williams, *op. cit.*, p. 11.
12 Article 3(4).
13 Article 3(3).
14 For excellent reviews of the Agreement, see David Palmeter, 'A Commentary on the WTO Anti-Dumping Code' (1996) 30 *J. of World Trade* 43, and Gary Horlick and Eleanor Shea, 'The World Trade Organization Antidumping Agreement', 29 *J. of World Trade* 5, including its negotiating history.
15 See M. Koulen, 'Some Problems of Interpretation and Implementation of the GATT Antidumping Code', in J.H. Jackson and E.A. Vermulst (eds) *Antidumping Law and Practice: A Comparative Study* (Ann Arbor: University of Michigan Press, 1989) p. 366.
16 *United States – Imposition of Anti-Dumping Duties on Imports of Fresh and Chilled Atlantic Salmon from Norway*, Report of the Panel adopted by the Committee on Anti-Dumping Practices on 27 April 1994, ADP/87.

17 *Korea – Anti-Dumping Duties on Imports of Polyacetal Resins from the United States*, Report of the Panel, 2 April 1993, ADP/92.

18 *EC – Imposition of Anti-Dumping Duties on Imports of Cotton Yarn from Brazil*, Report of the Panel, 4 July 1995, ADP/137; *Guatemala – Anti-Dumping Investigation Regarding Portland Cement From Mexico*, FB-1998-6, WT/DS60/AB/R, November, 1998.

19 Details of the Canadian regime are drawn from: R.K. Paterson, *Canadian Regulation of International Trade and Investment* (Toronto: Carswell, 1986) p. 106; p. A. Magnus, 'The Canadian Antidumping System', in Jackson and Vermulst *op. cit.*, p. 167; J. Buchanan, 'Antidumping Law and the *Special Import Measures Act*' (1985) 11 *Can. Bus. L.J.* 2; and M. Dutz, 'Enforcement of Canadian Trade Remedy Laws: the Case for Competition Policies as an Antidote for Protection', in J.M. Finger, *Antidumping* (Ann Arbor: University of Michigan Press, 1993). The US regime is described in G. Horlick, 'The United States Antidumping System', in Jackson and Vermulst *op. cit.*; G. Bryan, *Taxing Unfair International Trade Practices* (Lexington MA: Lexington, 1980) chs. 1–7; and J.M. Finger and T. Murray, 'Antidumping and Countervailing Duty Enforcement in the United States', in Finger, *op. cit.* For the USA and Canada, see Warner, *op. cit.* The description of the EC draws primarily on J.F. Bellis 'The EEC Antidumping System', in Jackson and Vermulst *op. cit.*, p. 41. For a more detailed account, see I. Van Bael and J.-F. Bellis, *Antidumping and Other Trade Protection Laws of the EEC* (Bicester: CCH, 1990). For a critical review of the experience under EC dumping laws, see P. Messerlin, 'The Antidumping Regulations of the European Community: The Privatization of Administered Protection', in Trebilcock and York *op. cit.*, and A. Eymann and L. Schuknecht, 'Antidumping Enforcement in the European Community', in Finger, *op. cit.*

20 An Act to Amend the Customs Tariff, 1897, S.C. 1904 ch. 11.

21 R.S.C. 1985, ch. S-15.

22 15 USC, ss 71–72 (1988).

23 19 USC, ss 1673 *et seq.* (1988).

24 Council Regulation 2423/88, OJ (1988) L209/1 governs the EC antidumping system. For a detailed description of the development of the EC antidumping regulations, see Beseler and Williams, *op. cit.*, p. 21.

25 SIMA, ss 38–41.

26 SIMA, s. 45.

27 The Financial Administration Act, R.S.C. 1985, ch. F11, gives the Minister this authority.

28 House of Commons Sub-Committee on Import Policy: *Report on the Special Import Measures Act*, Issue No. 31, 1st Sess., 32nd Parl., 1980–1–2, 9 June 1982; referred to in Paterson, *op. cit.*, pp. 125–6.

29 *Surgical Adhesive Tapes and Plasters, Excluding Plastic Tapes and Plasters, Originating in or Exported from Japan* (CIT-8-85) 4 December 1985; *Grain Corn Originating in or Exported from the United States of America* (CIT-7-86) 6 March 1987; *Fresh Whole Yellow Onions, Originating in or Exported From the United States of America* (CIT-1-87) 30 April 1987. (These cases include countervailing duty cases.)

30 Articles 11(1) and 12(1).

31 Beseler, *op. cit.*, p. 169; Michael Trebilcock, Marsha Chandler and Robert Howse, *Trade and Transitions* (London: Routledge, 1990) pp. 200, 201.

32 SIMA, s. 76(1).

33 *Id.* s. 76(2).

34 *Federal Court Act*, R.S.C. 1985, ch. F7, s. 28.

35 *Id.* s. 31. See Paterson, *op. cit.*, pp. 126–30 for a discussion of the various appeal provisions.

36 28 USC para 1581 *et seq.* (1988).

37 I. Van Bael, 'Lessons for the EC: More Transparency, Less Discretion, and, at Last a Debate', in Jackson and Vermulst *op. cit.*, 405 p. 407; Messerlin, *op. cit.*

38 *FTA*, Article 1907 contemplates the creation of a Working Group to propose new legal norms to govern government subsidies and unfair cross-border pricing.

39 *NAFTA*, Article 1902:2.
40 *NAFTA*, Article 1902:2.
41 *NAFTA*, Article 1903:1. Article 1903:2 requires that the panel conduct itself in accordance with the procedures set out in Annex 1903.2, which provides for procedures very similar to those used in Chapter 20. The Annex also allows the panel to make recommendations about how an offending provision can be brought into conformity with Article 1902.
42 *NAFTA*, Article 1903:3. Article 1907 requires each Party to designate one or more officials who are to be responsible for ensuring that consultations are as expeditious as possible.
43 *NAFTA*, Article 1904:10 provides that the Agreement is not to affect judicial review of other than 'final determinations'. 'Final determination' is a technical term defined by Article 1911 – it includes determinations made by administrative tribunals under the Special Import Measures Act (Canada) and the Tariff Act of 1930 (USA). See also Article 1904:15(f) regarding amendments to the Special Import Measures Act deeming certain determinations as final for the purposes of the Agreement. For a description of the relevant provisions, as well as the administrative procedures to which they relate see Johnson and Schacter, *op. cit.*, at ch. 9.
44 NAFTA, Article 1904:1–2. 'Law' here includes 'statutes, legislative history, regulations, administrative practice, and judicial precedents to the extent that a court of the importing Party would rely on such materials' (Article 1904:2). Article 1904:9 makes a panel decision binding on both Parties; Article 1904:11 precludes judicial review of a final determination if either Party has requested panel review; and Article 1904:11 also forbids either Party from allowing its courts to hear an appeal from a decision of the panel.

Article 1904:13 provides for the 'extraordinary' challenge of panel decisions if a Party alleges that: (a) a panel member was guilty of gross misconduct; (b) the panel flouted procedural rules; or (c) substantive limitations on panel powers were ignored; and any of these transgressions materially affected the panel decision and threatens the integrity of binational panel review. The challenge is heard by a panel of three chosen from a roster of ten judges. They will use the criteria of Article 1904:13 to decide the case (see Annex 1904:13). Article 1909 contemplates an exchange of letters by the two Parties which will establish a code of conduct for panellists and committee members operating under Articles 1903 and 1904.
45 *NAFTA*, Article 1904:3. The relevant statutes are set out in Annex 1911: they are in Canada, the Federal Court Act (s. 28(1)), in the United States the Tariff Act of 1930 (ss. 516A(b)(1)(A) and 516A(b)(1)(B)), and in Mexico, the Federal Fiscal Code (Article 238).
46 *NAFTA*, Article 1904:4. 'Publication' means publication in either the *Canada Gazette the Federal Register* or the Diario Oficio. If there is no publication of the determination, then the Party whose tribunal made it must notify the other Party, which then has thirty days to request a panel.

The Agreement is not as detailed as it might be about procedure; details are left to be worked out by the Parties at a later date (see Article 1904:14). However, the Agreement (Article 1904:14) is very clear about the time limits to be allocated to each phase of the panel process, and it sets an overall limit of 315 days, beginning from the date when a request for a panel is made, for the completion of dispute resolution.
47 *NAFTA*, Article 1904:15 sets out a number of amendments that had to be made to existing legislation to give persons standing so that they could ask a Party to request a panel. Thus, s. 28(4) of the Federal Court Act had to be modified, and rules added such that persons could ask Canada to request a panel if they were entitled to pursue judicial review.
48 *NAFTA*, Article 1904:7.
49 *NAFTA*, Annex 1901.2:5.
50 *NAFTA*, Article 1904:8. This provision also requires the panel to establish as brief a time as possible given the nature of the case for the administrative body to take action 'not

inconsistent' with the panel's decision. In no case can the time given be any longer than that provided by the relevant statute for a final determination by the relevant authority.

51 *NAFTA*, Article 1908: 1–2.
52 *NAFTA*, Article 1908: 3–4.
53 *NAFTA*, Annex 1901.2:1.
54 *NAFTA*, Annex 1901.2:1.
55 *NAFTA*, Annex 1901.2:2.
56 *NAFTA*, Annex 1901.2:3.
57 *NAFTA*, Annex 1901.2:4.
58 For a discussion of this literature, see T.M. Boddez and M.J. Trebilcock, *Unfinished Business: Reforming Trade Remedy Laws in North America* (Toronto: C.D. Howe Institute, 1993).
59 John Mercury, 'Chapter 19 of the United States – Canada Free Trade Agreement 1989–95: A Check on Administered Protection?' (1995) 15 *Northwestern J. of International Law & Business* 525.
60 William J. Davey, *Pine & Swine – Canada–U.S. Trade Dispute Settlement: The FTA experience and NAFTA prospects* (Ottawa, Can: Centre for Trade Policy and Law, 1996).
61 US General Accounting Office (GAO), *Issues in Binational Panel Review in the Canada–U.S. FTA*, GAO/GGD-95-175 BR, June 1995.
62 Davey, *op. cit.*, p. 134.
63 *Ibid.*, p. 287.
64 Article 1504, North American Free Trade Agreement.
65 Article 1907, North American Free Trade Agreement.
66 *J. Viner, Dumping: A Problem in International Trade* (Chicago: University of Chicago Press, 1933) p. 86.
67 A US Congressional subcommittee remarked: '[Antidumping laws are] designed to free US imports from unfair price discrimination practices [by foreign exporters]'. S. Rep. No. 93-1298, 93rd Cong., 2d Sess. 179, cited in W. Caine, 'A Case For Repealing the Antidumping Provisions of the Tariff Act of 1930' (1981) 13 *Law & Pol'y Int'l Bus.* 681 p. 682.
68 Competition Act, R.S.C. 1985, ch. C-34, ss 50(1)(a), (b).
69 Clayton Act, as amended by the Robinson–Patman Act, ss 2, 3; 15 USC para. 13 (1988).
70 B.J. Dunlop, D. McQueen and M.J. Trebilcock, *Canadian Competition Policy: A Legal and Economic Analysis* (Toronto: Canada Law Book, 1987) p. 208.
71 Price discrimination is impossible under perfect competition because sellers who charge a price which is higher or lower than the competitive price will be forced out of the market.
72 See Dunlop, McQueen and Trebilcock, *op. cit.*, pp. 208–10.
73 Since a monopolist has complete market power any losses from price discrimination will be highest if the discriminator is a monopolist.
74 Richard Posner, 'The Social Costs of Monopoly and Regulation' (1975) 83 *J. Pol. Econ.* 807.
75 The conflicting views are summarized in M.J. Trebilcock, *The Common Law of Restraint of Trade* (Toronto: Carswell, 1986) pp. 364–5.
76 Joan Robinson showed that the output effects of price discrimination depend on the shape of consumer demand curves. See *The Economics of Imperfect Competition* (London: Macmillan, 1933) pp. 188–93. R. Schmalensee, in 'Output and Welfare Implications of Monopolistic Third-degree Price Discrimination' (1981) 71 *Amer. Econ. Rev.* 242, and H. Varian, 'Price Discrimination and Social Welfare' (1985) 75 *Amer. Econ. Rev.* 870, find that welfare effects also depend on the shape of consumer demand curves. Hence, generalizations about the output and welfare effects of price discrimination are impossible.
77 It is not 'dumping' for the seller to charge lower prices in its home market than in its

export market and this practice is not prohibited by current legislation. See Deardorff, 'Economic Perspectives on Antidumping Law', in Jackson and Vermulst, *op. cit.*, p. 26.

78 See US International Trade Commission, 'The Economic Effects of Antidumping and Countervailing Duty Orders and Suspension Agreements', Investigation Nos 332–44, June 1995 estimating that the removal of ADD and CVD orders in 1991 would have created a welfare gain of US $1.59 billion in that year; Anderson, 'Antidumping Laws in the United States: Use and Welfare Consequences' (1993) 27 *J. of World Trade* 99, analysing eight antidumping measures and estimating the average consumer cost per dollar of increased profit to be US $8.00.

79 See Jorge Miranda, 'Should Antidumping Laws Be Dumped?' (1996) 28 *Law & Policy in International Business* 255; Clarisse Morgan, 'Competition Policy and Anti-Dumping: Is it Time for a Reality Check?' 30 (1998) *J. of World Trade* 61.

80 See Cars Produced By or Behalf of Hyundai Motor Co., Canadian Import Tribunal, 1987; Mathew Kronby, 'Kicking the Tires: Assessing the Hyundai Anti-Dumping Decision From a Consumer Welfare Perspective' (1991) 18 *Canadian Business L.J.* 95.

81 For proposals along these lines, see Bernard Hoekman and Petros Mavroidis, 'Dumping, Antidumping and Antitrust' (1996) 30 *J. of World Trade* 27.

82 Dunlop, McQueen and Trebilcock, *op. cit.*, p. 208. See generally J.A. Ordover and R.D. Willig, 'An Economic Definition of Predation: Pricing and Product Innovation' (1981) 91 *Yale L.J.* 8.

83 The original US antidumping law, the Antidumping Act of 1916, 19 USC 1673, made evidence of predatory intent an element of the dumping offence.

84 Competition Act, R.S.C. 1985, ch. C-34, ss 50(1)(b), 50(1)(c), and 79.

85 Sherman Act, 15 USC para. 2 (1988), s. 2. Occasionally predatory pricing is challenged under para. 2 of the Clayton Act, as amended by the Robinson–Patman Act. See Hovenkamp, *op. cit.*, pp. 188–90.

86 Articles 85 and 86 of the Treaty of Rome set out the basis for EC competition law.

87 This is not to say that predatory pricing will never occur. See Dunlop, McQueen and Trebilcock, *op. cit.*, pp. 220–4; Posner, *Antitrust Law, op. cit.*, pp. 183–6; Bork, *The Antitrust Paradox* (New York: Basic Books, 1978) pp. 144–60; and Hovenkamp, *op. cit.*, pp. 172–84.

88 See e.g. B.S. Yamey, 'Predatory Price Cutting: Notes and Comments' (1972) 15 *J. L. & Econ.* 129; F. Easterbrook, 'The Limits of Antitrust' (1984) 63 *Tex. L. Rev.* 1 p. 26 and 'Predatory Strategies and Counterstrategies' (1981) 48 *University of Chicago L. Rev.* 263 p. 268; J. McGee, 'Predatory Pricing Revisited' (1980) 23 *J. L. & Econ.* 289, pp. 295–7.

89 Hovenkamp and Silver-Westrick, 'Predatory Pricing and the Ninth Circuit' (1983) *Ariz.St.L.J.* 443 pp. 460–5.

90 McGee, *op. cit.*

91 P. Areeda and D.F. Turner, 'Predatory Pricing and Related Practices Under Section 2 of the Sherman Act' (1975) 88 *Harvard L. Rev.* 697 p. 698.

92 The marginal cost of one unit of output is the amount by which the seller's total costs (for all units of output) increase when that one additional unit of output is produced. Since accountants typically report average costs, not marginal costs, marginal cost is extremely difficult to calculate.

93 The seller's total costs are the sum of its fixed costs and its variable costs. Variable costs vary with the level of output; fixed costs do not. By definition, average variable costs are lower than average total costs.

94 For the Canadian approach see Dunlop, McQueen and Trebilcock, *op. cit.*, and R.J. Roberts, Anticombines and Antitrust (Toronto: Butterworths, 1980) pp. 218–29. For the US approach see Bork, *op. cit.*, pp. 144–60, and Hovenkamp, *op. cit.*, pp. 172–84.

95 Deardorff, *op. cit.*, p. 36.

96 For further support for this view, see J. Barceló, 'Antidumping Laws as Barriers to Trade – The United States and the International Antidumping Code' (1972) *Cornell L. Rev.* 491 pp. 501–3.

97 S. Hutton and M.J. Trebilcock, 'An Empirical Study of the Application of Canadian

Antidumping Laws: A Search for Normative Rationales' (1990) 24 *J. of World Trade* 123 p. 128.

98 See 'Attack on Antidumping Law Sparks OECD Row', *Financial Times*, 21 September 1995, p. 16, referring to a study by a team led by Robert Willig.

99 For a mathematical proof of this result see S.W. Davies and A.J. McGuiness, 'Dumping at Less Than Marginal Cost' (1982) 12 *J. Int'l Econ.* 169 pp. 171–6; see also P. Nicolaides, 'The Competition Effects of Dumping' (1990) 24 *J. of World Trade* 115 pp. 119, 120.

100 Antidumping duties were imposed in each case. Hutton and Trebilcock, *op. cit.*, p. 128.

101 Deardorff, *op. cit.*

102 This practice is widespread. Bulk mail, for example, often contains free samples. Sellers provide samples hoping customers will be willing to purchase goods after 'experiencing' samples.

103 It may be objected that dumped goods cannot be characterized as 'learning by doing' goods because any technological learning would have the same effect on both the home market and the export market. However, if home market sales were 'insufficient' within the meaning of antidumping legislation, antidumping investigations would examine only the 'fully-allocated costs' of the exporter. If those costs exceeded the export-market price, there would be a positive finding of dumping even if the exporter were merely pricing below-cost (in both markets) to gain technological know-how.

104 In the USA, the legality of aggressive pricing policies to increase market share has been upheld: *Telex Corp.* v. *IBM*, 510 F.2d 894 (10th Cir. 1975), *cert. dismissed*, 423 US 802 (1975); *Berkey Photo v. Eastman Kodak Co.*, 603 F.2d 263 (2d Cir. 1979). Canadian courts have also recognized the legitimacy of promotional sales: *R.* v. *Hoffman-La Roche Ltd.* (1981), 28 O.R. (2d) 164 at 196; 109 D.L.R. (3d) 5 at 37 (Ont. C.A.).

105 See Clarisse Morgan, *op. cit.*

106 See Miranda, *op. cit.*

107 Viner, *op. cit.*, pp. 30–1.

108 For a fuller discussion of intermittent dumping see F. Lazar, 'Antidumping Rules Following the Canada–US Free Trade Agreement' (1989) 23 *J. of World Trade* 45.

109 Four of the thirty cases studied exhibited indications of intermittent dumping (Hutton and Trebilcock, *op. cit.*, p. 61).

110 *Ibid.*

111 See Trebilcock and Quinn, *op. cit.*, pp. 108–11.

112 *Ibid.*

113 Several studies have shown that the cost of capital in markets with strong import competition and demand fluctuation exceeds its cost in markets with constant demand and weak import competition: see W. Wares, *The Theory of Dumping and American Commercial Policy* (Lexington MA: Lexington, 1977, pp. 67–73); Agnar Sandomo, 'On the Theory of the Competitive Firm under Price Uncertainty' (1971) 61 *Amer. Econ. Rev.* 65; and Albert Zucker, 'On the Desirability of Price Instability: An Extension of the Discussion' (1965) 22 *Econometrica* 437.

114 Hutton and Trebilcock, *op. cit.*, p. 130.

115 See e.g. Barceló, *op. cit.*

116 S. Rep. No. 249, 96th Cong. 1st Sess. 37 (1980); cited in Palmeter, *op. cit.*, p. 191.

117 *Bingham and Taylor Div. Va. Industries, Inc.* v. *United States*, 815 F.2d 1482, 1485 (Fed. Cir. 1987). See also *Matsushita Electric Industrial Co.* v. *United States*, 823 F.2d 505, 509 (Fed. Cir. 1987).

118 For a useful discussion of both the economic and political elements of unfairness claims see R.E. Hudec, 'Mirror, Mirror, On the Wall: The Concept of Fairness in United States Trade Policy', in *1990 Proceedings*, Canadian Conference on International Law.

119 Bhagwati, *op. cit.*, p. 50.

120 *Ibid.*, p. 68.

121 For a brief and incisive discussion of the welfare effects of low-priced imports see J.A.

Ordover, A.O. Sykes and R.D. Willig, 'Unfair International Trade Practices' (1983) 15 *Int'l L. & Pol'y* 323 pp. 330–4.

122 Hutton and Trebilcock, *op. cit.*, p. 124. The issue that is raised is whether antidumping laws are the appropriate tool for vindicating these concerns. Compared to antidumping actions, safeguard actions and domestic adjustment assistance policies are preferable policy instruments to address those impacts. This is discussed further in Chapter 9.

123 See e.g. John Rawls, *A Theory of Justice* (Cambridge MA: Belknap Press, 1971).

124 While shareholders often include pension plans and employee shareholders (and therefore workers) it is likely that pension plans would diversify their assets so that import competition would not significantly erode workers' savings.

125 See e.g. Michael Sandel, *Liberalism and the Limits of Justice* (Cambridgeshire NY: Cambridge University Press, 1982).

126 Hutton and Trebilcock, *op. cit.*, p. 143.

127 *Ibid.*

128 Alan Sykes, 'The Economics of Injury in Antidumping and Countevailing Duty Cases' (1996) 16 *International Review of Law and Economics* 5.

129 See Nicolaides *op. cit.*; B.M. Hoekman and M.P. Leidy, 'Dumping, Antidumping and Emergency Protection' (1989) 23 *J. of World Trade*, p. 27.

130 See *United Brands v. E.C. Commission* [1978] E.C.R. 207; 1 C.M.L.R. 429 C. Ct. of Justice.

131 Presley Warner, 'The Canada–U.S. Free Trade Agreement: The Case for Replacing Antidumping with Antitrust' (1992) 23 *Law and Policy in International Business* 791.

132 See Hoekman and Leidy, *op. cit.*

133 See more generally, Boddez and Trebilcock, *op. cit.*

8 Subsidies, countervailing duties, and government procurement

1 This is not the case among member countries of some free trade–common market arrangements, like the EC, where countervailing duties have been abolished.

2 P. Messerlin, 'Antidumping', in J.J. Schott (ed.) *Completing the Uruguay Round: A Results-Oriented Approach to the GATT Trade Negotiations* (Washington DC: Institute for International Economics, 1990), 108 at p. 110.

3 *Ibid.*

4 P. Messerlin, 'Public Subsidies to Industry and Agriculture and Countervailing Duties'. Paper prepared for the 'European Meeting on the Position of the European Community in the New GATT Round' (Spain, 2–4 October 1986) as cited in J.M. Finger, 'Antidumping and Antisubsidy Measures' in J.M. Finger and A. Olechavski (eds) *The Uruguay Round: A Handbook on the Multilateral Trade Negotiations* (Washington DC: The World Bank, 1987) 153 at p. 156.

5 See Michael Trebilcock, Marsha Chandler and Robert Howse, *Trade and Transitions: A Comparative Analysis of Adjustment Policies* (London: Routledge, 1990) p. 88.

6 Industrial subsidies as a percentage of GDP at market prices in Canada were 2.6% in 1980–4 and 2.2% in 1985–8. In the United States the same measures show a 0.5% contribution for 1980–4 and 0.7% for 1985–8.

7 E. Fry, *Subsidies and International Trade: The Provincial and State Dimension* (Halifax: Institute for Research and Public Policy, 1990).

8 Fry, *ibid.*; M.G. Smith, 'Overview of Provincial and State Subsidies: Their Implications for Canada–U.S. Trade', in *International Economic Issues* (Halifax: Institute for Research on Public Policy, April 1990).

9 J-F. Bence and M.G. Smith, 'Subsidies and the Trade Laws: The Canada–U.S. Dimension', *International Economic Issues*, May–June 1989.

10 *Ibid.*, pp. 31–2. OECD, *Economic Survey: United States (1991–1992)* (Paris: OECD, 1991) p. 148.

11 Article VI, GATT. Part V of the Uruguay Round Subsidies Code also governs countervailing duties.
12 In the USA, retaliation against certain unfair foreign producers is authorized under s. 301 of the *Omnibus Trade and Competition Act*, 1988.
13 Of course, if domestic producers in country C were being harmed then from the perspective of country C this situation is like the first.
14 There is some evidence that early commentators on trade were concerned about unfair trade and did not sharply distinguish the concepts of dumping and subsidization: J.H. Jackson, *The World Trading System: Law and Policy of International Economic Relations* (Cambridge MA: MIT Press, 1997, 2nd ed.) p. 285 [hereinafter *World Trading System*]. Even now, because of the overlap between countervailing duty and antidumping complaints, US producers will often initiate both actions against an exporter.
15 This distinction leads some commentators to conclude that countervailing duty actions are more legitimate: these duties offset distortions caused by government interference in a free market, while antidumping duties compound the distortion created by a producer with market power by forcing domestic consumers to pay monopoly prices. See for example, K. Dam, *The GATT: Law and International Economic Organization* (Chicago: University of Chicago Press, 1970) pp. 177–9.
16 Paragraph 4 of Article VI of the GATT.
17 Paragraph 7 of Article VI of the GATT.
18 R.R. Rivers and J.D. Greenwald, 'The Negotiation of a Code on Subsidies and Countervailing Measures: Bridging Fundamental Policy Differences' (1979) 11 *Law & Policy in International Bus.*, 1447 at p. 1460.
19 Section B is entitled, 'Additional Provisions on Export Subsidies'. However, there is no definition of export subsidies in the Section or Article.
20 Seventeen developed countries accepted the new section. G. Horlick, R. Quick and E. Vermulst, 'Government Actions Against Domestic Subsidies, An Analysis of the International Rules and an Introduction to United States' Practice' (1986) 12 *Legal Issues of European Integration*, pp. 1–51.
21 See Jackson, *World Trading System, op. cit.*, p. 286.
22 See J. Jackson, *Legal Problems of International Economic Relations* (St Paul, MN: West Publishing Co., 1977) p. 756. This list was updated during the Tokyo Round Subsidies Code negotiations.
23 G. Winham, *International Trade and the Tokyo Round Negotiations* (Princeton NJ: Princeton University Press, 1986) p. 116.
24 *Ibid.*, p. 119.
25 The nature of the policy differences and the way in which these differences were resolved is discussed in detail in Rivers and Greenwald, *op. cit.* In large part, the conflict on subsidies can be linked to the USA's dissatisfaction with the Common Agricultural Policy of the EC.
26 Article 4, Subsidies Code.
27 J.H. Jackson, *World Trading System, op. cit.* p. 288.
28 J.J. Barceló III, 'The Two Track Subsidies Code – Countervailing Duties and Trade Retaliation', in J. Quinn and P. Slayton (eds) *Non-Tariff Barriers After the Tokyo Round* (Montreal: Institute for Research on Public Policy, 1982) [hereinafter 'Trade Retaliation'] p. 121.
29 As was the case in the GATT, there is no definition of export subsidies. There is a revised 'Illustrative List of Export Subsidies' in the annex to the Code which is intended as an aid to interpretation. There is some debate about whether the list is relevant to Track I or only Track II of the Code. According to Jackson: 'The U.S. has taken the position that [it] is only useful in interpreting a definition of subsidies for purposes of Track 2 of the Code and does not in any way constrain national sovereigns in their definition of "subsidy" for purposes of Track 1' (*World Trading System, op. cit.*, pp. 259–60).
30 Article 11(1).

31 Article 11(1) of the Code.
32 Article 11(2).
33 According to Jackson: 'It is not surprising that the Subsidies Code has had a very difficult history subsequent to the completion of the Tokyo Round, since its very language reflects considerable ambivalence about its obligations' (*World Trading System*, *op. cit.*, p. 259).
34 Article 12(3).
35 The Committee is comprised of a representative from each signatory to the agreement.
36 *United States – Denial of Most-Favoured Nation Treatment as to Non-Rubber Footwear from Brazil*, Report by the Panel adopted on 19 June 1992 (DS18/R – 39S/128).
37 *United States – Imposition of Countervailing Duties on Imports of Fresh and Chilled Atlantic Salmon from Norway*, Report of the Panel adopted by the Committee on Subsidies and Countervailing Measures on 28 April 1994, SCM/153.
38 *Ibid.*, para. 351.
39 *Ibid.*, paras 235–41.
40 *Brazil – Imposition of Provisional and Definitive Countervailing Duties on Milk Powder and Certain Types of Milk from the European Economic Community*, Report of the Panel adopted by the Committee on Subsidies and Countervailing Measures on 28 April 1994, SCM/179.
41 For reviews of the Uruguay Round Subsidies Agreement, see Terry Collins-Williams and Gerry Salembier, 'International Disciplines on Subsidies: The GATT, the WTO, and the Future Agenda' (1996) 30 *J. of World Trade* 5; Americo Zampetti, 'The Uruguay Round on Subsidies: A Forward-Looking Assessment' (1995) 29 *J. of World Trade* 5; and Jeffrey Schott, *The Uruguay Round: An Assessment* (Washington DC: Institute for International Economics, 1994) pp. 86–93.
42 The application of the assistance must be limited to the following costs: personnel; instruments, equipment, land and buildings used exclusively and permanently for the research activity; consultancy and other similar services used exclusively for the research activity; other overhead costs; and running costs incurred directly as a result of the research activity.
43 *Brazil – Measures Affecting Desiccated Coconut*, AB-1996-4, WT/DS22/AB/R.
44 *Brazil – Measures Affecting Desiccated Coconut*, AB-1996-4, WT/DS22/AB/R, p. 20.
45 For an extensive review of government procurement under international agreements, see: Ari Reich, *Toward Free Trade in the Public Sector* (S.J.D. Thesis, Faculty of Law, University of Toronto, 1994).
46 S. Arrowsmith, *Government Procurement and Judicial Review* (Toronto: Carswell, 1988) p. 1.
47 For examples of this 'secondary' use, see W.F. Leimkuhler, 'Enforcing Social and Economic Policy through Government Contracts', in *Annual Survey of American Law* (1980) p. 539.
48 For this topic, see US General Accounting Office, Washington DC, *Government Buy-National Practices of the United States and Other Countries – an Assessment* (1976). On the discriminatory procurement practices of various governments see R. Baldwin, *Nontariff Distortions of International Trade* (Washington DC: Brookings Institution, 1970) pp. 59–70; M. Krauss, *The New Protectionism: The Welfare State and International Trade* (New York: New York University Press,1978) pp. 54–6.
49 For example, the Canadian Content Premium (see Deputy Minister of Supply and Services Directive 637 [10/02/89] Annex A-1) and the Buy American Policy (see the Buy American Act [41 U.S.C., 1976]).
50 See *Selling to Government, A Guide to Government Procurement in Canada* (Ottowa: Minister of Supply and Services Canada, 1989) pp. 48–50.
51 See Olivier Long, *The Tokyo Round of Multilateral Trade Negotiations*, Report by the Director General of GATT (Geneva, April 1979).
52 The Agreement on Government Procurement (the Code), Published in GATT BISD, 26th Suppl., p. 33. The amendments to the Code enacted in 1987 were published as

'Protocol Amending the Agreement on Government Procurement', BISD 34th Suppl. p.12.

53 This threshold was lowered from SDR 150,000 (Article 1:1(b)) by the 1987 amendments. SDR stands for Special Drawing Rights, the IMF's monetary units. The value of the threshold in the currency of each signatory is determined by the Committee established by the Agreement, in consultation with the signatory in question, and applies throughout a two year period until next determination. SDR 150,000 is approximately $US181,000.

54 See Article 1:1(a). Note that this has been changed under the Uruguay Round negotiations.

55 See Article 11:4.

56 See Article V.

57 See Articles V:2, V:6, and V:7.

58 Article V:16 limits circumstances for 'single tendering'. On collusion in tendering see: United Nations Conference on Trade and Development, *Collusive Tendering* (New York, 1985).

59 See Article V:15(f).

60 See Article VI:6. Usually, no effective remedy is provided. See US International Trade Commission, *Review of the Effectiveness of Trade Dispute Settlement Under the GATT and the Tokyo Round Agreements* (Washington DC: USITC, 1985).

61 See Article VII:14.

62 *Norway – Procurement of Toll Collection Equipment for the City of Trondheim*, Report of the Panel adopted by the Committee on Government Procurement on 13 May 1992.

63 *Ibid.*, para. 1.3.

64 For reviews of the Uruguay Round Government Procurement Agreement, see Arie Reich, 'The New GATT Agreement on Government Procurement: The Pitfalls of Plurilateralism and Strict Reciprocity' (1997) 31 *J. of World Trade* 125 and Schott, *op. cit.*, pp. 66–76. See also Report (1998) of Working Group on Transparency in Government Procurement to the WTO General Council.

65 Mission of Canada Geneva, '(draft) GATT Agreement on Government Procurement' (15/12/93).

66 *Ibid.*, Article I.

67 *Ibid.*, Article XVI.

68 *Ibid.*, Article XX.

69 See Reich, *op. cit.*

70 Treasury Board of Canada, Ottawa, Canada, *Administrative Policy Manual*, Chapter 305, 'Procurement Review' (March 1980).

71 See Minister of Supply and Services, Hull, Canada, *The Canada–U.S. Free Trade Agreement and Government Procurement: An Assessment*, 1989.

72 Most Favourable Treatment' obligation under Article 1305:1 of the FTA.

73 Compare Annex 1002.1 of NAFTA with Annex 1304.3 of the FTA.

74 See NAFTA Article 1006.

75 See Council Directive 71/305/EEC, *O.J.* 1971, L 185/5 ('The Works Directive') and Council Directive 77/62/EEC *O.J.* 1977 L 13/1 ('The Supplies Directive'). Also see Council Directive 88/295/EEC *O.J.* 1988 L 127 ('Amending Supplies Directive') and Council Directive 89/440/EEC *O.J.* 1989 L 210 ('Amending Works Directive'). For a recent study on public sector procurement in Europe, see The 'Cost of Non-Europe' *in Public Sector Procurement*, Research on the 'Cost of Non-Europe', Basic Findings, vol. 5, by W.S. Atkins Management Consultants (Commission of the European Communities, 1988).

76 For a list of these circumstances, see Article 9 in the Works Directive, and Article 6 in the Supply Directive.

77 Council Directive 89/665/EEC *O.J.* 1989 395/33–35.

78 Council Directive 90/531/EEC *O.J.* 1990 297.

79 Council Directive 92/13/EEC *O.J.* 1992 76, p. 14.

80 For a detailed description of the administration of countervailing duty laws in the USA see: T. Boddez and M. Trebilcock, *Unfinished Business: Reforming Trade Remedy Laws in North America* (Toronto: C.D. Howe Institute, 1993); R. Diamond, 'A Search for Economic and Financial Principles in the Administration of United States Countervailing Duty Law' (1990) 21 *Law and Policy in International Bus.* 507; and T.V. Vakerics, D.I. Wilson and K.G. Weigel, *Antidumping, Countervailing Duty and Other Trade Actions* (New York: Practising Law Institute, 1987) pp. 218–19.

81 The Tariff Act, 19 U.S.C. §§702(a) and 732(a) authorizes the ITA to initiate investigations. It rarely does so. Most investigations are initiated by complaints from domestic producers.

82 Tariff Act, 19 U.S.C. §1671.

83 Jackson, *World Trading System, op. cit.*, p. 293.

84 A.O. Sykes, 'Countervailing Duty Law: An Economic Perspective' (1989) 89 *Columbia L. Rev.* 199 at p. 203.

85 See Vakerics, Wilson and Weigel, *op. cit.*, pp. 218–19.

86 G.C. Hufbauer and J. Erb, *Subsidies in International Trade* (Washington DC: Institute for International Economics, 1984).

87 Vakerics, Wilson and Weigel, *op. cit.*, p. 221.

88 Tariff Act, §1677(5)(B).

89 See J. Bello and W. Homer, 'Subsidies and Natural Resources: Congress Rejects a Lateral Attack on the Specificity Test' (1984) 18 *George Washington J. of Int'l L. and Econ.* 297; Panzarella, 'Is the Specificity Test Generally Applicable?' (1986) 18 *L. and Policy in Int'l Bus.* 417; and Sussman, 'Countervailing Duties and the Specificity Test: An Alternative Approach to the Definition of "Bounty or Grant"' (1986) 18 *L. and Policy in Int'l Bus.* 475.

90 564 F.Supp. 834 (Ct. Int'l Trade 1983).

91 620 F.Supp. 722 (Ct. Int'l Trade 1985).

92 54 *Federal Register* 30774 (1989) at p. 30777.

93 These aspects are highlighted in Vakerics, Wilson and Weigel, *op. cit.*, p. 222.

94 The rationale for this rule is that in a non-market economy there is no valid distinction between government and industry. See, for example, *Carbon Steel Wire Rod from Czechoslovakia*, 49 Fed. Reg. 55014 (1983).

95 Upstream subsidies are defined in 19 U.S.C. §1671-1(a)(1) as subsidies paid or bestowed by a foreign government with respect to an input that is used in the manufacture, in the same country, of merchandise that is the subject of a countervailing duty proceeding.

96 See, for example, *Prestressed Concrete Steel Wire Strands from Spain*, 47 Fed. Reg. 28723, 28726 (1982).

97 Details of the approach of the ITA to these cases can be found in Vakerics, Wilson and Weigel, *op. cit.*, p. 230.

98 See, for example, *Certain Iron-Metal Castings from India*, 45 Fed. Reg. 34946 (1980).

99 19 U.S.C. §1671(a)(1)(B). An example of this is found in *Certain Steel Products from the Republic of Korea*, 47 Fed. Reg. 57535 (1982).

100 J. Terry, 'Sovereignty, Subsidies and Countervailing Duties in the Context of the Canada–U.S. Trading Relationship' (1988) 46 *University of Toronto Fac. L. Rev.* 48 at p. 69.

101 G.N. Horlick, 'Subsidies and Suspension Agreements in Countervailing Duty Cases' in *The Commerce Department Speaks on Dumping and Countervailing Duties* (New York: Practising Law Institute, 1982) p. 31.

102 *Certain Textile Products from Mexico*, 50 Fed. Reg. 10824 (1985).

103 Diamond, *op. cit.*, pp. 541–2.

104 See 19 U.S.C. §1677(b).

105 Vakerics, Wilson and Weigel, *op. cit.*, p. 221.

106 See Vakerics, Wilson and Weigel, *ibid.*, p. 239 for details on this aspect of US countervailing duty law.

107 Thus, many of the same problems arise that were discussed in Chapter 7.
108 Article 16.1.
109 19 U.S.C. §1677(4)(A).
110 19 U.S.C. §1677(4)(C).
111 19 U.S.C. §1677(10).
112 In *Certain Carbon Steel Products from Argentina, Australia, Finland, South Africa and Spain*, Inv. No. 701-TA-212, USITC Pub. No. 1510 (1984), there were five separate like products.
113 Article 15.4.
114 Tariff Act, 19 U.S.C. §1677(7)(A).
115 19 U.S.C. §1677(7)(C).
116 *Ibid.*
117 M.S. Knoll, 'An Economic Approach to the Determination of Injury Under United States Antidumping and Countervailing Duty Law' (1989) 22 *New York University J. of Int'l Law & Pol.* 37 at p. 52.
118 For a detailed criticism of ITC methodology see Boddez and Trebilcock, *op. cit.*, 73 at p. 57.
119 Article 15.5.
120 Knoll, *op. cit.*, p. 54; and R. Cass and A. Schwartz, 'Causality, Coherence, and Transparency in the Implementation of International Trade Law', in M.J. Trebilcock and R.C. York (eds) *Fair Exchange: Reforming Trade Remedy Laws* (Toronto: C.D. Howe Institute, 1990) [hereinafter *Fair Exchange*] 24 at p. 43.
121 Cass and Schwartz, *op. cit.*, p. 43.
122 *Ibid.*, p. 33.
123 See for example, *Matsushita Electric Industrial Co.* v. *United States*, 750 F.2d 927 (1984).
124 *Ceramica Regiomontana, S.A.* v. *United States*, 810 F.2d 1137 at 1139 (Fed. Cir. 1987).
125 See Boddez and Trebilcock, *op. cit.*, ch. 3 for a detailed analysis of binational panel decisions in antidumping and countervailing duty cases; also John Mercury, 'Chapter 19 of the United States – Canada Free Trade Agreement 1989-1995: A Check on Administered Protection?' (1995) 15 *Northwestern J. of International Law and Business* 525.
126 Boddez and Trebilcock, *op. cit.*, ch. 3. See also Chapter 5.
127 Boddez and Trebilcock, *op. cit.*, pp. 43–50.
128 For a similar proposal, see Charles Gastle and Jean-G. Castel, 'Should the North American Free Trade Agreement Dispute Settlement Mechanism in Antidumping and Countervailing Duty Cases Be Reformed in the light of Softwood Lumber III?' (1995) 26 *Law and Policy in International Business* 823.
129 Terry, *op. cit.*, p. 51; and W. Schwartz and E.W. Harper, Jr., 'The Regulation of Subsidies Affecting International Trade' (1972) 70 *Mich. L. Rev.* 831.
130 Schwartz and Harper, *op. cit.*, p. 844.
131 See Sykes, *op. cit.*
132 Schwartz and Harper, *op. cit.*, pp. 834–5. Predatory pricing and international price discrimination are discussed in detail in Chapter 5.
133 Robert Hudec, 'Mirror, Mirror on the Wall: The Concept of Fairness in the United States Foreign Trade Policy' in *Proceedings of the Canadian Council on International Law* 88.
134 See Countervailing Duty Law Symposium Issue (Ottawa: Canadian Council of International Law, 1990). (1990) 21 *Law & Policy in International Business.*
135 See Jagdish Bhagwati, 'Fair Trade, Reciprocity, and Harmonization: The New Challenge to the Theory and Policy of Free Trade' in A. Deardorff and R. Stein (eds) *Analytical and Negotiating Issues in the Global Trading System* (Ann Arbor: University of Michigan Press, 1993); Bhagwati, 'Challenges to the Doctrine of Free Trade' (1993) 25 *International Law and Politics* 219.
136 See Hudec, *op. cit.*, note 127.
137 J. Bhagwati, *The World Trading System at Risk* (Princeton NJ: Princeton University Press, 1991) pp. 21–2; see also James Bovard, *The Fair Trade Fraud* (New York: St. Martin's

Press, 1991).

138 This group would include unskilled, immobile or low-income workers. See, J. Rawls, *A Theory of Justice* (Cambridge MA: Belknap Press, 1971).

139 For an extensive comparative evaluation of attempts to regulate subsidies in international trade, see R. Behboodi, *The Regulation of Subsidies in International Trade* (London: Routledge, 1995).

140 Diamond, *op. cit.*; M.J. Trebilcock, 'Is the Game Worth the Candle? Comments on Diamond, "A Search for Financial and Economic Principles in the Administration of Countervailing Duty Law"' (1990) 21 *Law & Policy in Int'l Bus.* 723; Trebilcock, 'Throwing Deep: Trade Remedies in a First-Best World', in Trebilcock and York (eds) *op. cit.*; and M. Hart, 'Idealism *versus* Pragmatism: Policy and the Academic Analyst', in Trebilcock and York (eds) *op. cit.*

141 Diamond, *op. cit.*, pp. 158–9.

142 Diamond, *op. cit.*

143 C. Goetz, L. Granet and W. Schwartz, 'The Meaning of "Subsidy" and "Injury" in the Countervailing Duty Law' (1986) 6 *Int'l. Rev. of Law and Econ.* 17; see also R. Diamond, 'Economic Foundations of Countervailing Duty Law' (1989) 29 *Virginia J. of Int'l Law* 767.

144 Identifying predatory pricing or setting a reasonable rate of return for a natural monopoly are prominent examples.

145 These would include, for example, cases of inefficiency or mismanagement of domestic firms as well as threats from more efficient third country exporters. At the same time, the subsidy in question may have been conferred principally for home market reasons.

146 See Goetz, Granet and Schwartz, *op. cit.*, pp. 26–9; see also Alan Sykes, 'Second-Best Countervailing Duty Policy: A Critique of the Entitlement Approach' (1990) 21 *Law & Policy in International Business* 699.

147 J.J. Barceló, 'Subsidies and Countervailing Duties: Analysis and a Proposal' (1977) 9 *Law & Policy in Int'l Bus.* 779.

148 See Barceló, 'Trade Retaliation' *op. cit.*; and Sykes, *op. cit.*

149 See for example, Richard Harris, *Trade, Industrial Policy and International Competition*, Royal Commission on the Economic Union and Development Prospects for Canada Collected Research Studies 13 (Toronto: University of Toronto Press, 1985).

150 See, H. Milner and D. Yoffie, 'Between Free Trade and Protectionism: Strategic Trade Policy and a Theory of Corporate Trade Demands' (Spring 1989) *International Organization* 238.

151 The Commission has, however, employed some common-sense *de minimis* tests to dispose of cases where the aid in question could have little plausible impact on trade; see, in general, C. Quigley, 'The Notion of a State Aid in the EEC' (1988) 13 *European Law Review* 242; R. Howse, *Economic Union, Social Justice, and Constitutional Reform: Towards a High but Level Playing Field* (Toronto: York Centre for Public Law and Public Policy, 1992) Appendix III.

152 See A. Evans and S. Martin, 'Socially Acceptable Distortion of Competition: Community Policy on State Aid' (1991) 16 *European Law Review* 80.

153 See more generally, Boddez and Trebilcock, *op. cit.*

154 These panels hear disputes between Canada and the USA that are unrelated to unfair trade law.

155 T.L. McDorman, 'Using the Dispute Settlement Regime of the Free Trade Agreement: The West Coast Salmon and Herring Problem' (1991) 4 *Canada–U.S. Bus. L. Rev.* 117, p. 179.

156 See especially, *R.* v. *Oakes* (1986) 26 D.L.R. (4th) 200 (S.C.C.).

157 For a similar set of proposals, see Terry Collins-Williams and Gerry Salembier, 'International Disciplines on Subsidies: The GATT, the WTO and the Future Agenda' (1996) 1 *J. of World Trade* 5.

9 Safeguard regimes and domestic adjustment policies

1 Article XIX:1 lays out the grounds for invocation; XIX:2 the notification requirement; and XIX:3 the right to compensation.
2 Compensation usually takes the form of other trade concessions. In the absence of agreement on compensation, the exporting countries can impose import restraints of substantially equivalent value.
3 See G. Sampson, 'Safeguards', in J.M. Finger and A. Olechowski (eds) *The Uruguay Round: A Handbook on the Multilateral Trade Negotiations* (Washington DC: The World Bank, 1987) 143, Table 19.3 p. 147. Jeffrey Schott, *The Uruguay Round: An Assessment* (Washington DC: Institute for International Economics, 1994) pp. 94, 95.
4 From P.A. Messerlin, 'Antidumping', in J.J. Schott (ed.) *Completing the Uruguay Round: A Results Oriented Approach to the GATT Trade Negotiations* (Washington DC: Institute for International Economics, 1990) 108, Table 6.1 p. 110 [hereinafter *Completing the Uruguay Round*].
5 From M.J. Trebilcock, 'Throwing Deep: Trade Remedies in a First-Best World', in M.J. Trebilcock and R.C. York (eds) *Fair Exchange: Reforming Trade Remedy Laws* (Toronto: C.D. Howe Institute, 1990) 235, Table A-4 p. 273 [hereinafter *Fair Exchange*]. This figure includes voluntary export restraints, orderly marketing arrangements, export forecasts, basic price systems, industry-to-industry arrangements and discriminatory import systems.
6 These arrangements are not contemplated by the GATT but are generally believed to be inconsistent with GATT's policy on export restraints. It is difficult for the GATT to control these agreements unless a complaint is lodged; since both Parties usually have an interest in the ERA complaints are infrequent. See J.H. Jackson, *The World Trading System: Law and Policy of International Economic Relations* (Cambridge MA: MIT Press, 1997, 2nd ed.) p. 205 [hereinafter *The World Trading System*].
7 23 December 1942, Article XI, 57 Stat. 833 (1943); E.A.S. No. 311 (effective 30 January 1943).
8 William L. Clayton, *GATT: An Analysis and Appraisal of the General Agreement on Tariffs and Trade* (U.S. Council of the International Chamber of Commerce, 1955) p. 36, n. 8.
9 J.H. Jackson, *World Trade and the Law of GATT* (Ann Arbor: Bobbs-Merrill, 1969) p. 554 [hereinafter *World Trade*].
10 The historical description that follows draws primarily on G. Winham, *International Trade and the Tokyo Round Negotiations* (Princeton: Princeton University Press, 1986).
11 Jackson, *World Trade, op. cit.*, p. 557.
12 According to Sampson: 'Article XIX has rarely, if ever, been interpreted in a way that would appear to be consistent with the text' (*op. cit.*, p. 143).
13 This interpretation of 'increased' was adopted at the Second Session of the GATT Contracting Parties in 1948 (GATT, 2 BISD 39, pp. 44–5 (1952)). The allowance of safeguard actions when imports have not increased absolutely is controversial since it shifts the burden of an economic downturn to foreign producers (Jackson, *World Trade, op. cit.*, p. 558).
14 Jackson, *The World Trading System, op. cit.*, p. 197.
15 *Ibid.*
16 A.O. Sykes, 'Protectionism as "Safeguard": A Positive Analysis of the GATT "Escape Clause" with Normative Speculations' (1991) 58 *University of Chic. L. Rev.* 255 p. 288 [hereinafter 'Protectionism'].
17 *Ibid.*, p. 287.
18 See *Report on the Withdrawal by the U.S. of a Tariff Concession Under Article XIX of the GATT (the Hatter's Fur Case)* (Geneva, GATT/151-3, 1951).
19 Sampson, *op. cit.*, p. 143.
20 GATT L/76 (1953). The interpretation was developed as part of the negotiations on the International Trade Organisation which was never realized so it has only persuasive value.

21 The legal and practical requirement of nondiscrimination is the subject of some controversy. See Jackson, *The World Trading System, op. cit.* pp. 195–9; M. Bronckers, 'The Nondiscriminatory Application of Article XIX GATT: Tradition or Fiction?' (1981/2) *Legal Issues of European Integration (LIEI)* 35, 'Reconsidering the Nondiscrimination Principle as Applied to GATT Safeguard Measures' (1983/2) *LIEI* 113 and *Selective Safeguard Measures in Multilateral Trade Relations* (Deventer: Kluwer, 1985); and Koulen, 'The Nondiscriminatory Interpretation of GATT Article XIX(1): A Reply' (1983/2) *LIEI* 89.
22 See Jackson, *World Trading System, op. cit.*, p. 194.
23 Sykes, 'Protectionism', *op. cit.*
24 *The Canada–U.S. Free Trade Agreement* (Toronto: CCH Canadian, 1988) 364. For a discussion of the FTA provisions, see M.J. Trebilcock, 'Reforming the GATT Safeguards Regime' (1989) 15 *Can. Bus. L.J.* 234.
25 Article 1101. Once the transition period is over bilateral emergency action can only be taken with consent of the other country.
26 These measures contrast with ERAs which typically allow exporters to reap monopoly profits at the expense of domestic consumers.
27 Kenneth Dam, *The GATT: Law and International Economic Organization* (Chicago: University of Chicago Press, 1970) p. 106.
28 *Ibid.*, p. 99.
29 Sykes, 'Protectionism' *op. cit.* and A.O. Sykes, 'GATT Safeguards Reform: The Injury Test', in *Fair Exchange, op. cit.*, p. 203 [hereinafter 'The Injury Test'].
30 Sykes, 'Protectionism', *op. cit.*, p. 279.
31 If these two assumptions are false then there is no need for a safeguard clause since countries can either escape their obligations via a substitute for safeguard relief or else simply ignore their trade obligations.
32 Jackson, *The World Trading System, op. cit.*, p. 176.
33 G.C. Hufbauer and H.F. Rosen, *Trade Policy for Troubled Industries* (Washington DC: Institute for International Economics, 1986).
34 With the remaining four it was too early to make a determination. Successful adjustment cases included cases in which the industry requested further protection following the end of the relief and ITC denied such renewal on the grounds that trade was not causing the injury.
35 See M.J. Trebilcock, M.A. Chandler and R. Howse, *Trade and Transitions: A Comparative Analysis of Adjustment Policies* (London: Routledge, 1990) pp. 42–76.
36 R.W. Crandall, 'Import Quotas and the Automobile Industry: The Costs of Protectionism' (1983) 2 *Brookings Review* 4, p. 8.
37 Economic Council of Canada, *Managing Adjustment* (Ottawa: Economic Council of Canada, 1988) pp. 61,70,76.
38 Until midway through 1987 compensation was offered in twenty GATT safeguard clause cases and retaliation occurred in only thirteen. See E.-U. Petersmann, 'Grey Area Trade Policy and the Rule of Law' (1988) 22 *J. of World Trade* 23, p. 36.
39 See Sykes, 'Protectionism', *op. cit.*
40 R.Z. Lawrence, 'GATT Safeguards Reform: A Comment', in *Fair Exchange, op. cit.*, p. 203.
41 C. Hamilton and J. Whalley would include in these alternate measures antidumping and countervailing-duty actions. 'Safeguards', in *Completing the Uruguay Round, op. cit.*, 79 p. 89.
42 E-U Petersmann, 'Economic, Legal and Political Functions of the Principle of Non-Discrimination', 9 *World Economy*, March 1986, 113.
43 Marco Bronckers, *Selective Safeguard Measures in Multilateral Trade Relations: Issues of Protectionism in GATT, European Community* and *United States Law* (Deventer: Kluwer Law and Taxation Publishers, 1985) ch. 3.
44 For a fuller elaboration of these arguments, see Bronckers *op. cit.*
45 Winham, *op. cit.*
46 According to Winham, the USA adopted a middle ground. It was sympathetic to the

view of developing countries but also saw itself as vulnerable to sudden import increases from low cost suppliers (*op. cit.*, p. 199).

47 Winham, *ibid.*, pp. 243–4.

48 GATT Secretariat, *The Tokyo Round of Multilateral Trade Negotiations: Supplementary Report* (Geneva: 1980) p. 42.

49 Winham, *op. cit.*, p. 358.

50 A.W. Wolff, 'The Need for New GATT Rules to Govern Safeguard Actions', in W.R. Cline (ed.) *Trade Policy in the 1980s* (Washington DC: Institute for International Economics, 1983) 363 p. 383.

51 *Ibid.*

52 J. Zietz, 'Negotiations on GATT Reform and Political Incentives' (1989) 12 *World Economy* 39.

53 Sykes: 'Protectionism', *op. cit.*; and 'The Injury Test', *op. cit.*

54 Hufbauer and Rosen, *op. cit.*, p. 60.

55 Trebilcock, *op. cit.* (1989) p. 238; J.D. Richardson, 'Safeguards Issues in the Uruguay Round', in R.E. Baldwin and J.D. Richardson (eds) *Issues in the Uruguay Round* (Cambridge MA: NBER, 1988) 24 p. 33.

56 *Ibid.*

57 J. Tumlir, 'A Revised Safeguard Clause for GATT?' (1973) 7 *J. of World Trade Law* 404.

58 Wolff, *op. cit.*, p. 380.

59 Trebilcock, *op. cit.* (1989) p. 238.

60 See Trebilcock, Chandler and Howse, *op. cit.*

61 Report of the Advisory Council on Adjustment (De Grandpré Report) *Adjusting to Win* (Ottawa: Supply and Services Canada, 1989).

62 *Ibid.*, p. xvii.

63 L. Kaplow, 'An Economic Analysis of Legal Transitions' (1986) 99 *Harvard L. Rev.* 509.

64 For a discussion of the difficulties of predicting employment effects with precision, see Economic Council of Canada, *Venturing Forth: An Assessment of the Canada–U.S. Trade Agreement* (Ottawa: Supply and Services, 1988).

65 The evidence is presented in W. Wendling, *The Plant Closure Policy Dilemma: Labor, Law and Bargaining* (Kalamazoo MI: Upjohn Institute for Employment Research, 1984).

66 See more generally, R. Howse and M. Trebilcock, 'Protecting the Employment Bargain' (1993) 43 *University of Toronto L.J.* 751.

67 See, especially, G. Glenday, G.P. Jenkins and J.C. Evans, *Worker Adjustment to Liberalized Trade: Costs and Assistance Policies* (Washington DC: World Bank, 1980) pp. 50–5.

68 The seminal study on this phenomenon is J. Elster, *Sour Grapes: Studies in the Subversion of Rationality* (Cambridge: Cambridge University Press, 1983).

69 See C.R. Leana and D.C. Feldman, *Coping with Job Loss: How Individuals, Organizations and Communities Respond to Layoffs* (New York: Lexington Books, 1992) ch. 3 'Reactions to Job Loss'.

70 F. Michelman, 'Property, Utility and Fairness' (1967) 80 *Harvard L. Rev.* 1165.

71 G. Calabresi, *Ideals, Beliefs, Attitudes and the Law* (New York: Syracuse University Press, 1985) p. 109.

72 See Robert Foy 'Enhancing the Effectiveness of Active Labour Policies: Evidence from Programme Evaluations in OECD Countries', Labour Market and Social Policy Occasional Paper No. 18, OECD, Paris 1996; Duane Leigh, *Does Training Work for Displaced Workers?* (Kalamazoo MI: Upjohn Institute for Employment Research, 1990); Duane Leigh, *Asserting Workers Displaced by Structural Change* (Kalamazoo MI: Upjohn Institute, 1995).

73 M. Trebilcock, *The Political Economy of Economic Adjustment* (vol. 8, Research Study prepared for Royal Commission on Economic Union and Development Prospects in Canada, Toronto: University of Toronto Press, 1985).

74 R.Z. Lawrence and R. Litan, 'Living with the Trade Deficit: Adjustment Strategies to Preserve Free Trade' (1985) 4 *Brookings Review* 1, pp. 3–13.

75 Hufbauer and Rosen, *op. cit.*
76 P. Morici, 'Transition Mechanisms and Safeguards in a North American Free Trade Agreement', in L. Waverman (ed.) *Negotiating and Implementing a North American Free Trade Agreement* (Toronto and Vancouver: Fraser Institute and Centre for International Studies, 1992) p. 84.
77 See Daniel Tarullo, 'Beyond Normalcy in the Regulation of International Trade' (1987) 100 *Harvard L. Rev.* 546.
78 R. Howse, 'The Case for Linking a Right to Adjustment with the *NAFTA*', in J. Lemcoe and W. Robson (eds) *Ties Beyond Trade: Labor and Environmental Issues under the NAFTA* (Toronto and Washington DC: C.D. Howe Institute and National Planning Association, 1993) pp. 79–107.
79 See Richard Freeman, 'Are Your Wages Set in Beijing?', J. David Richardson, 'Income Inequality and Trade: How To Think, What to Conclude', Adrian Wood, 'How Trade Hurt Unskilled Workers' (1995) 9 *J. of Economics Perspectives* 151 (Symposium); William Cline, *Trade and Economic Distribution* (Washington DC: Institute for International Economics, 1997).

10 Trade in agriculture

1 See *Issues and Developments in International Trade Policy* (Washington DC: International Monetary Fund, 1992) ch. VI, 'Agricultural Trade Policies Recent Developments and Issues for Reform'.
2 K. Dam, *The GATT: Law and the International Economic Organization* (Chicago: University of Chicago Press, 1970) p. 260.
3 D. Hathaway, *Reforming World Agricultural Trade* (Washington DC: Institute for International Economics, 1988) p. 109.
4 But, note that it does not encompass prohibitions.
5 *Dairy Products from the Netherlands*, BISD, vol. II (1952) 116.
6 *Japan: Restrictions on Certain Agricultural Products*, BISD 35th Supp. (1989) 163.
7 *European Community: Restrictions on Imports of Apples*, BISD 36th Supp. (1990).
8 *France: Assistance to Exports of Wheat and Wheat Flour*, BISD 7th Supp. (1959) 46.
9 *European Community: Subsidies on Export of Wheat Flour*, SCM/42 (21 March 1983). See W.H. Boger III, 'The United States–European Community Agricultural Export Subsidies Dispute' (1984) 16 *Law & Policy in International Business* 173.
10 J. Jackson, *The World Trading System: Law and Policy of International Economic Relations* (Cambridge MA: MIT Press, 1997, 2nd ed.) p. 119.
11 *European Community: Subsidies on Exports of Pasta Products*, SCM/43 (19 May 1983).
12 *European Community: Payments and Subsidies on Oilseeds and Animal-Feed Proteins*, BISD, 37th Supp. (1989) 86.
13 See 'Introduction', in K.A. Ingersent, A.J. Rayner and R.C. Hine, *Agriculture in the Uruguay Round* (London: St. Martin's Press, 1994) pp. 5–6.
14 The following account of the agricultural provisions of the *NAFTA* draws extensively on R. Bartichello and T. Josling, 'Agriculture in the *NAFTA*: A Preliminary Assessment', paper presented at C.D. Howe Institute *NAFTA* Conference, Toronto, December 1992.
15 T. Grennes and B. Kristoff, 'Agricultural Trade in a North American Free Trade Agreement' (1993) 16 *World Economy* 483.
16 *Ibid.*, pp. 486–7.
17 B. Wilson and P. Finkle, 'Is Agriculture Different? Another Round in the Battle Between Theory and Practice', in G. Skogstad and A.F. Cooper (eds) *Agricultural Trade: Domestic Pressures and International Tensions* (Halifax: Institute for Research on Public Policy, 1990) p. 17.
18 L. Martin, 'Global Competition and Canadian Federalism: the Agri-Food Sector', paper presented at a Conference on Global Competitiveness and Canadian Federalism, Faculty of Law, University of Toronto, 16 September 1990, p. 3.

19 See J.C. Gilson, 'Agriculture and the Uruguay Round of the GATT', in *World Agriculture Changes: Implications for Canada* (Toronto: C.D. Howe Institute, 1988).
20 *Ibid.*
21 See, for example, OECD, *National Policies and Agricultural Trade* (Paris: OECD, 1987); World Bank, *World Development Report* (Washington DC, 1986).
22 'Grotesque: A Survey of Agriculture', *The Economist*, 12 December 1992, p. 7.
23 See M. Kelly and A.K. McGuirk, *Issues and Developments in International Trade Policy* (Washington DC: IMF, 1992) pp. 59–60. Empirical evidence cited in this study suggests that in the longer term virtually all developing countries would gain from liberalization of agricultural policies in the industrialized countries, as long as the developing countries themselves eliminated domestic distortions in both the agricultural and industrial sectors. See also the economic modelling in R. Tyers and K. Anderson, *Disarray in World Food Markets* (Cambridge and New York: Cambridge University Press, 1992).
24 The members of the Cairns Group were Argentina, Australia, Brazil, Canada, Chile, Colombia, Fiji, Hungary, Indonesia, Malaysia, New Zealand, the Philippines, Thailand and Uruguay. Although Canada was initially very active in the Group, out of concern for its Western grain farmers who have suffered greatly due to export subsidy wars between the USA and the EU, more recently Canada has sought to protect its own system of supply management, particularly with respect to poultry and eggs.
25 *The Economist*, *op. cit.*, p. 7.
26 It is important to note that the United States received strong support for its position that agricultural protection be disciplined in the GATT by the so-called Cairns Group, representing a number of agricultural exporting countries whose agricultural trade was affected by the subsidies wars between the USA and the EC. See A.J. Rayner, K.A. Ingersent and R.C. Hine, 'Agriculture in the Uruguay Round: An Assessment' (1993) 103 *Economic Journal* 1511 pp. 1516–17.
27 Cited in M. Plain, *Trade Negotiations in the OECD* (London: Kegan Paul, 1993) pp. 120–1.
28 *Ibid.*
29 *Ibid.*
30 A.B. Philip, 'The European Community: Balancing Domestic Pressures and International Demands', in G. Skogstad and A.F. Cooper (eds) *op. cit.*, p. 75.
31 Martin, *op. cit.*
32 See, for a discussion of the transitional gains trap problem, M.J. Trebilcock and J. Quinn, 'Compensation, Transition Costs and Regulatory Change' (1982), 32 *University of Toronto Law Journal* 117; see also G. Tullock, 'Achieving Deregulation – A Public Choice Perspective' (1978), *Regulation*, Nov.–Dec. 1978. See Gordon Tullock, 'The Transitional Gains Trap' (1975) 6 *Bell Journal of Economics* 671.
33 Significant work was done at the OECD between 1982 and 1987 with respect to developing methodologies for measuring and comparing levels of agricultural protection in various countries. See Plain, *op. cit.*, pp. 122–3.
34 For an excellent discussion of some of these methodological alternatives, see Gilson, *op. cit.*
35 Some European experts give credence to this US concern. Tarditi for instance suggests the European approach to shifting from price to income support for farmers would involve very significant administrative costs and complexities and be quite vulnerable to widespread fraud by farmers. S. Tarditi, 'Perspectives on EC Agricultural Policy Reform', in Ingersent, Rayner and Hine (eds) *op. cit.*, pp. 212–14.
36 See K.A. Ingersent, A.J. Rayner and R.C. Hine, 'Agriculture in the Uruguay Round: An Assessment', in Ingersent, Rayner and Hine (eds) *op. cit.*, pp. 268–9.
37 Substitution of income support for price support was a major ingredient in the so-called MacSharry Report on Reform of the CAP, which provided the basis for negotiation *within* the European Community in 1991–3 on liberalization of agricultural policies. Commission of the European Communities, 'The Development and Future of the CAP: Reflections Paper of the European Commission', COM (91) 285 (Final) Brussels, 1991.

38 See J.S. Marsh, 'An EC Approach to Decoupling' in Ingersent, Rayner and Hine (eds) *op. cit.*
39 Commission of the European Communities, *op. cit.*
40 'United States Department of Agricultural Statement on US–EC Accord on Oilseeds and the Uruguay Round' (1992) 9 *International Trade Reporter* 2028 (11 November 1992).
41 'Special Report: Progress Made in US–EC Trade Negotiations as of December 7' (1993) 10 *International Trade Reporter* 2042–3 (8 December 1993).
42 See the discussion of Annex 2 and Article 13.
43 *Brazil – Measures Affecting Desiccated Coconut*, Report of the Panel (17 October 1996) WT/DS22/R, para. 282.
44 *European Communities – Regime for the Importation, Sale and Distribution of Bananas*, Report of the Appellate Body (9 September 1997) WT/DS27/AB/R, para. 157.
45 *European Communities – Measures Affecting the Importation of Certain Poultry Products*, Report of the Panel (12 March 1998) para. 278.
46 *In the Matter of Tariffs Applied by Canada to Certain US-Origin Agricultural Products*, Secretariat File No. CDA-95-2008-01, Final Report of the Panel, 2 December 1996.
47 An egregious example is a document published simultaneously with the closure of the Uruguay Round by the Canadian Department of Agriculture, which emphasizes that the Canadian system of supply management for dairy and poultry products (which keeps prices far above world prices for these items) will remain in place despite the Uruguay Round Agreement, since the Agreement permits prohibitive tariffs to replace import quotas. The document notes approvingly the 'high level of protection' still allowed under the Agreement; it is completely silent as to any possible benefit to *consumers* from the reductions in protection required by the Agreement. Government of Canada, Department of Agriculture, 'GATT and Agri-food General Information Package', Ottawa, 15 December 1993.
48 Remarks of Peter Sutherland, Director General of the GATT, Centre for International Studies Forum on the Uruguay Round Results, University of Toronto, 21 March 1994.

11 Trade in services

1 K. Sauvant, 'The Tradeability of Services', in P.A. Messerlin and K.P. Sauvant (eds) *The Uruguay Round: Services in the World Economy* (Washington and New York: The World Bank and The United Nations Centre on Transnational Corporations, 1990) p. 117.
2 See R. Howse and M.J. Trebilcock, 'Protecting the Employment Bargain' (1993) 43 *University of Toronto Law Journal* 751, pp. 783–4.
3 Sauvant, *op. cit.*, note 1.
4 B. Hoekman, 'Market Access Through Multilateral Agreement: From Goods to Services' (1992) 15 *The World Economy* 707, p. 710.
5 See, in general, R. Howse, J.R.S. Prichard and M.J. Trebilcock, 'Smaller or Smarter Government?' (1990) 40 *University of Toronto Law Journal* 498.
6 See OECD, *Regulatory Reform, Privatization and Competition Policy* (Paris: OECD, 1992).
7 J.N. Bhagwati, 'Splintering and Disembodiment of Service and Developing Nations' (1984) 7 *World Economy* 133.
8 Sauvant, *op. cit.*, p. 116.
9 An excellent guide to these issues, accessible to the non-specialist, is to be found in J.N. Bhagwati, 'International Trade in Services and its Relevance for Economic Development', in *Political Economy and International Economics* (Cambridge MA: MIT Press, 1991) ch. 14. See also the review of these issues in P.W. Daniels, *Services in the World Economy* (London: Basil Blackwell, 1993) pp. 1–23.
10 Indeed, one of the main examples we drew upon to illustrate the theory of comparative advantage, that of the lawyer and her secretary is an example of the gains from trade of services.

11 See G. Feketekuty, *International Trade in Services: An Overview and Blueprint for Negotiations* (Cambridge MA: American Enterprise Institute and Ballinger, 1988).
12 P. Nicolaides, 'The Nature of Services' in Messerlin and Sauvant (eds) *op. cit.*
13 B. Hindley, 'Principles in Factor-related Trade in Services', in Messerlin and Sauvant (eds) *op. cit.*, note 1, pp. 13–15.
14 See M. Marconini, 'The Uruguay Round Negotiations on Services: An Overview', in Messerlin and Sauvant (eds) *op. cit.*, pp. 20–1.
15 See, for instance, I. Walter, *Liberalization of Trade in Financial Services* (Washington DC: AEI, 1988).
16 See Howse, Prichard and Trebilcock, *op. cit.*
17 See International Monetary Fund (Exchange and Trade Relations Research Departments) *International Capital Markets: Developments and Prospects* (Washington DC: IMF, 1989) particularly pp. 50–60.
18 *Ibid.*
19 See Howse, Prichard and Trebilcock, *op. cit.*
20 Given the conceptual difficulties in defining services discussed earlier in this chapter, it is not surprising that no definition of services appears in the *NAFTA*. Instead the scope of application of Chapter Twelve is defined in terms of a variety of 'measures relating to border trade in services by service providers'. These include, *inter alia* 'measures respecting . . . the production, distribution, marketing, sale and delivery of a service; . . . the purchase, payment or use of a service' and 'the presence in its territory of a service territory on a service provider of another territory' (Article 1201.1).
21 Organization for Economic Cooperation and Development, Code of Liberalisation of Current Invisible Operations, November 1990.
22 OECD, *Liberalisation of Capital Movements and Financial Services in the OECD Area* (Paris: OECD, 1990) p. 17.
23 The US effort to put services on the international trade agenda began to take shape in the OECD Trade Committee at the end of the 1970s. As early as the Autumn 1982 GATT Ministerial Meeting, the USA was pressing for GATT-based negotiations on services. See W.J. Drake and K. Nicolaidis, 'Ideas, interests and institutions: "trade in services" and the Uruguay Round' (1992) 46 *International Organization* 45.
24 See Marconini, *op. cit.*, note 14, pp. 19–20. See also, for a developing country perspective, R. Chakravarthi, *Recolonization: GATT, the Uruguay Round and the Third World* (London: Third World Network, 1990) ch. 5 'Services'.
25 J.N. Bhagwati, 'Splintering and Disembodiment of Services and Developing Nations', *op. cit.*; 'Trade and Services in the Multilateral Trade Negotiations' in *Political Economy and International Economics*, *op. cit.*, pp. 282–305. See also, B. Balassa, 'Interest of Developing Countries in the Uruguay Round', *World Economy* (March 1988), pp. 39–54.
26 B.M. Hoekman, 'Services-Related Production, Employment, Trade and Factor Movements', in Messerlin and Sauvant (eds) *op. cit.*, p. 32.
27 *Ibid.* This was the case for Cameroon, Colombia, South Korea, Mexico, Chile, India, Egypt, Kenya, Morocco, the Philippines, Senegal, Singapore, Sudan, Thailand and Tanzania.
28 For a brief explanation of the purported conceptual basis of this distinction, see 'The nature of services' (this chapter).
29 See Howse, Prichard and Trebilcock, 'Smaller or Smarter Government', *op. cit.* See also, R. Howse, 'Reform, Retrenchment or Revolution? The Shift to Incentives and the Future of the Regulatory State' (1993) 31 *Alberta Law Review* 455; and R. Daniels and R. Howse, 'Reforming the Reform Process: A Critical Analysis of Privatization Proposals in Central and East Europe' (1992) 25 *New York University Journal of International Law and Politics* 27.
30 See Marconini, *op. cit.*, pp. 20–1.
31 Feketekuty, *op. cit.*
32 It should be noted that some Members have, pursuant to the Understanding on

Commitments in Financial Services, already inscribed in their schedules commitments to permit temporary entry of certain specialized personnel in connection with the provision of financial services.

33 i.e. applicable even in the absence of specific multilateral disciplines based on the criteria, as contemplated in Article 6:4.

34 Since the National Treatment obligation applies only to sectors subject to specific commitments in Members' schedules, it appears in Part III of the GATS, to be discussed in the next section.

35 B. Hoekman, 'Assessing the General Agreement on Trade in Services', in L. Martin and A. Winters (eds) *The Uruguay Round and Developing Countries* (Cambridge: Cambridge University Press, 1996) pp. 88–124.

36 *Ibid.*, p. 105.

37 P. Sauve, 'Assessing the General Agreement on Trade in Services: Half-Full or Half-Empty?' (1996) 29 *Journal of World Trade* 125, p. 142.

38 Organization for Economic Co-operation and Development, Code of Liberalisation of Capital Movements, November 1990.

39 See p. A. Messerlin, 'The European Community', in Messerlin and Sauvant (eds) *op. cit.*, pp. 132–49.

40 'Large risk' commercial insurance. Messerlin, *Ibid.*, p. 147.

41 T. Kim, *International Money and Banking* (London: Routledge, 1993) pp. 318–21. The following discussion draws extensively on ch. 14 of this work, 'The EC Framework For Banking Services'.

42 See G. Hufbauer, 'An Overview', in G. Hufbauer (ed.) *Europe 1992: An American Perspective* (Washington DC: Brookings Institution, 1990).

43 Second Council Directive of 15 December 1989 on the Co-ordination of Laws, Regulations and Administrative Provisions Relating to the Taking Up and Pursuit of the Business of Credit Institutions and Amending Directive 77/80/EEC.

44 Kim, *op. cit.*, p. 319.

45 The following discussion of banking regulation in Canada and the USA draws on J.F. Chant, 'Free Trade in the Financial Sector: Expectations and Experience', Centre for International Studies/Fraser Institute Conference, 'How is Free Trade Progressing?', University of Toronto, 18–19 November 1991.

46 A clear and comprehensive presentation of Mexico's commitments under the Financial Services Chapter of *NAFTA* is to be found in B. Gonzalez-Hermosillo and P. Sauvé, 'Financial Services and *NAFTA*: Implications for Canadian Financial Institutions', paper presented at Conference on *NAFTA*, C.D. Howe Institute, Toronto, 5–6 December 1992.

47 'Negotiators Clear Path to GATT Pact by Sweeping Away Remaining Differences' (1993) 10 *International Trade Reporter* 2106 (15 December 1993) p. 2107.

48 World Trade Organization, 'The Results of the Financial Services Negotiations under the General Agreement on Trade in Services (GATS)', http://www.wto.org/wto/services/finance_background.html, p. 3.

49 'Non-attributable summary of the main improvements in the new financial services commitments', 26 February 1998, http://www.wto.org/wto/services/finsum.html.

50 *Ibid.*, p. 1.

51 M. Kono, P. Low, M. Luanga, A. Mattoo, M. Oshikawa and L. Schuknecht, *Opening Markets in Financial Services and the Role of the GATS* (Geneva: World Trade Organization, 1997) pp. 23–35.

52 Some of these proposals are summarized and discussed in R. Haas and R. Litan, Globalization and its Discontents' (1998) 77 *Foreign Affairs* 2 and in 'Towards a New Financial System', *The Economist*, 11 April 1998, pp. 52–4.

53 The Honourable Paul Martin, 'Statement Prepared for the Interim Committee of the International Monetary Fund', 16 April 1998.

54 S. Globerman, H.N. Janisch, R.J. Schultz and W.T. Stanbury, 'Canada and the Movement towards Liberalization of the International Telecommunications Regime',

in A.C. Cutler and M.W. Zacher (eds) *Canadian Foreign Policy and International Economic Regimes* (Vancouver: UBC Press, 1992) pp. 262–4.

55 J. Aronson, 'Telecom Agreement Tops Expectations', unpublished manuscript, School of International Relations, University of Southern California, 1997.

56 *Ibid*, p. 6.

57 M. Bronckers and P. Larouche, 'Telecommunications Services and the World Trade Organization' (1997) *Journal of World Trade*, pp. 21–2.

58 P. Sauve, 'Preparing for Services 2000 (Buy Ten Commandments, Get One Free!)', XIIth Conference of the Coalitions of Service Industries, Geneva, 25 June 1997, p. 9.

59 World Trade Organization, Council on Services, *Guidelines For Mutual Recognition Agreements or Arrangements in the Accountancy Sector* (29 May 1997) http://www.wto.org/wto/new/press73.html.

60 M. Bacchetta, P. Low, A. Mattoo, L. Schuknecht, H. Wager and M. Wehrens, *Electronic Commerce and the Role of the WTO* (Geneva: World Trade Organization, 1998). This excellent study surveys a very wide range of electronic commerce issues with WTO implications.

61 *Canada: Certain Measures Concerning Periodicals*, Report of the Panel, WT/DS31/R (14 March 1997) para. 5.18. Since Canada claimed that only the GATT was within the panel's terms of reference, the panel went on to consider only Canada's obligations under the GATT.

62 *European Communities-Regime for the Importation, Sale* and *Distribution of Bananas*, Report of the Appellate Body, WT/DS27/AB/R (9 September 1997) AB-1997-3, para. 219.

63 Howse, Prichard and Trebilcock, *op. cit.*

12 Trade-related intellectual property (TRIPs)

1 See R.A. Epstein, *Takings: Private Property and the Power of Eminent Domain* (Cambridge MA: Harvard University Press, 1985) and R. Nozick, *Anarchy, State* and *Utopia* (New York: Basic Books, 1974).

2 For an excellent discussion about the centrality and limits of the idea of private property in liberal democratic theory, in the American context, see J. Nedelsky, *Private Property and the Limits of American Constitutionalism* (Chicago: University of Chicago Press, 1990) pp. 216–64.

3 See the discussion of monopoly power and coercion in M.J. Trebilcock, *The Limits of Freedom of Contract* (Cambridge MA: Harvard University Press, 1993) ch. 4.

4 A good survey is to be found in C.A. Primo Braga, 'Guidance from Economic Theory', in W.E. Siebeck (ed.) *Strengthening Protection of Intellectual Property in Developing Countries: A Survey of the Literature* (Washington DC: The World Bank, 1990).

5 *Ibid.*, p. 22.

6 See C. Primo Braga, 'The Developing Country Case For and Against Intellectual Property Protection', in Siebeck (ed.) *op. cit.*, pp. 77–8.

7 A. Deardorff, 'Should Patent Protection Be Extended To All Developing Countries?' (1990) 13 *World Economy* 13, pp. 497–508.

8 Everson suggests that, with respect to developing countries, 'the literature does not show strong correlations between direct foreign investment and the strength of IPRs'. 'Global Intellectual Property Rights Issues in Perspective', in M.B. Wallerstein, M.E. Mogee and R.A. Schoen (eds) *Global Dimensions of Intellectual Property Rights* (Washington DC: National Academy Press, 1993) p. 366.

9 Binley challenges the link between strong intellectual property protection and higher levels of foreign investment. She notes: '. . . Korea benefited from technology transfer in numerous industries via licensing arrangements, sub-contracting agreements and the location of foreign subsidiaries during a period in which its intellectual property laws were as weak as any of the other LDCs'. M. Binley, 'Intellectual Property Rights: A Strategic Instrument of Developing Nations', International Business and Trade

Law Programme, Working Paper No. 46 (1992) Faculty of Law, University of Toronto, p. 25.

10 See L. Davis, 'Technology Intensity of US, Canadian and Japanese Manufactures Output and Exports', in J. Niosi (ed.) *Technology and National Competitiveness* (Kingston and Montreal: McGill-Queens, 1991).

11 See M. Borrus, 'Macroeconomic Perspectives on the Use of Intellectual Property Rights in Japan's Economic Performance', in F. Rushing and C. Brown (eds) *Intellectual Property Rights in Science, Technology and Economic Performance: International Comparisons* (Washington DC: U.S. Chamber of Commerce, 1990) pp. 261–7.

12 See J. Niosi, *Canada's Multinationals* (tr. R. Chodos) (Toronto: Between the Lines, 1983).

13 Deardorff, *op. cit.*, p. 497.

14 K. Maskus, 'Normative Concerns in the International Protection of Intellectual Property Rights' (1991) *World Economy*, 14 p. 403.

15 G. Grossman and E. Helpman, *Innovation and Growth in the Global Economy* (Cambridge MA: MIT Press, 1991) ch. 11 'Imitation'.

16 For a good discussion of this controversy see J.H. Jackson, 'Remarks of Professor John H. Jackson' (1989) 22 *Vanderbilt Journal of Transnational Law*, pp. 343–4.

17 This case is discussed more extensively below at pp. 318–19.

18 Paris Convention for the Protection of Industrial Property, 20 March 1883, 828 UNTS 107.

19 Commission of the European Communities, *Green Paper on Copyright and the Challenge of Technology: Copyright issues requiring immediate attention* (Brussels: European Commission, 1988) p. 233 [hereinafter, EC *Green Paper*].

20 Some commentators, however, read an MFN principle into the national treatment obligation on the basis of the history and general purposes of the Convention. See, for instance, J. Reichman, 'Intellectual Property in International Trade: Opportunities and Risks of a GATT Connection' (1989) 22 *Vanderbilt Journal of Transnational Law* 747, pp. 843–53.

21 W. Lesser, 'An Overview of Intellectual Property Systems', in Siebeck (ed.) *op. cit.*, p. 11.

22 M. Borrus, 'Macroeconomic Perspectives on the Use of Intellectual Property Rights in Japan's Economic Performance', in F. Rushing and C. Brown (eds) *Intellectual Property Rights in Science, Technology* and *Economic Performance: International Comparisons* (Washington DC: US Chamber of Commerce, 1990) p. 267.

23 C. Primo Braga, 'The Developing Country Case For and Against Intellectual Property Protection', in Siebeck (ed.) *op. cit.*, p. 75.

24 Berne Convention for the Protection of Industrial Property, 20 March 1883, 828 UNTS 107.

25 An exhaustive study of the evolution and contents of the Berne Convention is S. Ricketson, *The Berne Convention for the Protection of Literary and Artistic Works: 1886–1986* (London: Kluwer, 1986). The following section owes much to this work.

26 Hence, 'The expression "literary and artistic works" shall include every production in the literary, scientific and artistic domain, whatever may be the mode or form of its expression' (Article 2(1)).

27 See EC *Green Paper*, see also D. Llewellyn, 'Computers, Software and International Protection' (1986) 11 *VLA Journal of Law and the Arts* 183.

28 T. Stewart, 'Trade-Related Aspects of Intellectual Property Rights', in T. Stewart (ed.) *The Uruguay Round: A Negotiating History: vol. III* (Boston: Kluwer, 1994) pp. 2247–8.

29 Convention Establishing the World Intellectual Property Organization, 14 July 1967, 828 UNTS 3.

30 See E. Wolfhard, 'International Trade in Intellectual Property: The Emerging GATT Regime' (1991) 49 *University of Toronto Faculty L. R.* 106; See also, F.-K. Beier and G. Schricker (eds) *GATT or WIPO? New Ways in the Protection of Intellectual Property* (VCH: Weinheim, 1989).

31 International Convention for the Protection of Performers, Procurers of Phonograms and Broadcasting Organizations, 26 October 1961, 495–6 UNTS 44.
32 For a discussion of the rationale for the protection of intellectual property rights in the genetic material of plants, see R.L. Marguilies, 'Protecting Biodiversity: Recognizing International Intellectual Property Rights in Plant Genetic Resources' (1993) 14 *Michigan J. Int'l. L.* 322.
33 World Intellectual Property Organization: Treaty on Intellectual Property in Respect of Integrated Circuits, 26 May 1989, 28 *I.L.M.* 1477 (1989).
34 According to Goldberg, 'Chief among the problems that the United States found with the Washington Treaty were the inadequate terms of protection, the lack of specific protection for mask works incorporated in a finished product, broad provisions for compulsory licenses and excessively permissive treatment of so-called innocent infringers.' M.D. Goldberg, 'Semiconductor Chip Protection as a Case Study', in Wallerstein, Mogee and Schoen (eds) *op. cit.*, pp. 335–6.
35 But see W. Lesser, 'An Overview of Intellectual Property Systems', in Siebeck (ed.) *op. cit.* WIPO has an extensive web site where the texts of and detailed information about these agreements and their administration can be found: www.wipo.org.
36 See the discussion of US aggressive unilateralism in Chapter 8.
37 See VanGrasstek Communications, 'Trade-Related Intellectual Property Rights: Developing Countries and the *Uruguay Round*', in United Nations Conference on Trade and Development, *Uruguay Round: Further Papers on Selected Issues* (New York: United Nations, 1990) pp. 79–128.
38 GATT, United States-Section 337 of the Tariff Act of 1930, L 6439 (16 January 1989).
39 See VanGrasstek Communications, *op. cit.*, pp. 103–4.
40 The Instrument does not appear, however, to specify explicitly the nature or level of the retaliation contemplated.
41 See J. Bourgeois and C. Laurent, 'Le "nouvel instrument de la politique commerciale": un pas en avant vers l'élimination des obstacles aux échanges internationaux', *Revue trimestrielle de droit européen* (Jan.–Mar. 1985).
42 EC *Green Paper*, *op. cit.*, p. 235.
43 W. Brueckmann, 'Intellectual Property Protection in the European Community', in Rushing and Brown (eds) *op. cit.*, pp. 291–310.
44 As Stewart notes, the Conventions and WIPO offer the possibility of accepting the jurisdiction of the International Court of Justice with respect to settlement of disputes and WIPO itself has attempted to achieve some dispute settlement through the appointment of special informal committees of experts to address particular disagreements about the functioning of the Conventions. T. Stewart 'Trade-Related Aspects of Intellectual Property Rights', in Stewart (ed.) *op. cit.*, pp. 2247–8.
45 Primo Braga, 'The Developing Country Case For and Against Intellectual Property Protection', in Siebeck (ed.), *op. cit.*, pp. 73–5.
46 Indeed, extensive written reasons for a judicial decision are *a*typical of most legal systems in the world, which are based on the civilian approach to the role of courts in decision-making. The court is viewed as applying rules in a code and not as making law from case to case.
47 See G.B. Rathmann, 'Biotechnology Case Study', in Wallerstein, Mogee and Schoen (eds) *op. cit.*, pp. 319ff.
48 See W. Lesser, 'Seeds and Plants', in Siebeck (ed.), *op. cit.*, pp. 65–8.
49 United Nations Environmental Programme, Framework Convention on Biodiversity, 5 June 1992, Articles 15(1) and 16(2). The United States refused to sign the Convention. See Margulies, *op. cit.*, pp. 333–4.
50 These are discussed above at pp. 315–16.
51 See P. Samuelson, 'A Case Study on Computer Programs', in Wallerstein, Mogee and Schoen (eds) *op. cit.*, pp. 309–18.
52 An example would be a mark deemed obscene or associated with racial or religious hatred.

53 For a discussion of the nature of these exemptions and some concrete examples to which they might apply, see International Bureau of Intellectual Property, *The Paris Convention for the Protection of Intellectual Property from 1883 to 1983* (Geneva: WIPO, 1983) pp. 41–5.
54 See the above discussion of the Canada–USA FTA.
55 For instance the Convention permits member states to make exceptions to protection with regard to private and some journalistic use of recorded material, as well as use for purposes of teaching and scientific research (Article 15).
56 See, on these concerns, Stewart (ed.) *op. cit.*, pp. 2299–30.
57 See C.M. Correa, *Integrated Circuits: Trends in Intellectual Property Protection*, United Nations Industrial Development Organization (UNIDO) Doc. IPCT, 24 October 1989, pp. 21–3.
58 There are certain differences of wording between the Washington Treaty provisions and the applicable TRIPs Agreement provisions, but they are not major. For instance, where the TRIPs Agreement requires that 'adequate' remuneration be paid for a compulsory licence, the Washington Treaty uses the expression 'equitable remuneration' (compare TRIPs Agreement Article 31(h) and Washington Treaty, Article 6.3(a)).
59 Some adjustment costs may occur in developed countries as well where the Agreement requires extending protection (e.g. in the generic drug industry in Canada). However, no transitional or adjustment provision is available to them.
60 See R.M. Sherwood, 'Intellectual Property and Free Trade in North America', unpublished paper, Centre for International Studies/Fraser Institute Conference, University of Toronto, 18–19 November 1991.
61 See J. Dillon, 'Intellectual Property', in *Analysis of NAFTA Proposals and the Impact on Canada* (Toronto: Ecumenical Coalition for Economic Justice, 1992).
62 Document IP/C/2, November 1995.
63 Document IP/C/3, November 1995.
64 World Trade Organization, Council for Trade-Related Aspects of Intellectual Rights, *Annual Report (1997) of the Council for TRIPS*, 28 November 1997, IP/C/12, p. 5.
65 *India–Patent Protection for Pharmaceutical Products*, Report of the Appellate Body, WT/DS50/AB/R (19 December 1997) AB-1997-5, para. 58.
66 United States Trade Representative, *Annual Report 1997*, Office of the United States Trade Representative, Washington DC, 1997, p. 241.
67 Canada–Patent Protection of Pharmaceutical Products, Request for Consultations, 19 December 1997, WT/DS/114/1.
68 *World Intellectual Property Organization Provisional Treaty on Protection of Literary and Artistic Works* (1996).
69 Basic Proposal for the Substantive Provisions of the Treaty on Intellectual Property in Respect of Databases, WIPO Document CRNR/DC/6 (1996).
70 J. Boyle, 'A Politics of Intellectual Property: Environmentalism for the Net?' (1997) 47 *Duke Law Journal* 87, pp. 101–2.
71 CRNR/DC/95 (20 Dec. 1996).
72 See R.F. Martin, 'The WIPO Performances and Phonograms Treaty: Will the U.S. Whistle a New Tune?' (1997) 44 *Journal of the Copyright Society of America* 157.
73 M. Bacchetta, P. Low, A. Mattoo, L. Schuknecht, H. Wager and M. Wehrens, *Electronic Commerce and the Role of the WTO* (Geneva: World Trade Organization, 1998) p. 62.
74 United States Trade Representative, Press Release, 'Trade Preferences for Honduras Suspended', 30 March, 1998, citing 'widespread, blatant copyright piracy'.
75 R. Pechman, 'Seeking Multilateral Protection for Intellectual Property: The United States "TRIPs" over Special 301' (1998), 7 *Minnesota Journal of Global Trade* 179, pp. 202–4.
76 Bacchetta *et al.*, *op. cit.*, p. 64.
77 'Environment and TRIPS', WT/CTE/W/8 (8 June 1995), paras 76–8.

13 Trade and investment

1 N. Grimwade, *International Trade: New Patterns of Trade, Production and Investment* (London: Routledge, 1989) p. 144.

2 T. Stewart, 'Trade Related Investment Measures', in T. Stewart (ed.) *The GATT Uruguay Round: A Negotiating History* (Boston: Kluwer, 1994) p. 2003.

3 See E. Graham and M. Ebert, 'Foreign Direct Investment and U.S. National Security: Fixing Exon-Florio' (1991) 14 *World Economy* IP.245; see also, R. Kuttner, *The End of Laissez-Faire: National Purpose and the Global Economy After the Cold War* (New York: Knopf, 1991).

4 See S. Ostry, 'Globalization, Domestic Policies and the Need for Harmonization', Centre for the Study of Business and Public Policy, University of California (Santa Barbara) January 1993, pp. 12–18.

5 S. Strange, *States and Markets* (Cordar: Pinter, 1988).

6 See A. Rugman, *Inside the Multinational: The Economics of Internal Markets* (New York: Columbia University Press, 1981).

7 Recent empirical evidence, surveyed by Jenkins, suggests that a major effect of foreign direct investment in many sectors in developing countries is to make local enterprises more competitive, rather than making them fail for inability to compete with multinationals. In some instances, competition may have resulted in domestic enterprises adopting practices that were arguably regressive or distributively unjust – i.e. with respect to labour and employment practices. Here, foreign investment itself could hardly be considered the root problem as opposed to inadequate labour or other social regulation to which both multinationals and domestic firms operating in the jurisdiction would be subject. See R. Jenkins, 'The Impact of Foreign Investment on Less Developed Countries: Cross-Section Analysis versus Industry Studies', in P. Buckley and J. Clegg, *Multinational Enterprise in Less-Developed Countries* (London: Macmillan, 1991) especially pp. 123–30.

8 See A.J. Easson 'The Design of Tax Incentives for Direct Investment: Some Lessons from the ASEAN Countries', International Business and Trade Law Programme, University of Toronto, 1993.

9 OECD, *Investment Incentives and Disincentives* (Paris: OECD, 1989).

10 See, especially, D. Greenaway, 'Why Are We Negotiating on TRIMs?', in Greenaway *et al.* (eds) *Global Protectionism* (London: Macmillan, 1991).

11 For a discussion of the rationale for singling out export subsidies and its dubious merits, see Chapter 8.

12 See A. Barnea, R. Haughen and W. Senbet, 'Market Imperfections, Agency Problems, and Capital Structure: A Review' (1981) 10 *Financial Management*, Summer. See also, R. Caves, *Multinational Enterprise and Economic Analysis* (New York: Cambridge University Press, 1982). Gilpin notes, the application of the theory of the firm to explain foreign investment is relatively recent; before the 1980s, explanations of foreign investment depended upon assumptions about oligopolistic competition or invoked the 'product cycle' theory of production (according to which countries at different levels of development have a comparative advantage at different stages in the life history of a product, from research and invention downwards to standardized mass-production). R. Gilpin, *The Political Economy of International Relations* (Princeton NJ: Princeton University Press, 1987) p. 237. However, foreign investment has increasingly occurred in sectors not characterized by oligopolistic competition and the 'product cycle' theory cannot explain the existence of increasing foreign investment flows from developed countries to other developed countries.

13 Grimwade, *op. cit.*, pp. 178–92.

14 On the globalization of production through increasing use of international external contracting mechanisms such as sub-contracting, licensing and interfirm agreements, see OECD, *Globalisation of Industrial Activities Four Case Studies: Auto Parts, Chemicals, Construction and Semi-conductors* (Paris: OECD, 1993).

15 P. Nicolaides, 'Investment Policies in an Integrated World Economy' (1992) 15 *World Economy*, p. 123.
16 Although, of course, where a firm decided to choose the instrument of Foreign Direct Investment, it may encounter substantial agency costs in enforcing the various internal contracts in the jurisdiction in which it invests. The problem of the security of investors' assets and of expropriation will be discussed briefly later in this chapter.
17 See Grimwade, *op. cit.*, pp. 170–3.
18 J. Dunning, *Explaining International Production* (London: Unwin Hyman, 1988) especially ch. 2, 'The Eclectic Paradigm of International Production: A Restatement and Some Possible Extensions'. See also, J. Dunning, *Multinationals, Technology* and *Competitiveness* (London: Unwin Hyman, 1988).
19 M. Porter, *The Competitive Advantage of Nations* (New York: Free Press, 1990).
20 Transfer prices are the prices at which the firm buys and sells goods and services from and to itself.
21 See, for instance, J. Knubley, W. Krause and Z. Sadeque, 'Canadian Acquisitions Abroad: Patterns and Motivations', in L. Waverman (ed.) *Corporate Globalization through Mergers and Acquisitions* (Calgary: University of Calgary Press, 1991).
22 In general, recent economic literature seems to support the view that the consumer welfare losses from protection in these circumstances are likely to outweigh any gains to domestic welfare from rent-shifting. See A.E. Safarian, *Multinational Enterprise and Public Policy: A Study of the Industrial Countries* (Aldershot: Edward Elgar, 1993) p. 499.
23 See Safarian, *op. cit.*, pp. 467–70.
24 Indeed, Graham argues that protection-induced investment may actually result in a net loss to domestic economic development, where the foreign firm's access to a protected market reduces the pressure for it to invest in highly competitive production facilities in the host country. E. Graham, 'Strategic Trade Policy and the Multinational Enterprise in Developing Countries', in Buckley and Clegg, *op. cit.*, pp. 89–91. Hence, the economic development case for protection-induced investment depends upon capturing and channelling the rents from protection into directions that are beneficial to economic development.
25 A clear and balanced discussion of these and related concerns about foreign investment and multinationals can be found in Gilpin, *op. cit.*, ch. 6, 'Multinational Corporations and International Production'.
26 N. Machiavelli, *The Prince* (trans. M. Musa) (New York: St. Martin's Press, 1964) chs 6–7.
27 Stewart, 'Trade-related Investment Measures', *op. cit.*, pp. 2036–7. See also, UN Centre on Transnational Corporations, *National Legislation and Regulations Relating to Transnational Corporations*, UN Doc. ST/CTC/91 (1989).
28 50 U.S.C. app. §2170(a) (1990).
29 Stewart, 'Trade-related Investment Measures', *op. cit.*, p. 2038.
30 Nance and Wasserman note, for instance, a case where US industry interests complained to the CFIUS about the sale to a West German concern of a US company involved in manufacturing raw material for semiconductors. The transaction was eventually approved, but not before the German acquirer had sent a letter of intent to the US Government, undertaking, *inter alia*, to continue production in the USA for at least five years and to make its products available to the US semiconductor industry. D.S. Nance and J. Wasserman, 'Regulation of Imports and Foreign Investment in the United States on National Security Grounds' (1990) 11 *Michigan Journal of Intl. Law* 926, pp. 973–4. The CFIUS process is particularly suited to the exertion of pressure on foreign investors and to the striking of such deals or bargains because, as Nance and Wasserman also remark, the process is characterized by a 'complete lack of transparency': there are no hearings, no public submissions and no administrative record (p. 961).
31 Graham and Ebert, *op. cit.*
32 See, in general, A.L.C. de Mestral and T. Gruchalla-Wesierski, *Extraterritorial Application of Export Control Legislation: Canada and the United States* (Boston: Martinus Nijhoff, 1990).

33 See M. Leigh and P. Lichtenbaum, 'Law Without Borders: The Cuban Democracy Act of 1992' (1993) *The Canadian Law Newsletter* 13.
34 See Whitt, 'The Politics of Procedure: An Examination of the GATT Dispute-Settlement Panel and the Article XXI Defense in the Context of the U.S. Embargo of Nicaragua' (1987) 19 *Law & Policy in International Business* 63.
35 See J.G. Castel, A.L.C. de Mestral and W.C. Graham, *International Business Transactions and Economic Relations* (Toronto: Carswell, 1991) ch.10, 'Extraterritorial Application of Canadian and Foreign Laws Prohibiting Restrictive Business Practices'.
36 OECD, *Decision of the Council: Conflicting Requirements* (Paris: OECD, June, 1991).
37 See Chapter 17 on trade and competition policy.
38 For a discussion of these various options, see N. Campbell and M. Trebilcock, 'International Merger Review: Problems of Multi-Jurisdictional Conflict', in E. Kautzenbach, H.-E. Scharrer and L. Waverman (eds) *Competition Policy in an Interdependent World Economy* (Baden-Baden: Nomos Verlagsgesellschaft, 1993). For a somewhat more sceptical view of the possibility of establishing common rules to govern these inter-jurisdictional disputes, see S. Ostry, 'Globalization, Domestic Policies and the Need for Harmonization', Competition Policy in a Global Economy Project, University of California (Santa Barbara), January 1993 (unpublished).
39 These and related concerns are summarized and discussed in M.J. Trebilcock, *Public Enterprises in Papua New Guinea* (Port Moresby: Institute of National Affairs, 1982).
40 See, generally, for recent work, P.J. Buckley and J. Clegg, *Multinational Enterprise in Less Developed Countries* (London: Macmillan, 1991).
41 See J. Stopford and S. Strange, *Rival states, rival firms: competition for world market shares* (Cambridge: Cambridge University Press, 1991).
42 B. Emmott, 'Multinationals: Back in Fashion', *The Economist*, 27 March – 2 April 1993, p. 19.
43 International Chamber of Commerce and UNCTAD, *The Financial Crisis in Asia and Foreign Direct Investment* (Geneva and New York: ICC and UNCTAD, 1998), p. 2.
44 *Ibid.*, p. 1.
45 *Canada: Administration of the Foreign Investment Review Act (FIRA)*, BISD 30th Supp. 140 (1984).
46 See D. Greenaway, 'Trade Related Investment Measures: Political Economy Aspects and Issues for GATT' (1992) 15 *World Economy*, pp. 375–80.
47 An exhaustive discussion of the various conflicting perspectives that emerged in the Uruguay Round TRIMs negotiations can be found in Stewart, 'Trade-Related Investment Measures', *op. cit.*
48 *Final Act Embodying The Results of the Uruguay Round of Multilateral Trade Negotiations* (MTN/FA), Geneva, 15 December 1993, II.7 'Agreement on Trade-Related Investment Measures' [hereinafter, 'Agreement on TRIMs'].
49 See M. Gestrin and A.M. Rugman, 'The *NAFTA*'s Impact on the North American Investment Regime' (1993) 42 *C.D. Howe Institute Commentary* 1, p. 8.
50 There may be some difficult definitional problems as well. For instance, although public health care exists throughout Canada, for purposes of Canadian constitutional law, hospitals, although publicly-funded and regulated, are not viewed as part of government. Therefore, an argument could be made that they are not even covered by Article 1104.1.
51 J. Johnson, *International Trade Law* (Concord, Ont.: Irwin Law, 1998), p. 223.
52 See D. Schneiderman, '*NAFTA*'s Takings Rule: American Constitutionalism Comes to Canada' (1996) 46 *University of Toronto Law Journal*, p. 499.
53 Johnson, *op. cit.*, p. 223, text of fn. 16.
54 *Ibid.*
55 The investor-state dispute settlement process in *NAFTA*, which is described immediately below is based on commercial arbitration arrangements which allow for the particulars of proceedings to remain secret except by consent of both parties. Ethyl has not consented to public release of any documents in the proceedings and so accounts of this matter rely

on anecdotes. This account is from T. Clarke and M. Barlow, *The Multilateral Agreement on Investment and the Threat to Canadian Sovereignty* (Toronto: Stoddart, 1997), pp. 90–1.

56 With the exception of the Treaty of Rome, which is much more than a trade treaty and which may be rightly viewed as establishing the outlines of a supranational *government* that in many matters can act directly on individual citizens.

57 Annexed to OECD, Declaration on International Investment and Multinational Enterprises, Paris, 1976.

58 For a good discussion of the various Codes and guidelines and their perceived impact, see R. Grosse, 'Codes of Conduct for Multinational Enterprises' (1982) 16 *Journal of World Trade Law* 414; see also, M.A. Kwaw, 'Trade Related Investment Measures in the Uruguay Round: Towards a GATT for Investment?' (1991) 16 *North Carolina Journal of International Law and Commercial Regulation* 309, pp. 315–16.

59 See OECD (Committee on International Investment and Multinational Enterprises) *The OECD Declaration and Decisions on International Investment and Multinational Enterprises: 1991 Review* (Paris: OECD, 1992) pp. 42–54. See also, B. Blanpain, *The OECD Guidelines for Multinational Enterprises and Labour Relations 1982–1984: Experience and Review* (Boston: Kluwer, 1985).

60 The provisions of these Codes are discussed in the context of trade in financial services in Chapter 11 above.

61 OECD (Committee on International Investment and Multinational Enterprises), *National Treatment for Foreign-Controlled Enterprises* (Paris: OECD, 1993) p. 23.

62 OECD Council, National Treatment: Third Revised Decision of the Council (1991), Article 2(c).

63 *Ibid.*, Article 3.

64 OECD, Declaration on International Investment and Multinational Enterprises (1976), *op. cit.*, Article II.1.

65 See P.E. Bondzi-Simpson, *The Legal Relationship Between Transnational Corporations and Host States* (New York: Quorum, 1990).

66 See, for example, H.W. Baade, 'The Legal Effects of Codes of Conduct for Multinational Enterprises', in N. Horn (ed.) *Legal Problems of Codes of Conduct for Multinational Enterprises* (Deventer: Kluwer, 1980) pp. 32–7.

67 575 UNTS 159.

68 On the various theories concerning ICSID's very limited impact, see O. Unegbu, 'Dispute Settlement in International Investment: A Study of the ICSID Arbitral Regime', LLM thesis, Faculty of Law, University of Toronto, 1991 (unpublished).

69 What follows draws heavily on work in progress on the MAI by Robert Howse and Jonathan Feldman and a brief article by Feldman and Howse, 'A Brief Critical Overview of the MAI', *CanadaWatch*, Winter 1988.

70 M. Hart, 'A Multilateral Agreement on Foreign Direct Investment: Why Now?', in P. Sauve and D. Schwanen (eds), *Investment Rules for the Global Economy: Enhancing Access to Markets* (Toronto: C.D. Howe Institute, 1996), p. 82. See also the essay in the same volume by A. Rugman and M. Gestrin, 'A Conceptual Framework for a Multilateral Agreement on Investment: Learning from the *NAFTA*'. This volume also contains some more subtle and cautious but still positive assessments of the whole MAI project, including by the editors and Ed Graham.

71 *A Multilateral Agreement on Investment: Report by the Committee on International Investment and Multinational Enterprises (CIME)/and the Committee on Capital Movements and Invisible Transactions (CMIT)*, OECD, Paris, May 1995.

72 This overview is based on the Negotiating Text as of 24 April 1998, as posted to the OECD web site, www.oecd.org.

73 OECD Committee on Capital Movements and Invisible Transactions (hereinafter CCMIT), 'Movement of Key Personnel' (Working Paper), 1994, at 3.

74 *Ibid.*, at 12.

75 *Ibid.*, at 13.

76 OECD Directorate for Financial, Fiscal and Enterprise Affairs Negotiating Group on the MAI. *Multilateral Agreement on Investment: Consolidated Text and Commentary* 14 May 1997. Note that the scope of the agreement is quite wide and in Article II(I)(i) an investor is defined broadly as 'a natural person having the nationality of, or who is permanently residing in, a Contracting Party in accordance with its applicable law'.
77 For example, Canada, Mexico and the United States maintained a reservation on the coverage on the article concerning Senior Management [And Membership on Boards of Directors].
78 *MAI: Consolidated Text and Commentary* at 15. This demonstration of respect is found in the Special Topics section under Part 1 of the sub-section called *Temporary Entry, Stay and Work of Investors and Key Personnel.*
79 *Ibid.* [Part l(a)(i)]
80 *Ibid.* [Part l(a)(ii)]
81 *Ibid.* [Part l(b)(i)l]
82 *MAI-Chairman's Summary Report-Investment Protection*, OLIS, May 1995 at 3–4.
83 *Ibid.*
84 Because under the arbitration process adopted in *NAFTA* for Investor-Party dispute settlement, such proceedings are secret except by agreement of the Parties, the only information on this dispute that is reliable is through informal channels.
85 Ministerial Statement on the Multilateral Agreement on Investment, Paris, 28 April, 1998.
86 *Multilateral Agreement on Investment: Report by the MAI Negotiating Group*, OECD, Paris, May 1997.
87 T. Clarke and M. Barlow, *MAI: The Multilateral Agreement on Investment and the Threat to Canadian Sovereignty* (Toronto: Stoddart, 1997), pp. 4–5.
88 Ibid., pp. 5–6.
89 Thus, trade law specialists, including one of us (Robert Howse), testified before a Sub-Committee of the Canadian Parliament that the Canadian government should insist on this provision being amended to exempt general regulatory measures from the compensation requirement.
90 'Annex 2: Chairman's Proposals on Environment and Related Matters and on Labour', 9 March 1998.

14 Trade and developing countries

1 There is no agreed definition for the designation 'developing country'. Sometimes the term is used to refer to countries where per capita income is significantly below that of the major industrialized nations. The United Nations Development Programme (UNDP) has attempted to evolve indices of human development that take into account a broad range of factors, including education and literacy, the condition of women and children and the level of social infrastructure. The UNDP does not, however, attempt to define a human development threshold below which a country is considered a developing country. Instead, the UNDP classifies all countries other than Europe, Canada, the United States, Australia, New Zealand and Japan as 'developing', including a number of countries that have relatively high per capita incomes, such as Saudi Arabia and Singapore. See UNDP, *Human Development Report* 1991 (New York: Oxford, 1991). For purposes of certain GATT provisions, developing countries are defined as 'contracting parties the economies of which can only support low standards of living and are in the early stages of development' (GATT Article XVIII:1).
2 A.O. Krueger, 'Global Trading Prospects of Developing Countries' (1992) 15 *World Economy*, p. 9.
3 These were Burma, Ceylon, Chile, Cuba, India, Pakistan, Southern Rhodesia, South Africa and Syria.
4 R. Hudec, *Developing Countries in the GATT Legal System* (London: Gower, 1987).

5 See B. Balassa, 'The Importance of Trade for Developing Countries', in *New Directions in the World Economy* (New York: NYU Press, 1989) p. 17.
6 See J. Whalley (ed.) *The Uruguay Round and Beyond: The Final Report from the Ford Foundation Project on Developing Countries in the Global Trading System* (Ann Arbor: University of Michigan Press, 1989).
7 See Balassa, *op. cit.*
8 See R. Gilpin, *The Political Economy of International Relations* (Princeton NJ: Princeton University Press, 1987) pp. 298–302.
9 See, in general, M. Kelly and A.K. McGuirk *et al.*, *Issues and Developments in International Trade Policy* (Washington DC: International Monetary Fund, 1992) pp. 41–3.
10 See, for example, F. Fukuyama, *The End of History and the Last Man* (New York: Free Press, 1992) pp. 98–101.
11 B. Balassa, 'Liberalizing Trade Between Developed and Developing Countries', in Balassa, *op. cit.*, p. 360.
12 See Hudec (1987) *op. cit.*, pp. 24–5. See also, OECD (Centre for Cooperation with the European Economies in Transition) *Exchange Control Policy* (Paris: OECD, 1993) pp. 11–15.
13 Developing countries are defined, rather generally or imprecisely, as 'contracting parties the economies of which can only support low standards of living and are in the early stages of development' (XVIII:1).
14 Hudec (1987) *op. cit.*, ch. 2.
15 See Kelly and McGuirk *et al.*, *op. cit.*, Appendix I ('The GATT System' pp. 74–5).
16 Hudec (1987) *op. cit.*, ch. 4.
17 See B. Balassa, 'The Extent and Cost of Protection in Developed–Developing Country Trade', in Balassa (1989) *op. cit.*
18 Hudec (1987) *op. cit.*, p. 83.
19 J.H. Jackson, *The World Trading System: Law and Policy of International Economic Relations* (Cambridge, MA: MIT Press, 1988) p. 99.
20 See Kelly and McGuire *et al.*, *op. cit.*, Table A15, 'GATT Panels Established Since 1985', pp. 154–63.
21 See Jackson, *op. cit.*, pp. 278–9.
22 See Lomé I (1975) 14 *Intl. Leg. Mat.* 595; Lomé II (1980) 19 *Intl. Leg. Mat.* 327; Lomé III (1985) 24 *Intl. Leg. Mat.* 571.
23 See J.-G. Castel, A.L.C. DeMestral and W.C. Graham, *International Business Transactions and Economic Relations* (Toronto: Emond Montgomery, 1986) p. 35.
24 See Joseph McMahon, 'The EC Banana Regime, the WTO Rulings and ACP – Fighting for Economic Survival?', (1998) 32 *Journal of World Trade* 101.
25 *European Communities – Regime for the Importation, Sale, Distribution of Bananas*, WT/DS27.
26 'U.S. Seeks Talks on EU Banana Regime as WTO Confirms U.S. Win', *Inside U.S. Trade,* 12 September 1997.
27 J.H. Jackson, *The World Trading System* (Cambridge MASS: MIT Press 1997, 2nd ed.) p. 324.
28 Trade and Tariff Act of 1984, Section 505(b).
29 See R.E. Moore, 'The Level of Development and GSP Treatment' (1992) 26 *Journal of World Trade*, December, p. 21.
30 R.I. Meltzer, 'U.S. Renewal of the GSP' (1986) 20 *Journal of World Trade Law* 507.
31 See Jackson, *op. cit.* (1997) p. 325.
32 With respect to textiles, see the discussion below on the MFA.
33 B. Balassa, 'Liberalizing Trade Between Developed and Developing Countries', in Balassa (1989) *op. cit.*, p. 359.
34 See Kelly and McGuirk *et al.*, *op. cit.*, Table A11 in Statistical Appendix.
35 B. Balassa, 'The Extent and Cost of Protection in Developed–Developing Country Trade' in Balassa (1989) *op. cit.*, p. 335.
36 See M. Wolf, 'Managed Trade in Practice: Implications of the Textile Arrangements',

in W.R. Cline (ed.) *Trade Policy in the 1980s* (Washington DC: Institute for International Economics, 1983) pp. 457–9.

37 See Jackson, *op. cit.*, (1997) p. 207.

38 See Wolf, *op. cit.*, p. 457.

39 The nature of these competitive pressures and the costs and benefits to the restricting countries of import controls in the textile and clothing sectors are analysed in M.J. Trebilcock, M.A. Chandler and R. Howse, *Trade and Transitions: A Comparative Analysis of Adjustment Policies* (London: Routledge, 1990) pp. 50–9.

40 Jackson, *op. cit.*, p. 181.

41 G.C. Dao, 'The Developing World and the Multifiber Arrangement', in J. Whalley (ed.) *Developing Countries and the Global Trading System (vol. II)* (London: Macmillan, 1989) p. 85.

42 M. de P. Abreu and W. Fritsch, 'Market Access for Manufactured Exports from Developing Countries: Trends and Prospects', in J. Whalley (ed.) *Developing Countries and the Global Trading System (vol. I)* (London: Macmillan, 1989) p. 117. These estimates are based on UNCTAD, *Protectionism and Structural Adjustment* (Geneva: UNCTAD, 1986).

43 UNCTAD, *op. cit.*

44 Dao, *op. cit.*, pp. 87–8.

45 See N.A. Adams, *Worlds Apart: The North South Divide and the International System* (Atlantic Highlands, NJ: Zed, 1993) especially chs 4–5.

46 See A.O. Krueger, 'Trade Policy and Economic Development: How We Learn' (1997) 87 *American Economic Review* 1.

47 Hudec (1987) *op. cit.*, pp. 39–40.

48 See, particularly, *Charter of Economic Rights and Duties of States*, U.N.G.A. Res. 3281 (XXIX) (1974).

49 See M. Agarwal, 'South–South Trade: Building Block or Bargaining Chip?', in Whalley (ed.) *op. cit.*, pp. 196–9.

50 R.E. Hudec, 'The Structure of South–South Trade Preferences in the 1988 GSTP Agreement: Learning to Say MFMFN', in Whalley (ed.) *op. cit.*, p. 211.

51 *Ibid.*, pp. 213–14.

52 *Ibid.*, pp. 223–9. Space does not permit a discussion of the law of these regional South–South arrangements in this chapter. They include CARICOM (the Caribbean) the Latin American Free Trade Area, the East African Community, West African Economic Community and the Arab Common Market. For a survey of these arrangements and a detailed bibliography, see Agarwal, *op. cit.* In general they account only for a small percentage of the total trade of the member countries. This limited potential for South–South economic integration may reflect similarity of endowments among many of the countries concerned.

53 See H.D.B.H. Gunasekera, D. Parsons and M.G. Kirby, 'Liberalizing Agricultural Trade: Some Perspectives for Developing Countries', in Whalley (ed.) *op. cit.*, pp. 253–4.

54 T.A. Oyejide, 'Primary Commodities in the International Trading System', in Whalley (ed.) *op. cit.*, p. 104.

55 *Ibid.*, pp. 105–6.

56 As Ruggie notes, according to Ricardo's presentation of the theory of comparative advantage in the *Principles of Political Economy and Taxation*, 'specialization entailed no important dynamic implications for growth or development, but simply provided static gains from trade that made both parties better off than they would in its absence'. J.G. Ruggie, 'Introduction: International Interdependence and National Welfare', in J.G. Ruggie (ed.) *The Antinomies of Interdependence: National Welfare and the International Division of Labor* (New York: Columbia University Press, 1983) p. 6. The neo-classical trade theorists launched their analysis from this account of comparative advantage, with little attention to other work of Ricardo and his fellow classical political economists, that emphasized dynamic effects of trade liberalization. See R. Findlay, 'Growth and Development in Trade Models', in P.B. Kenen and R.W. Jones (eds) *Handbook of International Economics* (Amsterdam: North-Holland, 1984). Milner, as well, emphasizes

renewed attention to the work of the classical political economists on the dynamics of growth and development. C. Milner, 'Trade Strategies and Economic Development: Theory and Evidence', in D. Greenaway (ed.) *Economic Development and International Trade* (London: Macmillan, 1988) pp. 64–5.

57 See, for example, G.M. Grossman and E. Helpman, *Innovation and Growth in the Global Economy* (Cambridge MA: MIT Press, 1991).
58 See Gilpin, *op. cit.*, pp. 270–90.
59 R. Vernon, 'International Investment and International Trade in the Product Cycle' (1966) 80 *Quarterly Journal of Economics* 190.
60 Grossman and Helpman, *op. cit.*, p. 310.
61 See Kelly and McGuirk *et al.*, *op. cit.*, p. 404.
62 See A.O. Krueger, *Trade Policies and Developing Nations* (Washington DC: Brookings Institution, 1995).
63 See for a more recent elaboration of the theory, P. Evans, *Dependent Development: The Alliance of Multinational, State* and *Local Capital in Brazil* (Princeton: Princeton University Press, 1979).
64 See particularly the 1974 UN Charter of Economic Rights and Duties of States. Article 1 states 'that Every State has the sovereign and inalienable right to choose its economic system as well as its political, social and cultural systems in accordance with the will of its people, without outside interference, coercion or threat in any form whatsoever'. and Article 2(1) that 'Every State has and shall freely exercise free permanent sovereignty, including possession use and disposal over all its wealth, natural resources and economic activities.'
65 For the empirical evidence, see J. Bhagwati, 'Export-Promoting Trade Strategy: Issues and Evidence', in D. Irwin (ed.) *Political Economy and International Economics* (Cambridge, MA: MIT Press, 1991); B. Balassa, 'The Cambridge Group and the Developing Countries, in Balassa (1989) *op. cit.*; G. Feder, 'On Exports and Economic Growth' (1983) *Journal of Development Economics* 59; V. Thomas, K. Matin and J. Nash, *Lessons in Trade Policy Reform* (Washington DC: World Bank, 1990) p. 5.
66 B. Balassa, 'The Importance of Trade for Developing Countries', in Balassa (1989) *op. cit.*, Krueger (1995) *op. cit.*
67 B. Balassa, 'The Importance of Trade for Developing Countries', in Balassa (1989) *op. cit.*
68 J. Bhagwati, 'Export-Promoting Trade Strategy', in Irwin (ed.) *op. cit.*
69 *Ibid.*
70 See Kelly and McGuirk *et al.*, *op. cit.*, pp. 48–9.
71 Hong Kong is the only one of these countries that actually adopted a thoroughgoing *laissez-faire* approach. See Milner, *op. cit.*, pp. 72–3. The most dramatic contrast with Hong Kong is perhaps Korea, where systematic and pervasive industrial policy measures (including sectoral targeting) went hand-in-hand with liberalization of the external trade regime (i.e. tariffs and exchange rates). On the Korean case, see S. Haggard and C.-I. Moon, 'The South Korean State in the International Economy: Liberal Dependent, or Mercantile?', in Ruggie (ed.) *op. cit.*, pp. 147–52.
72 World Bank, *The East Asian Miracle: Economic Growth and Public Policy* (Oxford: Oxford University Press, 1993).
73 See *Canada, the International Financial Institutions and the Debt Problem of Developing Countries*, Report of the Standing Senate Committee on Foreign Affairs, Parliament of Canada, Ottawa, 1987.
74 Gilpin, *op. cit.*, pp. 318–19.
75 W.R. Rhodes, 'Third-World Debt: The disaster that didn't happen', *The Economist*, 12 September 1992, pp. 21–3.
76 Rhodes, *op. cit.*, p. 22.
77 J.I. Levinson, 'A Perspective on the Debt Crisis' (1989) 4 *Amer. University J. Intl. Law and Policy* 489, pp. 509–12.
78 Rhodes, *op. cit.*, p. 23.

79 Kelly and McGuirk *et al.*, *op. cit.*, pp. 41–7.
80 Thomas, Matin and Nash, *op. cit.*, p. 17.
81 Very recently, however, there are some signs of a change in outlook, although less in the context of assistance to LDCs than of support for the reform process in Central and Eastern Europe. Thus, the World Bank has approved a $100 million loan for labour adjustment in Poland.
82 See D. Papagerogiou, A. Choksi and M. Michaeli, *Liberalizing Foreign Trade in Developing Countries: Lessons of Experience* (Washington DC: World Bank, 1990).
83 B. Balassa, 'Interests of Developing Countries in the Uruguay Round' (March 1988) 11 *World Economy*, pp. 50–1.
84 For detailed reviews of different features of the Uruguay Round results for developing countries, see W. Martin and L.A. Winters (eds) *The Uruguay Round and The Developing Countries* (Cambridge University Press, 1996) especially introductory essay by Martin and Winters.
85 *Ibid.*, ch. 1.
86 L.A. Winters, 'The LDC Perspective', in K.A. Ingersent, A.J. Rayner and R.C. Hine (eds) *Agriculture in the Uruguay Round* (New York: St. Martin's Press, 1994) p. 159.
87 *Ibid.*
88 For descriptions and evaluations of the Uruguay Round Agreement on Textiles and Clothing, see M. Smeets, 'Main Features of the Uruguay Round Agreement on Textiles and Clothing and Implications for the Trading System' (1995) 29 *J. of World Trade* 97; N. Blokker and J. Deelstra 'Towards a Termination of the Multifibre Arrangement?' (1994) 28 *J. of World Trade* 97.
89 *United States – Restrictions on Imports of Cotton and Man-made Fibre Underwear*, WT/DS24/AB p. 3.
90 *United States – Measure Affecting Imports of Woven Wool Shirts and Blouses from India*, WT/DS33/AB.
91 'WTO Panel Rules Against U.S. on Shirts, Sidesteps Broader Issues', *Inside U.S. Trade*, 10 January 1997.
92 Judicial economy refers to, in this instance, the panel's refusal to rule on certain issues when rendered unnecessary by earlier decisions within the Panel Report.
93 See Chapter 15, on trade and the environment, Chapter 16 on trade and labour standards and the concluding chapter, on fair trade more generally.
94 See Michael Trebilcock, 'What Makes Poor Countries Poor? The Role of Institutional Capital in Economic Development', in E. Buscaglia, W. Ratliff and R. Cooter (eds) *The Law and Economics of Development* (Connecticut: JAI Press, 1997).

15 Trade and the environment

1 See generally, Daniel Esty, *Greening the GATT* (Washington DC: Institute for International Economics, 1994).
2 North American Agreement on Environmental Cooperation, 1993.
3 See GATT Secretariat, *Trade and the Environment* (Geneva: GATT Secretariat, 1992) p. 7; see also, E.-U. Petersmann, 'Trade Policy, Environmental Policy and the GATT: Why Trade Rules and Environmental Rules Should be Mutually Consistent' (1991) 46 *Aussenwirtschaft* 197.
4 S. Shrybman, 'International Trade and the Environment: An Environmental Assessment of the General Agreement on Tariffs and Trade' (1990) 20 *Ecologist*, p. 33.
5 S. Charnovitz, 'Exploring the Environmental Exceptions in the GATT' (1991) 25 *Journal of World Trade* 37.
6 The equivalent provision in the Uruguay Round Agreement on Technical Barriers to Trade, Article 2.2, contains identical wording.
7 *Canada – Measures Affecting Exports of Unprocessed Herring and Salmon*, BISD 35S (1988) 98.
8 Canada also argued (unsuccessfully) that the exemption in Article XI(2b) applied, since

quality control with respect to the marketing of processed fish required assuring access of the Canadian processing industry to unprocessed fish that were subject to Canadian quality control, implying the need to limit flight of these Canadian quality-controlled unprocessed fish to the United States markets.

9 *Ibid.*, p. 108.
10 *Ibid.*, p. 114.
11 *Thailand: Restrictions On Importation of and Internal Taxes on Cigarettes*, BISD, 37th Supp. (1990) 200–8.
12 *In the Matter of Canada's Landing Requirement for Pacific Coast Salmon and Herring*, Final Report of the Panel, 16 October 1989.
13 See note 7 of this chapter which follows it.
14 *Lobster From Canada*, Final Report of the Panel (25 May 1990) 3 T.C.T. 8182.
15 Of course, since it was exports and not imports that were affected in the *Salmon and Herring Landing Requirement* case, the panel could not have dealt with the matter under Article III, which applies only to internal measures affecting *imports*. However, the fact that the panel had a choice as to whether to apply Article III or Article XI in the *Lobster* case whereas it had no choice in *Salmon and Herring* does not go very far in reconciling the rather different views of Article XI itself that underlie these two decisions.
16 It should be noted, however, that while the panel found that Article XI did not apply to the ban on undersized Canadian lobster, it did not determine whether in fact the ban violated the National Treatment obligation in Article III. This is because the explicit terms of reference of the Panel did not include the issue of National Treatment.
17 *Canada – Import, Distribution and Sale of Certain Alcoholic Drinks by Provincial Marketing Agencies* (1992) 5 TCT 8003.
18 *Ibid.*, p. 8045.
19 *United States – Taxes on Petroleum and Certain Imported Substances*, BISD, 34th Supp. (1988) 136.
20 *Ibid.*, p. 161.
21 *United States – Prohibition of Imports of Tuna and Tuna Products from Canada*, BISD, 29th Supp. (1982) p. 99.
22 *Ibid.*, p. 102.
23 See Chapter 10 above.
24 *Ibid.*, p. 108.
25 *United States – Restrictions on Imports of Tuna* (1991) 30 I.L.M. 1594. The panel ruling was not formally adopted by the GATT Council, by mutual agreement of the USA and Mexico.
26 *Ibid.*, p. 1618.
27 *Ibid.*, p. 1620.
28 See GATT secretariat, *Trade and the Environment*, *op. cit.*
29 See Ted McDorman, 'The 1991 US–Mexico GATT Panel Report On Tuna and Dolphin: Implications for Trade and Environmental Conflicts' (1991) 17 *North Carolina J. Int'l. L. and Com. Reg* for a defence of the decision.
30 United States – Restrictions on Imports of Tuna, *op. cit*, pp. 1622–23.
31 See Charnovitz, *op. cit.* and accompanying text.
32 See for instance the Canadian Cultural Property Export and Import Act S.C. 1974–75–76, c 50.
33 See J.W. Kindt, *Marine Pollution and the Law of the Sea*, vol. IV (Buffalo NY: Hein & Co., 1986) pp. 2130–44.
34 In the *Nicaraguan Contra* case, the International Court of Justice found that there was no rule of customary international law prohibiting the use of economic measures, including a trade embargo, to influence the internal policies of another state; *Case Concerning Military and Para Military Activities in and Against Nicaragua (Nicaragua* v. *United States of America (Merits)* (1986) I.C.J. Rep. 14, 244.

35 33 I.L.M. 936 (1994) (known as the LaJolla Agreement).

36 *United States – Restrictions on Imports of Tuna: Report of the Panel* (1994) GATT Doc. DS29/R.

37 Supra, n. 34.

38 In exceptional circumstances, it might be possible to compensate for the loss of the US market by lowering the price of dolphin-unfriendly tuna in other markets to increase sales there; however, this would only be possible if tuna had been priced above marginal cost in these markets, which is a highly unlikely scenario.

39 *United States – Taxes on Automobiles*, Report of the Panel (29 September 1994) unadopted, DS31/R, 1–124.

40 Of course with globalization of automobile production and extensive cross-ownership between foreign and American automakers the whole basis for the distinction would have to be rethought. See Petrus van Bork, 'Victory in Europe: A Discussion Future Implications for Article III of the GATT', Discussion Paper, Nomos Corporation Consultants, to be posted in revised version to Nomos website, www.nomosconsulting.com.

41 A recent OECD document appears to take this view of the meaning of product-related PPMs. Thus, it claims that in that where the environmental damage is caused by the way in which the product is produced and not the product itself, the PPM is 'non-product related'. This analysis appears to be based on confused economic reasoning that non-product related PPMs do not address consumption externalities. Yet the kind of measure at stake in *Tuna/Dolphin*, at least the embargo does address consumption externalities. It is the consumption of dolphin-unfriendly tuna that leads to the dolphins in question being killed – the loss of dolphins is an externalized cost of consuming such tuna. By contrast a trade ban on let us say, straw hats, produced by countries that allow tuna to be caught in a dolphin unfriendly way does not address any consumption externality with respect to straw hats. OECD, *Processes and Production Methods (PPMs): Conceptual Framework and Considerations on Use of PPM-Based Trade Measures*, OCDE/GD(97)137, p. 15.

42 *Japan – Taxes on Alcoholic Beverages*, Report of the Appellate Body (4 October 1996) WT/DS 8/R, WT/DS10/R,WT/DS11/R, AB-1996-02, pp. 19–20. Followed in *Canada – Certain Measures Concerning Periodicals*, Report of the Appellate Body (30 June 1997) WT*/DS31/AB/R, AB–1997–2.*

43 Japan – Taxes on Alcoholic Beverages, *op. cit.*, p. 20.

44 *United States–Standards for Reformulated and Conventional Gasoline*, Report of the Panel, WT/DS2/R (29 January 1996).

45 *United States–Import Prohibition of Certain Shrimp and Shrimp* Products, Report of the Panel, WT/DS58/R (15 May 1998) [hereinafter in this chapter, *Turtles*).

46 Supra n. 41 and accompanying text.

47 *Report of (1996) the WTO Committee on Trade and Environment*, PRESS/TE 014, 14 November 1996, p. 7.

48 *Ibid.*, pp. 7–8.

49 O. Young, *International Governance: Protecting the Environment in a Stateless Society* (Ithaca: Cornell University Press, 1994) p. 20.

50 G. Hardin, 'The Tragedy of the Commons', in G. Hardin and J. Baden (eds) *Managing the Commons* (San Francisco: W.H. Freeman, 1977).

51 Young, *op. cit.*, p. 21.

52 G. Hufbauer, J. Schott and K. Elliott, *Economic Sanctions Reconsidered: History and Current Policy* 2nd ed. (Washington DC: Institute for International Economics, 1990). See also M. Miyagawa, *Do Economic Sanctions Work?* (New York: St. Martin's Press, 1992) and D. Baldwin, *Economic Statecraft* (Ithaca: Cornell University Press, 1985).

53 Nufbauer *et al.*, *op. cit.*, p. 93.

54 This is consistent with more recent work by Nossal, which found that sanctions by 'middle powers' such as Canada and Australia have been largely ineffective. See K.R.

Nossal, *Rain Dancing: Sanctions in Canadian and Australian Foreign Policy* (Toronto: University of Toronto Press, 1994).

55 In some cases such sanctions might, however, be aimed at goals that imply very significant regime change, for instance, in the case of China, sanctions aimed at inducing respect for the right of labour to organize and bargain freely.

56 S. Charnovitz, 'Encouraging Environmental Cooperation Through Trade Measures: The Pelly Amendment and the GATT', paper delivered at the Institute on Global Conflict and Cooperation (1993) cited in Chang, *op. cit.*, pp. 58–60.

57 GATT Secretariat, *Trade and the Environment*, GATT Doc 1529 (3 February 1992).

58 Chang, *op. cit.*, pp. 19–25.

59 K.A. Rodman, 'Public and Private Sanctions against South Africa' (1994) 109 *Political Science Quarterly* 313, p. 334.

60 There may also be a further alternative, akin to labelling, through which individual consumers by their investment choices can attempt to discipline socially irresponsible corporate behaviour. The phenomenon of socially responsible investing (SRI) refers to the 'making of investment choices according to both financial and ethical criteria'. For instance, individuals can choose to put their investments in firms that act in a manner consistent with their ethical values or they may choose to refrain from investing in those firms believed to be behaving in a socially unacceptable fashion. The two primary claims advanced by SRI adherents, that distinguish it from other strategies of investment, are: (i) that social screening does not entail a financial sacrifice (i.e. that advancing one's social agenda can be as profitable as investment for purely financial gain) and (ii) that SRI can later corporate behaviour in so far as it seeks to channel funds away from firms acting in a socially unacceptable way. While this phenomenon has become quite popular, there is good reason to be sceptical about its ability to deliver on its claims. Specifically, Knoll has suggested that, at best, only one of the claims can be true because each implies the negation of the other. As he explains, '[i]f markets are efficient, the first might be true but the second is false. If markets are inefficient, the second might be true but the first is false.' With respect to the second claim, Knoll found that 'regardless of the efficiency or inefficiency of the market, the impact of an investor's decision not to invest in a company will have little or no impact on the firm's ability to raise capital and therefore on its activities.' For a more thorough discussion, see Michael S. Knoll, 'Socially Responsible Investment and Modern Financial Markets' (18 March 1994, unpublished).

61 On environmental labelling, see R. Howse, 'Reform, Retrenchment or Revolution? The Shift to Incentives and the Future of the Regulatory State' (1993) 31 *Alberta Law Review* 486–7; D. Cohen, 'Procedural Fairness and Incentive Programs: Reflections on the Environmental Choice Program' (1993) 31 *Alberta Law Review* 554–74.

62 J. Bhagwati and T.N. Srinivasan suggest that environmental values, if sound, 'will spread because of their intrinsic appeal'. 'Trade and the Environment: Does Environmental Diversity Detract From the Case for Free Trade?', unpublished manuscript, July 1994. The fact that moral principles such as those prohibiting murder and theft are inherently sound does not, however, obviate the need to sanction non-compliance with them.

63 See R. Stewart, 'Environmental Regulation and International Competitiveness' (1993) 102 *Yale Law Journal* 2039.

64 See B.A. Langille, 'General Reflections on the Relationship of Trade and Labour (Or: Fair Trade is Free Trade's Destiny)', in J. Bhagwati and R.E. Hudec (eds) *Fair Trade and Harmonization: Prerequisites for Free Trade?* (Cambridge, MA: MIT Press, 1996).

65 See B.A. Langille, '"A Day at the Races": A Reply to Professor Revesz on the Race for the Bottom', unpublished manuscript, Faculty of Law, University of Toronto, 18 March 1994; R. Revesz, 'Rehabilitating Interstate Competition: Rethinking the 'Race to the Bottom' Rationale for Federal and Environmental Competition' (1992) 62 *N.Y.U. Law Rev.* 1216.

66 Laura Tyson, *Who's Bashing Whom?* (Washington: Institute for International Economics, 1992).

67 C. Rhodes, *Reciprocity, U.S. Trade Policy and the GATT Regime* (Ithaca: Cornell University Press, 1993).

68 M.J. Trebilcock, Chandler and R. Howse, *Trade and Transitions: A Comparative Analysis of Adjustment Policies* (London: Routledge, 1990 (1985)), pp. 211–15. This view of the legal order of liberal trade has been greatly influenced by the liberal internationalist perspective of Robert Axelrod and Robert Keohane. According to Axelrod and Keohane, 'The principles and rules of international regimes make governments concerned about precedents, increasing the likelihood that they will attempt to punish defectors. In this way international regimes help to link the future with the present. This is as true of arms control agreements, in which willingness to make future agreements depends on others' compliance with previous arrangements, as it is in the General Agreement on Tariffs and Trade, which embodies norms and rules against which the behaviour of members can be judged. By sanctioning retaliation for those who violate rules, regimes create expectations that a given violation will be treated not as an isolated case but as one in a series of interrelated actions.' R. Axelrod and R.O. Keohane, 'Achieving Cooperation Under Anarchy: Strategies and Institutions', in D.A. Baldwin (ed.) *Neorealism and Neoliberalism* (New York: Columbia University Press, 1993), p. 94.

69 In the case of labour rights, amending the actual text of Art. XX would seem to be necessary, because (apart from products manufactured with prison labour) Art. XX does not contain any explicit labour rights justifications for trade restrictions.

70 Convention on International Trade in Endangered Species of Wild Fauna and Flora, 3 March 1973, 27 U.S.T. 1087, 993 UNTS 243.

71 On the successes and limitations of CITES, see the excellent OECD study, *Experience with the Use of Trade Measures in the Convention on International Trade in Endangered Species of Wild Fauna and Flora (CITES)* OCDE/GD(97)106 (Paris: OECD, 1997).

72 This principle of customary international law is now codified in the Vienna Convention on the Law of Treaties, 23 May 1989, 1155 UNTS 331, Article 30, 3. Since the GATT predates the Vienna Convention, the principle applies to GATT by virtue of customary not treaty law. See K.C. Kennedy, 'Reforming U.S. Trade Policy To Protect the Global Environment: A Multilateral Approach' (1994) 18 *Harvard Environmental Law Review* 185, pp. 207–8.

73 Art. II.4, *Marrakesh Agreement Establishing the World Trade Organization.*

74 R. Hudec, 'GATT Legal Restraints in the Use of Trade Measures against Foreign Environmental Practices' in J. Bhagwati and R. Hudec (eds) *Fair Trade and Harmonization: prerequisites for Free Trade?*, Vol. 2 (Cambridge, MA: MIT Press, 1996) p. 121.

75 See K. Knop, 'Re/Statements: Feminism and State Sovereignty in International Law' (1993) 3 *Transnational Law and Contemporary Problems* 294, pp. 298ff.

76 In this sense, the *Reformulated Gasoline* AB decision, in breathing life into the 'chapeau' language, supports the claim of Chang that 'this proviso, properly interpreted and vigorously enforced, should provide sufficient protection against abuse of environmental trade measures'. H. Chang, 'Carrots, Sticks, and International Externalities' (1997) 17 *International Review of Law and Economics* 309, p. 324. In earlier work we ourselves placed greater emphasis on the conduct of a least-restrictive means test in determining whether measures are 'necessary' within the meaning of Art. XX(b) or 'relating to' the conservation of exhaustible natural resources in Art. XX(g). This was based upon the existing jurisprudence, which had largely ignored or read into insignificance the chapeau. However, we think that the Appellate Body was probably correct to adopt the approach it did, which fits more closely the actual words and textual structure of Art. XX.

77 For example, the United National Environmental Programme (UNEP) or in some instances the World Health Organization (WHO) as well as Secretariats responsible for implementation of specific international agreements.

78 See G. Feketekuty, 'The Link Between Trade and Environmental Policy' (1993) 2 *Minnesota Journal of Global Trade* 171. This article is especially illuminating on the relationship between trade and environment, and is notable for its clear, sophisticated, and sympathetic handling of both the environmental and the trade law values at stake.

79 For instance, the Montreal Protocol on Substances that Deplete the Ozone Layer provides developing countries with a period of time twice as long as that applicable to developed countries to achieve a given level of reductions in per capita consumption of ozone-depleting substances. See D.B. Magraw, 'Legal Treatment of Developing Countries: Differential, Contextual, and Absolute Norms' (1990) 1 *Colorado Journal of International Environmental Law and Policy* 69, pp. 73–81.

80 This interpretation is also suggested by W.G. Watson, *Environmental and Labor Standards in the NAFTA* (Toronto: C.D. Howe Institute, 1994) p. 14.

81 For a clear presentation of the nature of this paradigm, its limits, and some of the developments in international legal theory and practice that are putting into question traditional notions of sovereignty, see Knop, *op. cit.*

82 See Eco Region, Vol. 1, No. 1, Summer 1995, Newsletter of the Secretariat of the Commission for Environmental Cooperation.

83 The amounts specified for these projects range from US $77,000 for a plant biodversity Inventory and Information Network to $522,000 for a project on the sound management of chemicals. 'Record of Council Session 96-1', 25 January 1996. One can have little confidence that comprehensive and competent technical work, as opposed to consultants' reports full of generalities, can be done for these amounts.

84 See CEC News Release, 'The Commission for Environmental Cooperation (CEC) is Seeking Public Review and Comment on the Proposed Guidelines for a New Initiative: The North American Environmental Fund (NAEF)', undated.

85 See CEC Press Release, 11 April 1996, 'Three Additional Chemicals Targeted for Joint Action by Canada, the U.S. and Mexico'.

86 Submission No. SEM-95-001, 30 June 1995.

87 Determination of the Secretariat, 21 September 1995, p. 3.

88 Submission No. SEM-95-002, 31 August 1995.

89 Determination of the Secretariat concerning submission SEM-95-002, 8 December 1995, p. 3.

90 Submission No. SEM-96-001, 18 January 1996.

91 *Final Factual Record of the Cruise Ship Pier Project in Cozumel, Quintana Roo*, Commission for Environmental Cooperation, 1997.

92 *Ibid.*, Annex II.

93 CEC Secretariat Report on the Death of Migratory Birds at the Silva Reservoir, October 1995.

94 B. McKenna, 'NAFTA ecology watchdog quits', *Globe and Mail*, 14 February 1998, p. B4.

16 Trade and labour rights

1 The following draws extensively from R. Howse and M.J. Trebilcock, 'The Fair Trade – Free Trade Debate: Trade, Labour and the Environment' (1996) 16 *International Review of Law and Economics* 61. We have also learned much from conversations with Brian Langille and Sophie Dufour.

2 See H.F. Chang, 'Trade Measures to Protect the Global Environment', paper presented at the annual meeting of the American Law and Economics Association, Palo Alto, 9 May 1994, unpublished.

3 See, generally, B. Hepple, 'Equality: A Global Labour Standard', in W. Sengenberger and D. Campbell (eds) *International Labour Standards and Economic Interdependence* (Geneva: International Institute for Labour Studies, 1994).

4 *ILO Convention No. 138* (Minimum Age Convention) (1973).

5 We owe this point to our colleague Brian Langille.
6 J. Bhagwati, 'Policy Perspectives and Future Directions: A View From Academia', in United States Department of Labor, *International Labor Standards and Global Economic Integration: Procedings of a Symposium*, Washington DC, July 1994, p. 59.
7 M. Nussbaum, *Cultivating Humanity: A Classical Defense of Reform in Liberal Education* (Cambridge, MA: Harvard University Press, 1997) pp. 139–45.
8 A. Sen, 'Is Coercion a Part of Asian Values?', unpublished manuscript, cited in Nussbaum, *Ibid.*, p. 139-45.
9 See G. Hansson, *Social Clauses and International Trade: An Economic Analysis of Labour Standards in Trade Policy* (New York: St. Martin's Press, 1983) pp. 168–71.
10 Some economists have a generally sceptical view of the possibility that minimum standards, for instance in the case of occupational health and safety, can adequately correct for market failure. However, once this scepticism is put to the test through economic modelling, the results are ambiguous. Under some assumptions, minimum standards may be effective in correcting for market failure; under others (e.g. considerable heterogeneity in workers' risk preferences) minimum standards may actually result in greater market distortion. See D.K. Brown, A.V. Deardorff and R.M. Stern, 'International Labour Standards and Trade: A Theoretical Analysis', Fairness-Harmonization Project, July 1994.
11 See, generally, C. Sunstein, *After the Rights Revolution: Reconceiving the Regulatory State* (Cambridge MA: Harvard University Press, 1990).
12 *Trade, Employment and Labour Standards: A Study of Core Workers' Rights and International Trade* (Paris: OECD, 1996)[hereinafter in this Chapter, OECD Study) p. 40.
13 Thus, we would agree with some critics of labour rights based trade sanctions, such as Srinivasan, that de-restricting immigration may well be a first-best solution, a position consistent with that developed in Chapter 18 on the movement of people in this book; this, however, is unlikely to occur anytime soon. Cf. T.N. Srinivasan, 'International Trade and Labour Standards', in P. van Dyck and G. Faher (eds) *Challenges to the New World Trade Organization* (Amsterdam: Martinus Nijhoff/Kluwer, 1995).
14 See Albert Hirschman, *Exit, Voice and Loyalty: Responses to Decline in Firms, Organizations, and States* (Cambridge MA: Harvard University Press, 1970).
15 In the case of Mexico, for example, it is often suggested that gross violations of basic international labour rights norms are concentrated in the *maquiladora* region, while basic labour rights are respected throughout much of the country, particularly in unionized workplaces. See P. Morici, 'Implications of a Social Charter for the North American Free Trade Agreement', in J. Lemco and W.B.P. Robson (eds) *Ties Beyond Trade: Labour and Environmental Issues under the NAFTA* (Toronto and Washington DC: C.D. Howe Institute and National Planning Association, 1993) pp. 137–8. Morici notes that, even within the *maquiladoras*, 'many employers . . . provide workers with a wide range of benefits and a safe working environment, and they adhere closely to strict environmental standards' (p. 138). See also USITC, Review of Trade and Investment Measures by Mexico, USITC Report No. 2326 (October 1990).
16 M. Aggarwal, 'International Trade and the Role of Labor Standards', *International Economic Review*, United States International Trade Commission, August 1995.
17 K.E. Maskus, *Should Core Labor Standards Be Imposed Through International Trade Policy?*, Policy Research Working Paper 1817 (Washington DC: World Bank, 1997) pp. 19–21.
18 *Ibid.*, p. 26.
19 *Ibid.*, p. 50.
20 In the case of Poland, for instance, the beginnings of liberal revolution are to found in the gradual recognition of an independent trade union movement, which was able to mobilize broader social forces against the Soviet-bloc regime. See A. Pravaj, 'The Workers' in A. Brumberg (ed.) *Poland: Genesis of a Revolution* (New York: Vintage, 1983) pp. 68–91.
21 'Perpetual Peace' in Hans Reiss (ed.) *Kant's Political Writings*, trans. H.B. Nisbet (London: Cambridge University Press, 1970).

22 See Michael W. Doyle, 'Kant, Liberal Legacies and Foreign Affairs' (1983) 12 *Philosophy and Public Affairs* 205; and 'Liberalism and World Politics' (1986) 80 *American Political Science Review* 1151.
23 M.J. Trebilcock, M.A. Chandler, and R. Howse, *Trade and Transitions: A Comparative Analysis of Adjustment Policies* (London: Routledge, 1990 (1985) p. 45. See also R.E. Baldwin, 'The Ineffectiveness of Trade Policy in Promoting Social Goals' 8 *The World Economy* 109.
24 S. Dufour, *Les droits des travailleurs et les accords commerciaux* (Sherbrooke Que.: Presses de l'Universite de Sherbrooke, 1998) p. 60, fn. 161[hereinafter in this Chapter, *dimension sociale*].
25 L. Compa, 'Labor Rights and Labor Standards in International Trade' (1993) 25 *Law and Policy in International Business* 165, p. 170.
26 OECD study, *op. cit.*, p. 186.
27 G. Hufbauer, J. Schott and K. Elliott, *Economic Sanctions Reconsidered: History and Current Policy* 2nd ed. (Washington DC: Institute for International Economics, 1990). See also M. Miyagawa, *Do Economic Sanctions Work?* (New York: St. Martin's Press, 1992) and D. Baldwin, *Economic Statecraft* (Ithaca: Cornell University Press, 1985).
28 Hufbauer *et al., op. cit.*, p. 93.
29 Maskus, *op. cit.*, Srinivasan in van Dyck and Faher (eds) *op. cit.*
30 Maskus, *op. cit.*, p. 20.
31 Chang, *op. cit.*, pp. 19–25.
32 Srinivasan, in van Dyck and Faher (eds) *op. cit.*
33 For instance, the OECD notes: 'there are cases where the authorities, either at the national level (Korea, Singapore and Chinese Tapei) or at the local level (Kerala state in India) have given high priority to school enrolment and this has resulted in a drop in the levels of child labor'. OECD study, *op. cit.*, p. 47.
34 See note 60, Chapter 15.
35 See note 61, Chapter 15.
36 See note 62, Chapter 15.
37 International Labour Office, *The ILO, Standard Setting and Globalization*, Report of the Director General, International Labour Conference, 85th Session, 1997, Geneva, p. 20. Available at http://www.ilo.org/public/english/10ilc/ilc85/dg-rep.htm.
38 See note 68, Chapter 15.
39 B. Langille, 'Eight Ways to Think about International Labour Standards' (1997) 31 *Journal of World Trade* 27, p. 33.
40 Such an interpretation would have to hinge on the language of Art. XX(a) of the GATT, which refers to measures 'necessary to protect public morals.' In several respects, however, it would lack plausibility.
41 See *United States–Standards for Reformulated and Conventional Gasoline*, Report of the Appellate Body, WT/DS2/AB/R (29 April 1996) AB–1996–1. This case is discussed at length in the Trade and Environment Chapter.
42 International Labour Office, *The ILO, standard setting and globalization, op. cit.*, pp. 9–13.
43 See W. Sengenberger, 'Protection-participation-promotion: The systemic nature and effects of labour standards', unpublished manuscript, International Institute for Labour Studies, Geneva, Switzerland.
44 See B. Langille, 'General Reflections on the Relationship of Trade and Labour (Or: Fair Trade is Free Trade's Destiny)'.
45 See B.A. Langille, '"A Day at the Races": A Reply to Professor Revesz on the Race for the Bottom', unpublished manuscript, Faculty of Law, University of Toronto, 18 March 1994; R. Revesz, 'Rehabilitating Interstate Competition: Rethinking the 'Race to the Bottom' Rationale for Federal and Environmental Competition' (1992) 62 *N.Y.U. Law Rev.* 1216.
46 S. Charnovitz, 'The Influence of International Labour Standards on the World Trading System: A Historical Overview' (1987) 126 *International Labour Review* 565.
47 C.T. Feddersen, 'Focusing on Substantive Law in International Economic Relations:

The *Public Morals* of GATT's Article XX(a) and "Conventional" Rules of Interpretation' (1998) 7 *Minnesota Journal of Global Trade* 75, pp. 76ff.

48 *Ibid.*, p. 109. But see S Charhovitz, 'The Moral Exception in Trade Policy' (1998) 38 *Journal International Law* 68.
49 'ILO Chief Rebuffed by WTO On Trade-Labour Spat', Reuters Financial Service, 5 December 1996.
50 A proposal along these lines is discussed in Dufour, *Dimension Sociale, op. cit.*, pp. 337ff.
51 S. Charnovitz, 'Trade, Employment and Labour Standards: The OECD Study and Recent Developments in the Trade and Labor Standards Debate' (1997) 11 *Temple International and Comparative Law Journal* 131, pp. 162–3.
52 International Labour Organization Cross-Departmental Analysis and Reports Team, *The Social Dimension of the Liberalization of International Trade* (Geneva: ILO, 1998, p. 6).
53 *Omnibus Trade and Competitiveness Act of 1988*, Pub. L. 100–418, 102 Stat. 1107 (19880, 1101(b)(14)).
54 'Appendix. The Current Enforcement Authority and Procedures: 301, Super 301 and Special 301', in J. Bhagwati and H.T. Patrick (eds) *Aggressive Unilateralism: America's 301 Trade Policy and the World Trading System* (Ann Arbor: University of Michigan Press, 1990) pp. 39–40.
55 See Chapter 12 for an explanation of the GSP.
56 s. 503, General System of Preferences Renewal Act of 1984.
57 *Ibid.*, and see also, S. Weintraub and J. Gilbreath, 'The Social Side to Free Trade', in Lemco and Robson (eds) *op. cit.*, pp. 66–7.
58 Francis Wolf, 'Human Rights and the International Labour Organisation', in Theodor Meron (ed.) *Human Rights in International Law: Legal and Policy Issues*, Vol. II (Oxford: Clarendon Press, 1984) pp. 274–5.
59 OECD Study, *op. cit.*, p. 185.
60 *Ibid.*, p. 185.
61 S. Dufour, *Dimension Sociale, op. cit.*, p. 60.
62 *Ibid.*, pp. 49–54.
63 See Weintraub and Gilbreath, *op. cit.*, pp. 66–8.
64 *Ibid.*
65 See P. Morici, 'Implications of a Social Charter for the *NAFTA*', in Lemco and Robson (eds) *op. cit.*, pp. 137–8.
66 L. Compta, 'NAFTA's Labor Side Accord: A Three-Year Accounting', *NAFTA: Law and Busines Review of the Americas*, Summer 1997, pp. 19–21.

17 Trade and competition policy

1 For a useful introduction to the basic economics of antitrust, see H. Hovenkamp, *Federal Antitrust Policy* (St. Paul, MN: West Publishing Co., 1994) ch. 1.
2 See generally W. Landes and R. Posner, 'Market Power in Antitrust Cases' (1991) 94 *Harvard Law Review* 937.
3 The monopolist restricts output to the point where the marginal cost and marginal revenue curves intersect because, assuming it is able to charge only a single price for whatever output it produces (i.e. it cannot discriminate between price sensitive and price insensitive customers), lowering the price below PM in Fig. 17.1 in order to capture further sales means foregoing some of the profits on all sales up to that point. (This assumption is relaxed below.)
4 The extent to which the monopolist is able to price above PC is a function of the elasticity of demand which it faces. The more inelastic the demand at the competitive price, the greater the capacity to increase price above this level without losing large numbers of profitable sales.
5 See Richard Posner, *Antitrust Law: An Economic Perspective* (University of Chicago Press, 1976) p. 12.

6 However, it is not clear how these concerns can be rendered justiciable under competition law, and it seems likely that other public policies can better address inequalities of political influence: see B. Dunlop, D. McQueen and M. Trebilcock, *Canadian Competition Policy* (Toronto: Canada Law Book, 1987) pp. 67–8.

7 To return to Figure 17.1, if the monopolist were to raise the price for inelastic customers on the demand curve above PM and then set a separate price for more elastic customers on the demand curve below PM and above PC (i.e. set two prices) sales to the inelastic customers are likely to decline, while sales to the more elastic customers are likely to increase, with the net effect on output being unclear as a matter of logic (although in most cases it is likely to be positive).

8 See O. Williamson, 'Economies as an Antitrust Defence: The Welfare Trade-Offs' (1968) 48 *American Economic Review* 18.

9 We do not consider here the case of so-called 'natural monopoly' where scale effects are so large that for a single firm in an industry average total costs are falling in the region of total industry demand. Here some form of price regulation is more appropriate than a competition policy response, although it should be noted that in recent years industries or segments of industries traditionally viewed as natural monopolies, e.g. telecommunications, transportation, electricity, gas, are now widely viewed as contestable, leading to de-regulation, privatization and the application of competition policy to their contestable elements.

10 This section of the chapter is derived from Michael Trebilcock, 'Competition Policy and Trade Policy: Mediating the Interface' (1996) 30 *J. of World Trade* 71. For a comprehensive review of the international dimensions of competition policy, see WTO Annual Report, 1997, ch. 4.

11 See American Bar Association Antitrust Section, Report of the Special Committee on International Antitrust (1991); Report of the OECD Committee on Competition Law and Policy, 'Interim Report on Convergence of Competition Policies' (1994); Barry Hawk, *Antitrust and Market Access* (Paris: OECD, 1996). Alan Ballard and Kerrin Vautier, 'The Convergence of Competition Law with APEC and the CER Agreement', in Rong-1 Wu and Yun-Peng Chu (eds) *Business Markets and Government in the Asia Pacific* (London: Routledge, 1998).

12 Sylvia Ostry, *The Post-Cold War Trading System: Who's On First?* (University of Chicago Press, 1997).

13 For a more detailed review of the range of situations where this concern arises, see WTO Annual Report, 1997, *op. cit.*, Section IV: also Report (1998) of the Working Group on the Interaction Between Trade and Competition Policy to the WTO General Council.

14 See Americo Zampetti and Pierre Sauvé, 'New Dimensions of Market Access: An Overview', in OECD, *New Dimensions of Market Access in a Globalizing World Economy* (Paris: OECD, 1995) pp. 19–20; see also Eleanor Fox and Janusz Ordover, 'The Harmonization of Competition and Trade Law' (1995) 19 *World Competition* 5.

15 See Olivier Long, *Law and its Limits in the GATT Multilateral Trade System* (London: Graham and Trotman-Martinus Nijohff, 1987) pp. 1–2; Kenneth Dam, *The GATT* (Chicago: University of Chicago Press, 1970) ch. 2; Frank Stone, *Canada, GATT, and the International Trade System* (Montreal: Institute for Research on Public Policy, 1987) pp. 52–3; and John Jackson, *The World Trading System* (Cambridge MA: MIT Press, 1989, ch. 2; Eleanor Fox, *Competition Law and the Next Agenda for the WTO*, in OECD (1995), *op. cit.*, p. 169.

16 See George N. Addy, *International Co-ordination of Competition Policies*, in E. Kantzenbach, H. Scharrer and L. Waverman (eds) *Competition Policy in an Interdependent World Economy* (Baden-Baden: Nomos Verlagsgesellschaft, 1993) p. 292.

17 *The Set of Multilaterally Agreed Principles and Rules for the Control of Restrictive Business Practices*, 5 December 1980, UNCTAD Doc. TD/RBP/Conf. 10/Rev. 1.

18 See P. Ebow Bondzai Simpson, *Legal Relationships Between Transnational Corporations and Host States* (New York: Quorum Books, 1990) ch. 5.

19 Fox, in OECD (1995), *op. cit.*, p. 170.
20 See Edward Glynn, *International Agreements to Allocate Jurisdiction Over Mergers*, in Barry Hawk (ed.) *International Mergers and Joint Ventures* (New York: Fordham Corporate Law Institute, 1991) pp. 38–43; George N. Addy, 'International Co-ordination of Competition Policies', in Kantzenbach *et al.*, *op. cit.*, pp. 292–4.
21 See E.U. Petersmann, 'International Competition Rules for Governments and Private Business' (1996) 30 *J. of World Trade* 5.
22 For an overview of these agreements, see draft report by the International Chamber of Commerce, *Competition and Trade in the Global Arena* (February 1998), pp. 17–25.
23 Memorandum of Understanding Between the Government of Canada and the Government of the United States of America as to Notification, Consultation and Co-operation with Respect to the Application of National Antitrust Laws, 23 I.L.M. 275, 1984; see also the Treaty Between the Government of Canada and the Government of the United States of America on Mutual Legal Assistance in Criminal Matters, 24 I.L.M. 1092, 18 March 1985; see generally Lawson Hunter and Susan Hutton, *Where There is a Will There is a Way: Co-operation in Canada–U.S. Antitrust Relations*, paper presented in the American Conference Institute on Multinational Antitrust Enforcement, New York, 7 March 1994; Neil Campbell, Jeffrey Roode and William Rowley, *The Proper Framework for Co-operation Among National Antitrust Agencies*, paper presented at Roundtable on Competition Policy Reform, University of Toronto, 8 December 1995.
24 See *Notes* for an address by George Addy, Director of Investigation and Research, Canadian Bureau of Competition Policy, to ABA Section of Antitrust Law Annual Meeting, 6 August 1995.
25 Agreement Between the Government of the United States of America and the Government of Australia Relating to Co-operation on Antitrust Matters, 20 I.L.M. 702, 1982 (renegotiated in 1995).
26 Agreement Between the Government of the United States of America and the Government of the Federal Republic of Germany Relating to Mutual Co-operation Regarding Restrictive Business Practices, 1976.
27 Agreement Between the Commission of the European Communities and the Government of the United States of America Regarding the Application of their Competition Laws, Washington, DC, 23 September 1991. This Agreement was held invalid by the European Court of Justice as ultra vires the Commission's powers, but was subsequently approved by the Council.
28 See Organisation for Economic Co-operation and Development, *Revised Recommendation of the Council Concerning Co-operation between Member Countries on Restrictive Business Practices Affecting International Trade* [C(86)44(Final)] 1986, and predecessor versions referenced therein.
29 See Glynn, *op. cit.*, pp. 39–43.
30 See Valentine Korah, *An Introductory Guide to EC* Competition Law and Practice, 6th ed. (London: Sweet & Maxwell, 1997); Richard Whish and Brenda Sufrin, *Competition Law*, 3rd ed. (London: Butterworths, 1993); Vivien Rose (ed.) *Bellamy and Child: Common Market Law of Competition*, 4th ed. (London: Sweet & Maxwell, 1993); Ivo Van Bael and Jean-Frangois Bellis, *Competition Law of the EEC*, 2nd ed. (Bicester: CCH Editions, 1990).
31 See ABA *NAFTA* Task Force Report, *op. cit.*, Appendix.
32 These provisions are similar to the State-trading provisions in Article XVII of the GATT.
33 Eleanor Fox, 'Antitrust Trade and the Twenty-First Century: Rounding the Circle' *The Record* of the Association of the Bar of the City of New York, June 1993.
34 See Special Supplement, 64 BNA Antitrust and Trade Reg. Rep., 19 August 1993 (Special Supplement, No. 1628). For a review of the Code, see W.F. Kentscher, 'Competition Rules for Private Agents in the GATT/WTO System' (1994) 49 Aussenwirtschaft 281 (Code annexed).
35 It should be noted that several members of the Working Group (including Professor

Fox) dissented, favouring a more modest set of common minimum standards.

36 See Chapter 12.

37 See, e.g. J. Pelkmans, 'The Institutional Economics of European Integration', in M. Cappelletti, M. Seccombe and J. Weiler (eds) *Integration Through Law* (Florence: European University Institute, 1986); J. Pinder, 'Positive Integration and Negative Integration – Some Problems of Economic Union in the EEC' (1968) 24 *World Today* 88.

38 David W. Leebron, 'Lying Down with Procrustes: An Analysis of Harmonization Claims', in Jagdish Bhagwati and Robert E. Hudec (eds) *Fair Trade and Harmonization* (Cambridge MA: MIT Press, 1996) vol. 1, p. 41; Leebron, 'Claims for Harmonization: A Theoretical Framework' (1996) 27 *Canadian Business L.J.* 63.

39 See Robert Howse and Michael Trebilcock, 'The Fair Trade–Free Trade Debate: Trade, Labour and the Environment' (1996) 16 *International Review of Law and Economics* 61.

40 Fox and Ordover, *op. cit.*

41 Eleanor Fox, 'Competition Law and the Next Agenda for the WTO', in OECD (1995), *op. cit.*, pp. 181–3; 'Jurisdiction and Conflicts in the Global Economy: Crafting A Systems Interface', mimeo, N.Y.U. Law School, 3 March 1995.

42 EC Expert Group *Competition Policy in the New Trade Order: Strengthening International Co-operation and Rules* (Brussels: EC Commission, 1995); See Petersmann, *op. cit.*

43 M. Bacchetta, H. Horn and P. Mavroidis, 'Do Negative Spillovers from Nationally Pursued Competition Policies Provide a Case for Multilateral Competition Rules?', Working Paper, 14 August 1997; see also Edward Iacobucci, 'The Interdependence of Trade and Competition Policies,' (1997) World Competition S; Andrew Guzman, 'Is International Antitrust possible?' (1998) 73 N.Y.U.L.R. 150.

44 For a useful comparative review of the evolution and effects of these exemptions, see American Bar Association Antitrust Section, Report of the Special Committee on International Antitrust, 1 September 1991, chs. 3 and 4.

45 See Fox and Ordover, *op. cit.*, p. 15; Alan Wolff, 'The Problems of Market Access in the Global Economy: Trade and Competition Policy', in OECD (1995) *op. cit.*, ch. 19.

46 See Fox, 'Jurisdiction and Conflicts in the Global Economy: Crafting a Systems Interface', *op. cit.*, p. 34; Fox, 'Competition Law and the Next Agenda for the WTO' *op. cit.*, p. 182.

47 See John Mercury, 'Chapter 19 of the United States–Canada Free Trade Agreement 1989–95: A Check on Administered Protection?' (1995) 15 *Northwestern J. of International Law and Business* 525.

48 (1993) 1621 ATRR 30; for extensive discussions of this case, see Fox, 'Jurisdiction and Conflicts in the Global Economy: Crafting a Systems Interface', *op. cit.*; Kenneth Dam, 'Extraterritoriality in an Age of Globalization: The Hartford Case' (1993) *The Supreme Court Review* 289; Alan Swan, 'The Hartford Insurance Company case: Antitrust in the Global Economy – Welfare Effects and Sovereignty', in J. Bhandarai and A. Sykes (eds), *Economics Dimensions in International Law* (Cambridge University Press, 1997).

49 *United States* v. *Pilkington plc, and Pilkington Holdings Inc.* (IV No. 94-345 JVC CD Ariz. 1994).

50 Both the United States *Foreign Trade Antitrust Improvements Act* of 1982 and the recently released *Antitrust Enforcement Guidelines for International Operations* of the United States Department of Justice and Federal Trade Commission (April 1995) contemplate substantial United States extraterritorial jurisdiction over foreign restrictions on outbound United States trade.

51 See Neil Campbell, William Rowley and Michael Trebilcock, 'The Role of Monopoly Law in the International Trading System' (1995) 1 *International Trade Law and Regulation* 167.

52 See Norio Komuro 'The Kodak–Fuji Film Dispute and the WTO Panel Ruling', (1998) 32 *Journal of World Trade* 161.

53 See Sylvia Ostry, 'Challenges for the Trading System', in OECD (1995) *op. cit.*, 25 p. 31.

54 See Michael Gerlach, *The Keiretsu: A Primer* (New York: The Japan Society, 1992); Gerlach, *Alliance Capitalism: The Social Organization of Japanese Business* (1992); Ronald Gilson and Mark Roe, 'Understanding the Japanese Keiretsu: Overlaps Between Corporate Governance and Industrial Organization', Columbia University Law School, Working Paper No. 83, 14 September 1992.

55 See, e.g. Frank Mathewson and Ralph Winter 'The Law and Economics of Vertical Restraints', in F. Mathewson, M. Trebilcock and M. Walker (eds) *The Law and Economics of Competition Policy* (Vancouver: Fraser Institute, 1990) ch. 5.

56 See N. Campbell and M. Trebilcock, 'International Merger Review; Problems of Multi-Jurisdictional Conflict' in Kantzenbach *et al., op. cit.*; Campbell and Trebilcock, 'A Comparative Analysis of Merger Law: Canada, the United States, and the European Community' (1992) 15 *World Competition* 5; Campbell and Trebilcock, 'Interjurisdictional Conflict in Merger Review', in L. Waverman, W. Comanor and A. Goto (eds) *Competition Policy in the Global Economy* (London: Routledge, 1997); see also Richard Whish and Diane Wood, *Merger Cases in the Real World: A Study of Merger Control Procedures* (OECD: Paris, 1994).

57 See Fox and Ordover, *op. cit.*, p. 39.

58 (1990) No. 891-0098 Fed. Reg. 1614; and commentary by Deborah Owen and John Parisi, 'International Mergers and Joint Ventures: A Federal Trade Commission Perspective', in Barry Hawk (ed.) *International Mergers and Joint Ventures* (Fordham Corporate Law Institute, 1991) p. 11.

59 Aerospatiale-Alenia/de Havilland, Commission Decision 91/619 of 5 December 1991, 1 CEC at 2,034 (1992).

60 See Fox and Ordover, *op. cit.* for a similar approach.

61 *Ibid.*, pp. 13, 14.

62 See Campbell and Trebilcock, 'Interjurisdictional Conflict in Merger Review', *op. cit.*

63 *Ibid.*

64 See ABA *NAFTA* Task Force Report, *op. cit.*, chs. 4 and 5.

65 See Trebilcock, 'Competition Policy and Trade Policy: Mediating the Interface', *op. cit.*

66 See the Report of the OECD Committee on Competition Law and Policy, 'Interim Report on Convergence of Competition Policies' (1994) for a useful review of major commonalities and differences in OECD member countries' competition laws.

67 For a similar proposal, see I. Sharma, P. Thomson, and K. Christie, 'Delivering the Goods: Manufacturer-Retailer Relations and the Implications for Competition and Trade Policies', Policy Staff Paper, 1994/11, Dept. of Foreign Affairs and International Trade, Ottawa.

68 See Petros Mavroidis and Sally Van Siclen, 'The Application of the GATT/WTO Dispute Resolution System to Competition Issues' (1997) 31 *J. of World Trade* 5.

69 See Bernard J. Phillips, 'Comments on the Draft International Antitrust Code', and annexed Report of OECD Committee on Competition Law and Policy, 'Interim Report on Convergence of Competition Policies' (1994) 49 *Aussenwirtschaft* 327, for an initial statement of consensus views.

70 *Ibid.* This evolutionary approach to international harmonization of competition is also advocated by E.U. Petersmann, 'Proposals for Negotiating International Competition Rules in the GATT-WTO World Trade and Legal System' (1994), 49 *Aussenwirtschaft* 231 at 276, 277. A more sceptical view of whether there is any problem of significance is taken by David Palmeter, 'Competition Policy and "Unfair Trade": First Do No Harm' (1994) 49 *Aussenwirtschaft* 417. Palmeter notes that, according to research by Finger and Fung, in only one of the 82 Section 301 cases concluded in the United States between 1975 and 1992 was an affirmative determination based on anticompetitive provisions in a foreign country's laws and in only two other cases were competition issues even raised: see J.M. Finger and K.C. Fung, 'Can Competition Policy Control S.301?' (1994) 49 *Aussenwirtschaft* 379. Palmeter concludes that 'whatever might be limiting import competition in various national markets, the record suggests it is not likely to be lack of competition policy' (p. 421).

71 See Phillips, *op. cit.*

72 See T. DiLorenzo, 'The Origins of Antitrust: An Interest Group Perspective' (1985) 5 *International Review of Law and Economics* 73; M. Bliss, 'Another Antitrust Tradition: Canadian Anti-Combines Policy 1889–1910' (1973) 47 *Business History Review* 177.

73 See Michael Trebilcock and Thomas Boddez, 'The Case for Liberalizing North American Trade Remedy Laws' (1995) 4 *Minnesota J. of Global Trade* 1; see Palmeter, *op. cit.*, p. 422, for a similar view, although he regards this proposal as 'highly meritorious' but for the present and foreseeable future as 'highly utopian' (at p. 418). See also the Report of the Antitrust Section of the American Bar Association on the Competition Dimension of the North American Free Trade Agreement, 20 July 1994, ch. 6; and Fox and Ordover, *op. cit.*, p. 32, for similarly circumspect positions.

74 See Chapter herein.

18 The international movement of people

1 This chapter draws heavily on the contribution, 'Immigration Policy', by one of the authors (Trebilcock) in the Palgrave Dictionary of Economics and the Law (London: McMillan, 1998).

2 See Sharon Russell and Michael Teitelbaum, 'International Migration and International Trade' (Washington DC: World Bank Discussion Paper No. 160, 1992) pp. 36–41.

3 *Ibid.*, pp. 1, 9.

4 United Nations, *World Population at the Turn of the Century* (New York: United Nations, 1989) p. 61.

5 *The Economist*, 23 December 1989, p. 17; *The Economist*, 13 November 1993 p. 45.

6 Rachel M. Friedberg and Jennifer Hunt, 'The Impact of Immigrants on Host Country Wages, Employment and Growth' (1995) 9 *Journal of Economic Perspectives* 27.

7 Jane Badets and Tina Chui, 1994, *Canada's Changing Immigrant Population* (Ottawa: Statistics Canada, 1994), pp. 7, 10.

8 George J. Borjas, 'The Economics of Immigration' (1994) 32 *Journal of Economic Literature*, 1668.

9 Friedberg and Hunt, *op. cit.*, p. 27.

10 *Ibid.*, *op. cit.*, p. 26.

11 Alan G. Green, 'A Comparison of Canadian and US Immigration Policy in the Twentieth Century', in Don DeVoretz (ed.) *Diminishing Returns: The Economics of Canada's Recent Immigration Policy* (Toronto: C.D. Howe Institute, 1995).

12 Badets and Chui, *op. cit.*, p. 13.

13 Klaus Zimmerman, 'Tackling the European Migration Problem' (1995) 9 *Journal of Economic Perspectives* 45–62.

14 Richard Layard *et al.*, *East-West Migration: The Alternatives* (Cambridge MA: MIT Press 1992).

15 Zimmerman, *op. cit.*, p. 48.

16 Joseph Carens, 'Aliens and Citizens: The Case for Open Borders' (1987) 47 *The Review of Politics* 251.

17 *Ibid.*, pp. 252–4.

18 *Ibid.*, p. 255.

19 *Ibid.*, p. 256.

20 Joseph Carens, 'Membership and Morality: Admission to Membership in Liberal Democratic States', in *Immigration and the Politics of Citizenship in Europe and North America* (New York: University Press of America, 1989).

21 Carens (1987), *op. cit.*, p. 263.

22 Peter H. Schuck, 'The Transformation of Immigration Law' (1984) 84 *Columbia L.R.* 1 p. 6.

23 Michael Walzer, *Spheres of Justice* (New York: Basic Books, 1983) ch. 2.

24 *Ibid.*, pp. 61–2.

25 Robert L. Heilbroner, *The Worldly Philosophers – The Lives, Times, and Ideas of the Great Economic Thinkers* (New York: Simon and Schuster, 1980, 5th ed.) p. 76.
26 See Julian Simon, *The Economic Consequences of Immigration* (Oxford: Basil Blackwell, 1989); George J. Borjas, *Friends or Strangers: The Impact of Immigrants on the U.S. Economy* (N.Y.: Basic Books, 1990); Economic Council of Canada, *Economic and Social Impacts of Immigration* (Supply and Services, Ottawa, 1991); Lowell Gallaway, Stephen Moore, and Richard Vedder, 'Immigration and Unemployment: New Evidence' (USA: Alexis de Toqueville Institution, 1994).
27 Bob Hamilton and John Whalley, 'Efficiency and Distributional Implications of Global Restrictions on Labour Mobility: Calculations and Policy Implications' (1984) 14 *Journal of Development Economics* 61.
28 Alan O. Sykes, 'The Welfare Economics of Immigration Law', in Warren Schwartz (ed.) *Justice in Immigration* (Cambridge University Press, 1995).
29 Simon, *op. cit.*, ch. 14; Jagdish Bhagwati, *Political Economy and Economics* (Cambridge, MA: MIT Press, 1991), chapters 18–20.
30 Russell and Teitelbaum, *op. cit.*, pp. 18–32.
31 Arthur Schlesinger, *The Disuniting of America* (New York: W.W. Norton, 1992); Peter Brimelow, *Alien Nation* (New York: Random House, 1995).
32 Barry R. Chiswick, 'The Effect of Americanization on the Earnings of Foreign-Born Men' (1978) 86 *Journal of Political Economy* 897.
33 Simon, *op. cit.*
34 Borjas (1990), *op. cit.*
35 Borjas (1994), *op. cit.*; Borjas, 'The Economic Benefits from Immigration' (1995) 9 *Journal of Economic Perspectives* 3.
36 Borjas (1995), *op. cit.*, pp. 3–4.
37 Borjas (1994) *op. cit.*, p. 1685.
38 Borjas (1995), *op. cit.*
39 Borjas (1994), *op. cit.*, pp. 1704–8.
40 Friedberg and Hunt, *op. cit.*
41 Economic Council of Canada *op. cit*; Ather Akbari and Don DeVoretz, 'The Sustainability of Foreign Born Labour and Canadian Production Circa 1980' (1992) 25 *Canadian Journal of Economics.*
42 Ather Akbari, 'The Impact of Immigrants on Canada's Treasury Circa 1990', in DeVoretz (1995) *op. cit.*
43 Economic Council of Canada, *op. cit.*
44 Badets and Chui, *op. cit.*
45 Zimmerman, *op. cit.*
46 Economic Council of Canada, *op. cit.*, p. 25; Simon *op. cit.*, ch. 8.
47 Borjas (1995), *op. cit.*, p. 12.
48 Borjas (1994), *op. cit*; Borjas (1995), *op. cit*; DeVoretz (1995), *op. cit.*, pp. 23–9.
49 DeVoretz (1995), *op. cit.*, p. 8.
50 Alan G. Green and David A. Green, 'Canadian Immigration Policy: The Effectiveness of the Point System' (1995) 28 *Canadian Journal of Economics* 1006; Arnold DeSilva, 'Earnings of Immigrant Classes in the Early 1980s in Canada' (1997) 23 *Canadian Public Policy* 179.
51 Michael J. Trebilcock, 'The Case for a Liberal Immigration Policy', in Schwartz, *op. cit.*
52 Sykes, *op. cit.*
53 Roslyn Kunin and Cheryl L. Jones, 'Business Immigration in Canada', in DeVoretz (1995), *op. cit.*
54 Simon, *op. cit.*, pp. 315–18.
55 Simon, *op. cit.*, p. 302.
56 Sykes, *op. cit.*
57 See John Whalley, 'The North–South Debate and the Terms of Trade: An Applied Equilibrium Approach' (1984) 66 *Rev. of Economics and Statistics* 224, pp. 231–323.
58 See Russell and Teitelbaum, *op. cit.*, pp. 33, 34.

19 Conclusion: the future of the global trading system

1 The following is drawn from Michael Trebilcock and Robert Howse, 'Trade Liberalization and Regulatory Diversity: Reconciling Competitive Markets with Competitive Politics', (1998) 1 *European Journal of Law & Economics* 5.
2 See Sylvia Ostry, 'Beyond the Border: The New International Policy Arena', in E. Kantzenbach, H. Sharrer and L. Waverman (eds) *Competition Policy in an Interdependent World Economy* (Baden-Baden: Nomos; 1993) p. 261.
3 Miles Kahler, 'Trade and Domestic Differences' in Suzanne Berger and Ronald Dore (eds) *National Diversity and Global Capitalism* (New York: Cornell University Press, 1996) p. 299.
4 David Vogel, *Trading Up: Consumer and Environmental Regulation in a Global Economy* (Cambridge MA: Harvard University Press, 1995) p. 3.
5 *Ibid.*, pp. 14,15.
6 Alan O. Sykes, *Product Standards for Internationally Integrated Goods Markets* (Washington DC: The Brookings Institution, 1995) p. 117; see also Sykes, 'The (Limited) Role of Regulatory Harmonization in the International System' (unpublished manuscript, U. of Chicago Law School, 1997).
7 See Sykes, *op. cit.* p. 5; see more generally Douglas Irwin, *Against the Tide: An Intellectual History of Free Trade* (Princeton University Press, 1996).
8 For insightful discussions of the welfare effects of harmonization, see Jagdish Bhagwati, 'The Demands to Reduce Domestic Diversity Among Trading Nations', in Jagdish Bhagwati and Robert Hudec (eds) *Fair Trade and Harmonization: Pre-requisites for Free Trade?* (Cambridge MA: MIT Press, 1996), vol. I, ch. 1; Bhagwati, 'Fair Trade, Reciprocity and Harmonization: The Novel Challenge to the Theory and Policy of Free Trade', in Dominick Salvatore (ed.) *Protectionism and World Welfare* (NY: Cambridge University Press, 1993), ch. 2; David Leebron, 'Lying Down With Procrustes: An Analysis of Harmonization', in Bhagwati and Hudec *op. cit.*, ch. 2; Alan O. Sykes (1997), *op. cit.*
9 Albert Breton, *Competitive Governments* (Cambridge University Press, 1996).
10 Harold Demsetz, 'Why Regulate Utilities?' (1968) 11 *J. of L. & Economics.*
11 See also Donald Wittman, *The Myth of Democratic Failure: Why Political Institutions are Efficient* (University of Chicago Press, 1995) ch. 3.
12 See Michael Trebilcock and Robert Howse, *The Regulation of International Trade* (London, New York: Routledge, 1995) pp. 90–6.
13 R. Howse and M.J. Trebilcock, 'FTA/NAFTA, Regulatory Diversity and the Problem of Harmonization', Conference on the Canada–US Free Trade Agreement: Eight Years Later, Centre for International Affairs, Harvard University, 10 May 1996.
14 See e.g. Kalypso Nikolaides, 'Comments', in Sykes (1995) *op. cit.*, pp. 140–3.
15 An excellent overview of the issues and approaches of importance in consensual harmonization is to be found in OECD, *Regulatory Co-operation for an Interdependent World* (Paris: OECD(Public Management Service) 1994).
16 An example is the OECD test guidelines programme, which seeks to establish guidelines with respect to the collection of data on the basis of which regulations are made and enforced.
17 See, for instance the OECD Guidelines for Regulatory Decision-making, adopted 9 May 1995, requiring *inter alia* that regulation be based upon accurate analysis of the problem and that the distributive effects of the regulation be considered.
18 J. Braithwaite, 'Lessons for Regulatory Cooperation' in *Regulatory Cooperation for an Interdependent World*, p. 232. As Braithwaite observes more generally, certain minimum levels of harmonization may be needed to support regulatory competition (p. 235).
19 *The ILO, Standard-Setting and Globalization*, pp. 30–1.
20 Sykes (1995) *op. cit.*, pp. 110–17.
21 See Trebilcock and Howse, *The Regulation of International Trade, op. cit.* ch. 9.
22 *Ibid.*, ch. 1.

23 Kahler, *op. cit.*, p. 301.
24 See Kalypso Nikolaides, 'Comments', in Sykes *op. cit.* (1995) pp. 139–53.
25 See Kalypso Nikolaides, 'Mutual Recognition of Regulatory Regimes: Some Lessons and Prospects' in OECD Proceedings *Regulatory Reform and International Market Openness* (Paris: OECD, 1996) p. 181.
26 For a similar perspective, see Frieder Roessler, 'Increasing Market Access Under Regulatory Heterogeneity: The Strategies of the World Trade Organization', OECD, *ibid.*, ch. 10.
27 See the Canada – U.S. *Softwood Lumber* Case, *op. cit.*
28 *Thailand: Restrictions on Importations of and Internal Taxes on Cigarettes*, BISD 37th. Supp. (1990).
29 A.-M. Slaughter, 'The Real New World Order' (1997) 76 *Foreign Affairs* 183, pp. 196–7.
30 See D. Held, *Democracy and the Global Order: From the Modern State to Cosmopolitan Governance* (Stanford: Stanford University Press, 1995), particularly ch. 12, 'Cosmopolitan Democracy and the New International Order'.
31 B. Kingsbury, *'The Tuna-Dolphin Controversy, the World Trade Organization, and the Liberal Project to Reconceptualize International Law'*, Yearbook of International Environmental Law 1995 (Oxford: Oxford University Press, 1995) p. 17.
32 See the discussion of consideration and modification of contracts in M.J. Trebilcock, *The Limits of Freedom of Contract* (Cambridge MA: Harvard University Press, 1993) pp. 136–40, 168–70.
33 See Tyson, *op. cit.*
34 See M.J. Trebilcock, M.A. Chandler and R. Howse, *Trade and Transitions: A Comparative Analysis of Adjustment Policies* (London: Routledge, 1990) pp. 217–23.
35 See J. Grieco, 'Anarchy and the Limits of Cooperation: A Realist Critique of the Newest Liberal Internationalism' (1990) 42 *International Organization* 485.
36 See J. Gordley, 'Equality in Exchange' (1981) 69 *California Law Review* 1587.
37 Bhagwati, 'Fair Trade, Reciprocity and Harmonization: The New Challenge to the Theory and Policy of Free Trade', *op. cit.*, p. 28.
38 As did an FTA panel in the *Salmon and Herring Landing Requirement* case.
39 For the evidence, see Trebilcock, Chandler and Howse, *Trade and Transitions: A Comparative Analysis of Adjustment Policies*, *op. cit.*, ch. 2.
40 The following is drawn from M.J. Trebilcock, 'What Makes Poor Countries Poor? The Role of Institutional Capital in Economic Development, in E. Buscaglia *et al.* (eds) *The Law and Economics of Development* (Connecticut: JAI Press, 1997) pp. 15–52.
41 L. Frischtak, 'Governance Capacity and Economic Reform in Developing Countries', World Bank Working Paper, 1994.
42 World Bank, *Governance and Development* (Washington DC: World Bank, 1992).
43 L.J. Reynolds, 'The Spread of Economic Growth to the Third World: 1850–1980' (1983) *Journal of Economic Literature* 941, p. 976.
44 A. Talavera, 'The Future of an Illusion', in Diamond and Plattner (eds) *Capitalism, Socialism and Democracy Revisited* (Baltimore: Johns Hopkins University Press, 1993) p. 108.
45 R. Barro, *Determinanats of Economic Growth: A Cross-Country Empirical Study* (Washington DC: U.S. National Bureau of Economic Research, 1996).
46 M. Naim, 'Latin America: The Second Stage of Reform' (1994) 5 *Journal of Democracy* 32.
47 R. Putnam, *Making Democracy Work: Civic Traditions in Modern Italy* (Princeton: Princeton University Press, 1993).
48 Naim, *op. cit.*, pp. 41–2.
49 F. Weffort, 'The Future of Socialism', in Diamond and Plattner (eds) *op. cit.*
50 Barro (1996) *op. cit.*
51 C. Cadwell, *Implementing Legal Reform in Transition Economies*, paper presented at American Law and Economics Association Annual Meeting, Berkely CA, May 1995.
52 See Chapter 4.
53 See K. Nikolaides, 'Mutual Recognition of Regulatory Regimes', *op. cit.*
54 P. Cowhey and J.D. Aronson, 'A New Trade Order' (1993/4) 72 *Foreign Affairs*, p. 192.

Index